D0420178

STARLINGS
AND MYNAS

STARLINGS AND MYNAS

Chris Feare and Adrian Craig

Illustrated by Barry Croucher, Chris Shields and Kamol Komolphalin

Princeton University Press
Princeton, New Jersey

UNIVERSITY OF HERTFORDSHIRE
HATFIELD CAMPUS LRC
HATFIELD AL10 9AD   306426

BIB
0691004696X

CLASS
598.863 FEA

LOCATION
OWL

BARCODE
4405114771

© 1999 Chris Feare, Adrian Craig, Barry Croucher, Chris Shields and Kamol Komolphalin

Published in the United States, Canada, and the Philippine Islands
by Princeton University Press, 41 William Street, Princeton, New Jersey 08540

In the United Kingdom, published by Christopher Helm (Publishers) Ltd, a subsidiary of
A & C Black (Publishers) Ltd, 35 Bedford Row, London WC1R 4JH

ISBN 0-691-00496-X

All rights reserved. No part of this publication may be
reproduced or used in any form or by any means — photographic,
electronic or mechanical, including photocopying, recording,
taping or information storage and retrieval systems — without
permission of the publishers.

http://pup.princeton.edu

Printed in Singapore

10 9 8 7 6 5 4 3 2 1

DEDICATION

To our children
Adam, Simon, Roland and Andrew

We hope that these birds will be there for them and their children to see

CONTENTS

ACKNOWLEDGEMENTS

The seeds of this book were sown during the writing of the first chapter of the 1984 monograph *The Starling* (Feare 1984), but two subsequent events provided the impetus to commence what became a long gestation period; first, a chance meeting of the authors in the Natural History Museum in Tring, when both of us were working on starlings in the collection, and second, a stimulus from Christopher Helm ('If you don't do it, I'll find someone else!') to write a book for his series of identification guides.

During the gestation period, we have been fortunate to have been able to investigate some aspects of the biology and behaviour of several starling species, thereby giving us the opportunity to gain insight into some of the relationships between them. These studies involved both observations of birds in the wild and also in collections of captives. CF enjoyed valuable field trips with Kang Nee and Kamol Komolphalin in South-East Asia, and with Salvador Peris in Spain, and was able to study captive starlings with the help of Jim Irwin-Davies (Harewood Bird Garden, Yorkshire), Alan Martin (Merley Bird Gardens, Hampshire), Peter Olney (Zoological Society of London, Regents Park), and Roger Wilkinson (North of England Zoological Society, Chester). AC was assisted in field studies in Africa by Ludwig Coetzer, N Collins, Pat Hulley, Hanna Hofshi, Penn Lloyd, Gimme Walter and Francis White, and his research was funded by BirdLife South Africa (formerly the Southern African Ornithological Society), Rhodes University, and the Foundation for Research Development.

CF received considerable help from staff at the Natural History Museum, Tring, during studies of specimens and when consulting literature, and it is a pleasure to acknowledge the assistance at various stages of Robert Prys-Jones, Effie Warr, Michael Walters and Peter Colston. Michael Wilson (University of Oxford, Edward Grey Institute) kindly kept CF informed of publications in the Russian literature. Karl Schuchmann (Bonn), Michel Louette (Tervuren), Peter Colston and Anne Vale (Tring), Herbert Schifter (Vienna), Wesley Lanyon and Dave Willard (Chicago), Janet Hinshaw and Bob Payne (Michigan), Mary LeCroy and Bob Dickerman (New York), RW James and Charles MacInnes (Toronto), Phil Angle and Richard Zusi (Washington), Kit Hustler and Des Jackson (Bulawayo), Denise Brinkrow and the late JM Winterbottom (Cape Town), Aldo Berruti and John Mendelsohn (Durban), Carl Vernon (East London), Leon Bennun (Nairobi), Tamar Cassidy and Alan Kemp (Pretoria), and Joris Komen (Windhoek) enabled AC to examine material from museum collections.

Constructive help of many kinds has been freely given by many people, practically, in discussion and in correspondence, especially Geoff Carey, Roger Caton, Rene Dekker, Alec Forbes-Watson, Elaine Gill, Mike Grant, Julian Hume, Carl Jones, Kamol Komolphalin, Frank Lambert, Kang Nee, Juan Pascual, Salvador Peris, Richard Ranft and Yoram Yom-Tov. Neil Baker, Richard Brooke, Richard Dean, John Dittami, Francoise Dowsett-Lemaire, P Herroelen, Hanna Hofshi, Alan Kemp, Rick Nuttall, Vicky Roth, Roger Shanteau, Jack Skead, Walter Sontag, Jean Spearpoint, Warwick Tarboton and Carl Vernon contributed unpublished observations of African birds.

Carl Vernon and the late Richard Brooke read and commented on the text for the African species. Sections of the text on Asian species were read by Kang Nee, Juan Pascual and Salvador Peris, and some introductory chapters were read by Elaine Gill.

The authors are delighted to thank the artists for what we consider to be some of the best illustrations we have seen of starlings, some of whose characters are difficult to capture in artwork. The artists were able to examine specimens and discuss problems thanks to the help of staff at the Natural History Museum, Tring, Howard Mendel and David Lampard of Ipswich Museum, Mike Hounsome of Manchester Museum, Tony Parker at the National Museums and Galleries of Merseyside at Liverpool, staff of the American Museum of Natural History, Roger Wilkinson at Chester Zoo, Peter Hayman and Craig Robson.

CF is especially grateful to Elaine Gill for putting up with the disruption to our life during the writing of the book, and in particular for her encouragement and support throughout. AC appreciates Cheryl's tolerance of the many weekends away, and the help which she, Roland and Andrew have given on many occasions.

ABOUT THIS BOOK

Starlings range from familiar species such as Common Starling and Common Myna, which are closely associated with people and have been introduced to many parts of the world, to little-known forest birds with a very restricted distribution. The family is centred on tropical Asia and tropical Africa, where two separate evolutionary radiations have occurred.

The iridescent plumage of many glossy starlings makes them some of the most colourful birds, and presents a special challenge to artists. Blues and greens in this family are structural colours, produced by light reflected from the internal structure of the feather, and not by pigments. Thus colours change with light conditions and with the position of the observer, which often complicates identification.

This is the first monograph on the starling family, and summarises our current knowledge of all species, with a comprehensive bibliography. Information from the avicultural literature is included since for some species nesting and other behaviour have never been observed in the field. Many starlings are highly social, some even nest in colonies, and co-operative breeding ('helpers at the nest') occurs in a number of African species. This book highlights areas where information is lacking, particularly for those starlings whose existence is threatened by habitat destruction.

How to use this guide

While we hope that this book will enable readers to identify every starling species in the field, we do not expect that many people will carry a hamper of bird family handbooks with them on their travels! Since there has never been a single comprehensive account of the starling family, we have tried to assemble all of the literature on the group and provide a synthesis of information on their biology. For many species, little is known, and some of them are threatened with extinction, a fate that has befallen at least five in recent history. We hope that this book will stimulate an increased interest in and awareness of the many poorly studied starling species, and in places we have been deliberately controversial in the hope of stimulating research and discussion.

In its basic format, this book follows the style of earlier volumes in this series, and readers should consult them for details of avian morphology and terminology.

Plates

All living species are illustrated, and where sexes are separable in the field, or distinctive juvenile plumages are known, these are also depicted, as are some well-differentiated subspecies. Flight illustrations are included for those species which show distinctive markings on the wings, rump and tail. On each plate the birds are drawn to the same scale, but dependent on the number of species illustrated on each plate, the scales differ between plates. Body size is indicated in the text.

The caption to each plate and map includes a brief description of the geographical range and habitat, and key identification features.

Maps

The distribution maps follow the style of other books in this series. Where birds are resident, their distribution is shown in green. For migrants, the breeding ranges are shown in yellow and the non-breeding ranges are shown in blue.

Species sequence

The sequence of genera and the numbering of species should not be considered an indication of how closely they are related. Our ideas on the evolutionary relationships of the starlings are set out in the introductory chapters.

Measurements

In all cases these have been taken from museum specimens. For all African species, and for the genus *Saroglossa*, AC personally measured a sample of adult specimens. Wing and tarsus measurements were taken in the standard manner, but all bill lengths were measured to the skull, not to the feathers at the base of the bill (see Baker, *Warblers of Europe, Asia and North Africa*, Helm Identification Series, A&C Black, for illustrations). For remaining Asian species, measurements have, where possible, been taken from the literature and the source of the information is given. Where this was not possible, museum specimens in the Natural History Museum, Tring, were measured as described above. Body mass data have been taken from museum labels, or from published and unpublished sources. Body length measurements, at the beginning of the 'Field Identification' section, are taken from museum skins, and should be used only as a guide to comparative size (see Plates above), as skin preparation techniques vary.

References to published literature

In most cases, a reference is cited after the information to which it refers, but in species accounts where one or a few references are the main sources of information for that species, these are listed at the end of the species account to avoid repetition within the account.

THE STARLING FAMILY

Sibley and Ahlquist (1990) have recently reviewed the proposed relationships of the starling family. This family was traditionally associated with the corvids (Corvidae), although there was little evidence for such a link. Von Boetticher (1931a) suggested a link with the weaver family (Ploceidae) but his comparison of bill structure, vocalisations and nesting behaviour is unconvincing since it relies on shared primitive characters. Using egg-white protein data and some biological (nesting) characters, Sibley and Ahlquist (1974) suggested that the southern African sugarbirds *Promerops* might be derived from starlings, but this relationship has not been supported by subsequent work (Sibley and Ahlquist 1990). On the basis of DNA-hybridisation data, Sibley and Ahlquist (1990) concluded that starlings are not closely related to corvids or weavers, but that starlings, thrushes (Turdidae) and flycatchers (Muscicapidae) should be included in one superfamily. More controversial is their proposal that starlings are the closest relatives of the New World mockingbirds and thrashers (Mimidae) (Sibley and Ahlquist 1984, 1990). This is an intriguing possibility but, as with many of the conclusions based on DNA-hybridisation data, we may reserve judgement until further critical studies have been carried out.

The starlings are an entirely Old World family (apart from introductions to the New World by man), with the main concentrations of species in the Indo-Malayan and Afrotropical regions. The dichotomy between the Asian and African starlings appears to have occurred early in the family's history, for primitive features appear in both groups and there is wide divergence between them in certain aspects of their behaviour. There does, however, seem to have been repeated contact between the two regions as the Asian genus, *Saroglossa*, has a representative in Madagascar, and the Wattled Starling *Creatophora cinerea* of Africa and the extinct Bourbon Crested Starling *Fregilupus varius* of Reunion Island appear to show close relationships with more advanced Asian genera like *Sturnus*.

The intra-family classification accepted in most recent check-lists (e.g. Gruson 1976, Howard and Moore 1984, Sibley and Monroe 1990) is based on Mayr and Greenway (1962), which used the classification devised by Amadon (1943, 1956). This classification was based largely on the study of preserved skin collections and more recent studies of the ecology and behaviour of some species are revealing new and more complex relationships. For example, Marien (1950) stated that 'the one constant character by which *Acridotheres* differs from *Sturnus*, a tendency for the possession of a frontal crest, is too trivial in comparison with the many features which they share to warrant excluding *Acridotheres* from the enlarged genus *Sturnus*'. We now know that there are many behavioural features, including displays and voice, which distinguish these two genera. In this book we take the opportunity to revise the classification of starlings but, as studies of the various species' biology add to our knowledge, and as studies using recently developed genetic techniques are applied to relationships within the family, we expect further revisions to be necessary. We are currently experiencing a renewed bout of debate in taxonomy over the definition of 'species', and this has implications for many who may use this book. Our elevation of some formerly subordinate taxa to the species level may alarm some avian taxonomists, may excite some birders, and will almost certainly concern conservationists who will find a few more island endemics whose status is fragile. Above all, we hope that our decisions will stimulate further research and debate about the starling family.

English names

Several species of starlings have been given a wide variety of English names in the past, and we list many of them in the species text headings; for some species, the list is so great that we do not claim to be exhaustive. The names that we have selected for each species are those that we consider to be most appropriate, often based on common usage, but we have also tended to employ names that are descriptive, either of appearance, or of geographical origin where this is applicable. With many Asian members of the family, common usage dictates that they are called mynas or mynahs. This derives from the Hindi word 'maina', which is a term of endearment, often used towards children and favoured females, and more or less equivalent to the English word 'pet' (Bertram 1970). The centre of Hinduism is India, but the word 'myna' is commonly used to refer to starlings in other regions of South-East Asia that bear a resemblance to the Indian mynas of the genus *Acridotheres* and *Gracula*. We follow this usage, but accept that it is arbitrary and people will have their own preferences for different species.

The genera of Asian starlings

Aplonis

The genus *Aplonis* contains 21 currently recognised extant species and a further three species are known to have become extinct during the last two centuries. The members of the genus are entirely island species, reaching continental land masses only on the Malay Peninsula and in southern Vietnam, and in northeast Queensland. They are widely distributed over the islands of Indonesia,

Oceania and northern Australasia. In terms of the number of species, the centre of their present distribution is undoubtedly New Guinea and its associated islands.

Aplonis comprises species of different kinds of distribution, ranging from those with a wide distribution embracing many island groups, to single island endemics, suggesting a complex evolutionary history. There are six widespread species, Shining Starling *A. metallica* and Singing Starling *A. cantoroides* of Melanesia, Asian Glossy Starling *A. panayensis* of Indonesia and the Philippines, Short-tailed Starling *A. minor*, Micronesian Starling *A. opaca* and Polynesian Starling *A. tabuensis* (Fig 1). It is tempting to think that these are recent species and there are suggestions that Asian Glossy Starling is indeed so, and is still expanding its range (Deignan 1954). Polynesian Starling has, however, lost many of the characteristics regarded as typical of these starlings (in common with many island forms) and lacks the glossy iridescent plumage of most of its congeners, resembling more closely the immature plumages of these species. A further eight species have ranges that embrace groups of islands, these ranges overlapping those of some of the more widely distributed species above, especially in the New Guinea, Bismarck and Solomons areas (Fig 2).

At the other end of the scale, species endemic to single islands or island pairs (Fig 3) might be considered to be relicts of former more widespread distributions, having been outcompeted from some areas by more recent colonists, or having lost former breeding islands through rises in ocean levels, or through a variety of other causes including, of course, habitat modification and other factors associated with colonisation by man. The extinctions of Kusai Island Starling *A. corvina* and the Norfolk and Lord Howe Island Starling *A. fusca hulliana* in recent times are probably both attributable to the introduction of rats to these islands (Fuller 1987). Some of the island endemics display a number of features that deviate from more 'typical' congeners and might be taken to indicate a long history of isolation. Kusai Island Starling was large, as is Samoan Starling *A. atrifusca* and Brown-winged Starling *A. grandis*. White-eyed Starling *A. brunneicapilla* and Long-tailed Starling *A. magna* have some of the tail feathers exceptionally elongated. Tanimbar Starling *A. crassa*, Norfolk and Lord Howe Island Starling *A. fusca* and Striated Starling *A. striata* have developed a marked sexual dimorphism. Several species have entirely (Pohnpei Mountain Starling *A. pelzelni* and Rufous-winged Starling *A. zelandica*) or largely (Mountain Starling *A. santovestris*, Norfolk and Lord Howe Island Starling, Polynesian Starling, Samoan Starling, Mysterious Starling *A. mavornata* and Rarotonga Starling *A. cinerascens*) lost gloss in the plumage. Most *Aplonis* are lowland birds but, as the names of some imply, some occupy higher altitudes. Mountain Starling and Pohnpei Mountain Starling are birds of montane forest, as was Kusai Island Starling. The lowlands of the islands on which these species occurred were occupied by more widespread and, in the cases of the last two, more generalised forms. Deignan (1954) suggested that this process of competitive exclusion was currently occurring between Asian Glossy Starling and Short-tailed Starling *A. minor*. The former species is widespread in Indonesia and the Philippines, while the latter is much more localised on Mindanao (Philippines), central and southern Sulawesi and the Lesser Sundas. In most places, Short-tailed Starling is a lowland bird but on Mindanao, where both species occur, this species occurs in montane forest above 900 m. In Sulawesi, the ranges of the two species are mutually exclusive. Deignan (1955) considered that the range of Short-tailed Starling was formerly more extensive, but was contracting under the influence of the spread of the larger and more competitive Asian Glossy Starling. White and Bruce (1986) consider that these two species form a superspecies. It is possible that other *Aplonis* starlings are experiencing interspecific competition with congeners. For example on Rennell Island, there is habitat partition between Rennell Starling *A. insularis* and Singing Starling (Bradley and Wolff 1956). Perhaps more remarkable is the co-existence in parts of New Guinea of Shining and Yellow-eyed Starlings *A. mystacea*, between which there appear to be no ecological differences (Safford 1996).

The biology of many species of *Aplonis* is poorly known and the taxonomy of the genus is likely to change as more knowledge is gained. For the time being we follow the specific identities of Amadon (in Mayr and Greenway 1962) although we have changed the order of species. Our order reflects the present biogeography of species, for we feel that to look for relationships between widely separated species that have evolved on isolated island groups is unlikely to have much biological meaning.

Shining Starling is the widespread form of Melanesia, where its range embraces that of both Singing Starling and Yellow-eyed Starling. Shining Starling has differentiated into a number of races. The monotypic Yellow-eyed Starling shows many resemblances to Shining Starling and the little information available (Coates 1990, Safford 1996) suggests that the two species may also share ecological attributes. Singing Starling is also monotypic, but appears to form a superspecies with Tanimbar Starling, which has sometimes been regarded as a race of Singing Starling (Amadon in Mayr and Greenway 1962). Atoll Starling *A. feadensis* and Rennell Starling also appear closely related to Singing Starling, and the distributions of these species are largely complementary; however, both Singing and Atoll Starlings have been found together on an island in the Ninigo group, and Singing and Rennell Starlings occur together on Rennell Island (Coates 1990). Long-tailed and White-eyed Starlings have greatly elongated central tail feathers but differ in eye colour and the latter has a slight crest; perhaps this feature and the long tail led Amadon (1956) to consider White-

14

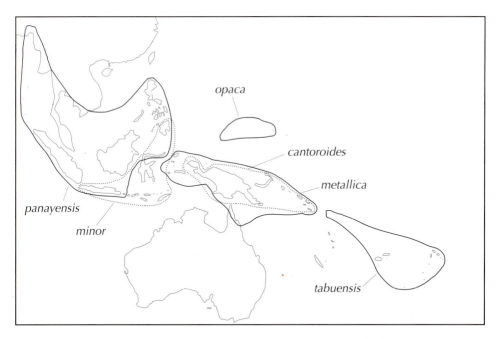

Figure 1. The distribution of the six wide-ranging species of Aplonis

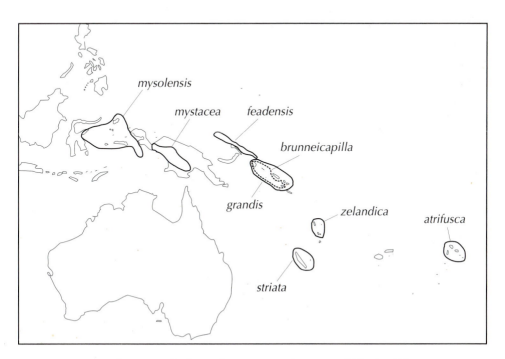

Figure 2. Eight species of Aplonis whose ranges embrace several islands within groups

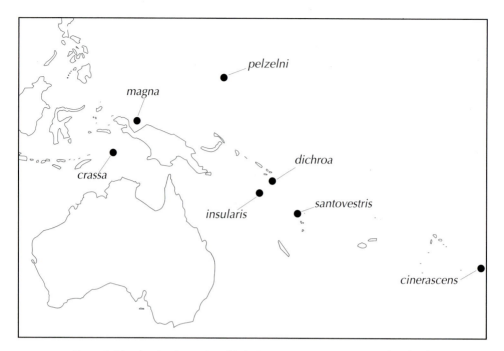

Figure 3. Island endemic species of Aplonis (magna occupies two nearby islands in Geelvink Bay, Irian Jaya)

eyed Starling to be closely related to Yellow-eyed Starling, which to an extent shares these characteristics, while Finch (1986) considered White-eyed Starling to be most closely related to Shining Starling. Amadon (1943) linked Long-tailed Starling in a superspecies with Moluccan Starling, which also has a brown iris and long graduated tail. These possible relationships need further investigation. Brown-winged and Makira *A. dichroa* Starlings have been considered to form a superspecies, but Finch (1986) casts doubt on a close relationship; he did, however, consider that *A. grandis malaita* should be given full specific status on the basis of its eye colour, longer hackles on the head and more glossy, greener plumage than the nominate form. The remaining three species of the Melanesian region, Rufous-winged, Striated and Mountain Starlings are unrelated to each other or to other species in the region.

The close relationship between Asian Glossy and Short-tailed Starlings of the Indonesian/Philippines region, and the possible competition between them, has been mentioned above. They share general features of the glossy plumage and brightly coloured eye of the mainland New Guinea species but differ from Shining and Yellow-eyed Starlings in lacking the long graduated tail. Hoogerwerf (1965) regarded a race of Moluccan Starling *A. mysolensis sulaensis* as a race of Asian Glossy Starling, but White and Bruce (1986) doubted the validity of this subspecies of Moluccan Starling, thereby casting doubt on the relationship between the two species. With its graduated tail, Moluccan Starling more closely resembles other New Guinea species.

In Micronesia, the widely distributed Micronesian Starling is a generalised *Aplonis* species, with reduced gloss compared with Asian and New Guinea species, and has differentiated into several subspecies. The other Micronesian species, Pohnpei Mountain Starling and the extinct Kusai Island Starling are island endemics, the former being a small, dull brown bird, while the extinct species was large and glossy black with a red iris, and with a distinctively long, curved bill.

The widespread starling of Polynesia, Polynesian Starling, has, as stated above, largely lost the glossy plumage of its more typical congeners, perhaps indicating a long period of isolation from them. The other Polynesian species also have much reduced gloss although the large Samoan Starling retains slight gloss on the body plumage. The two island endemics, Rarotonga Starling and the extinct Mysterious Starling, are both smallish, largely brown birds which may be related to Polynesian Starling.

Amadon (1943) linked Raratonga and Polynesian Starlings of Polynesia in a superspecies with Micronesian Starling and with Norfolk and Lord Howe Island Starling, from the southern Melanesian area. While similarities between birds of such wide distribution might reflect a common origin from an early radiation throughout the Pacific, such similarities could equally arise through convergence. Until there is evidence, e.g. from genetic studies, to support such a relationship, we treat these species along with their geographic congeners.

Mino

Species of the genus *Mino* inhabit New Guinea and its associated Bismarck and Solomon Islands. They are lowland arboreal frugivores. Some of their features, e.g. glossy black plumage and bare facial skin, are shared with many Asian starlings, while the presence of greatly elongated and degraded feather tips, vivid orange or gold in all forms, is characteristic of this genus and only occurs elsewhere in the genus *Enodes*. The primaries have white patches about halfway along their length, with the white restricted to the inner web of the outer primary, on both webs of most of the other primaries but only on the outer web of the inner primaries; this forms a prominent white patch on the wing, conspicuous in flight. This feature is shared with Golden-crested Myna *Ampeliceps* (in which the primary markings are yellow on the outer webs), and in *Gracula*. Amadon (1943) placed *Ampeliceps coronatus* in the genus *Mino*, but later revised this opinion (Amadon 1956), retaining *Ampeliceps* as a monotypic genus. Two species of *Mino*, *dumontii* and *anais*, were recognised by Amadon (1943) and Sibley and Monroe (1990). Schodde (1977), however, reported that the form of *M. dumontii* of the Bismarcks and Solomons, *kreffti*, differs both morphologically and in several behavioural traits from that on New Guinea, and we follow Schodde in recognising *kreffti* as a full species.

Basilornis

The genus *Basilornis*, of Sulawesi, the Moluccas and the Philippines, shares glossy black plumage and bare peri-orbital skin with the genus *Mino*, together with white patches on the breast of three species, tinged with orange in two of them. Three of the species also have white filoplumes around the head, as in *M. dumontii*. We thus agree with Amadon (1943, 1956) that the two genera are closely related. The genus *Basilornis* differs from the genus *Mino* in lacking white wing patches and in possessing a well-developed crest. The four species of *Basilornis* show a gradation of characteristics: Sulawesi Crested Myna *B. celebensis* has the least well-developed crest, which assumes a more pronounced form in Helmeted Myna *B. galeatus* and a remarkable erect structure of partially degraded feathers in Long Crested Myna *B. corythaix*. In Apo Myna *B. miranda*, the crest feathers are degenerate and the crest appears wispy. The first three species have white patches on the cheeks and sides of the breast, tinged orange in the first two. *B. miranda* differs from the other three species in lacking white on the sides of the neck and breast, but possesses a white rump, much more extensive, bare peri-orbital skin and a long tail. *B. miranda* is also restricted to montane forest, while *celebensis*, *galeatus* and *corythaix* inhabit lowland woodlands, extending into hills in some places. Eck (1976) considered that the latter three species comprised a single species, and that Apo Myna should be allocated to a separate genus *Goodfellowia*. We follow Amadon (1943) and White and Bruce (1986) in regarding them as congeneric, the first three forming a superspecies.

Sarcops

In some ways, the Coleto *Sarcops calvus*, a polytypic species of the Philippines, takes further some of the traits seen in the genus *Basilornis*, and also shows relationships with the genus *Streptocitta*. The area of bare skin on the head is considerably enlarged, some white feathers on the side of the lower neck are retained, but it possesses no crest and lacks gloss on the body plumage. While it does not have the white rump of the genus *Mino* or *B. miranda*, feathers of the upperparts are variously tipped silvery-grey in the three subspecies. The bill is black and the tail is wedge-shaped, but nevertheless very short in comparison with the genus *Streptocitta*.

Streptocitta

The two species of *Streptocitta*, of Sulawesi and Sula, the Moluccas, are magpie-like birds, with black and white plumage and very long tails. Both have bare facial skin, restricted to the peri-orbital region in the White-necked Myna *S. albicollis*, but more extensive in the Bare-eyed Myna *S. albertinae*, in which the throat is also bare. The black parts of the plumage of both species are glossed, but white plumage is more extensive than in the genera *Basilornis* and *Sarcops*, including the belly and breast, and extending round the back of the neck in *albicollis* and on to the crown in *albertinae*. None of the white feathers have any orange tinges, but the bill and legs of *albertinae* are orange-yellow, as in *Basilornis* species, while the bill of *albicollis* is largely black and the legs are black, as in *Sarcops*.

The four genera *Mino*, *Basilornis*, *Sarcops* and *Streptocitta* thus form a group with clear relationships between them, ranging over the area of New Guinea, Sulawesi and the Philippines.

Enodes and *Scissirostrum*

These two monotypic genera of Sulawesi were regarded by Amadon (1956) as specialised offshoots of the Sturnidae. The general similarity of plumage colour, absence of gloss, small legs and feet, and pointed tail suggested to Amadon that they were related, although there are substantial differences between them. Their life styles differ, and the Grosbeak Myna *Scissirostrum dubium* is clearly highly specialised as a colonial wood-boring starling, and the waxy red feathers of the rump and flanks are a peculiarity. The bristly orange feathers that form the superciliary stripe of the Flame-browed Myna *Enodes erythrophris* bear a resemblance to similar bristly feathers on the heads of some other starlings, especially *Sarcops*, and the elongated, degraded and golden-orange tips of the rump feathers bear a strong resemblance to those of *Mino* species. Although more remote, there are thus nevertheless links between these two genera and the complex of New Guinea, Sulawesi and Philippines starlings discussed above.

Saroglossa

Saroglossa was formerly a monotypic Asian genus, but Amadon (1943) expanded it to include the endemic Madagascar Starling, previously in its own monotypic genus *Hartlaubius*. He noted resemblances in the form of the bill and nostrils, the immature plumages, the white patch in the primaries, and the spotted eggs laid by both species. There are several other bird genera that link the Malagasy avifauna to that of Asia rather than Africa (Moreau 1966), including the extinct starling *Fregilupus varius*, from Reunion (Julian Hume, pers. comm.). Benson *et al.* (1977) accepted the generic placing, but disagreed with Moreau's (1966) comment that the genus is close to the Afrotropical genus *Cinnyricinclus*. On the basis of feather melanin granule structure, Durrer and Villiger (1970) placed Madagascar Starling in a group which included *Sturnus vulgaris* and *Creatophora cinerea*. However, they did not examine feathers from Spot-winged Starling *Saroglossa spiloptera*. Beecher (1978) investigated the jaw musculature of the Madagascar Starling and on this basis grouped it with Asian starlings, noting its close resemblance to Spot-winged Starling. He also commented on its frayed tongue, apparently adapted to drinking nectar. Sibley and Monroe (1990) retained both species in the genus *Saroglossa*, but there have been no studies of the DNA of this genus. We also retain this classification, thereby accepting the Asian affinities of Madagascar Starling, but the affinities of the genus *Saroglossa* with other Asian genera are less clear.

Ampeliceps

The form of the pale yellow patches on the primaries of the Golden-crested Myna is very similar to that of *Mino* species, and the golden crown of this myna is also present in *M. anais*. In Golden-crested Myna, however, the golden crown feathers are elongated into a crest, more reminiscent of some representatives of the genera *Acridotheres* and *Sturnus*. The black glossy plumage and the pale wing markings are more reminiscent of the genus *Gracula*, however, and Golden-crested Myna shares spotting on the eggs with this genus. This myna thus appears to form a link between the genera *Mino* and *Gracula* and its distribution in Indochina, Burma and Assam is remote from New Guinea, but within the geographical area occupied by *Gracula* species.

Gracula

Hill mynas *Gracula* are glossy black birds, renowned for their ability to mimic human speech in captivity. They are characterised by highly glossy plumage, the presence of white patches in the primaries, similar to those of the genera *Mino* and *Ampeliceps*, a heavy bill with a strongly curved culmen, and fleshy yellow wattles on the head, found in no other genus (apart from the temporary black wattles of the African *Creatophora*). Their distribution includes India, Sri Lanka, Malaysia, Indochina, the Greater Sundas, Borneo, Palawan and the Lesser Sundas east to Alor. Within this area two species are generally recognised (Mayr and Greenway 1962, Sibley and Monroe 1990), Common Hill Myna *G. religiosa* and Sri Lanka Hill Myna *G. ptilogenys*, the latter endemic to Sri Lanka. We follow Bertram (1976) and Wolters (1980) in recognising the southwest Indian and Sri Lankan form *indica* as a distinct species, Southern Hill Myna *G. indica*, on the basis of its different calls and shape of the wattles, and its failure to interbreed with *G. religiosa* in captivity. We also give full specific status to Nias Hill Myna *G. robusta* and Enggano Hill Myna *G. enganensis*, both of which Ripley (1944) synonymised with *G. religiosa*. However, both taxa outlie considerably the range of variation seen in remaining races of Common Hill Myna, and as both occur on islands off the southern coast of Sumatra, there is unlikely to be genetic exchange with the mainland form. *G. robusta* is particularly distinctive, being a large, crow-like bird with a massive red bill and a considerably more extensive white wing patch, which extends on to the secondaries, than in other members of the genus, and specific status was advocated by Finsch (1899) and Riley (1929). *G. enganensis* is similar in size to *religiosa*, again with more extensive white in the primaries (although less marked than in the preceding species) which extends to the first (inner) primary. This species shows a more turquoise gloss and a stubby bill. Hoogerwerf (1963) accepted that differences in the pattern of the wattles were sufficient to confer sub-specific separation, but we consider the characters outlined above to be of more fundamental importance. Nevertheless, more information is needed on these island forms and data on behaviour and social structure should be sought in confirmation of our classification.

Hill mynas are generally resident birds that may sometimes undertake local movements, and the classification proposed here recognises several races of Common Hill Myna *G. religiosa*, with four outlying taxa that have differentiated substantially from this stock. In one of these, *G. indica*, behavioural (voice) differences have also been described and studies of the behaviour of the other species may reveal other differences between them and the Common Hill Myna. *G. r. batuensis*, of Batu Island which also lies of the southwestern coast of Sumatra, is much larger than other races of *religiosa* (but not as large as *robusta*) and was regarded as a distinct species by Finsch (1899). It has the wattle arrangement similar to that of *robusta*, but has the white wing patch extending only to the 3rd primary, as in other forms of *religiosa*; its physical distinctiveness appears not to warrant full specific status but study of its behaviour may change this viewpoint.

Gracula hill mynas are largely arboreal frugivores and this habit, and their spotted eggs, link them to mynas from further east in Sulawesi and New Guinea.

Acridotheres

Acridotheres mynas have sometimes been included in *Sturnus* (Marien 1950, Medway and Wells 1976), but they differ from that genus in being larger and more stockily built, and display different behaviour. *Acridotheres* mynas demonstrate some relationship to *Gracula* mynas in that most species have largely dark plumage, all species have white patches in the primaries and give resonant fluty calls, and some have limited bare skin around the eye. There are, however, many departures from the *Gracula* form. *Acridotheres* mynas have lost most of the gloss on the plumage, retaining it only on the head, and there is a tendency towards the development of paler areas of plumage, especially on the underparts. *Acridotheres* mynas are much more terrestrial and, associated with feeding on the ground, they show some development of the 'prying' or 'open bill probing' feeding technique, which involves pushing the closed bill into the ground and then opening it in order to make a hole to expose concealed prey; this ability involves modifications of the skull structure and musculature (Beecher 1978). Also associated with their more terrestrial life, *Acridotheres* mynas walk, whereas *Gracula* mynas hop. *Acridotheres* mynas nevertheless also eat fruit and frequently visit trees in flower to take nectar; several species have well-developed frontal crests and, after feeding on nectar, the crests of these birds can often be seen to be covered in pollen. The crest may thus have a role in pollination, suggesting a co-evolution between these birds and those tree genera to which they are primarily attracted. *Acridotheres* mynas further differ from the preceding genera in laying unmarked blue eggs, and *Acridotheres* mynas frequently indulge in bowing displays, used in courtship and at other times, whereas *Gracula* mynas appear to have no visual displays other than copulation solicitation (Bertram 1970).

The taxonomy of the 'crested' mynas is confused. Amadon (1943) recognised this and commented that they must have had a complicated evolutionary history in Indochina. These complications are still evident today, with distributional changes promoted by habitat change, especially deforestation and urbanization, and introductions. The confusion within the 'crested mynas' is exacerbated by the non-uniform use of English names. For example, *A. javanicus* has been referred to as White-vented Myna in Singapore (Hails 1987), while in central and northern parts of Thailand this species has been referred to as Crested Myna by Lekagul and Cronin (1974) but White-vented Myna by Boonsong and Round (1991). The latter authors referred 'crested' mynas of the Thai peninsula to Jungle Myna *A. fuscus*, while Medway and Wells (1976) attributed these birds to 'Jungle or Buffalo' Myna, with the specific name *mahrattensis*. Deignan (1945) used the English name Crested Myna for northern Thai birds, but allocated to them the scientific name *A. critatellus grandis*. The 'crested' mynas of central and northern Thailand are clearly different from those in Singapore (CJF, pers. obs.), and we refer the Thai birds to *A. grandis*, the Great Myna. In northeastern India, Choudhury (1991a) and Ripley et al. (1991) reported the occurrence of Orange-billed Jungle Mynas, to which they ascribed the specific name *javanicus*, following Ali and Ripley (1972); this is unlikely to be the Javan White-vented Myna, which is endemic to Java and Bali but which has been introduced to Sumatra and Singapore, and doubtless refers to *A. grandis*. Kang Nee (*in litt.*) considers that *javanicus*, *grandis* and *fuscus* all now occur in the Malaysian peninsula, with interbreeding and hybridisation between them.

In the taxonomy we adopt here, we depart from Mayr and Greenway (1962) and follow Sibley and Monroe (1990) in giving full specific status to *javanicus*, on the basis of its more uniform colour than *fuscus*, and its uniformly orange bill. *Acridotheres* mynas are surprisingly absent from Borneo but a geographically disjunct population occurs in southern Sulawesi; this form, *cinereus*, is distinctively pale. Amadon (1956) regarded this form, together with *javanicus*, as conspecific with *fuscus*. However, *javanicus* and *cinereus* are more similar morphologically to *grandis*, and Inskipp *et al.* (1996) treated these three as conspecific. We follow Sibley and Monroe (1990) in allocating full specific status to *grandis* and *javanicus*. Furthermore, we consider that the geographical and morphological distinctiveness of *cinereus* warrant its treatment as a full species, as advocated by Meyer and Wigglesworth (1898). This separation of *cinereus* from *javanicus* renders redundant the problem of nomenclatorial precedence raised by Sibley and Monroe (1993).

Our acceptance of Jungle Myna *A. fuscus*, White-vented Myna *A. javanicus*, Great Myna *A. grandis*, Pale-bellied Myna *A. cinereus*, Crested Myna *A. cristatellus* and Collared Myna *A. albocinctus* as full species represents our attempt to simplify terminology to what appears sensible at present, but we accept that studies of their behaviour, genetics, distribution and interbreeding, are needed and that these studies might modify our perception of their taxonomy in the future. Such studies may indicate that *A. f. mahrattensis* may warrant specific status as an endemic of southwest India, in the way that we feel *Gracula indica* does.

On the basis of voice, wing shape and pattern, leg colour and courtship behaviour, we follow Feare and Kang (1992) and include Black-winged Myna *melanopterus* in the genus *Acridotheres*; in all of these features *melanopterus* differs substantially from *Sturnus* species. Feare and Kang (1992) suggested that Vinous-breasted Myna *burmannicus*, considered by Sibley and Monroe (1990) to form a superspecies with *melanopterus*, might also be allocated to the genus *Acridotheres*. As yet there have been no studies of the social behaviour of *burmannicus*, but K. Komolphalin (*in litt.*) has informed us that it performs bowing movements, is round-winged with a wing pattern resembling that of other *Acridotheres* mynas, and its calls have the fluty quality of Common Myna *A. tristis*. We therefore place *burmannicus* alongside *melanopterus* in the genus *Acridotheres*. This represents a departure from Mayr and Greenway's (1962) and Sibley and Monroe's (1990) classification, where these two species were placed in the genus *Sturnus*. The colour differences between these species and more typical *Acridotheres* species in fact simply take further traits that already exist in this genus, for Jungle Myna has pale lower underparts and Common Myna has pale underparts and browner plumage.

Leucopsar

Bali Myna *Leucopsar rothschildi*, with all-white plumage except for black-tipped primaries and a black tip to the tail, takes to an extreme form the lightening of the plumage seen in several *Acridotheres* species: *tristis*, *burmannicus*, *melanopterus*. Bali Myna shares with *Acridotheres* species a stocky body with rounded wings and short tail, unspotted eggs, bare skin around the eye, and courtship and contact behaviour involving raising and lowering the head, and is clearly closely related to that genus. Wolters (1980) included both Black-winged and Vinous-breasted Mynas in the genus *Leucopsar*; all three species have erectile crests but this is much larger in Bali Myna. Stresemann (1912) considered it to be structurally close to Black-collared Myna *Gracupica nigricollis*. We retain Bali Myna in the monotypic genus *Leucopsar*, rather than linking it with *Acridotheres*, since the species is extreme in several ways: the crest is greatly elongated and erectile, much more so than in any *Acridotheres* species; the plumage is largely white and has lost the distinctive wing pattern of the *Acridotheres* genus, formed by white bases to the primaries contrasting with an otherwise dark wing; the bill and legs are not yellow as in *Acridotheres*, and are proportientely more massive; display movements are more pronounced, and rather than bowing involve movements of the head which can be exaggerated to include bobbing of the entire body; and song differs markedly from that of *Acridotheres*, lacking the fluty resonant quality of that genus.

Gracupica

Amadon (1943), Greenway and Mayr (1962) and Sibley and Monroe (1990) included Black-collared Myna *nigricollis* and Asian Pied Myna *contra* in the genus *Sturnus*, although Amadon (1943) recognised that his definition of *Sturnus* contained a numbers of diverse forms. Wolters (1980) retained several genera which these other authors had synonymised with *Sturnus*, and allocated *nigricollis* to the genus *Gracupica* and *contra* to the genus *Sturnopastor*. Both species show affinities to each other and show closer affinities to the genus *Acridotheres* than to *Sturnus*. They both have similarly pied plumage, although there are differences in detail, and both are unusual among the starling family in building large domed nests with a side entrance. Affinities to the genus *Acridotheres* are shown by: calls which resemble those of that genus; they consort mainly in pairs throughout the year although larger groups sometimes form; display during courtship and at other times includes bowing; in flight the wings are rounded, rather than pointed; both genera have bare skin around the eye and yellowish legs. Furthermore, Beecher (1978) claimed that *nigricollis* is clearly related to the genus *Acridotheres* in its skull structure and musculature, although its bill is long and more typical of the genus *Sturnus*. On these morphological and behavioural grounds we accept that these two species are close to *Acridotheres* and more remote from the genus *Sturnus*, and on the basis of their similarities to each other place them together in the genus *Gracupica*.

Temenuchus

Brahminy Starling *Temenuchus pagodarum* was included in the genus *Sturnus* by Amadon (1943), Greenway and Mayr (1962) and Sibley and Monroe (1990). It differs from typical *Sturnus* species in having a crest, bare skin behind the eye and more rounded wings. It is also less gregarious, usually living in pairs or family groups, like birds of the preceeding two genera, but it does congregate in larger numbers where food is plentiful and at communal night roosts (Ali and Ripley 1972). Although it spends much time feeding on the ground, it also forages arboreally, eating fruits and visiting flowers, and has a brush-tipped tongue adapted for taking nectar (Beecher 1978). There appear to be no good descriptions of courtship, but Henry (1971) and Tyagi and Lamba (1984) mentioned head movements, perhaps allying this species closer to the genera *Acridotheres* and *Gracupica*, rather than to *Sturnus* in which wing movements are more evident. Structurally, the skull of *pagodarum* differs from *Sturnus* species, in particular showing little adaptation for prying (Beecher 1978). Sontag (1992) noted similarities between the behaviour of Brahminy Starlings and Chestnut-tailed Starlings and considered them to be closely related. On the basis of this evidence, we feel that *pagodarum* should be retained in the monotypic genus *Temenuchus*, but accept that its affinities are unclear.

Sturnia

Amadon (1943), Greenway and Mayr (1962) and Sibley and Monroe (1990) included in the genus *Sturnus* a group of small, pointed-winged starlings which are largely arboreal, unlike more typical *Sturnus* which spend much time on the ground. These are Purple-backed Starling *Sturnia sturnina*, Red-cheeked Starling *S. philippensis,* White-shouldered Starling *S. sinensis,* Chestnut-tailed Starling *S. malabarica*, White-headed Starling *S. erythropygia* and White-faced Starling *S. albofrontata* (this species has been referred to as *S. senex* in most texts, but Mees (1997) demonstrated that the species was originally described by Layard under the specific name *albofrontata*). White-headed, White-faced and Chestnut-tailed Starlings form a superspecies, and further information on the behaviour of the southwest Indian form of Chestnut-tailed Starling *S. malabarica blythii* may suggest that it should be elevated to an endemic species of that area. Beecher (1978) found that these species (and others) differed from *Sturnus* species in having broader, shorter skulls which are less well adapted for prying. These features render these species sufficiently different from *Sturnus* species to be placed in a separate genus and, while Wolters (1980) allocated them to several genera, we prefer to treat them all as *Sturnia*.

Pastor

Rose-coloured Starling *Pastor roseus* was lumped, along with *Sturnia* and others, in the genus *Sturnus* by Amadon (1943) and by Sibley and Monroe (1990), but has been retained in the monotypic genus *Pastor* by Beecher (1978) and Wolters (1980). We follow the latter authors in retaining the genus *Pastor*. Its reduced specialisation for prying may in fact represent a specialisation to its breeding season diet, which consists predominantly of surface-dwelling grasshoppers and locusts, and it is notable that another species with a similar diet, the Wattled Starling *Creatophora cinerea*, shows a similar reduced development of the skull for prying. The Rose-coloured Starling's courtship display, involving parading on the ground, has presumably evolved in association with its habit of breeding in holes in the ground, rather than higher in trees, as in *Sturnus* species. It shares many features with the genera *Sturnia* and *Sturnus*, for example its formation of large flocks and colonial breeding, its strongly migratory habit, and the juvenile plumage is very similar to that of Common Starling *Sturnus vulgaris*. A similar juvenile plumage is also seen in some *Acridotheres* species, however, and other resemblances to that genus include a well-developed glossy crest on the crown and nape and an arched culmen.

Sturnus

In the genus *Sturnus*, the evolution of the skull structure and musculature as an adaptation for prying is taken to its extreme in the starlings and mynas. This is associated with the terrestrial habit of the *Sturnus* genus, and doubtless facilitated the expansion of the geographical distribution of these species out of the humid tropics of South-East Asia to the more arid lands to the north and northwest. We include in the genus *Sturnus* Red-billed Starling *S. sericeus*, White-cheeked Starling *S. cineraceus*, Common Starling *S. vulgaris* and Spotless Starling *S. unicolor*. Common and White-cheeked Starlings share many attributes of structure and behaviour and are ecological counterparts in the East and West Palearctic. Their similarities, especially in the structure of the skull and its musculature, and its advanced adaptation for prying led Beecher (1978) to regard them as a superspecies, although Wolters (1980) allied White-cheeked Starling with Asian Pied Myna in the genus *Sturnopastor*. Red-billed Starling is relatively poorly known and shows some affinities with *Acridotheres* species in its white bases to the primaries and yellow-orange legs. Wolters (1980) included it in the genus *Sturnopastor* with *cineraceus* and *contra*. However, in flight it has pointed wings, it associates in large flocks and its calls are reminiscent of those of Common Starlings and unlike those of *Acridotheres* species (G. Carey, *in litt.*). Common and Spotless Starlings are clearly closely related and the latter may represent a relict of a population that survived in a refugium during a retraction of the range of *vulgaris*. Now that their ranges overlap in southwest France and northeast Spain, limited interbreeding demonstrates their close relationship.

The genera of African starlings

Some species of African starlings have spectacularly iridescent plumage. This iridescence is produced by the structure of the melanin granules within the feathers, and the resulting blues and greens are structural colours, not based on pigments (Durrer and Villiger 1967, 1970). Since the morphological basis of the colour should be a more reliable indicator of relationship than the superficial appearance of the plumage, all the African starling species have been investigated using transmission electron microscopy to reveal the structural patterns within the feathers (Craig and Hartley 1985). These data, together with unpublished studies of the surface structure of feathers by scanning electron microscopy (M. Smith, pers. comm.) and current investigations of skeletal characters, have been used to reassess the traditional generic arrangements. An analysis of 48 morphological and behavioural characters using both PAUP and HENNIG86 suggests the relationships among the genera shown in Figure 4 (Craig, in press b).

Creatophora

This is the only African starling which shows close links with Asian starlings, in particular the *Sturnus–Acridotheres* group. This is most striking in its jaw musculature and feeding behaviour, as it is the only African species which can perform open-bill probing or prying (Zirkeln of German authors) in the grass mat . The bare facial skin of the male is also a characteristic shared with several Asian starlings, but otherwise not found in the African representatives. The melanin granules show the primitive type of structure and patterning, so this is not suggestive of possible relationships (Craig and Hartley 1985).

Speculipastor

Speculipastor bicolor is a little-known nomadic East African starling. In general appearance and sexual dimorphism it is most like *Grafisia torquata*, though this link is not supported by melanin granule characteristics (Craig and Hartley 1985). Amadon (1943) placed this species in the genus *Spreo*, but subsequently recognised the genus *Speculipastor* (Amadon 1956), originally described by Reichenow (1879).

Grafisia

First described from Cameroon by Reichenow (1909) as *Spreo torquatus*, *Grafisia torquata* is a starling of central African woodland. Later a specimen from Zaïre was described as a new species, *Stilbopsar leucothorax* by Chapin (1916), who placed it in the same genus as *S. (Poeoptera) kenricki* and *stuhlmanni*. Bates (1926) noted that the latter two species belong in *Poeoptera*, and argued that *torquatus* is not in the genus *Spreo*, particularly in view of its sexual dimorphism, and he erected the genus *Grafisia*. Amadon (1943) initially returned White-collared Starling to the genus *Spreo*, but later reinstated *Grafisia* (Amadon 1956). However, its relationships remain obscure. The feather melanin granules are of the primitive, solid type according to Durrer and Villiger (1970), but Craig and Hartley (1985) found them to be of the same type as those of the typical members of the genus *Spreo*.

Neocichla

The sole member of the genus *Neocichla* is endemic to the belt of central African woodland known as *Brachystegia*. This species was originally described as a babbler in the genus *Crateropus* (Bocage 1871), and Sharpe (Layard and Sharpe 1884) retained it in the family Timaliidae, but erected a new genus for it on the basis of the very short first primary and the length of the tail coverts. Amadon (1943) excluded it from the Sturnidae, although Friedmann (1930) had suggested that it might be a starling. Chapin (1948) argued that *Neocichla* was a starling on the basis of morphology, juvenile plumage and the reports of its behaviour, and predicted that it would be found to nest in tree holes. Subsequently Amadon (1956) included the genus *Neocichla* in the Sturnidae, and this has been generally accepted. The feather melanin granule structure provides no new information on its relationships (Craig and Hartley 1985), and it certainly warrants further study. As noted by Chapin (1948), characters such as the white tail spots and pale-coloured legs are more typical of Asian than African starlings.

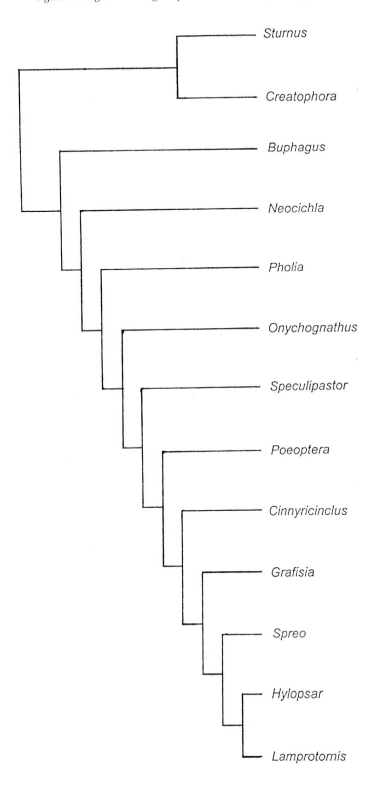

Figure 4. Diagram showing the possible relationships among the genera of African starlings

Cinnyricinclus

One of the most beautiful of all starlings is the male Amethyst Starling *Cinnyricinclus leucogaster*. This species has a unique feather melanin granule structure for the starling family, though similar to the arrangement found in peacocks *Pavo* sp. (Durrer and Villiger 1970, Craig and Hartley 1985). The female is dull-plumaged, but has a rufous patch in the wing feathers. Two other species have been included in the same genus, but we would prefer to place them in the genus *Pholia*.

Pholia

The genus *Pholia* was described by Reichenow (1900) for the species *Pholia hirundinea* (= *Pholidauges sharpii* Jackson 1898), and placed in the family Muscicapidae on the basis of the broad, flattened bill. The collector (Fuelleborn) reportedly wrote that the birds were seen flying in and out of holes in a steep rock-face, in the manner of swallows, and were apparently nesting there (Reichenow 1900). This observation must however refer to a different species. Later Reichenow (1903) placed the genus *Pholia* in the Sturnidae, with the single species *Pholia sharpii*.

Earlier Shelley (1889) had identified as *Pholidauges (Spreo) fischeri* a male specimen from Kilimanjaro. This is clearly the same species which Richmond (1897) described as *Pholidauges femoralis*. He commented that it was very similar in size to *Spreo fischeri* and *Cinnyricinclus leucogaster*, but it was unlikely to be the male of *S. fischeri* as Shelley (1889) had suggested. However, Reichenow (1903) placed *femoralis* in the genus *Spreo*, while Shelley (1906) used the genus *Cinnyricinclus* for *leucogaster*, *fischeri*, *sharpii* and *femoralis*.

Oberholser (1905) created a new genus *Arizelopsar* for the species *Pholidauges femoralis*, but the distinguishing features used are trivial, and no other authors have accepted this genus. Amadon (1943) placed the three species *femoralis*, *leucogaster* and *sharpii* in the genus *Cinnyricinclus*, although he admitted that *femoralis* and *sharpii* were much closer to each other than to *leucogaster* (Amadon 1956). Hall and Moreau (1970) retained these three species in the genus *Cinnyricinclus*, stressing the spotted juvenile plumage as a common characteristic. Sibley and Monroe (1990) and Dowsett and Forbes-Watson (1993) have also followed this arrangement. However, the feather melanin granule structure is very different (Craig and Hartley 1985), and together with the sexual dimorphism of Amethyst Starling, there are good grounds for placing them in separate genera, as was done by Sclater (1930).

Cosmopsarus

This genus formerly included two long-tailed species endemic to East Africa. Reichenow (1879) defined the genus by the bill shape, wing proportions and tail structure. He noted that species from this genus were similar to those of the genus *Lamprotornis* but were more slender with narrower rectrices, a smaller first primary, and were markedly different in colour (Reichenow 1903). Amadon (1943) included these two species in his enlarged genus *Spreo*, but later restored them to the genus *Cosmopsarus* (Amadon 1956). However, White (1962) placed both species in the genus *Spreo*. The close relationship between the brilliantly-coloured *C. regius* and the drab *C. unicolor* has never been questioned, and they have been grouped as members of a superspecies (Hall and Moreau 1970). However, the feather melanin granules of *C. regius* have the same structure and arrangement as those of *Lamprotornis* species, whereas those of *C. unicolor* are clearly different, like those of the typical members of the genus *Spreo* (Craig and Hartley 1985). Thus we propose transferring both species to these genera; such a radical re-arrangement is bound to stimulate debate and further study! Short *et al.* (1990) noted that *C. regius* and *unicolor* should not be placed in the same superspecies, but made no changes to the generic names, and Dowsett and Forbes-Watson (1993) retained both species in the same genus.

Lamprotornis

Lamprotornis is the largest genus of African starlings. Tail length is highly variable; formerly the group was split into the short-tailed *Lamprocolius* and long-tailed *Lamprotornis* (Hartlaub 1859, 1874, Sclater 1930). No recent authors have regarded this as good grounds for splitting the genus as long tails seem to have developed independently several times (Craig, in press a), and even Wolters (1975–82) includes 16 species in this genus, in eight subgenera. Stresemann (1925) argued that increasing tail length always produced a graduated tail, and even included *L. acuticaudus* in *L. chloropterus* on the basis of other similarities. Sibley and Ahlquist (1990) differ only in treating *L. (chloropterus) elisabeth* as a full species, and include some species usually placed in *Spreo* (see below). In a study of wing pterylography, Naik (1970) compared two species of *Lamprotornis* as defined here with members of the Asian genera *Aplonis*, *Acridotheres*, *Gracula* and *Sturnus*, but found no significant differences.

All *Lamprotornis* species are predominantly glossy blue or greenish dorsally, with a common pattern of hollow, oval, melanin granules arranged in a single layer close to the surface of the feather barbules, with other granules scattered within the barbule (Craig and Hartley 1985). The ventral surface may be dull, lacking iridescence, or coloured with brown or yellow pigments. On the basis of this definition, we would include in *Lamprotornis* four species formerly in the genus *Spreo* (i.e. *superbus, hildebrandti, shelleyi* and *pulcher*), as well as Golden-breasted Starling *Cosmopsarus regius* and Emerald Starling *Coccycolius iris*, together with 14 other species usually placed in this genus.

Oustalet (1879) erected the genus *Coccycolius* for a distinctive glossy starling from West Africa. Amadon (1943) placed it in *Lamprotornis*, as have many other authors, but he later recognised the genus *Coccycolius* (Amadon 1956). The melanin granule arrangement is unique in the African starlings, but can clearly be derived from the type found in *Lamprotornis* (Craig and Hartley 1985).

Hylopsar

The two glossy starlings *Lamprotornis cupreocauda* and *L. purpureiceps* have long been recognised as similar (cf. Hartlaub 1859, von Boetticher 1940, 1951). They were placed in a superspecies by Hall and Moreau (1970), and share a highly distinctive arrangement of solid, plate-like melanin granules (Craig and Hartley 1985). Thus similar colours have been produced by quite different internal structures, and we suggest that they should be placed in a separate genus until their relationships are clarified. For this purpose we have taken the name *Hylopsar*, introduced by von Boetticher (1940) for *purpureiceps* and subsequently used by Wolters (1975–82) as a subgenus for these two species.

Spreo

Membership of the genus *Spreo* has changed considerably over the years. Hartlaub (1859) used the genus *Notauges* for three species: *superbus* in one group, *bicolor* and *albicapillus* in another. In a later publication he retained these two groups, adding *chrysogaster* (= *pulcher*) to the first group (Hartlaub 1874). Oberholser (1930) created the new genus *Painterius* for *superbus* and *pulcher*, noting that *bicolor* and *fischeri* belonged together, while *albicapillus* was assigned to the genus *Poneropsar*. Sclater (1930) recognised six species in the genus *Spreo*, treating *shelleyi* as a subspecies of *hildebrandti*. Amadon (1943) included ten species, lumping the genera *Spreo*, *Cosmopsarus*, *Grafisia* and *Speculipastor*, but not recognising *shelleyi*. von Boetticher (1951) approved, but felt that Amadon had not gone far enough, and included all these genera in the genus *Lamprotornis*, using numerous subgenera. However, Amadon (1956) removed *Grafisia*, *Speculipastor* and *Cosmopsarus* from the genus *Spreo*, and followed this scheme in Peters' checklist (Amadon 1962). White (1962) recognised *shelleyi* as a separate species, and included *Cosmopsarus* in his genus *Spreo*. Clancey (1958) argued that the glossy members of the genus *Spreo* properly belonged in the genus *Lamprotornis*, and this was supported by Brooke (1971), who also proposed that *Cosmopsarus* should be included in the genus *Lamprotornis*. In Wolters (1975–82) *Spreo bicolor* is monotypic, as is *Poneropsar albicapillus*, while the other five species are placed in *Lamprospreo*, a genus created by Roberts (1922) to accommodate those species which he considered were closer to *Lamprotornis* than to *Spreo*. Short et al. (1990) retained a broad genus *Spreo*, on the grounds that no direct relationships with particular species or groups within the genus *Lamprotornis* have been demonstrated, while they considered the postures and behaviour of *superbus* and *hildebrandti* to be unlike those of *Lamprotornis* species. Finally Sibley and Monroe (1990) restrict the genus *Spreo* to the three species *bicolor, fischeri* and *albicapillus*, noting that DNA-DNA hybridization data support the placement of *superbus* in the genus *Lamprotornis*; this arrangement is also followed by Dowsett and Forbes-Watson (1993).

So currently seven species are generally recognised, but four of these have melanin granules identical in all respects to those of the genus *Lamprotornis*. Three others, *Spreo bicolor, S. fischeri* and *S. albicapillus*, share with *Cosmopsarus unicolor* round, hollow melanin granules which are scattered within the barbules without any stratification (Craig and Hartley 1985). We suggest that the genus *Spreo* should be restricted to these four species, three of which have hardly been studied.

Onychognathus

The red-winged starlings, black birds with rufous primaries in both sexes, were formerly divided into several genera. Hartlaub (1859) used the genus *Onychognathus* only for *fulgidus*, the genus *Oligomydrus* for *tenuirostris*, and the genus *Pilorhinus* for *albirostris*, with all the other species then known in the genus *Amydrus*. Subsequently he transferred *nabouroup* to the genus *Pyrrhocheira*. Sharpe (1891) created the monotypic genus *Galeopsar* for the distinctive species *salvadorii*. Reichenow (1903) transferred *tenuirostris* to the genus *Cinnamopterus*, and retained the genera *Galeopsar, Onychognathus, Pilorhinus, Pyrrhocheira* and *Amydrus*. This arrangement was soon criticised by Neumann (1904), who noted that the supposed generic characters were of little value, and he placed all species except *Galeopsar salvadorii* and *Pilorhinus albirostris* in the genus *Amydrus*.

Sclater (1930) retained these two monotypic genera, but returned all the other species to the earlier genus *Onychognathus*. Subsequent authors have included these two aberrant Ethiopian species in *Onychognathus* (Amadon 1943, 1962, Sibley and Monroe 1990), and a few have even expanded the genus to include those species usually placed in *Poeoptera* (von Boetticher 1951, Wolters 1975–82).

The eleven red-winged starlings in the present genus *Onychognathus* are medium to large birds, their plumage predominantly black with some gloss. The melanin granules are round, solid and scattered within the barbules, which represents the primitive condition (Craig and Hartley 1985). The genus is characterised by pigmented remiges in both sexes, forming a conspicuous reddish wing patch in flight. In one species, *O. nabouroup*, the inner vanes of the remiges are pale-coloured, so that in flight the wing-patch appears white. Females are duller, often grey, on the head, except in *O. frater* and *O. nabouroup*. Young birds initially resemble the male, and later acquire female plumage.

Nine species are African, one is endemic to the continental island of Socotra (*O. frater*), and one occurs east of the Red Sea rift, on the Arabian peninsula extending north to Israel (*O. tristramii*). Ethiopia has apparently been a centre of speciation, with three species endemic to this highland area. A preliminary phylogenetic analysis by Craig and Hulley (1992), based on morphology and some biological characters, shows that the three Ethiopian-based species *O. albirostris*, *O. blythii* and *O. salvadorii* form a cluster, together with the Sudanese and West African species *O. neumanni*. This last species was formerly treated as a race of *O. morio* (see Craig 1988a). *O. morio* is linked with *O. tenuirostris*, while the forest tree-hole nesters *O. fulgidus* and *O. walleri* are paired. The remaining species are not consistently associated with any other members of the genus.

Poeoptera

These three forest species, one in lowland forest and two in East African highland forests, are included in the genus *Poeoptera*. Snow (1981) lists *Poeoptera* as one of the specialised frugivorous genera of the African tropics. Bonaparte (1854) described the genus as close to the chats, but gave no reasons for this curious decision. Reichenow (1893) described the genus *Stilbopsar* on the basis of bill and wing characteristics, and noted that this genus was close to some of the red-winged starlings. Later Sclater (1930) placed the two short-tailed species *kenricki* and *stuhlmanni* in *Stilbopsar*, using *Poeoptera* only for *lugubris*. Amadon (1943) used *Poeoptera* for all three species, and noted that difference in tail structure was all that separated *lugubris* from the other two species. He also suggested a relationship to *Onychognathus*, the red-winged starlings (Amadon 1956), and Wolters (1975–82) included these species in *Onychognathus*, using *Poeoptera* and *Stilbopsar* as subgenera, following von Boetticher (1951). However, White (1962), Sibley and Ahlquist (1990), and Dowsett and Forbes-Watson (1993) have recognised *Poeoptera*, which can be characterised by rufous primary remiges in females only, and a highly distinctive feather melanin granule structure (Craig and Hartley 1985).

Buphagus

The generic name *Buphagus* indicates the close association of oxpeckers with cattle, noted by the first observers. Although these distinctive birds are sometimes placed in their own family Buphagidae (e.g. Clancey 1980), they are generally accepted as aberrant starlings. Amadon (1943, 1956) placed them in a separate subfamily within the Sturnidae, but both Wolters (1975- 82) and Sibley & Monroe (1990) included them in the Sturnidae without comment. No DNA-DNA hybridization data are available, and the melanin granule structure showed the primitive condition shared with numerous other starlings (Durrer and Villiger 1970). Beecher (1978) noted similarities in the jaw musculature of the Asian starling *Scissirostrum dubium* and Red-billed Oxpecker *Buphagus erthrorhynchus*, and in his phylogenetic tree of the family, he placed *Buphagus* as a specialised offshoot of a primitive glossy starling ancestor. This resemblance may however be convergence, since both genera use similar 'scissoring' movements of the beak, which presumably requires similar musculature. Raikow (1985) reported that dissection of the hindlimb musculature showed that the leg muscles of *Buphagus* were similar to those of other starlings, but two muscles showed modifications which would increase the grasping power of the feet. The karyotype of *B. erythrorhynchus* proved to be typical of the Asian and European representatives of *Sturnus* examined previously, suggesting that this could be a conservative character within the Sturnidae (Capanna and Geralico 1982).

DISTRIBUTION, HABITAT USE AND SOCIAL BEHAVIOUR

Distribution

The starling family is restricted to the Old World, except where man has introduced species elsewhere. Within the Old World, starlings have radiated into many geographic regions and occupied many habitats within them. Geographically, they range over the whole of Africa and west to the Azores, Europe north to *c.* 68°N, Asia north to *c.* 65°N, Japan and the Kurile Islands, the Indian subcontinent, Indonesia, New Guinea, islands of Micronesia east to *c.* 165°E, Melanesia south to *c.* 32°S, Polynesia east to *c.* 160°W, and in Australasia extend into northern Queensland. Within this range occur species of wide distribution, such as Amethyst Starling that occurs over most of sub-Saharan Africa and Common Starling that occurs over much of Europe and Asia, and species restricted to small islands.

This range embraces a wide diversity of habitats and starlings have penetrated most of them; these include forests, both evergreen and deciduous, humid and dry, and montane and lowland, although the absence of starlings in the highland forests of New Guinea is notable. Starlings also inhabit more open environments, including forest edge and open woodland, savanna, riparian valleys, arid semi-desert and of course cultivated areas.

Representatives are found in montane forest on Pacific islands, but these species are island endemics and most species in Oceania, New Guinea and Indonesia tend to be birds of the lowlands, where they inhabit forest, forest edge and clearings. Many of these species appear to be resident. In India and mainland South-East Asia, starlings occur throughout, with species in montane forest and extending into the Himalayan foothills; here again, however, most species occur in the lower areas, but including the Deccan plateau. The lowland starlings of India, Indochina and the large islands of Java and Sumatra have developed specialisations that enable them to exploit terrestrial food sources and this has been accompanied by a more insectivorous or even omnivorous habit. The evolution of these traits paved the way for starlings to enter more open, and especially more arid, areas and this enabled some forms to colonise the vast steppes of southeastern Europe and Central Asia, and ultimately the temperate grasslands so extensively expanded by man's activities. These areas possess rich food resources in terms of both invertebrates and fruit, but these resources are highly seasonal in their availability, and in response to this seasonality the starlings that colonised these more northerly areas evolved long-distance migrations.

These migrations are generally north-south, with birds that breed in eastern Europe and Asia returning to the tropics or subtropics in winter. In western Europe, Common Starlings sometimes winter to the southwest, or even west, of their breeding area and some populations, towards the west and southwest of their breeding area, are resident. After breeding, the young of several of the species that breed at higher latitudes undergo a dispersal, sometimes into habitats such as marshes and moorlands, which are not normally exploited by them. Some of these dispersals can be highly directional, e.g. Swiss-breeding Common Starlings move northwest to the North Sea and Atlantic seaboard prior to undertaking their autumn migration to the south. In India, Chestnut-tailed Starlings undertake movements, possibly migrations, so that at certain times of year the distinctive races *Sturnus malabarica malabarica* and *S. m blythii* may be found in the same area, even in mixed flocks (Ali and Ripley 1972); the nature of these movements is not understood. Brahminy Starling also undertakes movements in the monsoon, but again these are not fully understood except for the movement of northern populations which are known to be summer visitors to this breeding area. Spot-winged Starling is both an altitudinal and an east-west migrant, breeding in the western Himalayan foothills and migrating east through Nepal and Sikkim to winter commonly in Assam. This species is often associated with Chestnut-tailed Starlings both in the breeding and non-breeding areas.

Within Africa also, there are forest starlings and savanna starlings, and birds whose range is centred on high, rocky areas, although they will forage in various surrounding habitats. In contrast to Eurasia, only two species, African Pied Starling and Wattled Starling, occur regularly in treeless, grassy areas. The birds of high rocky ground may be found above 4000 m, and undergo extensive altitudinal movements, even on a daily basis in species such as Slender-billed Red-winged Starling. This group also includes several species which may be found in arid, desert areas. The forest starlings fall into two clear groups: birds of lowland forest, and those of montane forest. They are all primarily birds of the forest canopy, and only one species, the Black-bellied Glossy Starling of the coastal belt, is regularly found at low levels within the forest. Most of the African starlings occur within the savanna vegetation zone, and within this broad category they may be found in all areas from moist to arid regions.

The forest starlings are primarily West and Central African in their distribution, with three montane forest species in East Africa and only a single species ranging from eastern to southern Africa, in coastal forest. Purple-headed Glossy and Coppery-tailed Starlings show a distribution suggesting separation of the parental population and subsequent speciation when the forest was subdivided into western and eastern blocks at the Dahomey Gap in West Africa (Hall and Moreau 1970). The other lowland forest species today show a continuous distribution in the central area, with no morphological differences to confirm any past separation. The two East African montane species, Kenrick's and Stuhlmann's Starlings are separated by the Rift Valley, yet a third species, Waller's Red-winged Starling, has populations on both sides of the Rift Valley and also occurs on the Mount Cameroon massif in West Africa. This implies a longer history for Waller's Red-winged Starling, with a former distribution over areas which today represent unsuitable habitat.

The starlings of rocky habitats include Tristram's Red-winged Starling, apparently isolated on the Arabian peninsula by the formation of the Red Sea rift, and a species endemic to the island of Socotra. In this group, three species have a distribution centred on Ethiopia and another is restricted to eastern Africa. The most widespread member of the group is Red-winged Starling, with a range from temperate South Africa to Ethiopia, although the West African populations, formerly treated as a race of Red-winged Starling, are here regarded as a separate species, Neumann's Red-winged Starling, derived from one of the other Ethiopian species (Craig 1988a).

One savanna species, Amethyst Starling, is the most widespread African starling, with breeding populations in western, eastern, and southern Africa. Two other species, Greater and Lesser Blue-eared Glossy Starlings, also range over these three regions, but their southern African distribution is much more restricted than that of Amethyst Starling. The remaining savanna-woodland birds show four general patterns of occurrence: West African, in some cases extending as far east as the Nile valley; East African; Central African in the *Brachystegia* vegetation belt; and southern African, extending northwards to Central or East Africa. This group contains several species endemic to eastern Africa, with some such as Ashy Starling having an extremely restricted total range. The Rift Valley and the Ethiopian highlands seem to define the northern and western limits of an area in which these endemics have evolved; by contrast there is only a single endemic of southern African origin, African Pied Starling (Craig 1985). Pale-winged Starling, now virtually restricted to southern Africa, may have descended from an Angolan ancestor (Craig and Hulley 1992).

The movements of starlings within Africa are still poorly understood, although detailed seasonal data for several countries are now available in the form of bird atlases. The most recent attempt at a synthesis of such movements by Curry-Lindahl (1981) did little to advance our knowledge, and the best synopsis of migration within Africa remains the account by Chapin (1932). He mentioned the two species in which migration is best documented, Splendid Glossy Starling and Amethyst Starling. Traylor (1971) provides a good picture of the movements of Amethyst Starling, and these show some resemblance to the regional migrations of Red-billed Quelea *Quelea quelea* (Ward 1971, Elliott 1990), with the rainfall regime in different parts of Africa determining the movements between breeding and non-breeding areas. The Amethyst Starling's savanna woodland habitats are highly seasonal in terms of rainfall, and thus food availability, but its distribution does not extend into any temeperate regions. There is a small inter-continental component to its migration, with birds visiting the southern Arabian peninsula to breed.

In marked contrast to most other migratory species, Splendid Glossy Starling is found in tropical forest at all seasons. In this habitat many frugivores show irregular movements related to food abundance, but it seems clear that this species is a true migrant, at least in the southern populations, which are breeding visitors to Zambia and southern Zaïre. Much further study is required to provide a full picture of its movements.

The two species of semi-arid areas in East Africa, Magpie Starling and Hildebrandt's Starling, apparently show regular migratory movements linked to rainfall (Lewis and Pomeroy 1989). Other African starlings may be nomadic in the non-breeding season, but their movements are too localised and erratic to justify the term migration. This is supported by a detailed analysis of the seasonal occurrence of Wattled Starling, based on both museum specimens and on data from bird atlas schemes (Craig 1996).

Habitat use and social behaviour

Starlings show a wide variety of social behaviours, some of which vary with habitat and geographical location. Social behaviour during breeding is described in the chapter on breeding and its associated activities, while here we discuss social behaviour during activities that are not directly related to breeding, but are related to habitat use.

Few starlings live a solitary existence, Brown-winged and Shelley's Starlings being the only well-documented cases in which solitary breeding is usual, but out of the breeding season the latter species associates in flocks (Britton 1980). Others for which solitary behaviour has been described are mainly species living on islands, such as Mountain Starling and Pohnpei Mountain Starling, and which live in the forest canopy. These are comparatively rare and unknown species and our impression of their lack of social activity may reflect their scarcity or the difficulty of seeing them. The majority of Asian and Pacific starlings, including most species of *Aplonis*, and many African species display tendencies to be more gregarious, at least in some situations.

Most members of the genus *Aplonis* are largely frugivorous but also include insects in the diet. They are generally found in pairs or small groups but some gather in larger numbers at particularly good food sources, e.g. fruiting trees. Two species, Shining Starling and Asian Glossy Starling, depart from the typical *Aplonis* social behaviour in that they regularly occur in large flocks, and also roost communally in large assemblages at night. These traits are associated with a more opportunistic diet in these two species, and also with a geographical range encompassing larger land masses than in other species.

The members of the largely frugivorous genera *Mino*, *Basilornis*, *Streptocitta* and *Ampeliceps* also generally associate in pairs, although Yellow-faced Myna regularly feeds in larger flocks and sometimes groups of over 200 birds roost together at night. The monotypic and somewhat aberrant Sulawesi endemics, Flame-browed Starling and Grosbeak Myna, also frequently form large flocks; in the latter species this may be associated with their extreme form of colonial breeding, and the constant vocalisation within feeding flocks doubtless serves to maintain flock cohesion. The significance of the greater propensity of these two largely frugivorous species to form flocks will, however, be elucidated only when more is known of their general biology. Hill mynas tend to show a somewhat greater plasticity in behaviour in that, although largely frugivorous and feeding and roosting in pairs or small family groups, they demonstrate opportunism by, at times, congregating in large flocks to feed in fruiting or flowering trees.

The emphasis on opportunism is taken further by the *Acridotheres* and *Gracupica* mynas, and this is accompanied by a more omnivorous diet, involving a much higher proportion of insects and other animal matter and a greater tendency to feed on the ground. Terrestrial feeding has involved a switch from hopping, the form of locomotion used by arboreal frugivores, to walking and running. In these genera we also see the development of prying, the technique that permits the procurement of food items by probing in the surface vegetation or even into the soil. The ability to employ this feeding action has involved modifications of skull shape, eye position and movements, and jaw musculature. These developments have also been accompanied by changes in social behaviour, and although these mynas associate in pairs throughout the year, pairs coalesce into large flocks whenever suitable concentrations of food appear. These species usually roost communally at night (except when breeding), sometimes in huge assemblages and often in company with other starling species. *Acridotheres* and *Gracupica* mynas are also highly vocal, using a wide repertoire of calls throughout the day and indulging in intensive bouts of singing during preparation for roosting and during roost departure in the morning; the function of this song in roosts and pre-roost assemblies is not known. The adaptations that facilitated the opportunism of these mynas in exploiting transient abundances of food also permitted the birds to take advantages of similar locally abundant but transient food sources made available by man. These food sources take many forms - cultivation of land, ripening crops grown in monocultures, abundances of flowering and fruiting trees, facilities for storing and disposing of human waste - and the act of creating human settlements and their associated facilities has often involved the removal of forest and the creation of open ground dominated by herbaceous vegetation, thus making available the kind of habitat that these mynas are pre-adapted to exploit. In consequence, these mynas often live in close association with man.

The six species of *Sturnia* retain a more arboreal habit but nevertheless have a broad diet, including insects, fruit and seeds, and are also opportunistic in their exploitation of temporary superabundances of food. While White-faced and White-headed Starlings are island endemics and probably sedentary, other members of the genus are more mobile. Chestnut-tailed Starling undertakes local movements allowing it to capitalise on seasonally available food, while Red-cheeked, Purple-backed and White-shouldered Starlings exploit seasonally abundant food supplies, especially insects, in temperate regions by migrating north to breed. This trait is taken to its extreme by Rose-coloured Starlings which, in the breeding season, rely upon insect swarms, especially grasshoppers and locusts, in the more arid regions of Central Asia and eastern Europe. This is paralleled in Africa by Wattled Starling, whose movements are more nomadic in their exploitation of insect infestations, again primarily grasshoppers and locusts. As soon as breeding is over, these species revert to a broader diet, including fruits and seeds whose availability is temporary. In association with their exploitation of ephemeral resources, these species form large flocks and roost communally.

In the genus *Sturnus*, Common and White-cheeked Starlings have combined the opportunism and terrestrial habit seen in *Acridotheres* species with northward migration to breed, enabling them to exploit the spring flush of surface and sub-surface insects in temperate grasslands. Their opportunism also permits them to capitalise on other temporary superabundances of food made available by man's agricultural activities and his by-products. After the breeding season, juvenile and adult Common Starlings tend to segregate but both age groups become more omnivorous. In migratory populations both adults and young leave the breeding areas, form flocks and begin to roost communally at night. Communal roosts are largest in winter and at this time adults and 1st-winter birds roost together. The behaviour associated with communal roosting is spectacular and complex, however, involving assembly in ever larger flocks by birds approaching the roost site, coordinated aerial manoeuvres immediately prior to entry, much vocalisation while settling in the roost and before departure, segregation of age and sex classes within the roost and during morning departure, and extreme synchronisation of exoduses of groups of birds during departure (Summers and Feare 1995). The significance of this behaviour is not fully understood.

African starlings are mostly omnivorous, feeding opportunistically on whatever food is most readily available, and even some forest canopy species, which have been categorised as specialist frugivores by Snow (1981), take many insects as shown by their stomach contents. Nevertheless, there is certainly a division between arboreal species, with proportionately short legs and a large component of fruit in the diet, and the longer-legged terrestrial foragers which take a high proportion of animal food. As with Asian species, African starlings take seeds on occasion but none can be termed granivorous.

The most specialised African starlings, with respect to diet, are the oxpeckers, which feed almost exclusively on ticks and other ectoparasites plucked or combed from the body surface of large mammals. Using similar movements, they also feed on blood and body fluids from their hosts. Their legs and claws are modified for clinging in woodpecker-like posture, while the bill shape is distinctive and associated with the stereotyped feeding movements. Three other starlings of rocky areas, with relatively short legs and strong grasping claws have regular grooming associations with ungulates in Africa and Arabia: Red-winged, Pale-winged and Tristram's Red-winged Starlings (Gargett 1975, Tilson 1977, Yosef and Yosef 1991). However, some predominantly terrestrial starlings, such as African Pied Starling (Craig 1987) and the *Acridotheres* mynas will also remove ticks from both domestic and wild mammals.

African starlings are also sociable, to varying degrees, outside the breeding season. Commonly, family groups form at the end of the breeding period and in cooperative groups, e.g. in African Pied Starling, members of a breeding unit remain together throughout the year (AC, pers. obs.). These groups may link up while foraging to form flocks of up to 100 birds in many species, and in a few cases very large flocks may form at roosts; these often assemble from a wide area and are clearly not associated as feeding groups during the day. More than 1,000 birds may be found in roosts of Wattled Starlings (Liversidge 1961), African Pied Starlings (Every 1975), Lesser Blue-eared Glossy Starlings (A J Tree, pers. comm.), Purple Glossy Starlings (Thonnerieux *et al.* 1989), Burchell's Glossy Starlings (R K Brooke, pers. comm.) and Red-winged Starlings (AC, pers. obs.). The largest assemblages may be those of Splendid Glossy Starlings, for which Brosset and Erard (1986) reported that nocturnal roosts in Gabon during the dry season may contain tens of thousands of birds.

The sexually dimorphic Amethyst Starling seems to be the only species in which the sexes may form separate flocks (Traylor 1971). Long-tailed Glossy Starlings in savanna may join members of other bird families in mixed species feeding flocks (Moynihan 1978), and so do Splendid Glossy Starlings in forest (Prigogine 1978). These associations are assumed to provide extra security against predators, but there have been few studies of the correlates of mixed species flocking in Africa. Ground-feeding starlings may be found alongside other sympatric starlings, or birds such as weavers, and in this situation there may also be benefits in awareness of predators. Wattled Starlings sometimes roost in association with Greater and Lesser Blue-eared Glossy Starlings and, in South Africa, with African Pied Starlings (Liversidge 1961), but in this case the key factor is probably the choice of similar roosting habitat.

Vocalisations

Starlings are not normally thought of as great songsters, compared to families such as the thrushes whose voices are more musical to our ears. Nevertheless, the song of Common Starling is very complex and has been the subject of much research in recent years (for a review see Eens, 1977). Motifs from a captive bird were evidently used as a theme in a score by the composer Mozart (West and King 1990).

Vocalisation plays an important role in intra-specific communication, and during the breeding season is used by males to advertise status and possession of a nest site to females, but it may also attract potential rival males to the area (Mountjoy and Lemon 1991). Song is also used outside the breeding season. Many African starlings gather in trees during the middle of the day or at other times, and vocalise in 'choirs' for long periods. It is not known whether both sexes are involved, nor whether such choruses have any special function in the social organisation of the species. In winter, flocks of Common Starlings may be found throughout the day in the tops of bare trees near good food sources, and such flocks keep up a constant cacophony of song. Both sexes participate and although the function of this song is not known, Summers and Feare (1995) have suggested that it may be used by overflying birds to assess the extent of competition likely to be encountered if these birds attempted to feed at the site.

Many species of starling are also vocal in their communal night roosts, especially as the birds settle at the roost site and as they prepare to depart in the morning. Where birds roost in city centres, the noise made by the birds is sometimes regarded as a nuisance of sufficient importance to warrant some form of control, e.g. as in urban roosts of Common Starlings, and Common and White-vented Mynas. In Common Starlings, both sexes are known to participate in this song but its function is uncertain; however, it does seem to play a role in perch acquisition and defence (CJF, pers. obs.).

In Red-winged Starling, the musical whistling calls serve for communication between the members of a pair, and are likely to be individually distinct. Duetting has been noted between members of a pair in Brahminy Starlings (Sontag 1985b) and in Rüppell's Long-tailed Glossy Starling in Kenya

(Dittami 1987). Most starlings have distinctive flight calls in their vocabulary, but harsh alarm calls are very similar between species and are mutually recognisable. Mammals, such as the hosts of the oxpeckers, and the monkeys found alongside ground-feeding starlings in East Africa, can also learn to respond to starling alarm calls (Hauser 1988).

Hill mynas are renowned for their abilities to imitate human speech in captivity, but in the wild they do not imitate the calls of other species but do imitate the calls of neighbouring hill mynas (Bertram 1970). Sonographic analysis of their mimicry of the human voice shows that it is a very accurate representation of the trainer's voice (Klatt and Stefanski 1974). Vocal mimicry has been reported for several African starlings in the field (Vernon 1973) and is well-known in Common Starling (Hindmarsh 1984, Hausberger *et al.* 1991). Common Starlings are also capable of mimicking human speech but this ability seems to depend upon a very close bond between the bird and its foster parent (West *et al.* 1983). There is now clear evidence that Common Starlings are unusual among birds in continuing to learn new song elements, from sounds in their natural environment, throughout life (Bohner *et al.* 1990, Eens *et al.* 1992). Recently, neurological studies have identified the brain areas involved in such learning in this species (Uno *et al.* 1991).

BREEDING

Nest sites

Most starlings nest in holes, in trees, cliffs, river banks, rock screes, and also in holes that become available in man's artefacts, such as house roofs, walls and other structures, and in nestboxes. Some forest species nest in cavities found in the tangles of epiphytic ferns and other plants. Many species often nest in holes made by other species, especially woodpeckers (Picidae), barbets (Capitonidae) and kingfishers (Alcedinidae), but also other hole-nesting species like Sand Martins *Riparia riparia*; previously used holes may be adopted by starlings, or owners may be usurped from freshly made ones. In Africa, old nests of White-billed Buffalo Weavers *Bubalornis albirostris* may be used by Chestnut-bellied Starlings, while Superb Starlings sometimes breed in old nests of Red-billed Buffalo Weavers *B. niger* and Rufous-tailed Weavers *Histurgops ruficauda*. A few starlings make their own holes; Bank Mynas and African Pied Starlings do so regularly and Common Starlings have been recorded doing so on rare occasions, in areas where other cavities are scarce and where substrates are sufficiently soft. The Grosbeak Myna of Sulawesi bores its own holes in dead trees, woodpecker fashion, but as this species is densely colonial the occupied parts of trees become riddled with holes, weakening the trees (Wiles and Masala 1987). The Magpie Starling, of northeastern Africa, is unusual in nesting inside termite mounds.

A few species have foresaken hole-nesting. Black-collared and Asian Pied Mynas and Brown-winged, Wattled, White-crowned, Fischer's and Chestnut-bellied Starlings build bulky domed nests in trees and bushes, and Common Mynas and Superb Starlings sometimes do so. These nests usually have side entrances. Common Myna also sometimes builds cup-shaped nests, but this species most frequently nests in holes. Shining and Yellow-eyed Starlings, of New Guinea and Queensland, are unique among the starlings in building pendulous nests that hang from the branches of trees and are reminiscent of the nests of weaver birds (Ploceidae). Some of the red-winged starlings *Onychognathus* build cup-shaped nests on ledges, usually on cliffs but Red-winged and Tristram's Starlings are increasingly nesting on buildings, and Slender-billed Red-winged Starling achieves extra protection by nesting behind waterfalls.

Nest

Although most starlings nest in cavities, the majority of species build bulky nests inside the cavities, suggesting that hole-nesting is a secondary acquisiton in starlings. The nest is normally constructed from dried grasses, fine twigs, leaves and sometimes man-made products, often with a lining of finer materials including hair, feathers and soft vegetation. The amount of material used in nest construction is related to the size of the cavity to be filled, and also to the requirement for insulation; nests in colder regions tend to be larger than those in warmer regions, and some tropical species use very little nest material. Those species of red-winged starling that build cup-shaped nests incorporate mud into the structure.

In addition to these basic constituents, some species add other materials whose function is uncertain. Many *Acridotheres* mynas place pieces of sloughed snake skin in the nest, as do a few African glossy starlings, and ungulate dung is included in the nests of Red-billed Oxpeckers, Amethyst and Cape Glossy Starlings. Several species, both in Africa and Eurasia, add fresh green leaves, and sometimes flowers, to the nest lining and Clark and Mason (1985) proposed that Common Starlings selected plants that contained aromatic chemicals with insecticidal properties for this purpose. There has been much debate over the efficacy of this tactic in defence against insect parasites in the nests, and in Common Starlings the behaviour ceases before egg-laying, while nests are most susceptible to a parasite fauna when chicks are in the nest. The carrying of fresh green plant material into a nest by a male of this species appears to stimulate a female to follow, and this behaviour may thus also play a role in pair formation.

Eggs

The background colour of the eggs of most species is a shade of blue, and in most genera the eggs are marked with spots and blotches of a darker colour. The eggs are thus typical of birds which nest in exposed positions and this provides further evidence that hole-nesting in starlings is a secondary development and that starlings are derived from birds that built open, cup-shaped nests. In the genera *Acridotheres*, *Leucopsar*, *Gracupica*, *Sturnia*, *Temenuchus*, *Pastor*, *Creatophora* and *Sturnus*, however, the eggs are generally unmarked and resemble more closely birds with a more obligate hole-nesting habit.

Parental care of eggs and young

From those species for which there is adequate information, it appears that both members of the pair participate in rearing the young to independence. Both sexes participate in nest construction and in feeding the young, but it is in incubation that there is a dichotomy between Asian and African starlings. Apart from in Wattled Starlings and the two oxpeckers, in all African Starlings the female alone incubates, the male perching nearby, often warbling for long periods. In only a few African starling species has the male been seen to feed the female on the nest. In Asian Starlings, on the other hand, males participate in the care of the eggs by covering them for a part of the day, while the female incubates for most of the day and at night. In Common Starlings, and possibly others, the male does not incubate *sensu strictu* and has a poorly developed incubation patch; his role in sitting on the eggs is to reduce the rate of heat loss of eggs, rather than to apply heat to them (K Westerterp, in Feare 1984).

When feeding young, the limited information available indicates that Asian frugivorous starlings deliver food both by carrying food items in the bill and by regurgitation. The frequency of the latter may be underestimated, however, as detailed observations of food delivery have been made on only a few species. For example, casual observations indicate food carrying by Atoll and Micronesian Starlings, while more detailed observations of Shining Starlings showed that adults both regurgitated and delivered food in the bill. Common Hill Mynas usually feed nestlings by regurgitation but occasionally carry food in the bill. In the genera *Acridotheres*, *Sturnia*, and *Sturnus*, however, most food is carried in the bill although Red-cheeked Starlings sometimes regurgitate food for nestlings. In Africa, all starlings whose provisioning of nestlings has been observed carry food in the bill and do not appear to regurgitate. Starlings do not possess a crop and may not have a mechanism to prevent digestion of food items in transit, so that those species whose nestling diet is almost entirely insectivorous may be forced to carry food in the bill to prevent damage to such easily digested prey.

Starlings in most genera have been recorded removing the faeces of nestlings from the nest. This behaviour may be important from two standpoints, firstly to ensure that nest material remains dry and retains its insulating properties, especially before the young have developed homoiothermy, and secondly to avoid the accumulation in the nest of droppings that could provide a growth medium for pathogens and coprophagous infauna. The widespread occurrence of this behaviour in the family is doubtless related to nesting in holes, whose availability may be limited and which are therefore often re-used for successive broods both within and between breeding seasons. Starlings also frequently remove old nest material before starting to build a new nest and this behaviour may also help to prevent the build-up of potentially harmful organisms.

Social behaviour during breeding

Coloniality

Most starlings breed in colonies or in clusters of nests. In some species, such as Grosbeak Myna, Shining, Rose-coloured and Wattled Starlings, colonies are obvious due to the close proximity of nests, which in Rose-coloured Starlings may coalesce. This sometimes applies to other species, for example when several pairs of Asian Pied Mynas or White-crowned Starlings nest together in one bush; in the latter species, nests may even be joined together. Where the distribution of suitable nest cavities precludes breeding in dense colonies, colonial behaviour may nevertheless be evident. This is seen in Common Starlings, where pairs that breed in tree holes or nestboxes that are widely distributed in open woodland display a remarkable synchrony in the initiation of their first clutches each year (Feare 1984); this synchrony is presumably achieved through the birds' social behaviour although the exact mechanism is not understood. Nevertheless, such synchrony indicates that the birds are breeding as a colony, and when the opportunity arises both Common and Spotless Starlings can form dense colonies, as seen in the pantiled roofs of buildings in villages of northeast Spain.

Although breeding in groups is the norm in starlings, some species do breed solitarily. Shelley's and Brown-winged Starlings are examples, and Mountain Starlings, Golden-breasted and Yellow-faced Mynas may also prove to be solitary. Common Hill Mynas usually nest *c*. 1 km apart, but occasionally several nests are found in a single tree. This illustrates the flexibility exhibited by starlings, for many species demonstrate wide ranges of sociality in breeding, a feature that must have facilitated the expansion of starlings into new areas, both under natural circumstances and following introductions.

Pair bonds

The duration of the pair bond has received little study in most starlings but there are indications of differences within the family, and these differences have allowed the evolution of different reproductive strategies. In some Asian species, detailed study and casual observation suggest that birds may pair for life. The retention of a pair bond over successive seasons has been demonstrated in Common Hill Mynas and in Common Mynas (Bertram 1970, Sengupta 1982); in both these species paired birds remain together throughout the year. This may be widespread in Asian starlings as many species are reported to be normally found in pairs. This is especially noticeable in the genus *Acridotheres*, where even in large feeding flocks and in large night roosts, pairs are readily apparent. However, although pairs are also normally apparent in Asian Pied Mynas, one limited ringing study has suggested that pair bonds may not be long-lived (Tyagi and Lamba 1984). In these species, birds are thought to be monogamous but most studies have been insufficiently detailed to reveal polygyny and extra-pair copulations.

In Africa, pairs of Red-winged, African Pied and Cape Glossy Starlings may persist for more than two years.

In the genus *Sturnus*, however, pair bonds are frequently of short duration and mates may even be exchanged within a breeding season (Feare and Burnham 1978). Failure to retain a long-lived pair bond may be associated with long-distance migration and a with a higher annual mortality than in tropical species, although data on the latter are lacking in tropical Asian starlings.

The existence of a prolonged pair bond, together with limited opportunities for breeding if nest sites are limited, facilitates the evolution of breeding strategies that depart from the simple situation of a pair of birds raising its own broods. Similarly, the lack of a strong pair bond allows birds to practice breeding strategies that depart from strict monogamy, and both possibilities have been exploited during the evolution of the starling family.

Cooperative breeding

Grimes (1976) reviewed the occurrence of cooperative breeding in African birds, and listed four starling species for which this had been reported. Current information suggests that cooperative breeding occurs regularly in eleven African starlings, but only two, African Pied Starling in southern Africa and Chestnut-bellied Starling in West Africa, have been studied in any detail to date. In several cases only anecdotal reports are available, but certain patterns do emerge.

In most cooperative breeding birds, helpers assist in feeding the young, but play no part in nest construction or incubation (Brown 1987), and this appears to be true for all the African starlings except oxpeckers, in which helpers may bring in some nesting material. In a few cases, the helpers have been reported to feed the breeding female. Helpers are most often subadult birds which have yet to breed themselves, and commonly assist their parents in rearing siblings. However, since they may feed young at several nests, they are clearly not only assisting close relatives. Jamieson and Craig (1987) have suggested that attempts to find adaptive explanations for helping behaviour may be misguided: the strong motivation to feed begging young (as is shown by the readiness with which brood parasites such as cuckoos are fed by many birds) can by itself lead to feeding the offspring of other birds, when dispersal does not occur and not all members of a group are nesting.

There have been many attempts to establish a relationship between ecological conditions and the occurrence of cooperative breeding. Brown (1987) concluded that there are no general rules, but there may be a predisposition towards cooperative breeding in some bird groups. Since helping instead of breeding independently implies deferred breeding, the life expectancy of such species should be sufficient to offer a good chance of breeding in the future. This does seem to be supported by available ringing data, in particular for African Pied Starling (AC, unpub. data).

In the African starlings, helpers have been reported only from savanna species, many of which live in highly seasonal and semi-arid environments. In all cases the species are not sexually dimorphic in appearance, while immature birds may retain distinctive features. Nesting may be solitary or semi-colonial, and the birds associate in resident flocks throughout the year. These characteristics suggest that cooperative breeding may be found to occur in the following additional species, whose breeding biology is little known at present: White-crowned Starling, White-winged Babbling Starling, Emerald Starling, Bronze-tailed Glossy Starling and Shelley's Starling.

Among Asian species, Rowley (1976) suggested that Shining Starlings might breed cooperatively, and Draffan (1977) recorded three Yellow-faced Mynas carrying nest material into a cavity and thought that all three birds assisted in feeding the young. These are the only examples reported, suggesting that in Asian species cooperative breeding is rare and, in contrast to the African species, these two species are forest frugivores, rather than savanna species.

Polygyny and intra-specific nest parasitism

Among the Asian species that have adapted to more open habitats, different departures from the monogamous pair breeding system have been recorded. Polygyny has been described in Red-cheeked, Common and Spotless Starlings, and intra-specific nest parasitism, where a female lays one or more eggs in the nests of other females of the same species, has been recorded in Common and Spotless Starlings, and is suspected in Purple-backed Starlings. These behaviours may be found in other species, e.g White-cheeked Starling, when these receive appropriate study but at present most of our knowledge is derived from investigations of the behaviour of Common Starlings. In addition to polygyny and intraspecific nest parasitism, Common Starlings also demonstrate frequent exchange of mates (Feare and Burnham 1978), indulge in extra-pair copulations (Hoffenberg *et al.* 1988, Pinxten *et al.* 1993, Smith and Schantz 1993), and occasionally two females may nest communally. These departures from strict monogamy are all facilitated by the synchrony of behaviour that accompanies the onset of each breeding season.

Polygyny is widespread in Starlings and Pinxten *et al.* (1989a) found that 20–60% of males were polygynous each year in a Belgian colony. While most polygynous males have two mates, up to five females may be mated to a single male (Merkel 1978, Pinxten *et al.* 1989b). Polygynous males produce more fledglings than monogamous males (Pinxten *et al.* 1989a), but females of polygynous males produce fewer young than monogamous females (Pinxten and Eens 1990). This may result from a difference in the behaviour of monogamous and polygynous males, for polygynous males devote less time to the care of their eggs and young than do monogamous males (Pinxten *et al.* 1993b). The primary female of a polygynous male can compensate for the reduced contribution of her partner by increasing her own contribution of food to the nestlings, but secondary females appear unable to do this and they fledge fewer young than primary and monogamous females (Pinxten and Eens 1994).

Intra-specific nest parasitism was first described in Common Starlings by Yom-Tov *et al.* (1974) but this behaviour has also proved to be common and widespread. Up to 37% of first clutches have been found to contain an egg that was not laid by the female who owned the nest (Evans 1988, Karlsson 1983, Lombardo *et al.* 1989, Pinxten *et al.* 1991a, Romagnano *et al.* 1990) but estimates of the proportions of parasitized nests are likely to be under-estimates in view of the techniques used to identify parasitism (Feare 1996). The frequency of this behaviour suggests that it is a strategy adopted by some females, but an interpretation of the function of the behaviour requires identification of the females which parasitise, and this has proved difficult. Females may become parasites following disturbance during the laying period (Feare 1991). Parasitism may also be stimulated by competition for nest sites (Evans 1988), and some parasitic females might be unmated young birds who had been fertilised by an already paired male, but which did not possess nests of their own (Pinxten *et al.*1991a). Females might also operate a mixed strategy, rearing a clutch of their own but also depositing an egg in another Starling's nest (Evans 1988, Feare 1996), thereby spreading their potential offspring and insuring against total failure of their own clutch. Evidence for these suggestions is difficult to obtain.

Intra-specific nest parasitism is accompanied by behaviours that help to ensure the success of the parasitic female's egg, and which also help potential hosts to guard themselves against parasitism. Some parasitic females appear to avoid being close to hosts' nests at the time when hosts are most likely to be in the vicinity of their nest (Feare *et al.* 1982) and parasitic females lay their eggs remarkably quickly (Pinxten *et al.* 1991b). Some parasitic females remove a host egg when they lay their parasite egg (Lombardo *et al.* 1989, Pinxten *et al.* 1991a).

Communal breeding has been recorded twice in Common Starlings. Both instances involved two females laying in one nest, with both females and a single male assisting with incubation and feeding the young (Stouffer *et al.* 1988, Pinxten *et al.* 1994). Communal breeding in Common Starlings is probably rare, but unusually large clutches, assumed to have been laid by two females, have also been reported in Rose-coloured Starlings.

Brood parasites

The Great Spotted Cuckoo *Clamator glandarius* has been recording as parasitizing eleven African starling species, although starlings are not its only hosts, and there is no evidence that a high proportion of their nests are affected (Irwin 1988). Adult cuckoos are attacked by nesting starlings, but there is presumably no discrimination by adult starlings against cuckoo eggs, which do not match those of the host species. The egg pattern will only be relevant in the case of hosts such as Redwinged Starling, which builds an open nest not situated in a dark cavity. There are also records of three hole-nesting species parasitized by the Greater Honeyguide *Indicator indicator*, and two by the Lesser Honeyguide *Indicator minor* (Short and Horne 1988). However, many other bird species are parasitized by honeyguides, and brood parasitism is unlikely to represent a major source of breeding failure for most African starling populations.

In Eurasia there appear to be no records of brood parasites laying eggs in the nests of starlings.

MOULT

In all birds, feathers become worn and require replacement if the plumage is to function efficiently in the mechanical demands of flight, and in providing insulation for the body. The process of moulting the feathers follows a particular sequence, so that the normal functions are disrupted as little as possible, but the form which it takes will depend upon the lifestyle of the species concerned.

Growing new feathers involves protein synthesis, which leads to increased energy demands. Moult is thus a potentially stressful process in physiological terms, and would not be expected to occur at the same time as other activities with high energy demands such as breeding or migration. Wing moult will also affect the bird's flying ability, so that it should not occur during migration or other times when efficient flight is at a premium. General moult of the body plumage will make insulation less effective, and thus should not take place during the coldest months; in fact the bird would be better off with new plumage at times when the demands of thermoregulation are highest. These principles provide a starting point for reviewing our knowledge of moult in the starlings.

Recording moult

The recording system which has become established amongst bird-ringers focuses primarily on wing moult. Each feather is assigned a score on a 0–5 scale, with old feathers scoring 0 and new feathers 5. Since the moult is normally symmetrical on both wings, the resulting 'moult score' provides an indication of how far advanced the moult is, and by a graphical comparison with date, the time when moult starts and is completed in the population, and its duration in individual birds, can be estimated (Ginn and Melville 1983).

The moult score method is a quick and consistent means of recording wing and tail moult on both live birds or museum skins. For other feather regions, anything more than a crude assessment of the presence and extent of moult is extremely time-consuming. Some mathematicians have long been unhappy with the moult score as a basis for calculations, particularly since many authors claim better estimates of the duration of moult by regressing date against moult score, which is the reverse of the intuitively correct procedure - the date is surely the 'fixed' variable in this case! This has led to new models, based on the percentage feather mass grown (Underhill and Zucchini 1988). For birds, the total mass of the plumage is quite small, and less than half of it is made up by the wing and tail feathers: for instance in an African Pied Starling, with a total body mass (unplucked) of 95 g, the plumage constituted 7.8 g, with the contribution of the primary wing feathers being 1.3 g, the secondaries and tertials 0.8 g and the tail feathers 0.7 g (AC, unpub. data). Once these figures are known for a particular species, the moult score can be used to calculate the mass of primary wing feathers grown, and a much more accurate estimate of the duration of moult and indirectly of the extra energy requirements is possible. So far this method has been applied to one starling species only, the Common Starling in South Africa (Cooper and Underhill 1991).

The sequence and rate of moult

With very few exceptions, passerine species replace the primary feathers descendantly, from the innermost primary outwards to the wingtip. The secondaries are replaced from the first feather, adjacent to the first primary in the standard numbering system, inwards. Secondary moult generally starts when primary moult is about half complete. The three innermost wing feathers, the tertials, are renewed before secondary moult is completed, in a variable sequence. The tail feathers are often replaced from the innermost pair of feathers outwards, but tail moult is much less symmetrical than wing moult, and irregular sequences are common. Body moult commonly accompanies tail moult and wing moult, and for many species the period of primary wing moult spans the moult in all other body regions (Ginn and Melville 1983). Starlings have 19 flight feathers (remiges) on each wing; ten primaries, of which the outermost one is much reduced, six secondaries, and three tertials; and 12 tail feathers (rectrices).

Interrupted wing moult may occur, in which case birds will be found with some new feathers adjacent to old feathers, while there is no active moult. If moult is later resumed at the next feather which is due for replacement, the condition is termed 'suspended moult', whereas if 'arrested moult' a new moult cycle starts from the beginning, and the old feathers which have been retained are replaced in the new moult sequence (Ginn and Melville 1983). The condition in which more than one moult cycle is in progress in the same wing is termed 'Staffelmauser' (Stresemann and Stresemann 1966).

In several African starlings, interrupted wing moult was noted, but the only species in which it seems to be a common occurrence is Wattled Starling, which shows suspended wing moult (Craig 1983a, 1996). Suspended wing moult has been recognised as a regular part of the cycle in some long-distance migrants (Stresemann and Stresemann 1966) and Traylor (1971) found that interrupted moult occurred in some migrating Amethyst Starlings. Naik and Naik (1969) found a few cases of interrupted secondary moult in the migratory Rose-coloured Starling during the non-breeding season. In the Wattled Starling it also seems likely that suspension of moult coincides with periods when the birds are especially likely to be flying long distances, rather than periods when breeding occurs (Craig 1996). Local food shortages could be the trigger both for emigration and for moult suspension. Evans (1986) reported cases of interrupted moult in Common Starlings, in both migratory and resident populations, though it seemed to be most common in sedentary island birds from localities such as the Faroe and Shetland islands. He suggested that for some of these birds interrupted moult might occur for energetic reasons, during periods of temporary food shortage. However, Meijer (1991) demonstrated that under experimental conditions of restricted access to food, male Common Starlings started moulting later, but females did not, while there was no effect on the duration of moult in either group.

The rate at which moult is completed will clearly depend both on the growth rate of individual feathers, and on the number of growing feathers at any one time. This in turn will determine the effect which moult has on flying ability and energetics. The only passerines in which wing moult regularly occurs so rapidly that the birds may be temporarily flightless are the dippers *Cinclus cinclus* and *C. mexicanus* (Stresemann and Stresemann 1966). In the Common Starling, there is evidence that northern populations have a more rapid moult before migration than those in other areas (Lundberg and Eriksson 1984), and birds which start moult later, such as late breeders, also moult more rapidly (Meijer 1991). Based on the number of growing wing feathers, the rate of moult in starling species occurring in the same area may differ significantly (Craig 1983a).

The energetics of moult

The traditional view, based primarily on experience of birds in the north temperate region, was that the energy demands of moult are incompatible with breeding. However, research on tropical birds soon showed that moult-breeding overlap did occur in a significant number of species (e.g. Foster 1975). Detailed studies of the actual energy requirements during moult are now available for a few species of passerines, and these have shown that the energy costs of moult greatly exceed the mere costs of feather production, and require changes in diet to increase the intake of certain amino acids, as well as a higher overall food intake. This suggests that at high latitudes, with an increased daylength and thus feeding time, moult can be completed more rapidly so that moulting in these regions could be advantageous (Murphy and King 1991).

The starlings are predominantly a tropical group. Northern populations of the Common Starling and other species migrate to regions with a milder climate during the winter, so that the role of plumage in thermoregulation is less critical than for species which overwinter at high latitudes. The large communal roosts of the Common Starling do seem to be located at sites which provide a warmer environment to the birds using them (Yom-Tov *et al.* 1977). There has been very little physiological work done on any species other than the Common Starling, but it is probable that for most starling species the energy demands of moult are not the primary factor determining its timing in the annual cycle.

Age and plumage changes

When they first leave the nest, young birds often have a distinctive plumage, and only later come to resemble the adults, once they have undergone a moult. In species which take several years to mature, the young may have a series of immature plumage stages. There are also birds which change their plumage and appearance in the course of a year, alternating between a dull eclipse plumage and a brightly-coloured breeding or nuptial plumage, as is found in many members of the African weaver family (Craig 1983a).

The only starling species which shows seasonal changes in plumage related to breeding is Wattled Starling, but here the changes involve the loss of feathers which are then replaced in the course of the next moult, so that an 'extra' moult is not required. There also appear to be no cases in which plumage changes continue beyond the first year, although other features such as iris coloration may take more than one year to reach the adult condition, as in African Pied Starling (Craig 1983c).

The post-juvenile moult may be complete, which means that the wing, tail and body feathers are replaced, or partial, in which case it usually involves only the body plumage. Both forms are found within the starlings, and there appears to be a clear division based on systematic relationships. In the genus *Sturnus*, Common Starling (Bährmann 1964), Spotless Starling (Peris 1988), White-cheeked Starling (Kuroda 1963) and Rose-coloured Starling (Naik and Naik 1969) all have a complete post-juvenile moult, and so do Common Myna and Bank Myna in the genus *Acridotheres* (Naik and Naik 1969). Sometimes a few juvenile secondary feathers may be retained in Common Starling (Scott 1965). Under experimental conditions, juvenile Common Starlings kept on short days (10 hours light, 14 hours dark) did not undergo a post-juvenile wing moult, and showed only irregular moult of some body plumage (Williams *et al.* 1989). In Rose-coloured Starling, some juveniles show delayed moult (Roberts 1982, van den Berg 1982), and perhaps interrupted wing and tail moult (Roberts 1982, Herroelen 1987). Peris (1988) noted that the moult of young Spotless Starlings from second broods started much later than in the adults and young from first broods, so that these may represent late-moulting birds which are unable to complete wing moult.

Wattled Starling, which is closely related to the Common and Asian starlings, has a complete post-juvenile moult, whereas other African species apparently have a partial post-juvenile moult, in which the body plumage is replaced and sometimes some secondaries and rectrices. However, Wilkinson (1983) found evidence of a complete post-juvenile moult in Chestnut-bellied Starling.

The timing of moult

For most passerines there is a single complete moult, which takes place once a year. Seven species are known to show two complete moults within a year; these include both migrant and resident species, but none are starlings (Prŷs-Jones 1991). Individual feathers or groups of feathers can of course be replaced at any time if they are accidentally lost, but this does not entail starting a full moult cycle.

Often the complete annual moult follows directly after the breeding season, after which the birds may leave the area. This is particularly obvious in migratory species, and is clearly shown by Scandinavian populations of Common Starling (Lundberg and Eriksson 1984). In this case the moult is rapid, and in the wings several feathers will be growing simultaneously. However, in some migratory species the moult takes place in the non-breeding area, so that the post-breeding migration is undertaken with old plumage, while the birds will have fresh plumage on the return to the breeding grounds. This is evidently the case in Rose-coloured Starling (Naik and Naik 1969, van den Berg 1982), and probably also in Spot-winged Starling (Marien 1951). The timing of breeding and migration need not determine the timing of moult, as is shown in Amethyst Starling, an intra-African migrant in which breeding and migration times differ regionally, whereas the timing of wing moult appears to be consistent between the different populations. Thus some Amethyst Starlings breed, moult, then migrate; others breed, migrate, then moult; while some moult, and then migrate to the breeding area. This species is also unusual in that wing and tail moult are completed well before moult of the body plumage (Traylor 1971).

The Wattled Starling of Africa follows a nomadic life style. There is some indication that the main period of moult differs in eastern and southern populations, but the picture is confused by the frequent occurrence of suspended moult, which means that birds at very different stages of moult may be present in the same flock (Craig 1996).

Many non-migratory starlings show a regular post-breeding moult, and this seems to apply to most Asian species and many African species. There may be striking differences between resident birds in the same habitat. Thus Cape Glossy Starling has a fairly rapid moult directly after breeding, and there is no evidence of moult-breeding overlap in individual birds, whereas at the same localities in South Africa, African Pied Starlings start moult while breeding, and the moult proceeds more slowly with fewer wing feathers growing at the same time (Craig 1983b). Further north, both Burchell's Glossy Starling and Meves' Long-tailed Starling complete their moult before breeding (Brooke 1967a, 1967b, 1968). In East Africa, Dittami (1987) found sympatric populations of Rüppell's Long-tailed Glossy Starling, in which moult and breeding often overlapped, and Greater Blue-eared Glossy Starling, which moulted after breeding was completed. In West Africa, Chestnut-bellied Starling has two breeding seasons within the year, and moult starts toward the end of the first, overlapping with breeding in the second period (Wilkinson 1983). Specimens examined in the present study showed that moult-breeding overlap is likely in several other African species, such as Fischer's Starling.

If wing moult is very slow, extending over much of the year, it will inevitably occur at the same time as breeding. Red-billed Oxpecker has a very protracted wing moult lasting more than 300 days, even though this species inhabits a seasonal savanna environment and has a clearly defined breeding season (Stutterheim 1980c).

The control of moult

From the above account it appears that moult in starling species shows some correlation with systematic relationships, suggesting that inherited characteristics play a role. In passerine birds in general it appears that the form of the post-juvenile moult is genetically determined, and may be consistent at least at the generic level (Stresemann and Stresemann 1966), while the sequence in which wing feathers are replaced follows a limited number of alternative patterns, which may be common to many species.

What about the timing of wing moult? Breeding has often been regarded as the central event in the annual cycle, but moult could be the fixed point in the annual cycle, while breeding varies regionally in response to local conditions. This would imply a large hereditary component in the control of the timing of wing moult. It is also known that in many bird species, periodic events such as moult, breeding and migration are under the control of circannual rhythms, inborn patterns whose timing is set by particular environmental stimuli. Experimental studies of Common Starling have shown that manipulation of the circannual rhythm can induce several cycles of moult within a single year (Gwinner 1977). The moult season of Amethyst Starling discussed above, and the differing moult times of two populations of Red-winged Starling, which are concordant with the patterns of morphological variation (Craig 1988a), strongly suggest that the timing of moult is often under direct genetic control.

The role of hormones in the control of moult is much less clear. The Common Starling moults after breeding, and the male hormone testosterone will inhibit moult in male birds. Sustained high testosterone levels lead to a delay in the start of wing moult, which then commences not with the first primary but further along the wing, so that only the outer primary feathers are replaced (Schleussner et al. 1985, Schleussner 1990).

Later experiments applying testosterone during the moult led to interruption, which was usually resumed at the point where it had stopped, but in some cases a completely new cycle started. Simulating decreasing daylength generally increased the rate of moult (Dawson 1994). Testosterone treatment also delayed moult in male Wattled Starlings, although wing moult was not the focus of the investigation (Hamilton 1959). Hormone treatments which mimic precocious sexual development will also induce earlier development of adult plumage in many species. Testosterone seems to produce particularly strong effects, whereas the role of female hormones and of hormones which may stimulate, rather than inhibit, moult is not clear. Schleussner et al. (1985) suggested that in male Common Starlings moult is retarded by testosterone and stimulated by thyroxine produced in the thyroid gland, so that moult would be regulated by a push-pull action of these two hormones, within the limits of the 'moulting window', which is a set period in the annual cycle during which moult may occur. Their study showed that when moult started very late, it ended before all wing feathers had been replaced, apparently terminated by some pre-set deadline. In starlings which moult while breeding, either the response to hormones such as testosterone is different, or hormonal levels may have dropped below a certain critical threshold before moult starts. In both African Pied Starling and Red-winged Starling, wing moult occurs while the birds are attending second broods (Craig 1983b), and it is possible that hormone levels in the blood are significantly lower during this phase of the breeding season. Dittami (1987) found that in Greater Blue-eared Glossy Starlings moult did not occur during the period of peak levels of testosterone and luteinizing hormone in males, or luteinizing hormone and 17-ß-estradiol in females. However, there was no cyclic variation in the levels of these hormones in Rüppell's Long-tailed Starling, and moult apparently occurred in all birds at the same period, despite great individual variations in blood hormone levels.

The moult of the Mimidae

If the mockingbirds and thrashers are the starlings' closest relatives as suggested by Sibley and Ahlquist (1984), how similar are they in respect of moult? The ten North American species all have 10 primaries with the outer feather much reduced, 9 secondaries and tertials, and 12 rectrices. None of them has a pre-breeding moult, and the post-juvenile moult is usually partial except in two species, which sometimes have a complete post-juvenile moult. For five of the ten species, age-related changes in iris coloration have been reported (Pyle et al. 1987). Moult-breeding overlap has been recorded in Northern Mockingbird Mimus polyglottos (Zaias and Breitwisch 1990). There are no data on the moult of the other 20 Central and South American species. So although there are no striking differences from the moult pattern of the starlings, the known moult characteristics of the mockingbirds are also shared by other passerine families.

Bathing and anting

Starlings are keen bathers, and all the African species which have been observed in the wild bathe regularly and often daily fly several kilometres to visit water holes. Dust bathing has not been reported, however, except in oxpeckers. Starlings also sun themselves regularly, on the ground or perched in trees, adopting specific postures for this activity (Simmons 1989).

The behaviour known as anting, in which birds either passively 'bathe' in ants, allowing the insects to swarm over their plumage, or actively hold individual ants in the bill and pass them over the feathers, is much less common. Anting has been studied in detail in Common Starling (Querengässer 1973), and it has been observed in three African and three Asian species in the wild. There are also records of five African and 11 Asian starling species anting in captivity (Poulsen 1956, Simmons 1961, 1966). Only the active form of anting has been observed in starlings. The ants used in the process are apparently usually species which release large quantities of formic acid when molested, and this may reduce the number of ectoparasites on the plumage, although direct evidence is lacking. There are also reports of 'anting' with millipedes which produce defensive secretions (Clunie 1976), and even of starlings using other strong-smelling materials such as mothballs (Clark et al. 1990). Such behaviour may be associated with moult and feather care, though we lack a fully satisfactory explanation for its occurrence (Craig in press c).

STARLINGS AND MAN

A large number of starling species interact in some way with man's interests. Many species are lowland birds and thus live in the areas most commonly occupied by man, which predisposes these birds to live in close proximity to human habitation. The trend in the family's evolution from a forest frugivore lifestyle towards exploitation of more open and drier habitats, particularly involving foraging on the ground, further facilitated a commensalism with man for many species. The adaptability of some of the more 'advanced' species has allowed them to exploit benefits provided directly or as a by-product of man's activities, and these species in particular interact with man in several ways.

Commensalism and opportunism

Most members of the family nest in holes, and although originally these holes were found mainly in trees and cliffs, many species have been sufficiently adaptable to enable them to take advantage of cavities provided by man. The most commensal species, such as Common Starling and Common Myna, are sufficiently tolerant of man that they even nest in his houses. The Common Starling has utilised such cavities throughout recorded history, and it has been said that holes were left deliberately for these birds in the mortise and tenon joints of Stonehenge, the birds having religious significance to those who erected this monument (Atkinson 1956); alternatively, the birds' use of these cavities may have conferred upon Common Starlings a cultural importance which they formerly lacked. Brahminy Mynas (also referred to as Pagoda Mynas) and Common Mynas (sometimes called House Mynas) are also claimed to hold religious significance for Hindus, and this may similarly have been derived from the birds' propensity to nest in temples. Many of the *Acridotheres* mynas nest in a wide variety of man-made sites in buildings, walls, drainage holes, and Bank Mynas have been recorded nesting in stacks of sugar cane (Lamba 1981). Starlings are able to adapt to newer technologies, and Asian Pied Mynas use electricity and telegraph pylons to build their large domed nests, and occasionally nest in street lamps. Common Starlings have sought additional advantages by nesting in the 'triangles' of large satellite receivers; nests in such sites were believed to be so warm that the birds had to devote little time to incubation! The adoption of man's edifices as nesting sites by starlings is an ongoing process; Red-winged Starlings took to nesting in towns in eastern and southern Africa (Holub and von Pelzeln 1882), presumably when buildings became sufficiently similar to their more natural sites on cliff ledges. Most recently, Tristram's Red-winged Starlings have begun breeding in cities in Israel during the last 20 years (Hofshi *et al.* 1987a), and colonisation of new cities is continuing.

Starlings have also adopted town and city centres as roosting sites. Potts (1967) documented the history of urban roosting by Common Starlings in the British Isles. These birds began roosting in trees in central Dublin in the 1840s and many urban roosts begin in this way. After leaf-fall, however, the birds in some towns shift to roosting on buildings or other structures. Before entering the roost site, Common Starlings form large gatherings, 'pre-roost assemblies', nearby and man-made structures are often used by assembling birds. Communication antennae seem particularly attractive; a police station antenna in Bradford was reputed to lose its transmission and reception ability during the birds' assembly period each evening. On 12 August 1949, assembling Common Starlings selected the hands of London's famous clock, Big Ben, as a pre-roost site, and the weight of birds was sufficient to stop the clock. Such an unforgivable intrusion into the British lifestyle led to questions about Starlings being raised in Parliament, and included calls for their extermination. Perhaps their greatest accolade, however, was the devotion of an entire episode of a 1950s cult comedy radio programme, *The Goon Show*, to the starling problem! Urban roosting has now been recorded in cities in continental Europe and also in North America, but in Britain many former urban roosts have disappeared, probably as a consequence of the decline in the numbers of Common Starlings breeding and wintering in Britain in the 1980s and 1990s (Feare 1996). Common and White-vented Mynas, together with Asian Glossy Starlings and Amethyst Starlings, have also adopted the urban roosting habit in Singapore, but these birds continue to roost in trees (Hails 1984, Kang 1989) and have yet to transfer to buildings.

In their utilisation of feeding sites, starlings have shown themselves to be particularly adept at exploiting man's environment. In the tropics, forest frugivores have presumably taken wild fruits valued by man since pre-history, but whether this was ever regarded by man as serious competition is unknown. The cultivation of some of these fruits doubtless provided opportunities for some starlings to forage on new abundances of food, but forest frugivores did not possess the adaptability to take advantage of man's wider exploits. The species which inhabited more open areas, on the other hand, had evolved behaviours that allowed them to exploit patchy and temporary supplies of food which, when available, were often superabundant. Examples of such transient abundances of food include fruiting and flowering trees, insect swarms, and ripening seeds of grasses following seasonal rains. The behaviours that facilitated the location and exploitation of these resources included feeding in large flocks, possibly associated with communal roosting at night, the undertaking of widescale movements, including nomadism and migration, and the capability of eating a wide range of foods, including both animal and plant matter.

The ability of some starling species to form large concentrations quickly when suitable food appeared has led them to be held in high esteem. Rose-coloured and Wattled Starlings, in particular, are renowned for their sudden appearance at plagues of locusts. Other species of starling use the characteristics mentioned above to take advantage of resources provided by man. At picnic parks in eastern and southern Africa, Superb, Blue-eared Glossy, Cape Glossy, Burchell's Glossy, African Pied and Red-winged Starlings assemble rapidly on the arrival of parties of humans. On a larger scale, other species of starling accumulate in huge numbers to take advantage of the seasonal ripening of crops such as cherries, olives and grapes. These fruits are of course transient in their appearance, but some of the concentrations of food made available by man have become almost permanent, such as the cereal grains fed to livestock at feedlots, invertebrates present at sewage treatment works, and the wide array of food types at refuse tips. The 'expert' in exploiting these is Common Starling. In western France they revealed their adaptability when farmers began feeding cattle from clamps of maize silage. This presented Common Starlings with such a rich food source that they changed their wintering area; birds which had formerly wintered in southern France switched to winter in Brittany in order to take advantage of the 'new' food that had become available throughout the winter (Gramet and Dubaille 1983).

The features of the birds' biology that enable starlings to capitalise on such food concentrations has led some species to be regarded as beneficial to man, and others to be deemed pests; some species change status during the year, being beneficial in some months and pests in others, depending on the foods being exploited at the time.

Beneficial starlings

The most celebrated 'beneficial' starling is perhaps Rose-coloured Starling, whose value as a destroyer of locusts was recorded by Pliny. Both this species and Wattled Starling establish breeding colonies in places where swarms of locusts or grasshoppers appear, and the birds are widely believed to eat sufficient of the insects to be valuable in terms of crop protection. Rose-coloured Starling is a migrant, wintering in India and breeding in Central Asia. Within the breeding area, the location of colonies is dependent upon the presence of large numbers of insects, and areas that hold large breeding colonies one year may be deserted the next if insects fail to appear. Wattled Starlings are more nomadic and their breeding does not appear to show an annual regularity (Craig 1996), so that this species may be able to capitalise on the flush of insects that appear with renewed grass growth after rains.

Searches for biological control techniques for insect pests have involved several species of starling. Narang and Lamba (1984) undertook detailed analyses of the stomach contents of five species from India — Brahminy Starling, Asian Pied Myna, Common Myna, Jungle Myna and Bank Myna — and concluded, from the abundance of harmful insects that the birds had eaten, that these species were, on balance, beneficial to agriculture. The Common Myna was of marginal importance, however, since it ate crop seeds at sowing time and harvest, and this was assumed to represent damage to these crops. Akhmedov (1957) regarded the beneficial activities of Common Mynas as heavily outweighing damage caused in Tadjikistan, and recommended that their presence should be encouraged by the provision of nest boxes. In Korea, Won and Woo (1957) and Won (1961a) studied the diet of Purple-backed Starlings to discover whether this species might play a role in controlling insect pests of forestry. They concluded that the birds' consumption of insect pests was sufficient to be beneficial, and therefore recommended that nestboxes should be erected in forests to encourage the birds. In northern parts of their Eurasian breeding range, Common Starlings are similarly believed to benefit agriculture and forestry through their consumption of insect pests, and Feare (1984) was told that in the former Soviet Union, 25 million nestboxes had been erected to encourage Common Starling populations; these nestboxes also served an educational role, since the breeding of the birds was monitored by school children. Most introductions of Common Starlings to other parts of the world were for largely aesthetic reasons (Lever 1987), but Thompson (1922) claimed that insect pest control was also a factor in this species' introduction to New Zealand. It was here that the only detailed study of the Common Starling as a regulator of an insect pest population was undertaken. East and Pottinger (1975) concluded that only under exceptional coincidences of high sheep grazing pressure, high rainfall, high starling density and localisation of the insect pest — the grass grub, larva of the moth *Costelytra zealandica* — was any control likely to have been achieved. Adequate study may well reveal similar shortcomings of other forms of assumed pest control by starlings, although Whitehead et al. (1996) have shown that during the breeding season Common Starlings are capable of depleting local populations of leatherjackets (larvae of the cranefly *Tipula paludosa*). In the Netherlands, however, a farmer who suffered severe problems with flies in a cattle shed enclosed the shed in bird-proof netting and then released Blue-eared Glossy Starlings into the shed in the expectation that they would control the flies (Feare 1984); the outcome of this is unknown.

A by-product of the belief that starlings have a voracious appetite for insect pests has been the introduction of mynas, especially the Common Myna, to oceanic islands. These introductions were reputedly to control wasps, army worm, cut worm, ticks, grasshoppers and locusts. The only instance where success was claimed was on Mauritius, but Cheke (1987) claimed that other forms of control were also involved here. In most instances the effects of these introductions have been adverse (see below).

A more tangible benefit conferred by some starling species, especially in the Indo-Malayan region, involves pollination of flowers and seed dispersal. Many of the *Acridotheres* mynas regularly take nectar from flowering trees, and after bouts of such feeding the birds' frontal crests are often seen to be dusted with pollen, suggesting that one function of the crest may lie in pollination. These species may thus have co-evolved with the trees and aid their pollination. Although they lack frontal crests, pollen has also been seen on the heads of Samoan Starlings (Watling 1982) and Common Hill Mynas, and these species may also be important pollinators. Studies of seed passage through the guts of some of these species indicate that the birds may also be significant agents in the dispersal of seeds, and be of economic importance as dispersers of valuable trees like banyan *Ficus benghalensis,* sandalwood *Santalum album* and neem *Azadirachta indica* (Midya and Bramachary 1991, Mishra *et al.* 1987).

Starlings as pests

Conflicts with man's interests take several forms, affecting urban life (including public health), aviation and agriculture. The species that most commonly cause problems are of course those that live in closest proximity to man, and thus *Acridotheres* mynas and *Sturnus* starlings figure prominently in statistics of damage.

Urban pests

Although Asian Glossy Starlings and Purple-backed Starlings roost in trees in urban areas of Singapore, they are quiet in comparison with the Common and White-vented Mynas that dominate these roosting assemblages. It is the noise made by these birds, at dusk and dawn, and occasionally during the night, that constitutes the nuisance, since the noise is sufficient to disturb people living in nearby housing developments. Surprisingly, droppings do not appear to accumulate in sufficient quantity beneath the trees to pose a problem. Attempts to resolve the problem have included poisoning the birds, thinning or removing the trees, and scaring the birds. The two mynas are opportunistic in their foraging, especially in the case of White-vented Myna, and reduction of their food supply is regarded as impracticable; thus it seems unlikely that there will be a permanent reduction in the numbers of birds. Kang *et al.* (1990) concluded that removal of potential roost trees close to housing, coupled with provision of suitable trees where the birds would not be troublesome, may represent the best compromise.

In the British Isles, and more recently on continental Europe and in North America, the nocturnal roosting of Common Starlings in urban trees and on buildings and industrial structures is of concern in view of the quantity of droppings deposited by the birds overnight. The droppings smell, are unsightly, contribute to damage to masonry and pose a public health hazard in terms of rendering walkways and roads dangerously slippery. The droppings may also be hazardous through containing pathogens that are transmissible to man, and in parts of North America roosts of Common Starlings (together with several species of blackbird Icteridae) constitute foci of infection for a fungus *Histoplasma capsulatum,* which can cause pulmonary disease in man (Tosh *et al.* 1970). In the United States, attempts are made to eliminate roosts which become established near towns using poisons or detergent sprays (Feare 1984), while in London expensive daily cleaning of Leicester Square was required when all methods to scare the birds failed (Feare 1985).

Aviation

Birds that inhabit open grassland are attracted to airfields, where they may be involved in collisions with jet aircraft. These 'bird strikes' can cause considerable damage to aircraft but, as damage is usually related to the body mass of the birds and as starlings are relatively small, starlings do not figure prominently in bird-strike statistics. Nevertheless in India, Common Mynas, Asian Pied Mynas and Common Starlings are involved in a small proportion of bird strikes each year (Satheesan *et al.* 1990), and in Britain, Common Starlings were involved in several strikes between 1966 and 1976 (Rochard and Horton 1980). Since then, more detailed analysis has shown that Common Starlings are responsible for bird strikes at most British airports, although the incidence is low (Milsom and Horton 1995). When an aircraft with jet engines strikes a large number of starlings, the result can be catastrophic, and Common Starlings have been responsible for loss of human life in two incidents: 62 people were killed when a Lockheed Electra crashed following a collision with a flock at Boston Airport (USA) in 1960, and in 1996 a Hercules military transport crashed at Eindhoven (Netherlands) after hitting a flock of about 500 birds, killing 34 people (Anon 1996).

The techniques involved in protecting aircraft from birds involve scaring birds from airfields and rendering the grassland less attractive through appropriate management (Brough and Bridgeman

1980). Common Starling roosts that form near airfields are moved using a variety of scaring methods (Brough 1969), and aircraft engines are built to standards that will resist most bird impacts.

Agricultural damage

Although the Samoan Starling can cause considerable damage to cultivated guavas (Watling 1982), the species that are the most important agricultural pests are again those species that inhabit more open areas and are thus able to inhabit cultivated areas. In Africa, African Pied Starlings damage soft fruit (Mackworth-Praed and Grant 1963) and in Senegal Chestnut-bellied Starlings are thought to damage tomatoes and millet (Manikowski 1984). In Tanzania, Blue-eared Glossy Starlings and Superb Starlings damage grapes in vineyards, and the latter also digs up sprouting wheat (CJF).

The species responsible for most damage are the *Acridotheres* mynas in Indo-Malaya and the *Sturnus* starlings at higher latitudes; some of these species also cause agricultural damage where they have been introduced. In India, Jungle Mynas cause considerable damage to orchard fruits in the southern Indian Hills (Ali and Ripley 1972), and Bank Mynas damage ripening sorghum locally (Ali and Ripley 1972), and also cereals, vegetables and fruits (Simwat and Sidhu 1974, Sandhu and Toor 1984). The most serious damage by this species is in June, when they feed extensively in vineyards, taking up to 12.5% of some varieties (Toor and Ramzan 1974a). Common Mynas damage cereals, pulses and fruit. In Tadjikistan, Akhmedov (1957) regarded damage, especially by juveniles, to grapes, cherries, mulberries (and mulberry shoots), apples and myrobalan fruits to be relatively trivial. Toor and Ramzan (1974b), on the other hand, regarded Common Mynas to be the most serious pests of grapes in Punjab, but did not quantify the losses. They also reported damage to wheat, maize, millet, rice, ground-nuts and beans. In Tamil Nadu, Common Mynas contribute to losses of sorghum crops that can amount to 83% of the crop (Perumal *et al.* 1971).

In Japan, White-cheeked Starling is regarded as a major bird pest (Umeda *et al.* 1993), damaging orchard fruits including cherries, plums, peaches, pears and grapes (Shirota *et al.* 1983) and is responsible for total losses of cherries and over 40% of grapes. After the breeding season, Rose-coloured Starlings switch to a diet containing much fruit, especially mulberries and grapes (Serebrennikov 1931, Rustamov 1958, Korelov *et al.* 1974), upon which they inflict considerable damage. In their winter range in India, the variety of crops that they damage increases to include cherries, apricots, raspberries, dates and chillies (Ali and Ripley 1972). Spotless Starlings in Spain similarly damage cherries, and in winter join flocks of Common Starlings in causing extensive damage to olives and grapes (Feare *et al.* 1992). Common Starlings damage a wide variety of agricultural crops and estimates of losses include 7–100% of cherries, 20–30% of marketable apples, up to 15% of food put out for cattle, and £30,000 of poultry food per annum (Feare 1984, 1989). These losses were economically significant, but the recent decline in the northern European populations of Common Starlings (see species account) has led to reductions in the amounts of damage.

Techniques used to reduce damage by starlings have included the killing of large numbers of birds, using poisons, feather wetting agents and explosives, scaring by means of traditional scarers, tape recorded distress calls, and more sophisticated (but often no more efficient) electronic gadgetry, chemical repellents, physical exclusion of birds from areas where they cause damage, and changes in agricultural practice (Feare 1984, 1989). Although huge numbers of starlings have been killed in control operations, these operations appear to have had little impact on starling numbers and in many instances may not even have reduced damage. Scaring has considerable limitations as birds rapidly habituate to most scarers, although the use of recorded distress calls to move roosting birds is successful (Brough 1969), and balloons incorporating 'eye-spots' were claimed to be successful in deterring starlings from damaging fruit when the vulnerable period of the fruit was short (Shirota *et al.* 1983). The carbamate insecticide methiocarb was sometimes successful as a chemical repellent on fruit crops, but unacceptable residues on fruit led to its withdrawal in those countries where it had been registered for that use; a replacement has not yet become available. The recent decline in the European population of Common Starlings appears to be related to agricultural changes (Feare 1996), suggesting that these may be potent means of alleviating damage where this is serious and widespread (Feare 1995).

Starlings in captivity

The ability of some species of starling to mimic sounds in their environment, especially human speech, has led these species to be kept as captive companion animals. Greek and Roman literature indicates that Common Starlings were kept in cages over 2,000 years ago on account of their ability to recite phrases of human speech (Geikie 1912, Parmelee 1959). Pliny had heard of a Common Starling that could speak Greek and Latin, and which 'practised diligently and spoke new phrases every day, in still longer sentences'. Recent studies of mimicry suggest that this may have over-stated their abilities!

Common and Crested Mynas may also learn to utter phrases of human speech, but the species that holds the foremost reputation for this capacity are the hill mynas. There is a large international demand for these birds, few of which are bred in captivity (Bertram 1970). In Assam, a common method of capture of Common Hill Mynas involves providing the birds with artificial nest sites from which nestlings can be harvested when about three weeks old (Bertram 1968). Elsewhere in India, young are taken from natural nest holes in trees. Adult Common Hill Mynas are rarely taken, but in southern India, adult Southern Hill Mynas are caught as they feed in fruiting bushes. The alleged inferior ability of the latter species in mimicking human speech is due largely to the fact that the birds are caught as adults, rather than as nestlings like the Common Hill Myna (Ali 1963). Sri Lanka Hill Mynas are also popular cage birds and are taken as young from the nests (Henry 1971). Bertram (1970) thought that the extent of exploitation of hill mynas, which then involved thousands of birds each year and represented a valuable income to the communities that harvested the birds, could be adversely affecting populations locally. In Thailand, capture for the cagebird industry, together with forest destruction, have led to declines in populations of Common Hill Mynas (Boonsong and Round 1991) and similar events may be threatening the Nias Hill Myna on Nias and Banyak Islands (Dymond 1994).

Other species of starling are kept as cagebirds on account of their pleasant song or their decorative or distinctive plumage. Brahminy Starlings are kept as songsters in India and Coletos are commonly kept in cages in the Philippines, where they are reputed to mimic human speech (Delacour and Mayr 1946), while in South-East Asia a wider variety of species is readily available in bird shops. In Singapore in 1990, this included large numbers of Golden-breasted and Yellow-faced Mynas (CJF), doubtless valued for both their resonant calls and vivid appearances. In Java and Bali, Bali Mynas are apparently held as a status symbol by affluent and influential people, and the catching of birds to satisfy this market has led the species to its current status as the world's most endangered starling, and one of the world's most endangered birds. The adaptability of this species to captivity is a mixed blessing, however, as there is now a captive population in zoos and bird gardens around the world, and an international stud book to ensure that this population is maintained by outbreeding; in Britain confirmation of relationships has been confirmed using DNA fingerprinting (Ashworth and Parkin 1992). Some captive-bred birds have recently been released on Bali to augment the wild population, but even some of these released birds have later appeared in bird shops. In zoos and bird gardens, African starlings, especially Superb Starlings and Purple and Blue-eared Glossy Starlings, create spectacular images for visitors, and in Britain many of those on show are now bred in captivity. Recently, more unusual starlings have been imported into Britain, including Grosbeak Mynas, Sulawesi Crested Mynas, and Amethyst and Emerald Starlings.

Starlings for food

On Pacific islands, several species of *Aplonis* are eaten by indigenous people. Asian Glossy Starlings are trapped in large numbers in the Philippines (McClure 1974) and Micronesian Starlings are taken for food on several islands. Capture for food even extends to two threatened species, Mountain Starling and Pohnpei Mountain Starling; the impact that this has on populations is unknown. In northern India, Common Hill Mynas are trapped for food, a practice which is targeted mainly at adults, as juveniles are more valuable as birds for the avicultural markets (Bertram 1970). In Africa, White-winged Babbling Starlings are caught with lime sticks, presumably for food (Chapin 1948) but starlings do not appear to be a regular food item in Africa.

The species taken for food in the largest numbers is perhaps Common Starling. In the Netherlands, these birds were encouraged to nest in clay pots and the young were harvested, a practice that extended from the 14th to the 19th centuries (Hauff 1991). Exploitation of Common Starlings for food continues in southern Europe today. In Spain, cane fields are planted specifically as winter roost sites, and roosting birds are netted during the night (Parsons 1960). This harvest comprises mainly migrants from northern Europe, but Spotless Starlings are doubtless involved as well. In southern France, tinned Common Starling (paté de sansonnet) paté was available in many shops, including the Duty Free shop at Marseilles Airport, in the late 1980s (CJF). The source and method of capture of these birds was not stated on the tin!

Introductions

Starlings now occur in many parts of the world where they were formerly absent, due to deliberate introduction by man or through the escape of captive birds. All introductions have involved Asian and European species and details of their success or failure in naturalisation are given by Long (1984) and Lever (1987). Some of the intentional releases were aimed at biological control of insect pests but these, along with many introductions for other reasons, have usually led to conflict with man and with native wildlife. Furthermore, successful species have sometimes spread from the foci of introduction and colonised neighbouring regions, including islands. Coates (1970) reported the first occurrence of the Common Starling in Papua New Guinea, presumably as a vagrant from Australia, and noted the irony that this occurrence might presage the first occupation of the island by non-native birds. The starling species that have become successfully established following introduction are Common Hill Myna, Crested Myna, Jungle Myna, White-vented Myna, Common Myna and Common Starling.

Introduced populations of starlings are frequently claimed to have adverse effects on populations of indigenous birds. The most commonly expressed cause for concern relates to the possibility of competition for nest sites with native hole-nesting birds. This has been demonstrated in Nevada (USA), where Common Starlings displaced 11 species of native bird from a cottonwood site, including some species that did not nest in holes but nevertheless were harassed by the starlings; after elimination of the starlings, native birds returned to breed (Weitzel 1988). In North America and the West Indies, Common Starlings outcompete various woodpecker (Picidae) species and American Kestrels *Falco sparvarius* for nest sites (Kerpez and Smith 1990, Wiley 1986, Willimont 1990, Wilmers 1987) and Zeleny (1969) implicated Common Starlings in the national decline of the Eastern Bluebird *Sialis sialis*. In South Africa, Common Starlings displace Olive Woodpeckers *Mesopicos griseocephalus* (van der Merwe 1984), while in Australia competition with native parrots (Psittaciformes) is of concern, although the evidence for this is often circumstantial (Emison 1992, Green 1983). In attempts to prevent the spread of Common Starlings from South Australia into Western Australia, the W. A. Agricultural Protection Board operates a control policy where all individuals are shot or trapped. In 1987–88 these operations cost Aus $ 220,000, and are aimed at protecting the environment as well as agriculture (Hector 1989). In Australia, Common Myna is also regarded as a potential competitor with native hole nesting birds, but as mynas are still largely urban in their distribution, the threat is regarded as less severe than that of Common Starlings (Gregory-Smith 1985). In Polynesia, competition for nest sites and food from Common Mynas is believed to have contributed to declines in some endemic birds (Holyoak and Thibault 1984), and on St Helena, McCulloch (1991) thought that Common Mynas may be nest predators of the Wirebird *Charadrius sanctaehelenae*, and might also compete with this threatened species for food.

Introduced starlings may also have affected native avifaunas through the introduction of exotic diseases and parasites. Common Mynas may have contributed to declines and even extinctions of endemic birds in Hawaii (Warner 1968), where avian malaria *Plasmodium circumflexum* is thought to have been introduced with the mynas. However, the disappearance of endemic birds from areas inhabited by introduced birds such as the Common Myna is often indicative of a change of habitat; the endemic birds are unable to survive the change and become restricted to places where indigenous vegetation persists or they become extinct, whereas mynas adapt well to the new man-made habitats.

Nevertheless, there are examples of direct predation and interference by Common Mynas on island endemics. On Fregate Island, Seychelles, Common Mynas are believed to take eggs and young of the endangered Seychelles Magpie Robin *Copsychus sechellarum* (Watson *et al.* 1992) and the presence of mynas close to its nest has been shown to disrupt its incubation (Komdeur 1996). A myna control programme has now been implemented as part of the BirdLife International recovery programme for the Seychelles Magpie Robin.

Where two species of starling have been introduced to a given area, differences in ability to colonise become apparent. In South Africa, Australia and New Zealand, Common Starlings appear to increase more rapidly and to extend their ranges further than Common Mynas, and in North America, Common Starlings have been outstandingly successful whereas Crested Mynas continue to occupy only a small area around their point of introduction in British Columbia. Differences also appear where the two introduced species are more closely related, and in Singapore, White-vented Mynas appear to be more successful than Common Mynas, possibly because the former species is more adept at exploiting temporary abundances of food that are characteristic of urban areas (Kang 1989). In American Samoa, Jungle Mynas appear to be increasing more rapidly than Common Mynas (Trail 1994), and Engbring and Ramsey (1989) expressed concern that once established, Jungle Mynas might expand from urban into forest areas and threaten endemic forest birds. In Western Samoa, Jungle Mynas were introduced before Common Mynas, and the former species remains the more common (Trail 1994).

Conservation

Within recorded history, five species of starling are known to have become extinct, all of them island forms (Fuller 1987). Collar *et al.* (1994) list seven species as globally threatened: Mountain Starling, Pohnpei Mountain Starling, Rarotonga Starling, White-eyed Starling, Bali Myna, Socotra Starling and Abbott's Starling. In addition, a further 15 species are listed as near-threatened: Rufous-winged Starling, Tanimbar Starling, Rennell Starling, Yellow-eyed Starling, Helmeted Myna, Apo Myna, Bare-eyed Myna, Collared Myna, Black-winged Myna, Red-cheeked Starling, White-headed Starling, White-faced Starling and Red-billed Starling. For only one of these species, Bali Myna, is a conservation programme being implemented.

The major causes of decline of the Bali Myna have been habitat loss and capture for aviculture, and these threats continue. To reverse this decline, in 1987 the International Council for Bird Preservation (now BirdLife International), the American Association of Zoological Parks and Aquaria, the Jersey Wildlife Preservation Trust and the Indonesian Government began a recovery programme. This programme involves research on Bali Mynas in the wild, habitat protection and captive breeding with a view to rearing sufficient individuals for a release programme. In addition, the Indonesian Government has introduced a registration scheme for birds in captivity, and people found in possession of an unregistered Bali Myna are liable to imprisonment or to a substantial fine (Anon 1992b). Despite these attempts to prevent the capture of birds from the wild, individuals that have been reared in captivity, and fitted with transponders before release to augment the wild population, have been recovered in bird shops (van Balen and Gepak 1994).

PLATES 1–32

PLATE 1   NEW GUINEA *APLONIS* GLOSSY STARLINGS

1 Shining Starling *Aplonis metallica*   Text page 113

Lowland woodland and forest edge of New Guinea, Moluccas, Bismarck archipelago, eastern Lesser Sunda Islands, Solomon Islands, northeast Queensland.
a Adult: Black with high greenish gloss, long graduated tail, red eye.
b Immature: Dark above with variable gloss, pale below with dark streaks, long tail.

15 Moluccan Starling *Aplonis mysolensis*   Text page 125

Mainly lowland forest, mangroves, cultivated areas of the Moluccas, eastern Sulawesi, Banggai.
a Adult: Glossy black, long graduated tail, thick bill with strongly arched culmen.
b Immature: Dark above, heavily streaked underparts.

2 Yellow-eyed Starling *Aplonis mystacea*   Text page 115

Lowland forests of Irian Jaya/Papua New Guinea.
Adult: Glossy black, long tail, yellow eye (often appears whitish), tuft of feathers on forehead.

1a

1b

15b

15a

2

PLATE 2   *APLONIS* GLOSSY STARLINGS

3 Singing Starling *Aplonis cantoroides*   **Text page 115**

Mainly lowland forest, coastal woodlands, cultivated areas of New Guinea and offshore islands, Bismarck archipelago and Solomons.
a Adult: Black, glossed green, short square tail, reddish eye.
b Immature: Brown with some gloss above, underparts pale with darker streaking, eye brown but orange-red in older birds.

5 Atoll Starling *Aplonis feadensis*   **Text page 117**

Forest, woodland edge and coconut plantations of small outlying islands of the Bismarck archipelago and Solomons.
a Adult: Black with oily gloss, short square tail, yellow eye.
b Immature: Brown above, scaly underparts, greenish-yellow eye.

4 Tanimbar Starling *Aplonis crassa*   **Text page 117**

Woodlands and forest edge of Tanimbar Islands (Lesser Sundas).
a Adult: Dark charcoal glossed greenish, short square tail, large bill with arched culmen, eye dark brown.
b Immature: Brown above, buff underparts streaked darker.

6 Rennell Starling *Aplonis insularis*   **Text page 118**

Forest canopy, sometimes lower, on Rennell Island (Solomons).
a Adult: Glossy black, short tail, arched culmen, orange eye.
b Immature: Uniform chocolate-brown, grey-brown eye.

PLATE 3   *APLONIS* GLOSSY STARLINGS

7 Long-tailed Starling *Aplonis magna*   Text page 118

All habitats on Biak and Numfor Islands, off northwest Irian Jaya.
Adult: Large, glossy black, long lax tail, brown eye.

8 White-eyed Starling *Aplonis brunneicapilla*   Text page 119

Forest, forest edge and clearings of Bougainville, Choiseul, Rendova and Guadalcanal (Solomons).
a Adult: Glossy black with greatly extended central tail feathers (sometimes broken off), large arched bill, white eye and slight crest on forehead.
b Immature: Upperparts dark glossed green, underparts dark with white streaking, eye olive or brown.

9 Brown-winged Starling *Aplonis grandis*   Text page 120

Forest and secondary vegetation of the Solomon Islands (except Makira).
a Adult: Glossy black with pale wing patch, dark red eye.
b Immature: Duller with dull brown primaries, red or brown eye.

10 Makira Starling *Aplonis dichroa*   Text page 121

Forest of Makira Island (Solomons).
a Adult: Smaller than 9, primaries and secondaries pale, eye red.
b Immature: Browner than adult, eye orange.

PLATE 4   MELANESIAN ISLAND *APLONIS* GLOSSY STARLINGS

12 Striated Starling *Aplonis striata*   **Text page 123**

New Caledonia and Loyalty Islands.
a Adult male: Glossy black with square tail, stubby bill, orange-red eye.
b Adult female: Mousy brown, paler below, orange-red eye.

11 Rufous-winged Starling *Aplonis zelandica*   **Text page 122**

Primary forest, montane on larger islands, of the northern and central New Hebrides, Banks and Santa Cruz Islands.
a *A. z. zelandica*, Vanikoro: Dull brown with heavy bill and short tail, rufous patch in wing, eye brown, undertail tawny-chestnut.
b *A .z. rufipennis*, central and northern New Hebrides and Banks Islands: Brighter, paler chestnut in wing, more orange under tail.
c *A. z. maxwellii*, Santa Cruz Island: Thicker bill, rufous undertail.

13 Mountain Starling *Aplonis santovestris*   **Text page 123**

Cloud forest of Espirito Santo, Vanuatu.
Adult: Rusty-brown, warmer chestnut below, eye grey-green.

12a

12b

11a

11c

11b

13

PLATE 5   SOUTH-EAST ASIAN AND MICRONESIAN *APLONIS* GLOSSY STARLINGS

14 Asian Glossy Starling *Aplonis panayensis*   **Text page 123**

Widespread on Indonesian islands, west to Burma, Assam, southern Indochina, east to Philippines, in forest, cultivated areas and towns.
a Adult: Black, glossed green, short square tail, red eye.
b Immature: Dark brown above, heavily streaked below, yellow, orange or red eye.

17 Micronesian Starling *Aplonis opaca*   **Text page 127**

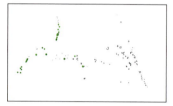

Most habitats on the Caroline Islands, Marianas and Palau Islands, Micronesia.
a Adult: Black with some gloss, yellow eye.
b Immature: Dark brown above, heavily streaked below, yellow eye.

16 Short-tailed Starling *Aplonis minor*   **Text page 126**

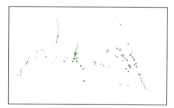

Lowland forest, forest edge and cultivated areas of Mindanao (Philippines), southern Sulawesi and islands, Java, Bali and Lesser Sundas.
a Adult: Very similar to 14, but head and neck glossed purple, red eye.
b Immature: Dark brown above, brown below with white streaking, red eye.

18 Pohnpei Mountain Starling *Aplonis pelzelni*   **Text page 129**

Montane forests of Pohnpei (Caroline Islands).
Adult: Sooty brown above, underparts paler olive-brown, no gloss, brown eye.

PLATE 6   POLYNESIAN *APLONIS* GLOSSY STARLINGS

19 Polynesian Starling *Aplonis tabuensis*   Text page 129

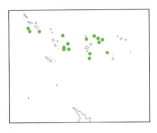

Islands of Fiji, Tonga and nearby groups, mainly forest on large islands but all habitats on smaller ones.

a A. t. tabuensis, southern Tonga and Lau archipelago: Medium size, brown above with purple gloss, paler below, pale wing patch, eye red-brown.

b A. t. brunnescens, Niue: Thinner bill, eye brown.

The eye may be yellow, red-brown or brown in different localities.

20 Samoan Starling *Aplonis atrifusca*   Text page 130

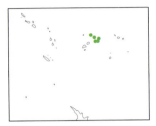

American and Western Samoa, lowland and coastal forest and plantations.

Adult: Large, dark brown with a long square tail and little gloss, heavy down-curved bill, dark brown eye.

21 Raratonga Starling *Aplonis cinerascens*   Text page 131

Montane forest on Raratonga (Cook Islands).

Adult: Mousy brown with pinkish/purplish gloss, pale edges to feathers on underparts, dark eye.

19b

19a

20

21

PLATE 7   *MINO* AND *AMPELICEPS*

24 Golden-breasted Myna   *Mino anais*   **Text page 133**

Lowland forest of New Guinea and Salawati Island.
a Adult *M. a. anais*, northwestern New Guinea and Salawati Island:
Glossy black with large areas of golden-yellow on breast, rump, creamy-
yellow on collar and lower belly, white wing patch.
b Immature *M. a. anais*: Lacks golden breast; breast and belly scaly yellow on black.
c Adult *M. a. orientalis*, northern New Guinea: Golden-orange crown
extends in stripes along side of nape to collar.
d Adult *M. a. robertsoni*, southern New Guinea: Entire top of head golden-orange.

23 Long-tailed Myna   *Mino kreffti*   **Text page 133**

Canopy of mainly lowland forest of islands of the Bismarck archipelago
and northern Solomons.
Adult: Large, glossy black with white rump, undertail and wing patch,
bright orange patch of bare skin around eye extends to point behind, long
tail.

22 Yellow-faced Myna   *Mino dumontii*   **Text page 132**

New Guinea and offshore islands, tree canopy of lowland and hill forest.
Adult: Large, glossy black with white rump, undertail and wing patch,
bright orange bare skin around eye, short tail.

36 Golden-crested Myna   *Ampeliceps coronatus*   **Text page 143**

Treetops of lowland forest from Assam and Burma to Yunnan, south to
northern Thailand and southern Indochina.
a Adult male: Glossy black with golden crown and face, yellow and
white wing patch, short tail, bill yellow with blue base.
b Adult female: Gold on head restricted to centres of crown and throat,
and bare skin around eye.
c Immature: Lacks gold on head, apart from bare skin around eye, gold
gradually acquired with age, bill dark.

24c

24a

24d

24b

23

22

36a

36b

36c

UNIVERSITY OF HERTFORDSHIRE LRC

PLATE 8 PHILIPPINE AND SULAWESI MYNAS

29 Coleto *Sarcops calvus* — Text page 137

Lowland and hill forest, plantations and secondary growth of the Philippines including Sulu archipelago.
a Adult *S. c. calvus*, northern Philippine islands of Luzon, Mindoro and neighbouring islands: Largely black with silvery-grey back, wedge-shaped tail, conspicuous pink bare skin covers much of face.
b Adult *S. c. melanonotus*, Philippines south of Panay and Samar, including Mindanao and Negros: Black mantle contrasts with silvery-grey collar and rump.
c Adult *S. c. lowii*, Sulu Archipelago: Paler than *S. c. calvus*

28 Apo Myna *Basilornis miranda* — Text page 136

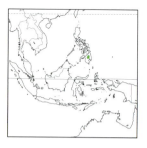

Montane forest of Mindanao.
Adult: Glossy black with long tail, white lower back, erect wispy crest, yellow patch of bare skin around eye.

26 Helmeted Myna *Basilornis galeatus* — Text page 135

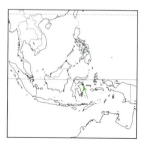

Mainly undisturbed forest on Banggai (Sulawesi) and Sula (Moluccas).
Adult: Glossy black with large white/ochre patches on the side of the neck and breast, rigid erect crest.

27 Long-crested Myna *Basilornis corythaix* — Text page 136

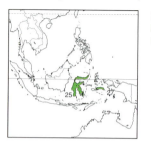

Lowland woodland on Seram (Moluccas).
Adult: Glossy black with a tall erect crest, small white patches on the sides of neck and breast.

25 Sulawesi Crested Myna *Basilornis celebensis* — Text page 134

Hill forest of Sulawesi and offshore islands. (Map above.)
Adult: Glossy black with white/ochre patch on the side of the neck and white patch on the side of the breast, short erect crest.

PLATE 9   SULAWESI ENDEMIC STARLINGS

31 Bare-eyed Myna *Streptocitta albertinae*   Text page 138

Open lowland forest of Sula Island (Moluccas).
Adult: Crown, nape and underparts white, back, wings and very long tail black, bare skin around eye blackish, bill and legs yellow.

30 White-necked Myna *Streptocitta albicollis*   Text page 138

Woodlands and forest of Sulawesi.
a Adult *S. a. albicollis*, southern Sulawesi: Breast and collar white, rest of body glossy black, very long tail, black bill with yellow tip.
b Adult *S. a. torquata*, northern Sulawesi: Bill all black.

32 Flame-browed Starling *Enodes erythrophris*   Text page 139

Mid-level forest of north and central Sulawesi.
Adult: Grey body, olive wings and tail, golden-yellow rump and undertail, vivid reddish-orange stripe above eye.

33 Grosbeak Myna *Scissirostrum dubium*   Text page 140

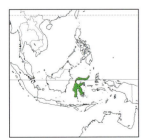

Lowland woodland and forest edge of Sulawesi.
a Adult: Slate grey, red tips to long feathers of rump, heavy yellow bill.
b Immature: Browner, thinner bill.
c Nest colony in dead tree.

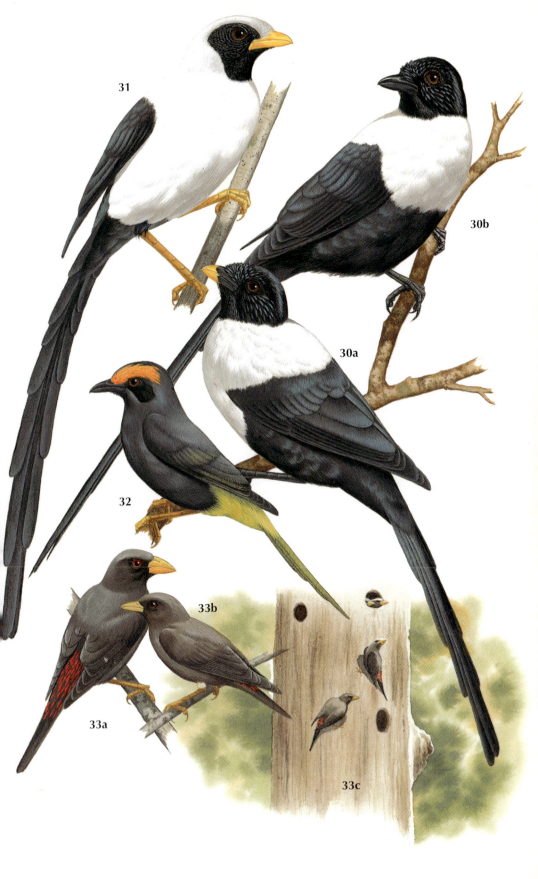

31

30b

30a

32

33b

33a

33c

PLATE 10   HILL MYNAS

37 Common Hill Myna *Gracula religiosa*
Text page 143

Moist forest from India east to southern China, Indochina, Thailand, Malaysia, Indonesia east to Alor, Palawan (Philippines).
a Adult: Black glossed with purple and turquoise, white wing patch, yellow wattles below eye and on hind-neck.
b In flight: Rounded wings, white wing patch.

38 Southern Hill Myna *Gracula indica*
Text page 146

Moist hill forest of southwestern India and southern Sri Lanka.
Adult: Smaller than 37, smaller wing patch and wattles extend from hind-neck up on to crown. Also differs from 37 in voice.

40 Nias Hill Myna *Gracula robusta*
Text page 147

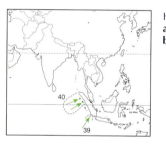

Hill forest of Nias and Banyak Islands, off western Sumatra.
a Adult: Large glossy black, crow-like, very large wattles.
b In flight: White wing patch more extensive than in 37.

39 Enggano Hill Myna *Gracula enganensis*
Text page 147

Endemic to Enggano Island off southwest Sumatra. (Map above.)
Adult: More turquoise above and duller below than 37, heavy stubby bill.

41 Sri Lanka Myna *Gracula ptilogenys*
Text page 148

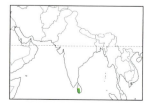

Humid forest of southwestern Sri Lanka.
Adult: Small glossy black myna, differs from 38 in lacking wattles on crown and below eye, black base to lower mandible.

37a

37b

38

40a

40b

39

41

PLATE 11   CRESTED MYNAS

43 Crested Myna *Acridotheres cristatellus*   **Text page 149**

Open spaces, cultivation, urban areas in southeastern and central China, Burma, east-central Laos, Vietnam and Taiwan.
Adult: Black, ivory bill, orange eye, long crest.

47 Collared Myna *Acridotheres albocinctus*   **Text page 154**

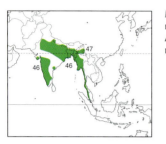

Moist open grassland and cultivations in northeast India (Manipur), northern Burma, southwest China (northwest Yunnan).
Adult: Short crest and distinctive buffish-white patches on sides of neck.

46 Jungle Myna *Acridotheres fuscus*   **Text page 153**

Mainly lowlands and foothills in well-wooded areas with open spaces, cultivations from Pakistan through India to Burma and central Malaysia. (Map above.)
a Adult *A. f. fuscus*, Pakistan, northern India: Grey-brown with medium crest, bill yellow-orange with blue base to lower mandible, eye yellow.
b Adult *A. f. mahrattensis*, western peninsular India: eye bluish-white or grey.

42 Great Myna *Acridotheres grandis*   **Text page 148**

Lowland grasslands, marshes in Nagaland east to Thailand (not peninsula), Indochina, southwestern China.
Adult: Black, long crest, chrome yellow bill, dark eye.

45 Pale-bellied Myna *Acridotheres cinereus*   **Text page 152**

Endemic to southern peninsula of Sulawesi, cultivations and lightly wooded areas. (Map above.)
Adult: Grey back, paler below, black head, wings and tail.

44 White-vented Myna *Acridotheres javanicus*   **Text page 151**

Lowland cultivation and urban areas, endemic to Java,Bali and southern Sulawesi, introduced Singapore and Sumatra. (Map above.)
Adult: Dark grey with short crest, orange-yellow bill and lemon-yellow eye.

43

47

46b

46a

42

45

44

PLATE 12   COMMON MYNA AND ALLIES AND *LEUCOPSAR*

49 Common Myna *Acridotheres tristis*   Text page 157

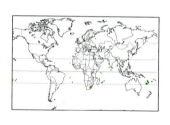

Iran through central southern Asia and India to southern China, Thailand, Indochina and Malaysia, in open country, cultivations and human habitation. Widely introduced.
a Adult: Brown with glossy black head, white wing patch, tip to tail and undertail, yellow bill, legs and patch around eye.
b Immature: Paler and duller than adult, especially head.
c In flight: Brown body, black wings and tail, white wing patch and tail tip, rounded wings.

48 Bank Myna *Acridotheres ginginianus*   Text page 155

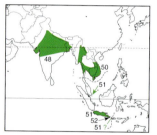

Cultivations and human habitation in plains of north and central India, Bangladesh, Nepal and eastern Pakistan.
a Adult: Blue-grey with black head and wings, buff wing patch and tail tip, orange patch round eye.
b Immature: Browner than adult, buff below.
c In flight: Grey body, black wings and tail, wing patch and tail tip buff, rounded wings.

50 Vinous-breasted Myna *Acridotheres burmannicus*   Text page 161

Largely terrestrial in short vegetation, Burma, Thailand, Indochina. (Map above.)
a Adult: Head and breast dirty white, dark grey-brown back, vinous below, white wing patch and tail tip.
b Immature: Duller and browner, brown crown.
c In flight: Whitish head and rump, white wing patch and tail tip, back dark, rounded wings.

51 Black-winged Myna *Acridotheres melanopterus*   Text page 162

Open ground and cultivation in Java and Bali, occasionally Lombok. (Map above.)
a Adult *A. m. melanopterus*, most of Java: White body, black remiges and tail, apart from white tip, yellow bill, legs and patch round eye.
b Immature: Browner above than adult, yellow patch round eye.
c In flight: White with black flight feathers and tail, apart from tip, rounded wings.
d Adult *A. m. tricolor*, southeastern peninsula of Java: White with black remiges and greater coverts, grey back, white rump.
e In flight: Grey back, more black in wings than 51c.
f Adult *A. m. tertius*, Bali: White with grey mantle, back and rump, black wings and tail, apart from tip, white wing patch.
g In flight: White, grey back and rump, black wings with white patch.

52 Bali Myna *Leucopsar rothschildi*   Text page 163

Endemic to northwestern Bali, Indonesia in open woodland with grass. (Map above.)
a Adult: White, long erectile crest, blue patch around eye.
b Immature: Mainly white but often with smoky and cinnamon tinges, crest short.
c In flight: White with black tips to wings and tail.

49a

49b

49c

48a

48b

48c

50a

50c

50b

1c

51e

51b

51a

51d

51f

51g

52a

52b

52c

KAMOL
MAY 97
BANGKOK

PLATE 13

63 Red-billed Starling *Sturnus sericeus*   **Text page 181**

Open areas with scattered trees, cultivations in China south of the Yangtze.
a Adult male: Grey back and underparts, head whitish sometimes tinged ochre/grey, bill red, usually with black tip.
b Adult female: Back brown, head and underparts tinged brown.
c In flight: Pointed wings, head and rump paler than back, wings dark with white patch.

54 Asian Pied Myna *Gracupica contra*   **Text page 167**

Open and lightly wooded areas and cultivations from Pakistan and northern India to Thailand, southwest China (Yunnan), Malaysia and western Indonesia.
a Adult: Pied myna with black throat and breast, white cheek and forehead, yellow bill with red base.
b Immature: Browner than adult, lacks white forehead and red bill.
c In flight: White head and rump, wingbar and belly, otherwise black, tail lacks white tip, rounded wings.

53 Black-collared Myna *Gracupica nigricollis*   **Text page 166**

Southern China, Indochina, Thailand and Burma in open areas including cultivations and urban areas, mainly terrestrial.
a Adult: Large black and white myna with yellow eye patch.
b Immature: Head and belly brownish-grey, lacks black collar.
c In flight: White head, rump and tail tip, white below with black collar, rounded wings.

63b

63c

63a

63a

54b

54c

54a

53b

53c

53a

KAMOL
MAY 97
BANGKOK

PLATE 14   SMALL ARBOREAL STARLINGS 1

57 White-shouldered Starling *Sturnia sinensis*   **Text page 172**

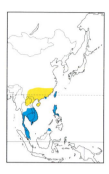

Open lightly wooded country, breeds southern China, winters Thailand, Indochina, Malaysia, northern Philippines and Taiwan.
a Adult male: Pale grey with prominent white shoulder patch, black wings and tail, pale eye, white areas sometimes with buff tinges.
b Adult female: Greyer than male, white shoulder patch, pale eye.
c In flight: Black wings with white shoulders, white tip to tail.

55 Purple-backed Starling *Sturnia sturnina*   **Text page 168**

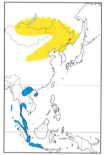

Lowland forest, villages of eastern Russia, Mongolia, northern China and North Korea, winters southern Thailand, Malaysia, western Indonesia.
a Adult male: Grey, paler below, purple mantle, black wings with white bars, dark eye.
b Adult female: Mousy brown, paler below, white wingbars, dark eye.
c In flight: Pale rump, black wings with bars, black tail lacks white tip.

56 Red-cheeked Starling *Sturnia philippensis*   **Text page 170**

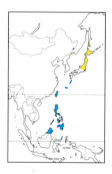

Open deciduous woodland of northern Japan, western Kuril Islands and extreme eastern Siberia, winters to south but main wintering area appears unknown.
a Adult male: Dark violet back, underparts pale, wings and tail black, white wing bar, reddish cheeks, dark eye.
b Adult female: Brownish grey above, paler below, brown wings with white bar, dark eye.
c In flight: Black wings with white bar, rump dark or with pale streaks, tail with pale outer edge.

57a

57c

57b

55c

55a

55b

56c

56a

56b

PLATE 15   SMALL ARBOREAL STARLINGS 2

58 Chestnut-tailed Starling *Sturnia malabarica*   Text page 173

Open woodland and open country in peninsular India east to western China, Thailand, Indochina.

a Adult *S. m. malabarica*, India except for southwest: Grey back, chestnut underparts, white face, broad rufous tip to tail, whitish eye, bill blue at base, yellow tip.

b Immature: Greyish-brown with darker wings, paler rufous tail tip.

c Adult *S. m. nemoricola*, eastern part of range: Paler head with white streaks on nape, paler below, some birds with small white shoulder patch.

d Adult male *S. m. blythii*, southwestern India: Brilliant white head with long hackles, white breast and upper belly, grey rump.

e Adult female *S. m. blythii*: Greyer than male on breast and head, nape with pale grey streaking.

59 White-headed Starling *Sturnia erythropygia*   Text page 174

Endemic to the Andaman and Nicobar Islands, forest and cultivated areas.

a Adult *S. e. erythropygia*, Andamans: Creamy white head and underparts, rump and lower belly chestnut, black wings, black tail with chestnut tip.

b Adult *S. e. andamanensis*, Car Nicobar: Rump, lower belly and tail tip white.

60 White-faced Starling *Sturnia albofrontata*   Text page 175

Endemic to Sri Lanka, hill forest.

Adult: White face, dark grey upperparts with white streaking on neck, underparts paler, vent greyish-white.

58a

58b

58c

58d

58e

59a

59b

60

PLATE 16   TERRESTRIAL STARLINGS 1

61 Brahminy Starling *Temenuchus pagodarum*   **Text page 175**

Peninsular India and Sri Lanka in open forest, cultivations and human habitation.
a Adult: Glossy black cap with long crest, grey above, cinnamon below.
b Immature: Dull black cap, body mouse-brown, darker wings and tail.
c In flight: Grey above, cinnamon below, dark primaries and tail, with tip and outer feathers white.

62 Rose-coloured Starling *Pastor roseus*   **Text page 177**

Arid central Asia from Turkey to western China, sometimes breeds outside this area. Winters open cultivated area of India.
a Adult spring: Pink with black head and neck, wings and tail.
b Adult in flight: Pink with black extremities.
c Juvenile: Brown, often with spotting on breast, yellowish bill, pale eye ring.
d Juvenile in flight: Buff margins to remiges and tail feathers, rump paler than back and tail.

64 White-cheeked Starling *Sturnus cineraceus*   **Text page 182**

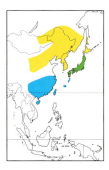

Lowland open woodland, cultivations and human habitation in eastern Russia, Mongolia, northern China and Japan, winters southern China, Taiwan. (See also plate 17, p. 80.)
In flight: White cheek patch, white rump, margins of secondaries white.

67 Wattled Starling *Creatophora cinerea*   **Text page 192**

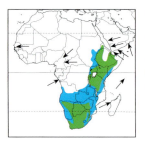

Eastern and southern Africa, vagrant to west Africa, southern Arabia and some oceanic islands; open savanna and thornbush. (See also plate 18, p. 82.)
a Breeding male in flight: Contrasting pale body with black remiges and tail, white rump.
b Non-breeding bird in flight: Grey-brown body, brown wings and tail without pale feather margins, white rump.

62b

64

67a

62d

62a

67b

62c

61c

61a

61b

PLATE 17   TERRESTRIAL STARLINGS 2

65 Common Starling *Sturnus vulgaris*

Text page 183

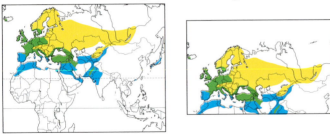

Western Europe and eastern Atlantic Islands, east to Lake Baikal, Lapland in north and Pakistan in south, in lowland wooded grassland, cultivations and human habitation. Winters south and west of breeding area, North Africa to northern India. Introduced North America, South Africa, southeast Australia, New Zealand; also Polynesia, Bermuda, Jamaica and Puerto Rico.

a Adult male spring: Glossy black, elongated throat feathers, limited spotting especially back and vent, yellow bill with bluish pase, dark eye.

b Adult female spring: Similar to male but more and larger spotting, pinkish base to yellow bill, pale eye ring.

c Immature female winter: Reduced gloss and heavy spotting, especially on underparts, bill dark.

d Juvenile: Sandy brown, whitish throat, usually dark streaking on underparts.

66 Spotless Starling *Sturnus unicolor*

Text page 189

Open woodland, cultivations, human habitation in Iberia, northwestern North Africa, Sardinia, Corsica, Sicily.

a Adult male spring: Black with some gloss, very long throat feathers, yellow bill with bluish base.

b Adult male winter: Black with fine white spotting as 'v'-shaped feather tips, mainly on back, sides of neck, breast and vent, dark bill, wings darker than in 65.

c Juvenile: Darker brown than 65, pale chin, underparts unstreaked.

64 White-cheeked Starling *Sturnus cineraceus*

Text page 182

Lowland open woodland, cultivations and human habitation in eastern Russia, Mongolia, northern China and Japan, winters in southern China, northern Philippines and Taiwan. (See also plate 16, p. 78.)

a Adult male: Brownish-grey above, grey below, blackish crown contrasts with white forehead and cheeks (but amount of white variable), rump white, orange bill.

b Juvenile: Buffish-grey, white throat, cheeks, belly and vent. For flight see Plate 16

65a

65b

65d

65c

66a

66b

66c

64a

64b

PLATE 18   STARLINGS LINKING AFRICA AND ASIA

34 Spot-winged Starling *Saroglossa spiloptera*   **Text page 141**

Himalayan foothills (breeding), to Assam, Bangladesh, Burma and northwestern Thailand (non-breeding); forested hills.
a Adult male: Upperparts grey with dark borders, red-brown throat, chestnut flanks, pale iris.
b Adult female: Grey-brown upperparts, underparts pale with brown streaking.
c In flight: White wing patch in centre of primary feathers.

35 Madagascar Starling *Saroglossa aurata*   **Text page 142**

Madagascar except highlands and southwest; woodland.
a Adult: Dull brown, darker on lower chest, white around vent, wings bluish with white outer edge, tail with white outer webs, dark iris.
b In flight: White patch in primary feathers, white margin on outer tail feathers and outermost primaries.

67 Wattled Starling *Creatophora cinerea*   **Text page 192**

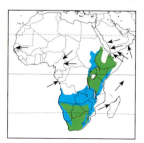

Eastern and southern Africa, vagrant to West Africa, southern Arabia and some oceanic islands; open savanna and thornbush. (See also plate 16, p. 78.)
a Adult male breeding: Body greyish, head with bald yellow skin and black wattles on forehead and throat, yellow bill, black wings with white coverts, black tail, dark iris.
b, d Adult male non-breeding: Feathered head except for yellow patch behind eye, dark moustachial streaks. In flight, white rump is conspicuous.
c Adult female: Like non-breeding male, but wing and tail feathers brown, little white on coverts.

34c

34b

35b

34a

35a

67d

67a

67b

67c

PLATE 19   SHORT-TAILED GLOSSY STARLINGS

68 Cape Glossy Starling *Lamprotornis nitens*   Text page 197

Angola and southern Zaïre south to Namibia, Botswana, Zimbabwe, South Africa and southern Mozambique; woodland and thornbush.
Adult: Glossy blue-green, lacking distinct ear patch or contrasting colour on underparts, coppery epaulet may be visible, orange-yellow iris.

69 Greater Blue-eared Glossy Starling *Lamprotornis chalybaeus*
Text page 199

Senegal to Ethiopia, south through East Africa to Angola, Namibia, Botswana, Zimbabwe and northeastern South Africa; open woodland.
Adult: Glossy blue-green with contrasting blue ear patch, violet wash on belly extending well forward past legs (contrast with Lesser Blue-eared), iris yellow or orange.

70 Lesser Blue-eared Glossy Starling *Lamprotornis chloropterus*
Text page 201

Senegal to Ethiopia, south to Uganda and northwest Kenya, southern population from southeast Kenya to southern Zaïre, Angola, Zimbabwe and northern Mozambique; savanna woodland.
a Adult: Very similar to Greater Blue-eared, but violet area on belly does not extend forward beyond legs.
b Juvenile: Upperparts with greenish sheen, underparts matt chestnut or dull brown, iris greyish.

71 Bronze-tailed Glossy Starling *Lamprotornis chalcurus*
Text page 203

Senegal east to Sudan, Uganda and western Kenya; open thornbush and savanna.
Adult: Glossy blue-green with purple on ear-coverts and belly, yellow iris.

68

69

70a

70b

71

PLATE 20   WESTERN AFRICAN GLOSSY STARLINGS

72 Splendid Glossy Starling *Lamprotornis splendidus* Text page 203

Senegal east to Ethiopia and East Africa, also on Bioko (Fernando Po) and Príncipe, south to Zaïre, Zambia and Angola; forested lowlands.
a Adult male: Upperparts glossy blue-green, underparts glossy purple with marked contrasts between plumage areas, bronze patch near ear-coverts, white iris.
b Adult female: Pattern like male, but duller, with less contrast.

73 Principe Glossy Starling *Lamprotornis ornatus*   Text page 206

Príncipe Island; forests and plantations.
Adult: Blue-green head and nape, contrasts with bronzy back and greenish underparts, white iris.

74 Emerald Starling *Lamprotornis iris*   Text page 207

Guinea and Mali to Ivory Coast; savanna woodland.
Adult: brilliant emerald green, with purple ear-coverts and belly, dark iris.

75 Purple Glossy Starling *Lamprotornis purpureus*   Text page 208

Senegal east to southern Sudan, Uganda and western Kenya; open woodland.
a Adult: Blue-green upperparts, deep purple underparts, yellow iris.
b Juvenile: Matt grey except for glossy wings and tail, grey iris.

PLATE 21   NORTHERN AFRICAN LONG-TAILED GLOSSY STARLINGS

76 Rüppell's Long-tailed Glossy Starling *Lamprotornis purpuropterus*
Text page 209

Southern Sudan, Ethiopia and Somalia through Kenya to northwest Tanzania; thornbush and savanna.
Adult: Bronzy head contrasts with glossy blue body, barring on tail, yellowish white iris (northern birds). In southern birds head is same colour as body.

77 Long-tailed Glossy Starling *Lamprotornis caudatus* Text page 210

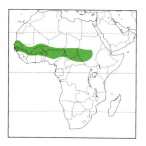

Senegal and southern Mauritania east to western Sudan; dry savanna.
Adult: Bronzy sheen on head, blue-green body, distinct barring on tail, yellowish iris.

78 Golden-breasted Starling *Lamprotornis regius*   Text page 211

Southern Ethiopia and Somalia to eastern Kenya and northeastern Tanzania; open thornbush in arid areas.
a Adult: Blue-green head and upperparts, purple collar on chest, golden underparts, bronzy tail, white iris.
b Juvenile: Matt grey head, chest and upperparts except for gloss on wings, dark iris.

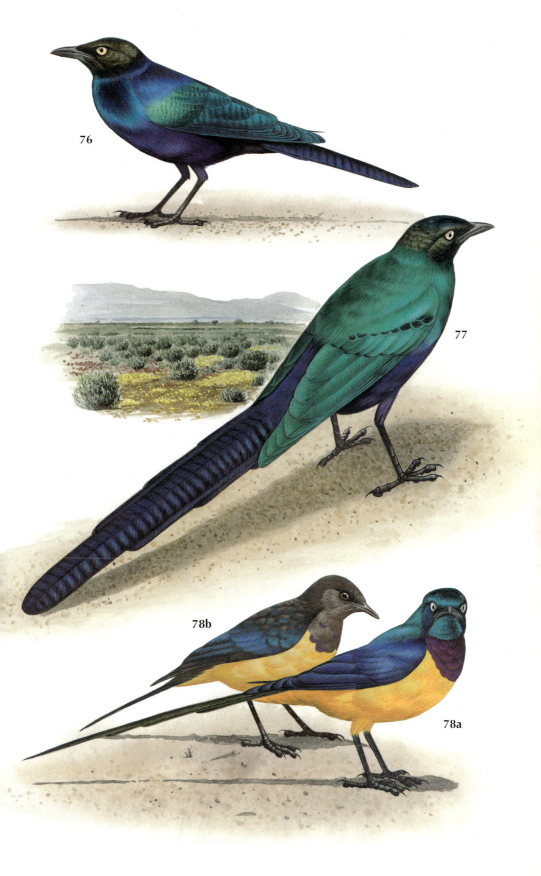

76

77

78b

78a

PLATE 22 SOUTHERN AFRICAN LONG-TAILED GLOSSY STARLINGS

79 Meves' Long-tailed Starling *Lamprotornis mevesii* Text page 212

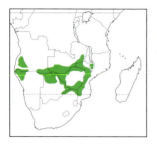

South Angola to Malawi, northern Namibia, Botswana, Zimbabwe, northern South Africa and central Mozambique; open areas with tall baobab or mopane trees.
Adult: Dark blue glossy plumage, obvious barring on long tail, dark iris.

80 Burchell's Glossy Starling *Lamprotornis australis* Text page 214

Southern Angola, western Zambia, northern Namibia, Botswana, Zimbabwe and northern South Africa; open woodland and savanna, especially with camelthorn trees.
Adult: Dark blue glossy plumage, heavy tail with dark barring, dark iris.

81 Sharp-tailed Glossy Starling *Lamprotornis acuticaudus* Text page 215

Southern Angola, northern Namibia east to southern Zaïre, Zambia and southwestern Tanzania; open miombo and mopane woodland.
a Adult: Glossy green with a pointed tail showing barring, red iris.
b Juvenile: Matt grey except for gloss on wings and tail, brown iris.

79

80

81a

81b

PLATE 23   FOREST GLOSSY STARLINGS

82 Black-bellied Glossy Starling *Lamprotornis corruscus*
Text page 216

Southern Somalia south to eastern South Africa, also on Zanzibar, Pemba and smaller offshore islands; lowland coastal thicket and forest.
a Adult male: Dark glossy green upperparts, underparts black with some sheen, iris yellow, sometimes red.
b Adult female: Like male, but underparts charcoal without gloss, iris yellow.

87 Purple-headed Glossy Starling *Hylopsar purpureiceps*
Text page 222

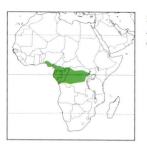

Southern Nigeria east to Uganda; canopy of lowland forest.
Adult: Glossy purple head and chest contrast with greenish-blue body, dark iris.

88 Coppery-tailed Starling *Hylopsar cupreocauda*   Text page 223

Guinea and Sierra Leone to Ghana; canopy of lowland forest and plantations.
Adult: Purple of head blends into turquoise-blue body, barring on tail not conspicuous, yellow iris.

82a

82b

87

88

PLATE 24   GLOSSY STARLINGS WITH BROWN BELLIES

83 Superb Starling *Lamprotornis superbus*   **Text page 218**

Western Uganda, southern Ethiopia and Somalia through Kenya to central Tanzania; open savanna and arid thornbush.
Adult: Crown bronzy-black, glossy blue-green nape, back, throat and chest, white band separates chest from chestnut-brown belly, white vent, creamy white iris.

84 Hildebrandt's Starling *Lamprotornis hildebrandti*   **Text page 219**

Southern Kenya and northern Tanzania; open thornbush.
Adult: Dark glossy blue crown, throat, chest and mantle, bronze collar on nape, greenish wings, belly and vent light brown, orange-red iris.

85 Shelley's Starling *Lamprotornis shelleyi*   **Text page 220**

Kenya, Somalia and southern Ethiopia; arid thornbush and open woodland.
Adult: Very like Hildebrandt's Starling, but crown not bluer than throat, bronze collar often very narrow, and underside much darker chestnut-brown.

86 Chestnut-bellied Starling *Lamprotornis pulcher*   **Text page 221**

Senegal east to northern Ethiopia; dry *Acacia* savanna of Sahel zone.
a, b Adult: Glossy bronze-green upperparts, throat and chest, chestnut brown belly and vent, pale iris. In flight, white patch in primary feathers.

83

84

85

86a

86b

PLATE 25   AMETHYST STARLING AND SIMILAR SPECIES

89 Amethyst Starling *Cinnyricinclus leucogaster*   Text page 224

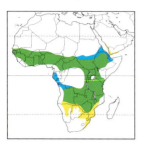

Africa south of the Sahara, southwestern Arabia; savanna woodland.
a Adult male: Head, back and upper chest iridescent purple; lower chest, belly and vent white, iris with yellow outer ring.
b, c Adult female: Head brown with dark streaks, back brown with paler margins to feathers; throat, chest and belly white with dark streaks; yellow outer ring on iris. In flight, shows some rufous in centre of primary feathers.

108 Sharpe's Starling *Pholia sharpii*   Text page 248

Southern Sudan and Ethiopia to eastern Zaïre, eastern Kenya and Tanzania; canopy of highland forest.
a Adult: Crown, nape and back glossy blue-black; throat and chest cream tinged with buff; belly and vent buff; iris yellow.
b Juvenile: Upperparts dull charcoal; throat, chest and belly creamy-white with arrow-shaped markings, buff towards vent; iris dark brown.

109 Abbott's Starling *Pholia femoralis*   Text page 249

Eastern Kenya and northeastern Tanzania, canopy of highland forest.
a Adult: Head, nape, back, throat and chest blue-black; belly and vent creamy white; iris white.
b Juvenile: Upperparts, throat and chest dark grey-brown; dark streaks on throat, chest and belly; dark brown iris.

89c

89a

89b

108a

109b

108b

109a

PLATE 26 *SPREO* STARLINGS

90 African Pied Starling *Spreo bicolor*

Text page 227

South Africa except northwest, and eastern lowlands; grassland, scrub and thornbush.
a Adult: Black with dull gloss, except for white around vent; conspicuous white iris, and yellow lower mandible and gape.
b Juvenile: Matt plumage, iris dark brown, gape dull yellow-white.

91 Fischer's Starling *Spreo fischeri*

Text page 229

Southern Ethiopia and Somalia to eastern Kenya and Tanzania; dry *Acacia* thornveld.
Adult: Dull ash-grey; white lower chest, belly and vent; white iris.

92 Ashy Starling *Spreo unicolor*

Text page 230

Central Tanzania; open wooded areas.
Adult: Dull charcoal grey, long tapered tail, yellow iris.

93 White-crowned Starling *Spreo albicapillus*

Text page 231

Northern Kenya, southern Ethiopia and western Somalia; arid thornbush.
Adult: White crown, dull bronze back and wings with white wingbar, grey throat and chest with white shafts to feathers, white belly and vent, pale yellow iris.

90a

90b

92

91

93

PLATE 27   MONTANE AND FOREST RED-WINGED STARLINGS

94 Red-winged Starling *Onychognathus morio*   **Text page 232**

Ethiopia and eastern Sudan southwards through eastern Africa to South Africa; rocky highlands, in south to sea-level, and in many urban areas.
a Adult male: Glossy black except for rufous wing feathers.
b Adult female: Head, nape and upper chest ash-grey with darker central streaks on feathers.
c In flight: Rufous patch almost to tips of primary feathers, moderately long wedge-shaped tail.

95 Slender-billed Red-winged Starling *Onychognathus tenuirostris*
Text page 234

Northern Malawi through eastern Africa to Ethiopia; montane forest and alpine zone of mountains.
a Adult male: Glossy black except for rufous wing feathers, long tapered tail.
b Adult female: Feathers of head, nape and throat have grey tips, producing a scalloped effect.
c In flight: Broad black tips to rufous primaries, very long, pointed tail.

96 Chestnut-winged Starling *Onychognathus fulgidus* Text page 236

Guinea east to Uganda, south to Angola, and on Bioko (Fernando Pó) and São Tomé; lowland forest.
a Adult male: Glossy blue-black with rufous wing feathers and red iris.
b Adult female: Head, nape and throat grey, heavily streaked with glossy dark green.
c In flight: Broad black tips to rufous primaries, and long, graduated tail.

97 Waller's Red-winged Starling *Onychognathus walleri*
Text page 237

Bioko (Fernando Pó) and Cameroon, also southern Sudan, western Kenya and adjacent Zaïre, and eastern Kenya and Tanzania to northern Malawi; montane forest.
a Adult male: Glossy black with rufous wing feathers, red iris and short, square tail.
b Adult female: Black plumage duller; head, nape and throat ash-grey, with dark central streaks on nape and crown.
c In flight: Rufous primaries with broad black tips, tail short and square.

PLATE 28 ARID-COUNTRY RED-WINGED STARLINGS

98 Somali Red-winged Starling *Onychognathus blythii* Text page 238

Ethiopia, Eritrea and Somalia, and Socotra Island; mountains and cliffs in arid areas.
a Adult male: Glossy black, rufous wing feathers.
b Adult female: Head, nape, throat and upper chest plain ash-grey.
c In flight: Rufous primary feathers with narrow black tip, long graduated tail.

99 Socotra Red-winged Starling *Onychognathus frater* Text page 239

Socotra Island; wooded areas near rocky outcrops.
a Adult: Glossy black except for rufous wing feathers; sexes alike.
b In flight: Rufous primary feathers with narrow black tips, graduated tail clearly shorter than in Somali Red-winged Starling.

100 Tristram's Red-winged Starling *Onychognathus tristramii* Text page 240

Yemen north to Sinai and Israel; rocky, arid regions, and in some urban areas.
a Adult male: Glossy black, rufous wing feathers, short, square tail.
b Adult female: Head, nape and throat grey with dark streaks on feathers of nape and throat.
c In flight: Rufous primary feathers with narrow black tips; short, square tail.

101 Pale-winged Starling *Onychognathus nabouroup* Text page 241

Southwestern Angola through Namibia to western South Africa; rocky hills and gorges in arid regions.
a Adult: Glossy black except for reddish brown edges to wing feathers, orange iris; sexes alike.
b In flight: White patch in primary feathers with broad black tips; short, square tail.

98a

98b

98c

99b

99a

100c

100b

100a

101b

101a

PLATE 29 **ETHIOPIAN AND WEST AFRICAN RED-WINGED STARLINGS**

102 Bristle-crowned Starling *Onychognathus salvadorii*
Text page 242

Ethiopia, Somalia and northern Kenya; arid, rocky highlands.
a Adult male: Projecting bristly feathers on forehead, very long, graduated tail.
b Adult female: Head duller than male, tail clearly shorter if seen together.
c In flight: Rufous primary feathers with narrow black tips; tail longer than body with very long central feathers.

103 White-billed Starling *Onychognathus albirostris*   Text page 243

Ethiopia; rocky areas in high mountains.
a Adult male: Glossy black plumage, white bill, short, square tail.
b Adult female: Head, nape and chest plain ash grey.
c In flight: Rufous primary feathers with narrow black tips; short, square tail.

104 Neumann's Red-winged Starling *Onychognathus neumanni*
Text page 244

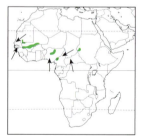

Western Sudan to Guinea and Mauritania; rocky outcrops and cliffs, primarily in the Sahel zone.
a Adult male: Glossy black, except for rufous wing feathers.
b Adult female: Head, nape and upper chest ash grey, with dark streaks on the feathers.
c In flight: Rufous primary feathers with narrow black tips; long graduated tail in eastern birds, but from Niger river westwards, birds are shorter-tailed.

102b

102c

102a

103b

103c

103a

104a

104c

104b

PLATE 30   FOREST CANOPY STARLINGS

105 Narrow-tailed Starling *Poeoptera lugubris*   **Text page 245**

West and Central Africa; lowland forest.
a Adult male: Dark blue plumage, yellow iris and long, narrow tail.
b, c Adult female: Dark grey plumage, yellow iris and long, tapered tail.
In flight, chestnut patch in the primary wing feathers.
d Adult male: Broad, flattened bill, seen from above.

106 Stuhlmann's Starling *Poeoptera stuhlmanni*   **Text page 246**

Southwestern Sudan to western Tanzania; montane forest.
a Adult male: Blue-black plumage, yellow iris.
b, c Adult female: Blackish plumage, yellow iris. In flight, chestnut patch
in the primary wing feathers.

107 Kenrick's Starling *Poeoptera kenricki*   **Text page 247**

Central Kenya to eastern Tanzania; montane forest.
a Adult male: Blackish plumage, yellow iris.
b, c Adult female: Less glossy than male, yellow iris. In flight, chestnut
patch in the primary wing feathers.

105a

105b

105c

105d

106a

106b

106c

107a

107b

107c

PLATE 31   SOME MONOTYPIC AFRICAN STARLINGS

110 White-collared Starling *Grafisia torquata*   **Text page 249**

Central Africa; open woodland.
a Adult male: Dark blue plumage except for broad white collar on chest, yellow iris.
b Adult female: Dark charcoal grey with no collar, yellow iris.

111 Magpie Starling *Speculipastor bicolor*   **Text page 250**

East Africa; arid thornbush.
a Adult male: Dark blue on back and upper chest, with a dark bib and white belly; iris yellow with red outer ring.
b Adult female: Dull grey head, chest and upperparts.
c In flight: White band at base of primary wing feathers.

112 White-winged Babbling Starling *Neocichla gutturalis*
Text page 251

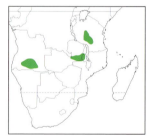

Western Angola, and western Zambia to eastern Tanzania; open miombo woodland.
a Adult: Grey-brown head and back except for white wingbar; dark bib in the throat, chest and belly buff; iris bright yellow.
b Juvenile: Mottled brown crown and back; whitish throat, chest and belly with tear-drop shaped streaks; iris grey; bill yellow with dark tip.
c In flight: White patch at base of secondary feathers.

110b

110a

111a

111b

111c

112c

112a

112b

PLATE 32   OXPECKERS

113 Red-billed Oxpecker *Buphagus erythrorhynchus*   Text page 252

Central Africa southwards to eastern South Africa; savanna with large game animals.
a Adult: Rump and back uniform olive-brown, red iris surrounded by yellow wattle, completely red bill.
b Juvenile: Dark eye and dull brown wattle, dark brown bill.

114 Yellow-billed Oxpecker *Buphagus africanus*   Text page 257

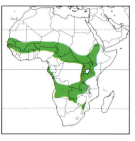

West Africa east and southwards to northern South Africa; savanna with large game animals.
a Adult: Pale rump contrasts with back, red iris but no yellow wattle, bill with broad yellow base and red tip.
b Juvenile: Dark eye, dark brown bill.
c In flight: Pale rump conspicuous.

114c

113b

113a

114a

114b

1 SHINING STARLING *Aplonis metallica*

Metallic Starling, Colonial Starling

Plate 1

Lamprotornis metallicus Temminck 1824

FIELD IDENTIFICATION 21–26 cm. Sexes similar. Adult Shining Starlings are all black but the plumage is highly glossed with metallic green, violet-purple and blue. The iris is bright red or orange-red. A useful distinguishing feature is the relatively long, graduated tail (see also Yellow-eyed and Moluccan Starlings). When breeding, the colonies of pendulous nests are diagnostic (but see also Yellow-eyed Starling). In young birds the upperparts and sides of the head are black or brownish-black with varying degrees of gloss according to age, and underparts are whitish or buffish-white, streaked with dark brown or black. Shining Starlings are often encountered in fast-flying flocks.

DESCRIPTION Adult: the forehead, crown, stripe on cheek, upper breast and mantle are glossy purple, throat and nape are glossy satin green, and scapulars, wing-coverts, back, rump, breast, and belly are glossy emerald green. The feathers of the head and neck are long and lance-olate. The wings are dark brownish-black with bluish iridescence on the outer margins of the primary coverts and secondaries. The tail is graduated, with the two central feathers *c.* 2 cm longer than the remainder, black with some gloss. The bill is black and fairly long with the culmen curved. The legs are black, and the iris bright orange-red or red, and sometimes with a fine inner yellow ring. **Immature**: Upperparts are chocolate-brown, wings blackish-brown showing a little gloss on the secondaries and scapulars. The tail is chocolate-brown. The chin and throat are buffish with brown feather shafts. The breast and belly are brown with broad pale buff margins producing streaking which is browner on the breast, more spotted on the belly. The iris of young birds changes from dark brown through olive-yellow, yellowish-green, greenish-orange to the orange-red of the adult. This description refers to the nominate form of Papua New Guinea, northeast Queensland and the Moluccas.

A. m. circumscripta, of the Tanimbar and Damar islands, is glossed reddish-purple on the head, mantle and breast.

A. m. nitida, from the Bismarcks, has the green iridescence more bronze.

A. m. purpureiceps, from the Admiralty Islands, is smaller with a shorter tail, and the purple in the head is less glossy and it lacks purple on the mantle.

A. m. inornata occurs on Biak and Numfor Islands.

MEASUREMENTS Male: wing (6)107–111, tail 92–108, tarsus 22–23, culmen 15–17. Female: wing (7)103–110, tail 90–101, tarsus 22–23, culmen 15–17. Weight 61 g.

VOICE Calls include a loud, unmusical, nasal, disyllabic downslur, and are said to resemble those of Moluccan Starling (Coates and Bishop 1997). Cain and Galbraith (1956) described the calls as being like those of White-eyed Starlings, but with less whistling and more harsh calling, and they recorded argumentative juveniles giving harsh chattering calls. Pizzey (1980) described the song as being canary-like, but briefer and more fluty. Coates has heard mimicry of other birds such as Hooded Pitta *Pitta sordida* and Common Koel *Eudynamis scolopacea*. Breeding colonies are noisy, continuously emanating a loud twittering. Birds approaching a colony give a high pitched twittering call. The flight call is a descending nasal note, frequently given by flock members.

DISTRIBUTION AND POPULATION Shining Starling is one of the more widely distributed *Aplonis* starlings. Its distribution is centred on New Guinea and its offshore islands, but its range extends west to the Moluccas, east to the Admiralty Islands, Bismarck Archipelago and the Solomon Islands, and south to northeastern Queensland. In this last locality it is a migrant (Blaker *et al.* 1984), presumably returning to New Guinea outside its breeding season, although Magarry (1987) claims that large flocks can be seen in the Cairns area for most of the year and it overwinters regularly in northern Queensland (Pavey 1991). In Papua New Guinea it is fairly common, being particularly abundant on some islands. On New Georgia (Solomons) it is the most abundant *Aplonis*. In the Moluccas it is common on Seram, moderately common on Ambon and the Kai Islands, locally common on Halmahera and uncommon or rare on the Sula Islands, Bacan, Obi and Buru. It is uncommon or rare on the Tanimbar Islands in the Lesser Sundas (Coates and Bishop 1997).

HABITAT Found in rainforest, forest edge, trees in clearings, coastal woodland and gardens. It also occurs in mangroves and fruiting trees in savanna. Most of its time is spent in the higher levels of tree canopies but it descends to lower levels at the forest edge. LeCroy (1981) recorded a flock of 15 birds feeding on the ground in a grassy area among cattle. It is essentially a lowland species although it does breed to 1100 m on mainland Papua New Guinea and has been recorded at over 3000 m.

FOOD AND FEEDING Essentially frugivorous, eating the fruits of forest trees. In a garden in Queensland, Magarry (1987) recorded them feeding on the fruits of native trees: Forest Mangrove *Carallia brachiata*, Native Nutmeg *Myristica insipida*, Umbrella Tree *Schefflera actinophylla*, *Terminalia seriocarpa*, *Glochidion harveyanum*, *G. ferdinandii*, *Polyscias elegans*, *P. murrayi*, the native palms *Phycosperma elegans* and *Archontophoenix alexandrae*, and an exotic palm *Pinanga khulii*. In addition, these garden birds were particularly partial to Birds-eye chillies *Capsicum frutescens*. Cain and Galbraith (1956) recorded berries and fig-like fruits in their diet. In addition to eating fruits, Shining Starlings take nectar, frequently visiting flowering trees with tubular blossoms (Bell 1984). They also eat insects and have been recorded hawking flying ants (Hymenoptera) (Rand 1942), and LeCroy (1995) saw them hawking insects, probably mayflies (Ephemeroptera), over water. They have been recorded as feeding on caterpillar infestations (Clapp 1987) and eating what appeared to be stout-bodied wasps (Cain and Galbraith 1956). Presumably the birds that LeCroy (1981) saw feeding among cattle in grassland were also taking insects. Shining Starling occurs in mixed species flocks with Moluccan Starlings on Seram (Coates and Bishop 1997) and with Yellow-eyed Starlings in parts of Papua New Guinea (Beehler and Bino 1995).

BREEDING Breeds colonially and usually the entire colony occupies a single tree. Nesting trees are often isolated in clearings, gardens or at the forest edge, but sometimes they occupy tall emergent trees in the forest. In the centre of Boro township, New Georgia (Solomons), a colony of this species nests in a tall tree (Blaber 1990). Colonies contain from four to 400 nests and sometimes groups of nests may coalesce to form a single structure. The weight of nests on some branches can be sufficient to break them (Blaker *et al.* 1984). Nests are domed with a side entrance and suspended from the end of twigs in the tree canopy. They are constructed of twigs, vine tendrils and stripped bark, and are lined with strips of palm frond.

One to three, sometimes four, eggs are laid. They are pale blue, variably spotted and blotched with dark rufous and pale greyish mauve, and measure 25.1–30.5 x 18.8–21.1 mm (11) (Schönwetter 1983). Incubation and fledgling periods are not known. LeCroy and Peckover (1983) described parents feeding chicks both by regurgitation and by carrying food in the bill. In Papua New Guinea, Shining Starlings breed at different times of the year in different locations. In most places they nest from July to October but in some areas from March to May. In the lowlands around Port Moresby, colonies are active from July-August to early February. In Queensland they begin nesting in August (Magarry 1987). Within a colony breeding is asynchronous, with nest building, incubation and the feeding of young occurring at the same time. There may be several broods in a season in a particular colony but it is not known whether the same breeding adults remain throughout. Coates reported that colonies comprise only adults and suggested that immatures were kept

away. However, LeCroy *et al.* (1984) described a colony of about 50 pairs, all in immature plumage, with around 30 nests and suggested that new colonies may be founded by young birds. Schodde (1977) thought that nests on Bougainville were used for both nesting and roosting, since nests were occupied for much of the year.

MIGRATION In northeast Queensland Shining Starlings are migratory, arriving in July–September and leaving in February–April. It is assumed that they spend the non-breeding season in New Guinea, although Magarry (1987) suggests that in recent years there has been a tendency for flocks to be present for much of the year. In the non-breeding season, birds in Papua New Guinea appear highly nomadic. In the Torres Strait they are nomadic throughout the year (Draffan *et al.* 1983).

BEHAVIOUR Early in the nesting season, single birds, presumably males, stand upright on top of their nests or on nearby branches and slowly flap their partially opened wings. During this display the bill is often open and sometimes holds an orange or red fruit. Cain and Galbraith (1956) witnessed this display in a flock of feeding juveniles, accompanied by a chattering call. At all times of year, Shining Starlings are gregarious, forming flocks of a few to several hundred birds. They fly in noisy and compact flocks over or through the treetops and flight is fast and direct. Flocks may comprise a mix of age groups, all or mainly adults, or mainly young birds. They roost communally in trees and have been recorded roosting in tall cane grass swamps (Gilliard and LeCroy 1966). When not feeding they sit on exposed perches in tall trees, where they also sit out rain showers.

RELATIONS WITH OTHER SPECIES They commonly feed in association with fruit doves, and Stephan's Emerald Dove *Chalcophaps stephani* feeds on the seeds of fruits voided by Shining Starlings in deposits of faeces beneath breeding colonies (Coates 1985). If nest colony trees have suitable holes, Eclectus Parrots *Eclectus roratus* will nest amongst the starlings (Sticklen 1981). Nesting colonies suffer predation by Variable Goshawks *Accipiter novaehollandiae* and possibly by Brahminy Kites *Haliastur indus*, and by snakes (Blaker *et al.* 1984). At the approach of a predator the adult starlings retreat to nearby trees.

RELATIONS WITH MAN In Papua New Guinea, Shining Starling nestlings are harvested for food by man, with individuals having rights to particular colonies. According to Bell (1986) this does not appear to affect the success of breeding colonies.

PRINCIPAL REFERENCE Coates (1990).

2 YELLOW-EYED STARLING *Aplonis mystacea*

Grant's Starling

Plate 1

Calornis mystacea Ogilvie-Grant 1911

FIELD IDENTIFICATION 18–19 cm. The sexes are similar. Yellow-eyed Starling is very similar to Shining Starling but is slightly smaller and has a thicker bill, a similarly long graduated tail, a small partially erectile crest on the forehead which can be a useful field character in flight, and a pale yellow iris which is said to appear startlingly whitish. In adults the plumage is glossy black with green and purplish iridescence, though in comparison with Shining Starlings in the field Yellow-eyed Starling appears duller and smoother owing to a brown tinge on the head and neck. Immatures have white underparts streaked with black, and conspicuously whitish eyes.

DESCRIPTION The feathers of the forehead are bristled. Feathers of the crown, nape, throat and upper breast are lanceolate and elongated. The head and mantle are black, glossed purplish, while the wing-coverts, back and rump are glossed bright emerald green. The gloss on the breast, belly and flanks is mauve bronzy-green. The primaries and secondaries are dark brown with some greenish iridescence on the outer webs, especially on the secondaries. The tail is dark brown with a hint of gloss, long and graduated. The small, stubby black bill has a strongly arched culmen. The legs are black and the iris pale yellow.

MEASUREMENTS Male (1): wing 101, tail 82, tarsus 21, culmen 18.

VOICE The calls of Yellow-eyed Starling have not been well described but are similar to those of Shining Starling, perhaps being rougher and more metallic than that species. They include harsh and bell-like notes. Birds at breeding colonies maintain a high pitched chattering.

DISTRIBUTION AND POPULATION This species is endemic to Irian Jaya and Papua New Guinea. It was thought to have a restricted range but recent observations in eastern Papua New Guinea suggest that it may be more widespread (Beehler and Bino 1995, Safford 1996). It has been recorded from the Wanggar and Mimika Rivers in Irian Jaya and from the middle Turama River, the upper Fly River catchment and the Nagore River. Its close resemblance to Shining Starling has led to it being overlooked and its status is uncertain. It may be locally common.

HABITAT Inhabits lowland alluvial forest where limited observations suggest that it is a canopy species, but there are also reports of its occurrence in hilly forest at 300 m (Beehler and Bino 1995).

FOOD AND FEEDING The only feeding observations are of birds feeding on fruit from the canopies of tall lowland forest trees, e.g. *Endospermum moluccanum*. Safford (1996) saw adults feeding young at entrances to nests with red berries.

BREEDING Only one breeding colony has been found, in structurally unaltered forest. This contained about 150 nests in a single 30 m tall tree somewhat isolated from other trees. Nests were globe-shaped, most of them suspended like those of Shining Starlings, although some were supported, and most were in clusters of about 15 nests, some of these were in contact with neighbouring nests. Nests were untidily made of strips of vegetation. Although Yellow-eyed Starlings commonly mix with Shining Starlings while feeding, no Shining Starlings were seen at this colony (Safford 1996).

BEHAVIOUR Has been observed in flocks of up to 100 birds but it usually occurs in smaller groups. Its behaviour is similar to that of Shining Starling, with which it occurs in mixed flocks, feeding in a constantly moving, nervous fashion (Beehler and Bino 1995). According to Safford (1996), no ecological differences between Yellow-eyed and Shining Starlings have been noted.

RELATIONS WITH MAN According to villagers, colonies are sometimes destroyed by cutting down the tree in order that eggs, chicks and adults can be eaten (Safford 1996)

PRINCIPAL REFERENCE Coates (1990).

3 SINGING STARLING *Aplonis cantoroides*

Little Starling

Plate 2

Calornis cantoroides Gray 1862

FIELD IDENTIFICATION 17–19 cm. Sexes similar. Adult Singing Starlings are black, glossed with oily green. They have thick bills and short, square tails. The iris is bright red or orange-red. Immatures have pale underparts, streaked with dusky brown. The iris is dark brown, changing through yellowish and orange-red as the birds age.

Singing Starlings are distinguished from Shining Starlings by their smaller size, deeper bills and square tails, while immatures are separated from that species by being less dark above and by having paler, less heavy streaking on the underparts. Singing Starlings are very similar to Asian Glossy Starlings, and are distinguished from the latter in having longer hackles especially on the throat, which in some lights gives a streaked appearance, and in being generally less glossy, especially on the lower belly, with the glossy tips to feathers on the underparts sometimes presenting a scaly appearance.

DESCRIPTION Adult: Entire body plumage is black with strong green iridescence. The feathers of the forehead are somewhat bristled and the crown feathers slightly hackled, the throat feathers more so. The remiges are black, with increasing green iridescence towards the inner feathers. The tail is black, short and square-ended. The thick bill is black, as are the legs. The iris is red or orange. **Immature**: Upperparts are dark brown, slightly glossed green. Throat feathers are hackled, pale buff with dark brown shafts. Breast and belly feathers have dark centres and buff margins; these buff margins become broader, with feathers increasingly buff-tipped, towards the central lower belly and vent. The iris of immatures is brown, becoming yellowish, orange-red or red in older birds.

MEASUREMENTS Male/female (8): wing 99–106, tail 62–70, tarsus 22, bill from nostril 13, weight 54–66 g (Mayr 1931).

VOICE Despite its name, Singing Starling is rather quiet but it does give a short tuneful whistle that Hadden (1981) described as more melodious than that of most starlings. Nesting birds give a *tiu tiu*. Common calls are a high-pitched, downward inflected *siiew* and a repeated, shorter, rising and slightly disyllabic *suweii* or *s'wei*. In flight, Coates describes a 'rusty rustling' call resembling a Papuan Cuckoo-shrike *Coracina papuensis*, while feeding birds give single creaking notes. Cain and Galbraith (1956) described feeding juveniles giving *pee wee* and *pee iu-ee* calls, similar to those of White-eyed Starlings.

DISTRIBUTION AND POPULATION Inhabits New Guinea and some of the offshore islands together with the Arus, the Bismarck Archipelago and the Solomons, although it is absent from some of the islands within these groups. Mayr (1931) considered it a straggler on Rennell Island (which has its own endemic species, Rennell Starling), but Bradley and Wolff (1956) found Singing Starlings breeding there. On the mainland of New Guinea it is widespread and can be common, although patchily distributed in the south and west. It is primarily a lowland bird but extends to 1700 m in cultivated mountain valleys and may be extending its range into Southern Highland Province of Papua New Guinea. It has also adapted to an urban existence and has colonised some montane towns (Finch 1986). On islands it is predominantly coastal. It has been reported once from Australian territory, on Boigu Island, Torres Strait, although this is only 3 km off the southern coast of Papua New Guinea (Anon 1988).

HABITAT On some islands Singing Starlings inhabit forest, but on New Guinea they are birds of forest edge, cleared areas, cultivated areas and gardens with trees, savanna, coastal woodland and coconut groves, and even urban areas. On New Georgia (Solomons) it is an abundant bird of secondary growth and villages, rather than primary forest (Blaber 1990).

FOOD AND FEEDING Largely frugivorous, eating figs, fruits from small forest palms, ripe papaya *Carica papaya* and birds-eye chillies *Capsicum frutescens*. It also hawks flying insects. Singing and Shining Starlings often feed together.

BREEDING Nests in holes, usually in dead or living trees but also in cliffs, buildings, including house roofs, and other structures such as power poles. Bradley and Wolff (1956) found them breeding in coral rock on Rennell Island. Where there are sufficient nest sites they are colonial, and they sometimes occupy the same tree as a colony of Shining Starlings. The nest material includes grasses and fibres. Two or three pale blue eggs, spotted with brown and violet, are laid and measure 25.0–30.0 x 18.2–21.6 mm (26) (Schönwetter 1983), although Bradley and Wolff (1956) found four young in a nest. Details of parental care are not known. Adults and even immatures attend nest holes for much of the year so that it is difficult to establish the breeding season. However, around Port Moresby breeding probably occurs mainly from September to December, in the late dry season, while other records from New Guinea reveal nesting up to at least February. On islands, breeding has been recorded in March and August.

MIGRATION Although Singing Starlings can be seen in the same places throughout the year, flocks of juveniles in particular give the impression that they are highly nomadic and Coates remarks that widespread diffusion may account for the lack of subspecific differentiation in this species. Diamond (1972) suggested that Singing Starlings might make post-breeding migrations from the lowlands to the highlands, where they are more numerous from April to early November.

BEHAVIOUR Gregarious, often occurring in pairs or small parties, but considerably larger flocks of immatures do occur. As mentioned above, they sometimes breed colonially and they roost communally, with thousands having been recorded roosting in the canopy of an isolated patch of trees.

In display activity seen in a captive pair, the male waved his wings in a manner similar to that of Common Starling. The female adopted an almost horizontal posture and fluttered her wings rapidly, giving repeated harsh *kar ka ka ka* calls (CJF).

RELATIONS WITH OTHER SPECIES Frequently seen feeding and sometimes breeding in the company of Shining Starlings and, apart from the selection of nest sites, the two species appear similar in their ecology and behaviour.

PRINCIPAL REFERENCE Coates (1990).

4 TANIMBAR STARLING *Aplonis crassa*

Plate 2

Calornis crassa Sclater 1883

FIELD IDENTIFICATION 20 cm. A smallish starling with a short tail and relatively large and heavy bill. It is similar to Singing Starling, with which it forms a superspecies (White and Bruce 1986), but adults are dark iron-grey glossed with steel green, greyer on the underparts. Wings and tail are black, slightly glossed with green. Immatures have underparts buff, streaked with black.

DESCRIPTION Sexes alike. **Adult**: Feathers of the crown and throat are lanceolate, and the entire body plumage is dark charcoal glossed with metallic greenish, slightly paler and more mousy below. The wings are dark brown with little gloss, and the short square tail is dark brown. The black bill is large with an arched culmen. The legs are black and the iris dark brown. **Immature**: Upperparts are mousy brown with a hint of greenish gloss on the margins of the crown feathers. The underparts are buff, the feathers of the throat with dark shafts and the breast and belly feathers with dark blackish-brown centres, producing heavy streaking.

MEASUREMENTS Male (1): wing 105, tail 72, tarsus 23, culmen 16.

VOICE Piping metallic notes are given repeatedly and flocks give a distinctive but jumbled cacophany of piping metallic calls.

DISTRIBUTION AND POPULATION Endemic to the islands of Tanimbar, towards the eastern end of the Lesser Sunda chain. On Yamdena it is common.

HABITAT Occurs in most wooded habitats, including secondary forest and woodland edge.

FOOD AND FEEDING Feeds in the dense crowns of flowering and fruiting trees, presumably taking nectar and fruits, and possibly insects.

BEHAVIOUR Occurs singly, in pairs, small groups and sometimes in larger flocks of up to 200 birds. Flies above the canopy with strong, direct flight.

PRINCIPAL REFERENCE Coates and Bishop (1997).

5 ATOLL STARLING *Aplonis feadensis*

Plate 2

Fead Island Starling

Calornis feadensis Ramsay 1882

FIELD IDENTIFICATION 20 cm. A smallish, heavy-looking starling with a square-ended tail. Its wings are broader and more rounded than those of Singing Starling, and its flight more hesitant. The plumage is black with an oily gloss and the iris is yellow or dark yellow. The bill varies between different island populations, being thick and heavy in some but slender in others. On Nissan Island, Atoll Starlings have distinct pale yellow eyerings. Immatures are duller with scaly markings on the underparts, and with a yellowish-green iris.

DESCRIPTION The forehead feathers are slightly bristled. The body plumage is black, glossed with oily turquoise-green. The wings are dark brownish-black, with slight iridescence on the outer webs of the secondaries and coverts. The square-ended tail is blackish-brown with some gloss. The bill is stout and black, and legs are black. The iris is yellow or dark yellow, while Finch (1986) described the iris as all dark, but with a bright pale yellow eyering. Immatures have pale feather edgings on the underparts, giving a scaly effect, the feathers of the upperparts lack gloss and they have a yellowish-green iris. This description refers to nominate *feadensis*, of Ontong Java, in the Solomon Islands, and Nissan and Nuguria Islands in Papua New Guinea.

A. f. heureka, of Ninigo and Hermit Islands (and possibly Wuvulu Island), has a thinner bill. Coates (1990) suggests that birds on Tench Island may be ascribed to a separate subspecies.

MEASUREMENTS Unsexed (1): wing 115, tail 78, tarsus 25, culmen 19.

VOICE Atoll Starlings on Nissan Island commonly give a loud ascending slur *wee-ee*, and softer notes resembling those of white-eyes (*Zosterops*). 'Starling-like' calls were heard on Tench Island. The most commonly given call is a loud rising slur *weeeee-eeeee* (Finch 1986).

DISTRIBUTION AND POPULATION Restricted to small outlying islands to the north and northwest of the Bismarck Archipelago where they occur on Ninigo, Hermit Islands, Tench, Nuguri (= Fead), Nissan and to the north of the Solomons on Ontong Java Atoll. There is also a doubtful record from Wuvulu Island. Coates points out that this distribution is almost complementary to the island distribution of the ecologically similar Singing Starling, although both species have been found on the same island in the Ninigo group. On Nissan Island, Atoll Starlings coexist with Shining Starlings.

HABITAT Inhabits forest, forest edge and coconut groves, where they usually frequent the canopy. At the forest edge they descend lower and they have been recorded on the ground.

FOOD AND FEEDING Eats insects, gleaned from leaves, and berries. Bayliss-Smith (1972) recorded them on all of the larger islands of Ontong Java atoll, generally as individuals or pairs, but near villages they congregated on open ground in small flocks.

BREEDING Nests in holes, 5–10 m high, in trees and in the tops of dead coconut trees. Eggs are pale blue with dark reddish-brown spots concentrated at the rounded end and measure 28.0 x 19.0 mm (clutch of 2); young were being fed in the nest in late July (Bayliss-Smith 1972). Apart from an observation of a pair feeding red berries to a chick

in a nest on Nissan Island in June (Hadden 1981) there is no further information.

MIGRATION Island endemics like Atoll Starlings are generally sedentary and the observation of a bird flying between islands in the Ninigo group (Bell 1975) is therefore noteworthy.

BEHAVIOUR Usually encountered in pairs or small groups and have not been recorded in large flocks (Finch 1986). There is no other information on their behaviour.

PRINCIPAL REFERENCE Coates (1990).

6 RENNELL STARLING *Aplonis insularis*   Plate 2

Aplonis insularis Mayr 1931

FIELD IDENTIFICATION 19 cm. Endemic to Rennell Island, Rennell Starling is glossy black with blue and green iridescence, duller on the underparts, and is very similar to Singing Starling, differing in its heavier bill, orange-yellow iris, rounder wings and bluer, rather than green, iridescence. Immatures are dark brownish-grey, lacking gloss, and have a pale brown iris.

DESCRIPTION The entire plumage is glossy black. Feathers of the forehead are slightly bristled, and those of the throat are lanceolate, those of the crown and hind neck less so. Body feathers are dark brownish-black, those of the head, mantle, back, rump, throat and breast edged glossy blue-purple, while those of the belly and under-tail-coverts lack gloss. Wings and tail are dark brown with a hint of gloss on the outer webs of the secondaries. Immatures are a uniform rich dark chocolate-brown, the narrow glossy feather edges producing a slight metallic sheen on the head. The black bill is slightly hooked and has a strongly arched culmen. In adults the legs are black and the iris orange-yellow or orange-red, in immatures the legs are dark grey and the iris brownish-grey.

MEASUREMENTS Male/female (8): wing 101–109, tail 53–62, tarsus 25–26, culmen 18–19, weight 66–74 g (Mayr 1931, Bradley and Wolff 1956).

VOICE In flight a sharp, metallic *chink chink* is given. The song is a musical series of notes, tinny as in Singing Starlings but more varied. When feeding in the canopy it is silent and unobtrusive.

DISTRIBUTION AND POPULATION Endemic to Rennell Island, in the south of the Solomons Islands, and neighbouring Bellona Island. It resembles Atoll Starling and is sometimes regarded as conspecific with it (Gruson 1976), although Mayr (1931) and Finch (1986) considered it to be more closely related to Singing Starling, which also occurs on Rennell Island. Rennell Starlings occur primarily on the mainland, around Lake Te-Nggano, while Singing Starlings occur mainly on the surrounding islets (Bradley and Wolff 1956). On Rennell Island it is fairly common.

HABITAT A bird of the forest canopy, although it readily comes down to feed in low shrubs.

BREEDING Nests in the stumps of coconut trees. Only one clutch of three eggs has been examined. These were pale blue-green with dark red-brown blotches concentrated at the obtuse end, and measured 30 mm x 20 mm (Bradley and Wolff 1956).

BEHAVIOUR Rennell Starlings are usually found in pairs.

PRINCIPAL REFERENCE Finch (1986).

7 LONG-TAILED STARLING *Aplonis magna*   Plate 3

FIELD IDENTIFICATION 28–41 cm. A large glossy starling with a long, lax graduated tail. The neck feathers are lanceolate but not elongated. The iris is brown. Its size and the long tail distinguish it from other sympatric starlings.

DESCRIPTION The feathers of the forehead are slightly bristled and the crown and throat feathers somewhat lanceolate. The entire body plumage is black, glossed oily green but with a hint of bronze on the head. The primaries and secondaries are blackish-brown, with some gloss on the secondaries. The tail is dark brown, with the central four feathers greatly elongated so that the tail is equal

to or even longer than the body. The bill is black with the culmen curved. The legs are black and the iris brown. This description refers to the nominate *magna*, of Biak Island.

A. m. brevicaudus, of Numfor Island, is similar but less glossy and with a shorter tail, about two-thirds of body length.

MEASUREMENTS Male (1): wing 126, tail 232, tarsus 29, culmen 19. Female (1): wing 126, tail 201, tarsus 28, culmen 19.

VOICE Gives a series of loud warbles, said by Beehler *et al.* (1986) to be incomplete. It also gives a shrill descending slurred call note *cheew*

(Harrison and Greensmith 1993).

DISTRIBUTION AND POPULATION Biak and Numfor Islands, off northern Irian Jaya, where it is abundant.

HABITAT Occurs at all altitudes in all habitats, especially tall secondary woodland, forest edge and gardens (Harrison and Greensmith 1993).

FOOD AND FEEDING Takes small fruits from trees and in the undergrowth (Harrison and Greensmith 1993).

BEHAVIOUR Occurs in pairs and in small parties. Feeds in fruiting trees and nests high in trees at the forest edge or in gardens.

PRINCIPAL REFERENCE Beehler *et al.* (1986).

8 WHITE-EYED STARLING *Aplonis brunneicapilla* Plate 3

Rhinopsar brunneicapillus Danis 1938

FIELD IDENTIFICATION 21–25 cm, 29–32 cm including the elongated central tail feathers. White-eyed Starling is similar to Shining Starling in its size and iridescent green and blue plumage. The major distinguishing features of White-eyed Starling are a much deeper bill with a strongly arched upper mandible, a slight crest of filamentous plumes on the crown and nape, a white iris, and a slightly graduated tail which is shorter than that of Shining Starling, except for the two central tail feathers which are elongated into tail streamers, up to three times the length of the rest of the tail, and which are flexible and blow about in the breeze (Kaestner 1987): these are slightly longer in males than in females but are often broken off, when the tail appears more rounded or wedge-shaped. When perched with Shining Starlings, Gibbs (1996) noted White-eyed Starlings to be slightly more heavily built. Immatures lack the crest and their bills are less arched (but still more so than in Shining Starling), the iris is dark or olive, and the underparts are duller with inconspicuous white streaking on the breast and belly.

DESCRIPTION The feathers of the forehead are degenerate and form a small frontal crest. The feathers of the crown and throat are elongate. The crown is slightly glossed bronze; the chin and throat are iridescent purple, the lores purple-bronze and the moustache area emerald green. The wing-coverts, mantle, back, rump, breast and belly are iridescent emerald-green, somewhat bluer on the uppertail-coverts. The primaries and secondaries are dark blackish-brown, with some purple gloss on the outer webs, extending to the inner webs of the secondaries. The tail is glossy blackish, of medium length but with the central two feathers elongated to up to three times the length of the remainder of the tail. The black bill is deep and the upper mandible strongly curved. The legs are black and the iris white. Females are slightly less iridescent, especially the emerald-green on the wing-coverts, and the elongated central tail feathers are slightly shorter. Immatures lack the frontal crest and the tail extensions, and the bill is less arched, but still larger than in *A. metallica*. The crown and the nape are dark purplish and the mantle, back and rump glossed green, except for the wings and tail which are dark blue. The underparts are blackish-brown with glossy green tips to some feathers and with fine whitish streaking on the breast and centre of the belly. The

iris is olive to dark grey-brown and the bill is black in older immatures, but grey in juveniles.

MEASUREMENTS Male (8): wing 110–114, tail 135–205 (80–87 discounting central feathers), tarsus 20–24, culmen 21–23, weight 63–76 g. Female (8): wing 98–111, tail 98–133 (68–86 discounting central feathers), tarsus 20–23, culmen 21–23, weight 59–73 g.

VOICE Calls have been generally described as a mixture of starling-like whistles and harsh cries (Cain and Galbraith 1956). These authors described specific calls that they associated with particular aspects of behaviour: a single harsh call *kwaitch*, regularly repeated by a single bird from the top of a dead tree on return to a temporarily deserted colony; a whistled *kwee kwee chee-er*, the last note harsher, given by birds about to return to a colony; a harsh chatter *chk chk chk chk* accompanied by wing-flicking and used in aggressive encounters; a whistled *kah, kwik-kwik-kwik-kwik chu-er* used in high flapping display (see below) at the nest; a soft repeated *chreep* used in courtship.

DISTRIBUTION AND POPULATION Endemic to the Solomon Islands and Papua New Guinea where it has been recorded only from Bougainville Island, Papua New Guinea and Rendova, Choiseul and Guadalcanal in the Solomon Islands. In the lowlands of Bougainville and on Choiseul it coexists with Shining Starlings, and on Bougainville also with Brown-winged Starlings, but on Guadalcanal it replaces Shining Starling in the hills. It is generally very uncommon or rare but can be locally plentiful (Gibbs 1996), possibly even nomadic, but due to pressures on its lowland forest habitat and to local people eating the nestlings, Collar *et al.* (1994) classify it as endangered.

HABITAT Inhabits forest, forest edge, gardens and trees in clearings. Both hill and lowland forest (including lowland swamp forest, Kaestner 1987) are occupied. In forest it is a bird of the canopy but in other areas it descends to lower levels, even near to the ground.

FOOD AND FEEDING Mainly frugivorous, eating figs and other soft fruit and berries. Some of the fruits eaten are large, *c.* 2.5 x 1.2 cm, with large stones which are probably regurgitated.

BREEDING A colonial nester, with the few colonies that have been reported containing between 10 and 40 nests. The trees in which colonies have been located have all been isolated as a result of forest clearance. Nests are built among dense growths of epiphytes on branches in the canopy, and consist of a short, horizontal tunnel lined with mosses. The eggs are whitish, speckled with coarse and fine grey and light chocolate-brown marks, and measure 25.5–27.1 x 18.4–18.9 mm (3) (Schönwetter 1983). Nothing is known of incubation or parental care, although parents have been observed carrying food in the bill. The breeding season is poorly known but active colonies have been reported from Bougainville in January and from Guadalcanal in July–August.

BEHAVIOUR Cain and Galbraith (1956) described the flight of White-eyed Starlings as swift and direct when birds were flying between feeding sites, whereas when foraging they closed the wings more frequently, as a result having an undulating flight. White-eyed Starlings breed colonially and feed in flocks, but their roosting has not been described. Cain and Galbraith (1956) reported that pairs often sat side by side on a perch, usually near to the nest entrance, and often entered the nest. These observations were made around the time of hatching and the authors describe some postures adopted at a breeding colony. Wing-flicking: nest site owners defended the area immediately around their nest by facing intruders with the head and shoulders lowered, neck stretched out and bill open, flicking the wings several times. When nest owners were threatened, they lunged at intruding birds. Such encounters sometimes resulted in fights, with combatants falling, interlocked, almost to the ground before separating. High flapping display: when a bird entered the nest cavity its mate, still on the perch,

stretched upwards and flapped its outspread wings several times while giving the *kah, kwik kwik kwik chu-er* call. Both sexes indulged in this display but it is presumed that males were more intense. This is similar to the display of Shining Starling. This display was also sometimes seen in feeding flocks. Probably courtship display: the presumed male crouched facing its mate with head lowered and crest raised; it cocked its tail up at a sharp angle and vibrated or wafted the tail streamers up and down, at the same time vibrating the wings and giving a metallic warble. On a vertical perch the presumed male stood above his mate, facing her but also pointing his tail downwards, again vibrating the wings and tail, but with the tail held up, down or even to the side. Pairs of birds often left the breeding colony and returned together and were sometimes away for long periods. On occasions the whole colony may appear deserted. On leaving the colony birds dropped vertically from their nests before levelling out, and on many occasions most or all of the birds left together. When they returned to the colony birds flew into the colony tree below the nests but then 'rocketed up to the nest with whirring wings and the tail fanned'. On one occasion, a bird that returned with moss in its bill passed this to its mate who then took it into the nest.

RELATIONS WITH OTHER SPECIES Cain and Galbraith (1956) were told by local people that colony trees were sometimes cut down in order that the nestlings could be taken for food. The authors also recorded Pied Goshawk *Accipiter albogularis* eating nestlings.

PRINCIPAL REFERENCES Cain and Galbraith (1956), Coates (1990).

9 BROWN-WINGED STARLING *Aplonis grandis*   Plate 3
Large Glossy Starling

Lamprocorax grandis Salvadori 1881

FIELD IDENTIFICATION 25–29 cm. Sexes similar. A large glossy starling with a square-ended tail and broad wings. The plumage is blackish with purple gloss on the head, greenish elsewhere, but the wings are brown and without gloss, and a pale brown wing patch is conspicuous in flight. The iris is red, dark red, dark brown or grey-brown, probably depending upon age. In immatures the plumage is duller. An important distinguishing feature is a loud fanning noise made by the wings in flight.

DESCRIPTION The feathers of the forehead are slightly bristled, while those of the crown, nape, throat and upper breast are lanceolate and greatly elongated, and iridescent purple. The upper mantle is glossed oily green, merging into a turquoise-purple iridescence on the back and rump. The breast is glossed oily green, and the belly, flanks and undertail-coverts are glossed bluish-purple.

The wing-coverts and scapulars are glossed bluish-purple. The secondaries are dark brown with some iridescence on the outer webs, and the primaries are similar but bleach to mid-brown when worn. The tail is square, dark brownish-black. The black bill is large with a strongly arched culmen, and is hooked at the tip. The legs are black and the iris dark red but in birds from some areas can be red-brown, dark brown or grey brown (Schodde 1977). Immatures are generally duller and the lanceolate feathers of the head and upper breast are less elongate, and the primaries are dull brown. This description refers to nominate **grandis** of Bougainville, Choiseul and Ysabel (Santa Isabel), in the Solomon Islands.

A. g. macrura, of Guadalcanal, is similar but with a much longer tail, especially in the male.

A. g. malaita occurs on Malaita and has a whitish iris, longer head and throat hackles, and is slimmer than *grandis*.

MEASUREMENTS Male (4): wing 135–147, tail 102–114, tarsus 30–34, culmen 19–20. Female (4): wing 135–139, tail 95–107, tarsus 29–33, culmen 19–20.

VOICE Brown-winged Starlings are quieter than most of the other Asian glossy starlings and their calls consist primarily of high-pitched whistles and squeaks. Coates described a high-pitched advertising call as a repeated smooth *hiiew*, and a loud *chik* or *tip* flight call. Other calls include a guttural chirp and a *click*, which may be contact calls, and a quiet, short, deep and musical *pink pink pink* given while feeding. Cain and Galbraith (1956) once heard a bird sitting upright give a low song like that of Common Starling and Finch described the song as a protracted, continuous string of warbles, chips, squeaks, shrill and chattering notes, and also commented on its similarity to the song of Common Starling. Hadden (1981) thought that some song might be above the range of human perception.

DISTRIBUTION AND POPULATION Endemic to the Solomon Islands, apart from Makira (= San Cristobal) where it is replaced by the Makira Starling. It is widespread on Bougainville and Buka and common in the lowlands. On New Georgia it is abundant in primary forest but also occurs in man-modified areas (Blaber 1990).

HABITAT Primarily birds of forest, Brown-winged Starlings also occur in secondary vegetation and trees in clearings, and also in villages and towns where there are tall trees (Blaber 1990). A common species in the lowlands, less abundant with altitude and does not usually occur above about 750 m, although on Guadalcanal they are common from sea level to 1200 m (Finch 1986). They inhabit the canopy but descend lower at the forest edge.

FOOD AND FEEDING Largely arboreal and frugivorous, eating figs and other soft fruit, berries and pieces taken from large fruits. Schodde (1977) recorded one eating fruits of *Cananga odorata*. Some insects are taken.

BREEDING The nest is a large bulky mass of twigs, dry leaves, moss and grass with a side entrance. It is usually built in a fork in the top of an isolated tree but sometimes in a cavity at the end of a broken branch. The breeding season may be prolonged since nest-building and fledging have both been recorded in September on Bougainville, and a pair that commenced building in May was still active at the nest in August. The eggs are pale green or blue, with large brown spots sometimes coalescing at the larger end, and (*malaitae*) measure 25.3–29.8 x 19.3–20.9 mm (24) (Schönwetter 1983).

BEHAVIOUR Usually encountered singly or in pairs. Finch (1986) thought that they might pair for life; he considered that groups of four, which were regularly seen, comprised a pair and two young. Unlike most of the Asian glossy starlings, they do not breed colonially and do not associate in flocks except on Guadalcanal, where associations have been seen in fruiting bushes. They commonly sit in exposed positions on dead branches in the tops of trees (Hadden 1961). Only one display has been described (Cain and Galbraith 1956). This involved posturing by one bird at another, probably feeding, nearby. The displaying bird sat upright with its tail down, craned its head forward and drooped its wings, shaking them vigorously.

PRINCIPAL REFERENCE Coates (1990).

10 MAKIRA STARLING *Aplonis dichroa*   Plate 3
San Cristobal Starling

Sturnoides minor Ramsay 1882

FIELD IDENTIFICATION 18–21 cm. Similar to the Brown-winged Starling and sometimes regarded as conspecific with this species. However, Makira Starling is much smaller, the bill is shorter and stouter, and the wings and tail are dark brown without the pale brown wing patch of *A. grandis* species. The tail is noticeably short and square and the feet are larger and more powerful than in most *Aplonis* starlings. The iris is dark red but may, as in other species, vary in colour with age.

DESCRIPTION The forehead feathers are lanceolate almost to the point of bristling. Feathers of the crown, throat and upper breast are lanceolate and glossed purple-green. The mantle, back, rump are dark brown, the feathers broadly tipped glossy bottle-green. The belly and undertail-coverts are blackish-brown without gloss. The wing-coverts are dark blackish-brown with some gloss, especially on the lesser coverts. The primaries and sec-ondaries are chocolate-brown with a hint of rust on the inner webs, and lack gloss. These flight feathers contrast with the remainder of the plumage in being paler and browner, and this contrast is accentuated when the remiges are worn and bleached. The tail is dark brown and square-ended, of medium length. The bill is black, with an arched culmen. The legs are black and the iris red, orange or tawny. Immatures are browner and less glossy, but the remiges contrast with the rest of the plumage, as in adults. The iris is tawny-orange.

MEASUREMENTS Male (4): wing 113–120, tail 76–81, tarsus 26–28, culmen 20–21. Female (3): wing 110–114, tail 67–69, tarsus 26–27, culmen 20–21.

VOICE Much more vocal than Brown-winged Starling and foraging birds give a variety of calls, including melodious whistles *wu-ee wu-ee tee*, a call with an oboe-like quality *te-eu te-eu*, a harsh chu-ai, a soft churr, a soft musical chattering and other harsh calls. High-pitched squeaks and clinks resemble the calls of Singing Starlings, and Makira Starlings have been heard to give a rising whistle (Finch 1986).

DISTRIBUTION, POPULATION AND HABITAT Endemic to the island of Makira, Solomon Islands. It is a forest bird and occurs at all altitudes, but is commonest in the ridge forest and scarcest near the coast. It may be more restricted to unbroken forest canopy than Brown-winged Starling.

FOOD AND FEEDING The only information suggests that Makira Starlings may eat more seeds and less fruit than Brown-winged Starlings but that, like them, it is predominantly frugivorous

(Cain and Galbraith 1956).

BREEDING The eggs are whitish, sparsely marked at the large end with soft pale flecks, and measure 26.1–27.2 x 20.1–20.5 mm (3) (Schönwetter 1983).

BEHAVIOUR Much more social than Brown-winged Starlings, being frequently encountered in parties of four to eight birds but also seen in a feeding flock of 20 to 30. They are agile and move nimbly among slender twigs, and hang by their feet to reach food items (Finch 1986)

There is no information on breeding or on other aspects of this species' biology.

PRINCIPAL REFERENCE Cain and Galbraith (1956).

11 RUFOUS-WINGED STARLING *Aplonis zelandica*   Plate 4
Rusty-winged Starling, New Hebrides Starling

Lamprotornis zelandicus Quoy and Gaimard 1830

FIELD IDENTIFICATION 19 cm. A smallish dull brown starling with a heavy bill and short tail. Upperparts are dull brown, and crown and nape indistinctly streaked; the lower back, rump and uppertail-coverts are tawny. The underparts are buffy-grey, and the flanks and undertail-coverts are tawny-chestnut. The wings are brown, but with a rufous-chestnut patch. The iris is brown. Females are slightly smaller and paler than males.

DESCRIPTION The forehead, crown and nape feathers are dark chocolate brown with paler edges. The lores and primary coverts are blackish. Hindneck, mantle and back are warm brown, shading into tawny on the rump and uppertail-coverts. When recently moulted, the back shows a slight greenish gloss. The chin, throat, breast, belly and vent are buffy grey-brown, paler on the upper throat and vent, and shading into tawny-chestnut on the flanks and undertail-coverts. Primaries and secondaries are dark brown, but the outer webs of the secondaries and inner eight primaries are rufous-chestnut, forming a wing patch. The square-ended tail is chocolate-brown. The bill is black and hooked at the tip. The legs are warm brown. The iris is pale brown. This description refers to the nominate form of Vanikoro Island, Santa Cruz Islands.

A. z. rufipennis, of Central and northern New Hebrides and Banks Island, is slightly larger, buffier and brighter than nominate *zelandicus*, and with paler chestnut in the wing, rusty flanks and orange undertail-coverts.

A. z. maxwellii, of Santa Cruz Island, is similar to *rufipennis* but has a thicker bill and rufous, not orange undertail-coverts, and browner, less buff,

underparts; bill dark brown.

MEASUREMENTS Male: wing 103–106, tail 59–61; female: wing 99–101, tail 55. Male/female tarsus 24–25, culmen 23–24 (sample sizes not given, Mayr 1942).

VOICE The most commonly given call is a short, melodious *zee-twee* or *twee*, frequently repeated, but metallic whistles are also given repetitively. In dense forest Rufous-winged Starlings are heard more often than seen.

POPULATION AND DISTRIBUTION Occurs on the central and northern New Hebrides, and Banks Islands, and on Santa Cruz and Vanikoro in the Santa Cruz Islands. On most islands it is more common in the highlands, or even restricted to them, but it occurs on the coast on smaller flat islands.

HABITAT On larger mountainous islands, Rufous-winged Starling is primarily a bird of montane forests, whereas on smaller islands it occurs in wooded gardens at lower altitudes. Although primarily a forest bird, it occurs in secondary growth and in partly cleared areas. It inhabits the lower canopy, occasionally descending lower.

FOOD AND FEEDING Fruits probably constitute the main food, but Rufous-winged Starlings have also been seen gleaning insects from foliage.

BREEDING According to local people, Rufous-winged Starlings nest in holes high above the ground.

BEHAVIOUR Rufous-winged Starlings are usually found singly or in pairs, but more may gather in fruiting trees.

PRINCIPAL REFERENCE Bregulla (1992).

12 STRIATED STARLING *Aplonis striata*   Plate 4
Striped Glossy Starling

Calornis striata Gmelin 1788

FIELD IDENTIFICATION 18 cm. A small starling with a short stubby bill and square tail. The male is glossy black with violet and green iridescence while the female is mousy-brown, paler below. In both sexes the iris is reddish-orange.

DESCRIPTION Adult male: Forehead and crown feathers are slightly hackled and glossed violet and green. The mantle, back, rump, breast and belly feathers are dark blackish-brown, tipped iridescent turquoise-green. Chin and throat feathers are hackled with green iridescence. The lower belly and undertail-coverts are dark brownish-black without gloss. Primaries, secondaries and tail are brown with slight iridescence on the outer webs of the feathers. **Adult female**: Slightly smaller, mousy grey-brown and slightly paler below. The forehead and crown show slight violet-green iridescence. The bill of both sexes is short, stubby and black, legs purple-blue and iris reddish-orange. This refers to **A. s. striata** of New Caledonia.

A. s. atronitens, of the Loyalty Islands, is larger with a heavier bill, and in the male the head iridescence is less violet, more green.

MEASUREMENTS Male (3): wing 99–107, tail 58–72, tarsus 23–26, culmen 14–15. Female (1): wing 95, tail 60, tarsus 20, culmen 13.

DISTRIBUTION AND POPULATION Endemic to New Caledonia and the Loyalty Islands. Nothing appears to have been recorded of its biology.

13 MOUNTAIN STARLING *Aplonis santovestris*   Plate 4

Aplonis santovestris Harrisson and Marshall 1937

FIELD IDENTIFICATION 17–18 cm. A small dark brown starling with a short square tail, found only on the island of Espiritu Santo, Vanuatu.

DESCRIPTION The forehead and crown are dark brown, with a slight hint of gloss on the crown feathers. The mantle, back and wing-coverts are dark rusty-brown, the underparts warmer chestnut. The primaries and secondaries are dark brown with dark rusty outer margins to the outer webs. The tail is short and square, dark brown with rusty margins to the outer webs, especially on the outer feathers. The bill is brownish-black, paler at the tip, and stout. The legs are brownish-flesh and the iris grey-green. The adult female has duller rufous plumage.

MEASUREMENTS Male (1): wing 97, tail 53, tarsus 20, culmen 17.

VOICE A thin hissing note, an unemotional harsh thrush-like call, a short and moderately loud *tzeet-zeetzee* or separate notes *tzee-tzee-tzee*, given when perched and in flight, have been described.

DISTRIBUTION AND STATUS Endemic to the island of Espiritu Santo in Vanuatu (New Hebrides). It appears to be rare, having been seen only in 1934 at *c.* 1200 m on Mount Watiamasan, in 1961 on Mount Tabwemasana and in 1991 above 1700 m on Peak Santo (Anon 1992a). According to S. Maturin (quoted in Collar *et al*. 1994), however, local people say that it is seen commonly in the mountains of southern Espiritu Santo.

HABITAT Inhabits cloud forest on the highest peaks of Santo, where it occurs in the understory, and is rarely seen more than 5 m off the ground.

FOOD AND FEEDING Fruit, seeds and insects are eaten.

BREEDING Mountain Starlings nest in holes in trees, close to the ground, and are said to lay two white eggs.

BEHAVIOUR Generally found singly or in pairs. Its flight is direct with rapid wingbeats.

RELATIONS WITH MAN Local people are claimed to eat Mountain Starlings regularly (S. Maturin, quoted in Collar *et al*. 1994). Collar *et al*. (1994) classify this species as 'vulnerable'.

PRINCIPAL REFERENCE Bregulla (1992).

14 ASIAN GLOSSY STARLING *Aplonis panayensis*   Plate 5
Philippine Glossy Starling, Indonesian Tree Starling

Muscicapa panayensis Scopoli 1753

FIELD IDENTIFICATION 17–20 cm. A medium-sized, slenderly built, black starling with green gloss, a short, square tail and a conspicuous red eye. The sexes are alike but immatures are dark brown above and buff, streaked brown, below. It is gregarious at all times; its posture at rest and its direct flight are strongly reminiscent of Common Starling. Distinguished from Short-tailed Starling by having the head glossed green, rather than purple in that species, and from Moluccan Starling by this species' longer, graduated tail. Asian Glossy Starlings are very similar to Singing Starlings, but the former species is generally more glossy except for the lower belly and undertail-coverts, which are devoid of gloss, and it has shorter hackles, especially on the throat.

DESCRIPTION Sexes similar. **Adult**: the forehead feathers are slightly bristled and the throat feathers are lanceolate. The entire body plumage is black, glossed bottle-green, apart from the lower belly and vent which lack gloss. The primaries are blackish with green gloss on the margins of the outer webs, the secondaries are similar but with much more gloss. The tail is square, black glossed green. The bill is black with the culmen curved. The legs are black and the iris red. **Immature**: Recently fledged young are dark chocolate-brown above with very little green gloss, mainly on the secondaries and wing-coverts; the chin and throat are mainly mousy-brown with paler margins producing indistinct streaking, while the breast and belly are brown with broader buff margins to the feathers, producing heavy streaking. Older immatures have the forehead feathers somewhat bristled and the crown and throat feathers lanceolate. The upperparts are dark brown, the feathers broadly edged glossy metallic-green. The chin and throat are buff with dark brown feather shafts, producing fine streaking, but on the breast feathers brown pigmentation is more extensive and the buff edges narrower, giving heavier streaking. The belly is largely buff with brown shafts producing little more than brown lines. The wings and tail are dark brown with a hint of green gloss, especially on the inner webs of the secondaries and the outer webs of the rectrices. The iris of immatures is yellow, orange or pink and apparently increases in intensity with age until the deep red of the adult iris is attained. This description refers to nominate *panayensis*, from the Philippines and northern Sulawesi.

A. p. sanghirensis, from the islands of Talaud, Sangihe, Siau, Tahulandang, Ruang and Biaro, off the northern tip of Sulawesi, has a more massive bill and the frontal feathers are longer, forming a crest.

A complex of subspecies has been described from various parts of Indonesia.

A. p. alipodis, from the islands of Panjang, Maratau and Derawan, to the east of Borneo, is slightly duller and slightly larger than the nominate form.

A. p. eustathis, from eastern Borneo.

A. p. gusti, from Bali.

A. p. strigata, from southern Thailand, Malaysia, Sumatra, Java and western Borneo.

A. p. heterochlora, from Aramba and Natura Islands, between Borneo and the Malay Peninsula.

A. p. enganensis, from Enggano Island, off southern Sumatra is larger than *strigata*.

A. p. altirostris, from Simeuluë, the Banyak Islands and Nias (western Sumatran Islands).

A. p. leptorrhyncha, from Batu Island.

A. p. pachistorhina, from Mentawai Islands (western Sumatran Islands). The descriptions of these subspecies have been made largely on the basis of size and sample sizes have often been small (Hoogerwerf 1965), so the reliability of these distinctions may be questionable, although birds from islands east of Java do appear larger than *strigata* (from measurements given in Hoogerwerf 1965).

From the western part of the species' range.

A. p. affinis, of Assam, Bangladesh and Arakan (Burma), has a crimson iris.

A. p. tytleri, from the Andamans and Car Nicobar, is darker than *A. p. affinis* and the green gloss is tinged bluish; it also has a larger bill and the iris is often brown, though variable, and may be pink or orange.

A. p. albiris, of the Great and Central Nicobars, has a white iris.

MEASUREMENTS Male (3): wing 107–109, tail 68–81, tarsus 21–23, culmen 18–19. Female (4): wing 101–107, tail 72–76, tarsus 21–23, culmen 17–19.

VOICE When in flocks the Asian Glossy Starling is noisy. Most descriptions of the call note its metallic quality and Hails (1987) described the voice as a series of plaintive metallic squeaks. In a mixed roost of Common and White-vented Mynas in Singapore, the voices of Asian Glossy Starlings were noticeably quieter than the other two species although they did call frequently, giving a repeated *tsuu tsuu* and a high-pitched weak trill (CJF).

DISTRIBUTION AND POPULATION
Predominantly an island species, it ranges from the Philippines through Sulawesi, Borneo, Bali and the Greater Sunda Islands into continental Asia in Indochina, Burma and Eastern India. It is resident throughout the Philippines in the lowlands (Dickinson *et al.* 1991), in northern and north-central Sulawesi and its offshore islands (White and Bruce 1986), and in coastal Borneo (Smythies 1960), throughout the lowlands of the Greater Sunda Islands (MacKinnon and Phillipps 1993), in peninsular Thailand (Boonsong and Round 1991), southern Vietnam (Wildash 1968) and in Tenasserim, Burma. In Sulawesi its precise southern limits are not known due to difficulties of distinguishing this species from Short-tailed Starling, with whose range it may overlap (Coates and Bishop 1997). In all of these areas it is common, but only locally so in Sulawesi. In the Andaman and Nicobar Islands it is resident but locally migratory on most islands (Abdulali 1967), occurs locally in Arakan, western Burma (Smythies 1981), is locally common in Bangladesh, and appears to be a summer visitor to the Garo, Khasi and northern Cachar Hills in Assam (Ali and Ripley 1972). It has occurred once as a straggler in Madras. In the Philippines, ringed birds have survived for over seven years, despite extensive hunting (McClure 1974).

HABITAT Inhabits forest, secondary growth and villages (Delacour and Mayr 1946). In Malaysia, it inhabits mangrove and other coastal vegetation, gardens and lowland plantations, and also lives on offshore islands (Medway and Wells 1976).

Coconut plantations are preferred in the Andamans and Nicobars and elsewhere, and it also occurs in towns and cities (Abdulali 1967, MacKinnon and Phillipps 1993). In forest it prefers the forest edge and clearings for cultivation, especially where there are tall trees (Ali and Ripley 1972). Throughout its range it is primarily a bird of the lowlands, occurring to about 700 m.

FOOD AND FEEDING Eats mainly fruit and large numbers of these starlings congregate in trees bearing ripe fruit, e.g. *Ficus* sp. They occasionally feed on ripe fruit that has fallen to the ground (Hails 1987). They also drink nectar from flowering trees such as *Salmalia* and *Erythrina* (Ali and Ripley 1972) and eat insects, including adult and larval beetles (Carabidae), mole-crickets (Gryllotalpidae) and immature grasshoppers (Orthoptera) (Smythies 1960).

BREEDING Breeds colonially, nesting in holes in trees or in the crowns of palm trees, in the eaves of houses, holes in cliffs and walls and in other artificial sites (Medway and Wells 1976), including nest boxes (Hails unpub.). They also use the holes of other species, including woodpeckers (Picidae) and kingfishers (Alcedinidae) (Abdulali 1967, Smythies 1960). In Assam the breeding season is believed to be from February to April (Ali and Ripley 1972). In Burma breeding extends from March to June (Smythies 1981) and in the Andamans and Nicobars occurs mainly in April (Ali and Ripley 1972). In Malaysia the season is somewhat longer, from February to July (Medway and Wells 1976), and in Java and Bali extends from January to June (MacKinnon and Phillips 1993), while in Borneo the season is prolonged, from January to October, although most occurs in June-September (Smythies 1960). The nest is built of roots, grass and leaves, forming a rough cup (Smythies 1981). The eggs have a blue or blue-green background on which are superimposed brown markings or spots (Delacour and Mayr 1946, Smythies 1981), and measure 24.6–27.4 x 19.0–20.1 (10) (Schönwetter 1983). Each clutch contains 3–4 eggs.

MIGRATION Asian Glossy Starlings disperse or undertake local migrations away from their breeding sites. These movements can sometimes be long and involve journeys over the sea, and may be nocturnal (Medway and Wells 1976). In the Philippines, McClure (1974) concluded from ringing studies that this species is a 'wanderer that borders on migratory'. Juveniles ranged widely with no distinct pattern to their movements. On the edge of its range in Assam it appears to be a summer migrant, and even on islands with endemic subspecies it appears to be locally migratory, arriving to breed in particular areas and then disappearing to unknown regions for much of the year (Abdulali 1967).

BEHAVIOUR Asian Glossy Starlings are highly social and almost invariably feed in flocks, breed colonially and roost communally. They frequently perch in flocks in the tops of tall dead trees. Asian Glossy Starlings roost communally, mainly in trees but also on high tension electricity wires (Medway and Wells 1976) and have been recorded roosting on tall radio antennae (Smythies 1960). In Singapore, they roost with other starlings, notably Common and White-vented Mynas, and Purple-backed Starlings (Kang 1989), but the Asian Glossy Starlings tend to select roosting trees away from these other species. Before roosting, this species performs aerial manoeuvres (Hails 1987), and in this behaviour, its posture at rest and its direct flight in tight flocks, it shows a close resemblance to Common Starling.

RELATIONS WITH MAN Asian Glossy Starlings are extensively trapped and hunted in the Philippines (McClure 1974), presumably for food but possibly as cagebirds. In Singapore, the communal roosts of this species and other starlings are regarded as problematical on account of the noise of the birds and the droppings which foul footpaths (Hails unpub. Kang 1989), although the *Acridotheres* mynas are responsible for most of this problem. In Burma, Asian Glossy Starlings can be a major pest of pepper (Smythies 1960).

15 MOLUCCAN STARLING *Aplonis mysolensis* Plate 1
Island Starling

Lamprotornis obscura Bonaparte 1851

FIELD IDENTIFICATION 20 cm. A small black starling with a long, graduated tail. The plumage is dull metallic green-purple, duller than that of Shining Starling, and the iris is dark red-brown. Immatures are brown above and streaked below.

DESCRIPTION Sexes similar. The feathers of the forehead are somewhat bristled and the throat and neck feathers lanceolate, but not greatly elongated. The entire body plumage is black, glossed green-purple and duller, more leaden, than in Asian Glossy Starling. The wings are dark brown, without gloss. The tail is dark blackish-brown, without gloss, and is long and graduated, the outer rectrices being 25–30 mm shorter than the central ones. The black bill is relatively heavy, long and with a strongly curved culmen. The legs are black and the iris brown. Immatures are chocolate-brown above, while the feathers of the underparts are chocolate-brown with pale margins, producing heavy streaking; immatures also have a shorter tail. This description relates to nominate *mysolensis*, of the Moluccan Islands Morotai, Ternate, Halmahera, Bacan, Obi, Seram, Ambon, Haruku, Saparua and Buru.

A. m. forsteni is doubtfully distinct from the nominate form (White and Bruce 1986).

A. m. sulaensis, of eastern Sulawesi, Banggai Islands and Sula Islands, is slightly more glossy and green, and with a purplish-bronze gloss on the throat and neck but White and Bruce (1986) also doubt the validity of this distinction, and regard the species as monotypic.

MEASUREMENTS Male (7): wing 98–110, tail 103–110 but up to 20 cm shorter when worn or during moult, tarsus 22–24, culmen 17–20. Female (4): wing 98–103, tail 89–100, tarsus 20–22, culmen 17–19.

VOICE A wide variety of calls is given, including piercing, sharp upwardly inflected notes, nasal whistles and chattering and squealing notes; Coates and Bishop (1997) suggest that *A. m. mysolensis* and *sulaensis* may give different calls. While feeding in fruiting trees they give loud, reedy high-pitched *teeck* calls, and in flight produce short *sqweow, sqweow* calls (Jepson 1993).

DISTRIBUTION AND POPULATION Inhabits the Moluccan islands of Morotai, Ternate, Halmahera, Bacan, Obi, Seram, Ambon, Haruku, Saparua, Buru, and the Sula Islands group, eastern Sulawesi including the Banggai Islands and Peleng, and the west Papuan islands of Misool,

Waigeo, Salawati, Batanta, Gebe, Ajoe and smaller islands. It is generally moderately common to common, but less so on Buru (Coates and Bishop 1997).

HABITAT Predominantly an island species, Moluccan Starling occurs in mangroves and coastal woodland, primary lowland and hill forest to 1000 m or more, and also in degraded forest, forest edge, cultivated areas and trees in towns.

FOOD AND FEEDING Feeds in flocks high in the trees, especially in fruiting figs *Ficus*, *Casuarina*, and in flowering sago palms *Metroxylon*.

BREEDING Nests colonially, excavating holes in large dead forest trees. Colonies normally comprise 15–50 nests, but up to 200 have been recorded. A noisy species at the colony.

BEHAVIOUR Moluccan Starlings are gregarious, breeding colonially and forming small and large flocks; it is only occasionally seen singly or in pairs. On Seram it forms mixed species flocks with Shining Starlings.

PRINCIPAL REFERENCE Coates and Bishop (1997).

16 SHORT-TAILED STARLING *Aplonis minor* Plate 5
Lesser Glossy Starling, Short-tailed Glossy Starling

Lamprotornis minor Bonaparte 1850

FIELD IDENTIFICATION 18 cm. This species is very similar to and difficult to separate from Asian Glossy Starling. It is a smallish glossy black starling with a strong oily-green gloss on the plumage, but glossed purple (compared with a greenish gloss in Asian Glossy Starling) on the hackle feathers of the neck and throat; the extent of this purple varies geographically. The tail is only slightly graduated, distinguishing this species from Moluccan Starling which has a longer and much more strongly graduated tail. The black bill is somewhat down-curved and the legs and feet are black. The iris is red. Immatures are browner than adults, with a slight green gloss, while the underparts are dull white, broadly streaked with black; the iris of immatures is also red.

DESCRIPTION The feathers of the forehead are slightly bristled and the throat feathers are lanceolate. The feathers of the forehead and crown are iridescent purple-bronze, and the throat, upper breast, sides of neck and nape are brighter purple. The rest of the body plumage is iridescent oily-green. The wings are black with some green gloss on the secondaries. The tail is short and square, black with a little greenish gloss on the outer margins. The black bill is relatively fine and short with a curved culmen. The legs are black and the iris vermilion. Immatures are dark brown above, showing some green gloss on the crown and back. The underparts are brown, paler on the throat and on the belly, with buffy or whitish margins pro-

ducing streaking. This description refers to nominate *minor*, of the Lesser Sunda Islands.

A. m. montosa, of Sulawesi, has purple in the plumage reduced.

A. m. todayensis, of the Philippines, almost lacks purple, but White and Bruce (1986) cast doubt on the validity of both subspecies and regard the Short-tailed Starling as monotypic.

MEASUREMENTS Male (2): wing 100–101, tail 65–68, tarsus 21, culmen 14. Female (4): wing 89–102, tail 57–66, tarsus 19–21, culmen 12–13.

VOICE The common call is a plaintive *seep*, but they also give a slurred, metallic *chilanc* and short chattering notes (Coates and Bishop 1997). A clear metallic shriek is given in flight (MacKinnon and Phillipps 1993).

DISTRIBUTION AND POPULATION Occurs in the Philippines, Sulawesi, Java, Bali and the Lesser Sunda Islands. In the Philippines it occurs only on Mindanao, where Dickinson *et al.* (1991) reported it to be fairly common but very locally distributed. In Sulawesi it is found in central and southern parts and on the islands of Tukangbesi, Pendek, Muna, Butung, Salayar, Tanahjampea, Kayuadi, Kalao and Kalaotoa, while in the Lesser Sundas it occurs on Lombok, Sumbawa, Flores, Paloe, Sumba, Timor, Wetar, Romang and Moa (White and Bruce 1986). It also occurs on Java and Bali where it is frequently encountered (MacKinnon and Phillips 1993) and apparently breeds (MacKinnon 1990), although White and

Bruce (1986) considered it to be a migrant there, and one which had only recently begun occurring there. Hoogerwerf (1965) found no evidence of breeding on Java or Bali. In western Timor, Coates and Bishop (1997) thought that it may be nomadic, since it was present locally in the wet season, but absent during the dry season.

HABITAT In Java, Bali, Sulawesi and the Lesser Sundas, Short-tailed Starling is a bird mainly of the lowlands, to 1500 m, and of smaller islands. In Sulawesi and the Lesser Sundas it occurs primarily in forest and forest edge, and is found only occasionally in cultivated areas and villages (Coates and Bishop 1997). In Java, especially the east, and Bali, MacKinnon and Phillips (1993) found it to favour cultivated areas close to forest. On Mindanao, however, Short-tailed Starling is a bird of mountain forest, both in the canopy and at the edge, occurring above 900 m (Dickinson *et al.* 1991).

FOOD AND FEEDING According to MacKinnon (1990) Short-tailed Starlings feed mainly in trees and bushes and eat fruit and berries, including coffee *Coffea*, and also a variety of insects. They can form large flocks in fruiting trees.

BREEDING MacKinnon (1990) reported that this species breeds in small colonies in holes in dead trees, while Coates and Bishop (1997) state that pairs nest solitarily and imply that they excavate the holes themselves. The eggs are similar to those of Asian Glossy Starling but are finely speckled, and measure 23.6–24.8 x 17.7–18.3 mm (3) (Schönwetter 1983).

BEHAVIOUR Short-tailed Starlings are gregarious, feeding in small flocks, breeding in small colonies and roosting communally.

17 MICRONESIAN STARLING *Aplonis opaca* Plate 5

Lamprothornis opaca Kittlitz 1833

FIELD IDENTIFICATION 24 cm. A fairly large glossy starling that is widely distributed on islands across Micronesia. Adults males are dusky black with limited greenish gloss but the underparts are duller, and females lack iridescence and are streaked below. The black bill is curved, feet are black and the iris is yellow. Young birds are duller with streaked underparts.

DESCRIPTION Adult: Plumage is entirely black with slight green iridescence on the head, mantle, back, and wing-coverts, less so on the breast. Females are slightly duller and smaller than the males. **Immature:** Upperparts, wings and tail are dark brown without iridescence. Feathers of the throat and breast are dark brown with pale buff outer margins to webs, producing heavy streaking. The lower belly feathers are progressively more broadly margined and tipped buffy-ochre. The large black bill is down-curved, the base horn-coloured in immatures. The legs are black and the iris yellow. As with breeding seasons, moult seasons vary on different islands, being recorded on Pohnpei in November–December, on Palau in August–September (and not in November–December) and on Ulithi in August (Baker 1951). Birds from different island groups are ascribed to separate subspecies.

A. o. opaca Caroline Islands — Kusai.

A. o. angus Caroline Islands — Truk, Ulithi, Fais, Wolea, Ifalik, Faraulep, Lamotrek, Nukuoro, Lukunor — larger than nominate with bill less deep, and with distinct greenish iridescence on both upperparts and underparts.

A. o. kurodae Caroline Islands — Yap — bill longer and thicker than in nominate *opaca*, and plumage more bronzy-green.

A. o. ponapensis Caroline Islands — Pohnpei — larger with longer bill and richer green iridescence then nominate *opaca*.

A. o. aeneus Mariana Islands — Alamagan, Pagan, Agrihan, Asuncion — smaller bill and bronze rather than green iridescence.

A. o. guami Mariana Islands — Guam, Rota, Tinian, Saipan — similar to *angus* but with shorter bill.

A. o. orii Palau Islands — Kayangel, Babelthuap, Koror, Garakayo, Ngesebus, Peleliu, Ngabad, Angaur — slightly larger and with longer and shallower bill than nominate *opaca*.

MEASUREMENTS Male (15): wing 121–125, tail 76–85, culmen 24–26; female (12): wing 115–125, tail 72–82, culmen 23–26 (Baker 1951).

VOICE Baker (1951) described Micronesian Starlings as noisy and conspicuous. Their usual call was described as a 'squawking', but during presumed courtship birds produced a sweet ascending song, reminiscent of a Red-winged Blackbird *Agelaius phoeniceus*. On Yap, birds frequently sang from the tops of coconut trees (Fisher 1950). On Guam the calls are highly varied, including a series of whistles and other notes often given in chorus with those of other individuals, a single clear whistle which is often inflected and repeated, and in flight a soft chipping call, possibly a contact call, is given (Jenkins 1983).

DISTRIBUTION AND POPULATION Resident on the Micronesian island groups of Palau, the Carolines and the Marianas. On all of the island groups these starlings are numerous and constitute the most conspicuous and abundant of all the land birds. However, the published descriptions of status appeared shortly after World War II (Baker 1951, Fisher 1950, Brandt 1962) and, as Baker pointed out, human occupation during the war and the dereliction of former agricultural areas might have provided suitable conditions for the starlings. On Guam, the population has declined and by 1990–1994 the population was probably less than 200 birds (Wiles *et al.* 1995). On all of the island groups, Baker (1951) reported that birds in immature plumage greatly outnumbered adults although on Guam, Jenkins (1983) found that just over half of the birds were in juvenile plumage, indicating either a high productivity or that juvenile plumage was retained for a long time.

HABITAT Occurs in most habitats available on the island groups, living on both coralline and mountainous islands. The birds occupy forest and disturbed areas, but apparently avoid low bush and savannah (Fisher 1950). According to Baker (1951) they prefer open woodland and marginal areas, and especially areas that have been cultivated and allowed to become derelict, largely on account of the abundance of papaya *Carica papaya*, on which the birds feed, in such areas. On Guam, Jenkins (1983) stated that Micronesian Starling formerly occurred in all habitats, but by the early 1980s was most commonly found in scrub, secondary growth, mixed woodland and mature forest, being most abundant in the last. By 1990–1994, the range on Guam was further restricted and the largest concentration of birds occurred in the northeast of the island.

FOOD AND FEEDING All accounts indicate that the Micronesian Starling is predominantly frugivorous, although Baker (1951) reported one specimen from the Marianas whose stomach contained a grasshopper (Orthoptera) and Jenkins (1983) found a wasp (Hymemoptera) and unidentified insect larvae in the stomachs of two individuals. Reichel and Glass (1990) recorded them eating the eggs of Black Noddies *Anous minutus* and those of a Red-footed Booby *Sula sula*. The fruit and seeds of *Carica papaya* constitute a major part of their diet but a range of other plants is also taken (Jenkins 1983).

BREEDING Nests in cavities, usually at least 4m above the ground and up to 15m, using holes in trees, in the tops of tree ferns and coconut palms and sometimes in holes in rocky cliffs and the tops of decaying telegraph poles. Brandt (1962) described the nest as being made of coarse sticks and grasses containing a shallow cup lined with fine grasses, while Jenkins (1983) found nests containing the leaves of broadleaved trees and needles from *Casuarina* trees. The breeding season appears to differ in different island groups, with eggs on Pohnpei in August, on Guam in all months, and in October and December on Truk (Brandt 1962). On Yap, Fisher (1950) found adults feeding young in August. The clutch is normally 2 eggs, but 1–4 have been recorded. Eggs are pale green or greenish-blue with black, russet, brown and purplish spots concentrated near the broad end (Baker 1951) Brandt (1962) found two clutches in which the eggs were unmarked. Eggs (*kurodae*) measure 25.5–33.0 x 19.5–23.0 (47) (Schönwetter 1983). Both sexes incubate, brood and feed the young and remove faeces from the nest. One bird usually stays near the nest while the other member of the pair forages. Young are fed by regurgitation and their diet includes insects and fruits of a number of plants. The young fledge after 21–25 days and become independent shortly afterwards, forming flocks (Jenkins 1983).

BEHAVIOUR Strictly arboreal (Jenkins 1983), and live in small flocks of 2–12 birds (Baker 1951). Baker recorded what may have been courtship behaviour, where one of two adults sitting on a palm frond fanned out its tail, spread its wings and at irregular intervals picked up and released part of the frond. Jenkins (1983) reported two birds in flight touching each other, and giving a single high-pitched call during the descending part of each undulation. Fisher (1950) found Micronesian Starlings most commonly in the tops of tall trees and noted that they were aggressive towards other species, notably Cardinal Myzomela *Myzomela cardinalis* and Yap Monarch *Monarcha godeffroyi*, and they aggressively defend their nest territories against monitor lizards (*Varanus indicus*), White-tailed Tropic Birds (*Phaethon lepturus*), Micronesian Kingfishers (*Halcyon cinnamomina*) and Mariana Crows (*Corvus kubaryi*) (Jenkins 1983)

RELATIONS WITH MAN On Pohnpei, Yap, Koror and Truk, people collect Micronesian Starlings for food (Baker 1951). Reichel and Grass (1990) thought that Micronesian Starlings followed humans in order to take eggs of disturbed seabirds on islands in the northern Marianas. On Guam the number of Micronesian Starlings has declined markedly and its range has contracted. Wiles *et al.* (1995) considered this decline to have resulted from the introduction of the Brown Tree Snake (*Boiga irregularis*) and that the birds' survival in the developed areas of the military base may be due to a reduced predation pressure from the snake in built-up areas, where snake density is lower than in forest, and where starling nests in the tops of telegraph poles and in buildings may be more inaccessible to snakes than are natural nest cavities.

18 POHNPEI MOUNTAIN STARLING *Aplonis pelzelni*   Plate 5
Pohnpei Starling

Aplonis pelzelni Finsch 1876

FIELD IDENTIFICATION 16 cm. A small dark starling with little gloss, paler and more olive below. Bill and feet are black and the iris brown. Juveniles are paler, especially on the underparts. The lack of gloss, brown iris and more slender bill of the adults and the lack of streaking in the immatures distinguish this species from the commoner Micronesian Starling *A. opaca*.

DESCRIPTION Adult: Entire plumage shows little iridescence. The upperparts are sooty brown, the head darker and the forehead and lores blackish. The wings, tail, rump and uppertail-coverts are paler and browner, and the underparts paler and washed with olive-brown. The bill and legs are black and the iris brown. **Immature**: Similar to adult but lighter brown, especially on the underparts.

MEASUREMENTS Male (10): wing 101–105, tail 63–67, tarsus 26–28, culmen 19–21; female (10): wing 97–102, tail 57–64, tarsus 26–27, culmen 19–20 (Baker 1951).

VOICE The call has been described as weaker and finer than that of Micronesian Starling (Baker 1951). Buden (1996) described its call as a plaintive, high-pitched, sibilant whistle.

DISTRIBUTION AND POPULATION Occurs only on the Caroline Island of Pohnpei in Micronesia. It is restricted to mountain forest and is now categorised as critically endangered (Collar *et al.* 1994). Baker (1951), however, reported that local people claimed that this starling formerly inhabited the whole of Pohnpei and that it also occurred on a nearby atoll, Ant. It was also sympatric with Micronesian Starling. There have been few recent sightings of this species and it was not seen in a survey undertaken in 1983. Rat predation may have contributed to its decline (Engbring *et al.* 1990, in Collar *et al.* 1994) but the procurement of a specimen in 1995 indicates that the species is not yet extinct (Buden 1996).

HABITAT Little information, except that Pohnpei Mountain Starling appears to be restricted to high forest.

BREEDING This starling is said to nest in holes in trees and to lay two eggs (Baker 1951). A female shot in July 1995 had enlarged follicles (Buden 1996).

BEHAVIOUR Coultas (in Baker 1951) states that Pohnpei Mountain Starlings usually occur in pairs.

RELATIONS WITH MAN According to Coultas (in Baker 1951), Pohnpei Mountain Starlings can easily be attracted to the calls of wounded birds or to man-made sounds (squeaking the lips against the hands) and that 'many were taken' (for food?) in fruit trees. According to Engbring *et al.* (1990), it was never abundant but underwent a severe decline in numbers after 1930. The reason for this is unclear, but predation by rats, hunting of birds for food and habitat loss may have contributed.

19 POLYNESIAN STARLING *Aplonis tabuensis*   Plate 6
Striped Starling

Lanius tabuensis Gmelin 1788

FIELD IDENTIFICATION 17–21 cm. Sexes similar. A medium-sized stocky starling with a comparatively stubby bill. The upperparts are brown with the crown glossed purple and the secondaries have white outer margins, producing a pale wing patch. The underparts are buffish, paler on the chin and lower belly, and show some streaking due to paler feather shafts. The bill is black and the legs and feet are horn-brown. The iris may be yellow, red-brown or brown, depending upon location. In flight, the broad, rounded wings suggest a fluttering movement.

DESCRIPTION The forehead and crown are dark brown with violet iridescence, the remaining upperparts are mid-brown. The underparts, especially the chin, are paler buffy-brown, the feathers of the throat and breast having white shafts, producing a slight streaking. The wings are dark brown but the margins of the outer webs of the secondaries are proximally paler, producing a pale patch in the closed wing. The tail is mid-brown and square-ended. The bill is black, short and thick, and slightly hooked at the tip. The legs are dark brown and the iris is red-brown. This description refers to the nominate form of most of southern Tonga and of the Lau Archipelago of Fiji.

Elsewhere in Tonga, **A. t. tenebrosus**, of Niuatoputapu and Tafahi, differs from nominate *tabuensis* in being almost uniformly dark sooty-brown, with the upperparts glossed greenish and the underparts with fine buffy shaft streaks.

A. t. nesiotes, of Niuafo'ou, is also darker than the nominate form but less so than *tenebrosus*, and has a yellow iris.

A. t. brunnescens, of Niue, is smaller with a thinner bill, with no iridescence on the crown, and with the iris red-brown or dark brown.

A. t. vitiensis, of Fiji is smaller, has a thinner bill and the streaking on the underparts is more pronounced, as is the pale wing patch, than in nominate *tabuensis*; iris colour varies according to location, being brown in birds from the northern and western islands, and yellow on birds from other islands, although on a few islands birds with irises of both colours are present.

A. t. fortunae, of the Horne Islands, is slightly smaller with a browner back and paler underparts with more pronounced streaking than in nominate *tabuensis*, but the pale outer margins of the secondaries are less prominent and confined to two feathers only; the iris is yellow.

A. t. rotumae, of Rotuma Island, has broad grayish margins to the back and rump feathers, a more extensive whitish area on the lower belly, and a slenderer, less curved bill than in *fortunae*.

A. t. tucopiae, of Tukopia Island, east of Santa Cruz, is uniformly brown without streaking on the underparts, with gloss confined to purplish-brown on the crown, and with a yellowish or brown iris.

A. t. pachyramphus, of the Reef, Swallow and Tinakula Islands in the Santa Cruz group, has a short heavy bill, darkish brown underparts with pear-shaped shaft streaks confined to the lower breast and flanks, and a brown iris.

A. t. brevirostris, of Western Samoa, is smaller and darker brown above and darker below, but with pronounced streaking; the pale wing patch is prominent, the bill stubby and paler brown than in the nominate form; the iris is yellow.

A. t. tutuilae, of Tutuila Island, American Samoa, is larger than *brevirostris*, with darker underparts, more pronounced light shaft streaks, and a large bill; the iris is yellow.

A. t. manuae, of the Manua Islands, American Samoa, has the back darker than in *tutuilae*, no wing patch and dark grey-brown underparts without shaft streaks; the bill is very small and the iris is yellow.

MEASUREMENTS Male: wing 108–118, tail 60–71; female: wing 105–112, tail 59–67; male/female tarsus 28–30, culmen 23–26 (sample sizes not given, Mayr 1942).

VOICE The advertising call is a fluty, high-pitched double whistle *twee-wee*, regularly repeated. Other whistles and a hissing call are given.

DISTRIBUTION AND POPULATION Widely distributed on islands in the Tonga, Fiji and Samoa groups, and on other central Polynesian islands where it has differentiated into several races. On many islands it is common.

HABITAT Found on large islands and also on the smallest islets. On smaller islands it is found in all vegetated habitats, including forest edge, regenerating scrub, coconut plantations and villages (Kinsky and Yaldwyn 1981), while on larger islands, such as Fiji, it is primarily a forest bird, inhabiting forest edge, clearings or well-wooded secondary habitats (Watling 1982). On islands where Samoan Starling occurs, Polynesian Starlings occur mainly in high forest where the former species is scarcer (Bellingham and Davis 1988).

FOOD AND FEEDING Active and sometimes acrobatic birds, Polynesian Starlings eat fruit and insects with the former probably predominant. They feed from the low scrub to the high canopy, taking fruits and berries, but also gleaning insects from foliage. Kinsky and Yaldwyn (1981) described this species' attempts to hunt in the cracks and crevices of bark by clinging to the tree trunk and supporting themselves, woodpecker fashion, using the tail. Rinke (1986) recorded them eating fruits of *Morinda citrifolia*, *Cassytha filiformis*, *Scaevola frutescens* and *Premna taitensis* on Niuafo'ou Island, Tonga.

BREEDING Nests at almost any height in holes in trees and in the tops of broken-off coconut palms. The nest is built of dry vegetable fibres. The clutch of two or three eggs are various shades of blue with brown or red-brown specks and blotches. Eggs (*vitiensis*) measure 26.0–28.4 x 17.8–20.7 mm (5) (Schönwetter 1983). Kinsky and Yaldwyn (1981) recorded nesting in August on Niue but breeding seasons elsewhere are not known. Parental care has not been described.

BEHAVIOUR Gregarious, feeding in small loose flocks, but solitary birds also occur. Flight is quick and direct with rapid wing beats.

PRINCIPAL REFERENCES Mayr (1942), du Pont (1976), Watling (1982).

20 SAMOAN STARLING *Aplonis atrifusca*   Plate 6

Lamprotornis atrifusca Peale 1848

FIELD IDENTIFICATION 30 cm. Sexes similar. A large starling with a long tail and heavy bill. The entire bird is dark brown with a slight purple-green iridescence on the head, mantle and breast; the head, chin, throat and breast are darker than the rest of the body.

DESCRIPTION The forehead, crown and nape, chin, throat and upper breast are dark brown with violet-green iridescence. The mantle is brown with the feather tips slightly iridescent green and pinkish-violet. The back, belly, wings and tail are mid-brown with a hint of rufous on the outer webs of the primaries. The tail is long and square. The bill is heavy, black and slightly down-curved, legs and feet are black and the iris dark brown. Immature birds are dull brown. Dhondt (1976) saw birds in wing moult in June.

MEASUREMENTS Male (36): wing 148–162, tail 100–115; female (19): wing 142–150, tail 97–105; male/female tarsus 35–36, culmen 34–36 (Mayr 1942).

VOICE The usual call is a harsh screech, but softer whistles are also given (Watling 1982).

DISTRIBUTION AND POPULATION
Endemic to the American Samoan islands of Ofu, Olosega, Tau and Tutuila, and on the Western Samoan islands of Savii and Upolu. It is a common bird at all elevations.

HABITAT Most abundant in coastal fringe and exotic plantations, but also frequently found in lower forests, especially those which have been partially logged, but is less abundant in forests at higher altitudes (Bellingham and Davis 1988). They also occur commonly in urban areas (Evans et al. 1992).

FOOD AND FEEDING The diet comprises mainly fruit but also insects, and guavas *Psidium* sp. are particularly attractive when trees are ripening (Watling 1982). It is one of the main pollinators of the liana *Freycinetia reineckei* (Cox 1982).

BREEDING Nests in holes in trees (Evans et al. 1992). The breeding season is not known, but Dhondt (1976) saw flying birds carrying food in May and June, and carrying a twig in July. The eggs are pale blue, measuring 30.6–35.6 x 22.0–23.1 mm (4) (Schönwetter 1983), but the clutch size is not known (Watling 1982).

BEHAVIOUR An aggressive bird, its ability to compete with the recently introduced Jungle Myna will be monitored with interest. Its flight is slow and laboured.

RELATIONS WITH MAN Watling (1982) states that Samoan Starlings eat guavas when in season, without describing the extent of any damage. They are important pollinators of some Samoan plants (Cox 1982) and are exploited for food by island inhabitants. Craig et al. (1994) stated that they were infrequently harvested but on Tutuila Island the population declined by 66% between 1986–7 and 1992; the 1992 census followed a hurricane in 1990, which made other animals, and possibly the bird itself, more readily available to local hunters.

21 RAROTONGA STARLING *Aplonis cinerascens* Plate 6

Aplonis cinerascens Hartlaub and Finsch 1871

FIELD IDENTIFICATION 21 cm. A medium-sized starling, generally grey-brown and with a long, curved bill. The head is brownish-grey with a slight purplish gloss. The undertail-coverts and vent are pale, and the tail and wings dark brown. Bill and legs are black, iris dark.

DESCRIPTION The forehead and crown are mousy brown with a hint of pinkish or purplish iridescence. The rest of the body is mouse-brown, the feathers of the back and rump edged with grey, and somewhat paler below due to broader pale tips to the breast and belly feathers. The lower belly and undertail-coverts are buff. Wings and tail are mid brown, the inner secondaries having narrow pale edges. The bill is horny black, long and down-curved. The legs are black and the iris black or dark brown, sometimes with a yellow outer ring.

MEASUREMENTS Male (7): wing 122–127, tail 70–77, tarsus 30–33, bill 27–29; female (5) wing 118–125, tail 69–74, tarsus 30–33, bill 27–29 (Holyoak and Thibault 1984).

VOICE This starling is said to produce soft whistles and a sweet song, and McCormack (1997) described it as the most melodious bird on Rarotonga. Most calls were heard when birds were disturbed and they rarely called in flight. Holyoak and Thibault (1984) recorded a series of strident whistles *skwii-skwii-skwii-skwae-skwae-skwae-ouae-oui-ouae-oui* which varied in length and intensity.

DISTRIBUTION AND POPULATION
Endemic to the island of Rarotonga, in the Cook Islands. In 1904 it was abundant and in 1973 there were estimated to be between 1,000–3,000 birds (Holyoak and Thibault 1984). In 1984 the population was estimated at only about 100 birds (Collar and Andrew 1988), but this figure has been revised to a few hundred birds (Collar et al. 1994), possibly around 500 (McCormack 1997). The reason for its rarity is not known and its status is regarded as vulnerable (Collar et al. 1994). However, McCormack (1997) thought that the large size of the birds' territories limited the number of pairs that could occupy the available habitat.

HABITAT Inhabits montane native forest and fringing disturbed forest in the rugged interior of the island, from 150 m to the highest peaks on the island at 600 m. In 1973 it occurred in all the main valleys and McCormack (1997) found it to be widespread, but it did not occur in coastal areas, which were almost totally cultivated.

FOOD AND FEEDING Limited information suggests a varied diet of insects, fruit and possibly nectar. It has been recorded feeding in flowers, on fruits from the canopy and by gleaning insects from leaves and tree branches.

BREEDING Two nests have been found, both in the same old tree in holes 4 and 6 m above the ground. Nest material comprised dead leaves and dry plant fibres.

BEHAVIOUR Most often seen singly or in pairs, rarely in larger groups. They are rarely seen as they remain in trees, making rapid flights above the canopy.

PRINCIPAL REFERENCE Holyoak and Thibault (1984).

22 YELLOW-FACED MYNA *Mino dumontii*

Plate 7

Orange-faced Grackle, Papuan Myna, Long-tailed Myna

Mino Dumontii Lesson 1827

FIELD IDENTIFICATION 23–26 cm. The Yellow-faced Myna is largely black, glossed with oily green or purple, but has a white rump and undertail-coverts, yellow lower belly and a white wing-bar, which is prominent in flight. The most distinctive feature, however, is a large orange-yellow patch of bare skin around and behind the eye. The bill, legs and feet are yellow.

DESCRIPTION Feathers on the head are lanceolate but small, and restricted to the forehead, along the base of the mandibles, in a broad stripe over the centre of the crown, in a stripe from the gape to the side of the neck, and in a triangle extending from the throat to a point on the gular skin. These feathers are black, slightly glossed bluish-purple. The remainder of the head is bare yellow-orange skin, comprising a large patch above, behind and below the eye, less extensive in front, and a gular patch at the front of the chin and on the sides of the throat. The neck, mantle and throat are black, glossed purple, and the back, breast and belly are black glossed greenish. Most individuals show small white flecks on the sides of the neck produced by white filoplumes, and on some birds this flecking extends to the hind neck and throat. The rump is white. Feather tips of the lower belly are elongated and degraded, deep golden and the undertail-coverts are white. The wings and the short, square tail are black, lightly glossed and the primaries have a white patch, restricted to the inner web of the outer large feather, both webs of primaries 8–4 and outer web only of primary 3. The bill and legs are yellow, and the iris is orange-yellow, flecked or mottled with black, although in southern New Guinea it is sometimes brown and in northern New Guinea may be dark brown with or without gold spots. Juveniles have paler facial skin and in immatures the golden lower belly is paler than in adults.

MEASUREMENTS Male (8): wing 145–155, tail 74–82, tarsus 35–39, culmen 23–27; female (7) wing 137–154, tail 68–76, tarsus 35–38, culmen 24–27; weight 217 g (sample size not given — Bell 1982).

VOICE Yellow-faced Mynas are noisy birds, giving distinctive loud nasal, growling and croaking calls with a sometimes human-like conversational quality. Both low and high-pitched calls are given. In the Port Moresby area, most calls are disyllabic with a wide variety of types. Elsewhere on the mainland tri- and polysyllabic calls predominate. A captive pair on St Johns Island, Singapore, gave disyllabic calls reminiscent of a squeaky hinge but with a deep, resonant fluty quality (CJF).

DISTRIBUTION AND POPULATION Occurs on New Guinea and many of the small islands offshore, but surprisingly not on those off the southeastern coast of the mainland. A generally widespread and common species in the lowlands and hills to about 800 m, exceptionally to 1800 m in Papua New Guinea.

HABITAT A tree canopy species although it descends lower at the forest edge. It inhabits rainforest, swamp forest, monsoon forest and gallery forest, forest edge and partly cleared areas, secondary growth, and also extends into savanna.

FOOD AND FEEDING Primarily frugivorous, eating fruit and berries of trees, often in company with Golden-breasted Mynas and other fruit-eating birds. They also eat animal food including caterpillars and they have been recorded sallying for insects from high perches. Coates saw a parent bring a long-legged animal, which he thought was a cricket or a frog, to its young.

BREEDING Nest in holes, usually 10 to 30 m above the ground, in living or dead trees at the forest edge or in a clearing. Bell (1972) recorded a nest in the base of a large Bird's Nest Fern *Asplenium nidus* on a horizontal branch of a dead tree. Nest material consists of dry sticks, and twigs with green leaves have also been seen to be taken into nest holes. The clutch consists of one or two eggs, which are light blue with pale grey and red-brown markings. The incubation and fledgling periods are not known. Draffan (1977) recorded three birds occupying and carrying nest material into a hole, and all three may have been involved in feeding the two young. The third bird may have been the youngster of a previous brood and these observations suggest that some nests have helpers. The breeding season is extended although the use of nest holes for roosting can give a false impression of the length of the season. Egg laying or feeding young have been recorded in August, September, January, February and April, suggesting that breeding extends from the middle dry to the early wet season.

BEHAVIOUR Usually seen in pairs and they may pair for life. They are also encountered in small family groups or flocks of a few pairs, but may occasionally be seen in larger flocks of up to 50 birds. Large roosting flocks of over 200 birds have been recorded in tall densely-crowned trees (Bell 1972, Peckover 1975). As mentioned above, Yellow-faced Mynas may breed cooperatively.

This species commonly perches for long periods on exposed branches in the tops of tall trees, announcing their presence with loud calls. Flight is direct with rapid wing beats and usually the pair fly together.

RELATIONS WITH MAN Yellow-faced Mynas were available in bird shops in Singapore in 1990 (CJF).

PRINCIPAL REFERENCE Coates (1990).

23 LONG-TAILED MYNA *Mino kreffti*

Gracula kreffti Schlater 1869

FIELD IDENTIFICATION 29–32 cm. A large myna with glossy black plumage, bare orange skin on the sides of the head, white wing patch, rump and undertail and narrow golden band on lower belly. It is larger than Yellow-faced Myna, with longer wings and a noticeably longer tail.

DESCRIPTION The forehead, crown, nape, throat and breast are black glossed purple, and the back and belly are black but glossed greenish-blue. Around the eye is a patch of bare skin, smaller than in Yellow-faced Myna, and which comes to a point behind the eye; this bare skin is orange-yellow to deep orange. The feathers of the head are not lanceolate. On most individuals there are a few white filoplumes behind the eye patch. The uppertail-coverts are white and elongated. Feathers of the lower belly are golden, forming a band which is narrower than in Yellow-faced Myna, and the undertail-coverts are white. The wings and tail are black with some gloss, and the primaries have white patches: on the inner web of primary 9, both webs of primaries 8–4, on the outer web of primary 3 with a spot on the inner web, and a spot on the outer web of primary 2. The white patches are larger than in Yellow-faced Myna, up to 4 cm broad on the inner webs of the inner primaries. The bill is orange-yellow to deep orange, hooked and deeper than in Yellow-faced Myna. The legs are deep yellow or yellow-orange, and the iris is orange-yellow to orange in adults, yellowish, tinted brown, in juveniles. Hartert (1929) attributed smaller birds on Guadalcanal and Malaita Islands to the race *sandfordi*, but Amadon (1956) noted variation in size and tail length in the Solomons and concluded that they were all best included in *kreffti*.

MEASUREMENTS Male/female (Solomons, 7): wing 154–166, tail 112–121, tarsus 38–43, culmen 28–33.

VOICE A wide variety of extended whistles and squawks, and the loud, high-pitched and sometimes nasal whistles are more reminiscent of those of Golden-breasted Myna. These calls may comprise a number of notes but they are distinctive of the species (Hadden 1981). In the eastern Solomons the whistles have an unmistakable liquid trilling quality and they sometimes end with a squawk (Cain and Galbraith 1956).

DISTRIBUTION AND POPULATION Occurs on the Bismarck Archipelago and in the northern and central Solomons, but not on San Cristobal. On Bougainville they are abundant.

HABITAT Inhabits the canopy of open forest, remnant pockets of forest in clearings, and plantations, usually to c. 500 m but exceptionally to 1050 m in the Solomons (Hadden 1981). In the Solomons it is one of the most obvious and vocal birds of primary forest (Blaber 1990), but it also occurs in coconut plantations and in secondary growth near towns and villages, but not in urban areas (Hadden 1981).

FOOD AND FEEDING Frugivorous. Cain and Galbraith (1956) found large slices of soft fruits and hard-seeded berries in stomach contents.

BREEDING Nests in holes in trees, and Cain and Galbraith (1956) found this species nesting in broken palm trees. Eggs are pale blue with fine reddish-brown and grey markings, and average 36 x 25 mm (2) (Schönwetter 1983). Nesting activity has been observed in November and January (Coates 1990).

BEHAVIOUR A much less gregarious species than Yellow-faced Myna, and occurs singly or in pairs. Pairs spend much time conspicuously perched on exposed dead branches of trees, calling frequently.

PRINCIPAL REFERENCE Schodde (1977).

24 GOLDEN-BREASTED MYNA *Mino anais*

Golden Myna

Sericulus anais Lesson 1839

FIELD IDENTIFICATION 22–25 cm. Sexes similar. A heavily built myna with the face, throat, back, belly, wings and tail black with an oily green gloss, while the crown, breast, collar, rump and uppertail-coverts are golden yellow. The lower belly is bright yellow and the undertail-coverts white. A white bar in the primaries is conspicuous in flight. There is a dark blue bare patch of skin around the eye and the iris, bill, legs and feet are yellow. In immatures the yellow plumage is less bright and mottled with black, and the underparts are black with yellow scaling.

DESCRIPTION The feathers of the forehead, crown, chin, throat, mantle, upper back and belly are black, broadly tipped with glossy oily-green. A broad collar on the sides and back of the neck is creamy-orange, without gloss. Tips of the breast feathers and those of the lower back and rump are elongated and degraded, deep orange with a slight gloss. The undertail-coverts are creamy. The wings are dark brown, each of the large primaries having a white patch, restricted to the inner webs of primaries 1 and 9, but on both webs of the others. The tail is short and square, black slightly glossed green. The iris, bill, legs and feet are yellow, and there is a patch of dark blue bare skin around the eye, extending to a point behind it. Immatures have the upperparts duller than adults and lack the creamy-orange collar and the orange breast. Orange on the lower back is less extensive and the underparts are black, the feathers having short degraded yellow margins giving a scaly appearance. This description refers to the nominate form of northwest New Guinea and Salawati Island.

M. a. orientalis, of northern New Guinea east to the Huon Peninsula, has a glossy orange crown, with glossy orange stripes extending backwards from the crown, above the eye, to join the neck collar which is also glossy orange.

M. a. robertsoni, of southern New Guinea east to Milne Bay, has the entire crown and nape glossy orange.

MEASUREMENTS Male/female (4): wing 135–148, tail 80–89, tarsus 32–34, culmen 17–20; weight 144 g (sample size not given — Bell 1982).

VOICE The calls of Golden-breasted Myna comprise a variety of hoarse, nasal, whistled or squeaky notes, including a short, sweetly whistled song (Beehler *et al.* 1986). Coates describes the song as 'a variable series of two to six high and low pitched, rising and falling, mellow and squeaky notes, the pattern repeated or sometimes changing from one utterance to the next, the result being reminiscent of the pedalling of a squeaky bicycle'. Coates also describes an alarm or scolding hoarse, rasping, buzzing, descending *whaaaa* or a rising and descending *whaiiiey*, and a high-pitched metallic *queelie* of parrot or drongo quality, given in alarm.

DISTRIBUTION AND POPULATION Endemic to New Guinea and Salawati Island, and may occur on Yapen Island. It does not occur along the north coast or the southeast, which Coates finds surprising, or in the Trans Fly region, but is widespread elsewhere.

HABITAT Primarily a lowland bird, where it inhabits forest, including monsoon forest, forest edge and partially cleared areas. In clearings, however, it does need the presence of tall trees. Its range extends to about 300 m in the foothills but at Ok Tedi it is found at 570 m.

FOOD AND FEEDING Frugivorous, taking fruits from the upper tree canopy. However, the kinds of fruit taken have not been described.

BREEDING Nests in holes in living or dead trees, the nest site usually being 10 to 30 m above the ground. Trees at the forest edge or isolated in clearings are selected for nesting. The eggs have not been described and the only information on clutch size relates to a nest in which two young were seen. Limited evidence suggests that chicks are fed entirely on fruit and that, typical of species in which chicks are frugivorous, the fledging period is long (Bell 1984).

The breeding season appears to be long, with activity recorded at nest holes from February to October, although such holes may be used for roosting as well as breeding. Coates considered that the breeding season begins towards the end of the wet season and extends through the dry season.

BEHAVIOUR Usually seen in pairs and they may pair for life. Members of pairs spend most of their time close together and they indulge in mutual allopreening. Even when feeding young the adults leave the nest as a pair and return together. Like other members of the family, they frequently sit in exposed positions in the tops of dead branches of tall trees. Small parties sometimes occur with flocks exceptionally numbering 25 or more birds. They sometimes join groups of Yellow-faced Mynas.

RELATIONS WITH MAN Golden-breasted Mynas were readily available in bird shops in Singapore in 1990 (CJF).

PRINCIPAL REFERENCE Coates (1990).

25 SULAWESI CRESTED MYNA *Basilornis celebensis* Plate 8

Sulawesi (Celebes) Starling, Sulawesi (Celebes) King Starling, Celebes Myna, Short-crested Myna

Basilornis celebensis G R Gray 1861

FIELD IDENTIFICATION 23–27 cm. A medium-sized glossy black starling with a permanently erect crest along the top of the head and white patches on the side of the neck and side of the breast.

DESCRIPTION Sexes similar, although the crest of the male is somewhat longer than that of the female. Feathers of the forehead, crown, nape and hindneck are directed to the central line to form an iridescent glossy violet-blue rigid crest extending from in front of the nostrils over the top of the head. The mantle, back, rump, breast, belly and undertail-coverts are black, the feathers broadly tipped with metallic green iridescence. A patch of white feathers behind and below the eye has the posterior feathers washed orange, and is surrounded by filoplumes with small white tips, giving a speckled appearance. Feathers on the side of the breast are white, washed buff, producing a small patch. The tail is black, slightly glossed on the outer webs and the wings blackish-brown. The underwing-coverts are glossy greenish-black, the primaries and secondaries dull grey below, paler towards the bases and darker towards the tips. The bill is pale greenish-blue; the legs are lemon-yellow; bare skin around and behind the eye is blue-black and the iris is brown-red. Immatures are chocolate brown with only a little greenish iridescence. Underparts comprise dark feathers with paler edges, some with iridescent tips, producing a streaked appearance. White patches on the sides of neck and breast lack the orange or buff wash. Feathers of the forehead, but not the crown or nape, are directed towards central line. Monotypic. Juveniles undergo a complete moult (Stresemann 1940), but nothing else is recorded.

MEASUREMENTS Male (sample size not given): wing 138, tail 88, tarsus 29, bill from nostril 16 (Meyer and Wigglesworth 1898).

VOICE Watling (1983) reported a wide repertoire of whistles, squeaks, grunts and warbles. Calls, mainly high-pitched whistles and prolonged nasal notes, include 4 types: a series of 3 very high-pitched descending whistles of decreasing volume; a single high-pitched whistle; a nasal descending *meeow*; intermittent soft brief squeak and *chip* calls (Coates and Bishop 1997).

DISTRIBUTION AND POPULATION Endemic resident of the Sulawesi archipelago, inhabiting Sulawesi, Lembeh, Muna and Butung (White and Bruce 1986). It is a bird of the hill forests and while Meyer and Wigglesworth (1898) and Stresemann (1940) described it as the rarest of the Sulawesi starlings, Watling (1983) found it 'not uncommon' up to 1200 m, and Coates and Bishop (1997) described it as widespread and generally moderately common. In suitable habitat, it occurs throughout the island of Sulawesi.

HABITAT A forest bird, preferring wooded parts of open mountain country, although it is occasionally found in lower thick primary forest (Stresemann 1940). On Sulawesi, Watling (1983) recorded it from secondary forest, forest edge and clearings. This species may therefore not have suffered, or may even have benefited, from the destruction of primary forest that has taken place in much of the region. On Muna and Butung, which are not mountainous and which are, according to de Haan (in van Bemmel and Voous 1951), dry savanna and grassland with patches of evergreen trees, it inhabits the woodlands.

FOOD AND FEEDING Little is known of this species' feeding habits, Meyer and Wigglesworth (1898) simply stating that it eats fruit. Watling (1983) recorded it feeding in the upper parts of trees but did not describe food items. Van den Berg and Bosman (1986) saw single immatures eating berries in tree tops.

BREEDING Nothing is recorded.

BEHAVIOUR Usually found in pairs or family groups (Stresemann 1940) but van den Berg and Bosman (1986) recorded solitary immatures feeding in the tops of trees among large flocks of Flame-browed Mynas. Regularly associates with other frugivores. Watling (1983) recorded groups of 3–6 birds. When giving the nasal *meeow* call, it fluffs up its back feathers and throws the head forward with each call (Coates and Bishop 1997).

26 HELMETED MYNA *Basilornis galeatus*   Plate 8
Greater King Starling, Sula Starling

Basilornis galeatus Meyer 1894

FIELD IDENTIFICATION 24–25 cm. A largely glossy black starling with white patches on the sides of the neck and breast. It has a round-ended tail but its most prominent feature is the tall permanently erect crest, with crest feathers about three times as long as those in the Sulawesi Crested Myna.

DESCRIPTION Sexes similar. Feathers of the forehead, crown and nape are directed towards the mid-line and central feathers are elongated to form a tall black crest with purple iridescence. The mantle, back, rump, middle of the breast, belly and undertail-coverts are black with green iridescence. On the side of the neck, a white patch, with feathers towards the posterior ochreous, is congruent with a large white patch on the side of the breast, the ventral feathers of which are tinged ochre. The primaries, secondaries and tail are dark chocolate-brown, the tail rounded. The bill is creamish; legs and feet yellow. In immatures the crest is shorter, the plumage generally less glossy with the chin brown, and the upper mandible dark.

MEASUREMENTS Male/female (5): wing 137–149, tail 93–100, tarsus 30–34, bill from nos-

tril 16–20 (Meyer and Wigglesworth 1898).

VOICE Coates and Bishop (1997) describe 3 deep resonant booming *poo poo poop* calls, repeated at 5–7 sec intervals.

DISTRIBUTION AND POPULATION Confined to the Banggai islands, off Sulawesi and the Sula islands in the Moluccas, where it is scarce to moderately common. It occurs from sea level to at least 1000 m.

HABITAT Occurs most frequently in the least disturbed forests, but is also found in degraded forest and cultivations, often in fruiting trees but also in tall dead or leafless trees in reedswamp (Davidson *et al.* 1995), and in tall mangroves (Coates and Bishop 1997).

FOOD AND FEEDING Fruit and berries are the only food items recorded.

BEHAVIOUR Usually seen in pairs, although Davidson *et al.* (1995) recorded a flock of 22 birds in a fruiting tree. It is usually seen in the upper parts of tall trees but sometimes descends to lower levels (Coates and Bishop 1997). Nothing is known of its breeding.

RELATIONS WITH MAN Listed as near-threatened by Collar *et al.* (1994), and is particularly vulnerable in lowlands where large trees are being lost. Its montane forest habitat in Sula, however, is now given a degree of protection, although we do not know how effective this is likely to be.

27 LONG-CRESTED MYNA *Basilornis corythaix* Plate 8
Moluccan Starling, Ceram King Starling

Basilornis corythaix (Wagler) 1827

FIELD IDENTIFICATION 24–26 cm. A glossy black starling with a tall wispy crest and small white patches on the sides of the neck and breast. **DESCRIPTION** Feathers of the crown and nape are directed towards the mid-line, and are elongated to form a tall crest of degenerate plumes without iridescence. Feathers of the forehead, sides of the crown, nape, throat and breast have purple iridescence, and some throat feathers of some individuals are finely tipped white, but this is a variable character. The mantle, back, rump, breast and belly are black with green iridescence. The side of the neck has a small white patch, as does the side of the breast. Primaries are brown, tinged rusty, with pale buffy inner webs; secondaries are blackish brown. The tail is black, tinged purple on the outer webs but not glossed; the outer rectrices are shorter than the inner feathers, producing a wedge shape. The bill is cream, legs yellow, and the bare circum-orbital skin is dark. **MEASUREMENTS** Male/female (3): wing 136–137, tail 94–100, tarsus 31–32, culmen 17–19. **VOICE** Gives a series of 5 loud, piercing rising whistles. Other calls include a variety of nasal ascending and descending notes interspersed with occasional short piping notes (Coates and Bishop 1997). **DISTRIBUTION AND POPULATION** Endemic to the Moluccan island of Seram. Found in primary and degraded forest (F. Lambert *in litt.*) **FOOD AND FEEDING** Probably largely frugivorous, it visits fruiting trees. **BEHAVIOUR** Found singly, in pairs and occasionally in small groups. They are noisy and often sit for long periods on exposed branches. In garden areas it consorts with flocks of Moluccan Starlings (Coates and Bishop 1997).

28 APO MYNA *Basilornis miranda* Plate 8
Goodfellowia miranda Hartert 1903

FIELD IDENTIFICATION 28–30 cm. A glossy black starling with a long tail and peculiar erect crest of down-like feathers, and white lower back. Around the eye and extending onto the cheek is a patch of naked yellow skin. Bill and legs are yellowish. **DESCRIPTION** Sexes similar. The head, mantle, upper back, breast, belly and undertail-coverts are black, the feathers broadly tipped glossy blue-black. The feathers of the forehead are compressed towards the mid-line to form a ridge, extending as short degenerate plumes on the fore-crown and longer degenerate feathers on the crown to form a permanent crest. The lower back is white. The tail is long and graduated, brownish black and the wings dark chocolate brown. The bill is yellow, shading to greenish-yellow at the base, and the legs and feet are olive-yellow. The iris is yellow-brown or dark brown, and bare skin around the eye and extending on to the cheek is bright lemon yellow. Monotypic. **MEASUREMENTS** Male/female (sample size not given): wing 124, tail 173, tarsus 30, bill 25 (du Pont 1971). **VOICE** Nothing recorded. **DISTRIBUTION AND POPULATION** Endemic to Mindanao in the Philippines, where it is recorded from Mount Apo, Mount Katanglad and from Daggayan, Misamis Oriental. It is common but very local. **HABITAT** Inhabits forest and forest edge over 1250 m. **FOOD AND FEEDING** Nothing recorded **BREEDING** A nest was found in July. **BEHAVIOUR** Occurs singly, in pairs and in groups. **PRINCIPAL REFERENCES** du Pont (1971), Dickinson *et al.* (1991).

29 COLETO *Sarcops calvus*
Bald Starling

Plate 8

Gracula calva Linnaeus 1766

FIELD IDENTIFICATION 26–28 cm. Characterised by its largely black and white plumage and bald pink head. The bald head in fact comprises two large patches of bare pink skin surrounding the eyes and separated on the crown by only a thin line of bristly black feathers. The back and rump are silvery-grey, in one race with a black patch on the back. The wings and tail are black glossed with blue-green and the underparts are dull black. The bill and feet are black. The sexes are similar.

DESCRIPTION Flesh pink (which gets redder when the bird is excited — Peck 1983) bare skin covers most of the face, from the base of the bill back to the cheeks, and up on to the top of the head behind, above and in front of the eyes. The upper mandible behind the nares bears short bristly black feathers, and similar feathers extend as a thin black line over the centre of the crown. Feathers of the upper nape and hindneck are matt black, extending on to the throat and chin. The lower nape is silver-grey. The mantle is black suffused with silver-grey, and the back shows increasing amounts of grey on feather tips posteriorly towards the rump, where all feathers are black, tipped grey. The breast, belly and undertail-coverts are dull black, flanks black with grey tips to feathers. The side of the breast, behind the carpal joint of the closed wing, has a small white patch. The primaries are dark brown, blacker on the outer webs, the secondaries dark chocolate-brown. The tail is black and wedge-shaped, the outer feathers 3–4 cm shorter than central feathers. The wings and tail are glossed blue-green. The bill is black, legs dark brown, and the iris is pink or brownish-red. This description refers to the nominate **calvus**.

S. c. melanonotus, of Mindanao, Cebu, Panay, Negros, Bohol, Samar and Ticao, is smaller with a black back, so that the grey mantle appears as a pale collar.

S. c. lowii, of the Sulu archipelago, has the nape, mantle, back, rump and flanks more extensively silver-grey, paler than in *calvus*, and the wings and underparts are brownish black.

Other races have been described (Gilliard 1949, Parkes 1952) but, as there is much regional and even inter-individual variation, Amadon (1956) considered that the simpler classification into three subspecies adequately described this variation, a view accepted by Dickinson *et al.* (1991).

Examples of one subspecies are sometimes found on islands dominated by another; the origin of these birds is unclear, but they may be escaped cagebirds or wandering individuals (Ripley and Rabor 1958).

MEASUREMENTS Male/female (sample size not given): wing 124, tail 173, tarsus 30, bill 25 (du Pont 1971).

VOICE The call is a metallic click, followed by a high-pitched *kliing-kliing* (Gonzales and Rees 1988).

DISTRIBUTION AND POPULATION Endemic to the Philippines and the Sulu Archipelago, where it occurs on all of the major islands and many of the smaller ones (du Pont 1971). One ringed bird survived five years (McClure 1974).

HABITAT Common in indigenous forests, forest edge, coconut groves, secondary growth and clearings with isolated trees, in coastal areas and inland, below 1500 m.

FOOD AND FEEDING A frugivorous species, feeding actively in fruiting trees, flying from branch to branch. They also eat insects (du Pont and Rabor 1973).

BREEDING has been reported on different islands between May and September (Dickinson *et al.* 1991). No information on breeding biology appears to have been reported from the wild. Eggs are blue with brown and mauve blotches, more heavily marked around the large end and measure 32.0–32.5 x 22.4–22.9 mm (2) (Schönwetter 1983). Peck (1983) thought the incubation period to be in the range 16–24 days in captive birds.

MOVEMENTS Most ringed birds have been recovered close to the ringing site, but one bird moved 175 km (McClure 1974).

BEHAVIOUR Usually found in pairs, sometimes singly, and occasionally in groups of 12 or more in fruiting trees; birds assembling in such trees usually fly in from different directions, rather than as a cohesive flock. They also frequently sit in the tops of dead trees. In display, the nape feathers are erected and the tail is held horizontal (Delacour and Mayr 1946).

RELATIONS WITH MAN McClure (1974) claimed that Coletos were hunted in large numbers, mainly for food. They are commonly kept as cagebirds on account of their ability to mimic human speech (Delacour and Mayr 1946).

30 WHITE-NECKED MYNA *Streptocitta albicollis*   Plate 9
Priest Bird, Sulawesi Magpie Starling, Celebes Starling

Corvus caledonicus Latham 1801

FIELD IDENTIFICATION 42–50 cm (head/body 20–22 cm). A large magpie-like starling, black and white with a long, graduated tail. The breast and a broad collar around the neck are white. The rest of the body is glossy black with steel-blue and green iridescence. The wings and tail are dusky black. The bill is black with a yellow tip (all black in northern birds), and the legs and feet are black. Young birds are similar but with a shorter tail and less well-developed feathering of the head.

DESCRIPTION Sexes similar. The head is black with a purple and blue gloss, with feathers lengthened and waxy. The feathers of the lores and nostril area are directed upwards to produce an erect crest on the forehead. The mantle, sides of breast and breast are pure white, forming a broad collar. Black plumage of the remainder of the body is strongly glossed with steel blue and green, the latter being most pronounced on the rump and underparts. The wings are dusky black with slight purplish iridescence. The long graduated tail is black, with slight gloss, and is crossed with close, narrow bars throughout its length, although these are visible only in some lights. The bill is black with the distal half yellow, and slightly decurved with a slight hook; the legs and feet are black, the iris brown and the bare orbital skin dark. Immatures have poorer development of the crest and a shorter tail, and less yellow on the bill.

S. a. torquata, of northern Sulawesi, has the bill all black, and slightly shorter wing and tail, and longer bill.

MEASUREMENTS Male/female (7): wing 145–158, tail 251–300, tarsus 36–37, bill from nostril 17–19 (Meyer and Wigglesworth 1898).

VOICE Holmes (1979) described the call as a loud melodious whistle, interrupted by short pauses. The most commonly heard call comprises 2–3 medium-pitched, slightly twangy, nasal notes described by Coates and Bishop (1997) as unmu-

sical. White-necked Myna produces a wide variety of calls, reminiscent of a drongo *Dicrurus*, and the song, given from an exposed branch at the top of a tree, is a clear whistling *towee*; it also produces a penetrating alarm call *keee* (Watling 1983), and a harsh rasping note (Coates and Bishop 1997). When making its 'harsh cry' it waves its tail up and down (Meyer and Wigglesworth 1898). In addition to their vocalisations, the wings of flying birds make an 'almost metallic whirring' (Stresemann 1940).

DISTRIBUTION AND POPULATION Endemic to Sulawesi and occurs throughout the island in the lowlands to about 1000 m (Stresemann 1940) or higher (Coates and Bishop 1997). In the north, Meyer and Wigglesworth (1898) recorded it as common and Watling (1983) found it common in central Sulawesi at forest edge and in open woodland.

HABITAT A bird of primary and secondary lowland and hill forest, forest edge, swamp forest, wooded bushland, and isolated thickets and groups of trees. It has a special preference for dead and isolated trees.

FOOD AND FEEDING According to Stresemann (1940), the diet of White-necked Myna appears to comprise solely fruit. They generally forage in the middle height of the canopy, and according to Harrison and Greensmith (1993) take other foods in addition to fruit, but these authors do not specify the foods taken. They sometimes join mixed species feeding flocks (Coates and Bishop 1997).

BREEDING Nests in cavities in old dead trees and Watling (1983) found a nest in the rotting stump of an *Arenga* palm, and recorded breeding in September–October.

BEHAVIOUR Generally found in pairs and trios, occasionally in groups of up to five birds. Flies readily and strongly over open areas.

31 BARE-EYED MYNA *Streptocitta albertinae*   Plate 9
Sula Magpie, Sula Starling, Bare-eyed Starling, Albertina's Starling

Charitornis albertinae Schlegel 1866

FIELD IDENTIFICATION 42–45 cm (head/body 19–20 cm). Like White-necked Myna on Sulawesi, Bare-eyed Myna is largely black and white and has a long, graduated tail. The crown, nape and underparts are white, except for the lower flanks, lower belly and undertail-coverts which are glossy black. The back is glossy black with a greenish iridescence. The wings and tail are

black. The side of the head and the throat are bare blackish skin. The bill, legs and feet are yellow.

DESCRIPTION Sexes similar. The forehead, crown, hindneck, breast and belly are pure white. The mantle, back, lesser and median wing-coverts are glossy greenish-black, with some purple iridescence. The lower flanks, lower belly and undertail-coverts are glossy black with green iridescence. The skin of the chin, upper throat, cheeks and lores, and an area above and behind the eye is bare and corrugated, blackish. The forehead has no crest. The wings and tail are black, the feathers edged with a greenish wash. The central tail feathers are long, the rectrices becoming progressively shorter towards the outer feathers. The bill, legs and feet are yellow and the iris is light brown, light grey or red. In immatures, the forehead is mottled with dark brown feathers.

MEASUREMENTS Male/female (5): wing 135–151, tail 280–303, tarsus 35–39, culmen 25–28.

VOICE The call is an irregular series, usually of 5 notes, with the first two given together, descending and reminiscent of a squeaky gate (Coates and Bishop 1997), often given from a favoured tree.

DISTRIBUTION AND POPULATION Endemic to the Sula Islands, Moluccas, where Meyer and Wigglesworth (1898) thought it may be rare. It is now regarded as uncommon (Coates and Bishop 1997), recorded in small numbers from sea level to about 250 m.

HABITAT It is recorded from heavily degraded, selectively logged and open forest, lightly wooded swamps and cultivated areas, but its status in intact forest is unknown as it is surprisingly inconspicuous (Davidson *et al.* 1995). It is most commonly seen in the largest trees in degraded forest.

BEHAVIOUR Most often seen in pairs, but singles and trios occur.

RELATIONS WITH MAN Listed as near-threatened (Collar *et al.* 1994) and is probably susceptible to habitat loss, especially of large fruiting trees in the lowlands. Davidson *et al.* (1995) consider that more information on its occurrence in forest is needed, especially at higher altitudes. Hunting and trapping is not currently regarded as a threat, although F. Lambert (*in litt.*) found one for sale on Ambon. Nothing appears to be known of the biology of Bare-eyed Myna.

32 FLAME-BROWED STARLING *Enodes erythrophris* Plate 9

Flame-browed Myna, Fiery-browed Myna, Celebes Enodes Starling, Red-browed Starling

Lamprotornis erythrophrys Temminck 1824

FIELD IDENTIFICATION 27–29 cm. Body slate-grey, contrasting with golden yellow rump, upper and undertail-coverts. Wings and tail olive-greenish-yellow, the long tail tipped cream. On each side of the head is a broad reddish-orange superciliary stripe. The bill is black and the legs sulphur-yellow.

DESCRIPTION Sexes similar. The centre of the forehead and crown, nape, mantle, back, chin, throat, breast and belly are dark charcoal-grey. Feathers at base of bill behind nares and extending over and behind eye are bristled and bright reddish-orange. Feathers below and behind eye are black. The rump feathers are elongated and degraded, brilliant golden. The thighs and undertail-coverts are gold. The short rounded wings are dark brown with olive-yellow outer webs to primaries and secondaries; the olive-yellow is restricted to the base of the outer large primary but becomes more extensive on the inner primaries and secondaries. The greater coverts are olive-yellow. The long graduated tail is brown, tinged olive-yellow, brightest on the long central pair of rectrices on which the terminal 2 cm are pale cream. The bill is black, with the culmen strongly curved and hooked at the tip. The legs and feet are sulphur-yellow and the iris pale yellow or sepia with a darker line in the centre. Young birds are browner than adults, with the supercilliary stripe narrower and yellower, and the iris brown. This description refers to nominate *erythrophris*, of the northern peninsula of Sulawesi.

E. e. centralis, of northern Central Sulawesi and the southeast peninsula, has the brow stripe yellower and the bill longer and more ridged.

E. e. leptorhynchus, of the southern and central parts of Central Sulawesi, has the brow stripe as in the nominate form but the bill as in *centralis*.

MEASUREMENTS Male/female (11) wing 106–116, tail 106–120, tarsus 25–28, bill from nostril 12–13 (Meyer and Wigglesworth 1898)

VOICE Watling (1983) heard a high-pitched *peeep* interspersed with a variety of guttural calls, together with *tik tik* calls in flight. Stresemann (1940) described the song, given by a male from the topmost twig of a forest tree, as a monotonous, repeated metallic *zeek zeek*, with similar calls given in other contexts.

DISTRIBUTION AND POPULATION Endemic to Sulawesi, but does not occur in southern Sulawesi. It is particularly numerous in forest between 1000 and 1500 m (Stresemann 1940), but occurs from 500–2300 m (Coates and Bishop 1997).

HABITAT Unlike other starlings in Sulawesi, this species inhabits dense montane rain forest (Stresemann 1940), where it is common. It also occurs in lowland and elfin moss forest, sometimes at the forest edge (Watling 1983) and in selectively logged areas (Coates and Bishop 1997).

FOOD AND FEEDING Flame-browed Starlings eat fruit and invertebrates, feeding in a wide range of habitats, gleaning insects in the forest canopy and also eating berries from branches only 1 m off the ground; it commonly scales tree trunks and larger branches, oxpecker-fashion (Watling 1983), and may cling partially upside down when pecking at loose bark or searching for inverbrates under epiphytes (Coates and Bishop 1997). Van den Berg and Bosman (1986) reported large flocks eating berries in tree tops. While feeding, Flame-browed Starlings are agile (Stresemann 1940). At fruiting trees they may flock with Sulawesi Crested Mynas and Grosbeak Mynas.

BEHAVIOUR Generally found in pairs or small groups (Stresemann 1940) but they sometimes form large flocks (van den Berg and Bosman 1986). Coates and Bishop (1997) described a display in which a lone bird repeatedly raised its plumage and then briefly bowed well forward, thereby showing to maximum effect its eyebrows to a bird directly in front.

33 GROSBEAK MYNA *Scissirostrum dubium* Plate 9
Finch-billed Starling, Scissor-billed Starling

Lanius dubius Latham 1801

FIELD IDENTIFICATION 17–21 cm. A slaty-grey bird with black wings and tail. The rump feathers have long stiff red tips. The bill is bright yellowish-orange, very strong with the upper mandible strongly decurved. The legs and feet are yellow-orange. Young birds are browner, with the tips of rump feathers sometimes paler. The bill is more slender than in the adult.

DESCRIPTION Sexes similar. The entire body plumage is mouse-grey, darker blackish on the wings and tail. The feathers on the rump and uppertail-coverts, and some on the flanks, are elongate with stiff, waxy, bright vermilion, narrow tips. On some birds, some of these feathers are orange, possibly faded. The tail is wedge-shaped. The bill is massive, yellowish-orange and has a strongly curved culmen, and the nostrils lie in a deep groove. The legs and feet are orange-yellow and the iris reddish. Immatures are mouse-brown but with red or orange-tipped feathers on the rump, uppertail-coverts and flanks; the bill is more slender and paler than in the adult, and the iris is blackish.

MEASUREMENTS Male/female (20) wing 94–101, tail 78–86, tarsus 21, bill from nostril 14 (Meyer and Wigglesworth 1898).

VOICE Grosbeak Mynas are very noisy both at breeding colonies and in feeding flocks, and they call continuously in flight. The call is harsh and rasping, described by Stresemann as a *schirr schirr*. At rest, captive birds gave a soft chirruping, similar to that of Zebra Finches *Poephila guttata* (CJF). The song comprises a series of chuckles and whistles (see BEHAVIOUR). In flight, a liquid *churip* and a nasal chatter are given, together with a moderately loud, clear, moderately high-pitched single *sweee* which is repeated; while in fruiting trees a whistled *wrriu* is heard (Coates and Bishop 1997).

DISTRIBUTION AND POPULATION Endemic to Sulawesi, where they occur at lower levels but also in some upland valleys to 1100 m. They are widespread and common, sometimes locally abundant (Coates and Bishop 1997).

HABITAT Occur mainly in forest edge or lightly wooded country and swamp forest, and rarely travel far into dense forest.

FOOD AND FEEDING Meyer and Wigglesworth (1898) reported that Grosbeak Mynas eat grain and fruit. They generally feed in the canopy of fruiting trees including *Ficus* and *Albizzia*, but also eat birds eye chilli *Capsicum frutescens* and insects (Coates and Bishop 1997).

BREEDING Grosbeak Mynas are highly colonial, boring their own nest holes, woodpecker-fashion, in rotten standing or dying tree trunks 30–40 cm diameter. Colonies can contain hundreds of nests, generally above 10 m above the ground but extending from this height to the top of the trunk. Stresemann (1940) described a colony as being reminiscent of a beehive, with continuous bustling activity. The concentration of nests may on occasions weaken the nesting tree so much that the tree breaks, destroying the colony (Wiles and Masala 1987). Nest cavities are tear-drop shaped, 25–30 cm long and angled downwards at 30–60 degrees; the entrance is about 4 cm diameter (Wiles and Masala 1987). Within the cavity, a rough pad is built of dry grasses and leaves, sometimes with some green leaves. Eggs are pale blue with fawn and brown speckles or reddish-brown patches concentrated at the broad end, and average 26 x 20 mm. The clutch is normally two eggs, the eggs laid 24 hours apart (Kraus 1985) (in captivity, clutches of 4 eggs were laid by two females in the same nest). Eggs are incubated for 13–14 days by both parents. Both members of a captive pair were observed taking food to chicks in a nest (Peck 1983) and young fledge at 21–23 days old. In captivity, parents continue to feed the young for at least five weeks after leaving the nest. In the wild, only one young appears to be produced from each nest (Wiles and Masala 1987).

BEHAVIOUR Breeds colonially with colonies often containing more than 100 pairs. They feed in flocks which wheel noisily around the forest edge. Many activities, e.g. preening, bathing, feeding, and especially breeding, are closely synchronised, such that all nestlings in a colony are at about the same developmental stage (Wiles and Masala 1987). Grosbeak Mynas defend only a small area around the nest; defence usually comprises mild threat, with the beak closed, or open-billed threat when more aggressive. When not involved in other activities, members of a pair sit close together, often in contact. Mutual allopreening of the head area is common. In courtship, a male approaches a female and makes a long series of chuckling notes with the throat feathers extended; as display progresses the chuckles are interspersed with loud whistles which come to dominate the song. During this time, the male raises his beak with the throat feathers extended, then slowly raises his body into an erect posture, whistling with the bill wide open. The head is then rapidly lowered and the whole body drops below the horizontal. This display is repeated several times in a succession of nodding movements. Grosbeak

Mynas sometimes roost at night with Asian Glossy Starlings and on Butung it commonly feeds with Short-tailed Starlings in fruiting trees (Coates and Bishop 1997).
RELATIONS WITH MAN Grosbeak Mynas are increasingly being kept by aviculturists in Europe.
PRINCIPAL REFERENCES Kraus (1985), Stresemann (1940), Watling (1983).

34 SPOT-WINGED STARLING *Saroglossa spiloptera*   Plate 18

Lamprotornis spilopterus Vigors, 1831

FIELD IDENTIFICATION 19 cm. A slender starling with grey or brownish upperparts, contrasting with dark chestnut throat, rufous breast and flanks and whitish belly. In flight, it has pointed blackish wings with a conspicuous white wing patch, and the chestnut rump is prominent.
DESCRIPTION Adult male: Grey crown and nape feathers, bordered with charcoal-grey. The mantle and back feathers are also grey with dark borders, and the rump is dark red-brown. The sides of the head are dark grey, the chin and throat dark red-brown. The chest, flanks, belly and undertail-coverts are chestnut-brown, with pale edges to feathers in the centre of the belly, so that a variable white patch is formed. The thighs are grey. Tail feathers and tertials are brown, the other wing feathers blackish with an olive-green sheen. The primaries have a central white patch on each feather and the underwing-coverts are white. The iris is whitish to pale yellow. The bill is black with a brown base, pale yellow margins, slender and slightly down-curved; the legs are dark brown.
Adult female: Grey-brown dorsally, with smaller pale areas like spots on the feathers. The chin, throat and chest feathers are pale with dark central streaks, while the flanks, belly and undertail-coverts are dull white. An immature female was described as paler than the adult, with brown tips to the tertials and wing-coverts, more streaky below, and washed with brown on the flanks. Marien (1951) concluded that there were two forms of immature plumage in males, one resembling the female but with a more extensive white area on the abdomen, the other with unstreaked rufous underparts and glossy black wings like the adult male. At three months, a juvenile male had a dark brown head, with the dorsal surface lighter brown, particularly at the edges of the feathers. Uppertail-coverts were reddish-brown, the tail feathers dark brown. The primaries were black and the white wingbar was present. The underparts were whitish, mixed with brown at the sides of the chest and belly. The iris was dark grey, the bill and legs black. A juvenile female from the same brood was similar but duller, the iris dark brown with a faint pale ring around the pupil (Scamell 1969). A second race *S. spiloptera assamensis* has been described, but it is poorly defined and is not generally recognised.
    None of the 100 specimens examined showed

wing moult, but of these, only five were birds collected between July and November, when wing moult might be expected. Marien (1951) found no specimens in moult in the collection which he examined, but there were birds in fresh plumage from November, whereas specimens from February to June had worn feathers. Whistler (1923) had also noted that birds collected in June had worn plumage, and concluded that the moult had not yet started. Since this species appears to be on passage in June-July, this suggests that the moult may take place in the non-breeding quarters, probably from August to October.
MEASUREMENTS Male (10): wing 105–112, tail 57–62, bill 24.6–26.5, tarsus 23.0–24.7. Female (10): wing 95–106, tail 51–57, bill 23.0–24.6, tarsus 21.7–24.1. Weight (male) 48 g.
VOICE Gives noisy chattering calls, reminiscent of mynas. An aggressive *chek-chek-chek* was directed at birds feeding in the vicinity, and perched birds gave a soft *chik-chik* chirruping call.
DISTRIBUTION AND POPULATION The breeding range is the foothills of the Himalayas from Kangra (Himachal Pradesh) to Garhwal and Kumaon (Uttar Pradesh) and Nepal. Birds are recorded in Nepal and Sikkim on passage, and winter in Assam, Bangladesh, Burma and NW Thailand. They are locally common, but the species is listed in the 'near-threatened' category by Collar *et al.* (1994).
HABITAT These starlings are found in open forest in hilly country at 700–1000 m, rarely to 1800 m in Nepal (Inskipp and Inskipp 1991), and are primarily arboreal. In winter in Thailand they often occur in trees in cultivated areas.
FOOD AND FEEDING Food includes insects such as red tree ants (Formicidae) and winged termites (Termitidae), which may be taken in the air (Whistler 1923). Spot-winged Starlings are very fond of nectar, which is taken from *Salmalia, Bombax, Erythrina* and *Grevillea* trees, and also feed on berries and figs. A captive pair ignored nectar, and took live food only while nesting (Scamell 1969).
BREEDING Nest in natural tree holes or barbet (Capitonidae) holes, 6–10 m above ground, lining the cavity with a pad of green leaves and debris. Privet leaves were used by captive birds (Scamell 1969). The eggs are pale grey or bluish-green with small reddish-brown specks and blotches, measur-

ing 23.7–28.5 x 16.2–19.7 mm (36), weight 4.4 g (Schönwetter 1983). The clutch is 3–4. No observations of nesting birds have been recorded in the field, but in captivity both sexes fed the young on mealworms, gentles and maggots, and both removed faecal sacs (Scamell 1969). The breeding season is mainly April to June.

MIGRATION Within Asia, Spot-winged Starlings appear to migrate on an east-west axis, breeding above 1000 m in the western Himalaya area, passing westward at 700–1200 m through Nepal and Sikkim in March-April, and eastward in June-July. It winters at lower altitudes, to 1000 m, mainly in Assam. In Burma it has been recorded erratically between December and February (Smythies 1953).

BEHAVIOUR This species forms flocks which may number several hundred, and often associates with Chestnut-tailed Starlings and Jungle Mynas in India. Spot-winged Starlings appear to be shy, restless birds; they are strong fliers, and periodically perform well-coordinated aerial manoeuvres (Whistler 1923). They remain in the canopy, and seldom come to the ground (Whistler 1923, Smythies 1953). Wintering birds in Thailand are often associated with flocks of Chestnut-tailed Starlings (Boonsong and Round 1991).

PRINCIPAL REFERENCE Ali and Ripley (1972).

35 MADAGASCAR STARLING *Saroglossa aurata*   **Plate 18**

Turdus auratus Müller 1776

FIELD IDENTIFICATION 20 cm. A medium-sized brownish starling, slender, with a long thin bill and longish legs. There is some sheen on the wings and tail, a white belly, white outer tail feathers, and a white bar on the folded wing, forming a white patch in flight.

DESCRIPTION Adult male: Head, nape, mantle, rump, chin, throat and a bib-shaped area in the centre of the chest are dull brown. The rest of the chest and flanks are a darker chocolate-brown. The centre of the belly, thighs and undertail-coverts are white, but the extent of white on the ventral surface seems to be variable. The tail feathers are dark blue-green with a slight gloss; the outermost feathers have a white outer web and are also the longest, producing a swallow-tailed appearance. The underwing-coverts are white, and the six outer primary feathers have a broad white strip on the outer vane, and a small oval white patch on the inner vane about halfway along their length. The alula also has a white outer vane, while the secondary and tertial feathers are uniform dark blue with some violet gloss. The iris is brown, the bill and legs black. **Adult female**: Resembles the male in pattern but the wings are less glossy; the crown and nape are brown with paler edging to the feathers, the chin, throat, chest and flanks are grey-brown with dark central streaks on the feathers. Immature birds resemble the female.

A total of 45 specimens was examined, and birds with wing moult had been collected from January to May, which suggests that the moult follows the breeding period.

MEASUREMENTS Male (10): wing 100–104, tail 70–75, bill 23.7–26.3, tarsus 21.3–23.2. Female (10): wing 95–100, tail 64–71, bill 22.0–24.6, tarsus 21.2–22.7. Weight (male) 41 g.

VOICE A high-pitched song *chee chreetee* is delivered continuously for several minutes from a conspicuous perch.

DISTRIBUTION AND POPULATION This starling is endemic to Madagascar, where it is widespread in the western and eastern coastal areas to 1800 m, but is absent from the south-western corner of the island. It is still common.

HABITAT Madagascar Starlings favour humid areas with woodland, where they are mostly found in the treetops. They are often seen on the fringe of open areas, even near villages and rice paddies.

FOOD AND FEEDING The stomach contents of seven birds were composed entirely of fruit (Rand 1936), though insects have also been reported (Milon *et al.* 1973). Fruits, including *Ficus* sp., and berries, with occasional insects were noted in the field. There appear to be no observations of nectar feeding, despite Beecher's (1978) comments on the frayed tip of the tongue.

BREEDING Madagascar Starlings nest in holes in trees, but the nest has not been described. The eggs are pale blue with rusty-brown spots (Milon *et al.* 1973), and measure 22.1–27.0 x 16.5–17.8 mm (8), weight 3.8 g (Schönwetter 1983). Clutch sizes and behaviour at the nest have not been recorded. On the basis of gonadal development, Rand (1936) suggested that the breeding season was September-November. Benson *et al.* (1977) noted birds entering nest holes in September. However, there is also a juvenile specimen from September.

BEHAVIOUR Although keeping mainly to the canopy, the birds are reportedly not shy (Milon *et al.* 1973), and are generally to be found in flocks of 4–20 individuals (Rand 1936). In a recent study, Madagascar Starling was the only passerine seen regularly in the study area which did not join mixed-species flocks (Eguchi *et al.* 1993), although this had been reported by other observers. Kunkel (1962) noted that captive birds moved on the ground almost exclusively by hopping.

RELATIONS WITH MAN The local name 'vorontainaomby' is translated by Milon *et al.* (1973) as meaning a bird which is associated with cow dung, which implies observations of the birds foraging for insects on the ground. Madagascar Starlings do come to clearings and cultivated areas, and do not appear to be threatened by human activities.

PRINCIPAL REFERENCE Langrand (1990).

36 GOLDEN CRESTED MYNA *Ampeliceps coronatus*   Plate 7

Ampeliceps coronatus Blyth 1842

FIELD IDENTIFICATION 19–21 cm. A glossy blue-black myna with the crown, forehead and throat golden yellow, the crown feathers extended into a long crest. The wings sport a white and yellow patch comprising white inner and yellow outer webs to the inner 6 primaries. The periorbital skin is naked and orange-yellow. The bill is pale orange with a blue base and the legs and feet are dull orange or waxy-yellow. In females the yellow on the head is restricted to the forecrown and in young birds the head is black, becoming progressively yellower with age.
DESCRIPTION Adult male: Bristly feathers at the base of the upper mandible are directed forward over the nares. The forehead, crown, nape, chin and centre of the throat are golden-yellow. The rest of the body plumage is black, glossed with purple on the sides of the face, mantle and breast, glossed blue-green on the belly, back and rump, less glossy on the lower belly and flanks. The wings are black with little gloss on the primaries, more on the secondaries. The outer primary has a white patch on the inner web, the next 5 primaries have this white patch accompanied by a pale yellow patch on the outer webs, and the next primary has only a yellow patch on the outer web; these form a pale patch about half-way along the primaries. The tail is black with little gloss, and is short and square. The bill is yellow with a bluish base to the lower mandible (bill may be variable, yellowish-horn or greenish-yellow in some birds). The legs and feet are dull orange or chrome-yellow, the claws brown. The iris is dark brown; the circum-orbital bare skin is orange-yellow, extending to a point behind the eye. **Adult female**: Less extensive gold on the top of the head and especially on the chin and throat, where it is restricted to the centre. Gold on the head seems to be acquired gradually in young birds, and in juveniles the head is black.

MEASUREMENTS Male/female (sample size not given): wing 121–133, tail 59–63, wt 78–99 g (Ali and Ripley 1972).
VOICE The calls are said to resemble those of Hill Myna, but are higher-pitched and also include a high, metallic bell-like note.
DISTRIBUTION AND POPULATION Extends from Cachar District in Assam and Manipur through Burma south of Mogok into Yunnan (China) and south to northwestern Thailand and southern Indochina, to 1000 m. In eastern India and over much of Burma it is uncommon, possibly more abundant in northern Tenasserim (southern Burma) and common in parts of northern Thailand. It is believed to be resident.
HABITAT Occurs in dense lowland evergreen forest, moist deciduous woodland, open forest and cultivated clearings with tall relict trees. It is a bird of tree tops.
FOOD AND FEEDING Thought to be mainly frugivorous but also to eat insects.
BREEDING In Burma and Thailand nests have been recorded in April–May and juveniles in April–June. Nests are built in holes 5–15 m high in trees. The nest is built of grasses and the eggs are blue-green with brown blotches concentrated around the broader end of the egg, measuring 24.8–28.8 x 20.0–21.0 mm (Schönwetter 1983). A captive pair laid 4 eggs, two of which hatched after an estimated 14–15 days, incubation being by the female alone. Males may assist in feeding the chicks or may feed the female on the nest. Young fledged in captivity after 25–26 days (Partridge 1966).
BEHAVIOUR Usually occurs in pairs or small groups.
PRINCIPAL REFERENCES Ali and Ripley (1972), Lekagul and Round (1991), de Schauensee (1984), Smythies (1953).

37 COMMON HILL MYNA *Gracula religiosa*   Plate 10
Common Grackle, Talking Myna

Gracula religiosa Linnaeus 1758

FIELD IDENTIFICATION 28–30 cm. The Hill Myna is a stocky glossy black myna. The sides and back of the head bear bright, yellow bare skin and wattles, the arrangement of which varies between races. The central crown, nape, mantle and breast are glossed purple, the sides of the face velvety-black while the rest of the body is glossed greenish. The central parts of the primaries are white, forming a broad white band conspicuous in flight. The bill is orange, sometimes reddish, and the legs and feet are yellow. The iris is dark brown. The sexes are similar. In young birds the upperparts are less glossy than in the adult, while the underparts are dull brownish-black. The head bears patches of yellow bare skin but the wattles are not developed. The iris is grey-brown.
DESCRIPTION Sexes similar. Feathers of the forehead and centre of the crown are black, glossed purple; those on the sides of the forehead are directed upwards to form a small crest, while those of the crown are flattened. Feathers on the sides of the crown back to the post-orbital wattles,

143

and over and in front of the eye are dull black and velvety. The chin, throat, neck, mantle, back and belly are glossed purple. The rump and upper breast are more turquoise with hints of bronze, and the lower belly is glossed turquoise. The wings are black, with purple gloss on the secondaries and scapulars. The 9th (outer large) primary has a white patch on the inner web, primaries 4–8 have white patches on both webs and primary 3 a white patch on the outer web. The tail is black, short and square. Below the eye is a patch of bare yellow skin, narrowly separated posteriorly from a line of bare skin extending from just behind the eye round the nape, where it extends into two pendulous bright yellow wattles. The bill is large with the culmen strongly curved and hooked at the tip; the bill is red with a yellow tip. The legs and feet are large, chrome yellow, and the iris brown. Immatures lack gloss on the head and belly, and gloss is much reduced on the back. The areas of yellow bare skin on the head are as in the adult, but the wattles are smaller. This description refers to *G. r. religiosa*, from Malaysia, Sumatra, Java, Bali, Borneo and Bangka Island.

G. r. batuensis, from Batu and Mentawai Islands off the northwest coast of Sumatra, is considerably larger.

G. r. palawanensis, from Palawan Island (Philippines), is more bluish and bronzy on the underparts and especially on the back and rump. It is slightly smaller than *religiosa*, and the bill is shorter but deep; the bare skin patches below and behind the eye are separated and the wattles on the back of the nape are slightly separated; there is very little white on the outer margin of the 3rd primary.

G. r. venerata, of Sumbawa, Flores, Pantar and Alor Islands in the Lesser Sundas, is more glossy green than the nominate form; the bare skin patches below and behind the eye are separated, but that behind the eye forms a broader patch which extends posteriorly into large broad wattles, and anteriorly on to the sides of the crown.

G. r. intermedia, of northern India, Burma, Thailand and Indochina, and southern China, is smaller than the nominate form, with the upper breast and upper back more bronzy; the band of flattened feathers in the centre of the crown is broader and the dull velvet feathers over the eye accordingly reduced; the bill is smaller with the culmen less curved, and the eye and nape skin patches are joined, but the nape patches do not continue round the back of the nape.

G. r. peninsularis, of northeastern peninsular India, is similar to *intermedia* but slightly smaller, and has a shorter and finer bill.

G. r. andamanensis, of the Andaman and Nicobar Islands, has the eye and nape skin patches joined or narrowly separated, and the wattles are widely separated; the bill is longer and the culmen less curved than in *religiosa*; the white on the primaries extends on to the 2nd primary in some birds, but is much reduced there compared with other primaries.

Abdulali 1967 noted that a further subspecies *halibrecta* might be distinguishable on Little and Great Nicobar, with two large lappets on the back of the neck, joined together at the top. This possibility does not appear to have been subsequently examined. We follow White and Bruce (1986) in regarding *mertensi* as synonymous with *venerata*. The differences between *intermedia* and *peninsularis* are very slight and the two may be synonymous, *intermedia* taking precedence (Majumdar 1978).

MEASUREMENTS Male: wing 174–186, tail 70–89, culmen 26–32; female: wing 169–185, tail 70–87, culmen 23–32 (Hoogerwerf 1963, Ripley 1944, sample sizes not known as compiled from several sources, but at least 30 birds).

VOICE Common Hill Mynas make a diverse range of calls which Bertram (1970) categorised into four types. 'Chip-calls' are very loud, piercing, short, descending squeaks, made by all adults when alarmed or when communicating with other mynas some distance away; the call is made with the bill open and is accompanied by jerking movements of the body. 'Um-sounds' are soft nasal noises made most of the time when birds are close together. 'Whisper-whistles' are soft high-pitched sounds made by inactive birds. 'Calls' comprise the huge variety of whistles, croaks, wails and shrieks given when mynas see or hear each other. Many calls are low-pitched and reminiscent of the human voice. In the wild, individuals imitated calls of other Common Hill Mynas but did not mimic sounds made by other birds or animals.

DISTRIBUTION AND POPULATION In India, Common Hill Mynas occur in eastern Madhya Pradesh and northern Andhra Pradesh; and in the Himalayan foothills from eastern Himachal Pradesh through Nepal, Sikkim, Bhutan east to Manipur and Nagaland. The range then extends eastwards through Burma, Thailand and Indochina to southern China and Hainan, south to the Andaman and Nicobar Islands, through Malaysia to the Greater and Lesser Sundas east to Alor, and through Borneo to Palawan in the Philippines. Common Hill Mynas are mainly resident throughout their range but they do undertake local movements. According to Ripley (1944) they are common to abundant and large numbers can congregate in fruiting trees, while Bertram (1970) said that they were rarely abundant, except temporarily when in roaming flocks. Common Hill Mynas have been introduced and become established in Florida, Puerto Rico and Hawaii. An introduction to Christmas Island (Indian Ocean) was unsuccessful and it is uncertain whether they were introduced to St Helena, where Common Mynas now occur; reports of Common Hill Mynas may have resulted from misidentification (Lever 1987). They are frequently kept as cage birds and escapes can survive for long periods, as in England (CJF).

HABITAT Primarily birds of areas of high rainfall and humidity, especially the edge of moist evergreen or semi-evergreen forest, but sometimes also occur in wet deciduous forest. They occur most commonly in hills between 300 and 2000 m, but do occur at sea level. They inhabit dense jungle but are more commonly found, and are certainly more noticeable, at forest edges, thinned areas and clearings. In some areas (e.g. the Lesser Sundas) this species can be found in cultivated areas, especially where large flowering trees are grown as shade trees in tea and coffee plantations, and in mangroves.

FOOD AND FEEDING Mainly frugivorous but also eat nectar, insects and other animals. Figs *Ficus* predominate among the fruits eaten but Common Hill Mynas also eat other berries and the seeds from a wide variety of trees and shrubs, taking fruits up to 2 cm diameter. Several fruits may be swallowed in quick succession and the stones of these are regurgitated soon afterwards. Nectar is taken from flowers of *Salmalia, Bombax, Erythrina, Grevillea* and the forest shrub *Helicteres isora*. Most of the insects that are eaten are gleaned from the foliage of trees but winged termites are often taken in the air, flycatcher-fashion. The diet also includes lizards (Reptilia) which, together with insects, are taken especially when feeding young (Bertram 1976).

BREEDING The breeding season varies throughout the range. In northern India they breed mainly in April–July and in Thailand from January–July (Archawaranon 1994). Nests are in holes in tall trees, at least 10 m above the ground. The holes selected are small, the birds often having to squeeze themselves through the entrance. The trees selected for breeding are at the forest edge, in a clearing or isolated in cultivated areas. In Garo (Assam), however, Hill Mynas breed in artificial nest sites made of split bamboo covered with straw and erected in trees; this allows people to collect the nestlings for the cagebird trade (Bertram 1968). Within the tree cavity, usually about 0.5 m deep, a rough nest is built of small twigs, leaves and feathers, all of the material being collected in trees. The nest is built by both sexes. The clutch is 2–3 eggs, sometimes only 1, and the eggs are blue, light blue or greenish-blue with variable reddish-brown and chocolate spotting and blotching, measuring 31.8–37.6 × 23.1–27.1 mm (25) (Schönwetter 1983). Both sexes incubate for 13–17 days but the female spends more time on the nest and undertakes more incubation shifts than the male. Nestlings are fed by both sexes, usually by regurgitation although food may also be carried in the bill. Parents tend to feed together, leaving the chicks unattended (Archawaranon 1994). Parents also remove faeces from the nest, placing the droppings on a branch, rather than dropping them in flight. The young fledge after 25–28 days. After the young have fledged they probably gain independence quickly, as parents soon return to begin another clutch. In Thailand, two to three broods are raised annually.

BEHAVIOUR Common Hill Mynas are thought to be monogamous and to pair for life. They usually occur in pairs but larger groups of 10–12 birds are formed in the non-breeding period and much larger flocks sometimes congregate at fruiting trees; even in such flocks, pairs are apparent. They are not aggressive to other mynas and several pairs may nest in the same tree, although more usually neighbouring nests are about 1 km apart. Females solicit copulation by adopting a horizontal posture, but not crouched, raising the tail and quivering it up and down rapidly (Bertram 1970). No other visual sexual displays have been recorded. They do not roost communally, but roost individually, in pairs or family groups, on leafy branches or in tree holes. Prior to roosting, Hill Mynas become very vocal from high perches in tree tops.

They are almost strictly arboreal and frequently perch on the tops of exposed dead branches. Flight is rapid and direct, although they sometimes fly in undulating woodpecker-fashion, particularly when one pair chases another. In trees, they move around branches by sideways hops, rather than adopting the jaunty walk of other starlings and mynas, and on their rare visits to the ground they also hop, rather than walk.

RELATIONS WITH MAN In Nagaland, northeastern India, Hill Mynas used to be caught in order for Naga people to eat them, curried myna being a great delicacy (Bertram 1969). Hill Mynas are among the most popular of cagebirds, largely on account of their great powers of mimicry, when in captivity, of the human voice. The demand for these birds has led to the development of local 'cottage industries' for the capture of young birds and adults. In the Garo Hills, Assam, they are encouraged to nest in artificial sites from which the young can be easily harvested (Bertram 1968). Bertram (1969) reported that in the 1960s over 10,000 Hill Mynas were captured annually for sale to the cagebird industry from Nepal, Assam and Orissa. The rate of capture has been so extensive that concerns have been expressed about over-exploitation and in Thailand capture for the cagebird trade, along with forest destruction, is thought to have been responsible for population declines (Lekagul and Round 1991). Considerable trade in Common Hill Mynas occurs in Indonesia, Thailand, Malaysia, Singapore and Vietnam, and although the export of these birds from India was banned in 1972, an illegal trade continues (Menon 1994), with an estimated 15,000–25,000 birds captured in northeast India alone in 1979 (Sane 1983). In the Lesser Sundas, populations are believed to have declined markedly due to excessive trapping for the captive bird trade (Coates and Bishop 1997). Common Hill Mynas commonly feed in flowering trees and are frequently seen with pollen on the face; they may be important pollinators of forest trees. Their regurgitation of the stones of fruits may also assist seed dispersal.

PRINCIPAL REFERENCES Ali and Ripley (1972), Bertram (1970).

Eulabes indicus Cuvier 1829

FIELD IDENTIFICATION 23–24 cm. Very similar to Common Hill Myna from which it differs mainly in its voice and behaviour. It is smaller than Common Hill Myna and has a finer bill and less extensive white wing patch. The nape wattles differ from those of Common Hill Myna in extending in tongues up on to the crown. It is distinguished from Sri Lankan Hill Myna by the presence of bare skin on the cheeks and crown, and by the lack of black on the bill.

DESCRIPTION Feathers of the forehead and centre of the crown are black, glossed purple, and those of the sides of the crown are matt black and velvety. The body plumage is glossed purple and oily-green, but the breast and belly are less glossy than in *religiosa*. The wings are black. The 9th (outer large) primary has a white patch on the inner web, primaries 4–8 have white patches on both webs and primary 3 has a white patch on the outer web. The bare skin patch below the eye is clearly separated from the post-orbital bare skin, which extends posteriorly on to the nape, but with long forward projections over the crown to a point level with the back of the eye, and with two wattles on the nape. Neither the wattles nor the forward projecting bare skin make contact in the mid-line. The orange bill with a yellow tip is considerably finer than in *religiosa*, even than that in *G. r. intermedia*, and the culmen is less curved.

MEASUREMENTS Male (sample sizes not known): wing 139–155, tail 55–72, tarsus 29–33, bill 29–32; female: wing 140–149, tail 60–70, tarsus 31–33, bill 28–31; weight (1) 126 g (Ali and Ripley 1972).

VOICE The voice of Southern Hill Myna is higher-pitched and considerably less variable than that of Common Hill Myna, consisting of wheezes, screeches and chuckles (Ali and Ripley 1972), some of the sounds resembling a squeaky door hinge (CJF). Flock members give piercing but musical whistles, interspersed with harsh guttural notes (Henry 1971). Southern Hill Mynas completely lack the low-pitched calls of Common Hill Mynas. The alarm call of Southern Hill Myna is a loud squeaky wheeze, whereas that of Common Hill Myna is a sharp *chip*, and the close contact call of Southern Hill Myna is a soft lilting squeak, very different from the soft nasal grunts of Common Hill Myna.

DISTRIBUTION AND POPULATION Inhabits the Western Ghats in southwest India and southern parts of Sri Lanka, most commonly between 300 and 1300 m. In the Western Ghats they occur from about 17°N in the Sahyadri Mountains, south through western Mysore and Kerala and in Sri Lanka throughout the wet zone and in the southern and eastern forests of the dry zone. It is resident although some seasonal local movements have been recorded; it occasionally reaches Bombay.

HABITAT Occurs in wooded areas, including evergreen forest and well-wooded cultivated areas, especially the edges of coffee plantations and tall shade trees planted in other cultivated areas.

FOOD AND FEEDING The diet consists primarily of fruit and nectar. Fruits include figs *Ficus*, berries and the seeds of the Sapu tree *Michelia champaca* (Henry 1971). Nectar is taken from *Salmalia*, *Bombax*, *Erythrina* and *Grevillea*, and also from the flowering forest shrub *Helicteres isora*.

BREEDING In southwestern India, Southern Hill Mynas breed mainly from February to May; in Sri Lanka the breeding season is longer, from March to August though mainly in April and May. Nests are built in deep holes in trees, usually at great height. The nest consists of a scant lining of leaves and grasses. The clutch is normally two eggs, occasionally three, which are greenish-blue with brown spots and measure 30.4–35.5 x 21.8–24.8 mm (46) (Schönwetter 1983).

BEHAVIOUR An arboreal species, active in tree tops where it usually occurs in pairs and small flocks, but can sometimes form large flocks, especially where nectar-producing flowers are in profusion. Flight is direct and the wings produce a hum, described by Henry (1971) as pleasant and musical.

RELATIONS WITH MAN Although reputed to be inferior to other Hill Mynas in their ability to imitate human speech, and to be consequently less valuable, Southern Hill Mynas are nevertheless caught in large numbers for the cagebird trade. They are often caught using bird lime when numbers descend to feed in flowering *Helicteres isora* shrubs. Ali and Ripley (1972) argued that this apparent inferiority to mimic speech stemmed from the catching of Southern Hill Mynas as adults, rather than as nestlings as is the case with Common Hill Mynas; a small sample of Southern Hill Mynas collected as nestlings did become proficient talkers although they lacked the lower frequencies required to produce more accurate renditions of human speech.

Gracula enganensis Salvadori 1899

FIELD IDENTIFICATION 27 cm. Similar to Common Hill Myna, but with a stronger turquoise gloss on the back, duller below, and a stubby bill.
DESCRIPTION The feathers of the sides of the forehead, in front of the eye, are larger than those of Common Hill Myna and are directed upwards to form tufts at the base of the upper mandible. The head, neck and mantle are strongly glossed purple, while the lower back and rump are glossed turquoise. The underparts are duller. The wings and tail are brownish-black, and white patches are present on the inner web of primary 9 and on both webs of all other primaries; these are broader than in Common Hill Myna, especially on the inner primaries. The patch of bare yellow skin below the eye is small and separated from the post-orbital stripe that leads to large wattles which almost join on the back of the nape. The bill is deep, more stubby than in other forms. The iris is dark brown, the bill red with a yellow tip, and the legs yellow.
MEASUREMENTS Male (8): wing 163–177, tail 80–92, culmen 24–27, tarsus 38; female (1): wing 173, tail 86, culmen 25 (Hoogerwerf 1963).
DISTRIBUTION AND POPULATION Endemic to Enggano Island, west of the southern tip of Sumatra.

Gracula robusta Salvadori 1887

FIELD IDENTIFICATION 30–36 cm. A large crow-like myna with a massive red bill and large white wing patches.
DESCRIPTION Feathers of the forehead and crown are black, glossed purple; in front of the eyes the feathers are directed inwards and upwards, while on the crown they are flattened down the central line and on to the back of the crown. In front of, behind and above the eye, almost to the centre of the crown, the feathers are dull black and velvety. The rest of the body plumage is black with a strong purple gloss, tinged bronzy-turquoise on the rump and breast. Feathers of the lower belly of some birds are tipped buffy-white, producing an inconspicuous barring. The wings and tail are brownish-black. White patches on the primaries are more extensive than in other hill mynas, extending almost to the bases of these feathers; the outer large primary (9th) has white on the inner web while primaries 8 to 2 have white on both webs. The secondaries also have white patches but these are close to the rachis and do not extend to the feather margins, and occur only on the inner web of secondary 6. The bill is massive with a strongly curved culmen, and is red, but orange-red at the base and yellow at the tip. The bare skin behind the eye is separated from a large wattle on the hindneck; the wattles overlap in the mid-line. The legs are deep yellow and the iris brown.
MEASUREMENTS Male/female: wing 200–213 (sample sizes not given, Finsch 1899), tail 99–108 (6), culmen 31–34 (sample sizes not given, Finsch 1899); tarsus 44–50 (8).
DISTRIBUTION AND POPULATION Endemic to the islands of Nias, Pulan, Babi, Tuangku and Bangkaru, off the southwest coast of Sumatra.
HABITAT According to Ripley (1944), these are birds of the hills away from the coast. They are found in the forest, usually in small flocks.
BREEDING Ripley (1944) found Nias Hill Mynas in breeding condition in June.
Nothing appears to have been recorded on this species' voice, feeding habits, breeding habits or behaviour.
RELATIONS WITH MAN During a 17-day visit to Nias in 1990, Dymond (1994) did not see this species, even at nestboxes provided for them. Nias Hill Mynas are, according to local people, famous for their quality as talking birds, and in 1990 commanded a good price (Rp 100,000 = £30) for an untrained bird. They are under much pressure from trappers on both Nias and Banyak, and have doubtless also suffered from habitat modification, since most indigenous forest has been destroyed.

41 SRI LANKA HILL MYNA *Gracula ptilogenys*   Plate 10
Ceylon Hill Myna, Ceylon Grackle

Gracula ptilogenys Blyth 1846

FIELD IDENTIFICATION 23–25 cm. Sexes similar. Very similar to Hill Myna. It is glossy black, more glossy than Common and Southern Hill Mynas, with a white patch in the wing which is smaller than that of Common Hill Myna. Sri Lanka Myna has only one pair of yellow wattles, on the back of the head, and the base of the reddish-orange bill is black. The legs and feet are yellow.

DESCRIPTION The feathers of the forehead project upwards and anteriorly, forming small tufts. A narrow strip of matt black, velvety feathers extends from the nares over the eye, and from the base of the lower mandible to beneath the eye, giving a masked appearance. The remainder of the body plumage is highly glossed purple. The wings and tail are black, the tail relatively shorter than in Common Hill Myna. The 9th (outer large) primary has a white patch on the inner web, primaries 8 to 4 have white patches on both webs, but on primary 3 that on the inner web is much reduced. There are no bare skin patches on the head, but there is a pair of yellow wattles on the nape, separated by feathers; the bill is reddish-orange with the base black; the culmen is strongly curved, and the bill is finer than in Common Hill Myna, but deeper than in Southern Hill Myna. The iris of the male is greyish-white speckled with brown, while that of the female is yellowish-white.

MEASUREMENTS Male/female (4): wing 147–158, tail 66–69, tarsus 33–35, bill (from skull) 31–33 (Ali and Ripley 1972).

VOICE Produces a variety of piercing whistles, together with croaking and guttural notes. Captive birds are good mimics.

DISTRIBUTION AND POPULATION Endemic to Sri Lanka, where it inhabits the Wet Zone of the southwest. It is locally common, especially in the hills.

HABITAT In the wetter parts of the southwest, Sri Lanka Myna extends to over 2000 m. It is a bird of forest or well-wooded areas where it occurs primarily in tall trees, but it also ventures into estates and village gardens, and in some places is sympatric with Southern Hill Myna.

FOOD AND FEEDING The diet consists mainly of forest fruit, especially figs *Ficus*. It also eats wild nutmegs *Myristica* and seeds.

BREEDING Sri Lanka Mynas breed in February–May, sometimes again in August–September. They nest in holes in trees, usually at great height, in dense forest or in cultivated areas. Nest cavities are sometimes unlined, but usually grasses and other materials are used. The clutch is normally 2 eggs which are prussian blue, blotched with purplish-brown. Eggs average 33.3 x 22.9 mm. There is no information on parental care or times of incubation and fledging.

BEHAVIOUR Gregarious, but less so than Common Hill Myna. They are arboreal, rarely settling on the ground, and usually occur in pairs in scattered colonies. In flight the wings produce a musical hum which can be heard over a considerable distance.

RELATIONS WITH MAN This species, like Common Hill Myna, is a popular cagebird and nestlings are frequently taken. In captivity, it is an excellent mimic, capable of imitating human speech.

PRINCIPAL REFERENCES Henry (1971), Ali and Ripley (1972).

42 GREAT MYNA *Acridotheres grandis*   Plate 11
Buffalo Myna, Thai Crested Myna

Acridotheres grandis Moore 1858

FIELD IDENTIFICATION 25 cm. Similar to Jungle, White-vented and Crested Mynas but is generally blacker and the crest on the forehead is longer than in Jungle and White-vented Mynas. In adults the plumage is glossy black on the crown, nape and crest, duller elsewhere. The wings are black, glossed with bronze and with broad white bases to the primaries, forming a large white wing patch in flight. The tail is black, with white tips to the feathers becoming broader towards the outer rectrices. The shortest undertail-coverts are black, the remainder white with concealed black bases. The bill is bright chrome-yellow, paler towards the

tip, and the legs and feet are also chrome-yellow. The iris is bright red-brown but in most views appears dark, differentiating it from its close relatives. Juveniles are browner.

DESCRIPTION The feathers of the forehead are greatly elongated, hackled and erect, forming a frontal crest that may curve backwards or in some birds appears lank and unkempt. Feathers of the crown and nape are elongate and hackled, jet black with a slight gloss. The body plumage is uniformly black, in fresh plumage with a hint of gloss especially on the back and wings, and there is a bronzy wash on the scapulars and secondaries.

The undertail-coverts are white. The bases of the primaries are white and the tips of the rectrices are white, narrower on the central feathers and progressively broader (c. 2.5 cm) on the outer feathers. The legs and feet are deep yellow, and the bill chrome-yellow. The iris is reddish-brown, appearing dark at a distance. Immatures are dark brown with a very short frontal crest. The chin and throat feathers sometimes have buffy-white bases, producing a spotted appearance. The undertail-coverts are buffy, and the white wing patch is smaller, and the white tail tip narrower than in the adult, sometimes absent when the feathers are abraded. This species is monotypic and includes *A. fuscus infuscatus* of Nagaland, Manipur and Bangladesh. There is some geographical variation. Some birds from Burma show pale tips to feathers of the lower belly, producing a slight barring, and the undertail-coverts are black, broadly tipped white, producing a mottled vent, and some birds from Manadalay are somewhat greyer on the underparts but have white undertail-coverts.

MEASUREMENTS Male (4): wing 129–136, tail 78–79, tarsus 38–42, culmen 18–20; female (5): wing 126–139, tail 77–83, tarsus 36–40, culmen 18–20.

VOICE Produces a variety of calls similar to other mynas, involving repeated notes which are generally higher-pitched and less fluty and resonant than those of Common Myna. In Thailand, they commonly give a high-pitched, disyllabic *chuur-chuur* call (CJF), and Deignan (1945) described song as a harsh *queeter, queeter, queeter, queeter, queeter*. On take-off they give a soft *piu* flight call, and the alarm call is a harsh *kaar* (CJF).

DISTRIBUTION AND POPULATION Occurs from Nagaland through Bangladesh and Manipur to Burma, Thailand (but only the very northern part of the peninsula) to Cambodia, Laos and Vietnam, and in southern China in Guangxi and Yunnan. Throughout this range it is common and widespread, especially in the lowlands. It appears to be spreading southwards down the Malay Peninsula.

HABITAT Inhabits cultivated areas and other open habitats, especially grasslands and marshes where birds frequently accompany cattle. They are tolerant of man and are relatively unwary, occurring in parks, gardens and on golf courses.

FOOD AND FEEDING Feed in grassland on insects that they obtain from the sward by open bill probing. Great Mynas walk on mats of tall grasses in marshes in order to pick insects from the leaves and also take larger items; one, probably a leech, was taken to a tree where it was repeatedly beaten against a branch before being swallowed whole. They commonly sit on the backs or heads of cattle and buffalo, catching insects disturbed by the grazing animals. They also remove insects from the animals themselves, and have been observed clinging to the skin in order to remove parasites from the anus and inner thighs of buffalo (CJF). After harvest, Great Mynas glean grain from rice stubbles. There appear to be no records of them taking nectar but in all probability they do so, and in Bang Phra, Thailand, they were seen eating unidentified green berries in a tree (CJF).

BREEDING Nests in holes. In northern Thailand, Deignan (1945) found a nest in a hole in a tree at a height of about 5 m, and another in the crown of a coconut tree *Cocos nucifera*. He also found them breeding in the roofs of houses. These breeding records were in April–July. In Kuala Lumpur, Great Mynas nest in drainage holes located high in the retaining walls of houses (D Wells pers. comm.). The eggs are similar to those of Common Myna, but are darker blue and measure 25.4–32.0 x 19.0–23.0 mm (50) (Schönwetter 1983).

BEHAVIOUR Like other *Acridotheres* mynas, Great Mynas bow and Kang Nee (pers. comm.) noted that when the head was dipped low in bowing, the position was held for a short while, exposing the crest.

43 CRESTED MYNA *Acridotheres cristatellus*   Plate 11
Chinese Crested Myna, Chinese Jungle Myna, Tufted Myna, Chinese Starling

Gracula cristatella Linnaeus 1766

FIELD IDENTIFICATION 22–26 cm. Crested Myna is a typical *Acridotheres* myna, with largely black plumage, white-tipped tail, narrower than in other species, and conspicuous white wing patches. It is distinguished from the similar Jungle and White-vented Mynas in having a larger frontal crest, an ivory-coloured bill with a reddish base, and black undertail-coverts edged with white giving a scaled effect. The feet and legs are dull yellow and the iris dull orange. The sexes are similar, but young birds have a smaller crest, are browner, have a blue iris, and the white tail tip and scaling on the undertail-coverts are much less conspicuous or even absent.

DESCRIPTION The feathers of the forehead are elongated but broad, rather than lanceolate as in other 'crested' mynas, and orientated towards the mid-line to form a compact crest. The crown and nape feathers are hackled but shorter than in Great Myna. The remainder of the plumage is black, slightly glossed on the upperparts but duller below. The undertail-coverts are black, narrowly tipped whitish in fresh plumage. The wings are brownish-black, the white bases to the primaries forming a conspicuous wing patch. The tail is narrowly tipped white, broader on the outer feathers but only c. 0.5–0.75 cm wide. The legs and feet are dull yellow. The iris is dull orange and the bill ivory-white. Immatures are uniformly browner with a much less well-developed frontal crest and the white terminal tail band is narrower than in the adult. The iris of the immature is bluish. This description refers to nominate *A. c. cristatellus*, of eastern Burma to southeastern and central China.

A. c. brevipennis, of Hainan, has the feathers of the forehead narrower than in the nominate form, more like *A. grandis*.

A. c. formosanus occurs on Taiwan and is slightly smaller with a greenish-yellow bill, a slight green tinge on the crown and back, and white undertail-coverts (Hachisuka and Udagawa 1950).

MEASUREMENTS Male/female (10): wing 133–146, tail 79–92, tarsus 36–43, culmen 18–22.

VOICE The calls are very similar to those of Common Myna, but are less fluty and resonant, having a more whistled quality. The most common call is a trisyllabic myna-like call, usually with a downward inflection but in a few individuals upwardly inflected. Sometimes this call is repeated many times. Occasionally croaking calls are produced. On take-off, Crested Mynas often give a trilling flight call. (CJF). Crested Mynas mimic other species, including Red-winged Blackbird *Agelaius phoeniceus* in Canada (Mackay and Hughes 1963), and mimic other sounds, including human speech, in captivity (Vaughan and Jones 1913).

DISTRIBUTION AND POPULATION Resident in southeast and central China, occurring in the Yangtze valley west to southeast Jiangxi and lowland Sichuon, and south of the Yangtze to Guandong, Guangxi and south Yunnan, from where it extends eastwards to northern Indochina, and it has been recorded in eastern Burma. They also occur on Taiwan and Hainan, and as accidental visitors to western Japan, especially the Yaeyama Islands. Throughout their range they are common and widespread. They are popular cagebirds and have been successfully introduced in Penang, Singapore, Manila, Japan, Vancouver and Argentina. They are established in Penang (Lever 1987) and appeared to be increasing in Singapore (Hails 1987) but by 1995 seemed to have disappeared (Kang Nee, pers. comm.); in Kuala Lumpur they are seen periodically but do not yet appear to have become established. In the Philippines they breed on Luzon and have been recorded on Negros (Dickinson *et al.* 1991). In Japan a small population breeds ferally in the Tokyo area of Honshu. They may also breed in small numbers in Borneo (Smythies 1981). Crested Mynas were introduced to Vancouver, Canada, in the 1890s and by the mid 1920s numbers had increased to an estimated 20,000 and the species had spread south from Vancouver to Washington, USA. Thereafter, numbers decreased to 2–3,000 in the 1950s (Mackay and Hughes 1963) but since then it has remained common but in fluctuating numbers in the Vancouver area; in 1979 the Christmas Bird Count recorded only 270 birds (Godfrey 1986). Crested Mynas were first reported in Buenos Aires Province, Argentina in 1982, but are increasing in numbers and geographical distribu-

tion, with flock of 100 or more birds now being seen (Chiurla and Martìnez 1995). From 1983 to 1991, a flock that reached a maximum of 14 birds was present in suburban gardens, parks, orchards and pasture on the outskirts of Graz, Austria, and up to three pairs nested in tree cavities and nest-boxes; the origin and reason for the demise of this group are not known (Hagemeijer and Blair 1997).

HABITAT Crested Mynas occur mainly in open country, avoiding woodland and mountains, and inhabit cultivated areas, suburban parks and gardens, and playing fields. This species spends much of its time on the ground where it frequently feeds in grassland, especially where moist, and often among cattle.

FOOD AND FEEDING Feeds mainly on the ground by prying (open-bill probing) in the grass sward, taking food items from the vegetation and also dashing after more mobile prey. The diet here presumably consists primarily of insects, as in other members of the genus. Crested Mynas also take insects from the backs of buffalo, upon which they often settle. They also eat fruit, for example the berries of *Lantana camara* (CJF) and have been seen scavenging dead fish on the shore in Singapore (CJF). On Stonecutters Island, Hong Kong, adults took large caterpillars and adult moths into nest cavities (CJF). In a colony of Chinese Pond Herons *Ardeola bacchus* at Mai Po, Hong Kong, a Crested Myna harassed a recently-fed pond heron chick until the chick regurgitated food, which the myna picked up and carried away as if feeding young (Leader 1995).

BREEDING Nests in holes and, where the distribution of suitable holes permits, the mynas are colonial. Holes in rock faces, trees, buildings and other man-made structures are used, but in addition they have been recorded nesting in the disused holes made by kingfishers and in the old nests of Magpies *Pica pica* and Black-collared Mynas (Vaughan and Jones 1913). The introduced population in Vancouver additionally nests in telephone pole cavities, bird houses in urban areas, and also in nest boxes, nest sites varying from 1–20 m above the ground (Mackay and Hughes 1963). The nest is untidy and is made of straw, dry grasses, pine needles, feathers, wool, paper and other material and, in South East Asia, almost invariably contains pieces of sloughed snake skin (Vaughan and Jones 1913). In Vancouver, pieces of cellophane were regularly found in nests, many of which also contained green leaves (Mackay and Hughes 1963). In Hong Kong, breeding occurs from April to July, with most birds breeding in May, and Vaughan and Jones (1913) considered most to be double brooded. In Vancouver, nesting also occurred from April to July. Clutch size ranges from 4–7 eggs, 4 being the most common in Hong Kong (Vaughan and Jones 1913), while 5 was more common in Vancouver (Mackay and Hughes 1963). The eggs are pale blue or blue-green, varying in shade, with occasional clutches of white eggs, and measure 28.5–33.7 x 19.0–23.0 mm (46) (Schönwetter 1983). Eggs are unspotted, although Vaughan and Hughes reported some eggs with spots in later clutches; these spots may have been spots of blood resulting from parasite bites on the incubation patches of the adults. The eggs are incubated for 14 days and chicks fledge at about 21 days old. In Vancouver, in two years of study, hatching success was poor with only 35–40% of eggs laid surviving to hatch, but 79–87% of chicks fledged successfully.

BEHAVIOUR Gregarious, but even in large flocks pairs remain close together, and when not in flocks they are usually found in pairs or trios. Where the distribution of nest holes allows, they breed colonially, and out of the breeding season they roost communally at night, sometimes in groups of several hundreds and often in reedbeds. Prior to roosting, Crested Mynas sometimes perform aerial evolutions like Common Starlings, and they are similarly noisy. Like other members of the genus, Crested Mynas frequently bow, both when alone and in pairs.

RELATIONS WITH MAN Often kept in captivity where their ability to mimic, especially human speech, is admired. Populations that have become established outside the native range have probably resulted from birds that have escaped or been deliberately released from captivity.

44 WHITE-VENTED MYNA *Acridotheres javanicus* Plate 11

Javan Myna

Acridotheres javanicus Cabanis 1850

FIELD IDENTIFICATION 21–23 cm. A dark grey myna with a short crest on the forehead and white undertail-coverts. The bill, legs and feet are orange-yellow and the iris lemon-yellow. Juveniles are paler and browner, often appearing streaky on the underparts, and the iris is white. White-vented Myna is distinguished from Jungle Myna by the former lacking the blue base to the bill and by its greyer, rather than browner, plumage, and from Great Myna by the latter's blacker plumage, yellower bill and orange-brown iris.

DESCRIPTION Feathers of the forehead are hackled and erect, forming a frontal crest. Feathers of the crown and nape are elongated and hackled, black and slightly glossed. The ear-coverts are black. The mantle, back and rump are ashy-black, somewhat paler and slaty on the underparts, except for the undertail-coverts which are white. The wings are brownish-black, the bases of the primaries white but with very little white on the outer large (9th) primary and less extensive generally than in Jungle and Great Mynas. The tail is black with white tips to the rectrices, narrow on the inner feathers and broader (*c.* 1.5 cm) on the outer feathers. The bill, legs and feet are orange-yellow and the iris lemon-yellow. Immatures are generally browner, with a shorter brown frontal tuft. The crown feathers are hackled but shorter than in the adult and lack gloss. The remainder of the upperparts are dull brown, including the wings and tail. The underparts are somewhat paler and more mousy, sometimes with pale feather margins producing a streaky appearance, but with white undertail-coverts. The white bases to the primaries and the tail tip are as in the adult, but are narrower.

MEASUREMENTS Male/female (7): wing 123–128, tail 70–78, tarsus 36–39, culmen 19–22.

VOICE The calls are very similar to those of Common Myna but are distinguishable with considerable experience of both together (Kang Nee pers. comm.).

DISTRIBUTION AND POPULATION Endemic to Java and Bali, where it is common and widespread. It has also been introduced to Sumatra and Singapore. In Singapore, during the last 25 years it has become widespread and is now the commonest myna and one of the most conspicuous birds on the island, and is extending its range northwards through the Malay Peninsula (Kang *et al.* 1994). It occurs throughout the lowlands of mainland Sumatra, where it is assumed to have been introduced, and is locally common (van Marle and Voous 1988). It was first recorded in the Lesser Sundas on Sumba in 1987 and Flores in 1990; it is assumed to have been introduced there (Coates and Bishop 1997). It has also recently been introduced to Puerto Rico (Raffaele 1989).

HABITAT In all parts of its range, White-vented Myna occurs in cities and in cultivated areas. Studies in Singapore suggest that it is better able to exploit urban areas than Common Myna, since the former readily feeds at sites where food is temporarily superabundant but unpredictable in its occurrence (Kang 1992). It feeds mainly on the ground, especially in grassy areas and cultivated fields, but also in streets and on the shore. It is especially attracted to flooded or freshly-mown grassland, such as found on playing fields and airfields. It also feeds in trees and roosts communally in trees.

FOOD AND FEEDING Omnivorous, eating seeds, fruit, nectar, insects and other animal matter, and human refuse. The diet has not been studied in detail, but Kang (1992) recorded them eating wild figs *Ficus* and berries, together with cultivated fruits such as pawpaw *Carica papaya* and banana *Musa*. They feed with some agility at the terminal rosettes of *Casuarina* branches and take ovules from the cones of this tree. They take nectar from flowers such as coral *Erythrina*, and eat arthropods, including flying ants (Hymenoptera), termites (Isoptera) and maggots (Diptera), and earthworms (Annelida). A wide variety of human refuse is eaten; this is obtained at tips, where spilt on streets and birds will enter rubbish bins in order to take food from within. White-vented Mynas also eat carrion, for example animals killed on roads or washed up on beaches.

BREEDING Like other mynas, this species nests in holes. In Singapore, sites include holes in trees or among fruit clusters in the crowns of palms, gaps in the rooting pad of Birds' Nest Fern *Asplenum nidus,* drainage holes in retaining walls, and holes in buildings, bridges and other man-made structures, including lamp posts, holes in deep monsoon drains, and even in a bus involved in routine journeys (Kang *et al* 1990). Medway and Wells (1976) recorded a nest in a hole about 10 m high in a tree, during May. Eggs are uniform bluish-glaucous and measure 27.5–33.1 x 19.5–22.5 mm (64) (Schönwetter 1983). In aviaries, clutches of 2–5 eggs were laid and these were incubated for 13–14 days (Kang Nee pers. comm.).

BEHAVIOUR White-vented Mynas are social birds throughout the year. They generally occur in pairs but pairs frequently associate in larger groups, especially where food is abundant, as at flowering or fruiting trees. White-vented Mynas in Singapore are more opportunistic than Common Mynas, and appear better able to exploit temporary abundances of food (Kang 1992). At night they roost communally in large groups in trees. Prior to entering the roost they gather nearby on buildings, in trees or on the ground, arriving singly, in pairs, or more frequently in small parties. From these assemblies birds fly to the roost trees, which in Singapore are often lines of amenity trees in residential areas. White-vented Mynas commonly roost with Common Mynas, although there appears to be some segregation between species within the roost (CJF). They are sometimes joined by Asian Glossy Starlings and Purple-backed Starlings, which also seem to segregate in different parts of the roost. As birds arrive at the roost in the evening, prior to morning departure, and sometimes during disturbance during the night, White-vented Mynas sing loudly. During departure in the morning, Kang and Yeo (1993) found that each departure was accompanied by a short period of

silence, as occurs in Common Starlings. At a Singapore roost in November 1990, a few birds flew into the roost carrying green leaves. Trees selected for roosting are generally those with dense canopies and in Singapore *Pterocarpus indicus, Eugenia grandis* and *Terminalia catappa* are frequently used (Hails 1985, Kang and Yeo 1993), although other trees, including coconut *Cocos nucifera* are used in some areas; in these the mynas roost among the bases of the fronds. Kang (1992) found that individual White-vented Mynas used several night roosts over a nine month period and that on average they ranged over an area of about 3 km^2. By contrast, individual Common Mynas used only one roost and ranged over a much smaller area. Non-feeding birds sometimes form large daytime roosts, for example in trees near rubbish tips, in which there is much song. Like other *Acridotheres* mynas, White-vented Mynas bow periodically both when alone, and also in the company of other birds, generally their mates. Such bowing occurs on feeding sites and in daytime roosts, and during assembly in night roosts.

RELATIONS WITH MAN This species is kept in captivity in Malaysia and Indonesia and escapes from cages have doubtless accounted for the birds' introduction to Sumatra and Singapore. They became established in Singapore some time before 1925 and in the 1960s, Ward (1968) described them as shy birds of the suburbs. Since then, its population has increased dramatically and it is now bold and tolerant of man; this increase has probably been facilitated by waste from man's increasing population. The main complaints about mynas in Singapore result from their night roosts in trees close to human habitation, where the noise of the roosting birds, and to a lesser extent droppings deposited beneath the roosts, are cause for concern among local inhabitants. This has led to calls for management and attempts have been made to remove the birds by scaring, poisoning, and thinning or removing the trees (Hails 1985, Kang *et al.* 1990). Such methods have met with only temporary success (Kang *et al* 1990).

45 PALE-BELLIED MYNA *Acridotheres cinereus*　　Plate 11
White-vented Myna

Acridotheres cinereus Bonaparte 1851

FIELD IDENTIFICATION 22–25 cm. A crested myna with black crown and cheeks, dark blackish wings and tail, but with a grey back and ashy-grey breast paling to buffy-grey on the belly and with a white vent. It has the white wing patch typical of crested mynas but the white tip to the tail is broader than in other species.

DESCRIPTION Feathers above the nares and of the forehead are blackish-charcoal, lanceolate and erect forming a frontal crest. The crown feath-

ers are lanceolate and elongated, black with a slight gloss, while those of the cheeks are less elongate and duller black. The mantle and back are grey with a hint of silvery gloss, paler on the rump where some feathers have white shafts. The chin and throat are ashy-grey, becoming paler posteriorly to buffy-grey on the belly and white on the vent. The primaries are dark brown except for white bases, and the primary coverts are white, forming a white patch in the wing. The secondaries are also dark brown, but slightly paler than the primaries. The tail is brownish-black with broad white tips to the outer feathers (extending to about one-third of their length), becoming narrower, c. 1 cm wide, on the inner rectrices. On these white tips, the dark feather shaft is prominent, and is spine-like when the white tip has become abraded. The bill is yellow with a small grey-blue patch at the base of the lower mandible; the legs are yellow and the iris is lemon-yellow to brownish-orange.

MEASUREMENTS Male/female (5): wing 121–135; tail 71–82; tarsus 34–39; culmen 19–21.

VOICE A variety of unmusical nasal squeaky rattles and whistles.

DISTRIBUTION AND POPULATION Restricted to the southern peninsula of Sulawesi, north to Rantepao, from sea level to 1500 m. It is locally common.

HABITAT Inhabits dry fallow paddyfields, scrubby edges of wet paddyfields, lightly wooded cultivated areas and trees in villages.

BREEDING Nests solitarily in holes in trees.

BEHAVIOUR Occurs singly and in pairs, but are more usually found in groups of 3–10 birds. They feed on the ground, often among cattle and sometimes perch on their backs. They are conspicuous and approachable.

PRINCIPAL REFERENCE Coates and Bishop (1997).

46 JUNGLE MYNA *Acridotheres fuscus*   Plate 11
Buffalo Myna

Pastor fuscus Wagler 1827

FIELD IDENTIFICATION 22–24 cm. A grey-brown myna with a tuft of feathers forming a small crest on the forehead and at the base of the bill. The head is black, the upperparts grey-brown; the chin, breast and belly are dark ashy-grey, paling into a buffish-white lower belly and undertail-coverts. It possesses white bases to the primaries, forming a white wing patch, and has a white-tipped tail typical of *Acridotheres* mynas. The bill is yellow-orange, but the base of the lower mandible is leaden-blue, differentiating it from Great and White-vented Mynas. The legs and feet are yellow. In northern India, the iris is yellow, while in southern India it is bluish-white or grey. Juveniles are browner.

DESCRIPTION The feathers of the forehead are elongated and hackled, and directed upwards and towards the mid-line to form a short frontal crest. The feathers of the crown, nape and sides of the neck are elongate, lanceolate and glossy black. The mantle and upper back are brownish-charcoal, becoming paler on the lower back and rump. The chin, throat and breast are slaty grey, the belly paler and tinged buffish, increasingly so on the lower belly. The undertail-coverts are white. The wings and tail are brownish-black, with the secondaries and scapulars and their coverts washed iridescent bronze. The primaries have white bases, comprising 20–25% of the largest outer primary (9), and increasing to about half the length of the inner primaries. The rectrices are tipped white, narrowly on the innermost feathers but becoming broader on the outer feathers. The bill is orange with a bluish-black base to the lower mandible, and the legs and feet are waxy orange. The iris is bright yellow. Immatures are browner, with feathers on the head less hackled and lacking gloss. The wings and tail are also browner, the tail with less distinctive white tips to the feathers. The underparts lack grey on the throat and breast, the

feathers of the throat are mid brown, those of the breast have dark brown centres and pale margins giving a slight streaked appearance which becomes more pronounced on the belly. This description refers to *A. f. fuscus*, from Pakistan through the lower Himalayas to Assam and with southern limits from Rajasthan to northern Orissa.

A. f. mahrattensis, mainly of western peninsular India from Rajasthan south to Kerala, east to western Mysore and western Tamil Nadu, and possibly in Orissa and Madhya Pradesh, is browner and the iris is bluish-white or grey.

A. f. fumidus, of Nagaland and eastern Assam, is darker than nominate *fuscus*, more sooty on the upperparts and more smoky on the abdomen and belly, with a yellow iris.

A. f. torquatus, of northern and central Malaysia, has the crown hackles somewhat longer and more glossy, the belly is darker, especially on the flanks, and the undertail-coverts are dirty white.

MEASUREMENTS Male (sample sizes not given): wing 122–130, tail 72–76, bill 26–28; female: wing 120–125, tail 67–75, bill 25–27; male/female weight (2) 78–94 g (Ali and Ripley 1972).

VOICE Calls are similar to those of Common Myna, but are higher pitched and less resonant. In Goa the most commonly heard call was an often repeated disyllabic or trisyllabic *tiuck-tiuck-tiuck* (CJF).

DISTRIBUTION AND POPULATION Throughout its range, Jungle Myna is resident and patchily distributed, but in some areas it undertakes seasonal movements. Its range extends from Murree in west Pakistan eastwards through the lower Himalayas, through parts of Nepal (where it appears to undertake movements which are not understood (Inskipp and Inskipp 1991) to Assam, Burma and south to Malacca in central Malaysia.

Here, it may hybridise with *A. javanicus* as this species spreads up the Malay Peninsula (Kang *et al.* 1994). Within peninsular India it occurs mainly on the western side, with a disjunct population on the eastern side in southern Orissa. Jungle Mynas have been successfully introduced on Fiji, purportedly to control armyworm, and they are now present on Viti Levu and its offshore islands and rare on Vanua Levu (Watling 1982). They have also occurred on islands in the Tonga and Samoa groups, possibly storm-driven from Fiji (Lever 1987).

HABITAT Occurring to over 2000 m in the Himalayas and Tamil Nadu, they are primarily birds of lowlands and foothills where they inhabit well-wooded deciduous areas with open spaces, especially near cultivation, tea plantations, villages and coastal plains. They feed mainly on the ground, especially in grassland grazed by cattle, and in stubble, but also in flowering trees.

FOOD AND FEEDING Eat insects, fruit, seeds and nectar. Insects are sought mainly on the ground, foraging birds parting surface vegetation or soil by open-bill probing. They regularly feed among cattle and take insects disturbed by the animals' feet and mouths, and also flutter up to take insects from the flanks and mouth of the cattle, upon which they frequently perch (CJF). In Fiji, Watling (1982) did not record them taking insects from the bodies of cattle, simply using the cattle as observation platforms. Analysis of stomach contents showed that grasshoppers, mole crickets and crickets (Orthoptera), termites (Isoptera), beetles (Coleoptera), ants (Hymenoptera), caterpillars (Lepidoptera), bugs (Hemiptera) and fly larvae (Diptera) were taken, grasshoppers being commonly eaten (Narang and Lamba 1984). Plant matter taken includes a variety of figs *Ficus,* berries of *Lantana camara,* chilli *Capsicum,* and *Litsea,* flower parts of *Grevillea,* seeds of *Albizia,* coriander *Coriandum,* cloves *Syzygium* and ground-nuts *Arachis.* Jungle Mynas are commonly seen feeding in flowering trees, taking nectar from *Salmalia, Erythrina, Bombax, Butea, Careya* and *Spathodea.* While drinking nectar, the crest acts as an efficient pollen brush and Jungle Mynas are important cross-pollinators (Ali and Ripley 1972). Seeds eaten include cereal grains, and Jungle Mynas also feed on human food scraps and at refuse dumps.

BREEDING Jungle Mynas nest in holes, often in natural cavities in trees or in old woodpecker holes, usually 2–6 m above the ground. They also nest in man-made sites and form large colonies in drain holes in walls and in bridges; these colonies may be used year after year. Less commonly they nest in the roofs of houses. The nest is made of twigs, roots, feathers and man-made materials, and often includes pieces of snake slough. The breeding season in southern India is from February to May, April to June–July further north. Two broods are often raised. The clutch is normally 3–6 eggs. Eggs are turquoise-blue, without markings and slightly glossed, and measure 26.0–32.8 x 19.0–23.0 mm (124) (Schönwetter 1983). Both sexes participate in nest-building, incubation and care of the young (Ali and Ripley 1972).

BEHAVIOUR This species is social throughout the year. When feeding, they often occur in pairs but pairs frequently coalesce into small flocks where food is abundant or concentrated. Where the availability of nest holes permits, Jungle Mynas breed colonially and they roost communally at night in reedbeds, sugarcane fields and trees, sometimes in the company of other birds including Common Mynas and Rose-coloured Starlings. During courtship, Jungle Mynas indulge in much bowing and head-bobbing (Ali and Ripley 1972). At other times of year they bow occasionally when perched and while feeding, both when alone and when landing near another bird, although bowing appeared less frequent than in Common Mynas (CJF) and White-vented Mynas (Kang Nee pers. comm.).

RELATIONS WITH MAN Jungle Mynas cause considerable damage to fruit in orchards in the southern Indian hills (Ali and Ripley 1972) and to the plumules of ground-nut *Arachis* crops in Fiji (Watling 1975). There is concern in Samoa that successful colonisation by Jungle Mynas could lead to competition for nest sites with the Blue-crowned Lory *Vini australis* (Lever 1987). Introduction to Fiji was deliberate, aimed at controlling grasshopper pests in sugarcane plantations (Lever 1987). Narang and Lamba (1984) noted that many of the insects taken were agricultural pests, but also that Jungle Mynas damaged cloves *Syzygium.*

47 COLLARED MYNA *Acridotheres albocinctus* Plate 11

Acridotheres albocinctus Godwin-Austen and Walden 1875

FIELD IDENTIFICATION 22–25 cm. This myna is glossy slate-black above and greyish-black below, and is distinguished from all other 'crested' mynas by a buffish-white collar comprising prominent patches on the sides of the neck which extend less distinctly around the back of the neck. The wings have a prominent white wing patch and the tail is tipped white. The forehead sports a short crest. The bill is orange-yellow, the legs and feet are yellow and the iris bluish. The sexes are similar. Young birds are dark brown, paler on the throat and belly.

DESCRIPTION The feathers of the forehead are hackled and erect but short, forming a small frontal crest. The crown and nape feathers are elongated and lanceolate, black and slightly glossed. The remainder of the body plumage is black, slightly glossed on the upperparts but duller below. The feathers of the sides of the neck are buffish-white, white when abraded, extending ventrally to the sides of the throat, and posteriorly as white feather tips that form a narrow broken collar, partly overlain by the elongated nape feathers. The undertail-coverts are black, tipped white, producing a barred effect. The wings are black, the bases of the primaries white forming a white patch, smaller than in Great and Crested Mynas. The rectrices are tipped white, narrowly or sometimes absent, on the inner feathers but broader towards the outer feathers, c. 1 cm wide. The bill is orange-yellow and legs and feet are yellow. The iris is pale blue or azure-blue. Immatures are browner with a pale throat and the feathers of the sides of the neck are tipped dirty buffish-white forming a small pale patch; the feathers of the forehead are bristled but do not form a crest. This species undergoes a complete postjuvenal moult.

MEASUREMENTS Male/female (sample sizes not given): wing 110–120, tail 72–76, bill (from feathers) 23–25 (Ali and Ripley 1972).

VOICE Apparently not described.

DISTRIBUTION AND POPULATION Restricted to the Manipur Valley, northern Burma and northwest Yunnan. It may be locally migratory (Ali and Ripley 1972).

HABITAT Inhabits moist areas, open elephant grass country, cultivated areas and villages, mainly between 800 and 1200 m. It often accompanies cattle.

FOOD AND FEEDING This species eats grasshoppers (Acrididae) and other insects, and also small frogs (Amphibia) and lizards (Reptilia). Foods of plant origin include fruits of *Ficus*, nectar and cereal grains.

BREEDING Ali and Ripley (1972) state that its breeding habits are similar to those of Jungle Myna, but give no details. Eggs measure 26.1–29.6 x 20.0–22.0 mm (42) (Schönwetter 1983).

BEHAVIOUR Frequently occurs in pairs, family groups or flocks of 30–50 birds.

PRINCIPAL REFERENCE Ali and Ripley (1972).

48 BANK MYNA *Acridotheres ginginianus* Plate 12

Turdus ginginianus Latham 1790

FIELD IDENTIFICATION 20–23 cm. Slightly smaller than Common Myna but is a similarly 'jaunty' bird. This species is generally bluish-grey with a black head and wings, and pinkish-buff centre of the belly, wing patch and tips of the tail feathers. Behind and below the eye is a brick-red patch of bare skin. The forehead bears a small tuft of erect feathers. Bill, legs and feet are yellow. The sexes are similar and young birds are browner with buff edgings to the flank and breast feathers.

DESCRIPTION Feathers of the forehead are slightly bristled and directed centrally to form a short frontal crest. Feathers of the crown and nape are elongate and lanceolate and, together with the forehead and hindcheek, are glossy black. The mantle, back and rump are grey, the mantle suffused with brown. The chin is grey, the breast grey tinged cinnamon, the centre of the belly and undertail-coverts cinnamon, and the flanks grey with a cinnamon wash. The wings are glossy black, the secondaries with a slight metallic-green iridescence. The bases of the primaries are white, becoming chestnut on the inner feathers. The primary coverts and underwing-coverts are chestnut, the underwing in flight appearing banded — chestnut coverts, white bases to primaries and remainder of the wing black. The tail is black, slightly glossed, and with chestnut tips to the rectrices, narrow on the inner feathers but progressively broader towards the outer feathers, and extending half-way along the outer web of the outermost rectrix. The bill is orange-yellow and the legs and feet yellow. The iris is orange-red and the bare skin behind and below the eye, coming to a point posteriorly, is brick-red. Immatures are dun-brown above, paler buffish below. The wings and tail are brown, with buffish primary coverts, bases to the primaries and tips to the rectrices, narrower than in adults. The iris is red-brown, duller than in adults, the bill and bare facial skin dull orange and the legs golden-brown.

MEASUREMENTS Male (sample sizes not given): wing 118–129, tail 65–74; female wing 114–123, tail 60–71; male/female tarsus 36–38, bill 24–25; weight (6) 64–76 g (Ali and Ripley 1972).

VOICE Ali and Ripley (1972) described the voice of Bank Myna as being similar to, but softer than, that of Common Myna. During bowing displays, males give what Schlee (1993) described as croaking sounds, together with song that included low croaks and high-pitched whistles and warbles. After copulation, Schlee (1993) heard a female produce high-pitched staccato sounds. Calls that are not associated with pair maintenance include a *wheek* contact call or flight call when a bird moves, usually by flying but sometimes when hopping, a raucous alarm call given during disturbance or when a bird is threatened, and a high-pitched scream given by young when caught and by parents when mobbing (Schlee 1993).

DISTRIBUTION AND POPULATION Occurs in the plains of northern and central India from the foothills of the Himalayas, including southern Nepal, southwest to Sind and south to Bombay, and east to Bangladesh. Within this range, Bank Mynas are resident but undergo regular seasonal movements and nomadic movements in some areas (Ali and Ripley 1972). In Punjab, the population has increased (Dhindsa 1984).

HABITAT Inhabits areas frequented by man, both in agricultural areas and in cities. In farmland, they prefer moister parts such as fields bordering rivers and canals, and also irrigated fields. The birds follow the plough and attend cattle, sometimes settling on them. In cities they frequent refuse dumps and sewage farms, and also occur wherever man is likely to drop potential food items, such as railway stations and near street vendors' carts (Ali and Ripley 1972).

FOOD AND FEEDING Eat fruit, seeds and insects, and also human food waste. Seeds include ripening cereal crops (see below) and invertebrate food includes ticks taken from the backs of cattle. Adults eat cereal grains, including millet *Pennisetum*, maize *Zea mays* and wheat *Triticum* from September to January in Punjab, and also eat ground-nut *Arachis* kernels during this period. Fruits, especially the figs of banyan and peepal *Ficus benghalensis* and *F. religiosa* are eaten in most months, while mulberries *Morus* appear in the diet in May and grapes *Vitis* are eaten in large quantities in June and July (Simwat and Sidhu 1974). In northern Uttar Pradesh, Narang and Lamba (1984) also recorded peas (*Pisum*), chillies (*Capsicum*), berries of *Lantana camara* and *Zizyphus*, and flower parts of nectar-rich trees. Insects are eaten throughout the year, including ants and wasps (Hymenoptera), a wide variety of beetles (Coleoptera), adult and larval flies (Diptera), caterpillars and butterflies (Lepidoptera), grasshoppers, crickets and mole crickets (Orthoptera) termites (Isoptera), bugs (Hemiptera), earwigs (Dermaptera), cockroaches (Dictyoptera), ticks (Ixodidae), spiders (Araneae), earthworms (Annelida), molluscs (Gastropoda) and centipedes (Diplopoda) (Simwat and Sidhu 1974, Narang and Lamba 1984). Grasshoppers, beetles and caterpillars predominated, with ticks more important during droughts (Narang and Lamba 1984). They take human food waste, and Ripley (1983) recorded Bank Mynas riding on airport catering vehicles, presumably to capitalise on any spillages. In a study of the diet of nestlings, Parasara *et al.* (1990) found only small quantities of plant food, including figs *Ficus benghalensis*, kernels of neem *Azadirachta indica* and human food waste; over 95% of the food brought to the nestlings was of animal origin, mainly insects. Grasshoppers and butterflies/moths and their larvae predominated, but the diet also included beetles, ants, wasps and bees (Hymenoptera), termites (Isoptera), bugs (Homoptera), flies (Diptera), cockroaches and mantids (Dictyoptera), together with millipedes (Myriapoda), spiders (Arachneae), earthworms (Annelida) and frog tadpoles (Amphibia). Mollusc (Gastropoda) shells and hen's egg shells were brought occasionally by the parents.

BREEDING Bank Mynas have a well-defined breeding season, mainly from April–June, but with occasional breeding activity from March–August. They are colonial and excavate tunnels in the banks of rivers, brick kilns, bridges, and wells, so deep that birds have to rise vertically when leaving the nest (Ali and Ripley 1972). Exceptionally, they have also nested in stacks of crushed and dried sugarcane (Lamba 1981). Within a colony, holes

may be as close as 14.5 cm. The tunnels average *c.* 1 m long, but may be longer in softer soils, are slightly upward-sloping, *c.* 7–10 cm wide but somewhat deeper, and end in a broadened chamber, *c.* 21 cm long and *c.* 18 cm in diameter (Jior *et al.* 1995). In this chamber the nest is built, comprising a pad of straw, feathers and often pieces of sloughed snake skin, and Jior *et al.* (1995) found pieces of polythene in most nests. Schlee (1993), observing captive birds, found that the male excavated the nest and contributed straw and dry grass, but that the female completed the final stages, in particular adding fresh green leaves. The clutch consists of 3–6, exceptionally 8, eggs which are glossy pale blue or greenish-turquoise, without markings. Eggs measure 24.2–29.8 x 18.3–22.1 mm (165) (Schönwetter 1983). Incubation, lasting about 13 days, is by both sexes (Simwat and Sidhu 1974) but females take the greater share (Khera and Kalsi 1986a). Throughout incubation, Schlee (1993) reported that fresh green leaves were placed in the nest and dried leaves were removed. Eggs are partially covered with nest material when the female leaves of her own accord (Schlee 1993). Chicks fledge at about 20–22 days old (Simwat and Sidhu 1974). Both parents feed the chicks and remove faecal material from the nest.

BEHAVIOUR Gregarious throughout the year, Bank Mynas breed in colonies, feeding in flocks and roosting at night, often with Common Mynas and other birds. Bank Mynas are relatively unwary of man. Communal roosting occurs throughout the year but incubating and brooding females roost in the nest. Winter roosts are often in sugarcane and reedbeds while roosts at other times of year occur in tall trees (Khera and Kalsi 1986b) and sometimes on buildings. Conspicuous behaviour used in courtship and pair maintenance involves bowing and head-bobbing, usually accompanied by vocalisations. When bowing, belly feathers are often ruffled and the tail is spread. Both sexes may indulge in bowing (Schlee 1993).

RELATIONS WITH MAN Bank Mynas can eat sufficient ripening sorghum to cause local damage (Ali and Ripley 1972), and in Punjab they damage grapes and millet (Sandhu and Toor 1984, Simwat and Sidhu 1974). Bank Mynas are often considered beneficial, however, since they eat large numbers of insects which are regarded as pests (Narang and Lamba 1984), including the larvae of a noctuid moth *Ophiusa melicerte* which is regarded as a serious pest of castor oil plants *Ricinus communis*. They may be important predators of an insect *Helicoverpa armigera*, whose larvae infest Egyptian clover *Trifolium alexandrium*, an important fodder crop in northern India; the birds may also be involved in the spread of a virus disease of the insect (Singh *et al.* 1990). Dhindsa (1980, 1984) considered them to be beneficial in destroying insect pests, including House Flies *Musca domestica*. Bank Mynas may also be important dispersers of banyan *Ficus benghalensis* seeds (Midya and Bramachary 1991).

49 COMMON MYNA *Acridotheres tristis*   **Plate 12**
Common Mynah, Indian Myna, House Myna, Locust Starling

Paradisea tristis Linnaeus 1776

FIELD IDENTIFICATION 25–26 cm. Medium-sized but heavily built starling with predominantly brown plumage. The head, neck and upper breast of the adult is glossy black, the undertail-coverts and tip of the tail, especially the outer feathers, are white, as are the bases of the primaries, forming a conspicuous patch in the open wing; the remainder of the primaries are dark brown and the tail is brownish-black. The back, flanks and lower breast are rich vinous-brown, paling on the belly. The bill, legs and feet, and a patch of bare skin behind and below the eye are bright yellow. The iris is brown or reddish-brown, mottled with white. Juveniles are paler and duller, with the head ashy brown rather than black. Common Mynas walk 'jauntily' on the ground and are noisy, frequently giving a variety of loud calls.
DESCRIPTION Feathers of the forehead are slightly bristled but short. The feathers of the crown and nape are glossy black, elongate and lanceolate. Feathers of the hindcheek are black, slightly glossed, becoming duller and greyer on the chin, throat and upper breast. The mantle, back and rump are brown with a warmer chestnut tinge on the back. The flanks are similar with a vinous tinge, becoming paler buff on the central belly, and white on the lower belly and undertail-coverts. The wings are brownish-black, with the secondaries browner. The primary coverts and the bases of the primaries are white. The tail is brownish-black with white tips to the rectrices, narrow on the central feathers but progressively broader towards the outer feathers. The bill is yellow with the base of the lower mandible brownish-green; the legs are yellow and the bare skin behind and below the eye, coming to a point posteriorly, is bright yellow; the iris is brown or reddish-brown mottled with white. Immatures are similar but the head feathers are browner, lack gloss and are less hackled; the chin, throat and upper breast are brownish-black, and the tips to the rectrices are narrower than in adults and tinged buff. Adults undergo one complete annual moult but the exact timing in relation to breeding is not known. In South East Asia there is some overlap between moult and breeding (Medway and Wells 1976) but this does not occur in New Zealand (Wilson 1973), suggesting that Common Myna is adaptable in its moult schedule. This description refers to nominate **tristis**, but according to Ali and Ripley (1972), birds in the northwest of India tend to be paler, those in the south darker, and in Kerala birds intergrade with the endemic **A. t. melanosternus**, of Sri Lanka. This is darker brown on the upperparts with a rufous tinge on the back. It is also darker on the underparts with brownish-black feathers extending on to the upper belly, while the flanks and sides of the belly are warm rufous-brown and the centre of the belly cream. The

white tips to the rectrices are narrower than in the nominate form.
MEASUREMENTS Male (sample sizes not given): wing 134–153, tail 79–95, tarsus 34–42, bill 24–30, weight 120–138 g; female: wing 133–147, tail 75–88, tarsus 35–41, bill 24–28; weight 111–143 g (Ali and Ripley 1972, Sengupta 1982).
VOICE Highly vocal throughout the year. This species has a variety of calls including loud whistles, somewhat fluty notes, harsh calls and snarling noises; the calls are often repeated and different calls may be given in combinations. They also mimic other birds and can imitate human speech (Ali and Ripley 1972). Both sexes sing throughout the year but song production is greatest during the breeding season; song is used in territorial defence and in pair formation. Many notes and combinations of notes are used in song, including melodic phrases and harsher calls: a common sequence is rendered as *hee hee chirk-a chirk-a chirk-a* (Counsilman 1971) or *krr krr krr ci ri ci ri krrup krrup krrup chirri chirri chirri weeu weeu*. In these phrases most notes are repeated. Counsilman (1971) described other notes as *pen hawn heal*, *pip-e* and a throaty *donck*. Pairs sometimes duet and neighbouring pairs may also match song types. Courtship displays, such as bowing (see BEHAVIOUR), include song and other calls and song is also given in night roosts, when the singing of large numbers of birds can produce a cacophony of sound, pleasing to the ornithologist but annoying and disturbing to humans living close to roosts (Hails 1984). *Chip* calls are given during aggressive encounters and on take-off a flight call, a weak and querulous *kwerrh*, is usually heard (Roberts 1992). High-pitched screams, distress calls, are given when a myna is caught by a predator, when severely attacked by another myna or sometimes when handled by a human. A harsh, scolding *chake chake* alarm call is given when predators, such as snakes, are seen and these calls are recognised by other mynas and also other species as indicating danger (Ali and Ripley 1972). Parents sometimes give a rich honky trill when approaching the nest with food; this stimulates the young to beg (Cousilman 1971).
DISTRIBUTION AND POPULATION Widely distributed in India and Central and southern Asia. They extend eastwards from southeastern Iran and Afghanistan into Pakistan, India and Sri Lanka, through Nepal, Sikkim and Bhutan to west and south Yunnan and Hainan in southern China, in South East Asia in Burma, Thailand, Vietnam, west Malaysia and Singapore. In Central Asia they inhabit Turkmenistan, Uzbekistan, Tadzhikistan and into southern Kazakhstan (Ali and Ripley 1972, Dement'ev and Gladkov 1960, de Schauensee 1984, Hollom *et al.* 1988, Boonsong and Round 1991, Medway and Wells 1976,

Sagitov *et al.* 1990). In Central Asia the Common Myna's range is extending northwards (Akhmedov 1957, Mauersberger and Möckel 1987, Sagitov *et al.* 1990), and a self-sustaining population in southern European Russia, with further extension into Turkey, may be part of this natural range expansion or may stem from introductions (Cramp and Perrins 1994). Colonisation of southern Malaysia and Singapore is relatively recent, following forest clearance, cultivation and urbanisation (Hails 1987). In addition, Common Mynas have been introduced successfully to many parts of the world, both deliberately in the name of insect, especially locust, control, and accidentally through the escape of cagebirds (Lever 1987, Long 1984). As a result, Common Mynas now live in South Africa, the North Island of New Zealand, eastern and southeastern Australia and northern Tasmania, Hong Kong, Brunei and Sumatra. In Australia, the geographical range continues to expand, although expansion north of 40°S and into colder regions of the southeast may be limited by climate (Martin 1996), a factor that may also be restricting spread in South Africa (Craig 1997). Introduced populations also occur in the Caucasus, Tashkent and Alma-Ata, regions now also being reached through natural range expansion in Central Asia. They occur locally in Saudi Arabia, United Arab Emirates and Iraq, probably also as a result of introduction. On many tropical and subtropical oceanic islands, Common Mynas are among the commonest and most conspicuous birds, occurring in the Atlantic (Ascension, St Helena, and recently on Tenerife in the Canary Islands), Pacific (Hawaii, Solomons, Vanuatu, New Caledonia, Fiji, American Samoa, Western Samoa and many islands in Polynesia in the Cook, Society, Tuamotu and Marquesas groups) and Indian Oceans (Madagascar, Comores, Mascarenes, Seychelles, Agalega, Chagos, Lakshadweeps, Maldives, Andamans and Nicobars) (for reviews of this distribution see Cramp and Perrins 1994, Lever 1987, Long 1984). Birds seen in Sumatra are assumed to have escaped from captivity (van Marle and Voous 1988) and a pair has been seen recently near Jakarta airport, Java (R. Grimmett, per F. Lambert). Common Mynas have recently been found breeding in the wild in Dunkirk, northern France (Hars 1991). Throughout most of its range the Common Myna is indeed common, but its conspicuousness is increased by its preference for proximity to human habitation.

HABITAT Inhabits more open country, often cultivated and close to human habitation. They avoid dense forest. Where indigenous, they are common residents of flood plains and river valleys, grasslands, cultivated areas, plantations, villages, towns and cities where they rely heavily on human by products. They also live in desert oases with few humans, and in the foothills of mountain ranges, breeding to 3000 m in the Himalayas (Ali and Ripley 1972, Dement'ev and Gladkov 1960). Where introduced, Common Mynas are usually restricted to towns and cities but on oceanic islands they inhabit coastal mangroves, open land

(especially airstrips), secondary forest and areas of human habitation.

FOOD AND FEEDING Feed predominantly on the ground but will feed in flowering or fruiting trees and bushes and also sometimes hawk flying insects. The structure of their skull and bill musculature adapts them well to seeking food in the upper few centimetres of soil and grassland (Dubale and Patel 1975), and much of the food is sought while walking, though more mobile prey may be chased by running or by flying. Feeding sites include open grassland, such as pastures, lawns, parks and airfields, and cultivated land; they sometimes follow grazing livestock and agricultural machinery (Ali and Ripley 1972, Kang 1992). Common Mynas also feed around buildings, especially farms and food processing areas, and scavenge at rubbish tips and other sites where human waste accumulates, and by roads and on the foreshore where carrion may be found. In trees and bushes they catch insects but visit vegetation primarily to exploit fruit and nectar. The diet is very broad and Common Mynas are highly adaptable, so that in the extensive geographical range where they are indigenous and in places where they have been introduced, they eat a wide range of plant and animal foods. The precise make-up of the diet varies with time and location (Cramp and Perrins 1994) but for most of the year insects form the bulk of the diet, with fruit, nectar and scavenged items being more important when insects are scarce (Narang and Lamba 1984, Sengupta 1976). A wide variety of invertebrates is eaten, including worms (Oligochaeta and Polychaeta), snails (Gastropoda), crustaceans (Decapoda and Amphipoda), ticks (Acarina), spiders (Araneae), centipedes (Chilopoda), millipedes (Diplopoda) and insects. Representatives of most insect orders have been recorded in the Common Myna's diet but beetles and their larvae (Coleoptera), grasshoppers and crickets (Orthoptera), moths and butterflies and their larvae (Lepidoptera), flies and their larvae (Diptera), bees, wasps and ants (Hymenoptera) and bugs (Hemiptera) predominate. The Common Myna's capacity for eating grasshoppers and locusts lies behind the bird's introduction to some countries in the expectation that the mynas would control these pests. Vertebrates also appear in the diet, including frogs (Amphibia), geckos and lizards (Reptilia), eggs and nestlings of birds (Aves) and mice (Mammalia). Many other vertebrates are eaten in the form of carrion, and Davidar (1991) observed Common Mynas catching fish in drying pools.

Plant foods include the fruits and seeds of a wide variety of wild species, especially figs (*Ficus*), and the nectar of trees whose showy flowers attract birds, notably Silk Cotton (*Salmalia*), Coral (*Erythrina*) and Palas (*Butea*). Common Mynas also eat the fruits and seeds of many cultivated plants: Papaya (*Carica*), Dates (*Phoenix*), Apple (*Malus*), Pear (*Pyrus*), Tomato (*Solanum*), Strawberry (*Fragaria*), Grapes (*Vitis*), Guava (*Psidium*), Mango (*Mangifera*), Breadfruit and Jackfruit (*Artocarpus*), Maize (*Zea*), Wheat (*Triticum*) and Rice (*Oryza*) (Ali and Ripley 1972, Moeed 1976, Narang and

Lamba 1984, Sengupta 1976). Some of these fruits and seeds are eaten in sufficient quantity for farmers to regard Common Mynas as agricultural pests. In addition to these foods, Common Mynas forage at garbage dumps, taking offal and waste food (Kang 1989). Common Mynas drink frequently, sometimes even resorting to sea water from rock pools (Feare 1994a). After hatching, nestlings are fed for the first five or six days on soft insects and insect larvae. After this period other insects, including dragonflies (Odonata), butterflies, beetles, bugs and earthworms are brought by the parents and after the tenth day soft fruit is included in the nestlings' diet (Sengupta 1976).

MOVEMENTS Common Mynas are sedentary throughout their range. There is no information on the extent of dispersal of the young after fledging, but the movements of adults are very limited: ringed adults have been observed feeding 3 km from the roost while in Singapore radio-tagged birds flew on average only 0.4 km from the roost to feeding sites and occupied a home range of only 0.10 km² (Kang 1992).

BREEDING The breeding season of Common Mynas varies according to locality. The season extends from March–August in Central Asia (Dement'ev and Gladkov 1960). Over much of India breeding occurs mainly between April and July, the time of peak breeding perhaps depending on the onset of monsoons (Lamba 1963). For example, in Kerala breeding is concentrated in March–April, with some clutches as early as January (Lamba 1963) while in the plains of the lower Ganges breeding lasts from April to June (Sengupta 1982). In Dhaka, Bangladesh, breeding occurs in January–March, May–June and sometimes in September–November (Rahman and Hussain 1988). In west Malaysia, the breeding season lasts from February to August (Medway and Wells 1976) and is similar in Singapore, although Kang (1991) noted that courtship and pair-bonding occurred during much of the remainder of the year. In the introduced populations in Australia and New Zealand, breeding occurs from October to March–April (Macdonald 1973, Counsilman 1974). Common Mynas usually nest in holes. Natural nest sites include holes in trees, cliffs and earth banks, together with holes made by other birds and mammals. They also nest among the dense vegetation provided by the flowers of palm trees, such as coconut *Cocos nucifera* and oil palm *Elaeis* sp. In addition, they use man-made structures, like the eaves of houses, holes in walls and bridges, drain pipes, air conditioning vents, lamp posts, and used and obsolete vehicles and machinery (Ali and Ripley 1972, Kang 1989, 1990, Lamba 1963, Medway and Wells 1976, Sengupta 1982). Cup-shaped or domed nests are occasionally built in trees (Ali and Ripley 1972, Dhanda and Dhindsa 1996). Nest sites are usually 1.5–40 m above the ground (Cramp and Perrins 1994). The nest itself is an untidy mass of twigs, grass, leaves, straw and roots and may also contain animal hair, paper, cloth, string, plastic and other artefacts. The nest is built by both sexes, usually taking 1–2 weeks to complete. The eggs are clear

pale blue, sky blue or greenish-blue, glossy and without markings and measure 26.5–35.0 x 19.2–24.2 mm (125) (Schönwetter 1983). The clutch is normally 4–5 eggs but can vary from 2–6. Eggs are laid in the morning at about 24 hour intervals (Lamba 1963). Up to three clutches may be laid each year, the interval between clutches being 1–2 weeks (Dement'ev and Gladkov 1960, Lamba 1963). Incubation, by both sexes, lasts 13–18 days. Females incubate all night and take a greater share of daytime duties, but during the day, especially during the hotter part, eggs may be left uncovered (Counsilman 1974, Sengupta 1982, Dement'ev and Gladkov 1960). The eggs often hatch asynchronously and earlier hatched chicks are fed more and grow faster than later-hatched young (Sengupta 1968). The young fledge after 22–35 days but continue to beg food from the parents for several weeks (Eddinger 1967). Dhanda and Dhindsa (1996) found that birds that nested in nestboxes laid earlier and laid larger clutches than birds that nested in natural sites; nestbox breeders had a higher breeding success than birds in natural sites, but the difference was not significant.

BEHAVIOUR During the day Common Mynas generally live in pairs or are solitary. Larger aggregations into small or large flocks sometimes occur at feeding sites where food is plentiful, for example rubbish tips and trees in flower or fruit, and in pre-roost assemblies, but even here pairs are often distinguishable by their proximity to each other (Ali and Ripley 1972, Kang 1989, Lamba 1963, Sengupta 1982). Common Mynas roost communally at night, usually in trees (Hails 1984); these roosts may be small, comprising a few tens of birds in a single tree, or may be large with several thousand individuals occupying a group of trees (Counsilman 1974, Greig-Smith 1982, Kang 1989, Mahabal and Vaidya 1989). In some communal roosts, however, pairs clearly roost together (Feare *et al.* 1994). Roosts undergo seasonal variations in size, and the feeding areas used by birds from different roosts may overlap (Mahabal *et al.* 1990). Prior to roosting in the evening, birds gather nearby in pre-roost assemblies, which may be in trees, on the ground, especially in grassy areas (Mat and Davison 1984) such as playing fields and airfields and sometimes on buildings (CJF). During departure in the morning, birds may leave the roost singly, as pairs or in larger groups (Mat and Davison 1984). Common Mynas also roost communally with other species, especially other members of the starling family: White-vented Mynas and Asian Glossy Starlings (Hails 1987), Common Starlings (Counsilman 1974) and Rose-coloured Starlings (Ali and Ripley 1972). In addition, roosts with crows *Corvus*, parakeets *Psittacula* and sparrows *Passer* have been recorded (Ali and Ripley 1972, Gadgil 1972).

Breeding pairs defend territories around their nests but they sometimes nest close to each other (Eddinger 1967), occasionally even in large nesting colonies (Dement'ev and Gladkov 1960). Although Wilson (1963) reported Common Mynas in New Zealand both breeding and feeding within their territories, in most cases food is sought within a home range outside the boundaries of the defended territory around the nest (Kang 1992). In disputes, the most common form of threat involves crouching with the head and neck extended towards an opponent, and with the bill open; a bird in this posture may jab at the opponent. In disputes at territorial boundaries and sometimes in pre-roost assemblies, competing birds may jump into the air, apparently attempting to grasp each other with the claws. Overt fighting is unusual but involves pecking at each other, usually at the head, and sometimes wrestling on the ground when the two combatants have grasped each other (Counsilman 1977, Cramp and Perrins 1994). One of the most conspicuous behaviours of Common Mynas is bowing (Counsilman 1977). Both mated and unmated birds bow while foraging and in communal roosts, but bowing displays are most frequently performed by mated pairs within their territories. Bowing involves a lowering of the head with the scapulars, breast, neck and head feathers fluffed, the last producing a short crest. The wings are drooped and the tail spread. The extent of head lowering is variable, with the bill sometimes pointed downwards as though the bird was looking at something below, while other movements are more exaggerated with the bill down towards the feet or as if intending to preen the lower breast feathers. Head lowering and raising may be repeated several times in rapid succession, sometimes with much calling but at other times in silence. Bowing may be stimulated by the sudden landing of one bird close to another, but it is more usually performed when pairs are close together and both birds participate: in this context bowing appears to be a part of the pair-bonding process and may be followed by copulation. A second display between mated pairs, called 'placing' by Counsilman (1977) and 'billing' by Sengupta (1982), involves the pair standing together with their open bills touching or almost so, while crouching with necks stretched and calling: this behaviour may be followed by bowing.

Immediately before copulation the female crouches and remains still (Sengupta 1982) or raises her head and vibrates her tail from side to side (Counsilman 1977). The male mounts, balancing himself with partially spread wings, and lowers his tail to effect what Sengupta (1982) described as a 'cloacal kiss'. Pair-bonding may also be helped by allopreening, where members of a pair preen each other, usually on the head and especially the bare yellow skin around the eye. During courtship, male Common Mynas have been reported to present straw, grass and feathers to their mates (Eddinger 1967, Sengupta 1982), and green leaves have been seen to be taken into the nest and also to be carried into a roost (CJF). Common Mynas are believed to be monogamous and to pair for life (Wilson 1963).

RELATIONS WITH MAN In India, Common Mynas are so closely associated with man that reference to them is found in early literature and they play a part in traditions, legend and folklore, and even in some semi-religious customs (Sengupta 1982). They have also been held to be beneficial

to agriculture on account of their appetite for insect pests (Akhmedov 1957) but more recently, studies of economic losses of crops to birds have implicated Common Mynas in serious damage to ripening grapes *Vitis*, and they also damage other crops including cereals, pulses and fruit (Akhmedov 1957, Perumal *et al.* 1971, Toor and Ramzan 1994b, AICRP 1992). Concern has even been expressed that they destroy beneficial insects (Dupont 1930). Mishra *et al.* (1987) considered Common Mynas to be important seed dispersal agents of the neem tree *Azadirachta indica*, a tree valued for the ability of extracts to repel insects and other pests.

In Singapore, night roosts (in company with White-vented Mynas) are generally in trees but where these are close to human habitation, the loud noise of calling mynas as they enter the roost in the evening, as they prepare to leave in the morning, and sometimes as they wake for a chorus during the night, can be annoying to the human residents (Hails 1984). As a result, mynas are regarded as an urban pest and a variety of attempts has been made to deter them (Kang *et al.* 1990). The close association between Common Mynas and man has led this species to be introduced to many parts of the world, especially in the tropics. Introductions have been accidental, following escapes of cage birds, and deliberate, both for aesthetic reasons (for example by Acclimatisation Societies in Australia and New Zealand) and as a potential agent of biological pest control. In Mauritius, they were introduced to control plagues of grasshoppers and were alleged to have been successful in this, although other forms of control also contributed to the decline of the insect pests (Cheke 1987). They were introduced to the Seychelles from Mauritius, ostensibly for the same reason, although grasshoppers and locusts had never been a problem there (Dupont 1930). Pest control also lay behind introductions to some Polynesian islands (wasps), Madagascar (grasshoppers and other insects), Agalega (insects), Ascension (insects), St Helena (cattle ticks), Fiji (grasshoppers) and Hawaii (army worm and cutworm) (Lever 1987, McCullogh 1991). In the Andaman Islands, they were apparently introduced as scavengers to aid waste removal. Common Mynas have spread naturally to Tadjikistan, but once established, Akhmedov (1957) recommended the provision of nestboxes to encourage an increase in numbers, in the belief that they would control agricultural and forest insect pests.

Rarely have these beneficial aspects been realised and in many places mynas became crop pests, largely through their eating cultivated fruits (Hawaii, St Helena, Mauritius, Seychelles, Australia, New Zealand, South Africa) and groundnuts (Fiji). In Hawaii, they were implicated in the spread to pest proportions of an introduced fruiting plant *Lantana camara* (Storer 1931). Common Mynas eat the eggs of seabirds (terns *Sterna* and noddies *Anous* in Fiji and the Seychelles, gulls *Larus* in New Zealand), and even attack adult Black Noddies *Anous tenuirostris* and White Terns

Gygis alba on Midway Atoll (Grant 1982), but it is doubtful whether this predation has a serious impact on the seabird populations. However, at Kilauea Point on Kauai, Hawaii, Byrd (1979) found that 23% of Wedge-tailed Shearwater *Puffinus pacificus* eggs were taken by Common Mynas, which had entered their burrows. In New Zealand, Common Mynas also eat the eggs of other birds, but mainly of other introduced species (Lever 1987). Elsewhere, Common Mynas may have contributed to declines and even extinctions of endemic birds in Polynesia (Holyoak and Thibault 1984) and Hawaii (Warner 1968) where competition for food and nest sites, and the introduction of exotic parasites (e.g. the mite *Ornithonyssus bursa*) and diseases (e.g. avian malaria *Plasmodium circumflexum*) are considered to have been among the processes involved. On St Helena, McCullogh (1991) thought that Common Mynas may be nest predators of the Wirebird *Charadrius sanctaehelenae*, and might also compete with this threatened species for food.

An example of direct predation and interference by Common Mynas on island endemics occurs on Fregate Island, Seychelles, where Common Mynas are believed to take eggs and young of the endangered Seychelles Magpie Robin *Copsychus sechellarum* (Watson *et al.* 1992) and the presence of mynas close to its nest has been shown to disrupt its incubation (Komdeur 1996). Part of the BirdLife International recovery programme for the Magpie Robin involves augmenting the birds' food supply when breeding, and Common Mynas compete for some of this food (Adam Gretton pers. comm.). As a result, a myna control programme has now been implemented. On Mauritius, Common Mynas compete for nest holes with the critically endangered Echo Parakeet *Psittacula eques* (Jones 1996), and Jones (pers. comm.) has also recorded an instance where a myna attacked a half-grown young Echo Parakeet which subsequently died, and has recorded mynas displacing Mauritius Kestrels *Falco punctatus* from nest sites. In South Africa, Common Mynas have been linked to outbreaks of dermatitis in humans, caused by the mite *Ornithonyssus bursa* (Liversidge 1975).

50 VINOUS-BREASTED MYNA *Acridotheres burmannicus* Plate 12

Jerdon's Starling, Vinous-breasted Starling

Sturnia burmannica Jerdon 1862

FIELD IDENTIFICATION Length 21–24 cm. The head nape and breast are dirty white. The back and wing-coverts are dark grey-brown and underparts purplish or wine-coloured. The primaries and tail are blackish, but the bases of the primaries are white, producing a white wing patch which is conspicuous in flight. The rectrices are broadly tipped white or buff, especially towards the outer feathers. The bill is red with the lower mandible black at the base. The iris is pale, appearing white. Immatures are duller with a brown crown. According to Smythies (1953) the plumage varies seasonally.

DESCRIPTION The feathers of the forehead and crown are hackled and elongate, dirty white. Chin, throat and upper breast are white. Lower breast and belly are vinous, becoming paler in the central belly and undertail-coverts, greyer on the flanks. Mantle, back and rump greyish-brown, sometimes showing a little gloss on the back. Tail brown, outer feathers increasingly blackish but with progressively broader white tips. Primaries chocolate brown, darker proximally but with white bases. Secondaries and secondary coverts pale brown with dark margins. Underwing-coverts white. Bill orange-red with basal half of lower mandible dark blackish; legs orange-yellow or orange-flesh; iris brown and bare skin in front of, below and behind the eye slaty-black.

In *A. b. leucocephalus*, of southern Thailand, Cambodia and southern Indochina, the top of the head is greyer, producing a pale collar round the hindneck. Back, tail and wings are darker, but the rump is vinous-white or white, the breast and belly pinker, and the tail tip is often buff or vinous; the bill is yellow with a red base and the iris variable in colour — yellow, brown, pale brown, grey or black. There is some variability in birds from different areas. Some specimens from southern Shan State, Burma are largely mouse-grey, darker on the throat and grey-brown, less vinous, below, and with dark wings, while some birds from Tenasserim, Burma, have the forehead and crown chocolate-grey, dark grey throat and pale rump.

MEASUREMENTS Male (5): wing 112–122, tail 72–87, tarsus 31–34, culmen 19–20; female (4): wing 111–115, tail 73–78, 31–33, culmen 19–20.

VOICE Described as a chattering note given when feeding (Smythies 1953). Calls are very similar to those of Common Myna (Komolphalin pers. comm.)

DISTRIBUTION AND POPULATION An endemic resident of Burma, southwest, northeast, southeast and central Thailand, Cambodia, Cochinchina, southern Annam and south and central Laos (King *et al.* 1975), and rare in western Yunnan, China (Cheng 1987). It is widely distributed in Burma, where it occurs to 2000 m (Smythies 1953). In Thailand it is a locally common resident, but is uncommon in some areas (Boonsong and Round 1991). It may be spreading into peninsular Thailand following deforestation (Round *in litt.*).

HABITAT It is a predominantly ground-dwelling species, inhabiting open grassland, gardens, cultivation and scrub (Smythies 1953), and favours especially well-watered short grass on lawns and playing fields (Boonsong and Round 1991).

FOOD AND FEEDING Feeds mainly on the ground but also in trees (Baker 1926).

BREEDING Nests in holes in trees, under eaves and in thatched roofs. The breeding season is concentrated in April–June but second broods occur up to August (Smythies 1953). The nest is described as untidy. The eggs are dark 'thrush-like' blue with some gloss (Baker 1926) and measure 23.6–29.5 x 18.9–23.0 mm (74) (Schönwetter

1983). Nothing is known of parental care.

MIGRATION While generally thought to be resident, Smythies recorded movements to Rangoon in cold weather, and in Thailand it may also make local movements as its presence in a given area cannot be predicted (Komolphalin pers. comm.).

BEHAVIOUR Vinous-breasted Mynas feed in flocks and roost communally in reedbeds, bamboo and sugar cane (Smythies 1953). In the evening they assemble in large noisy flocks (Baker 1926).

51 BLACK-WINGED MYNA *Acridotheres melanopterus*   Plate 12
Black-winged Starling, White-breasted Starling

Gracula melanoptera Daudin 1800

FIELD IDENTIFICATION 22–24 cm. A largely white myna with black wings and tail. The head feathers are elongated to form an erectile crest. The bases of the primaries are white, forming a white patch in the open wing, and the tip of the tail is white, increasingly so on the outer feathers. The bill, legs and feet are yellow, as is a circumorbital ring of bare skin that extends behind the eye as a triangle. The sexes are alike but in juveniles the crown, nape and mantle are grey. It differs from Bali Myna in having yellow, not blue, bare skin around the eye, yellow bill and legs, and a black tail with a white tip, rather than a white tail with a black tip, more black in the wings, and, in some areas, grey or black on the mantle and back.

DESCRIPTION The head, mantle, back, wing-coverts, breast, belly and undertail-coverts are white, the head sometimes suffused ochre. Feathers of forehead, crown and nape are hackled, and those of the nape are elongate. The primaries are black, slightly glossed bronze-green, but with white bases, and the primary coverts are white. The secondaries are black, as is the largest alula. The tail is black with white tips progressively broader towards outer rectrices. The bill is yellow; legs yellow, and iris dark brown. The circumorbital skin is yellow, extending behind the eye in a small triangle. In immatures, the feathers of the forehead, crown and centre of the nape are grey-brown, while the sides of the crown, nape, chin and cheeks are dirty white. The mantle and median coverts are grey-brown, edged with buffish-grey, giving a somewhat mottled appearance, and some mantle feathers have dark shafts. The bases of the primaries are white, but the primary coverts are white with black tips to the inner webs. The breast, belly, lower back and rump are white. This description refers to **A. m. melanopterus**, which occurs over most of Java, except for the southeast peninsula, and on Madura.

A. m. tricolor, of the southeastern peninsula of Java east of Tosari (Mees 1996), has the lower back grey and broad black edges to the otherwise white upperwing-coverts.

A. m. tertius, of Bali, has the mantle, back, and

wing-coverts charcoal-grey, the rump and upper-tail-coverts slightly paler, and the thighs and flanks smoky. Mees (1996) reported an individual of *tricolor* in west Java, within the range of the nominate form, concluding that this was an escaped cagebird, but on Bali J S Ash (*in litt.*) found substantial variation in plumage; further studies of large numbers in the field are needed to verify the current subspecific taxonomy.

MEASUREMENTS Male (4): wing 126–129, tail 76–81, tarsus 36–39, culmen 19–21; female (5): wing 120–127, tail 72–80, tarsus 36–37, culmen 18–19.

VOICE Calls have been described as harsh scratchy notes (J S Ash *in litt.*) and harsh whistles (Harrison 1963b). Feare and Kang (1992) described the calls as loud and varied, of the same quality and often very similar to those of Common and White-vented Mynas. They included a repeated *cha cha cha*, each note with a downward inflection, a throaty *tok* or *chok*, a harsh *kaar kaar*, a harsh drawn out *kreeer*, a frequently given disyllabic *kishaa kishaa* and other whistles and squawks. On take-off, a high-pitched whistling *tsoowit* or *tsoowee* flight call was given and a *kaar* alarm call was heard once. Bursts of calling often interrupted feeding bouts, the calls often consisting of disyllabic notes similar to those of Common Myna and calling by one bird often stimulated the presumed mate to duet in response.

DISTRIBUTION AND POPULATION Resident on Java, Bali and Lombok, Indonesia. They are common and widespread on Java and Bali but only accidental visitors (White and Bruce 1986) or local residents (J S Ash, *in litt.*) on Lombok. A breeding population, most likely derived from escaped cagebirds, has survived for some time on St John's Island, Singapore (Hails 1987), although the population in 1990 was much reduced (Feare and Kang 1992) and by 1994 was thought to be extinct (Kang Nee pers. comm.); it has been recorded breeding on Singapore (C J Hails *in litt.*).

HABITAT It frequents cultivated areas (de Wiljes 1957), fruit farms, fallow fields, grass lawns

162

(MacKinnon 1990) and open grass savannas but not (contrary to Delacour 1947) gardens (van Helvoordt *in litt.*). In Java, Mees (1996) claimed that it is 'not rare', especially in the northern lowlands, but it is more patchily distributed inland. It is common and widespread to 1200 m on Bali but occurs mainly at lower and middle altitudes and especially in the cultivated areas of the southern peninsula and adjoining areas (J S Ash *in litt.*). However, it is spreading in Bali as man's cultivations expand and its range there now overlaps with that of Bali Myna in the northwest of the island (Sieber 1978).

FOOD AND FEEDING In Singapore, Hails (1987) regarded Black-winged Myna as mainly arboreal but on St Johns Island they spent much time feeding on the ground in grassland and on the beach, but also took fruit and insects in trees and bushes (Feare and Kang 1992). On the ground Black-winged Mynas pecked at items in the vegetation and made dashes at more mobile prey. They probed in the ground near a termite mound and on the beach pecked at small items on the strand line and chased prey in *Ipomoea* bushes at the top of the beach. In trees and bushes they took nectar, especially from the Madras Thorn *Pithecellobium dulce*, fruits from *Fagraea fragrans* and *Eugenia longiflora* and insects gleaned from leaves. They also probed into the bases of terminal rosettes of *Casuarina* and into ripe pods of the Madras Thorn. A 5 cm mantid (Orthoptera) was taken from a bush and dismembered on the ground before being eaten. On Java and Bali it eats ripe fruits of *Morus indica*, *Manilkara kauki*, *Passiflora foetida* and *Strychnos ligustrina* (Sieber 1978) and is believed to compete for the same foods as Bali Myna in areas of overlap on Bali.

BREEDING Nests are built in holes in rocks (de Wiljes 1957) and in holes in *Acacia* trees (van Helvoordt *in litt.*). The nest itself has not been described. Eggs are clear blue without markings, measuring 26.5–27.9 x 19.0–20.0 mm (9) (Schönwetter 1983). Clutches of 3 or 4 eggs have been recorded (Sody 1930; Hoogerwerf and Hellebrekens 1967). Black-winged Mynas breed in March-May in west Java (Hoogerwerf and Hellebrekens 1967), June in east Bali (Sody 1930) and February on Bali (van Helvoordt *in litt.*).

BEHAVIOUR Black-winged Mynas breed colonially (de Wiljes 1957). They occur mainly singly or in pairs on Bali, although flocks of 3 to 10 are common and up to 50 have been recorded (J S Ash *in litt.*). They roost communally in tall trees and, now that ranges overlap, they have been recorded roosting with Bali Mynas (Sieber 1978). In a captive pair one bird, believed male, stood erect between song bouts, fluffed its belly and flank feathers, spread its tail, raised its crown feathers and repeatedly bowed its head until its bill almost touched the lower belly. This behaviour appeared to be accompanied by subdued vocalisation (Harrison 1963b). On St Johns Island, Singapore, Feare and Kang (1992) frequently saw Black-winged Mynas bowing. *Tok* calls were often accompanied by bobbing of the head with the short crest erected and the cheeks puffed out. While preening and resting, members of a pair periodically came together and sometimes one of the birds (sex unknown) pointed its bill down towards the breast and at the same time bobbed its body up and down. A more exaggerated form of this behaviour was seen in a pre-roost assembly and during song, when the crest was raised, the bill pushed down into the breast feathers and the whole body bobbed at each bow; these bows seemed to elicit little response from the other member of the pair. Immediately prior to roosting, one pair sat on a branch with bodies touching and touched bills briefly. Harrison (1963) recorded allopreening in captive birds.

RELATION WITH MAN This species is commonly sold in markets in Java (Morrison 1980) and is kept as a cagebird. It is imported for this purpose into Britain (Trollope 1987).

Concern has been expressed that Black-winged Mynas may compete for food and nest sites with the endangered Bali Myna. A study of the two species and their relationships in the area of range overlap is clearly needed.

52 BALI MYNA *Leucopsar rothschildi*   Plate 12
Bali Starling, Rothschild's Myna

Leucopsar rothschildi Stresemann 1906

FIELD IDENTIFICATION 25 cm. A largely white myna with black tips to the wings and tail, a blue patch of bare skin around the eye and a long erectile crest. In flight, the Bali Myna is stocky, with rounded wings and a short tail, similar in silhouette to *Acridotheres* mynas. The black tips to the primaries appear as a black band around the end of the rounded wing, clearly differentiating Bali Myna from Black-winged Myna. The sexes are similar but the crest is longer in the male than in females. Young birds lack or have a much shorter crest.

DESCRIPTION The entire body is white. Feathers of the forehead and on the upper mandible down to the nares are bristled. The feathers of the crown and nape are hackled and greatly elongated, especially in males, to form a long erectile crest. The tail is white except for a black tip, c. 1.5 cm broad on the central feathers and somewhat narrower towards the outer rectrices. The secondaries are white, the primaries are tipped black, with only a small area of black on the inner primary, increasing to c. one-third of the inner margin and half of the outer margin of the outer large (ninth) primary. The inner webs of the primaries have inwardly directed notches. Bright cobalt or lavender blue bare skin around the eye extends to a point behind the eye. The heavy bill has a strongly curved culmen and is grey or brown, paler yellow or horn towards the tip. The legs are pale leaden blue, the iris grey, whitish or brown. Immatures are similar to adults but with a much shorter crest; in fledglings it is little more than a fluffy appearance to the crown feathers. Immatures may also show a smoky tinge to the back and a cinnamon tinge on the wings.

MEASUREMENTS Male (4) wing 132–133, tail 82–88, tarsus 35–40, culmen 25–26; female (3): wing 132–135, tail 79–87, tarsus 36–37, culmen 23–27.

VOICE The song consists of a wide variety of loud chattering notes, including chuckles, squawks, whistles and piercing high-pitched notes. All of these lack the fluty resonance and repetitive di- and trisyllabic notes of *Acridotheres* mynas (CJF), although von Plessen (1926) likened the calls to those of Asian Pied Myna, but interspersed with shriller and more piercing notes. Song is given by both sexes and is often delivered without display. During bobbing display, a quieter chattering may be given, and a captive male sometimes gave a resonant, throaty, repeated *kwo-kwo, kwo-kwo, kwo-kwo* when the female emerged from the nest hole. On take-off, a *creer* flight call, similar to that of *Acridotheres* mynas is given, and in flight a louder *kwuk-kwi*, with a squeaky quality is sometimes delivered. A captive female gave a harsh *kraar-si*, the last syllable being very loud and piercing. The alarm call is a loud *tshick tshick tshick*. A fledgling made a *schwick* call in the presence of its parents.

DISTRIBUTION AND POPULATION
Endemic to the island of Bali, Indonesia. At the time of the species' discovery in 1911 (Stresemann 1912), it occurred along the northwestern coastal strip of Bali from the northwest tip to Bubunan, a distance of about 50 km. In the 1920s, von Plessen (1926) found it 'in hundreds', occasionally up into high mountains but never in areas inhabited by man. Its range has now contracted to about 60 km² in the Bali Barat Nature Reserve in the northwestern point of Bali. The population is very difficult to estimate. There are no estimates of numbers in the early part of this century but it appears that the bird has never been numerous. In the late 1970s and early 1980s, the population appeared to be about 200 birds (de Iongh *et al.* 1982, van Helvoordt *et al.* 1985). Since then, the population declined to 47 birds in 1988 and 28 individuals in 1989, largely as a result of illegal trapping (MacKinnon and MacKinnon 1991). The wild population decreased further to c. 15 individuals in 1990, this figure including 13 birds which had been released as part of a recovery programme (van Balen and Gepak 1994). Numbers subsequently increased, post-breeding censuses in 1991 and 1992 revealing c. 35 and 55 birds respectively. Some of the captive-bred birds that

were released after being fitted with transponders have been found in the possession of a local bird dealer (van Balen and Gepak 1994) and in 1998 only 14 were thought to survive in the wild (Anon 1998). Bali Mynas survive in captivity and in zoos, bird parks and private collections, the captive population may be more than 700 individuals (van Balen and Gepak 1994).

HABITAT The main habitat occupied by Bali Mynas in northwest Bali comprises open woodland with a grass understory, ranging from tree savannah (tall grass with solitary trees) to woodland (dominated by trees but with tree crowns not touching and with an understory of grass). Seasonal and evergreen forest are avoided (van Helvoordt *et al.* 1985).

FOOD AND FEEDING Eats seeds, fruit and animal food, mainly insects but including worms and small reptiles. Plant food includes small berries of *Lantana camara* and *Deeringia amaranthoides*, larger berries of Passion Fruit *Passiflora foetida* and *Manilkara kauki* to larger fruits of figs *Ficus* sp., *Morus* sp. and pawpaw *Carica papaya*, and seeds of the deciduous tree *Sterculia foetida*. Insects include caterpillars, ants (Hymenoptera) and termites (Isoptera), dragonflies (Odonata) and grasshoppers (Orthoptera), these being eaten mainly during the rainy season (de Iongh 1983).

BREEDING Breeds during the rainy season, January–March (de Iongh 1983) or April (van Helvoordt *et al.* 1985). They nest in holes, often in trees where old woodpecker holes are most commonly used. Nest holes have been recorded at 4–10m above ground level and the nest is lined with dry twigs. The clutch usually consists of 2–3 eggs which are pale blue, without spots or rarely with faint brown spots (Sieber 1983). Generally only one chick survives to fledging (de Iongh 1983). In captivity, breeding can continue over several months, with repeat and replacement clutches leading to up to four young produced annually per pair (de Iongh *et al.* 1982). They adapt well to nest boxes of various kinds, in which they usually place some lining, using a wide variety of material (van Helvoordt *et al.* 1985). Both sexes usually participate in building with the male playing the greater part; the female may complete the lining (van Helvoordt *et al.* 1985). Clutch size in captive pairs is usually 3 eggs but 1–5 are recorded (Sieber 1983, van Helvoordt *et al.* 1985). Eggs measure 27.2–33.4 x 19.0–24.0 mm (69) (Schönwetter 1983, Sieber 1983). Incubation lasts normally 12–14 days and is performed mainly by the female; she incubates throughout the night and plays the greater part during the day. Only the female broods the young chicks at night but both sexes share the feeding, approximately equally. The fledging period ranges from 21–28 days although 22–24 days appears usual (van Helvoordt *et al.* 1985). After fledging, young continue to be fed by the parents but at 4–5 weeks old the young begin to feed themselves, and at 6–7 weeks parental feeding stops. There appears to be a decline in fecundity with age, and females older than 11 years have not been recorded laying eggs (West and Pugh 1986).

BEHAVIOUR More arboreal than other mynas, although they do sometimes feed, drink and bathe on the ground (Sontag 1992). From April to December, Bali Mynas can be gregarious, forming flocks numbering up to 40 birds (de Iongh 1983), although even during this period pairs spend most of their time together. At night they roost communally, arriving at the roost site in flocks of 2–6 birds. Overnight roosts may be in tall trees, such as the Tamarind *Tamarindus indicus* (de Iongh 1983) and dense Coconut *Cocos nucifera* (van der Zon 1980), or in shrubby undergrowth at a height of 2–4 metres (van Helvoordt *et al.* 1985). Black-winged Mynas sometimes roost with Bali Mynas but the two species generally occupy different parts of the roost; aggression is sometimes seen between the two species. Within communal roosts, pairs of Bali Mynas roost together (van Helvoordt *et al.* 1985). Bali Mynas also roost communally during daytime and Ash (1984) recorded 26 birds roosting with Black-winged Mynas and Asian Pied Mynas. During the breeding season, Bali Myna pairs become territorial and communal roosts largely disappear, suggesting that the birds roost on their territories. At this time of year Bali Mynas are reported to be aggressive and to defend large territories but this requires substantiation. Between members of pairs allopreening is common. This is often directed towards the blue periorbital skin (Harrison 1963a) and to the throat, back and sides of the neck and to the crest (West and Pugh 1986). Allopreening also occurs between unmated males (Hughes and Turner 1975). Pairs also perform bobbing displays in which the birds stand upright with belly and flank feathers fluffed out. The head is thrown back so that the bill points upwards, the bill is then thrust forward and finally brought down almost to the horizontal while the crest is erected. This movement is reminiscent of choking or regurgitation, and movements of the throat sometimes accentuate this impression (CJF). During this display the bird bobs up and down (Harrison 1963b); bobbing may be restricted to the head and breast, but in intense display the entire body may bob up and down, vigorously shaking the branch upon which the bird is sitting (CJF), and 1-10 bobs may be made in succession (West and Pugh 1986). While both members of a pair may perform this display, males are more active. Bali Mynas may also bob alone, and it is often performed by a bird when its mate emerges from the nest (Hughes and Turner 1975, CJF). According to Harrison, neither bird calls but CJF heard a low chattering from displaying pairs, and Hughes and Turner (1975) and West and Pugh (1986) described calls that accompanied bobbing, concluding with a low growl.

Bali Mynas sometimes make bowing movements but these are never as ritualised as in *Acridotheres* mynas and are often followed by preening. When standing close to a mate, a bird exposes its crest by bowing (which West and Pugh (1986) called 'head-dipping'), or by turning its bill away from the mate, thereby presenting the back of the head and the erected crest (West and Pugh 1986). These authors thought that allopreening, bowing and turning away were behaviours involved in pair maintenance, while bobbing may be more concerned with advertisement of territory ownership. Females solicit copulation by sideways vibration of the tail (Hughes and Turner 1975), as in the genera *Gracula, Acridotheres* and *Sturnus.*

RELATIONS WITH MAN While Bali Mynas have never been widely distributed since their discovery in 1912, their distribution and population size have been reduced by man's activities. Their habitat has been eroded by forest destruction as human settlements have encroached on their breeding area and collection of firewood within protected areas continues to be a threat (van Helvoordt 1987). In 1925, von Plessen (1926) reported that other myna species were rare in the region occupied by Bali Mynas, but now Black-winged Mynas are common in the area and van Helvoordt (1987) considered that the two species may compete for nest sites; the numbers of Black-winged Mynas may have increased in response to habitat modification. Illegal collecting of birds for the captive bird trade, however, probably constitutes the main threat. To counter the decline in numbers, a survival programme was inaugurated in 1987, involving the International Council for Bird Preservation (now BirdLife International), the American Association of Zoological Parks and Aquaria, the Jersey Wildlife Preservation Trust and the Indonesian Government. This programme involves research on Bali Mynas in the wild, management within the Bali Barat reserve and captive breeding, aimed at maintaining genetic diversity within the captive stock (Ashworth and Parkin 1992) and at rearing sufficient individuals for a release programme. In addition, the Indonesian Government has introduced a new law that decrees that all protected animals are the property of the state and had to be registered before 31 October 1992; people found in possession of an unregistered Bali Myna after that date are liable to imprisonment or to a substantial fine (Anon 1992b). Despite these attempts to prevent the capture of birds from the wild, individuals that have been reared in captivity, and fitted with micro-tags before release to augment the wild population, have been recovered in bird shops (van Balen and Gepak 1994). The wild population now stands at only 14 birds (Anon 1998), and until the birds' security within the reserve can be guaranteed, conservation actions by international organisations and by the Indonesians themselves will be fruitless.

53 BLACK-COLLARED MYNA *Gracupica nigricollis*   Plate 13
Black-collared Starling, Black-necked Starling

Gracula nigricollis Paykull 1807

FIELD IDENTIFICATION 26–30 cm. Adult: A large pied starling. The head, throat, belly and rump are white, the back dark brown (almost black), and the collar black. The tail is black with a white tip; wings black but with white bases to the primaries, producing a white wing patch. White areas of the plumage usually appear dirty. The orbital skin, legs and feet are yellow. Immature: Upperparts are browner than in the adult, the head and belly are brownish-grey with some white streaking, and there is no black collar. Differs from Asian Pied Myna in its large size and white, rather than black, head.

DESCRIPTION Sexes similar. The forehead, crown, chin and throat are white. Feathers of the forehead and crown are hackled. The collar on the hindneck, sides and front of neck are black with slight iridescence. The mantle and back are dark chocolate-brown, almost black in fresh plumage, and the rump white. The lower breast, belly and undertail-coverts are white. White areas are often tinged with grey-brown, looking dirty. The tail is chocolate-brown, rectrices tipped white, these tips becoming progressively broader on outer feathers. The primaries and secondaries are chocolate brown, secondaries tipped with white. The primary coverts are white, secondary coverts blackish-brown but with outer feathers tipped white and median coverts blackish-brown, tipped white. The bill is blackish, legs and feet yellowish and the iris is pale grey. Bare yellow skin around eye extends to a triangle behind the eye. Young birds lack the black collar, the head, neck and breast are brownish-grey, streaked white, and the back is browner than in the adult. Monotypic.

MEASUREMENTS Male (8): wing 153–160, tail 93–104, tarsus 39–44, culmen 25–29; female (8): wing 146–162, tail 86–99, tarsus 37–41, culmen 25–29.

VOICE Very vocal with shrill rattles and melodious notes. Bourlière (1953) reported a disyllabic *tiu tiu* given during displays between two birds. Smythies (1981) described a harsh *kraak kraak* reminiscent of a Jay *Garrulus glandarius*.

DISTRIBUTION A resident of southern China, from northern Fukien west to south and west Yunnan, Burma, Laos, Vietnam, Cambodia and Thailand apart from the southernmost part of the peninsula. Deforestation appears to be allowing the species to extend its range down the peninsula. There is a single record from Brunei (Elkin *et al.* 1993), though the possibility of this being an escaped captive must be recognised.

HABITAT The Black-collared Myna is a ground living starling of open grassland, rice stubbles, lawns, cultivated areas and human habitation. It also occurs in dry stunted forest. It is mainly a bird of the plains in Burma but occurs to 2000 m

(Etchécopar and Hüe 1983, Deignan 1945, Smythies 1981).

FOOD AND FEEDING In Burma, the diet consists primarily of grasshoppers and crickets (Smythies 1981) while in Thailand Deignan (1945) recorded them eating seeds, earthworms and other small items obtained primarily on the ground. He also noted that Black-collared Mynas fed among grazing cattle.

BREEDING In northern Thailand, breeding occurs throughout the hot dry season, from February to May, while Herbert (1923) stated that breeding followed the rains. In China, Black-collared Mynas breed from March to July (Etchécopar and Hüe 1983) while in Burma the season extends from April to June, with second broods until August (Smythies 1981). The nest is a large, untidy domed structure placed in the tops of trees in fields or around field edges. Black-collared Mynas often nest in colonies in China (Etchécopar and Hüe 1983) and the same nests may be used in successive years (Smythies 1981). Nests are built of fine twigs, rice straw and grasses, lined with feathers, grass and flowers (Wang *et al.* 1983). Eggs measure 29.3–37.4 x 21.5–25.0 mm (132) (Schönwetter 1983) and are unmarked blue or blue-green. The clutch consists of 3–5 eggs. Parental care has not been described but breeding may be synchronised within colonies as in May–June Deignan (1945) reported that recently-fledged birds were everywhere.

BEHAVIOUR Bourlière (1953) described two kinds of behaviour seen in Thailand in late March. These were performed in the early morning among small groups of birds, most of them apparently paired, on the ground. The first involved two birds standing facing each other, with ruffled breast feathers and open bills, almost touching. This posture was held for about 10 seconds and was accompanied by song, although Bourlière was unable to ascertain whether the two notes of the song were given by one bird or whether the two birds duetted. In the second display, two birds faced each other or stood side by side with feathers fluffed out, wings drooped and bills pointing slightly downwards. In this position both birds bowed their heads. Harrison (1963) recorded bowing in a captive individual, in which the bill was lowered towards the breast and sometimes touched it, and he remarked on the conspicuous raising of the crown feathers during this display. Between the two behaviours described by Bourlière, the members of duos, presumably pairs, chased each other on the ground or in flight, and also indulged in mutual allopreening. Black-collared Mynas roost communally at night (Smythies 1981).

54 ASIAN PIED MYNA *Gracupica contra*

Plate 13

Pied Starling

Sturnus contra Linnaeus 1758

FIELD IDENTIFICATION 21–24 cm. Asian Pied Mynas are about the same size as Common Mynas and are superficially similar to Black-collared Mynas in having a contrasting black and white plumage, but are smaller than this species. Differs from White-cheeked Starling in having clearer white cheeks, blacker back, wings and tail, and a clear demarcation between the black breast and white belly. The head, neck, throat and breast are black, but the cheeks are white. The rump and underparts are white, shading to greyish on the lower breast. The wings and tail are blackish-brown although the white edges to the median coverts form a white line on the closed wing. The bill tip is pale yellow or horn while the base of the bill and a patch of bare facial skin around the eye are bright orange-red. Juveniles lack the white on the forehead and are browner. The legs and feet are pale yellow or straw-coloured. The iris is white or straw. In flight Asian Pied Myna is round-winged and flight is slow and butterfly-like.

DESCRIPTION Sexes similar. The head, back, tail, throat and upper breast are black. Feathers of the forehead and crown are hackled, those of the hindcrown and nape slightly elongated but not hackled; these feathers have slight iridescence, as do those on the chin and throat. On the sides of the neck and nape some feathers have white shafts and greyish webs, producing faint streaking. The cheeks are white behind the eye, forming a white patch. The mantle is dark chocolate-brown. Lower breast, belly and undertail-coverts greyish-white; rump white. Tail black. Wings black, but white edges to secondary coverts and white median coverts form white wingbar. Bill red with light horn or yellow tip; legs and feet yellowish-brown; iris brownish-orange or orange-buff; bare skin around eye orange. Young birds are generally browner and lack iridescence, and the cheek patch is dirty white and browner to the lower and posterior borders.

G. c. sordidus, of northern Assam, has less pronounced streaking to the sides of the neck and none on the nape, and the underparts are greyer.

G. c. superciliaris, of Manipur and Burma south to Tenasserim, has the forehead and forecrown streaked with white, and the lower breast and belly are smoky-grey.

G. c. floweri, of southern Burma, Thailand and Laos, has the hackled feathers of the forehead and crown buffy-white, and the black feathers of the mantle, throat and upper breast are more glossy, legs paler.

G. c. jalla, of Sumatra, Java and Bali, is whiter below and has more extensive bare orange skin around the eye.

MEASUREMENTS Male (sample sizes not given): wing 116–126, tail 63–75, tarsus 32–35, bill 30–35; female: wing 114–120, tail 64–72, tarsus 32–34, bill 31–33; wt (7 male/female) 72–82 g (Ali and Ripley 1972).

VOICE The song is a prolonged sequence of phrases, similar to but more melodic than that of Common Myna. Other calls consist of wheezing and chuckling notes, and long whistles and high-pitched warbling. They also mimic the calls of other birds (Roberts 1992). In Thailand, they give myna-like disyllabic *cheek cheurk* calls and pairs when sitting side by side and bowing gave trisyllabic descending *treek treek treek* calls, again myna-like; on take-off they gave trisyllabic flight calls (CJF). Both sexes sing, and loud warning calls *staar-staar* and shrill alarm calls *shree-shree* or *keet-keet* are given (Meier 1988).

DISTRIBUTION AND POPULATION Extends from Lohore, Pakistan, east across the northern plains and south to Karnataka State, India. Further east it occurs in Bangladesh, Burma, Malaysia, western Yunnan, western Thailand and northern Laos, and western Indonesia (Sumatra, Java and Bali). Asian Pied Mynas are thought to be resident but they appear to be currently extending their range westwards into Pakistan (Roberts 1992). They are inhabitants mainly of plains and foothills to 700 m (Ali and Ripley 1972). In Sumatra they may have spread in response to the extension of cultivation and deforestation (van Marle and Voous 1988). An introduced population breeds in the United Arab Emirates, and may also do so in Jeddah, Saudi Arabia (Jennings 1991).

HABITAT Occur in open areas with scattered trees, usually with moist ground and often near human habitation and cultivation, but enter built up areas less than Black-collared Starlings (CJF). They frequent wet grazing areas and feed among cattle, but rarely settle on their backs. They are frequently seen at sewage farms and refuse tips.

FOOD AND FEEDING Feed predominantly on the ground, in marshy grassland, lawns and fields, especially rice stubbles, where they eat mainly insects and cereal grain. They follow cattle, eating insects they disturb, and also follow the plough. They eat figs *Ficus*, fruits of *Zizyphus*, *Syzygium* and *Lantana camara* and take nectar from flowers of *Salmalia* and *Erythrina*. They also take flower parts of *Butea* and *Grevillea*. Potato *Solanum tuberosum* may come from human waste, and wheat grains *Triticum* originate from stored grain and from germinating crops. Asian Pied Mynas have been recorded eating frogs (Amphibia), earthworms (Annelida) and snails (Mollusca). Invertebrates eaten include grasshoppers, crickets and mole crickets (Orthoptera), earwigs (Dermaptera), cockroaches (Dictyoptera), termites (Isoptera), bugs (Hemiptera), flies (Diptera), a variety of beetles (Coleoptera), ants, bees and wasps (Hymenoptera), cutworms and caterpillars

(Lepidoptera), ticks (Ixodidae) and spiders (Araneae) (Ali and Ripley 1972, Narang and Lamba 1984, Roberts 1992).

BREEDING In India, the breeding season lasts from late February to late August and may start later in years when winter rains are prolonged. Most nests are active in May. The Asian Pied Myna is unusual among starlings in building a large domed nest, 60–80 cm wide and 35–50 cm high with a 6–8 cm diameter entrance hole in the side. Nests are built 5–15m high in tall trees of many species (Pandey 1991). Nests may also be built on telegraph or electricity poles, especially in urban areas (Gupta and Bajaj 1991) and Naik (1987) recorded a nest in a street lamp in Bombay. Nests are built of a wide range of materials, including twigs, stems, grasses, feathers and materials of human origin, such as plastic wires and bags, wool, string, clothing, cellophane, wire etc. (Gupta and Bajaj 1991). The nest chamber is lined with finer material of similar origin. Rarely, bulky open nests may be built. Both parents are involved in nest construction, mainly in the early morning, but the male devotes more time to collecting materials while the female does most of the building. Nests are completed in 11–22 days. The clutch consists of 3–6, normally 4–5 eggs which are pale blue and unmarked, with a slight gloss, and measure 24.2–31.8 x 18.3–21.1 mm (170) (Schönwetter 1983). Most eggs are laid in the morning and the interval between eggs is 24h. Incubation, mainly by the female during the day and entirely by her at night, takes 14–15 days (although Meier (1988) recorded an incubation period of only 12 days in captivity). Hatching success is high, 87–92% over 4 years. Chicks are fed by both parents but the female plays the greater part and both parents remove faecal sacs, which they eat during the early days of the nestlings' life. Older nestlings defaecate out of the nest entrance.

They fledge at 21–25 days. Fledging success over five years was 52–58%. Second broods occur occasionally, in late June and early July.

BEHAVIOUR Usually found feeding in pairs or small parties of 3–6 birds, and in groups of up to 30 birds when not breeding (Ali and Ripley 1972, Roberts 1992). At night they roost communally, Roberts (1992) recording a roost of 300 birds. Asian Pied Mynas defend a relatively large territory around the nest. While two pairs may nest in a single tree, nests are in this instance 10–12m apart, and generally nests are 14–300m apart. In the presence of potential predators, members of neighbouring pairs cooperate in defence. Evidence from ringed birds suggests that Asian Pied Mynas do not pair for life. Male courtship display involves fluffing out the feathers and head-bobbing (Tyagi and Lamba 1984). Apparent pair-bonding behaviour is common out of the breeding season: in Thailand, pairs frequently sat close to each other and indulged in bowing, often with one bird sitting slightly above the other. The upper bird bowed more frequently and more intensively than the lower. Asian Pied Mynas were also seen to sing with the bill held open and the head rocking backwards and forwards. Birds sitting alone periodically looked down as if bowing but this lacked the intensity of display when another bird was present (CJF). Ara (1953) described copulation on the ground, in which a (presumed) female crouched with one wing extended, tail fanned and crown feathers erected in solicitation; the male called during the brief mounting.

RELATIONS WITH MAN Narang and Lamba (1984) concluded that Asian Pied Myna was a beneficial species to agriculture due to its consumption of various species of insect pest.

PRINCIPAL REFERENCE Tyagi and Lamba (1984).

55 PURPLE-BACKED STARLING *Sturnia sturnina*   Plate 14
Daurian Starling

Gracula sturnina Pallas 1776

FIELD IDENTIFICATION 16–17 cm. Purple-backed Starlings are sexually dimorphic, small, gregarious starlings. Adult males are largely grey, paler on the belly, but with a metallic purple nape patch and mantle. The tail and wings are blackish glossed metallic green and there is a variable, white barring on wings. The rump is pale and this is particularly conspicuous in flight, especially when flocks wheel in preparation for landing or during pre-roosting aerial manoeuvres. Females are duller and browner with a less pronounced pale rump and with less pronounced pale barring in the wing. Immatures are greyer, with a browner back and lack the nape patch.

DESCRIPTION Sexually dimorphic. **Adult male:** Forehead, crown and cheeks are grey, the chin

and breast paler grey, and this also extends on to the flanks. Glossed purple feathers on the nape produce a small patch in the otherwise grey feathering, and purple glossy feathers may also be variably interspersed with grey on the lower neck and upper mantle. Feathers on the head are not hackled. The lower mantle and back are glossy purple. The rump is pale, whitish or brownish, and the belly and undertail-coverts are creamy-white. The tail is black glossed green, with white outer webs to the outer rectrices. The primaries are brown with increasing green gloss on the inner feathers and the secondaries are glossed green. The primary coverts are glossy green, and the secondary coverts glossy purple and broadly tipped white. The median coverts are dark purple, broadly tipped white. The bill is horn, paler at the base; the legs are greenish-grey; the iris dark brown. **Adult female**: Forehead, crown, mantle and back are mousy-brown, the chin, throat, breast and flanks paler, and the belly is white. The rump is pale, browner in the centre. The tail is brown, lightly glossed mauve. The primaries and secondaries are brown, the inner secondaries paler and the secondary coverts are variable buffy-white. Adults may commence moult immediately after their chicks fledge, but juveniles probably moult mainly after they have left the breeding area (Winter and Sokolov 1983). Some juveniles undergo a partial moult after fledging, suspend moult on migration and complete feather renewal in the wintering area. Other juveniles, possibly later-hatched birds, complete the migration in juvenile plumage (Riddiford *et al.* 1989). Medway and Wells (1976) found birds still in moult in January.

MEASUREMENTS Male: wing (46) 103–112, tail (18) 48–54, tarsus (19) 25–28, bill (to skull — 19) 18–20; weight (53) 103–110 g; female: wing (33) 101–110, tail (20) 47–54, tarsus (20) 25–27, bill (to skull — 20) 18–20; weight (34) 100–109 g (Cramp and Perrins 1994).

VOICE Various whistling and whickering notes (Medway and Wells 1976). It is less vocal than other starlings but has a well-developed song, comprising notes peculiar to this species. During song the throat feathers are puffed out and the wings are fluttered. In Singapore during the winter it is remarkably quiet for a starling. The most frequently heard vocalisation was a flight call, a soft *prrrp* when birds took off, but a similar call is heard occasionally from many flock members while a flock was in flight (CJF)

DISTRIBUTION AND POPULATION Breeds in eastern Mongolia, the middle Amur, Ussuriland, south and central Manchuria and the northern provinces of China, and in northern Korea. The northern limits of its range in Russia are unclear. It presumably migrates through China and winters in the Andaman and Nicobar Islands, southern Burma, southeast, central and peninsular Thailand, Malaya and Singapore south to Sumatra, Java, Cochinchina, Tonkin, northern Laos and Hainan. It is a vagrant to Hong Kong (King *et al.* 1975). Records in Britain and Norway (Riddiford *et al.* 1989, Bentz 1987) are presumably escaped captives. In Russia it is nowhere abundant but it is a reasonably common winter visitor to Singapore (Hails 1987).

HABITAT It breeds in low altitude forest steppe, mixed forest, forest clearings, villages and on the outskirts of towns (Won 1961a, Etchècopar and Hüe 1953). It prefers broad leaved woodland edge or small clumps of trees in open, often cultivated, areas to dense forest. On migration it inhabits woodland edge (Medway and Wells 1976) but winters in coastal vegetation, derelict land, farmland, gardens and parks (Medway and Wells 1976, Hails 1987).

FOOD AND FEEDING Purple-backed Starlings are mainly insectivorous. Earthworms are taken from tilled land and seeds and berries are also eaten (Dement'ev and Gladkov 1960, Won

1961a). On Fair Isle, Shetland, a bird (presumed escape) spent much time flycatching from a perch, but in bad weather foraged by probing on the ground around sheep droppings (Riddiford *et al.* 1989). Caterpillars (Lepidoptera) and locusts and grasshoppers (Orthoptera), collected at woodland edges, in meadows and marshy areas, are brought to nestlings (Winter and Sokolov 1983). In winter the diet includes insects and fruit, and in Singapore birds were seen hawking insects, including large moths, from perches; gleaning under the leaves of *Terminalia catappa* trees; prying in the bases of rosettes of *Casuarina* leaves, involving acrobatic manoeuvres at the ends of fine branches; feeding among flowers at the top of a tall *Albizzia* tree; eating the orange fruits of *Fagraea fragrans* from the tops of trees. All of these birds fed in flocks of 10 to 50 individuals and were completely silent while feeding (CJF). Purple-backed Starlings also eat the fruit of cultivated trees, such as *Sambucus latipinna*, in Korea (Won 1961b).

BREEDING Nests in holes, usually in trees, walls of houses and in nestboxes. They do not breed in large colonies (Dement'ev and Gladkov 1960, Won 1961a, Etchècopar and Hüe 1953). They also nest in holes made by White-backed Woodpeckers *Dendrocopus leucotos* (Winter and Sokolov 1983). Nests are generally 3 to 10 m above the ground. Winter and Sokolov (1983) found that they nested at comparatively low densities, normally 50 to 80 m apart: they attributed this to competition for nest holes with other species, including White-cheeked Starlings, which lay 24–26 days earlier than Purple-backed Starlings and may therefore have an advantage in nest site acquisition. White-cheeked Starlings sometimes lay eggs in the nests of Purple-backed Starlings (Won 1961b). The nests are built from dry grasses, sedges, leaves, roots and paper and sometimes have a sparse lining of feathers. The eggs are various shades of blue, glossy and without markings, measuring 23.0–26.0 x 16.8–20.0 mm (17) (Schönwetter 1983). Clutches are usually of 5 to 6 eggs but clutches of 3 and 7 have been recorded. In Korea, laying occurs in the second half of May while in the Amur region of Russia, eggs are laid somewhat later, from 28 May to 13 June. Both sexes share in nest building. Eggs are laid at daily intervals although there are exceptions to this normal routine, raising the possibility of intra-specific nest parasitism as in Common Starling. Both sexes incubate but the female takes a greater part. Incubation begins after the laying of the third or fourth egg so that hatching is asynchronous. Both sexes feed the chicks and remove their faeces from the nest (Won and Woo 1957, Won 1961a, Winter and Sokolov 1983).

MIGRATION Purple-backed Starlings arrive in Korea in late May and reach the Burenskaya Khingan plain (Amur Region) around 20 May. They leave these Russian breeding grounds almost as soon as the chicks leave the nest and the last birds leave in late July. Korean birds leave in September–October. Wintering birds are present in Singapore from October to April (Hails *in litt.*).

Most birds that visit the Andaman and Nicobar Islands are immatures (Abdulali 1967).

BEHAVIOUR In winter, Purple-backed Starlings feed in flocks, usually small (Medway and Wells 1976) but sometimes flocks of several hundreds may occur (Hails *in litt.*). Non-feeding flocks sit in exposed positions in dead branches in the tops of trees, where they preen. Flocks are very active, however, and after brief periods of preening and sitting such flocks take wing, flying fast and directly through the treetops either to feed or simply returning to their exposed perches (CJF). For about a week after arrival on the breeding areas they remain in small flocks, sometimes in the company of White-cheeked Starlings. Towards the end of the breeding season flocks of 30–40 occur. Young birds are sometimes taken by Sparrowhawks *Accipiter nisus*. Purple-backed Starlings roost communally in reedbeds and trees in winter, and in Singapore join roosts of Common and White-vented Mynas and Asian Glossy Starlings (Hails 1987). In such mixed roosts, Purple-backed Starlings tend to segregate into a group of their own species. Arrival at a roost in a row of trees in a Singapore street was in compact flocks of 20 to 100 birds, flying fast and directly to the roost site.

Over the site arriving birds joined others in brief aerial manoeuvres before entering the trees but the entire period of arrival and entry was brief in comparison with the other sturnids and, unlike them, the process appeared to be accomplished in silence (CJF). Courtship behaviour has not been described.

RELATIONS WITH MAN The extensive studies of Won and Woo (1957) and Won (1961a,b) in Korea were designed to assess how beneficial Purple-backed Starlings might be in controlling insect pests in forests. They concluded that insect consumption could reach beneficial proportions and as a result nestboxes are erected in forests to encourage the birds to breed. In Singapore, the mixed roosts of mynas and starlings that Purple-backed Starlings join are regarded as troublesome on account of the noise of the birds and the droppings deposited on pavements beneath roost trees (Kang 1989), but the comparatively small numbers of Purple-backed Starlings in these roosts presumably contribute little to the problem.

PRINCIPAL REFERENCES Won and Woo (1957), Dement'ev and Gladkov (1960), Winter and Sokolov (1983).

56 RED-CHEEKED STARLING *Sturnia philippensis*   Plate 14

Violet-backed Starling, Red-cheeked Myna, Chestnut-cheeked Starling, Japanese Small Starling

Motacilla Philippensis Forster 1781

FIELD IDENTIFICATION 16–18 cm. Red-cheeked Starlings are small, sexually dimorphic members of the family. In males the head is creamy-white and the cheeks, ear-coverts and sides of neck reddish-chestnut, sometimes extending around throat to form a collar. The mantle and back are glossy metallic dark violet and this colour extends on to the rump where it is variably interspersed with pinkish-white. The wings are blackish, glossed on the coverts and with a white bar at the shoulder. The upper breast is vinous, the rest of underparts grey but whiter on the central belly. The female is duller, with head and upperparts dull brownish-grey and underparts greyish-white with breast and sides of body more grey and undertail-coverts vinous-chestnut. The wings are brownish-grey, the inner feathers glossed with metallic grey-green and the median coverts broadly tipped with white. The tail is black glossed green, the outer feathers edged with red-brown. The bill is grey and the legs olive.

DESCRIPTION Sexually dimorphic. **Adult male**: the forehead and crown are buffy white, the chin and throat white, the former suffused with orange; the feathers are not hackled. The cheeks and sides of the neck are brick red, variably extending on to the nape and upper breast. The mantle and back are glossy violet, the rump pale salmon, variably interspersed with purple feathers and often purple

without paler feathers. The upper breast and flanks are pale grey, the belly whitish-buff shading to buffy-salmon on the lower belly and undertail-coverts. The tail is black, glossed green; the outer web of the outer rectrix is pale salmon, extending almost to the tip. The primaries are dark brown with buffy outer margins to the outer three large feathers; the outer webs of the remaining primaries are glossed green. The secondaries are glossed purple and green, with the outer webs of the outer secondaries white at the base. The primary coverts and inner remiges are dark glossy bronze-green. The greater coverts are white. **Adult female**: lacks red cheeks. The crown and back are buffish-grey, tending to ochreous on the rump. The underparts are buffy-white. The primaries, secondaries and tail are dark brown, the primaries with a little gloss on the outer webs, and the secondaries with a little gloss on the outer feathers and pale edges proximally to the outer secondaries, producing a narrow bar in the closed wing. The wing-coverts are variably tipped white, producing a suggestion of a wingbar. The bill is grey or blackish, the legs olive, dark green or bluish-horn, and the iris is dark brown.

MEASUREMENTS Male (3): wing 103–114, tail 48–54, culmen 12–14, tarsus 26; female (4) wing 102–106, tail 46–50, culmen 12–14, tarsus 24–26.

VOICE The calls are not particularly striking or loud. The song is a simple sequence of calls, which Jahn (1942) described as a babbling of moderately loud call notes. Adults produce *airr* or *tshairr* calls when excited and a penetrating alarm call *tshick*, sometimes repeated. The flight call is a soft melodious *chrueruchu*. When rearing young, adults give a long, drawn-out hoarse alarm call *dsha-a-a* (Jahn 1942). Young in the nest produce a soft chirping *tsirr* or *tsieee*. Calls become louder closer to fledging, a loud *shuu-eee*, a trisyllabic *shipshuu shipshuushuu shuu-uu-uu* and a *choodi-vit*.

DISTRIBUTION AND POPULATION Breeds in cooler parts of northern and central Japan, on the islands of Hokkaido, central and northern Honchu, Rishiri-tō, Teuri-jima, and Sado. They also breed in the Kurile Islands northeast to Iturup, in south Sakhalin Island and on the island of Askold, southeast of Vladivostok. They are not known to breed on the Asian mainland. The wintering area includes the Philippines where it is uncommon (Dickinson *et al.* 1991), although du Pont and Rabor (1973) reported small flocks in the south Sulu islands, northern Borneo where numbers are irregular but large flocks are sometimes recorded (Kidd 1978, Smythies 1981), with some wintering on southern Japanese islands. (According to Dement'ev and Gladkov (1960), the main wintering area is in the Philippines, but Dickinson *et al.* (1991) report that it is uncommon there; since it only occurs in reasonable numbers, but irregularly, in northern Borneo, it appears that the main wintering area has yet to be discovered). On migration it occurs on the southern Japanese islands and the Ryukyu Islands, and passes through eastern China from Jiangsu to Fujian. In China it is rare on the mainland but common on Taiwan (Cheng 1987, although de Schauensee (1984) regarded it as a vagrant there). It has been recorded from the coast of eastern Russia, and occurs as a vagrant in Hong Kong (Chalmers 1986) and in northern Sulawesi and the Moluccas (White and Bruce 1986). Red-cheeked Starling is on the list of migratory birds of the United States (Fish and Wildlife Service 1985). Records in Malaya and Singapore may be of escaped captives (Parish and Prentice 1989). In Sakhalin and the Kurile Islands it is scarce (Dement'ev and Gladkov 1960). In the Tokyo area of central Honshu numbers appear to have declined over the last 50 years (Brazil 1990).

HABITAT Occurs in the breeding season in open and mixed deciduous woodland, often in agricultural land, orchards and sometimes in urban parks and around villages, nesting in woodland edge or in clearings. In Honshu they breed mainly between 800–1500 m but further north in Hokkaido they occur in the lowlands (Brazil 1990). Jahn (1942) thought that breeding recorded at higher altitudes in Honshu might be a response to the presence of White-cheeked Starlings, competitors for nest sites, in the lowlands. They avoid higher mountains and forest. In winter in the Philippines it occurs in open country (Delacour and Mayr 1946) but also in cities (Temme 1979).

FOOD AND FEEDING There appears to be no information on the diet of adults in the breeding areas, although Thiede and Thiede (1971) thought that Red-cheeked Starlings preferred to feed in the tops of trees, where they appeared to be skilful in procuring caterpillars and other insects. In the autumn, Red-cheeked Starlings feed in berry-bearing bushes (Jahn 1942). In the Philippines, Temme (1979) recorded them feeding on the figs of *Ficus religiosa* and fruits of the Max Arthur palm *Actinophloeus macarthur* and Smythies (1981) reported them feeding in berry-bearing shrubs. On migration in the Ryukyu Islands they eat mulberries *Morus* (Hachisuka and Udagawa 1953). The main foods brought to nestlings are caterpillars (Lepidoptera), dragonflies (Odonata), adult daddy-long-legs (Tipulidae) and cherries *Prunus*, the last only in the nine days before fledging. In addition, bees, ants and ichneumon flies (Hymenoptera), beetles and their larvae (Coleoptera), flies (Diptera), grasshoppers and bush crickets (Orthoptera), adult butterflies (Lepidoptera), shield bugs (Heteroptera) and cocoons of spiders (Araneae) have been reported.

BREEDING Red-cheeked Starlings breed from May to July, in holes in trees and in man-made structures, including roofs of buildings and nest-boxes. The nest may or may not contain nest material; where nests are built, both sexes collect material, mainly in the morning (Koike 1988); the male does most of the building (Haneda and Ushiyama 1967). Males sometimes sing while holding green leaves in the bill, and both sexes incorporate green leaves into the nest, some females continuing to do this after the eggs have hatched. The clutch contains 3–7 (usually 5) azure eggs, measuring 24.4–27.2 x 17.0–19.3 mm (12) (Schönwetter 1983). Later clutches are smaller (Koike 1988). Incubation takes 10–14 days, mainly by the female who also incubates at night (Haneda and Ushiyama 1967, Koike 1988). Nestlings are fed by both parents and both remove faecal pellets; insects are brought by the adults to young nestlings, but later fruit is brought (Koike 1988). Thiede and Thiede (1971) found that Red-cheeked Starlings sometimes regurgitated food for the nestlings, often after offering food that had been carried to the nest in the bill. Fledging occurs after 15–22, usually 18, days and adults continue to feed young after they have left the nest (Koike 1988). In two studies, 45.3% and 47.1% of eggs produced fledged young (Haneda and Ushiyama 1967, Koike 1988); in the latter study losses were due to predation by Blue-green Snakes *Elaphe climacophora* and starvation.

MIGRATION On northward migration in spring, Red-cheeked Starlings arrive in southern Japan in late March, moving north to the breeding area in April and early May (Brazil 1990). In the Kurile Islands they begin to arrive in mid-May, and are a few days later arriving in Sakhalin (Dement'ev and Gladkov 1960). Older birds arrive in advance of yearlings (Koike 1988). They leave the breeding area from August to October, assembling in hundreds of thousands in Kyushu before flying south. They have been recorded in Borneo from

September to early April and in the Philippines from October to late April.

BEHAVIOUR Appear to be less colonial than *Sturnus* starlings. They appear to be mainly monogamous (Haneda and Ushiyama 1967) but nests are sometimes visited by birds other than the occupying pair, especially later in the breeding cycle (Thiede and Thiede 1971), and Koike (1988) recorded extra-pair copulations and instances of bigamy where a male had two nests. Koike (1992) found that 1% of males were polygynous and recorded a polygynous male with three mates; the male assisted incubation of all broods but fed nestlings of the first only, resulting in higher breeding success in the first female than in the others. Haneda and Ushiyama (1967) described birds defending territories of 150–250 m² and nests can be widely dispersed, over 100 m apart, but Nakamura (1986) and Koike (1988) found that they defended only a small area around the nest and in a beech forest lived at the high density of 140 birds per square kilometre. Older birds arrive on the breeding grounds first in the spring, and dominant males initially occupy several nest sites. Out of the breeding season, Red-cheeked Starlings form flocks, commonly of up to 50 birds and of hundreds of thousands on migration. They roost communally at night in trees, especially *Casuarina*, often in company with Asian Glossy Starlings. Prior to roosting, flocks perform aerobatic manoeuvres but when they settle they tend to roost in separate trees from other starling species (Kidd 1978, Koike 1988).

PRINCIPAL REFERENCES Brazil (1990), Thiede and Thiede (1971).

57 WHITE-SHOULDERED STARLING *Sturnia sinensis* Plate 14

Chinese Starling, Grey-backed Starling

Oriolus sinensis Gmelin 1788

FIELD IDENTIFICATION Length 17–18 cm. Adult male: A generally pale starling with whitish-cream crown, throat, belly, underwing- and undertail-coverts. These areas are sometimes tinged rusty. Head, back and breast are grey. White upperwing-coverts and scapulars form a conspicuous white patch on the closed wing, contrasting with black flight feathers which are tinged metallic-green. The tail is black with white tips to the outer feathers. The bill is blue-grey, the legs leaden-grey, and the iris pale. Adult female: Parts which are white or cream in the male are grey in the female.

DESCRIPTION Sexually dimorphic. **Adult male:** Forehead is buffy white, often extending on to the crown but the crown is sometimes pale grey. The cheeks are grey-brown, chin and throat buff, breast buffy grey and the belly and undertail-coverts ochreous; the nape, mantle and back are silver-grey, the rump buffish-ochre. The tail is black, slightly glossed and with white or buff tips to the rectrices becoming progressively broader towards the outer feathers; in these pale tips the rachis is dark, and the pale tips to the rectrices become abraded to the extent that some birds have short dark tails without pale tips to the feathers. The primaries are dark brown, blackish on the outer webs; the secondaries are black, slightly glossed green. The upperwing-coverts are white, sometimes washed ochre, forming a large white shoulder patch. The underwing-coverts are white, washed buff. The legs are grey, the bill blue-grey and the iris silver or white. **Adult female:** Most are greyer than the male, with less contrast; the rump is only marginally paler than the back, and the tips of the rectrices are dirty buff. Some are more like the male but with brown wings showing a small white shoulder patch, and ochreous rump and tips to the rectrices. No subspecies are recognised but there is some regional variability. Males from central Thailand are generally greyer with white shoulders and tips to tail, but birds from Burma and China show more buff or ochre on the paler parts of the plumage, exceptionally tinged cinnamon with rich cinnamon tips to the rectrices, when the tail resembles that of Chestnut-tailed Starling.

MEASUREMENTS Male (9): wing 101–107, tail 54–68, culmen 15–17, tarsus 25–28; female (6) wing 100–105, tail 55–66, culmen 14–17, tarsus 24–28.

VOICE The song has not been described. In Thailand feeding flocks were silent, but birds gave a soft *preep* flight call on taking off. One bird was heard to give a harsh *kaar* before taking off, resembling an alarm call of Common Starling (CJF).

DISTRIBUTION Breeds in southern China from east Yunnan to Fujian, Hong Kong, Hainan and northern Indochina. Breeding has not been confirmed on Taiwan but it winters there (de Schauensee 1984). It winters to the south in Thailand, Laos, Cambodia, Vietnam and Malaya occasionally as far south as Singapore, west to Burma and Manipur and accidentally east to Borneo and the Philippines (Harrison and Smythies 1963, Dickinson *et al.* 1991). It is resident in Hong Kong (King *et al.* 1975). In China it was formerly common but has decreased markedly in recent years (Cheng 1987).

HABITAT It inhabits open country, scrub and towns where it is largely arboreal, rarely descending to the ground (Etchécopar and Hüe 1983)

FOOD AND FEEDING No observations on food have been made from the breeding areas. In winter in Thailand a flock of six birds flew from an exposed perch in a dead tree to feed on the ground among cattle in a grassy marsh. A party of eight birds fed in a *Casuarina* tree. These birds walked along twigs to reach into terminal rosettes of leaves, where they could stretch acrobatically or hang upside down on the tips of fine twigs. They made short direct flights between twigs and were apparently silent while feeding (CJF).

BREEDING Nests, often in large colonies and sometimes with other species, in holes in trees and rocks and also often in pagodas. The nest is a large accumulation of various kinds of vegetation. The clutch consists of 4 eggs, blue-green and without markings, measuring 24.2–27.4 x 17.1–19.0 mm (10) (Schönwetter 1983). Nothing further appears to be known.

BEHAVIOUR White-shouldered Starling is a gregarious species and, like other members of the family, non-feeding birds sit in exposed positions in the tops of dead trees. In Hong Kong, winter flocks of up to 300 birds occur (Chalmers 1986). Flight of birds wintering in Thailand was noted as direct but more leisurely than that of Purple-backed Starlings (CJF).

58 CHESTNUT-TAILED STARLING *Sturnia malabarica* Plate 15

Grey-headed Starling, Grey-headed Myna, Ashy-headed Starling, Ashy-headed Myna, White-winged Myna, Blyth's Myna

Turdus malabaricus Gmelin 1789

FIELD IDENTIFICATION 17–22 cm. A small, slim and agile starling, whose plumage can be variable. The face and forehead are pale whitish-grey. The nape and back are ashy brownish-grey and the underparts are rufous-chestnut, paler on the upper throat and chin. Feathers on the crown, nape and upper throat are elongated into hackles with whitish shafts, giving a streaked, silvery appearance. The wings are blackish with silvery grey outer margins to the primaries, the tail also blackish although with silvery-grey central feathers, all rectrices broadly tipped with chestnut. The sexes are similar although females are less rufescent on the underparts. Juveniles are more greyish-brown with paler wings and tail than adults, but with rufous tinges on the uppertail-coverts and tail tip. The bill of adults is bright blue at the base, passing through greenish-yellow to yellow at the tip. The legs and feet are yellowish-brown. The iris of adults is whitish while that of juveniles is bluish.

DESCRIPTION The forehead and chin are white. The crown, hindneck and sides of face are silver-grey, the feathers elongate and hackled, with pale shafts producing streaking. The throat is cinnamon with feathers elongate and hackled, with white shafts producing streaking. The breast, belly and vent are rich cinnamon, the undertail-coverts white. The back and wing-coverts are grey, tinged brownish, and the rump orange-brown. The primaries are brown, blacker on the outer webs and slightly glossed green. The primary coverts are black, glossed green. The secondaries are brown with grey margins to the outer webs, these margins broader on the inner secondaries. The underwing-coverts are whitish. The tail is grey tipped chestnut, the extent of chestnut increasing towards the outer rectrices and the outer feathers are entirely chestnut. The bill is yellow at the tip, green in the middle and blue at the base; the legs are brownish-yellow or olive-brown; the iris is greyish-white. The sexes are practically indistinguishable.

S. m. nemoricola, of eastern India, Burma, Thailand, southwest China and Indochina, has the head and breast greyer but with white streaking and the underparts dirty white, in some birds slightly tinged cinnamon. The underwing-coverts are dirty white. The primary coverts are variable, grey in some birds, white in others forming a white shoulder patch.

S. m. blythii, of southwest India, has the head and breast brilliant white, with feathers on the nape markedly elongate and hackled. The rump is grey, washed cinnamon and the flanks, lower abdomen and undertail-coverts rufous. The primary coverts are black, the base of the primaries white. Adult female *blythii* differs from the male in that pure white is restricted to the forehead, fore-crown, chin and throat; the rest of the crown and nape are grey, like the back, but with paler grey streaking, and the sides of the face and neck are grey; the breast is greyish and merges into creamy-rufous on the lower abdomen and flanks, and the undertail-coverts are greyer and less rufous than in the male. The iris is greyish-white, legs and feet pale yellow or yellowish-olive.

Immatures of all races have the upperparts grey-brown, paler on the head, with an indistinct pale supercilium, and the uppertail-coverts are tinged rusty; the sides of the head and the underparts are dirty buffish-white; the wings and tail are dark brown with paler brown edges to the flight feathers and coverts, while the tail has narrow rufous tips (narrower than in adults) becoming broader on the outer rectrices; the iris is bluish.

MEASUREMENTS Male (sample sizes not given): wing 98–106, tail, 59–65, tarsus, 23–25, bill 21–24; female: wing 94–104, tail 55–65, tarsus 22–24, bill 20–22; weight male/female (21) 32–44 g (Ali and Ripley 1972).

VOICE In Thailand generally silent while feeding (CJF) but Roberts (1992) reported a constant chattering and starling-like squabbling when two birds approached the same flower. The flight call is reported to be disyllabic and metallic and the song a pleasant warble.

DISTRIBUTION AND POPULATION Occurs over much of peninsular India south of a line from southeastern Rajasthan to Chandigarh, then east along the lower Himalayas in Nepal (where it is a summer migrant to the Kathmandu Valley (Inskipp and Inskipp 1991)), Sikkim and Bhutan, Bangladesh and Burma and east to southern Sichuan and Yunnan east to Mengtsu in China, Indochina and Thailand except the southern part of the peninsula. It appears to be extending its range northwest into Pakistan. In most of its range it is generally resident but undertakes erratic movements and local migrations, and in Thailand the resident population is augmented by large numbers of immigrants in the northern winter (Deignan 1945, Lekagul *et al.* 1992). It does not occur in Sri Lanka.

HABITAT Occurs in lowlands and foothills to about 800 m, in open woodland and open country with scattered trees. They occur both close to and remote from human habitation, and commonly frequent young forestry plantations.

FOOD AND FEEDING One of the most arboreal of starlings, feeding in treetops and at the ends of small branches with tit-like agility, although it also feeds in low bushes and occasionally on the ground. It is especially attracted to flowering trees and according to Deignan (1945), the timing of its appearance in northern Thailand is closely related to the flowering of *Butea* and Silk-cotton *Bombax*. They also take nectar from Coral *Erythrina, Salmalia, Grevillea* and occasionally *Loranthus* trees and probably eat pollen and flower buds. Berries of *Lantana, Zizyphus* and the Madras Thorn *Pithecelobium dulce* are eaten when avail-able, together with figs *Ficus,* and seeds of *Albizzia* and other wild plants. Devasahayam and Rema (1991) reported them eating *Acacia auriculiformis* seeds exposed when pods split open. Insects, taken by gleaning flowers, leaves and fine twigs, include termites (Isoptera), bees (Hymenoptera), caterpillars (Lepidoptera), flies (Diptera), bugs (Hemiptera), earwigs (Dermaptera) and beetles (Coleoptera). Nestlings are given mainly insects, including caterpillars (Lepidoptera) and beetles (Coleoptera)(Mason and LeFroy 1912).

BREEDING In India, the breeding season extends from February–July, with local variation in the precise timing. Chestnut-tailed Starlings nest in holes in trees, often those made by woodpeckers and barbets, usually 3–12 m above the ground. The nest is built by both parents of grasses, rootlets and twigs. The clutch is of 3–5 eggs which are pale blue-green and unmarked, measuring 20.0–26.2 x 16.0–19.1 mm (80) (Schönwetter 1983). The incubation and fledging periods are unknown, but both sexes participate in incubation and feeding of the young.

BEHAVIOUR Feed in pairs or small groups, occasionally in flocks of 20 or more birds. Larger flocks assemble to feed on emerging winged termites. When feeding in trees they can be extremely acrobatic, gleaning insects or other items from the tips of thin twigs or the terminal rosettes of *Casuarina* branches by reaching out or hanging upside down in actions reminiscent of tits (*Parus*). They roost communally in bushes, sometimes with other starlings, e.g. Asian Pied Starlings.

Flight is fast and direct, rapid beats of the pointed wings being followed by short glides.

PRINCIPAL REFERENCES Ali and Ripley (1972), Narang and Lamba (1982).

59 WHITE-HEADED STARLING *Sturnia erythropygia*   Plate 15

White-headed Myna

Sturnia erythropygia Blyth 1846

FIELD IDENTIFICATION 19–22 cm. Endemic to the Andaman and Nicobar Islands, and appears to be closely related to the similar Chestnut-tailed Starling. The entire head, neck and underparts are creamy-white, the back and scapulars pale grey, and the wings and tail black glossed with green. The rump, uppertail-coverts and vent vary between subspecies. The bill is greenish-yellow, bluish or pinkish at the base, the legs and feet are dull yellow. The iris is pale. The sexes are similar.

DESCRIPTION The forehead, crown, nape, chin and throat are dirty white, with the crown of some birds greyish-white. The feathers are not hackled. The upper mantle is white, the lower mantle and upper back grey with purplish suffusion. The rump is chestnut. The tail is black, slightly glossed green, with chestnut tips becoming larger towards the outer rectrices and the outer feathers almost entirely chestnut. The primaries are blackish with some gloss on the outer webs. The secondaries are black, glossed green. The breast and belly are white, the vent chestnut. The underwing-coverts are white. The bill is yellow with a small blue area at the base; legs and feet yellow; iris opalescent white, grey or bluish. Young birds have the head streaked brown and the wing-coverts have tawny edgings.

In *S. e. andamanensis,* of Car Nicobar Island, the plumage is greyer, with less gloss on the wings. The rump and vent are white or tinged rufous and the tail lacks chestnut.

In *S. e. katchalensis,* of Katchall Island, the rump is pale but the undertail-coverts are rufous.

MEASUREMENTS Male (3): wing 110–112, tail 76–78, bill 23–24; female (2): wing 106–108, tail 65–71, bill 22–23 (Ali and Ripley 1972).

VOICE Not recorded.

DISTRIBUTION AND POPULATION An

endemic resident on the Andaman and Nicobar Islands, in the latter restricted to the islands of Car Nicobar and Katchall, although introduced on Camorta. On the Andamans and Car Nicobar it is common.

HABITAT On the Andamans, White-headed Starlings inhabit forest and secondary jungle, forest edge, open grassland and cultivated areas including coastal coconut plantations.

FOOD AND FEEDING Eats fruit, nectar and insects, including a caterpillar (probably the larva of *Pyrausta coclesalis*) which rolls itself in narrow bamboo leaves; in obtaining these it displays a tit-like agility.

BREEDING The breeding season is March–May. White-headed Starlings breed in tree holes 2–10 m above ground, building a nest of small twigs lined with small green leaves. Clutches contain 4 eggs which are uniform blue, without markings, and measure 25.0–32.3 x 18.0–19.7 mm (8) (Schönwetter 1983).

BEHAVIOUR Forms both small and large flocks, and roosts communally at night in trees. They join other species, such as drongos (Dicruridae), cuckoo-shrikes and minivets (Campephagidae) in foraging guilds.

PRINCIPAL REFERENCES Abdulali (1967), Ali and Ripley (1972).

60 WHITE-FACED STARLING *Sturnia albofrontata*　　Plate 15
Ceylon White-headed Myna, White-headed Starling

Heterornis albofrontata Layard 1854

FIELD IDENTIFICATION 19–22 cm. A small, slim starling similar to Grey-headed Starling of peninsular India, and most easily seen at flowering forest trees. The face is white, while the crown and the rest of the upperparts are dark; the feathers of the nape and neck are streaked white. The breast and belly are smoky lavender grey streaked with white and the undertail-coverts white. The bill is pale greyish-green with a dull blue base and the legs are bluish-grey. The sexes are similar. Juveniles are browner and lack white streaking on the breast.

DESCRIPTION The forehead, sides of face, chin and throat are white, sometimes tinged grey. The crown, hindneck and upper mantle are dull greyish-black, the feathers elongate and hackled. On the forecrown, sides of neck and upper mantle these feathers have white shafts, producing white streaking. The back, wings and uppertail are black, slightly glossed greenish. The breast, upper belly and flanks are brownish-grey with a lavender tinge, the feathers with white shafts producing streaking, extending onto the lower belly in most birds. The vent and undertail-coverts are dirty white. The bill is greyish-green or horn at the tip shading to a blue-grey base; the legs and feet are leaden blue-grey; iris brown with grey outer circle, white with red-brown inner circle, or white. Bluish bare skin

around the eye is visible in some birds.

MEASUREMENTS Male/female (sample sizes not given): wing 105–112, tail 69–75, bill (from feathers) 20–21 (Ali and Ripley 1972).

VOICE White-faced Starling is said to be relatively silent, the only calls reported being a starling-like chirp, and a *cheow* with the tone of a grackle.

DISTRIBUTION AND POPULATION A rare bird, endemic to Sri Lanka. It is confined to tall forest and adjacent clearings of hills in the southwestern wet zone, to about 1300 m.

HABITAT Strictly arboreal, foraging in the tops of tall trees.

FOOD AND FEEDING Eats fruit, including cinnamon *Cinnamonum* berries and several species of fig *Ficus*, flower nectar of *Salmalia* and *Grevillea*, and insects.

BREEDING There appears to be only one recorded breeding observation. The nest was in a hole in a tree and the eggs were laid on the bare wood, without nest material. The two eggs were pale blue, without markings, and measured 25.6 x 20.0 mm (Baker 1926).

BEHAVIOUR Little is known, but White-faced Starlings are said to bow like a myna.

MOULT There is a complete post-juvenile moult.

PRINCIPAL REFERENCES Henry (1971), Ali and Ripley (1972).

61 BRAHMINY STARLING *Temenuchus pagodarum*　　Plate 16
Brahminy Myna, Pagoda Myna, Black-headed Myna

Turdus pagodarum Gmelin 1781

FIELD IDENTIFICATION 19–20 cm. Brahminy Starling has a grey back and the underparts are cinnamon. The forehead, crown and nape are glossy black with the feathers elongated into a

long crest. The wings are black and the tail brown with white on the outer margins and on the tip, conspicuous in flight. The bill is yellow with a steel blue base, and the legs and feet are yellow.

The sexes are similar. Young birds are browner, with the head sooty brown and without a crest. Adults are most easily distinguished from the similar Rose-coloured Starling by the absence of black on the throat and upper breast, and in flight the Brahminy Starling's wings are more rounded whereas those of Rose-coloured Starling are pointed.

DESCRIPTION The forehead and crown are glossy black, the crown feathers elongate and hackled, longer in males and sometimes extending to the mid-back, when the crest hides the chestnut nape feathers. The chin, throat, upper breast, sides of neck and nape are cinnamon with feathers of the upper breast and nape hackled and with pale shafts, producing streaking. The belly is cinnamon, becoming greyer on the flanks. The mantle, back, wing-coverts and rump are grey tinged brownish. The primaries are brownish-black without gloss. The base of the primaries and the under-wing-coverts are white. The tail is grey-brown with white tips on all but the central feathers, and becoming broader on the outer feathers, and especially on the outer web of the outer rectrices. The bill is yellow, the base of upper mandible greenish and the base of the lower mandible bluish; the legs and feet are lemon yellow and the iris pale greenish. Behind the eye is a small bare patch of whitish skin. Young birds are dull and browner on the back, and the top of the head is brown, without a crest, and with the feathers not hackled; the underparts are buffer, the legs flesh and the bill lacks the blue base; the iris is grey. Brahminy Starlings undergo a complete moult in October–November. Post-juvenal moult is complete and 1st-winter birds are indistinguishable from adults.

MEASUREMENTS Male (sample sizes not given): wing 99–115, tail 60–75, tarsus 26–30, bill 20–24; female (sample sizes not given): wing 99–109, tail 58–68, tarsus 28–29, bill 20–21; weight (9 male/female) 40–54 g (Ali and Ripley 1972).

VOICE Ali and Ripley (1972) describe the song as a pleasing, rambling warble which incorporates mimicry of other birds' calls; Roberts (1992) found the song more musical than that of the Common Myna. According to Ali and Ripley (1972) and Roberts (1992), the song is given from a shady perch, usually high in a tree, the male partially raising his crest and with the plumage ruffled; Tyagi and Lamba (1984), however, refer to Brahminy Starlings singing on the ground. Brahminy Starlings also produce a variety of croaking and chattering notes. Sontag (1985) described a loud territorial song, delivered in short phrases, a softer 'advertising' song, and a song of complicated structure given by both members of a pair before and during copulation. In captive pairs, CJF heard a squawk *kwa-chu* and a *Acridotheres* myna-like *kchu*; when perched they gave a soft *krrr krrr* and the song comprised a wide variety of notes, with short phrases repeated, and was more musical, lower pitched and softer than song of Common Starling. The alarm call is a series of short grating churrs.

DISTRIBUTION AND POPULATION Occurs throughout peninsular India north to southern Kashmir, Himachal Pradesh and the foothills of the Himalayas (but only in western Nepal, and not in Sikkim and Bhutan), west to the Indus Valley in Pakistan and to eastern Afghanistan, and east to the longitude of Calcutta. It is widely distributed in Sri Lanka. It occurs rarely in Assam and Bangladesh. Over most of its range, Brahminy Starling is resident, but may make seasonal movements, especially during the monsoons. In Goa, it is scarce during the late dry season (December–April), but occurs during the monsoon. In the northern parts of its range in Pakistan and Kashmir it is a summer migrant, occurring mainly between 900–1800 m, but occasionally to 4400 m (Akhtar 1990). In Sri Lanka it is mainly a coastal species (Henry 1971), but is now said to be rare (Kotagama and Fernando 1994). Throughout its range it is locally common and it may be expanding its range in Pakistan, although Roberts (1992) thought that its numbers there might be limited by competition for nest holes with more aggressive mynas. There are few records outside its normal range but there is a single record, of four birds in company with White-shouldered Starlings, in central peninsular Thailand in 1977 (Lekagul and Round 1991) and it is accidental in Yunnan, China (Cheng 1987).

HABITAT In India, Brahminy Starlings occur principally in open deciduous forest, scrub jungle, in cultivated areas and near human habitation. They avoid arid semi-desert and desert, and also humid forest. In Pakistan they occur mainly in valley bottoms with rice cultivation interspersed with fruit orchards and clumps of taller trees, while in Sri Lanka they are most commonly found round the northern and eastern coasts in open scrub or cultivated areas (Henry 1971).

MIGRATION In the north where they are summer migrants, Brahminy Starlings arrive in April–May.

FOOD AND FEEDING Feeds in flowering and fruiting trees, occasionally foraging for insects in the canopy, and also feeds on the ground, especially among cattle grazing in moist grassland and marshes. Adults eat fruits and berries of a wide variety of shrubs and trees, including figs *Ficus* sp., *Lantana camara*, *Salvadora persica* and *S. oleoides*, *Zizyphus*, *Syzygium*, *Bridelia*, *Litseal*, *Mimusops hexandra* and the poisonous fruits of Yellow Oleander *Thevetia neriifolia*. They also eat the fleshy flowers of Mhowa *Madhuca indica*, flower parts of *Butea* and *Grevillea*, and nectar from the flowers of *Salmalia*, *Erythrena*, *Butea* and *Capparis*. The tongue of this species ends in a brush-like tip, which is probably an adaptation to the exploitation of this food source (Beecher 1978). Adults also eat insects, especially grasshoppers, crickets and mole crickets (Orthoptera), earwigs (Dermaptera), cockroaches (Dictyoptera), termites (Isoptera), bugs (Hemiptera), butterflies and moths and their caterpillars (Lepidoptera), flies (Diptera), ants and bees (Hymenoptera), beetles (Coleoptera) and also spiders (Araneae) and snails (Mollusca) (Narang and Lamba 1984). Parents feed their young mainly animal food, especially insects. In a study of nestling food in cultivated land at Gujarat, the diet was dominated by termites (Isoptera), moths (Lepidoptera) and grasshoppers (Orthoptera) but beetles (Coleoptera), flies (Diptera), bugs (Hemiptera), ants, bees and wasps (Hymenoptera), earwigs (Dermaptera) and cockroaches (Dictyoptera) were also taken, together with other invertebrates including spiders (Araneae), millipedes (Myriapoda) and earthworms (Annelida). Smaller quantities of plant matter were brought to the nestlings, including seeds and pulp of Neem *Azadiracta indica*, figs *Ficus* sp., seeds and fruit of *Lantana camara*, gourd *Luffa cylindrica*, and leaves of *Peltoforum pterocarpum* (Patel *et al.* 1992).

BREEDING Brahminy Starlings are thought to be monogamous. They breed earlier in the south than in the north, but overall they breed from February/March to August/September. The nest is built in a hole in a tree, often one which has been taken over from a tit (Paridae), barbet (Capitonidae) or woodpecker (Picidae); sometimes holes in walls or house roofs are used and they will nest in nestboxes. If sufficient holes are available close together, Brahminy Starlings may nest colonially. The nest is untidily built from dry grasses, dead leaves, feathers, paper etc. and lined with finer materials, though according to Baker (1926) has little material. The clutch is of 3–5 eggs, normally 4 eggs which are pale or prussian blue and unmarked, measuring 21.8–29.2 x 16.8–20.3 mm (100) (Baker 1926). Eggs are laid at 24 h intervals, mainly in the early morning. Nest building takes 12–25 days. Both sexes build the nest and incubate the eggs, but the female plays a greater part in both activities than the male. According to Tyagi and Lamba (1984), the male collects food and feeds the incubating female through the nest entrance: this is unusual behaviour in starlings. Incubation takes 12 days and Tyagi and Lamba found hatching success to be high, from 91–95%

over four years. Both parents feed the young, the female contributing more than the male. Egg shells and faecal sacs are removed by the parents, but larger nestlings raise the cloaca to the nest entrance and eject their faeces. Chicks leave the nest after 18–21 days and overall nesting success was found by Tyagi and Lamba (1984) to be 67%. Second clutches are common and three broods are sometimes reared.

BEHAVIOUR Less gregarious than many starlings, normally occurring in pairs or small family groups, forming larger flocks in the non-breeding season and at food concentrations. When the distribution of nest holes permits, they will nest colonially and they roost communally in large congregations in trees and shrubs, and in reedbeds. Henry (1971) described singing birds nodding their heads and raising the crest, and Tyagi and Lamba (1984) described courtship display taking place on the ground, the male starting to sing while standing erect on the grass, puffing out his plumage and raising the crest when the head was thrown back, and fanning his tail. Copulation usually takes place on the ground, but sometimes in a tree or on a house roof. Brahminy Starlings spend much time feeding on the ground where, like other starlings and mynas, they walk rather than hop. They feed readily with other sturnids, such as the more arboreal Chestnut-tailed Starling when taking nectar and fruit, and with Asian Pied Mynas, and Jungle and Common Mynas when feeding on grassland insects. The flight of this species is less swift than that of Common or Rose-coloured Starlings, Roberts (1992) describing it as more like that of *Acridotheres* mynas.

RELATIONS WITH MAN Brahminy Starlings are kept as cagebirds in India on account of their pleasant song. Whistler (1928) described them as being important in local folklore, but did not go into detail.

PRINCIPAL REFERENCES Ali and Ripley (1972), Tyagi and Lamba (1984), Roberts (1992).

62 ROSE-COLOURED STARLING *Pastor roseus*   **Plate 16**
Rosy Pastor

Turdus roseus Linnaeus 1758

FIELD IDENTIFICATION 19–22 cm. A medium-sized starling with a somewhat shorter bill and more domed crown than Common Starling. The adult is unmistakable with glossy blue- or purple-black head, wings and tail and with a long erectile crest; the mantle, belly and flanks are pink. This adult plumage is achieved through wear of new feathers, for in fresh plumage the tips of black feathers are dull buff-grey while those of pink feathers are brown, giving a duller mottled appearance. The entirely black head most readily distinguishes this species from Brahminy Myna. Juveniles are pale dun-brown with a pale chin, eyering and belly, and the rump is paler than the

back and tail; the primaries and secondaries are darker brown than the body, but have prominent pale margins; yellowish base to the bill, with the upper mandible decurved. The contrast between the dark wings and tail with the rest of the plumage, and the pale rump in flight are good distinguishing characters from Common Starling. According to Cramp and Perrins (1994), the behaviour of Rose-coloured Starlings is less frenetic and more placid than in Common Starlings. Juveniles are distinguishable in flight from non-breeding Wattled Starlings by the latter's broad white rump and its lack of pale edges to the primaries and secondaries.

DESCRIPTION The head and upper breast are black, glossed purple, with the nape feathers hackled and elongate to form a long erectile crest. The mantle, back, lower breast and belly are pale pastel pink. The tail is blackish-brown with slight green/purple iridescence. The primaries are blackish-brown, the secondaries similar but with green/purple iridescence. The bill is yellow, with the base of the lower mandible black; legs bright pink. This plumage of the adult male is attained by abrasion of feather tips; when fresh after the complete late summer moult, tips of the black feathers are buffish-grey, while those of the pink feathers are pale brown on the underparts, darker on the back, giving a much duller appearance; the under-tail-coverts are dull black, variably tipped buff; the primaries and secondaries are margined buff, while the wing-coverts are margined buff or whitish. The underwing is black, mottled with white. The bill is dark brown or even blackish in summer and autumn, and brownish-pink in winter; the legs are dull yellowish-horn. Females in spring retain buffish feather tips and are always duller than males. Juveniles are sandy grey-brown, paler buff below. Chin feathers are paler, as are the throat feathers, but these have darker centres producing a slight spotting. A pale eyering and pale ear-coverts contrast with the crown. The rump is paler, tinged pinkish or buffish, and contrasts with the back and tail in flight. The tail is brown, the outer feathers with narrow buff margins to the outer webs. The primaries, secondaries and upper-wing-coverts are brown with buff margins, most pronounced on the inner secondaries and coverts. The underwing-coverts are pale buff, contrasting with darker axillaries and leading edge. The bill is horn with a bright yellowish or orange base; legs pinkish-yellow or straw-coloured. After the post-juvenile moult, from August in the wintering area but later in vagrants in the west, 1st-winter birds have dull black heads with feathers tipped brownish and crown feathers not elongated; the back and underparts are also browner than in adults, and the undertail-coverts are dull black with buff tips.

Adults undergo a complete post-breeding moult, usually after arrival in the winter quarters in India. Most birds commence moult in August and moult is completed in October, although some secondaries may be retained until March or even until after the following breeding season. Juveniles arrive in the wintering area in their juvenile plumage and moult into their first adult plumage between August and January–February, although some delay moult until later, not completing primary moult until May (Cramp and Perrins 1994). In fresh plumage, the tips of the major contour feathers are tipped buff-grey or brown (see FIELD IDENTIFICATION); these tips are abraded to leave the glossy black and pink plumage characteristic of this species.

MEASUREMENTS Male: wing (43) 127–139, tail (26) 65–75, tarsus (34) 29–34, bill (to skull — 35) 22–26, weight (43) 59–90 g; female: wing (15) 125–135, tail (7) 64–74, tarsus (16) 29–32, bill (to skull —16) 22–26, weight (19) 60–88 g (Cramp

and Perrins 1994).

VOICE Few calls of the Rose-coloured Starling have been described. The song of the male consists of a long series of bubbling, warbling, whistled and grating phrases, of a similar character to that of the Common Starling but apparently without any mimicked calls (Witherby *et al.* 1938, Roberts 1992). The most frequently given sequences of song consist of a short series of low-pitched squeaks *kitch kitch kitch* (Cramp and Perrins 1994). During courtship (see BEHAVIOUR), males give a jarring *trrr trrr* and a shrill *tjitjitji* and sometimes a call resembling the peeping of nestlings (Serebrennikov 1931, Schenk 1931–4). During the early stages of courtship females are quiet, but Schenk (1907) reported them giving a loud *zilij-zilij-zilij* in the later stages. Flocks settling into winter roosts keep up a continuous excited chattering, very similar to Common Starling and feeding flocks also chatter and give discordant squeaking and grating notes (Roberts 1992). On take-off, Rose-coloured Starlings give a short flight call similar to that of Common Starling and the alarm call is also similar to that species (Roberts 1992). Other calls reported include feeding and copulation calls of females (Serebrennikov 1931) but these have not been described. Nestlings give a weak chirp.

DISTRIBUTION AND POPULATION A starling of the more arid regions of Central Asia but which migrates to the Indian subcontinent for the winter. The breeding range typically extends from Turkey and Asia Minor eastwards through Iran and Afghanistan, the Caspian and Aral regions to the Pamirs in Kazakhstan and western and northern Xinjiang in China; to the north the range includes southern Ukraine, the steppes of the lower Volga and southern Ural mountains, and east to the western Altai; it usually does not breed north of 50°N, but occasionally the range extends to Barnaul and east to the Yenisey (Vaurie 1959). Within this area, the location of breeding colonies is determined largely by the abundance of the main food, locusts and grasshoppers (Orthoptera: see FOOD AND FEEDING). Periodically, large numbers of Rose-coloured Starlings appear outside this main breeding area and, if locusts and grasshoppers are sufficiently plentiful, breeding colonies may be established. Such erratic breeding has been recorded in Czechoslovakia, Hungary, Italy, Yugoslavia and Greece (Schenk 1931–4, Hölzinger 1992a) and now may breed annually in Bulgaria (Cramp and Perrins 1994). The entire population winters in the Indian subcontinent, most abundantly in the north from Gujarat east to Bihar and south through the Deccan. It is less abundant to the east and south of this area, although it is sometimes common in southern Kerala (CJF) and occurs periodically in Sri Lanka; small numbers winter irregularly in Oman (Gallagher and Woodcock 1980) and it occurs as a vagrant or irregular visitor in the Andamans (Ali and Ripley 1972). In China it occurs as a migrant in western Xinjiang and Gansu Province, and as a vagrant in Shanghai (Cheng 1987). Rose-coloured Starlings have been recorded as accidental visitors in Iceland, Faeroes, Britain, Ireland, France, Spain, Germany, Denmark, Norway, Sweden, Finland, Poland, Austria, Switzerland, Malta, Albania, Algeria, Tunisia, Libya, Egypt, Lebanon, Jordan, Kuwait, Seychelles and Thailand.

HABITAT During the breeding season, Rose-coloured Starlings feed in open steppes where locusts and grasshoppers are abundant. They may fly considerable distances, up to 10 km or more, from the colony to feed but colonies are usually established close to sources of water. Breeding colonies are often in valleys, usually among stones in screes, but nests are also built in cracks in cliffs, in man-made structures, in holes made by other species or in holes in trees. After the breeding season, colony sites are vacated and adults and young move to more wooded areas, for example orchards and vineyards, where they feed on fruit (Korelov *et al.* 1974, Serebrennikov 1931, Stepanov 1987). In winter Rose-coloured Starlings inhabit a wide variety of habitats including open country and wooded areas (Ali and Ripley 1972).

FOOD AND FEEDING During the breeding season, Rose-coloured Starlings are predominantly insectivorous, with locusts and grasshoppers often forming a major part of the diet. After the chicks fledge the diet switches to one consisting more of fruit, while in winter these starlings broaden their diet even further to include insects, fruit, seeds and nectar. While many accounts of breeding Rose-coloured Starlings emphasise the importance of locusts in the diet (Serebrennikov 1931, Dubinin 1953, Korelov *et al.* 1974, Shi-Chun *et al.* 1975) and comment on the importance of these birds in the biological control of locusts, detailed study of the diet shows that Rose-coloured Starlings eat a wide variety of insects. These include, in addition to grasshoppers, locusts and crickets (Orthoptera), bugs (Hemiptera), beetles (Coleoptera), ants (Hymenoptera), moths (Lepidoptera) and other orders, together with spiders (Araneae), woodlice (Isopoda) and snails (Mollusca) (Serebrennikov 1931, Rustamov 1958, Pek and Fedyanina 1961, Stepanov 1987). Rose-coloured Starlings have also been recorded flying from the steppe into forest during the breeding season in order to eat larvae of the winter moth *Operophtera brumata*, an insect also regarded as an important pest (Dubinin 1953). This suggests that these starlings will take whatever is most readily available; however, there is no doubt of their special attraction to areas of high locust abundance, a feature noted by Pliny the Elder who described their spectacular appearance during locust plagues. An individual Rose-coloured Starling can eat 120–200 locusts per day and they are said to continue killing locusts even after their appetites are satiated; however, this observation was made with captive birds which may not represent behaviour typical of wild birds (Serebrennikov 1931). While a few locusts may be caught in the air, most are taken on the ground. Large flocks of Rose-coloured Starlings run through locust swarms with all birds moving in one direction. Birds from the back of the flock fly over others to feed at the front, so that the whole flock moves forward in 'roller-feeding' fashion (Serebrennikov 1931, Korelov *et al.* 1974). The wings and legs of winged adult locusts are broken off before the insects are taken back to the nestlings but adult starlings swallow locust larvae on the feeding grounds without any prior treatment. Small snails, complete with shell, may be fed to the young and the shells of these, together with mulberry seeds and chitinous parts of locusts, are regurgitated in pellets (Hölzinger 1992b). Rose-coloured Starlings sometimes accompany cattle but, unlike other members of the family, they do not settle on the backs of the animals (Salikhbaev and Bogdanov 1967).

After leaving the breeding colonies, Rose-coloured Starlings disperse to areas where fruit is abundant. In particular, they visit mulberry *Morus* plantations and vineyards, where they can cause considerable damage (Serebrennikov 1931, Rustamov 1958, Korelov *et al.* 1974). At this time it is likely that birds also eat insects but no data are available. On migration, insects certainly comprise an important element of the diet but much plant material is also eaten (Kekilova 1978). In winter a wide variety of insects continues to be eaten but plant material, mainly fruit, seeds and nectar, assumes greater importance. Fruits of both wild plants (for example figs *Ficus*, nightshade *Solanum* and honeysuckle *Lonicera*) and cultivated trees and bushes (cherry and apricot *Prunus*, raspberry *Rubus*, dates *Phoenix* and chillies *Capsicum*) are taken, and in addition to wild grasses and other plants, Rose-coloured Starlings eat seeds of cultivated cereal, in particular sorghum *Sorghum*, millet *Pennisetum* and wheat *Triticum* (Ali and Ripley 1972). Rose-coloured Starlings frequently visit, along with other members of the family, the flowers of *Bombax, Erythrina, Salmalia, Butea* and *Careya* to drink nectar (Ali and Ripley 1972). In India, fruits of *Pithecelobium dulce* seem to be particularly important during the fattening period preceding departure in the spring (George 1976).

MIGRATION Rose-coloured Starlings are migratory, but true autumn migration to the wintering area in peninsular India follows a post-breeding dispersal. After breeding, colonies are deserted rapidly and adults and young move to areas of abundant food. The age groups soon separate, however, and during this dispersal phase flocks may roam widely or even be nomadic (Kovshar' 1966, Korelov *et al.* 1974, Kazakov 1976). Summer dispersal changes gradually into migration, adults leaving before the juveniles. In the west of the breeding range, migration is almost due west-east, but further east, the predominant direction of movement is southeasterly. Migration through Pakistan into India is on a narrow front between the Kangra Valley in the northeast and Baluchistan in the southwest. Thereafter, the birds spread widely over India. Spring migration takes the reverse direction and is more synchronised than the autumn movements. Birds migrate, mainly in the mornings, in flocks of up to a thousand, but millions can pass in a few days (Rustamov

1958, Ali and Ripley 1972). Summer dispersal begins as soon as most of the nestlings have fledged, usually in June–August. Autumn migration through Afghanistan involves huge numbers, adults passing from early July and the young later; passage is completed by mid-October (Hüe and Etchècopar 1970). Rose-coloured Starlings are among the earliest winter migrants to reach India, with the main passage through northwest India from early July to September. They remain in India until March–April (Abdulali 1947) and are among the latest migrants to reach their breeding areas, doing so from mid-April to early June, depending on locality (Korelov et al. 1974, Rustamov 1958, Salikhbaev and Bogdanov 1967, Schenk 1931–4, Hölzinger 1992a).

BREEDING The breeding season of Rose-coloured Starlings is closely tied to the availability of locusts and grasshoppers and is fairly short. Descriptions of breeding all suggest that it is accomplished in a hurry and as soon as most chicks have fledged, colonies are deserted, even though this often means that nestlings that are not yet ready to fly are also deserted by their parents. In most parts of the breeding range, breeding commences in May or early June (Schenk 1931–4, Korelov et al. 1974, Shi-Chun et al. 1975, Hölzinger 1992b) but rarely, possibly as a result of bad weather, breeding may occur in July (Ivanov 1969). Where an orthopteran food supply fails, due to cold weather or to depletion by the birds, a breeding colony may be deserted (Stepanov 1987). Rose-coloured Starlings breed in holes. The site most frequently used is the interstices between stones on scree slopes, ideally where stones are 10–15 cm (Ivanov 1969) or 20–50 cm (Buzun 1987) in diameter. They also nest in cracks in cliffs and rocks, among stones on railway embankments, in holes and crevices in walls, buildings, bridges and ruins, and under roofs and in thatch. Occasionally, they nest in holes made by Sand Martins *Riparia riparia* and sometimes nest in holes in trees, especially willows *Salix*. The nests are usually deep among the stones, and therefore difficult for the human observer to gain access, but sometimes they may be nearer the surface or even exposed (Serebrennikov 1931, Schenk 1931–4, Korelov et al. 1974, Buzun 1987, Hölzinger 1992b). In some colonies nests are built so close together that they coalesce. The nest itself is roughly made of grasses and twigs and is lined with finer grasses and feathers, usually of the starlings themselves. In addition, fresh Wormwood *Artemesia*, Giant Fennel *Ferula* and a grass *Aeluropus* are sometimes incorporated into the nest cup (Rustamov 1958); it is possible that these may be used on account of their insecticidal properties, as has been claimed for Common Starlings (see that species), which could be important in those areas where Rose-coloured Starlings breed annually and use the same nest sites each year (Salikhbaev and Bogdanov 1967).

Nest building begins very soon after the arrival of the birds and is accomplished rapidly. According to Serebrennikov (1931) only the female builds, but Schenk (1907) and Ivanov (1969) reported both sexes building. The eggs are pale blue or pale azure, slightly glossy but without any markings. They measure 25.0–33.0 x 18.5–22.7 mm (306) (Schönwetter 1983). The clutch consists of 3–6 eggs but up to 10 have been recorded, larger numbers probably being the result of two females laying in the same nest. Both sexes incubate, probably for about 15 days but there is no precise information. The young remain in the nest for about 24 days and are fed by both parents. Parental feeding continues after fledging but the duration of this parental care is not known; it is likely to be short however, as flocks of independent juveniles form soon after fledging. There are no data on breeding success but colonies attract avian, mammalian and possibly reptilian predators (Serebrennikov 1931, Korelov et al. 1974, Buzun 1987).

BEHAVIOUR Rose-coloured Starlings are gregarious at all times, feeding and migrating in flocks, breeding in colonies and roosting communally. Feeding flocks in the breeding season range from tens to hundreds (Rustamov 1958) while in winter flocks can be larger, sometimes described as of swarm proportions (Ali and Ripley 1972). On migration flock size is similarly variable, from tens to hundreds of thousands (Serebrennikov 1931, Rustamov 1958). Rose-coloured Starlings feed and roost communally with other species, notably other starlings, mynas *Acridotheres*, parakeets *Psittacula*, crows *Corvus*, weavers *Ploceus* and sparrows *Passer*. Rose-coloured Starlings congregate in daytime roosts near drinking and bathing sites, while night time roosts in winter can comprise thousands of birds in thorn bushes, trees, including roadside avenues, coconut plantations and reedbeds (Ali and Ripley 1972). Breeding colonies are rarely small; frequently they contain hundreds of nests and occasionally tens of thousands and may extend over large areas, up to 4 km^2 having been recorded (Serebrennikov 1931). The distance between nests depends on the nature of the colony site, but up to five nests per m^2 are commonly found and, in some scree slope colonies, nests may be contiguous (Schenk 1931–4, Korelov et al. 1974). In a colony in eastern Crimea, Buzun (1987) recorded many birds in immature plumage carrying food, but he could not confirm that they were breeding. Males arrive at the colony before females and presumably select the nest site. A territorial song is given by the male, usually while standing in the colony close to his nest site; this song is given with the crest raised and the throat feathers ruffled, and the bird adopts an erect posture. Unlike other members of the starling family, courtship display is performed on the ground. In this display the crest is raised, and the wings are partly extended and shaken, highlighting the contrasting black and pink plumage. At greater intensity the male may circle round the female and Schenk (1907) described the male, in crouched posture but with the head up, walking around the female while continuously vibrating his wings and tail; the female, in a similar but more horizontal posture and with her short crest raised, also began to circle so that both birds walked around each other. This occurred with increasing speed until both birds stopped and copulation occurred, always on the ground. Serebrennikov (1931) and Shenk (1931–4) also described courting males flapping their wings, bowing and gaping widely with the bill. Throughout these displays, a variety of calls may be given (see VOICE). Buzun (1987) commented on the lack of aggression between neighbouring pairs in dense colonies, even between birds whose nests share a common entrance. Flights of birds setting out on foraging trips, usually in flocks of 20–80 birds, were highly synchronised, but returning birds were in smaller flocks.

RELATIONS WITH MAN The great capacity of Rose-coloured Starlings for locusts and grasshoppers has led them to be regarded as highly beneficial birds. Although Stepanov (1987) mentioned an instance of apparent prey depletion by the birds, he also commented that (unspecified) pest control measures had been employed, and the real benefit of the predation of Rose-coloured Starlings on locusts and other insect pests has yet to be demonstrated. After breeding, when the diet is widened to include fruit, severe damage to mulberries and grapes *Vitis* has been reported (Serebrennikov 1931, Rustamov 1958, Korelov *et al.* 1974) and in India they damage cultivated fruits and cereals (Ali and Ripley 1972).

63 RED-BILLED STARLING *Sturnus sericeus*   Plate 13
Silky Starling

Sturnus sericeus Gmelin 1788

FIELD IDENTIFICATION 21–24 cm. Adult males are largely grey with the head and nape white tinted with grey or ochre. The belly and undertail-coverts are white. Feathers of the head, neck and especially the upper breast are long and lanceolate. Wings and tail are black with blue-green iridescence. The bases of the primaries are white, forming a white patch on the wing. Females are duller and browner. The bill is red tipped black, the legs and feet dull orange to chrome-yellow. In flight, the wings are pointed, as in Common Starling.

DESCRIPTION Sexually dimorphic. **Adult male:** Forehead and crown are dirty white, the chin and throat white. The forehead, crown and hindneck feathers are somewhat elongate and hackled, the upper breast less so. The mantle and back are slate grey, paler on the rump. The breast and flanks are grey, the belly and undertail-coverts white. The feathers of the upper mantle, sides of the lower neck and, to a lesser extent, the upper breast, are somewhat darker than more posterior feathers, producing a slightly darker collar which contrasts sharply with the whiter head. The tail is black, glossed green. The primaries are black, glossed blue and purple on the outer webs of the inner feathers, and the bases of the primaries are white; the secondaries are black with green and purple gloss on the outer webs. The lesser wing-coverts are slate grey but with white margins to the outer feathers; the primary coverts have white outer webs, forming a white patch. The bill is red or red with a black tip; the legs and feet are chrome-yellow to dull orange; the iris is bluish with a white ring. **Adult female:** Similar to adult male but the tail and wings are browner but with gloss, and the head, breast and underparts are tinged brown, so that there is less contrast between the head and the rest of the body. The back is browner, rather than grey, but the rump is paler buffish. The brown of the back extends on to the nape as mottling, and on to the sides of the crown as a greyish-

brown superciliary stripe. The sides of the chin have a greyish-brown moustachial stripe.

MEASUREMENTS Male/female (sample sizes not given): wing 118, tail 60, tarsus 29, bill 26 (du Pont 1971).

VOICE The song is described as sweet and melodious (Etchécopar and Hüe 1983). In flocks they make a chattering like Common Starlings (G Carey pers. comm.).

DISTRIBUTION AND POPULATION Resident in most of China south of the Yangtze, including Hainan and west to Sichuan Province (Cheng 1987). It does not occur in western Yunnan, but appears in Vietnam and Hong Kong in winter, and has occurred as a vagrant in the Philippines and in Japan, where it may now occur annually (Brazil 1990).

HABITAT Inhabits hilly country and low altitude cultivated areas with scattered trees and groves, gardens and scrub, especially by the coast. They feed in trees and on the ground, but have not been observed associating with cattle (Carey pers. comm.).

BREEDING Nests are built in holes in trees and walls and also in the roofs of houses (Cheng 1987). Eggs are pale blue-green, without markings, and average 28.5 x 20.5 mm (ranges and sample size not given — Schönwetter 1983). No other details of breeding are recorded.

MIGRATION Resident in most of China south of the Yangtze and in Hainan. In Hong Kong and Vietnam they are winter visitors; in the former, fairly common from November to late March, mainly in the northwest of the colony (Chalmers 1986).

BEHAVIOUR In winter Red-billed Starlings are gregarious, regularly seen in flocks of 100 birds and roosting communally at night, one roost containing 350 birds (Chalmers 1986) although in 1994 a roost of 3–5,000 birds was recorded in Hong Kong (Carey pers. comm.).

PRINCIPAL REFERENCES Etchécopar and Hüe (1983), Meyer de Schauensee (1984).

Grey Starling, Ashy Starling

Sturnus cineraceus Temminck 1835

FIELD IDENTIFICATION 20–23 cm. Adult male: Upperparts brownish-grey but crown blackish, forehead and cheeks white with dark streaks and narrow white rump. Underparts dark grey. Eyes brown, bill orange with dark tip, legs and feet dull orange. Adult female: Similar but browner and paler. Immature: Buffish grey with whitish cheeks, throat, centre of belly and undertail. Distinguished from immature Rose-coloured Starling by distinctly pale cheeks, by finer, whiter edges to secondaries and, in flight, by narrow white rump.

DESCRIPTION Adult male: Forehead is black with some gloss and some feathers have white tips. The crown and nape are black, slightly glossed greenish-blue and the nape feathers are hackled and elongate. The cheek feathers, from the lower mandible, below the eye and on to the ear-coverts, are white, with variable black running the length of the hackled feathers, producing streaking of this white area. The head plumage is variable and in some birds is largely dirty white, with variable amounts of black, giving a white head with variable streaking and white cheeks. In birds with white heads, the crown and elongated nape feathers are not glossed. The mantle and back are brownish-grey; uppertail-coverts white. The throat is dark grey, with feathers hackled but not elongated. The breast is grey, sometimes (in white-headed birds) with white-tipped or even largely white feathers irregularly distributed over the breast. The breast shades to smoky grey on the lower breast and flanks and to off-white on the belly and white on the undertail-coverts. The tail is dark brown, the outer webs of rectrices with a slight greenish gloss; the tips of the inner webs are white, becoming progressively broader towards the outer feathers. The primaries and secondaries are mid-brown, the secondaries and tips of the inner primaries slightly glossed greenish-bronze. The outer webs of the secondaries are narrowly fringed white, forming a white wingbar in the closed wing. The bill is orange with a dark base to the lower mandible in spring, in winter it is orange or yellow with a dark brown tip to the upper mandible and distal half of the lower mandible; the legs are yellow-orange, the iris brown, sometimes with a pale yellow inner ring. **Adult female**: Generally browner than the male and lacks the black cap, but has white cheeks, rump and tips to the inner webs of the rectrices. **Juveniles** are similar, but the white cheeks have brown streaking, the rump is whitish, and the remiges and rectrices are as in the adult but without gloss. The bill is dark horn, darker at the tip and the legs are horn. Monotypic.

MEASUREMENTS Male: wing (29) 124–135, female wing (19) 121–134 (Dement'ev and Gladkov 1960); male/female tail 70, tarsus 32

(sample sizes not given — du Pont 1971); culmen male (8) 23–27, female (7) 21–24.

VOICE The call is described as a monotonous, creaking *chir-chir-chay-cheet-cheet* (Brazil 1990). Young chicks produce a trilling note after being fed, but after nine days the voice changes and increases in intensity with hunger (Kuroda 1961).

DISTRIBUTION AND POPULATION Breeds from southeast Transbaikalia to the Ussuri River (although the northern limits of its range are not known precisely), eastern Mongolia, Manchuria, northern China west to eastern Qinghai and Sichuan Provinces, Korea, southern parts of Sakhalin, southern Kurile Islands and Japan. In southern Japan it is resident, but in most breeding areas it is a summer migrant. On the four main islands of Japan it is one of the commoner lowland birds, very common in central and northern Honshu, a summer visitor to Hokkaido and a winter visitor from northern Honshu southwards (Brazil 1990). It also winters in southern China, Hong Kong and Taiwan and has occurred accidentally in Burma, the Philippines (Dement'ev and Gladkov's (1960) map showing it wintering in the Philippines is erroneous, as is the statement by du Pont (1971) that it winters on Luzon, since, according to Dickinson *et al.* (1991), it occurs in the Philippines only accidentally) and in the United States (Dement'ev and Gladkov 1960, Tomek 1984, Fish and Wildlife Service 1985). In China it is common throughout its breeding range (Cheng 1987).

HABITAT Kuroda (1964) claims that White-cheeked Starling was originally a wet field insectivore. It is mainly a bird of low altitudes where it inhabits cultivated areas, fields and cattle pastures, open woodland, parks, and towns and cities. It avoids dense forest. It is also sometimes found in sparse, boggy larch forest and in summer it visits fruit orchards (Dement'ev and Gladkov 1957, Jahn 1942, Nechaev 1975). In Japan it also occurs in lowlands and inhabits villages more than in Russia, but it also occurs commonly to 1200 m on Honshu. In winter, White-cheeked Starlings feed commonly in subtropical rice-growing areas (Jahn 1942).

FOOD AND FEEDING White-cheeked Starlings seek much of their food on the ground and obtain prey from the surface vegetation or just below the soil surface by prying (Kuroda 1975), an action which 18-day old chicks begin to use (Kuroda 1961). They follow the plough and are attracted to recently-mown grassland (Dement'ev and Gladkov 1960). Fruits are taken from bushes and trees. White-cheeked Starlings are omnivorous but, like Common Starlings, prefer invertebrates when given a choice between animal- and plant-based foods. Adults are predominantly insectivorous, beetles (Coleoptera) comprising a large part of their diet, while nestlings are given caterpillars of butterflies (Lepidoptera), beetles and grasshoppers (Orthoptera) (Nechaev 1975). During the breeding season, Japanese White-cheeked Starlings preferentially select mole-crickets *Gryllotalpa* for the young, but bring back to the nest a wide variety of prey types, including pupae and caterpillars of butterflies and moths (Lepidoptera), fly (Diptera) larvae and imagines, including leatherjackets, beetle larvae (Coleoptera), ants and bees (Hymenoptera), grasshoppers (Orthoptera), spiders (Araneae), isopods (Isopoda), crayfish (Crustacea), earthworms (Annelida), frogs (Amphibia), lizards and geckos (Reptilia) and vegetable matter including cherries *Prunus*, mulberries *Morus* and strawberries *Fragaria* (Kuroda 1963). The diversity of prey brought back to nests in urban areas is greater than that in rural areas, where mole-crickets predominate in the chicks' diet (Kuroda 1963a). In winter a greater range of fruits is eaten, especially Bead Tree *Melia azedarch, Sapium sebiferum,* Camphor *Cinnamonum camphora,* Date-plum *Diospyrus kaki* and Chinese Privet *Ligustrum lucidum* (Hashiguchi and Ueda 1990).

BREEDING Nests in holes, within which an untidy nest is built of dry grasses and feathers. Tree holes are commonly used, but they also nest under eaves and in roof cavities, and will also use nestboxes. It has recently begun to nest in city houses (Brazil 1990). Exceptionally it makes nests in the open, with no cover. Nests are usually in colonies of up to 30 pairs, in groups of trees scattered in open country (Dement'ev and Gladkov 1960). Eggs are laid in the second half of April in Japan (Kuroda 1964a, b) and in late April–early May in Russia (Dement'ev and Gladkov 1960). Within a colony, first clutches are initiated synchronously. Replacement clutches are laid after the loss of the first clutch (Winter and Sokolov 1983), and in Japan second clutches are sometimes laid from mid-June to late July (Kuroda 1964a, b, Brazil 1990). Eggs are pale blue-green or azure, without markings, and measure 25.8–30.5 x 19.5–22.0 mm (53) (Schönwetter 1983). The most common clutch size is 5 eggs, but 2–10 (possibly by two females) have been recorded. Clutches are larger in urban than in rural areas, but clutch size varies between years and declines during the course of a breeding season (Kuroda 1964a, b). Eggs are incubated for 12–13 days by both sexes, but males, which lack a brood patch,

spend less time on the nest than females. Young are fed by both parents, but according to Dement'ev and Gladkov (1960) initially only by the male; parents collect food, mainly mole-crickets, within 800 m of the nest, and also remove chick faeces, unhatched eggs and dead chicks from the nest. Chicks fledge after 21–22 days, when they weigh 77–78 g (Kuroda 1959). Hatching success exceeds 80% and 67–77% of hatchlings fledge (Kuroda 1963b). White-cheeked Starlings sometimes lay eggs in the nests of Purple-backed Starlings (Won 1961b).

MIGRATION An early migrant in most of its breeding area, with arrival beginning in late March and most birds appearing in early April. After breeding it forms nomadic flocks, so that some breeding sites are deserted in July. The main autumn migration occurs later, however, with most departures from the breeding range in October and stragglers remaining until mid-November (Dement'ev and Gladkov 1957). On the wintering area in Hong Kong most birds arrive in October and remain until March–April (Chalmers 1986).

BEHAVIOUR Gregarious at all times of year, breeding in colonies, feeding in flocks and roosting communally at night. Flight is swift and noisy and on the ground they walk with long paces, occasionally making long hops. During the day, they normally consort in small flocks of up to 30 birds, occasionally up to 100. In the evening, flocks are larger, and exceptionally 1,000 birds may be present in pre-roost assemblies 1.5–2 km from a roost. Winter roosts, used from November to mid-March, may contain up to 50,000 birds, with some individuals flying up to 40 km from the roost to feed each day. There is some overlap in the feeding areas of birds from different roosts (Kuroda 1960, 1962). Winter roosts normally occur in bamboo *Bambusa* while summer roosts, which form after the breeding season from June to October, are found in a wider variety of vegetation types and contain 6,000–30,000 birds (Takenaka and Takenaka 1994); they are invariably found near rivers (Kuroda 1973). White-cheeked Starlings also roost communally during the breeding season, the birds involved presumably being non-breeders or non-incubating partners of nesting birds.

RELATIONS WITH MAN This species is regarded as one of the major bird pests in Japan (Umeda *et al.* 1993), presumably on account of its

65 COMMON STARLING *Sturnus vulgaris* Plate 17
European Starling, Purple-winged Starling

Sturnus vulgaris Linnaeus 1758

FIELD IDENTIFICATION 21–22 cm. Adults are blackish with pale tips to the body feathers after the post-nuptial moult, but these tips are abraded, leaving adults in the breeding season largely

blackish but with strong iridescent green and purple sheens. The wings and tail are dark brown, the straight, pointed bill is yellow with a steel blue (male) or pinkish (female) base in the breeding season but all brownish-black at other times of year, the legs deep pink in the breeding season but browner at other times of year, and the iris brown in males but brown with a paler ring in females. In flight the pointed wings and short tail are characteristic, and on the ground Common Starlings walk 'jauntily'. Juveniles are brown with a pale chin and throat.

DESCRIPTION Adult male: After post-nuptial moult, the forehead and crown feathers are black with purplish-green iridescence, largely masked by buff tips to feathers, these tips being darker in the mid-line but becoming paler towards the cheeks. Feathers of the crown and on to the nape are increasingly lanceolate. Feathers of the chin and throat are less glossed purplish and the tips of these feathers are white; these feathers become increasingly lanceolate posteriorly. On the nape and breast these lanceolate feathers are glossed green. The feathers of the mantle, back and rump are glossed green and are tipped buff, these tips being darker anteriorly and paler, almost white, posteriorly, but with much variation between individuals. Some mantle feathers may also have some purplish gloss. Feathers of the breast and belly are dark brown, glossed green and with white tips; the amount of gloss decreases posteriorly and the feathers of the lower belly and undertail-coverts largely lack gloss but have increasingly large white tips, these becoming buffer posteriorly and on the flanks. On the flanks, the gloss tends to become more turquoise and purple. The primaries and secondaries are brown with fine buff outer margins. The primaries have hints of gloss on the outer webs and as spots towards the feather tips, while on the secondaries, purple/green iridescence is much more pronounced and the buff margins to the outer webs extend around the feather tips. The tertials are highly glossed green. The underwing is paler brown with pale buff margins to the coverts. The tail is brown, the feathers finely margined with buff and also with a hint of gloss towards the margins. The bill is black with brown or grey hues, the legs are reddish- or chestnut-brown and the iris a uniform dark or liver-brown. By April, most of the pale feather tips, especially on the breast, become abraded, leaving the glossy parts of the feathers exposed, so that the breeding male is highly glossed purple on the nape, cheeks and throat, more black with less purple on the crown and forehead, and highly glossed green on the mantle, back, rump (although the rump feathers tend to retain their buff tips) and breast, less glossy on the belly and undertail-coverts (which also retain pale tips), and more turquoise/purple on the flanks. The feathers of the throat and upper breast are noticeably elongate and hackled when erected in display. Attainment of this state is gradual over the winter. The bill is yellow with the basal third steel-blue; attainment of this is also gradual over the winter, the timing of change varying between populations. The legs are deep pink.

Adult female: Similar to the adult male but tends to have more extensive pale tips to the body feathers, and the lanceolate feathers of the chin, throat and upper breast, and to a lesser extent the

crown and nape, are shorter than in the male and with less extensive gloss. Females also have less gloss on the belly and undertail-coverts. Towards the breeding season, the pale feather tips abrade but remain more extensive than in the male, especially on the rump, belly and undertail-coverts, and there is noticeably less gloss on the crown, nape, throat and breast. The bill in autumn and winter is as in the male, but in the breeding season it is yellow with the base paler, usually pale pink. The iris is dark brown but normally has a narrow pale ring; this ring may be on the inner or outer margin of the iris, and its colour is variable; cream, whitish, greyish, pale brown, pale yellow and sometimes more orange-brown.

First year birds: In both sexes, these are generally less glossy and the body feathers have more extensive pale tips than in the adults, but the ageing of Common Starlings, especially females, can be difficult and there may be geographical differences in characteristics used for ageing. First year birds can be ascribed to sex using the eye and (in the breeding season) bill characters described for adults. First year birds tend to have more rounded tips to the rectrices than adults, have less well-defined pale margins to the rectrices and less contrasting dark areas on the brown parts of the rectrix. The pale tips to the feathers of the underparts of first year birds are not divided by a pointed extension of the dark part of the feather along the rachis, which is apparent in adults. The longest throat feathers are shorter in first year birds than in adults but there is some overlap, especially in females. All of these features should be used in ascribing a bird to a sex/age category and for more detail Svensson (1992) and Cramp and Perrins (1994) should be consulted.

Juvenile: Entire upperparts, including wings and tail, are mid-brown. The lores may be darker brown or blackish, and the chin is whitish although the feathers have browner tips. Feathers of the breast are buffish-white but with mid-brown tips, while feathers of the belly have brown shafts and tips with paler buff webs, giving a streaked or sometimes blotched appearance, especially along the mid-line. Primaries, secondaries and rectrices are usually narrowly margined with pale buff. The underwing is paler brown, the coverts having darker shafts and paler margins. The bill is brownish-black, with yellow gape flanges disappearing with age. The legs are usually pinkish-brown but sometimes greyer and rarely red. During moult, juveniles become very variably patterned as the brown juvenile feathers are replaced with dark feathers broadly tipped white or buff. This transition begins on the wing-coverts and sides of the belly, and is completed with the head.

Adults undergo a complete moult after breeding. This begins with the inner primary in late May–early July and is completed in *c.* 80 days with the growth of primary 9. The fresh plumage appears spotted due to pale tips to the body feathers and the glossy appearance of the following breeding season is attained through abrasion of these pale tips. Juveniles also undergo a complete moult, although exceptionally some juvenile feathers may be retained or moult may be suspended. Moult begins in early–mid June with replacement of scattered feathers on the sides of the belly and mantle, followed by the shedding of the inner primary, and is completed in *c.* 90 days. Moult of both age classes is later in the north and east, and moult of migratory populations may be more rapid than that of residents.

The above description refers to nominate ***S. v. vulgaris***, from the Canary Islands and Iceland (and possibly the Azores) in the west, to the Ural Mountains in the east, where it occurs south to *c.* 48°N and west to northern Ukraine and south-eastern Europe. Other races recognised by Vaurie (1959) are as follows.

S. v. faroensis, a resident of the Faeroes, is larger and heavier than nominate *vulgaris*, with larger legs and feet, and a broader gape, and juveniles are much darker.

S. v. zetlandicus, from the Shetlands, also has a dark juvenile plumage but is less heavily built than *faroensis* and is intermediate between this and nominate *vulgaris*.

S. v. tauricus, from eastern and southern Ukraine, the Crimea and Asia Minor east to Stavropol, has the head green, the mantle bluish and the back and breast purplish, with bronze on the abdomen, flanks, wing-coverts and secondaries.

S. v. purpurascens, of western Transcaucasia east to Tbilisi, northern Black Sea to Sochi, Georgia, Russian and Turkish Armenia, and northern Iraq, has the head and throat coppery and the back and rump bluish-green.

S. v. caucasicus, of the Volga Delta, northern Caucasus and eastern Transcaucasia, Azerbaijan and around the southern Caspian to northern, western and southern Iran, has the head and upperparts green, and the abdomen purplish-violet.

S. v. nobilior, of Afghanistan, Transcaspia and Khorasan, has the head more purplish, but is otherwise similar to *caucasicus*.

S. v. poltaratskyi, from the eastern Ural mountains to Lake Baikal, south to eastern Kazakhstan, the northern Kirghiz Steppes, and through northern Dzungaria to western Mongolia, has the head more purple than in *vulgaris*, the underparts bluer, the underwing-coverts paler, and the gloss on the upperwing-coverts is part green, part purple.

S. v. porphyronotus, from southern Dzungaria, Tien Shan, and west through the Pamirs, Tadzhikistan to Samarkand, has the head green, sharply demarcated from reddish-purple upperparts and bronzish-purple underparts; during the breeding season it is virtually unspotted, especially the adult male, but is much more brightly and colourfully glossed than Spotless Starling.

S. v. humii, of the western Himalayas from Kashmir to Garhwhal, has the head bluish.

S. v. minor, a local resident of Sind, is considerably smaller than other forms with a wing length of only 108–118 mm.

S. v. granti, of the Azores is doubtfully separable from nominate *vulgaris* (Feare 1984, Vaurie 1959).

MEASUREMENTS Male: wing (574) 124–138, tail (27) 60–68, tarsus (58) 29–32, bill (to skull — 127) 26–32, weight (742) 52–108 g; female: wing (556) 118–136, tail (19) 58–65, tarsus (50) 27–31, bill (to skull — 91) 25–31, weight (657) 58–101 g (Cramp and Perrins 1994).

VOICE Highly vocal and males sing in most months, being relatively silent only during the early stages of the moult in July–August. The song is complex and incorporates mimicry of a wide variety of calls of other species of bird, sometimes together with other sounds, some of them man-made. Male song is organised into a sequence of song types, beginning with relatively simple whistles, often with a downward or upward inflexion, progressing through complex song types which include mimicked calls of other species, rattles and squawks, and ending with high-pitched trills or screams (Adret-Hausberger and Jenkins 1988, Eens and Verheyen 1989, 1991a, b). Both whistles and mimicked calls are also sung outwith these song sequences. The latter are learned both directly from the mimicked species and also from other starlings; unlike most other bird species, European Starlings are capable of learning new songs as adults (Eens *et al.* 1992). Male song serves primarily to attract a female (Cuthill and Hindmarsh 1985) but is also used to incite the female to solicit copulation (Eens and Pinxten 1990). European Starlings sing in daytime roosts and also in night roosts, especially after arrival in the evening and in the morning before departure; at this time the volume of song can be spectacular and may serve to synchronise the departure of groups of birds (Feare 1984). In autumn and winter females may also sing but the function of this song is unknown.

European Starlings give a variety of other calls in different contexts. On taking flight a soft *prurrp* is often given. Birds in post-breeding flocks frequently give a harsh high-intensity call similar to that given between parents and young shortly after fledging; this was called the 'flock call' by Hartby (1969). During fights, when two or sometimes more birds jump up to about a metre high grappling with each other, a repeated *chackerchackerchacker*, called by Hartby (1969) an 'attack call', is given and a similar call is given by males as they chase females in flight during mate-guarding (see BEHAVIOUR). When grasped by a predator (including ornithologists), and sometimes when grasped by another starling or when caught in a mist net, a high-pitched scream, called a 'distress call' is given. A short metallic *chip* call or mobbing call is often produced when starlings descend into a roost in the evening and when they drop from flocks on arrival at feeding areas in the morning; they are also given by many of the later birds to leave a roost in the morning, and are given by starlings on seeing a predator. At the approach of the predator, groups of birds may take off in a tight flock and fly towards it, giving *chip* calls with increasing frequency. *Chip* calls are sometimes incorporated into song and whenever given by perched birds may be accompanied by flicks of the wings. *Chip* calls in most contexts may reflect a state of anxiety (Feare 1984). When predators approach nests, especially when containing young, parents give a repeated harsh *caaar*, which Hartby (1969) called a 'snarl'; this call may also be incorporated into song bouts.

DISTRIBUTION AND POPULATION The breeding distribution extends from the Azores in the west to Lake Baikal in the east, and from Lapland in the north to Sind, Pakistan, in the south (Cramp and Perrins 1994). The western limits of distribution include the Azores, the Canary Islands, southwest Iceland, the Faeroes and the British Isles. On continental Europe it breeds from northeast Spain (Catalonia) and southwest France through the Low Countries to northern Norway. In northern Russia it breeds north to about 68°N in the west and to about 65°N in the Urals. Further east its northern limits are less precisely known but it extends eastwards to Lake Baikal and northern Xinjiang Uygur Autonomous Region in China. In addition, Dement'ev and Gladkov (1960) suggested that Common Starlings might breed in the east of the then Soviet Union and since the 1970s, small numbers have wintered in Hong Kong (Chalmers 1986) and Japan (Brazil 1990); the origin of these wintering birds in the Far East is not known. In the south, Common Starlings breed in southern France, to central Italy, northern Greece, central Turkey, across northern Iran and Afghanistan, where limits are imprecisely known, to Pakistan, where it is restricted to valleys associated with the Indus River (Cramp and Perrins 1994, Roberts 1992). Common Starlings breed occasionally in the Balearic Islands, Corsica and Sicily, and breeding has been recently reported in Iraq (Al-Dabbagh *et al.* 1992). Northern and eastern populations are migratory, wintering to the south, southwest and west of their breeding areas, while some of the southern and western populations are resident, as in Britain, parts of western Europe, around the Black Sea and in Pakistan (Cramp and Perrins 1994, Roberts 1992). The winter range includes western and southern Europe, the Canary Islands, Mediterranean islands, North Africa north of the Sahara, Egypt, Arabian Gulf States, Iraq, northern Iran and the plains of northern India. It occurs irregularly in Oman, rarely in Yemen and accidentally in Ethiopia and the Cape Verde Islands (Cramp and Perrins 1994).

Common Starling is established, following introduction, in New Zealand, Australia, South Africa and North America, and there are recent breeding records from Buenos Aires Province, Argentina (Rivero *et al.* 1996). In North America, it breeds from east-central Alaska through northern Manitoba to Newfoundland in the north, to Baja California in Mexico, southern Texas and the Gulf coast to southern Florida in the south (AOU 1983). In Australia it breeds in New South Wales and Tasmania, and is extending the range north into Queensland and west through South Australia to Western Australia. In South Africa it occurs in Cape Province and the Transkei, and is spreading into southern and eastern Orange Free State, with occasional records from Natal and Namibia. From these introduced populations, birds have become established on Fiji (Watling 1982), Jamaica (Downer and Sutton 1994) and Puerto Rico

(Raffaele 1989), with records on Antarctic islands and in Papua New Guinea (Coates 1970). In western Europe, the Common Starling's geographical range is currently contracting in the north, with considerable reductions in numbers; these changes are being reflected in declines in the numbers of birds wintering in southwestern France, Spain and North Africa (Feare *et al.* 1992, Feare 1996), and declines in winter in Israel (Y Yom-Tov, *in litt.*) and Jordan (Andrews 1995) suggest that there may be similar reductions in numbers of breeding birds in Central Europe. In southwestern and southern Europe, however, the breeding range is expanding and in southwestern France and northeastern Spain the range now overlaps with that of Spotless Starling (Motis 1992). In North America, the spread is continuing in the southwest, and numbers fluctuate in different states; overall the North American population is practically stable (Peterjohn *et al.* 1994). In Jamaica, numbers have increased rapidly over the last 25 years (Downer and Sutton 1990).

HABITAT Primarily birds of lowlands, although they breed to 1500 m in Switzerland (Glutz von Blotzheim 1962) and at 1850 m in Russia (Dement'ev and Gladkov 1960). During their relatively brief breeding season, they require holes for nesting and open land with short vegetation for feeding. Such conditions are provided by open woodland and woodland edge, especially where the surrounding grassland is grazed, and of course by man's cultivations, where trees, buildings and other structures provide nest sites. Cliff crevices also provide nest sites where suitable feeding areas occur nearby. Outside the breeding season a wider range of habitats is used. In summer, open moorland and salt marshes are used, especially by juveniles, and in autumn and winter, fruiting trees and sources of seeds are exploited. Fruiting trees exploited include wild and cultivated species, the latter involving orchards, vineyards and olive groves, while seeds, especially cereals, are taken from stubbles and from food provided for domestic stock. Common Starlings also feed on sea shores and mudflats, at refuse dumps and on other waste, and on food deliberately put out for birds in gardens. Throughout autumn and winter, however, Common Starlings need sources of invertebrates which are usually provided by grassland or cultivated land, although sewage treatment works are also regularly visited. In places where Common Starlings are resident throughout the year, birds may remain close to their breeding sites and roost in nest sites or other cavities nearby. Elsewhere, birds gather in large communal roosts for the night from a catchment extending for up to 50 km, sometimes more, from the roost site. Such roost sites include reedbeds, patches of scrub, young plantations, man-made structures such as bridges and piers, and even trees and buildings in town centres.

FOOD AND FEEDING Common Starlings are adaptable in their foraging techniques but their particular specialisation involves 'prying' or 'open-bill probing', in which the closed bill is inserted into the substrate where food items are sought, and the bill is then opened to make a small hole, exposing potential prey. This feeding technique is used in grassland to search for invertebrate prey beneath the soil surface or among grass roots, but also on settling beds at sewage treatment works, and among stones and seaweed on beaches, in germinating cereal fields to expose buried seed, and when feeding on cereal seed fragments in feed troughs, possibly in the search for fragments of particular size, and also when searching for ectoparasites in the pelts of ungulates. In addition, Common Starlings chase insects disturbed in grassland, hawk aerial insects, glean insects from vegetation, pluck whole small fruits from trees, peck fragments of larger fruits, drink nectar and peck at large food items where food is put out for birds, including taking peanut fragments from feeders (Cramp and Perrins 1994, Feare 1984, 1993). As expected from the wide geographical distribution, range of habitats used and adaptability of foraging techniques, the diet is diverse, and includes both plant and animal foods. Animal foods predominate during the breeding season and are given almost exclusively to nestlings, but are required throughout the year (Feare and McGinnity 1986). They include arthropods of the subsoil or soil surface, especially the larvae of insects such as craneflies (leatherjackets — Tipulidae) and moths (Lepidoptera). Animal foods also include vertebrates (lizards, frogs and newts, Reptilia and Amphibia), mayflies (Ephemeroptera), dragonflies and damsel-flies (Odonata), grasshoppers etc. (Orthoptera), earwigs (Dermaptera), bugs (Hemiptera), lacewings (Neuroptera), caddis flies (Trichoptera), flies (Diptera), sawflies, ants, bees and wasps (Hymenoptera), beetles (Coleoptera), spiders (Araneae), harvestmen (Opiliones), millipedes (Diplopoda), centipedes (Chilopoda), woodlice (Isopoda), earthworms (Annelida) and snails (Gastropoda). Plant foods include berries and seeds of yew *Taxus*, oak *Quercus*, apple *Malus*, pear *Pyrus*, cherry, plum etc. *Prunus*, rowan *Sorbus*, elder *Sambucus*, nightshade *Solanum*, bryony *Bryonia*, sea buckthorn *Hippophae*, and plants of economic importance such as olive *Olea*, grape *Vitis*, wheat *Triticum*, oats *Avena*, barley *Hordeum*, maize *Zea*, millet *Panicum* and sorghum *Sorghum*. Leaves and flowers of some plants are occasionally taken, as are some fungi (Cramp and Perrins 1994).

BREEDING The duration of the breeding season depends upon how many breeding attempts are made. In southern England there are often three phases: first clutches are begun highly synchronously within a colony; second clutches, laid by females who have already successfully reared a first clutch and by some females that begin breeding late in the year, are begun less synchronously 40–50 days later; between first and second clutches other clutches, 'intermediate' clutches, are begun with little synchrony, including replacement clutches of birds which lost their first clutch, mates of polygynous males that already have a female rearing a first clutch, and birds commencing their breeding season late. In the south and

west of the breeding area, second clutches are normally laid and the breeding season lasts from late March–early April to early July. In the north and east of the geographical range breeding may not commence until late May, second clutches are rarely or never laid, and the breeding season is shorter. In the southern hemisphere, breeding occurs in September–December. The nest site is a hole, which may be in a tree, cliff, building or other structure and occasionally, in the absence of alternatives, a hole in the ground. Nestboxes are readily used. While existing holes, including woodpecker holes, are normally used, exceptionally Common Starlings may make their own holes in sand dunes or soft rocks (Stevenson 1866, Summers 1989). Inside the hole a bulky, untidy nest of dry grasses, pine needles, fine twigs, string and other man-made materials is made. The nest cup, sited away from the entrance to the nest, is lined with softer material including grass feathers, moss, wool, hair and paper. In the later stages of construction, fresh green leaves and flowers are often placed in the cup; these may play a role in mate attraction (Feare 1984) or in defence against nest parasites (Clark and Mason 1988). The male builds the bulk of the nest and, where migratory, this may occur before the arrival of the females; the female contributes to the lining.

Eggs are unmarked, various shades of pale blue and sometimes white, and slightly glossy. Some eggs, mainly from second broods, may have reddish-brown or blackish spots, these being blood spots from the bites of ectoparasites on the incubating bird's brood patch (Feare and Constantine 1980). Eggs of nominate *vulgaris* measure 26.5–34.5 x 20.0–22.5 mm (1549) (Schönwetter 1983). Incubation lasts 11 days (rarely up to 14 days) and is by the female, who has a well-developed incubation patch and incubates throughout the night and for most of the day; the male spends about 25% of the day sitting on the eggs but has a poorly-developed incubation patch, and simply reduces the rate of heat loss from the eggs in the female's absence. When eggs are left unattended, they are often covered with a leaf or other material (Feare 1984). Young are brooded by the female for the first 5–8 days and are fed by both sexes, although when deserted by her mate the female can feed the chicks alone, sometimes with reduced fledging success. Young fledge at about 21 days and are fed by the parents for some days after leaving the nest.

MIGRATION In the north and east of the geographical range Common Starlings are migratory, although in some urban areas they remain throughout the year. In the south and west they tend to be resident. In spring, returning birds are among the earliest summer migrants, reaching breeding areas in Belgium in February, Poland and Sweden in February–March, and Archangel'sk (65°N) in April. Further east, arrival is later, birds reaching Kazakhstan in March, and Perm (58°N) in April. In the east of the range, autumn migration is north-south but towards the west there is a more westerly component in the direction of migration, and birds from Scandinavia migrate WSW. Birds from different breeding areas migrate at different times, along different routes, and have different winter destinations (Perdeck 1967, Fliege 1984). Juveniles of resident British birds disperse after gaining independence from their parents, but in migratory populations independent juveniles may undertake a directional summer migration: Swiss juveniles migrate northwest to the Low Countries and northern France in summer, later travelling south on autumn migration to North Africa and Iberia (Studer-Thiersch 1962). In South Africa Common Starlings are highly sedentary (Craig 1997) but in North America birds that breed in the north have established migrations, with birds in the east migrating north-south, while birds breeding further west migrate southwest in autumn.

BEHAVIOUR Common Starlings are gregarious at all times of year, breeding in colonies, feeding and migrating in flocks and roosting communally, although during the breeding season communal roosts are smaller than at other times of year. Typical song posture of the male involves the bird adopting a more or less erect stance, with the bill elevated above the horizontal and the tail oriented downwards; the long throat feathers and belly feathers are fluffed, and similar fluffing of the rump feathers produces a hunch-back appearance. In spring, males attract females using a peculiar display in which the wings are half-extended and then rotated around the shoulder joint, and which Feare (1984) called 'wing-waving'. This movement is usually performed during song from an exposed song perch, and is also performed by Spotless Starlings. Male courtship also includes flying into the nest hole in view of a female and singing in the cavity, building the bulk of the nest, and 'decorating' the nest lining with fresh green leaves or flowers (see BREEDING). Females solicit copulation by adopting a submissive horizontal posture close to their mate, and vibrating the tail from side-to-side (Eens and Pinxten 1996). The high degree of synchrony of initiation of laying within colonies is achieved through a combination of photoperiod, food supply and social stimulation (Feare 1996). During the female's fertile period, she is closely guarded by her mate who follows her to feeding sites, frequently giving *chackerchackerchacker* calls; at the feeding site the guarding male may cease feeding and sing quietly very close to his female. Many males are monogamous but polygyny is common (Pinxten *et al.* 1989a); most polygynous males have two mates but up to five have been recorded (Pinxten *et al.* 1989b). Some female Common Starlings behave as parasites, laying eggs in the nests of other females; associated with this behaviour, some parasitic females remove an egg of the host at the time of laying the parasite egg (Pinxten *et al.* 1991).

Feeding flocks are generally smallest and least cohesive during the breeding season, when birds feeding nestlings continually join and leave flocks, and the birds within a flock may be widely dispersed on the ground. After gaining independence, juveniles disperse and form flocks, sometimes numbering thousands, on upland rough pasture and moorland, on salt marshes and in

orchards. These flocks are much more cohesive, entire flocks taking wing together and flying in coordinated groups. In winter, daytime feeding flocks on grassland usually contain fewer than 50 birds, but larger flocks occur on stubble fields, at sewage treatment works and at cattle feedlots. In these winter flocks, individuals feed closer together than in the breeding season (Williamson and Gray 1975). Flocks are larger, however, immediately after arrival from the roost in the morning and also as birds gather prior to roosting in the evening, when feeding flocks may contain many thousands of birds. Non-feeding birds roost during the day at sites close to the feeding area. These sites are often on exposed perches, such as the tops of leafless trees, but are sometimes in dense cover. While in such roosts birds sing, preen and sleep and may leave for brief periods to drink or bathe, and for longer periods to feed. Towards dusk, Common Starlings leave their feeding areas and fly towards the communal night roost. As they approach the roost site, flocks from different feeding areas coalesce and huge flocks, of hundreds of thousands of birds, may form, usually within *c.* 1 km of the roost site. In these flocks individuals feed, preen, bathe and rest. These flocks eventually fly towards the roost site, usually in a stream of birds, and often perform spectacular aerial evolutions before entering the roost. In the roost social groups segregate, adult males predominating in the centre, young females towards the periphery. In the morning, birds depart for the feeding areas in groups at about three minute intervals, adult males leaving in earlier departing groups than young females (Summers and Feare 1995).

RELATIONS WITH MAN Common Starlings have been introduced by man to South Africa, New Zealand, Australia and North America, for aesthetic reasons (Lever 1987), although some of these introductions were also claimed to control outbreaks of insect pests (Thomson 1922). In northern parts of their Eurasian range, Common Starlings are believed to be beneficial in controlling insect pests and, to encourage the species, 25 million nestboxes were claimed to have been erected for them in the former Soviet Union (Feare 1984). East and Pottinger (1975) found that only under exceptional circumstances did starlings control an insect pest, the grass grub *Costelytra zelandica*, in New Zealand. Common Starlings are exploited as a human food source in some Mediterranean countries; in Spain they are trapped in winter roosts (Parsons 1960), and in southern France they are sold as pâté in tins (CJF). In Greek and Roman times they were kept as cagebirds, and there are some references to this species in classical literature and music (Feare 1984). Common Starlings are often regarded as pests. In North America and Australia they compete with native hole-nesting birds, but of more widespread concern is the damage they cause in agricultural and urban areas. They eat a great variety of foods of economic importance to man and his domestic stock (see FOOD AND FEEDING), and are capable of transmitting some diseases of domestic animals. In rural winter roosts, the weight of birds and of their droppings is sufficient to flatten reedbeds and damage young tree plantations. In towns, the droppings of roosting birds deface buildings and can render footpaths and roads dangerously slippery, and in the United States the droppings that accumulate beneath roosts provide a growth medium for the fungus *Histoplasma capsulatum*, the causative agent of histoplasmosis in man (Tosh *et al.* 1970). Common Starlings frequently forage on airfield grassland and are involved in bird strikes (Rochard and Horton 1980), and have been the cause of major loss of human life (Feare 1984). The Common Starling's omnivorous diet, ability to exploit food resources in grassland and tolerance of proximity to man have undoubtedly contributed to the species' wide distribution, in particular through man's creation of habitats, in terms of cultivated areas, suitable for the birds. It now appears, however, that extreme intensification and specialisation of agriculture are inimical to Common Starlings, and the current decline in populations in Britain and northern Europe (see DISTRIBUTION AND POPULATION) may be a reflection of these developments (Feare 1994b, 1996).

PRINCIPAL REFERENCES Cramp and Perrins (1994), Feare (1984).

66 SPOTLESS STARLING *Sturnus unicolor*   Plate 17

Sturnus unicolor Temminck 1820

FIELD IDENTIFICATION 22–23 cm. Very similar to Common Starling and has been regarded by some authors as conspecific (Dement'ev and Gladkov 1960) but most regard it as a distinct species (Vaurie 1959, Howard and Moore 1980, Wolters 1980, Cramp and Perrins 1994). The plumage of adult males is uniform black but with purplish iridescence in the throat feathers, breast, nape and mantle; the gloss on the rest of the body is oily-green. The throat and upper breast feathers are considerably longer than those of Common Starling, a feature which is conspicuous when these feathers are fluffed out during song. Adult females are also more uniformly black than Common Starlings but are slightly spotted on the undertail-coverts and to a lesser extent on the body feathers. After the annual moult, both sexes show a greyish bloom. As in Common Starlings, the bills turn yellow as the breeding season approaches; in the male the yellow bill has a blue-black base, while the base of the female's bill is pinkish. The legs of breeding Spotless Starlings are paler pink than those of Common Starlings. In winter, when Spotless and Common Starlings can occur together, separation of the species is more difficult but the former are blacker, less spotted and with smaller, greyer, arrow-shaped spots, and with blacker wings. Outside the breeding season the bills of both sexes are dark brown and the legs vary from light to dark brown. On the wintering areas of southern Europe in spring, the bill of Spotless Starling becomes yellow in February or sometimes earlier, while that of Common Starling remains black until later in the spring.

DESCRIPTION Adult male: In fresh plumage after the completion of the post-nuptial moult, feathers of the head, nape and upper breast may show a grey bloom produced by grey edges to the longer feathers; these feather edges wear away so that the grey bloom gradually disappears. The entire body plumage is black with metallic iridescence, nowhere as bright as in Common Starling. The head and upper breast have purplish tints, while the back, rump and belly are glossed grey-ish- or oily-green, but these areas show a mauvish wash in some lights. Mauve gloss is more pronounced on the outer webs of the inner secondaries and the tertials. The feathers of the crown, nape, throat and upper breast are considerably elongated, up to twice the length of those of Common Starling, and some are tipped with small white 'v' markings (Assertions that adult males are always spotless (Cramp and Perrins 1994, Hiraldo and Herrera 1974, Svensson 1992) are erroneous — CJF personal observations and J A Pascual, unpub. data). The wings are blackish-brown, paler on the inner webs, and the tail is blackish-brown. The underwing is uniform brown, darker than in Common Starlings and the coverts lack pale margins. The bill is blackish-brown, the legs reddish-brown and the iris uniform dark brown. Abrasion of the feather edges causes the breeding male to be more glossy, but never as glossy as with Common Starling, and entirely devoid of spots. Breeding males have the bill yellow with the base bluish-black. Leg colour becomes greyer during the moult of the tarsal scales in July–September, and the legs become paler in older birds (Peris 1983). In spring the legs become pinker, but paler than in Common Starlings, and the seasonal change in leg colour is not as marked as in that species.

Adult female: Similar to the male but less glossy and with shorter feathers on the head and upper breast. The feathers of the vent and undertail-coverts are finely tipped white, but these tips abrade so that females are entirely spotless in the breeding season. After completion of the moult in September–October, most body feathers of the female are fringed grey, giving the bird a greyish bloom. The iris is brown but with a pale inner or outer ring. In the breeding season the bill is yellow with a pinkish-brown base.

First year: Less glossy than adults and body feathers, especially on the back, belly and undertail-coverts, are more extensively tipped with 'v' marks, especially in females. In both sexes the elongated feathers of the head and upper breast are shorter than in adults, and they are shorter in 1st-year females than in males. The white spotting is retained, but reduced, in the breeding season. Cramp and Perrins (1994) and Svensson (1992) give criteria on which sexes and ages of Spotless Starlings can be determined.

Juvenile: Uniform brown, darker than juvenile Common Starlings, on the upperparts, but some have pale outer margins to the primaries and secondaries. The chin and throat are whitish, the feathers having white bases and browner tips. The breast and belly are as the upperparts, usually lacking any sign of streaking.

After breeding, adults undergo a complete moult, usually lasting from June to October. In fresh plumage both sexes may show a greyish bloom but the feather edgings responsible for this abrade to leave the glossy black appearance of the breeding adults. Juveniles also undergo a complete moult, beginning to replace their brown juvenile feathers 4–6 weeks after fledging. Young from first broods complete their moult by early October but young from second broods may not complete the moult until November (Peris 1988).

MEASUREMENTS Male: wing (314) 119–143, tail (280) 54–80, tarsus (12) 29–32, bill (to skull, 12) 28–31; weight 80–115 g; female: wing (249) 117–138, tail (226) 54–77, tarsus (13) 29–32, bill (to skull —12) 27–30, weight 70–100 g (Cramp and Perrins 1994).

VOICE Like Common Starlings, Spotless Starlings sing in most months. Song is louder than in the former species (Feare 1986), especially the long whistles, and comprises a similar variety of phrases, including mimicry of other species and other sounds. Outside the breeding season the most frequently given calls are whistles and in winter both sexes sing. The organisation of song is similar to that of Common Starling, usually beginning with whistles and progressing through more complex warbling, including rattling and mimicked calls, to high frequency calls (Cramp and Perrins 1994, S J Peris and A Motis, pers. comm.). Harsh alarm calls are given, especially when humans or predators approach nests containing young, and when Spotless Starlings are grasped by predators, humans or even conspecifics, they may give high-pitched distress calls.

DISTRIBUTION AND POPULATION The breeding distribution of Spotless Starling is localised around the western Mediterranean, embracing Spain, Portugal, Morocco south to about 31°N, Algeria (possibly to about the same latitude although there is no information), coastal Tunisia, Sardinia, Corsica and Sicily. This species is mainly sedentary but has occurred accidentally in Greece, Malta, Libya, Madeira and the Canary Islands (Cramp and Perrins 1994, Etchècopar and Hüe 1964), and occurs occasionally in the Balearic Islands (Parrack 1973). Spotless Starlings are common and widely distributed in Spain, Portugal and northern Morocco, locally common in Sardinia but only sparsely distributed in Corsica and Sicily; their status in Algeria and Tunisia is unknown. In Iberia they are expanding their range, an expansion that probably began in the

1950s when they were confined to the central and western parts of the peninsula. This eastward range extension was probably a response to agricultural change, especially increasing irrigation. Range extension is continuing and small numbers of Spotless Starlings have now become established as breeding birds in southwestern France. As a result of this northeast extension of their range, and a southwesterly extension of the breeding range of Common Starling, the breeding ranges of the two species now overlap in northeastern Spain (Ferrer *et al.* 1991) and southwest France (Cambrony and Motis 1994), with limited evidence of hybridisation (Motis 1992).

HABITAT Feeds mainly on the ground and nests in holes, mainly in trees and buildings. They prefer open woodland with expanses of short grass and frequently occur in association with cattle and other grazing animals. They are found in many types of Mediterranean woodland, in farmland, parks and gardens, and in cities. In autumn and winter they inhabit more open country, including open fields, especially where these are irrigated (Peris 1981). In summer they occur at higher altitudes, to 2200 m in the Gredos mountains in Spain and to 2500 m in the Atlas Mountains in Morocco (S J Peris, pers. comm.).

FOOD AND FEEDING Spotless Starlings are omnivorous but in spring and summer their diet comprises mainly insects, while in autumn and winter fruit and seeds predominate (Peris 1980a, b). A wide variety of invertebrates is eaten by adult and larval beetles (Coleoptera) are numerically the most important, especially dung beetles (Scarabidae), weevils (Curculionidae), leaf beetles (Chrysomelidae), ground beetles (Carabidae) and grain beetles (Tenebrionidae). Grasshoppers (Orthoptera), ants and wasps (Hymenoptera), bugs (Hemiptera), adult and larval flies (Diptera), caterpillars of butterflies and moths (Lepidoptera), cockroaches (Dictyoptera) and dragonflies (Odonata) are also eaten, together with small snails (Mollusca), earthworms (Lumbricidae), spiders (Araneae), ticks (Acarae) and millipedes (Myriapoda). Some vertebrates are eaten, including small frogs and toads (Amphibia), lizards and skinks (Reptilia), and shrews and mice (Mammalia). Fruits and seeds of a wide variety of plants are eaten, including seeds of docks and knotweeds (Polygonaceae), fruits of nightshade *Solanum*, mastic *Pistacea* and bramble *Rubus*, acorns *Quercus*, and buds and inflorescences of elm *Ulmus* and poplar *Populus*. Spotless Starlings also eat the fruits of cultivated plants, such as cherries and plums *Prunus*, grapes *Vitis* and olives *Olea*, and the seeds of sunflower *Helianthus*, maize *Zea* and smaller cereals, especially oats *Avena* (Bernis 1960, Peris 1980a, b). In Gibraltar, Spotless Starlings have been recorded drinking nectar from sisal *Agave* flowers (Cortès 1982). The foods brought to nestlings vary between colonies, between years and during the breeding season. Despite this variation insects and earthworms are important food items, especially moth caterpillars, but beetles, mole-crickets (*Gryllotalpa*), and grasshoppers and crickets are also brought to the nest in large numbers. Spiders are fed to very young nestlings, and vertebrates (young frogs, toads and lizards) are occasionally found in the nestlings' diet (Peris 1980b, Pascual 1992, pers. comm.). Most food is taken from the ground, especially in grassland, where prey in the surface soil or among grass roots are obtained by 'open-bill probing' or 'prying' (Beecher 1978, Feare 1984). Spotless Starlings also feed among cattle where they catch insects disturbed by the grazing animals, take insects and seeds from their dung, and take ticks and flies from their backs and eyes (Bernis 1960, Peris 1981). Flocks in winter often move in 'roller-feeding' fashion, with birds from the rear of the flock flying forward to the front so that the whole flock moves continuously forward; this is often done in company with Common Starlings (Peris 1981). Spotless Starlings feed in trees and bushes on defoliating caterpillars during the breeding season and during the summer take fruit and commonly hawk insects.

MIGRATION The movements of Spotless Starlings are poorly known but they appear to be largely sedentary, ring recoveries indicating that few birds move large distances from their birth places. Recoveries in winter tend to be further from the ringing site than at other times of year and young birds tend to be recovered further from the ringing site than adults; these patterns suggest dispersal or nomadism, rather than migration (Peris 1991). However, the finding that densities of Spotless Starlings in southern Spain are greater between September and November than at other times of year suggests that a short migration cannot be ruled out.

BREEDING In Spain the breeding season usually extends from early April to mid-July but there is local variation (Gallego and Balcells 1960, Motis 1985, Peris 1984a). In central Morocco laying begins about a month earlier than in Spain (Whitaker 1898). Many females lay two clutches each year but, as with Common Starlings, between these two periods of laying other clutches, 'intermediate' clutches, many of which are replacements, are laid (Peris 1984a, b). Spotless Starlings nest in holes. These may be in trees, sometimes in the holes made by Green and Great Spotted Woodpeckers (*Picus viridis* and *Dendrocopus major*). Nests are also made in the disused burrows of European Bee-eaters (*Merops apiaster*) and Sand Martins (*Riparia riparia*), and in the old nests of White Storks (*Ciconia ciconia*), Jackdaws (*Corvus monedula*) and sparrows (*Passer*) (Walter and Demartis 1972). Man-made sites are frequently used, the most common site in Spain being beneath roof tiles, but holes in walls, buildings, monuments and stacks of wheat are also used, and Spotless Starlings will nest in nestboxes (Cramp and Perrins 1994, Pascual 1993). Nest sites in trees range from 1–15 m above ground (Peris 1984b) but can be somewhat higher in buildings in towns (Feare 1986). Where the availability of holes permits, as in pantile roofs, Spotless Starlings can nest in dense colonies. Both sexes help to build the nest, which is made mainly of dry grasses, lined with grass, roots, leaves and feathers. Flowers,

often yellow, are sometimes taken into the nest (Cramp and Perrins 1994) and fresh green leaves of *Eucalyptus* were seen by Feare (1986) to be broken from trees close to the nest site by a male and taken into the nest hole. The eggs are pale blue, smooth and glossy and without markings (although some eggs, especially in second clutches, may have small reddish spots, possibly due to specks of blood from parasite bites on the brood patches of incubating adults). The eggs measure 28.1–34.2 x 20.5–22.6 mm (86) (Schönwetter 1983). Clutches normally contain 4–5 eggs but 2–9 have been recorded, the larger clutches possibly resulting from two females laying in the same nest. As in Common Starlings, some females lay eggs in other starlings' nests; this intraspecific nest parasitism is particularly common in first clutches (Pascual 1992, Verheyen 1994). Incubation, mainly by the female, lasts about 11 days and the young remain in the nest usually for 21–22 days, during which time they are fed by both parents, but the female takes the greater share of parental duties (Cramp and Perrins 1994); this includes removal of faecal sacs which during the first few days are swallowed, thereafter they are dropped by the parents as they leave the nest. After fledging, the young remain in the nesting area for a few days and continue to be fed by the parents, but after about a week juveniles begin to form large flocks and roam away from the breeding area.

BEHAVIOUR Gregarious throughout the year, feeding in flocks, roosting communally and breeding in colonies. Feeding flocks in the breeding season are small, usually containing only 8–12 birds, while summer, autumn and winter flocks are generally larger, usually 90–110 birds. They commonly flock with other species, especially Common Starlings, and feed alongside cattle, sheep, horses and pigs (Peris 1981). They roost communally at night throughout the year but communal roosts are largest, numbering 1,000–20,000 birds, from mid-June to late March. In summer, some roosts contain almost entirely juveniles. From November to March, Spotless Starlings form large mixed roosts with Common Starlings, mainly in coastal areas or in cities, containing up to 100,000 birds (Peris *et al.* 1991). Before settling in the roost site in the evening, Spotless Starlings perform aerial evolutions in the same manner as Common Starlings (Smith 1965, Ruthke 1971). Spotless Starlings breed in loose colonies. The density of nests within colonies is highly variable, with low densities in buildings in cities (Feare 1986), but up to 45 nests per hectare in holm oak woodland and 1 nest per m^2 in roof tiles in old farm buildings in villages (Peris 1984a). In the breeding season the male adopts a characteristic song posture, with the tail depressed and the rump feathers fluffed out to give a hunch-backed appearance; at the same time the long throat, nape and upper breast feathers are erected. This posture is the same as that adopted by Common Starlings. Males sing close to the nest site and territorial song is usually delivered from an exposed perch, such as a tree branch, television aerial, telegraph pole or roof tile (Cramp and Perrins 1994). Singing males also perform 'wing-waving' displays similar to those of Common Starling. Immediately prior to egg-laying, males follow females closely so that birds are most commonly seen in pairs, but after clutch initiation this mate-guarding decreases in intensity and males may attempt to mate with a second female (Feare 1986). Peris (in Cramp and Perrins 1994) describes females soliciting copulation by sleeking their feathers and holding the tail up, while Feare (1986) recorded females adopting a crouched submissive posture, with sleeked feathers, and a sideways vibration of the tail. Copulation, mainly in the morning and evening, is brief. It occurs usually on branches, telegraph wires, roofs or other perches but sometimes takes place on the ground.

RELATIONS WITH MAN Spotless Starlings eat olives *Olea* and cherries *Prunus* and are said to cause economic damage (Feare *et al.* 1992).

67 WATTLED STARLING *Creatophora cinerea* Plates 16 & 18

Rallus cinereus Meuschen 1787

FIELD IDENTIFICATION 21 cm. A small greyish starling, with a white rump, pale bill and legs. In flight, the pointed wings and short tail are very reminiscent of the silhouette of Common Starling.
DESCRIPTION Adult male: Dorsal plumage light grey, paling to white on the rump, with the uppertail-coverts grey. The chin, throat, chest and thighs are light grey, becoming paler to off-white on the belly, flanks and undertail-coverts. The primaries and secondaries, including the alula, are black with a slight bronzy-green sheen, and some or all of the coverts are white. There is considerable individual variation in the pattern of wing-covert coloration, partly age-dependent. The tail feathers are also black with a bronzy sheen. There is a small triangular patch of bare yellowish skin below and behind the eye, and two bare, dark streaks on the throat, extending from the base of the lower mandible on either side. The iris is brown, the bill pale brown to flesh-coloured, and the legs light brown. In breeding condition, males may lose all the feathers of the head, chin and throat, and develop pendulous wattles of variable size. In this condition, the skin of the forehead, lores, centre of the head, chin and throat is black, while the posterior crown of the head, ear-covert region, and the area below the eye is bright yellow. One or two small wattles may develop on the black areas on top of the head, while paired pendulous wattles grow from the bare streaks on the throat. These may be fused to form a single large 'dewlap', and there is great variability in the development of this breeding plumage. The base of the bill as far as the nostrils is black, and the bill colour is more yellow than at other times.
Adult female and juvenile: Resemble the male in non-breeding condition, except that the wing feathers, including the primary coverts, and the tail feathers are dark brown with a slight gloss in fresh plumage, and the wing-coverts are grey. However, some old females may have plumage resembling that of males, and even develop bald, pigmented areas and wattles. Recently-fledged young have a yellow bill, which darkens gradually.
Wing moult in Wattled Starling follows the normal descendant sequence, but there is usually only one primary feather growing at a time, and suspended moult is frequently recorded. This is most common outside the breeding period in southern Africa, with a peak of both active and suspended wing-moult from May to October. In East Africa, both breeding and moulting are less clearly seasonal, but moult is less common in the months when nesting has been recorded. More than 1,000 specimens were examined in this study. Dean (1978) examined a sample of birds apparently going into breeding condition, and concluded that they would complete primary moult before breeding; this may well occur in cases of opportunistic breeding, but in most cases a post-breeding moult is likely. In captive birds, Crandall (1949) noted a single annual moult at the time when male breeding condition regressed. Suspension of the primary moult may be related to movements of these nomadic birds, rather than breeding activity. The spectacular appearance of male Wattled Starlings in full breeding condition, with bald pigmented heads and pendulous wattles, has always attracted attention, but such birds are not often encountered; only 75 of 560 male museum specimens were in full breeding condition. There are two records of breeding colonies at which males were indistinguishable from females (Friedmann 1937, Uys 1977), and Britton (1980) commented that in East Africa the occurrence of birds with wattles was extremely irregular and apparently dependent on exceptional rain in arid or semi-arid areas.
Van Someren (1922) kept several birds in aviaries in Kenya for two years, and found no correlation between gonads and the state of the wattles. He noted that the bare skin behind the eye was bright yellow in the breeding season, but the birds did not shed their head feathers and the small wattles which did develop on some individuals were concealed by the feathers. However, in zoos in the Northern Hemisphere, seasonal baldness was observed in captive birds (De Schauensee 1928, Webb 1951), while Dean (1978) did find a correlation between male plumage state and testis size in birds collected in South Africa. The plumage state of captive birds was documented by Crandall (1949). He noticed that in a male bird's first spring, the throat wattle became enlarged, but no feathers were shed. The

following year there was a bald patch on the head, and the crown wattles were evident. In the third spring, the bird developed a fully bald head and large wattles, and maintained this condition for about three months. This seasonal change occurred annually in four males for nine to ten years, whereas a female specimen showed no baldness at any time. The difference between the sexes was investigated by Hamilton (1959), who was interested in the problem of baldness in humans. He showed that although the extent of the bare areas was not closely correlated with gonad size, baldness in both sexes could be induced by treatment with male hormones, which also enhanced the black pigmentation. Sontag has emphasized the great individual variability in the head appearance of Wattled Starlings, and found that baldness and wattles may develop in old females, but to a lesser extent than in males. Age, season and social stimulation (presence of receptive females) influenced the development of breeding plumage, and during behavioural interactions wattles could be retracted to some extent, and bare areas such as the patch behind the eye covered by feathers. This suggests that in the field the breeding population will also include birds in a wide range of plumage conditions, which may reflect the social hierarchy of the colony or flock.

MEASUREMENTS Male (12): wing 116–123, tail 65–73, bill 25.0–27.7, tarsus 29.6–31.6. Female (11): wing 111–124, tail 65–73, bill 25.0–27.5, tarsus 29.2–31.7. Weight of male (67) 64–85, of female (53) 51–83 g.

VOICE Observers have compared the wheezy song of male Wattled Starling to that of Common Starling (Joubert 1945, Chapin 1954, Harrison 1963), or Rose-coloured Starling (CJF pers. obs.). The song occurs in two contexts, as undirected song when the male is perched, and during both lateral and frontal courtship approaches to the female. Undirected song may be accompanied by waving movements of the wings. The song is uttered in long phrases of more than 20 seconds duration, although it is relatively quiet and evidently has no territorial function, unlike the songs of other starlings. While the birds are moulting their song alters, as though the voice is breaking, with normal song resuming once the moult is completed. Joubert (1945) reported that the song included imitations of other birds, but this has not been noted by other observers in the field, and Sontag could not detect any imitation in the song of captive birds. Females solicit males with high-pitched twittering (Liversidge 1961). Although the male sings less during the incubation period, in a few cases captive birds sang when coming to relieve the female at the nest. Chapin (1954) reported that flocks kept up a continuous clinking chatter, and Skead (1995) saw groups of about 50 birds singing in 'choirs'. Liversidge (1961) described the alarm call in flight as a double squeak, and also heard a less harsh trisyllabic phrase from birds in flight. At a breeding colony, adults gave harsh grating calls to which nestlings responded by high squeaks (Fuggles-Couchman and Elliott 1946). In captive birds, the harsh

screaming when one bird was grasped by its pursuer seemed to be a part of 'sexual chasing', and a sign that the two birds involved were engaged in pair formation.

DISTRIBUTION AND POPULATION
Wattled Starlings occur throughout eastern, central and southern Africa, from Ethiopia and Sudan through East Africa, southern Zaïre and Angola to the southern coasts of South Africa. The first records for West Africa were from the Gambia in January 1976 (Gore 1990). Subsequently small groups were seen in Cameroon in March and December 1990 (Robertson 1992), and then flocks of up to 60 birds in February 1992 (Robertson 1993). There have also been sightings in Congo and Gabon, and perhaps in the Central African Republic (Dowsett and Forbes-Watson 1993). This probably represents a recent range extension, as it is unlikely that the species could have been overlooked for so long. Meinertzhagen (1954) mentioned their occurrence in Arabia only in a footnote referring to two nineteenth century records, but Wattled Starlings have recently been recorded in winter in North Yemen (Brooks et al. 1987) and in Oman (Gallagher and Woodcock 1980). A bird, which had presumably been blown out to sea, landed on a trawler 100 km off the west coast of South Africa (Grindley 1964), and there is a specimen in the British Museum taken at sea off Aden. Their ability to cross open sea is confirmed by a recent record of a small flock on the west coast of Madagascar (Langrand and Sinclair 1994), and a bird which reached the Seychelles (Feare and Gill 1997). Wattled Starlings are generally common to abundant, but appear irregularly in many areas.

HABITAT They favour lightly wooded or open and cultivated habitats, usually with short grass. Although they have been recorded to 3000 m in East Africa, they are more often found below 2000 m, and often in quite arid country.

FOOD AND FEEDING Wattled Starlings have often been termed 'locust birds' (e.g. Thomsen 1907), and Stark (1900) described them as largely dependent on locusts (Acrididae), but commented that they would eat almost any insect food, especially grasshoppers (Orthoptera) and small beetles (Carabidae), and occasionally took berries and seeds. Friedmann and Northern (1975) found only insect remains in the stomachs of birds collected in Namibia, but Andersson and Gurney (1872) described the food of Wattled Starling in Namibia as berries, caterpillars, beetles and other insects. Birds in North Yemen were seen feeding on locusts (Brooks 1987). Hoesch and Niethammer (1940) reported that the stomachs of four birds collected in the vicinity of locust swarms held only berries of Ziziphus mucronata. Chapin (1954) examined ten specimens, which all contained berries or small fruit, and also reported a grasshopper, a cricket (Orthoptera), termites (Termitidae) and a tiny snail (Pulmonata). The birds investigated by Dean (1978) had been shot to protect grapes Vitis, and they had also been feeding on Ziziphus mucronata and insects, while one stomach contained a small lizard (Reptilia). A sample of 27 birds collected in central South Africa contained no locusts in their stomachs, and beetles were the only insects recorded; most of the birds had been feeding on grapes, and a few contained seeds of *Pollichia campestris* (Kok and van Ee 1990). Cantharid and tenebrionid beetles, short-horned grasshoppers (Acrididae), caterpillars probably of cut-worm *Euxoa segetum* and seeds of berries identified as *Azima tetracantha* were found in specimens from the Eastern Cape (Skead 1995). Specimens from Namibia (Fleck 1894) and Mozambique (Pinto 1965) had also eaten both seeds and insects. Wattled Starlings will feed on fruit such as figs *Ficus* sp. in gardens, take crushed maize *Zea* at feedlots (AC pers. obs.), and eat the arils of *Acacia cyclops* (Uys 1977). Observations at breeding colonies show that the young birds are fed on abundant insect prey such as locust-hoppers (Acrididae) (Hoesch 1936, Webb 1951, Brooke 1989), crickets (Uys 1977, Paxton and Cooper 1986), karoo caterpillars *Loxostege frustalis* (AC pers. obs.), mopane worms *Gonimbrasia tyrrhea* (Paxton and Cooper 1986), caterpillars of the lucerne butterfly *Colias electo* (Broekhuysen *et al.* 1963) and caterpillars of *Laphygma exemta* (Chapin 1954). Other food brought to the young included praying mantids (Mantidae) (Paxton and Cooper 1986), berries of *Azima tetracantha*, worms (Oligochaeta), moths (Lepidoptera), lacewings (Neuroptera) and various insect larvae (Liversidge 1961). Nectar is taken from *Erythrina caffra* (Jacot Guillarmod *et al.* 1979), *Schotia brachypetala* (R.K. Brooke pers. comm.), Kenya coffee trees *Acrocarpus fraxinifolius*, at which flocks gathered in successive winters in Zimbabwe (Cooper 1976), and also from sisal *Agave sisalana* flowers in East Africa (Cunningham-van Someren 1974).

On the South African coast, Wattled Starlings have been observed foraging in the rocky intertidal zone alongside Common and Pied Starlings (Robinson *et al.* 1957, Skead 1966). They will also scavenge at abbatoirs and rubbish heaps, according to Roberts (1932). Wattled Starlings feed in association with many species of wild and domesticated mammals, and they have been seen perched on sheep and white rhinoceros, but Dean and Macdonald (1981) knew of no observations of Wattled Starlings removing ectoparasites. However, in Kenya, Wattled Starlings were found alongside Greater Blue-eared Glossy Starlings, perching on the backs of sheep, catching insects on the ground, and removing ectoparasites from the ears of the sheep (Bennun *et al.* 1990). At Lake Nakuru, a bird was once seen perched on a common waterbuck *Kobus ellipsiprymnus*, and small flocks often foraged on the ground near ungulates. By contrast, at Masai Mara up to five Wattled Starlings were observed perched on blue wildebeest *Connochaetes taurinus* and Burchell's zebra *Equus zebra*, spending long periods perched alert on the back or rump, but also foraging for ectoparasites (Koenig 1994). Prigogine (1971) saw a small flock accompanying cattle from which they appeared to be removing ticks (Ixodidae), but the two birds collected had only spiders (Arachnida),

bugs (Hemiptera) and grasshoppers in their stomachs.

BREEDING Wattled Starling nests are always built in trees or bushes. They may be no more than 1 m off the ground such as those found in small *Acacia* bushes, or more than 10 m off the ground, as found in eucalypt trees, which are a common nest site in South Africa. The birds may nest alongside Cape Weavers *Ploceus capensis* in eucalypt trees (Uys 1977). Knobthorn *Acacia nigrescens* trees were used in Zimbabwe (Irwin 1981) and in the Kruger National Park, South Africa (AC pers. obs.), and *Acacia karoo* is also a common site in South Africa (Liversidge 1961, Brooke 1989), while in Namibia a colony was found in *A. luederitzii* and *Colophospermum mopane* (Paxton and Cooper 1986), and in Tanzania in *Balanites* trees (Fuggles-Couchman and Elliott 1946). The nests are ball-shaped, built of twigs and thorn branches, which may be up to 30 cm long and 5 mm in diameter (Every 1981). Both sexes build the nest, with lining and egg-laying taking place before the dome is complete, so that building continues during incubation. Birds stole nesting material from neighbours, and some nests were totally demolished (Liversidge 1961). In captive birds, the male made the major contribution to nest-building, and in two cases Wattled Starlings in the aviary utilised projecting material from one nest as a basis for an adjoining nest (Sieber 1980). The lining may be grass (Webb 1951) or feathers (Liversidge 1961). The nests may be single, or clustered together so that the individual structures can hardly be distinguished and several chambers can be found in a single nest mass (Hoesch 1936, Webb 1951, Liversidge 1961, Uys 1977). The nest entrance is usually at the side, but may be near the top. Stark (1900) stated that birds which could not find room in the nesting bushes would build on the ground, either under stones or in holes, but it is not clear whether he was reporting what he had been told, or whether he had seen this himself.

Breeding attempts are generally associated with abundant insect food in the area, and if this food scource fails, the birds will abandon the nests, even if eggs and young are present (Haagner and Ivy 1907, Pringle 1970). Smith (1957) described how a colony in Eritrea, begun in June 1953, was abandoned a few weeks later when the swarms of desert locusts in the area were destroyed in control operations. Barber (1880) reported that in the Eastern Cape, Wattled Starlings had followed a locust swarm, and built a large colony the following spring, in an area where locusts had laid their eggs. However, this breeding attempt was mistimed, as by the time the chicks had hatched, the locusts were well-developed and the winged phase was already appearing. Finally, when the nearest locusts were no closer than 20 miles to the colony, it was abandoned, leaving chicks in the nests. On another occasion Barber saw so many nests packed into scattered thorn trees, that the trees collapsed during a storm, breaking the nests apart and spilling the eggs. This colony was also abandoned. It seems likely that the description, quoted by Godfrey (1922) of 'huge conglomerations of separate nests ... in some cases so heavy that they broke the supporting branches', at Alice, South Africa in 1869, refers to this same event. Webb (1951) quoted observations from Nanyuki, Kenya, where a locust invasion was followed by massive breeding of Wattled Starlings, and in Namibia nesting followed egg-laying by locusts, with two successive broods raised (Hoesch 1936). Breeding in the Karoo, South Africa, in 1986, was associated with an outbreak of karoo caterpillar and locust hoppers only appeared later (AC pers. obs.). In the same year in Namibia, an influx of Wattled Starlings occurred into an area infested with mopane worm and breeding followed. However, in Bushmanland in 1989, breeding was associated with a locust outbreak (Brooke 1989). In captive birds, Sontag reported that the provision of locusts as food was followed by a marked upsurge in courtship and sexual activity. Under such artificial conditions of abundant food throughout the year, breeding cycles occurred at short intervals, several times a year.

The eggs are pale blue, either plain or with faint brown spots. They measure 24.9–32.1 x 18.3–22.0 mm (76), weight 6.5 g (Schönwetter 1983). Clutch sizes are 2–5 eggs (Maclean 1993), typically three or four (Hoesch and Niethammer 1940, Fuggles-Couchman and Elliott 1946, Webb 1951). One nest contained seven chicks and one egg, presumably a result of more than one female laying in the same nest (Paxton and Cooper 1986). Both sexes incubate and feed the young, both in the field and in captivity (Liversidge 1961, Sieber 1980), and the incubation period is about 11 days (Maclean 1985). Hatching is closely synchronised within the colony. The young birds leave the nest at 13–16 days and clamber about in the trees for several days, still unable to fly (Liversidge 1961). At this stage they are especially vulnerable to predators, and many are taken by Tawny Eagles *Aquila rapax* (Webb 1951, Paxton and Cooper 1986), Secretary Birds *Sagittarius serpentarius*, Gabar Goshawks *Micronisus gabar* and Lanner Falcon *Falco biarmicus* (Paxton and Cooper 1986).

There are no breeding records for Sudan (Cave and Macdonald 1955, Nikolaus 1987), nor for Zambia (Benson *et al.* 1971) and Malawi (Benson and Benson 1977). Ash and Miskell (1983) gave no records for Somalia, but Archer and Godman (1961) reported Wattled Starlings nesting in May, and Proud (1987) saw birds feeding flying young in August. Breeding occurs in Ethiopia from May to August, according to Urban and Brown (1971). For Kenya, Uganda and Tanzania there are breeding records for March to July, December and January (Brown and Britton 1980). Chapin (1954) suggested that Wattled Starlings in eastern Zaïre might be in a condition to breed from March to June, but there are no nesting records from that country, despite the statement in Mackworth-Praed and Grant (1973) that breeding occurs from September to December in southeastern Zaïre. A breeding colony has been found in Rwanda in May (Vande Weghe 1973). Traylor (1963) reported birds in breeding condition in Angola in October, and Günther and Feiler (1986) saw males in breeding

plumage in August and October, but there are no confirmed breeding records. There do not appear to be any records of Wattled Starlings in breeding condition from Mozambique. In southern Africa there are breeding records for all months of the year, and Wattled Starlings evidently have the ability to respond to unusually favourable conditions. Thus Uys (1977) found colonies in May in the western Cape during an exceptionally wet period. However, breeding is predominantly seasonal, with a peak in the austral spring (September–October) in the winter rainfall area of the western Cape, and from January to March in the summer rainfall region (Craig 1992). Some sites may be used annually, particularly in the western Cape, but in other localities the birds may reappear after long absences; the colony observed by Liversidge (1961) was at a site where Wattled Starlings had nested six years previously. There are remarkably few documented breeding records for such a conspicuous colonial species, which suggests that breeding often occurs in areas with few observers.

MIGRATION AND MOVEMENTS Wattled Starlings have often been categorised as 'local migrants' (Curry-Lindahl 1981, Nikolaus 1987). In Kenya, Britton (1980) referred to large non-breeding flocks in the Lake Victoria basin from June to October and in the Nairobi area from July to October, with birds caught at night at Ngulia, apparently on passage. They appear to be present in Sudan only fom August to March (Nikolaus 1987). Jackson and Sclater (1938) quoted observers in Uganda who saw flocks of tens of thousands of birds, mostly adult, in July, whereas flocks in October and November contained mostly immature birds. Despite some regularity in their appearance at breeding sites and other areas, it seems clear that their status is correctly described as nomadic in this region. The birds reaching the Arabian peninsula probably come from Ethiopia and Somalia, and represent irregular forays by small groups rather than migration as is found in Amethyst Starling. There are no breeding records from Zambia or Malawi, and Wattled Starling is very largely a dry season visitor to Zambia; since the rainfall in these areas is highly seasonal, the birds' movements may be more predictable than in semi-arid habitats, and thus more like a regular migration (Aspinwall 1986). For southern Africa, there appear to be certain core areas where Wattled Starlings are always found and breeding probably occurs annually, although there is no proof that the same birds are involved. In the eastern coastal areas and in Zimbabwe it is mainly a non-breeding visitor in winter, while it is a summer breeding visitor to the Transvaal lowveld in South Africa; its movements are however nomadic rather than migratory (Craig 1992, Craig and Herremans 1997).

BEHAVIOUR Apart from body proportions and general appearance, the relationship between Wattled Starlings and the genus *Sturnus* is highlighted by the trait of open-bill probing (or prying to some authors) in this species. This was first observed by Kramer (1930) at Berlin Zoo, and he commented that no other African starlings showed such '*Zirkeln*', as it is termed in the German literature. Harrison (1963) described the behaviour of a solitary captive male Wattled Starling, which directed its activities towards other species, and noted similarities in behaviour to the Common Starling and some Asian starlings. The behaviour of captive breeding groups of Wattled Starlings has been described in detail by Sontag, and the following account represents a synopsis of his observations. No allopreening was observed. The birds bathed daily, and also sunned themselves regularly, in characteristic postures. They would ant intensively, taking up ants in the bill and passing them through the feathers. Anting by captive birds was also reported by Simmons (1961). Dominance and social status depended in part on breeding condition, and individual differences in plumage appeared to play a significant role in 'status signalling'. In threat, the ventral plumage was fluffed out, and the bill directed towards the opponent. The wings were often raised above the body, particularly in the case of birds with conspicuous black and white wing feathering. Audible bill-snapping often accompanied aggressive interactions. Captive birds appeared to be monogamous with long-term pair bonds, but males would also court and copulate with other females in the cage; such opportunities are presumably rare under natural conditions. Either sex could initiate courtship; females used two postures: the 'thrush', in which the bird showed a rounded, fluffed belly, with the tail lifted and the head stretched forward horizontally with the feathers sleeked and the bare ocular patch prominent; or the 'vulture', in which the wings were pressed against the body but drawn forwards so that the shoulders appeared hunched, while the neck was stretched forwards with head and bill directed downwards. Females would approach males with frequent head movements and tails quivering, which indicated sexual readiness. Males commonly started courtship with a lateral display, in which the wing facing the female was spread slightly to reveal the white coverts, but held against the body. Song accompanied all male courtship displays. Males soon switched to a frontal approach, crouched with the head and bill directed upwards and towards a female, with the body feathers fluffed out, and the wings raised and quivered. In this posture the white rump feathers were conspicuous against the black rectrices, and individual differences in wing feather coloration became obvious. The male, still singing, then followed the female but if she was unresponsive, he might switch to attack or chasing. In soliciting copulation, the female moved the tail vigorously from side to side, and quivered the body and the wing feathers. Copulation occurred on the ground or on a perch. The female adopted a sleeked posture with the legs stretched out, and the tail raised to expose the cloaca. The head was extended vertically, and she sometimes pecked at the bald pate or wattles of the male. When mounting, the male grasped the head region of the female with his bill, and beat his wings to maintain his balance. The female gave soft calls before and during copulation, while the male sometimes uttered a harsh cry. After copulation the male flew off, perched a short distance away, and adopted the 'vulture' posture.

Huge roosts may be formed in reedbeds or in trees. Liversidge (1961) described marked differences in the behaviour of breeding and non-breeding birds at the roost: when not breeding, the birds flew in directly and were virtually silent, whereas breeding birds held aerial manoeuvres before entering the roost, and then called in chorus once settled. Wattled Starlings often associate with African Pied Starlings; where few birds are present, they are incorporated into Pied Starling flocks, and use the same roost sites (AC pers. obs.). Flocking and roosting with Red-winged Starlings (Thomsen 1907, Godfrey 1922) and Indian Mynas (R.K. Brooke pers. comm.) has also been reported in South Africa, and at Port Elizabeth, Wattled Starlings shared a roost with Common Starlings and Cape Weavers (Nixon 1971). Liversidge (1961) commented that Wattled Starlings often associate with African Pied Starlings, and sometimes with Cape Weavers, but in the eastern Cape, South Africa, Wattled Starlings are not found with Cape Glossy Starlings. However, in Namibia these two species were regularly seen together (Paxton and Cooper 1986). In Zimbabwe, large winter roosts in reeds were shared with Greater and Lesser Blue-eared Glossy Starlings, with the birds arriving in mixed parties (R.K. Brooke pers. comm.). Both Vincent (1936) in Mozambique and Cheesman and Sclater (1936) in Ethiopia observed Wattled Starlings in flocks of Greater Blue-eared Glossy Starlings, and Chapin (1954) saw a small party foraging with Bronze-tailed Glossy Starlings in Zaïre. Zambian records report foraging with Lesser Blue-eared Glossy Starlings, Sharp-tailed Starlings and Amethyst Starlings (Aspinwall 1986). Birds at Tsavo, Kenya, joined flocks of Fischer's Starlings and Superb Starlings (CJF pers. obs.). Of their association with locusts, one early observer remarked that the real locust birds were the pratincoles (*Glarcola* sp.), although Wattled Starlings occasionally accompanied locust swarms in large numbers (Barber 1880). During a locust invasion of the Eastern Cape, South Africa, in 1869, there were reportedly thousands of Wattled Starlings and White Storks *Ciconia ciconia* in attendance, but neither species appeared during a locust outbreak in 1909 (Godfrey 1922). Similarly, Priest (1936) related that one year during extensive travel in Zimbabwe he had often encountered locust swarms, yet had seen no Wattled Starlings; and in northern Mozambique, Vincent (1936) observed only one small group of Wattled Starlings, which were not associated with locusts, although these were common.

RELATIONS WITH MAN Wattled Starlings spend much of their time in regions of low human population density. They were formerly highly regarded for their attacks on locusts, and Godfrey (1922) noted that local authorities imposed a ban on egg-collecting to protect a breeding colony established during a locust invasion, but this role is of little significance today. In South Africa, birds are sometimes shot to protect grape crops (Dean 1978).

PRINCIPAL REFERENCES Sontag (1978–1991), Craig (1996).

Turdus nitens Linnaeus 1766

FIELD IDENTIFICATION 25 cm. A blue-green glossy starling, with no contrasting colours on the ear-coverts or flanks. The iris is bright yellow, but is duller in immature birds. There is a small bronzy-purple patch on the epaulet, and generally two rows of dark spots are visible on the wing-coverts. It is most likely to be confused with Blue-eared and Lesser Blue-eared Glossy Starlings, but the ear-coverts, flank colour and voice are the best characters to separate them (cf Newman 1986). The wings make a loud swishing noise in flight.

DESCRIPTION The frons, crown, nape, ear-coverts and chin are glossy blue, with the ear-coverts not forming a distinctive patch. Mantle, back and uppertail-coverts are blue-green, with the uppertail-coverts having faint blue fringes. Throat and upper chest have a blue sheen, but it is greener on the chest, belly and undertail-coverts. There is a bluish sheen on the underwing-coverts and thighs, while the wing feathers are blue-green with small dark spots or bluish tips to some of the lesser coverts, and a distinct bronzy-purple epaulet. Primaries 6 to 9 are strongly indented on the inner webs. The tail feathers are blue-green, the iris bright orange-yellow, the bill and legs black. The sexes are alike. A partial albino in South Africa had a pure white head, neck, mantle and chest, with scattered white feathers elsewhere. The plumage was light blue-green, and non-iridescent (Penzhorn 1982). Juvenile birds are initially very dull with virtually no gloss on the ventral surface, which appears matt black, and with a dull grey eye. According to Woodward and Woodward (1899) young birds have milky-white eyes, which remain this colour for about a year, before becoming orange as in the adult. G. Ranger (unpub. notes) recorded the eye colour of newly-fledged chicks as 'blue', then dull a yellow after three months old, while at five months of age it was barely distinguishable from the adults. It appears that by six months old the eye is orange-yellow like that of the adults (AC pers. obs.).

Three subspecies are commonly recognised, *nitens* from Angola, *phoenicopterus* from Botswana and northern South Africa to Zimbabwe and Mozambique, and *culminator* from the southernmost part of the range in South Africa. White (1962) noted that *nitens* was the smallest in regard to wing length and also more purple in colour, whereas southern birds were greener. However, Clancey and Holliday (1951) found that colour criteria were unsatisfactory and used only measurements to separate the different populations. It appears that southern birds are larger than those further north, but recognition of different subspecies in a bird with a continuous distribution and intergradation between different populations serves little purpose.

In southern Africa there is a complete moult after the breeding season, with wing moult occurring primarily from December to May. Both tail and body moult are concentrated between March and May, so that they may be completed after wing moult. However, some degree of body moult can be found on individual birds at any time of year. Juveniles replace the body plumage and some of the tail feathers. There is no evidence of overlap between moult and breeding, and most birds are growing two wing feathers simultaneously (Craig 1983b).

MEASUREMENTS Male (10): wing 130–137, tail 84–93, bill 24.9–29.0, tarsus 32.6–35.6. Female (10): wing 119–134, tail 77–90, bill 23.7–28.5, tarsus 31.0–34.0. Weight of male (17) 65–116, of female (12) 67–98 g.

VOICE The flight call is a slurred rolling *turr-rreeu*, the song a sustained warbling including varied notes, along with the flight calls (Maclean 1993). Birds mobbing Red-billed Woodhoopoes *Phoeniculus purpureus* included imitations of bulbul (Pycnonotidae) alarm calls in their cries (Vernon 1973). Cape Glossy Starlings may sing at the roost on moonlit nights (G. Ranger, unpub. notes), and often sing in chorus in trees in the hot part of the day (Skead 1995, AC pers. obs.). Godfrey (1922) noted that these starlings sang throughout the year, and stated that the male sang at dawn and dusk from a regular call site, and would also go there to sing during a rain storm. It is not clear how he established the sex of the birds which were singing.

DISTRIBUTION AND POPULATION Found from the mouth of the Congo River south through Angola, southwestern Zaïre, western Zambia, Namibia, Botswana, Zimbabwe, southern Mozambique and South Africa except for the southern and southwestern Cape. Old reports from Gabon and a sighting from Congo require confirmation. Localised in arid areas and absent from forest, but otherwise common.

HABITAT They occur in savanna and riverine bush, and in arid regions are restricted to water courses and other taller vegetation. These birds are also found on forest edge, in plantations, parks and gardens.

FOOD AND FEEDING Eat fruit and insects, 'though at bird tables they will take bread, bonemeal and other scraps. The stomachs of museum specimens contained seeds and small insects, including ants' (Formicidae) (Hoesch and Niethammer 1940); insect fragments, fig *Ficus* remains and fruit pulp reported by Friedmann and Northern (1975), and termites (Termitidae), ants and beetles (Carabidae) by Benson (1960). In the Eastern Cape, short-horned grasshoppers (Acrididae), termites, wasps (Sphecidae), caterpillars (Lepidoptera), beetles and millipedes (Spirostreptoidea) were noted. Fruit taken included *Azima tetracantha*, *Lycium*, *Rhus*, *Olea*, *Scutia myrtina*, *Diospyros pubescens* and *Atriplex bacifera*; the large seeds were regurgitated singly (Skead 1995). Ants *Plagiolepis custodiens* filled with honeydew were eaten (Newman 1971). Nectar was taken from *Aloe candelabrum, davyana, ferox, marlothii, spectabilis, vandalenii* and *Boscia albitrunca* (Oatley and Skead 1972), and also from *Erythrina caffra* (Godfrey 1922), and *Protea subvestita* (Skead 1995). Cape Glossy Starlings are regularly associated with ungulates, including cattle, blue wildebeest *Conochaetes taurinus*, white rhinoceros *Ceratotherium simum* and impala *Aepyceros melampus*. They usually feed on the ground near the mammals, but may perch on impala and white rhinoceros, where they will hawk flies (Diptera). Birds on cattle may glean ectoparasites, and this behaviour has also been noted on sable antelope *Hippotragus niger* and gemsbok *Oryx gazella*. Cape Glossy Starlings have also been seen feeding on mammalian carrion (Dean and Macdonald 1981).

BREEDING Nests are usually in holes in trees, but Cape Glossy Starlings may nest in holes in river banks (Taylor 1951), or in man-made structures such as metal pipes (Taylor 1951, Cole 1963), under roofs, and even in a wooden post-box which was in daily use (Kannemeyer 1951). Birds using nestboxes in Namibia selected those which were above 2 m off the ground (Riekert and Clinning 1985). In hollow trees or pipes, twigs and other material may be used to fill up the hollow before the nest is built closer to the entrance hole (Plowes 1944). In Namibia, the birds nested mainly in tree holes in *Boscia pechuelii* and *Albizzia* sp. The nest material included horse and cow dung, dry grass and feathers. Both sexes built the nest (Hoesch and Niethammer 1940). Various soft materials including shed snakeskins may be used (Maclean 1993). Feathers may be added to the nest during incubation, and even during the nestling period (Skead 1995). The eggs are light greenish-blue, speckled with light red, and measure 25.4–32.5 x 19.0–22.5 mm (128). Clutches of 2–6 have been recorded, with three being the most common clutch size (Maclean 1993). Eggs weigh 6.1 g (Schönwetter 1983). A record of six eggs suggested laying by two females (Donnelly 1967). Incubation lasts for 12–14 days, and is carried out by the female only, and the nestling period is about 20 days with the chicks fed by both adults and up to three helpers (G. Ranger, unpub. notes). The breeding season is from September to February in southern Africa, from mainly October to December in the north, and later in the arid western region; there are also some winter breeding records in the low-lying eastern regions (Craig 1983b, Maclean 1993). There are apparently no breeding records for Zambia or Zaïre; a female specimen collected during October in Angola was about to lay eggs (Bannerman 1948). Günther and Feiler (1986) described breeding as likely in February and March in Angola, and saw juvenile birds in August. Cape Glossy Starlings are parasitised by Great Spotted Cuckoos *Clamator glandarius* (Hoesch and Niethammer 1940, Jensen and

Jensen 1969, Kemp *et al.* 1972), and there is one record of a nest containing an egg of Greater Honeyguide *Indicator indicator* (Friedmann 1955). Priest (1936) saw a group of starlings mobbing a Great Spotted Cuckoo in Zimbabwe.

BEHAVIOUR The first hint of cooperative breeding is an anecdote in Woodward and Woodward (1899), who described a tame bird kept by a railwayman. This bird attracted two wild companions, which nested in a box provided by the owner, and all three raised the young. Later, observers reported four adults feeding a single brood of chicks (Donnelly 1966), and one nest site in an *Agave* had been used for some 20 years, with a single brood each year fed by a group of five to eight birds (Donnelly 1967). The statement by Haagner and Ivy (1907) that five or six pairs will build in the hollow branches of one tree may be a misinterpreted observation of cooperative breeding. G. Ranger (unpub. notes in Transvaal Museum) followed a group of Cape Glossy Starlings in his garden over more than ten years; some of these birds were ringed. Two females nested in the garden for four years, one with the same mate for at least two years. One nestling remained in the family group and helped at the nest for four years; it was apparently a male bird. Ranger noted that the female often took food from the helpers and then fed it to the chicks, but in her absence other birds would enter the nest. Helpers sometimes brought feathers to the nest while the female was incubating. One male bird was aggressive towards helpers, and often chased them away when they came to the nest with food. Observations at another nest site suggested a dominance hierarchy in the group, with some birds regularly displaced by others, and only able to feed the young when no other birds were present at the nest (AC pers. obs.). Stark (1900) quoted a report from Ayres that Cape Glossy Starlings had taken over a woodpecker's nest and destroyed the eggs before laying their own. Chasing of one bird by another prior to the breeding season is often observed, and may form part of courtship (Skead 1995). Godfrey (1922) noted that Cape Glossy Starlings used a regular roost site in small numbers, and called in chorus in the evening and the morning. Roosting in small flocks seems to be typical in the Eastern Cape, South Africa. In Zimbabwe, Priest (1936) described a gathering of more than 700 glossy starlings at a winter roost, but from his description most of these birds seem to have been Lesser Blue-eared Glossy Starlings. He also commented on local movements of birds at this time of year. Flocks of up to 80 birds were noted in Angola (Günther and Feiler 1986). On the ground, the birds both run and hop (AC pers. obs.).

RELATIONS WITH MAN Andersson and Gurney (1872) noted that these birds were very destructive in fruit gardens, but were 'not unpalatable', which suggests that they were hunted and eaten.

69 GREATER BLUE-EARED GLOSSY STARLING
Lamprotornis chalybaeus
Green Glossy Starling

Plate 19

Lamprotornis chalybaeus Ehrenberg 1828

FIELD IDENTIFICATION Length 22 cm. A highly glossy, blue-green starling, with dark blue ear-coverts (often appearing black) and a yellow eye. The flanks and belly are royal blue to well in front of the legs, and the wings generally show two full rows of dark spots on the coverts; these characters help to separate this species from the Lesser Blue-eared Glossy Starling (Milstein and Newman 1981, Newman 1986). The voice also differs.

DESCRIPTION The frons, crown, nape, mantle, back and uppertail-coverts are blue-green, with a blue sheen on the uppertail-coverts, which also have faint dark spots near their tips. The lores are black, the ear-coverts glossy blue, forming a marked patch. The chin, throat, chest and undertail-coverts are glossy blue-green, with the flanks, thighs, belly and underwing-coverts blue with some violet tones. The wing feathers are blue-green, with the primary coverts bluish and a bronzy-purple epaulet on the joint of the wing; dark spots are present on the tips of the greater and lesser coverts, and on the tertials. Primary feathers 6 to 9 have clear indentations on the inner webs. The tail feathers are distinctly bluer than the rest of the dorsal plumage. The iris is yellow or orange, the bill and legs black. The sexes are alike. Juvenile birds are much duller, with an underlying brownish coloration, more gloss on the dorsal than the ventral surface. The eye colour of juveniles is described as reddish-brown, with a grey outer ring (Bannerman 1948). Adamson (1953) noticed that some birds had yellow eyes and others had orange eyes. Wilkinson (1984) reviewed the eye colour of adult Greater Blue-eared Glossy Starlings; he found that it could be white, yellow, orange or red. It appeared that yellow eye colour was commoner in northern populations, and orange eye colour was commoner in southern birds, but there was also considerable variation within a single region. Benson (1946) commented that the indentations on the primaries were very small on the females and immatures collected. Two immature birds collected in July had brown irides. First year birds could be recognised in the hand by the yellow colour of the inside of the mandibles, which darkened progressively up until about 14 months old. The eye was fully yellow at four to five months. A specimen from Zambia had almost completely white plumage except for a normally-coloured feather in the secondaries of each wing. The bill and legs were black, and the iris pale orange (Benson 1962).

There is variation in size in the northern part of the range, with the larger East African birds often being treated as a separate subspecies **L. chalybaeus cyaniventris**. According to White (1962) the wings of West African male birds are 133–147 as opposed to 144–156 in East Africa, but he notes

that the two populations intergrade. Birds from southern Kenya southwards are smaller, with a brighter, greener head and neck; the measurements listed above are all taken from this population. There does seem to be some geographical or habitat separation in Kenya, and the race **L. chalybaeus sycobius** is recognised for these southern birds. The race *L. c. nordmanni* reportedly differs in having a coppery rather than violet shoulder patch, but this subspecies is not recognised here.

Adults in Kenya underwent a complete moult two to six weeks after the young had hatched, and there was no moult-breeding overlap. The peak months for this moult were July to November. Juveniles underwent a moult of the body plumage at the same time, but did not replace the wing feathers until their second year. When hormone levels were compared with moult timing, it became clear that gonadal hormones declined at the onset of moult, and that there were separate moulting and breeding seasons for individual birds. All the birds collected in Zambia in January were moulting (Traylor 1965), and Brooke (1968) referred to a complete moult after the breeding season; of the specimens examined for measurements, birds in March and May showed wing-moult. Juveniles were acquiring their first glossy plumage in August in Ethiopia (Cheesman and Sclater 1936), whereas in Tanzania, Lynes (1934) noted post-nuptial moult in January and February.

MEASUREMENTS Male (10): wing 127–143, tail 89–97, bill 23.8–27.3, tarsus 33.6–35.4. Female (10): wing 116–128, tail 79–93, bill 22.4–25.2, tarsus 32.1–33.5. Weight of male (191) 74–112, of female (109) 61–96 g.32.1-33.5. Weight, male (191) 74-112, female (109) 61–96 g.

VOICE The characteristic call of Greater Blue-eared Glossy Starling is a drawn-out nasal *skweer*, and the same whining tone is found in the rambling song. Flocks will sing in chorus from trees (Maclean 1993). Jackson and Sclater (1938) reported various call notes, some high-pitched and jarring, others quite musical. Archer referred to a 'cheery little song' (Archer and Godman 1961), while Vincent (1936) described the flight call as *kwee-kwee*, followed by a shrill, rattling whistle.

DISTRIBUTION AND POPULATION From Senegambia eastwards to Ethiopia and northern Somalia, then southwards to western Angola, northern Namibia and Botswana, Zimbabwe and northeastern South Africa. This is one of the most widespread glossy starlings, and is common to abundant.

HABITAT This bird is typical of open woodland, and in West Africa it is found well into the desert belt, as at Air in Niger (Fairon 1975). In Kenya, however, Greater Blue-eared Glossy Starlings avoid the dry northeast with one breeding population largely above 1500 m and in the region with rainfall above 500 mm, whereas the coastal population is found below 500 m, but also in high rainfall localities (Lewis and Pomeroy 1989). They are common on the high Ethiopian plateau (Cheesman and Sclater 1936), and in Somalia are not found on the coast, but inland from 600 to 2000 m (Archer and Godman 1961).

FOOD AND FEEDING Greater Blue-eared Glossy Starlings ate figs *Ficus* sp. in large numbers, but fed mostly on the ground, taking grasshoppers (Orthoptera), beetles (Carabidae) and seeds (Archer and Godman 1961). Birds in Ethiopia were feeding on the fruit of *Trichilia emetica* (Duckworth *et al.* 1992). Lack (1985) saw them feeding on fruit of *Salvadora persica*, but most of the food items he recorded were insects collected on the ground. Kenyan birds took nectar from the flowers of sisal plants *Agave sisalana* (Cunningham-van Someren 1974). In Kenya, Greater Blue-eared Glossy Starlings were observed perching on the backs of sheep, from which they flew down to collect insect food, and they also removed ectoparasites from the ears of the sheep (Bennun *et al.* 1990). Koenig (1994) saw birds perching on the backs of buffalo *Syncerus gaffer*, blue wildebeest *Connochaetes taurinus* and Burchell's zebra *Equus burchelli*, but did not observe any feeding on the mammals. Locust hoppers were fed to chicks in Eritrea (Smith 1957), and Cheesman and Sclater (1936) saw birds at locust swarms and catching termite alates. Brooke *et al.* (1972) also noted this species feeding on termite alates. Bates (1934) found insects in the stomachs of birds collected, and saw them hawking termites; there were berries and insects in stomachs of birds from Ethiopia (Desfayes 1975). Benson (1960) recorded fruit of *Syzigium* and *Guibourtia coleosperma*, small black ants, beetles, large termites and grit in the stomachs of birds collected in Zambia. A captive bird killed and ate frogs (Amphibia), lizards (Reptilia) and baby mice (Mammalia) (Delpy 1972).

BREEDING Nests are in tree holes, 3–13 m above the ground; either natural holes, or old barbet (Capitonidae) or woodpecker (Picidae) holes in dead trees may be used (Short and Horne 1985b). A nest 3 m above the ground in a natural hole of *Pseudolachnostylis maprounifolia* was lined with grass, leaves and bits of plastic (Meyer 1959); feathers have also been reported (Vincent 1949). Nests in Somalia were seldom more than 3 m above the ground, and some were unlined (Archer and Godman 1961). According to Smith (1957), in Eritrea, Greater Blue-eared Glossy Starlings nested in tunnels in vertical banks. Lamarche (1981) stated that in Mali, these birds often used old nests of buffalo weavers (Ploceidae), Sacred Ibis *Threskiornis aethiopicus* and Abdim's Storks *Ciconia abdimii*, presumably nesting within the structure of these stick nests. A pair in the Gambia used a hollow fence post (Gore 1990). The eggs are greenish-blue, varying a lot in shade and spotted with purple or umber-brown, in clutches of 3–5 (Archer and Godman 1961). Eggs measure 23.4–30.7 x 18.3–20.9 mm (34) (Maclean 1993), weight 5.9 g (Schönwetter 1983). Some eggs are almost unmarked (Jackson and Sclater 1938, Vincent 1949). In captive birds, the incubation period was 13–14 days, with only the female incubating, and the nestling period 23 days, during which the male rarely fed the young (Adamson 1953). Short and Horne (1985b) saw both adults feeding the young on insects, and later the adults also took berries to the nest.

Breeding occurred in Senegal from June to October (Morel and Morel 1982), and there is a record for the Gambia in May (Gore 1990). In Nigeria, the birds were in breeding condition in June and July (Paludan 1936), and breeding has been recorded in August (Elgood 1982). A female collected in Niger had an egg in the oviduct in June (Bates 1934), and Giradoux *et al.* (1988) reported nesting in June and August, while Fairon (1975) found a pair feeding young in July. Birds were also nesting from June to August in Mali (Lamarche 1981). Breeding occurs from April to June in Sudan (Nikolaus 1987), and from May to September and possibly in March and April in Ethiopia (Urban and Brown 1971, Dorst and Roux 1973). Birds were feeding chicks in July in Eritrea (Smith 1957), while Ethiopian birds collected in May had enlarged gonads (Desfayes 1975). Archer found eggs in Somalia in May and June (Archer and Godman 1961), but Phillips (1896) had found the birds nesting in March, and Clarke (1985) saw fledged young in April. Breeding occurred in western Kenya and Uganda in March and April, in Tanzania from October to January, while in central and coastal Kenya there were records for most months, but primarily March to June (Brown and Britton 1980). At Nakuru, Kenya, breeding of Greater Blue-eared Glossy Starlings in the savanna was highly seasonal, restricted to between April and June, whereas from July to January there was some breeding in acacia forest. Lynes (1934) collected juvenile birds in January in Tanzania. In Uganda, birds were nesting in January and July, and feeding chicks in March (van Someren 1916). In southeastern Zaïre, breeding was reported from September to December (Lippens and Wille 1976), and from October to January in Rwanda (Vande Weghe 1973). Breeding occurred in Zambia and Malawi in October and November (Benson *et al.* 1971, Benson and Benson 1977), and also primarily in these months in Zimbabwe and the Transvaal, South Africa, although there are records from August to January (Irwin 1981, Tarboton *et al.* 1987, Craig 1997). In Kenya, there was individual variation in the hormonal cycles of Greater Blue-eared Glossy Starlings in relation to breeding and moult, which appeared to correspond to the two groups nesting early in savanna or later in acacia forest. Each group had clearly defined annual cycles. In southern Africa, Greater Blue-eared Glossy Starlings were parasitised by Great Spotted Cuckoos *Clamator glandarius* (Meyer 1959, Jensen and Jensen 1969), and in one case by the Greater Honeyguide *Indicator indicator* (Friedmann 1955).

MIGRATION At Nakuru, Kenya, there was a marked exodus of Greater Blue-eared Glossy

Starlings during October and November, with very low numbers of birds in the study area from November to January. Elsewhere in Kenya, wandering flocks of several hundred birds have been reported during the non-breeding months (Lewis and Pomeroy 1989). In West Africa, Grimes (1987) referred to this species as a non-breeding migrant to northern Ghana, and it occurs in large mixed flocks in the Gambia (Gore 1990).

BEHAVIOUR Greater Blue-eared Glossy Starlings were observed anting on the ground and perched in a tree, using the ant *Anoplolesis custodiens*. Each ant was used briefly, then apparently dropped (Whyte 1981). Anting has also been recorded in captive birds (Poulsen 1956, Simmons 1961). Large roosts were formed in leafy trees after the breeding season in Ethiopia, with the chatter of the birds audible for some distance, and aerial evolutions before the birds settled down (Cheesman and Sclater 1936). Later visitors to Ethiopia noted this species roosting in villages (Dorst and Roux 1973). Belcher (1930) mentioned flocks roosting in reedbeds in Malawi, but was not certain of the species involved. Brooke (pers. comm.) saw up to 400 Greater Blue-eared Glossy Starlings at a roost in Zimbabwe, where the birds roosted in reedbeds, and sometimes in thorny bushes or *Acacia* trees from March to August. They were often associated with Lesser Blue-eared Glossy Starlings, and sometimes with Wattled Starlings. In Senegal, Greater

Blue-eared Glossy Starlings were seldom seen singly, but usually in flocks of up to 30 birds (Günther and Feiler 1986), sometimes with Purple Glossy Starlings or Chestnut-bellied Starlings (Schifter 1986). This species' flight is noisy, as a result of the indentations of the primary feathers. At Lake Naivasha, Kenya, Jackson and Sclater (1938) saw them with Superb Starlings and Wattled Starlings, and noticed that Greater Blue-eared Glossy Starlings hopped, but did not walk or run. When breeding, the birds are never colonial, and only a single pair was ever seen at the nest (Archer and Godman 1961). There are no records of cooperative breeding. In aviaries Greater Blue-eared Glossy Starlings may be aggressive towards other species, but single birds can become very tame (Delpy 1972, Michaelis 1977). A captive male threatened birds in the adjoining cage, adopting an upright posture, with head stretched upward and the wings held so that the dark spots on the secondaries were visible, and quivered slightly. The irides contracted and dilated rapidly. By contrast, the pair greeted by lowering the head and uttering a call reminiscent of the begging call of the young (Adamson 1953).

RELATIONS WITH MAN Van Someren (1916) commented that this species does well in captivity.

PRINCIPAL REFERENCES Dittami (1983, 1987).

70 LESSER BLUE-EARED GLOSSY STARLING
Lamprotornis chloropterus   **Plate 19**

Lamprotornis chloropterus Swainson 1838

FIELD IDENTIFICATION 18 cm. A glossy blue-green starling, with dark blue ear-coverts, and with magenta shading on the flanks and belly extending a little beyond the legs, and a yellow eye. The flank colour, and the single complete row of spots on the wing-coverts help to separate this species from Greater Blue-eared Glossy Starling (see above). Immatures with rusty-brown underparts will confirm the presence of this species; the calls also differ from those of similar species.

DESCRIPTION The frons, crown, nape, mantle, back and uppertail-coverts are glossy blue-green, with some darker spots near the tips of the uppertail-coverts. The lores are black, with the ear-coverts glossy blue, forming a distinct patch at the posterior border of the eye. Chin, throat, chest, much of the belly and the undertail-coverts are glossy blue-green. The flanks, thighs and a variable patch on the belly are violet-blue, as are the underwing-coverts. Wing feathers are blue-green, but the primary coverts have a blue gloss, while both greater and lesser coverts and the tertial feathers have dark velvety spots at their tips, and there is a purple-bronze epaulet patch on the bend of the wing. The tail feathers are glossy blue-green. The iris is orange-yellow, the bill and legs black. The sexes are alike, and there are no inden-

tations on the inner webs of the primaries. Juvenile birds of the race *elisabeth* have the entire ventral surface light-chestnut brown, whereas in the nominate race it is fawn-coloured. The dorsal plumage has a metallic-green sheen, but initially lacks the dark spots on the coverts and the epaulet, while the ear-coverts are dull. According to Bannerman (1948), the iris of the young bird is greyish-cream. Benson (1959, 1962) collected male birds in breeding condition which had retained juvenile chestnut plumage on the belly.

There are two distinct populations, with the nominate race north of the equator and the race *L. chloropterus elisabeth* to the south. In southern birds the juvenile has a distinctive rufous-brown ventral plumage, whereas in the northern population this is paler. Stresemann (1925) included *L. acuticaudus* as a race of *L. chloropterus*, but this has not been accepted by subsequent authors.

Lesser Blue-eared Glossy Starlings have a complete moult at the end of the breeding season (Brooke 1968); the specimens measured were all from the months May to October, and none showed wing moult. A juvenile specimen from Zambia in July has some glossy green feathers on the ventral surface, but is still mostly brown. In Zimbabwe, Irwin (1953) found that juveniles began to moult into adult plumage in May, and most had completed this moult by the end of June, although a few retained some rufous feathers on the flanks.

MEASUREMENTS Male (12): wing 114–127, tail 67–78, bill 22.0–25.0, tarsus 26.7–29.9. Female (10): wing 111–124, tail 65–76, bill 21.4–24.0, tarsus 25.7–28.7. Weight, unsexed (7) 52–66 g.

VOICE The flight call is a clear *wirri-gwirri*, while a harsh *chair* is given in alarm. The song is a phrase of six to twelve notes, rendered as *chip chirrew kwip kreeup kwip krip cheeu* (Maclean 1993).

DISTRIBUTION AND POPULATION

Distributed from Senegambia eastwards to Ethiopia, south to Uganda and northwest Kenya. There is a second population from southeastern Kenya, Tanzania, Zambia, Malawi, southern Zaïre, Angola, to northern Mozambique and Zimbabwe. This is one of the commonest glossy starlings in the northern part of its range, although there often appears to be uncertainty as to which species was observed when no specimens were collected.

HABITAT While breeding, Lesser Blue-eared Glossy Starlings occur primarily in miombo woodland, but later wander into woodland of all types, where they are commonly found alongside Greater Blue-eared Glossy Starlings. In Ethiopia they occur only in the lowlands (Cheesman and Sclater 1936), but in Kenya one population is found only above 1000 m, while the other is coastal, below 500 m (Lewis and Pomeroy 1989).

FOOD AND FEEDING Lesser Blue-eared Glossy Starlings eat fruit, nectar and insects, and often feed on the ground. Birds feeding on the red flowers of a thorn tree were presumably taking nectar (Serle 1943). Chapin (1954) found only insect remains, including fragments of beetles (Carabidae), in eleven stomachs which he examined. Fuggles-Couchman (1984) observed flocks in the cotton fields, apparently feeding on insects. He reported that locust-hoppers (Acrididae) were certainly eaten, and one specimen contained grasshoppers (Orthoptera), beetles and caterpillars (Lepidoptera). Brooke *et al.* (1972) noted this species as feeding on termite alates occasionally. Belcher (1930) reported that the local people regarded this bird as responsible for the spread of the Mpepho tree *Sterculia quinqueloba*, the green seeds of which were dropped by Lesser Blue-eared Starlings after feeding on the fruit.

BREEDING The nests are in tree holes, built of a pile of straw and leaves with a bowl-shaped hollow in the top (Maclean 1993). Brooke (1965b) reported nesting in a woodpecker's hole, and several sites where the dead bark was peeling off a branch, but no hole as such was present. The eggs are light blue-green, sparingly spotted with rusty red and grey (Maclean 1993). They measure 26.0 x 19.2 mm (3), weight 5.1 g (Schönwetter 1983). A clutch of three is apparently common (Brooke 1965b), and both birds feed the young (Irwin 1953). There are no confirmed breeding records for the Gambia (Gore 1990) nor for Senegal (Morel and Morel 1990), but Lesser Blue-eared Glossy Starlings breed in Nigeria from February to April (Elgood 1982). Grimes (1987) saw birds carrying nesting material in April in Ghana, and dependent juveniles with dark eyes in June. Breeding occurred in March in Uele, Zaïre (Chapin 1954), but in September and October in the Shaba region (Lippens and Wille 1976). In East Africa breeding has been recorded in March, May and June (Brown and Britton 1980), and in May and June in Ethiopia (Urban and Brown 1971). The breeding months are September and October in Zambia (Benson *et al.* 1971), October in Mozambique (Maclean 1993), October and December in Malawi (Benson and Benson 1977). Eggs were found from September to November in Zimbabwe (Irwin 1981), but recent data suggest that breeding may continue until March (Tree 1997).

BEHAVIOUR Priest (1936) noted large numbers of this species at winter roosts in Zimbabwe, and Irwin (1953) saw up to 500 at a single roost. Reedbeds are the commonest roost, but msasa trees *Brachystegia spiciformis*, thorny bushes or *Acacia* trees are also used (R.K. Brooke pers. comm.). Greater Blue-eared Glossy Starlings and Wattled Starlings often join Lesser Blue-eared Glossy Starlings at such roosts, and there is a short vocal display once the birds have settled in the evening. They may also vocalise in trees or on open ground before flying to the roost. On the Kafue River, Zambia, about 1,200 Lesser Blue-eared Glossy Starlings roosted in reedbeds on islands (A.J. Tree pers. comm.). Flocks of more than 20 birds were seen in Ghana (Lowe 1937). Small parties often mixed with Greater Blue-eared Glossy Starlings in Ethiopia (Cheesman and Sclater 1936). Seasonal movements in some areas are suggested by Nikolaus' (1987) comment that the Lesser Blue-eared Glossy Starling was a common visitor to Khartoum from late July to October. In Zambia there was some indication that this species was mainly a dry-season visitor except in the south (Aspinwall 1978). Captive birds ran on the ground, and were not seen hopping (Kunkel 1962).

71 BRONZE-TAILED GLOSSY STARLING *Lamprotornis chalcurus*
Plate 19

Lamprotornis chalcura Nordmann 1835

FIELD IDENTIFICATION 21 cm. A blue-green glossy starling, with a yellow eye, purple wash on ear-coverts and belly; the central tail feathers are bronzy, and the tail noticeably shorter than in Greater or Lesser Blue-eared Glossy Starlings. It is however difficult to distinguish from similar species except at close range.

DESCRIPTION The crown, nape and mantle are iridescent blue-green. The back and uppertail-coverts are blue with a purple tinge. The ear-coverts are purple; the chin, throat, chest, thighs and undertail-coverts blue-green. The belly is purple. The wings are blue-green, with dark blue tips to coverts and tertial feathers, and a blue and purple epaulet. There is a slight indentation on the inner webs of primaries 7–9. The underwing-coverts are purple, the tail feathers purple with a bronzy gloss and faint cross-barring; the outermost feathers are blue. The iris is yellow, the bill and legs black. The sexes are alike. A juvenile specimen is matt grey, with gloss only on the wings and tail, and a grey iris. Van Someren (1922) described the juvenile as blackish above with a slight blue tinge, the underside dull sooty-black with a greenish-blue sheen on the breast. The tail feathers were greenish, but the basal half of the central feathers were violet-purple. There is one record of a complete albino bird, with pink eyes and legs, in a flock of normal-plumaged birds (Davey 1982). Three birds labelled 'summer' have wing moult, as have 6 birds from May, June and July. There are no other specimens showing moult, among 37 birds from all months expect August, October and December. This suggests that moult occurs during the northern summer.

MEASUREMENTS Male (20): wing 129–145, tail 75–86, bill 25.6–29.0, tarsus 32.0–35.2. Female (13): wing 119–134, tail 70–80, bill 25.0–27.8, tarsus 29.6–32.8.

VOICE Harsh nasal and throaty chattering reported by Zimmerman *et al.* (1996).

DISTRIBUTION AND POPULATION Have been recorded from Senegambia to Sudan, Uganda and western Kenya. They are probably common but overlooked in mixed groups of glossy starlings.

HABITAT These birds are found in open bushed and wooded country, in Kenya above 1000 m and in high rainfall areas (Lewis and Pomeroy 1989).

FOOD AND FEEDING Chapin (1954) found insects in four stomachs, berries in two. Bolster (1935) reported, at second-hand, observations from Kenya of Bronze-tailed Glossy Starlings taking meat of cattle which had been slaughtered.

BREEDING A nest was found in a natural hole in the bole of a tree, 2 m above the ground. The cavity was stuffed with grass, with a large pile of feathers on top, most of them evidently collected from a nearby Cattle Egret *Bubulcus ibis* colony (Serle 1943). Chapin (1954) found a nest in an old tree stump, lined with leaves and grass. The eggs were pale blue, plain or very finely speckled with orange-brown, measuring 27.5 x 20 mm (Serle 1943); Schönwetter (1983) gives the measurements of a single egg as 27.0 x 17.0, weight 4.1 g. Clutch sizes have not been reported. Breeding occurred in Senegal in August (Morel and Morel 1982), and in June in Nigeria (Serle 1943), while Elgood (1982) reported juveniles in May and a pair entering a nest hole in March. There are no dated breeding records for Sudan or for East Africa, but Lewis and Pomeroy (1989) mentioned breeding in Kenya, with a recently-fledged bird found in May. Chapin (1954) found a chick in the nest in March in Zaïre.

MIGRATION Nikolaus (1987) listed this species as an intra-African migrant in Sudan, noting that it was present from September to April. Grimes (1987) also suggested that it might be a non-breeding migrant in northern Ghana, while in the Gambia, Bronze-tailed Glossy Starlings have been observed in large transient flocks during Oct–Nov (Gore 1990). However, its movements have not been adequately documented so far, and its distribution is poorly known because of confusion with similar species.

BEHAVIOUR Flocks of more than 100 Bronze-tailed Glossy Starlings were seen in Ghana (Lowe 1937), and this species may associate with Greater and Lesser Blue-eared Glossy Starlings (Lippens and Wille 1976). Chapin (1954) commented that Bronze-tailed Glossy Starlings were noticeably larger than Lesser Blue-eared Glossy Starlings, and their noisy flight was also obvious.

72 SPLENDID GLOSSY STARLING *Lamprotornis splendidus* Plate 20

Turdus splendidus Vieillot 1822

FIELD IDENTIFICATION 28 cm. Primarily a forest species, with brilliantly iridescent plumage with many variations on blue and green. The tail is dark with a broad greenish terminal band, and the pale eye is conspicuous.

DESCRIPTION Adult male: Glossy blue-green crown, sharply demarcated from the glossy green nape and mantle. The back is iridescent blue tinged with purple, the uppertail-coverts glossy blue-green, sometimes with cross-barring near the tip. The lores and frons are velvety black, while the sides of the head and ear-coverts are dark blue, tipped with iridescent blue. There is a small, triangular, golden-bronze patch between the ear-coverts and the throat. The chin, throat, chest and upper belly are purple with a bronze sheen, passing into violet on the flanks. The thighs are purple. The lower belly and undertail-coverts are iridescent blue. The wings are basically glossy green, but the coverts have large subterminal velvet-blue spots, and blue tips. The secondaries and tertials have blue tips and dark purple outer webs. Primaries 6–9 have a prominent notch on the inner vane. The underwing-coverts are purple. The tail feathers are purple at the base, with a broad terminal band of blue-green. Iris is yellowish white, the bill and legs black. **Adult female**: Like the male in pattern but is clearly duller. The crown is green, not contrasting with the nape; there is no purple gloss on the back, which has a smaller blue area. Ventrally, the plumage is bronze only in the centre of the belly, and the purple is partly replaced by blue. **Juvenile**: Initially has gloss only on the wing and tail feathers, with a matt-grey belly and a brown iris, but the adult pattern and iris coloration seems to appear quite soon. Sawyer (1982) reported that the young could be sexed on leaving the nest, as males were duller versions of the parents, whereas young females had blackish-brown ventral plumage with no blue gloss. Benson (1962) also noted that sexual dimorphism in plumage was quite marked in southern birds.

Several races have been described, but since the seasonal movements of the species are poorly understood, these all require further study.

L. s. lessoni, from the island of Bioko, is larger (wing of male 159–168), but birds from Princípe appear to be indistinguishable from the nominate race (Amadon 1953).

L. s. chrysonotis, from Senegal to Ghana, has a green crown and a blue rather than purple throat.

L. s. bailundensis, from Zaïre south to Zambia and Angola, seems to differ consistently in that the lesser coverts are blue, not green, and the crown is green as is the nape and back.

In a sample of 138 birds collected from all months, only 15 showed wing moult: one from March, three from December, and the rest during May to September. However, these represent only a small proportion of the birds collected in those months, and it is likely that different populations have different annual cycles. Van Someren (1916) stated that Splendid Glossy Starlings in Uganda were moulting in August, while Friedmann and Loveridge (1937) collected birds in fresh plumage in December in Tanzania.

MEASUREMENTS Male (19): wing 146–163, tail 110–130, bill 27.1–32.0, tarsus 30.4–37.4. Female (12): wing 128–149, tail 102–114, bill 25.5–30.7, tarsus 28.5–37.7. Weight of male (47) 111–155, of female (25) 96–139 g.

VOICE Large flocks produce a cacophony of varied sounds, which may include imitations of other birds and even of primates, especially during the hot part of the day when the birds gather in large trees (Marchant 1953). According to Chapin (1954) the voice is striking, very nasal or metallic, and he considered that the birds had a penchant for the most marvellous discords. Basilio (1963) compared its song with that of the Rook *Corvus frugilegus*, while Günther and Feiler (1986) described the voice as reminiscent of a rusty windmill. A loud ringing call, and also a sweet piping note were reported by Bates (1909). Captive birds showed a remarkable ability to mimic the human voice (Sawyer 1982). Harsh alarm calls attracted numerous birds to mob African Harrier-Hawks *Polyboroides typus* (Maclatchy 1937).

DISTRIBUTION AND POPULATION Occurs from Senegal and the Gambia westwards to Ethiopia, Uganda, western Kenya and Tanzania, Zaïre, Angola and Zambia. It was not observed on Princípe by Snow (1950), but de Naurois (1983, 1994) stated that it was abundant but irregular in occurrence; birds on Bioko are apparently resident (Basilio 1963). It is seasonally abundant in most areas.

HABITAT Birds occur both in primary and secondary forest, and even in parks and gardens. They are usually found in the treetops, but will come down to feed on lower berried bushes when food is scarce. Splendid Glossy Starlings may roost in coastal mangroves at times (Altenburg and von Spanje 1989). On Princípe they occur throughout the low altitude forests, from which they appear to displace Princípe Glossy Starlings, and also in plantations and other disturbed areas near people (de Naurois 1983, 1994); similar habitats are utilised on Bioko (Basilio 1963).

FOOD AND FEEDING An analysis of stomach contents revealed fruit or berries in the stomachs of 17 birds and insects in the stomachs of three (Herroelen pers. comm.); similarly Friedmann and Williams (1970, 1971) found insect fragments in only one of nine stomachs analysed, but fruit remains in all of them. Germain et al. (1973) reported fruit and beetles in the stomachs of three birds collected in Cameroon. Fruits of *Ficus* sp. (Eisentraut 1963, Dean et al. 1987, Dowsett-Lemaire 1996), *Pycnanthus*, *Rauwolfia*, *Dacryodes*, *Polyalthia*, *Trichoscypha*, *Coelocaryon*, *Xylopia*, *Beilschmiedia*, *Musanga* and Myrstacaceae were noted. Animal material was rare, but insects including wasps (Hymenoptera) and termites (Termitidae), and a small frog (Amphibia) were found by Chapin (1954), ants (Formicidae), beetles (Carabidae) and small tree snails (Pulmonata) by Basilio (1963), also grasshoppers (Orthoptera) and a lizard (Reptilia). In trees with a heavy crop of fruit, the birds may remain in the tree all day, and a veritable rain of falling seeds will be regurgitated as the fruit is eaten.

BREEDING Nests are placed high in the dead or moribund trunks of oil palms in Nigeria (Pettet 1975). On an offshore island in Guinea-Bissau, numerous nests lined with grass were found in mangrove trees (de Naurois 1969). A nest in a natural tree hole in Zambia was lined with twigs and stems of creepers (White 1943), while one brought to Bates (1909) was composed entirely of leaf petioles; Basilio (1963) reported a sparse lining of twigs and leaves. In Gabon, nests were found at heights ranging from 1.8 to 37 m, and several were occupied during the same month in successive years. One nest was lined with a cup of dry grass. The eggs are blue-green spotted with red, three clutches contained two eggs each. Only the female incubated, with the male perched on guard nearby, but both sexes fed the young. The eggs measure 25.7–31.5 x 20.5–24.5 mm (12), weight 7.7 g (Schönwetter 1983). In captivity, the incubation period was about 18 days, with only the female incubating, and the nestling period was also 18 days (Sawyer 1982). Breeding occurred in Zambia in September and October (Benson *et al.* 1971). Birds were in breeding condition in October and February in Angola (Traylor 1963), and courtship was noted in February (Heinrich 1958). Günther and Feiler (1986) observed juveniles in January in Angola. In Uganda, van Someren (1916) reported eggs in March, and while there are breeding records for East Africa from January–August most are from March, with February and April the only other months with several records (Brown and Britton 1980). There are no breeding records for Ethiopia (Urban and Brown 1971). Male birds in Gabon were singing and visiting nest holes in December, with active nests found from January–March. Chapin (1954) suggested breeding from September–January in southern Zaïre, and Lippens and Wille (1976) stated that this species nested in July and August in southwestern Zaïre. For the Itombe region, Prigogine (1971) indicated breeding in January. There are juvenile specimens from Kasai, Zaïre, from December, January and March; other specimens from Zaïre include a newly-fledged juvenile from September, while other juveniles were collected from August–October. In Rwanda, Splendid Glossy Starlings were nesting from November to March (Vande Weghe 1973). In Nigeria, eggs were found in December and February, and two clutches were destroyed by Broad-billed Rollers *Eurystomus glaucurus* (Pettet 1975). Another pair of Splendid Glossy Starlings was seen building in an old woodpecker hole in January (Marchant 1953), and Elgood (1982) gave the breeding season as December to March. In Ghana, birds were seen entering nest holes in February and April (Grimes 1987). Nesting was recorded in Togo in February and in May (Walsh *et al.* 1990) and in Guinea-Bissau in May (de Naurois 1969). Eggs were noted in June in Senegal (Morel and Morel 1982). Gore (1990) ascribed reports of breeding in the Gambia to misidentification. Breeding occurred in Cameroon in February and March (Serle 1981), while Bates (1909) reported a nest in August. On Princípe the birds may not breed every year; active nests were found in December (de Naurois 1994).

MIGRATION In an early discussion of migration in this species, Chapin (1932) stated that in parts of Nigeria, the birds were present only from September to January, and in the Ituri Forest, Zaïre from October to February, yet they were resident further northwards and eastwards in Zaïre. In the Itombe region of Zaïre, Prigogine (1978) found

Splendid Glossy Starlings common from November to March, although there were some records from June, suggesting that not all individuals migrated. He speculated that birds from Itombe might move north. Marchant (1953) noted that in southern Nigeria, some birds were present in the forest throughout the year, but flocks were noticed mainly in the second half of the year. Elgood (1982) considered that there was no evidence of migration, and classified Splendid Glossy Starling as resident in Nigeria, as did Grimes (1987) for Ghana. Gatter (1988) listed this species as a breeding resident, possibly migratory, in Liberia, while in Mali this species was scarce in forested areas in June and November (Lamarche 1981). Gore (1990) referred to local movements, and reported that in the Gambia this species was a dry season visitor from December to June. In southern Cameroon, Splendid Glossy Starlings were recorded from January to June, and in October and November, forming large flocks in the dry season (Germain *et al.* 1973). The populations in Gabon appeared to be nomadic over a very large area, but not truly migratory; regular movements, at least on a local scale, were reported by Maclatchy (1937). In Burundi, Gaugris *et al.* (1981) described the birds as resident. In Kenya, Splendid Glossy Starling appears to be a regular migrant, usually absent from June to October or November (Lewis and Pomeroy 1989). In East Africa as a whole, Britton (1980) commented that the movements of this species appear to be regular, though they are not well understood. Cave and Macdonald (1955) listed Splendid Glossy Starling as resident in Sudan, while Nikolaus (1987) noted it as uncommon, possibly resident. Benson (1982) considered that only the southern populations were migratory, in particular the race *bailundensis*. Birds attributable to this race were noted in Angola, Zambia, Tanzania and Upper Shaba, Zaïre, during June–October, and apparent non-breeding records came from northern Zaïre (Prigogine and Benson 1979). Gunther and Feiler (1986) saw birds in northern Angola from December to April, but they did not identify the race involved. Penry (1979) reviewed the records for Zambia, and noted that in the north Splendid Glossy Starlings arrived at the end of June, moving southwards by mid-August. There were a number of records for December and some for January, but the birds were clearly absent from February to early June. Prigogine (1983) reported two specimens of *bailundensis* from Burundi in May and November, but it was not clear whether these represented wintering or passage birds.

BEHAVIOUR Typically found in small flocks of a dozen or more individuals, but during the dry season in Gabon they may concentrate in tens of thousands of birds at nocturnal roosts. During the day, the flocks disperse over a radius of 15–20 km from the roost site and the evening assembly is marked by the noisy wingbeats of the birds and much vocalisation. Chapin (1954) compared the noise of their wings to the churning of a sternwheel steamer in the distance! Dean *et al.* (1987) saw feeding flocks of up to 20 birds in Angola, while Friedmann and Williams (1971) found more than 100 birds in a single group of fruiting trees. The species will join mixed-species flocks when feeding (Prigogine 1971). In Nigeria, no seasonal movements have been reported, but there are conspicuous daily movements between large roosts and the feeding areas (Elgood *et al.* 1973), and large dry-season roosts are also reported from Cameroon (Germain *et al.* 1973). Jackson commented that he had never seen Splendid Glossy Starlings settle on the ground. He also noted competition for nest holes with Broad-billed Rollers in Uganda (Jackson and Sclater 1938). Birds perching in the top of the canopy in sunlight may have been sunbathing (Basilio 1963). Captive birds were noted to be aggressive while breeding, and killed a young bird of the previous year which was still in the same aviary (Sawyer 1982).

RELATIONS WITH MAN Bannerman (1948) was informed that Splendid Glossy Starlings had been collected on a large scale for their beautiful plumage, and had become quite scarce in Senegal by the outbreak of the First World War. On Bioko, Basilio (1963) had the impression that numbers had declined during the 1950s.

PRINCIPAL REFERENCE Brosset and Erard (1986).

73 PRINCIPE GLOSSY STARLING *Lamprotornis ornatus* Plate 20

Sturnus ornatus Daudin 1800

FIELD IDENTIFICATION 30 cm. A large, spectacularly iridescent glossy starling, endemic to the forests of this island.

DESCRIPTION The crown, nape and upper mantle are bright metallic-green. The ear-coverts and sides of the head have green feathers tipped with turquoise. The back is glossy golden-bronze, edged with violet at the margins. The uppertail-coverts are turquoise tinged with violet. The chin, throat, chest, belly and flanks are a glossy bronze-green. The thighs and undertail-coverts are turquoise with violet tips to feathers. The wing has turquoise lesser coverts with violet centres, the greater coverts are velvet-black with violet tips, the tertials and secondaries are golden-bronze with dark cross-barring, and the primaries are blackish with turquoise and violet edges and tips. The underwing-coverts are bronze-green. The tail is dark bronzy-black with some cross-barring, while the tip is violet and turquoise. The iris is white, and the bill and legs black. The sexes are alike, but the metallic gloss is reduced on the female. A juvenile specimen is matt grey ventrally, with some sheen on the dorsal plumage. A bird collected during September was in heavy moult while one from November had almost completed wing moult; five birds from February, one from March and two from June had no wing moult.

MEASUREMENTS Male (7): wing 151–162, tail 108–120, bill 29.3–33.4, tarsus 33.1–37.9. Female (8): wing 141–146, tail 101–112, bill 28.8–32.0, tarsus 30.8–33.6. Weight of female 130 g.

VOICE The commonest call is a double caw, *waakyaa*, sometimes followed by musical *tu-ping*, and a pair at the nest called *pee-to-woo*. Possibly the caw is an alarm call, and the other notes contact calls and song respectively. Keulemans (cited in Bannerman 1948) compared the calls to those of Eurasian Golden Oriole *Oriolus oriolus*, and noted that around midday, flocks gathered in the trees, calling incessantly. De Naurois also referred to dozens of birds, concealed by the foliage, calling from a single tree, and compared the calls to those of Splendid Glossy Starling, though deeper in tone.

DISTRIBUTION AND POPULATION Endemic to the island of Príncipe in the Gulf of Guinea, where it was described as abundant by de Naurois (1983).

HABITAT These starlings occur in forest, in some areas also in plantations, with the birds spending most of their time in the trees. They were found throughout low and medium altitude forest (de Naurois 1983), and were common in plantations and other man-modified habitats (Jones and Tye 1988).

FOOD AND FEEDING Berries, bananas, spiders (Arachnida), caterpillars and small snails (Mollusca) were reported by Keulemans (in Bannerman 1948). Insects have also been recorded, and the birds were seen eating berries, such as those of *Dracaena draco*.

BREEDING A nest was located in a hole in a dead tree limb, 10 m above ground. The eggs were described by local inhabitants as white, spotted with red and black towards the thick end (Keulemans, in Bannerman 1948). A pair was seen nest-building in September. Chicks have been reported in January and February (Dohrn, in Bannerman 1948), and there is a juvenile specimen from August.

BEHAVIOUR Príncipe Glossy Starlings were encountered either in pairs or small parties of up to ten birds. In flight the wings make a loud noise. The birds were rarely seen on the ground. When Splendid Glossy Starlings were also present on the island, they were restricted to low altitude forests, while Príncipe Glossy Starlings occupied exclusively the higher forests.

PRINCIPAL REFERENCES Snow (1950), de Naurois (1994).

Coccycolius iris Oustalet 1879

FIELD IDENTIFICATION 21 cm. A brilliant emerald-green starling, dark (purple in good light) on the belly and the sides of the head, with a medium length tail.

DESCRIPTION The crown, nape, back, rump, wings, tail, chin, throat, upper chest and undertail-coverts are a brilliant emerald green. The belly is glossed with purple, while the thighs are grey with no iridescence. A curved patch from behind the eye over the ear-coverts, down towards the throat is glossy purple. In the hand, blue tones are apparent where green feathers border on the purple areas. The iris is dark brown, the bill and the legs black. The sexes are alike. Juveniles were described as a duller, more yellow-green than the adults, with the purple areas replaced by dark brown (Shelton 1982, Pyper 1994), but Bruch (1983) stated that the dorsal plumage was glossy olive-green, the ventral feathers a uniform matt grey, with no brown markings. One year after hatching, young birds were indistinguishable from their parents according to Pyper (1994), but Wilkinson (1996) noted that two young birds retained patches of the dull ventral plumage at 12 months, losing it gradually over the next few months. The specimens examined were all from the months December to March, and none showed wing moult.

MEASUREMENTS Male (9): wing 102–111, tail 74–82, bill 22.7–24.0, tarsus 24.6–27.0. Female (8): wing 99–108, tail 70–75, bill 21.2–23.7, tarsus 25.5–26.9.

VOICE Wheezy and squeaky calls have been reported (Bannerman 1948).

DISTRIBUTION AND POPULATION Has a very restricted range, from Guinea to Mali and Ivory Coast in West Africa, but it may be locally common.

HABITAT It occurs in savanna woodland, often perching on dead trees, but has never been reported in forest (Bannerman 1948, Thiollay 1985).

FOOD AND FEEDING The seed and pulp of small fruits, insect remains, and numerous small black ants were recorded, and the birds were seen feeding on the ground (Bannerman 1932, 1948). Captive birds ate ants which were attracted to nectar in the aviary (Shelton 1982).

BREEDING Nesting has not been described in the wild, but Emerald Starlings presumably nest in tree holes. Captive birds nested in a tree-hole lined with green leaves and pine needles (Bruch 1983, Robiller and Gerstner 1985); another pair used grass, coconut fibres and green shoots (Pyper 1994); a third nest contained leaves only (Wilkinson 1996). The eggs were pale blue, with red-brown blotching (Pyper 1994). The incubation period was about 14 days for clutches of three to four eggs, by the female alone, and the nestlings left the nest after 21 days (Robiller and Gerstner 1985, Pyper 1994). Bruch (1983) reported a clutch of three eggs, with the single surviving chick fledging after 20 days. Both parents fed the young on mealworms and crickets (Shelton 1982; Robiller and Gerstner 1985; Pyper 1994). Insects were brought to the nest by three captive adults, and in the following year by two adults and two immature birds (Wilkinson 1996). A male with large testes was collected in February, although the ovary of a female on the same date was undeveloped (Bannerman 1932). This is the only indication of the breeding season in West Africa.

MIGRATION Curry-Lindahl (1981) listed the Emerald Starling as a local migrant without providing any information. One of Bannerman's (1948) correspondents suggested that this species was not resident throughout the year, but local movements seem the most likely explanation.

BEHAVIOUR Green leaves may play a significant role in courtship. Ellis (1980) noted that a pair of Emerald Starlings frequently carried green leaves, which they sometimes took to nestboxes although they failed to breed. Similarly, Shelton (1982) saw the birds holding pieces of green leaves in their beaks, and referred to this as a 'pair-bonding ritual'. Pieces of green leaves may be cut out of living plants (Wilkinson 1996). Anting has been observed in captivity (Simmons 1966). In a captive group of three birds, Bruch (1983) had the impression that all three birds fed the young, but later the pair attacked the third bird, which died of its injuries. Pyper (1994) also reported the death of a third conspecific, in this case before the pair began nesting. This suggests that the birds are territorial while nesting. Wilkinson (1996) noted a third adult feeding one brood, while in the following season this bird did not feed the young, but the two immatures hatched the previous year did so, together with the putative parents. However, in the absence of observations on breeding wild birds it is premature to conclude that this species is a cooperative breeder. In West Africa, the birds were often seen in groups of 4–5 (Bannerman 1932), though flocks of 20–50 were also reported (Bannerman 1948). Demey and Fishpool (1991) noted groups of up to 10 Emerald Starlings in Ivory Coast.

Turdus purpureus Mueller 1766

FIELD IDENTIFICATION 27 cm. A large-bodied, short-tailed glossy starling, purple ventrally, with a prominent yellow eye.

DESCRIPTION The frons and crown are purple, the lores matt black. The nape and a band to the back of the eye is blue with some purple gloss. The mantle and back are blue-green, the rump and uppertail-coverts are purple. The chin, throat, chest, belly, flanks, thighs and undertail-coverts are purple. The wings are blue-green with dark spots on the tips of the coverts, and a blue and violet epaulet. The tail feathers are purple, but the two outermost feathers have a blue outer vane. The iris is golden-yellow, and the bill and the legs are black. The sexes are alike. Juveniles are matt grey except for gloss on wings and tail; the first body feathers are blue rather than purple. In captive birds the first glossy feathers appeared on head and body at three months, and at four months the iris became light grey (Thomson 1969). One specimen collected had a white patch across the abdomen (Lowe 1937).

Western birds have been distinguished on the basis of bluer dorsal plumage and longer tails, but the status of this race *L. purpureus amethystinus* has not been assessed.

In a sample of 21 specimens, there were birds with wing moult from May, July, August, September and October, but no moult in others from November to January and April to July.

MEASUREMENTS Male (11): wing 136–154, tail 77–95, fbill 28.5–31.8, tarsus 30.6–37.8. Female (11): wing 134–143, tail 70–86, bill 26.2–31.0, tarsus 29.3–33.7. Weight, unsexed (3) 91–140 g.

VOICE The flight call has been described as *twee-twee*, and flocks gathered in trees during the hot part of the day keep up a continuous chatter (Bannerman 1948).

DISTRIBUTION AND POPULATION Common and often abundant from Senegambia to Nigeria, Chad, southern Sudan, Uganda and western Kenya.

HABITAT These birds are found in open parkland, and also burnt and cultivated areas.

FOOD AND FEEDING Purple Glossy Starlings feed on fruit and berries, seeds and insects, which may be collected in the bushes or on the ground. They are especially attracted to fig trees *Ficus* (Jackson and Sclater 1938). Stomachs contained *Zizyphus* fruit and termites (Termitidae) (Bates 1934), black ants (Formicidae) in another individual (Lowe 1937). In Nigeria, Purple Glossy Starlings occasionally fed on the nectar of *Bombax costatum* (Pettet 1977). Captive birds took many insects and other live food, though they also ate fruit (Thomson 1969). Specimens from Sudan contained insects and bits of charred grass, apparently picked up when feeding on the ground after a bush fire.

BREEDING The nests are in tree holes, about 4 m above ground in one case; the nest lining has not been examined (Bannerman 1948). The birds will also nest under the eaves of houses and in drain pipes (Grimes 1987). The eggs are pale blue, finely freckled with reddish-brown, measuring 22.3–30.5 x 18.8–23.0 mm (7), weight 5.9 g (Schönwetter 1983). A record of captive breeding was wrongly attributed to *L. purpureiceps* — the birds concerned had bright yellow eyes (Thomson 1969), and the common name 'purple-headed starling' is evidently often used by aviculturalists for *L. purpureus* (cf editor's note, in Boosey 1959). The captive pair used a nestbox, in which a shallow cup of dried grasses was lined by pieces of leaves, both green and dried. The female continued carrying in leaf fragments for a week after the young had hatched. There was a clutch of three eggs, blue-green and mottled all over. Only the female incubated, but both birds fed the young, on live food only; the incubation and nestling periods were not reported (Thomson 1969). Nestlings in West Africa were fed on caterpillars (Bannerman 1948). Breeding was recorded in Uganda in February and April (Brown and Britton 1980). Lynes (1924) saw fledged young in August in Sudan, but Nikolaus (1987) recorded nesting from March to May. In Nigeria, Hutson (in Bannerman 1948) gave the breeding season as April to July, and reported chicks in June; Pettet (1975) found Purple Glossy Starlings feeding chicks at a hole in a *Parkia* tree in April. Breeding was reported from Ghana from April to July (Grimes 1987), in the Gambia in May to July (Gore 1990). In Burkina Faso, flying juveniles were seen in July, and birds with duller plumage than the adults were noted in October (Thonnerieux 1988). There are juvenile specimens from West Africa in June, July, August, September and December.

BEHAVIOUR In West Africa, flock size ranged from groups of twelve to flocks of more than a hundred. Groups were seen to mob both owls and hawks (Bannerman 1948). Labels on specimens from Uganda in August and September 1923 refer to vast flocks feeding in short grass areas and roosting in thorn trees. Flocks of hundreds of birds were noted in Mali (Lamarche 1981), while in Ouagadougou in Burkina Faso, Purple Glossy Starlings were present all year, with communal roosts containing thousands of birds (Thonnerieux *et al.* 1989). Anting behaviour has been observed in captive birds (Simmons 1961).

RELATIONS WITH MAN According to Bannerman (1948) this species was collected on a large scale for the trade in bird plumage, which was centred in Senegal and the Gambia.

Lamprotornis purpuropterus Ruppell 1845

FIELD IDENTIFICATION 35 cm. A dark blue, long-tailed glossy starling with a pale eye, lacking any dark spots on the wings. It is smaller than Long-tailed Glossy Starling but largest in the zone of sympatry (where it is found alongside *L. caudatus*), where the birds also have proportionately longer tails.

DESCRIPTION There appear to be two colour phases of Rüppell's Long-tailed Glossy Starling throughout its range, one of which closely resembles Long-tailed Glossy Starling. In this type, the crown, sides of the head and chin are blue-green with a bronzy sheen. The nape is blue with a purple sheen, the mantle and back are blue, the rump and the uppertail-coverts are purple. The throat and chest are blue-green; the belly, flanks, thighs and undertail-coverts are purple with a bronzy sheen in the centre of the belly. The wings are blue-green, with dark cross-bars on the coverts, tertials and outer vanes of the primary feathers, and a small purple shoulder patch. The tail feathers are purple with distinct cross-bars. In the second plumage type, except for a bluish sheen on the wings, the plumage is predominantly purple with some bronzy sheen on the uppertail-coverts and tail feathers, and very marked cross-barring on both. In both forms the iris is yellowish-white, the bill and legs black, and the sexes are not distinguishable. Juveniles lack this glossy plumage, and have a dark iris. Van Someren (1922) described the juvenile as black, with a faint purple lustre on the crown and mantle. The wings are bluish, and the underside slaty-black with slight bluish tips to the feathers. There is a record of a bird with a white head and tail feathers from East Africa (Dyer 1971).

Birds from Sudan and Ethiopia, **L. p. aenocephalus**, are very distinctive, and much larger than the nominate race, with a longer tail (160–217). White (1962) treats this species as a race of *L. caudatus*, while Sclater (1930) and Wolters (1975-82) consider *aenocephalus* a race of *purpuropterus*. The status of these populations requires further field studies.

At the same localities, some birds had wing moult in January and February, others in June, and there is no clear pattern from the 113 specimens examined which were collected from all months of the year; 25 birds were in moult, records from all months except August and September. In Uganda, Ogilvie-Grant (1910) noted birds in fresh plumage in May and others in very worn plumage in December, while Bowen (1931a) found two birds moulting in June in Tanzania, and Friedmann and Loveridge (1937) noted that one of two specimens collected during August had wing moult. In Kenya, moult started around April and was usually completed in February, thus taking nine or ten months to complete. There was a great deal of moult-breeding overlap, but no breeding birds

were found with active wing moult and it appeared that moult was suspended during this time. Thus some birds showed two concurrent waves of moult in the wings.

MEASUREMENTS Male (10): wing 150–166, tail 147–166, bill 25.2–27.4, tarsus 36.7–41.8. Female (10): wing 130–140, tail 120–143, bill 24.0–26.2, tarsus 35.0–39.4.

VOICE Vocal birds, with a variety of call notes. The song is described as 'quite musical' by van Someren (1916), and Jackson and Sclater (1938) also referred to a short, pleasing song. Both males and females had a simple song of four to ten notes, and members of a pair often sang in duet. Peaks of duetting coincided with nesting. The female's song was almost always preceded by male song, and then followed at a fairly constant interval. Birds sing for extended periods during the heat of the day (Zimmerman *et al.* 1996).

DISTRIBUTION AND POPULATION This long-tailed starling is distributed from southeastern Sudan through western Ethiopia, southern Somalia, Kenya, Uganda, Rwanda and northwestern Tanzania. It is common, but may be nomadic in some of those areas.

HABITAT The birds are found in bushed and wooded grassland, and also in cultivated areas to 1800 m. They are usually found near water in arid areas.

FOOD AND FEEDING Feeds predominantly on the ground and are commensals at camp sites, where they accept many scraps. Mackworth-Praed and Grant (1960) state simply that the species is 'almost omnivorous', but no detailed information seems to have been recorded.

BREEDING According to Lippens and Wille (1976), Rüppell's Long-tailed Starlings nest very high up, and may take over the nests of other species. Birds were seen nesting in old woodpecker holes in *Hyphaene* palms in Eritrea (Smith 1957). The eggs may be plain blue or bluish-green, or marked with rusty spots and blotches, measuring 26.0–28.4 x 20.3–20.8 mm (4), weight 6.2 g (Schönwetter 1983). Captive birds built a nest of leaves, rootlets and mud inside a nestbox and laid two clutches of three eggs. The incubation period was about 14 days, and the nestling period 25 days, with the female doing most of the feeding (Ezra 1933). In Kenya, both parents and helpers may feed the young at some nests (Dittami pers. comm.). In Sudan, the race *purpuropterus* breeds in December, while the race *aenocephalus* breeds in October (Nikolaus 1987); in Ethiopia, the nominate race has been found breeding in March, April and September, whereas *aenocephalus* breeds in June and July (Smith 1957, Urban and Brown 1971). In Rwanda, this species nests from August to November, and February to April. Breeding occurs in Tanzania and eastern Kenya in October and November, in Uganda and western Kenya chiefly from March to May, although there are also records from June, August, September, October and January (Brown and Britton 1980). Jackson and Sclater (1938) reported nesting in northern Kenya in August and September, and van Someren (1916) recorded eggs in April and juveniles in June from Uganda. There are juvenile specimens from Kenya from March (3), July and September. At Nakuru, Kenya, there was no clearly defined breeding season, and this corresponded to a lack of seasonal variation in hormonal levels. Individual pairs appeared to synchronise their breeding activity by duetting behaviour, and some pairs nested up to three times within six months.

BEHAVIOUR Rüppell's Long-tailed Glossy Starlings spend most of their time on the ground, both hopping and running (Jackson and Sclater

1938, AC pers. obs.). On landing either on the ground or on a branch, one wing was regularly raised in a folded position, pointing upwards and backwards; occasionally the second wing was also raised later. One individual consistently used the same wing, suggesting that this may be a display (Wickler 1966). Pairs at Nakuru, Kenya, occupied stable territories and juveniles remained on their parent's territory for up to a year. They were usually forced out to the periphery of the territory during breeding attempts by the adults. However, in some cases the juveniles were tolerated at the nest, and fed their younger siblings (J. Dittami pers. comm.). It seems likely that in this species cooperative breeding may be more common in some populations than others, perhaps in relation to the availability of suitable breeding habitat.

PRINCIPAL REFERENCE Dittami (1987).

77 LONG-TAILED GLOSSY STARLING *Lamprotornis caudatus*
Plate 21

Turdus caudatus Mueller 1776

FIELD IDENTIFICATION 40 cm. A very large, extremely long-tailed blue-green glossy starling, with a pale eye.

DESCRIPTION The crown, sides of head and chin are blue-green with a bronze sheen. The lores and frons are matt-black. The nape, mantle, back, throat and chest have a blue-green gloss, while the rump and uppertail-coverts are blue-violet with a purple gloss. The belly, flanks, thighs and undertail-coverts are blue-violet with a central bronzy patch. The wings are blue-green with prominent velvety-black spots near the tips of the lesser coverts. The tail is strongly graduated, with the feathers arranged in pairs in a step-like manner; purple with dark cross-barring. The iris is creamy-white, the bill and legs black. The sexes are alike in plumage, but males are clearly larger. Juvenile birds lack the gloss of the adults, and retain a dark iris for at least one year.

Sclater (1930) treated *L. caudatus eytoni* as a synonym of the nominate race. Louette (1981) found birds matching the description of *L. c. eytoni* alongside 'normal phase' birds, and he regarded those merely as a plumage variant. However, White (1962) treated both *L. purpuropterus* and *L. mevesii* as conspecific with *L. caudatus*, and consequently included five races in this species. No other authors have followed this lead. There are clear differences in biology between these populations, as well as major morphological differences, and *L. caudatus* and *L. purpuropterus* are locally sympatric in Sudan, apparently without interbreeding.

There is very clear seasonality in the specimens examined, with all 29 birds from April to July showing evidence of moult, with no wing moult apparent in the 18 specimens collected from October to February. Thus it appears that for the population as a whole, moult may start in March,

and is usually completed by August. A moult season of March to October was suggested by observations in Nigeria.

MEASUREMENTS Male (10): wing 173–199, tail 261–362, bill 28.1–30.0, tarsus 40.5–45.0. Female (10): wing 161–182, tail 250–300, bill 27.0–28.6, tarsus 38.8–42.3. Weight, unsexed (16) 102–133 g.

VOICE Bates (1934) referred to 'horrible screechings', but Wilkinson described the commonest call of Long-tailed Glossy Starlings as a sing-song *elekele*, and also mentioned a hoarse coughing *chuc-chu-chu* and raucous alarm calls. He considered the birds extremely vocal.

DISTRIBUTION AND POPULATION Found from southern Mauritania (Browne 1981) and Senegambia eastwards through Chad and the Central African Republic to western Sudan. They appear to be common residents in most areas.

HABITAT This is a species of dry savanna country, which may also occur in wooded suburbs in West Africa.

FOOD AND FEEDING Feed mainly on the ground, but also take fruit and insects in trees. The ripe fruit of *Azadirachta indica* and large terrestrial ants *Mesor galla* were noted as food items in Nigeria. Ants were recorded in the stomach contents (Bates 1934), and Moynihan (1978) saw the birds hawking for winged ants (Formicidae) and termite (Termitidae) alates.

BREEDING Several pairs were found nesting in close proximity in baobab trees in Nigeria (Serle 1943). The nests were in tree holes, lined with the spines of leaves. The eggs are plain blue, slightly glossy, in clutches of 3–4 (Shuel 1938), with measurements of 26.5–28.6 x 19.1–20.6 mm (9), weight 5.5 g (Schönwetter 1983). The incubation period was not determined in captive birds, but only the female was seen incubating. The nestling period was 17 and 21–22 days, with young fed by both parents and helpers, but only the female brooded young or removed faecal sacs. Breeding was recorded in Senegambia from September–November (Morel and Morel 1982, Gore 1990), from September to October in Nigeria (Shuel 1938, Serle 1943), and in June in Burkina Faso (Thonnerieux 1988) and Niger (Bates 1934, Giradoux et al. 1988). Birds were nesting in Mali between August and October (Lamarche 1981). In Sudan, Lynes (1924) found eggs in October at Darfur, while Nikolaus (1987) reported breeding in September. There is an old report of nesting in Ghana, but no modern records (Grimes 1987). There are two juvenile specimens from Nigeria in December.

BEHAVIOUR Usually seen in small groups of four to eight birds, with sometimes flocks of up to 25 individuals (Schifter 1986). From observations in Nigeria, Wilkinson concluded that this species lives in stable groups which defend group territories; large groups of up to 20 birds were only seen during June and July. In captive birds there was a clear dominance hierarchy, with the female dominating the male near the nest or the young, and always taking priority when feeding the young,

pushing the helpers aside. The female fed the young most frequently, with the male 'on guard', but once the chicks had left the nest, feeding was more evenly shared. Young of previous broods helped the parents under captive conditions, and it seems likely that groups of birds observed in the field are cooperative breeding units, similar to those found in Chestnut-bellied Starlings. Moynihan (1978) observed the activities of Long-tailed Glossy Starlings in a mixed-species flock in Senegal. These birds set out from a communal roost in small groups, which initially foraged alone. Later they were joined by groups of Red-billed Hornbills *Tockus erythrorhynchus*, with which other species such as Yellow-billed Shrikes *Corvinella corvina*, Senegal Coucals *Centropus senegalensis* and Hoopoes *Upupa epops* were already associating. The hornbills appeared to be strongly attracted by Long-tailed Glossy Starlings, which became the leaders of the group, and all species reacted to alarm calls given by the starlings. This species runs swiftly along the ground (Kunkel 1962). Anting has been observed in captive birds (Poulsen 1956, Simmons 1961).

PRINCIPAL REFERENCE Wilkinson (1988).

78 GOLDEN-BREASTED STARLING *Lamprotornis regius*   Plate 21

Cosmopsarus regius Reichenow 1879

FIELD IDENTIFICATION 30 cm. A slender, long-tailed starling, brilliantly iridescent green and blue on the upperparts and throat, with a golden-yellow chest and belly.

DESCRIPTION The crown, nape, chin, throat and cheeks are glossy greenish-blue, the ear-coverts are turquoise. The mantle, wings and underwing-coverts are greenish-blue glossed with purple; there are dark terminal spots on the wing-coverts. The rump and uppertail-coverts are turquoise-blue, the tail feathers bronze with faint transverse bars. The chest has a half-moon shaped purple patch, passing into blue at the base of the throat. The rest of the chest, flanks, belly, thighs and undertail-coverts are golden-yellow. The iris is white, and the bill and legs black. Primaries 6–9 are strongly indented on the inner web. The sexes are alike, but some observers suggest that females are less brilliantly coloured and have visibly shorter tails (Boosey 1959). Newly-fledged birds were described as dull blackish-blue dorsally, with fawn chests; later the yellow plumage developed ventrally, along with glossy blue-green head (Wavertree 1930). Young birds bred in captivity had dark eyes and duller plumage though in pattern like that of the adults; when first fledged they had pale pinkish beaks (Risdon 1990). Juvenile birds (two months old) have the head, throat and chest matt grey; there is some greenish gloss on the back and rump, and a violet gloss on the remiges and rectrices; the ventral plumage is buffy-yellow. The iris, bill and legs are dark brown, but the edges of the gape are pale whitish. At six

months old, the plumage resembles that of the adult, but the iris is pale grey, not creamy-white.

Van Someren (1924) proposed that northern birds could be distinguished by their more brilliant colours, with more purple on the throat, but *C. r. magnificus* does not seem to be separable from other populations.

It appears that at least one complete moult is necessary to attain adult plumage; according to van Someren (1956) the young birds moult at about three months old, and at six months old resemble the adults. Captive birds aged three months showed obvious head and body moult and were acquiring glossy plumage on the head and chest. Birds in immature plumage were collected in January, February, March, July, August, September, November and December; two immatures from November showed wing moult. However, a complete post-juvenile moult is not yet known for any African starling. Of a sample of 55 birds, birds were in moult in every month of the year except for April, September and October — but only two specimens were available from these three months. It is not known how often individual birds breed, and the moult cycles of breeders and helpers may differ.

MEASUREMENTS Male (10): wing 120–140, tail 186–247, bill 23.7–25.6, tarsus 32.0–34.4. Female (9): wing 120–125, tail 179–218, bill 21.0–24.8, tarsus 30.0–31.8. Weight, unsexed (12), 46–63 g.

VOICE During the hot part of the day the birds perch in trees, preening and warbling for long periods. The flight call or contact call is rendered as *cheeo cheeo*, the alarm call as *chiarr* (van Someren 1956).

DISTRIBUTION AND POPULATION A locally common resident in southern Ethiopia, Somalia, eastern Kenya and northeastern Tanzania. It is apparently nowhere sympatric with Ashy Starling (Lewis and Pomeroy 1989). Some seasonal fluctuations in the numbers of birds were noted in Tsavo (Lack 1985).

HABITAT The birds frequent open bush country in arid and semi-arid areas, mostly below 1000 m (Lewis and Pomeroy 1989).

FOOD AND FEEDING Golden-breasted Starlings are almost entirely insectivorous, but take some fruit (van Someren 1956). The stomach contents of one specimen included a beetle (Carabidae), termites (Termitidae), ants (Formicidae), a *Commiphora* seed, plant matter and grit (Lack and Quicke 1978); termites were also recorded by Fischer (Reichenow 1903). In Tsavo, 76% of 394 items were insects, and 97% of these were collected on the ground (Lack 1985). Captive birds preferred pupae to mealworms, and took ants readily, but ate little fruit (Risdon 1990).

BREEDING The nest is in a hole in a tree, either a natural hole, or a disused barbet (Copitonidae) or woodpecker (Picidae) hole 3–7 m above ground, lined with dry grass, felted hair and feathers (van Someren 1956); sometimes cast snake skins are included (Archer and Godman 1961), and leaves (Erlanger 1905). The eggs are pale greenish-blue with very small reddish-brown speckles (Wavertree 1930, Bell 1984). They measure 25.0–28.8 x 17.2–19.0 mm (19), weight 4.7 g (Schönwetter 1983). The clutch size is 2–6, according to Mackworth-Praed and Grant (1960). Up to nine birds have been seen feeding chicks (van Someren 1956, Huels 1981). Captive birds used a nestbox, in which a nest of leaves and moss, lined with feathers was built. Clutches of 3–4 eggs were laid; only the female sat on the nest (Wavertree 1930). In captivity, incubation lasted 14 days, the nestling period 19-22 days (Wavertree 1930, Risdon 1990, V. Roth pers. comm.). Captive-bred young were independent after three to four weeks (Bell 1984). Hybrid young were produced by a male Golden-breasted Starling and a female Superb Starling (Hopkinson 1932). Breeding has been recorded during both rainy seasons in Kenya, from March–May and November–December (Brown and Britton 1980), and from April to June in Somalia, where Archer suggested that the birds might be double-brooded (Archer and Godman 1961). Erlanger (1905) found nests with eggs and chicks in April in Ethiopia, and Benson (1946) suggested that breeding occurred from March to May in southern Ethiopia. Juvenile specimens from April and May were still in the process of growing wing and tail feathers.

BEHAVIOUR Golden-breasted Starlings spend much of their time on the ground, both hopping and running. The birds are shy and restless, and when disturbed will fly a short distance to the next clump of vegetation, seldom flying more than 3 m above the ground (Jackson and Sclater 1938, Archer and Godman 1961). The tail is raised when the bird stops or flies up to a perch (van Someren 1956); in flight it is often fanned slightly (Elliott, quoted in Reichenow 1903). Golden-breasted Starlings are often loosely associated with Fischer's Starlings (Fuggles-Couchman and Elliott 1946), and are most commonly found in pairs, or groups of up to eight birds (Jackson and Sclater 1938, Archer and Godman 1961). Captive birds dust-bathed, but were not seen to bathe although they would sit out in light rain and ruffle the feathers (Risdon 1990); they spent less time on the ground than other species such as Superb Starlings (V. Roth, pers. comm.). Anting has been reported in captivity by Simmons (1966). Van Someren (1956) noted three adult Golden-breasted Starlings feeding a brood of four chicks on moth and beetle larvae, and removing faecal sacs. He concluded that one male and two females were involved. Cooperative breeding was confirmed by Huels (1981), who observed five nests at which five to nine adult birds were seen, and at least five birds were seen to feed the same brood of chicks. He ringed two birds, one sexed as a female by laparotomy, and it appeared that only the female incubated, but other group members brought nesting material and fed the female on the nest. After the chicks hatched, the female would beg food from other adults, which she then fed to the chicks.

79 MEVES' LONG-TAILED STARLING *Lamprotornis mevesii*
Plate 22

Juida mevesii Wahlberg 1857

FIELD IDENTIFICATION 30 cm. A dark-plumaged, dark-eyed glossy starling, slender with a very long, tapered tail, which has distinct black barring. The tail is not broad and rounded as in Burchell's Glossy Starling, which is also much more heavily built.

DESCRIPTION In southern birds the frons, crown, nape and mantle are blue-green with some purple overtones. The lower back is purple tending to bronze on the rump, with the uppertail-coverts purple. Chin, throat and chest are blue-green with slight purple gloss; the lores and ear-coverts are velvety-black. The centre of the belly is bronze, bordered by purple on the flanks and undertail-coverts. The thighs are blue with purple tones. The wings are blue-green with a purple sheen on the outer webs of the primaries, while some coverts and mantle feathers have a dark blue central patch, surrounded by a blue-green margin. Cross-barring is evident on all the wing feathers, but is not strongly developed. Tail feathers are blue-violet with strong dark cross-barring. Ventrally the tail is black, strongly graduated, with the central feathers longest. The iris is dark brown, the bill and legs black. The female is like the male, but may be duller. In northerly populations, as from Namibia and Zambia, a purple tone dominates in all the body regions which are blue-green in the above description, and the bronze sheen extends over the lower back and uppertail-coverts. The juvenile is matt black ventrally, with some sheen on the dorsal plumage. Brooke (1971) described a female specimen which was entirely grey, except for a slight purplish gloss, mainly on the wing and tail feathers, and a solitary leucistic bird which was a uniform pale silvery-grey was sighted in Zimbabwe (Guy 1976). A non-iridescent bird with dull grey plumage and yellow eyes was seen feeding in a group of normal-plumage birds (Wilson 1975), and a normal-plumaged bird with some white secondaries in the left wing has also been sighted (Penzhorn and Cassidy 1985). A bird in Zambia was white across the mantle and middle of the back, and its lower abdomen was mostly white (Berry 1976).

White (1962) treats this bird as a race of Long-tailed Starling, but this does not seem justified to us. Irwin and Benson (1967) discussed this issue at length. They also reviewed local variations in size and coloration, and concluded that the birds from lower altitudes appeared to be smaller, but neither wing length nor coloration provided an adequate basis for distinguishing races. There is a distinctive local population in Angola, **benguelensis**, which differs primarily in colour (Hall 1960). This race also shows some habitat differences, favouring miombo rather than acacia and mopane woodland, and Hall and Moreau (1970) accorded it 'near-species' status. This race requires further study.

Traylor (1965) noted that January birds were in fresh plumage, whereas those from August had very worn plumage. Brooke (1967a) found that there was a partial post-juvenile moult from May to June, then the first complete moult from July to November. He assumed that the birds would breed at one year old; in subsequent years there was a partial moult of the dorsal plumage and tail feathers after the breeding season. However, the complete moult of adult birds apparently took place from October to February, before breeding.

MEASUREMENTS Male (10): wing 146–157, tail 188–225, bill 22.6–24.7, tarsus 38.3–42.0. Female (10): wing 131–149, tail 184–207, bill 21.3–24.0, tarsus 34.6–40.1. Weight, unsexed (15) 66–85 g.

VOICE The churring call notes are rendered as *chwirri-chwirr chwee chwirr chweer* (Maclean 1993).

DISTRIBUTION AND POPULATION Occurs in Angola, Zambia, Malawi, central Mozambique, the northern parts of Namibia, Botswana and Zimbabwe; also along the southern border of Zimbabwe and in the northern Transvaal, South

Africa. It is sparsely distributed in suitable habitat.

HABITAT The birds favour areas with tall trees, especially mopane and baobabs, and bare ground; often areas which are seasonally flooded (Tarboton *et al.* 1987).

FOOD AND FEEDING Meves' Long-tailed Starling forages mostly on the ground taking insects, but will also eat fruit such as *Diospyros mespiliformis* (Dean *et al.* 1987) and also feed in *Acacia albida* trees, either on flowers or fruit. Termites (Termitidae), primarily workers, and a scarab beetle (Scarabaeidae) were found in one stomach (Borrett 1973), and Benson (1959) reported termites, beetles (Carabidae), black ants (Formicidae) and mole-crickets (Gryllotalpidae) from specimens collected in Zambia. In Botswana, birds were seen feeding on nymphs of Psylloidea on the leaves of mopane trees (Herremans-Tonnoeyr *et al.* 1995). The birds followed moving elephants *Loxodonta africana* in the Kruger Park, foraging on the ground and presumably catching insects disturbed by the elephants (Dean and Macdonald 1981).

BREEDING The nests are normally in tree holes up to 4 m above the ground, but also in fence posts and even in a ventilation pipe (Maclean 1993). Benson (1953) reported nests in baobab, mopane, and *Hyphaene* palm. Three pairs were apparently nesting in separate holes in a single tree, about 10 m above ground (Jubb 1952), but no other instances of colonial nesting have been reported. Brooke (1965a) summarised the available breeding data: the eggs are plain blue, measure 24.0–30.0 x 18.2–20.0 mm (11), the nest is a cup of dead vegetable matter without feathers. The clutch is 3–4 eggs. Schönwetter (1983) gives the egg weight as 6.3 g. A female excavated a nest hole in rotting wood, about 4 m above the ground. Both male and female birds fed the nestings on insects and caterpillars. In captive birds, the incubation period was 18 days, and the chicks left the nest after 23 days (Richard 1975). Breeding in Zambia occurred in February and March (Benson *et al.* 1971), in Malawi in February (Benson and Benson 1977), in Zimbabwe chiefly in February and March, but there were also records from November to April (Irwin 1981), and in the Kruger Park birds were seen nesting in January (Tarboton *et al.* 1987). Brooke (1965a, 1967a) concluded that the breeding season was December to March. A specimen from Namibia in October is evidently a juvenile moulting into adult plumage (Rudebeck 1955b). In Zimbabwe, Great Spotted Cuckoos *Clamator glandarius* attempted to enter a nestbox while the starlings were building. They were attacked, and one of the cuckoos was jammed in the nest entrance. A cuckoo egg was ejected by starlings, which later nested successfully (Thomson 1975). Parasitism by Great Spotted Cuckoo has also been reported in Zambia (Colebrook-Robjent and Greenberg 1976), Botswana (Gargett 1984) and South Africa (Tarboton *et al.* 1987).

BEHAVIOUR During nest-building, a young bird from a previous brood was associated with the pair and not chased away, but there is no evidence of cooperative breeding. The nesting birds were aggressive towards other conspecifics and also mobbed a Woodland Kingfisher *Halcyon senegalensis*. Out of the breeding season, flocks of up to 150 birds were seen, and large communal roosts were found in *Acacia* trees in Zimbabwe and in Botswana (R.K. Brooke pers. comm.).

PRINCIPAL REFERENCE Dowsett (1967).

80 BURCHELL'S GLOSSY STARLING *Lamprotornis australis*
Plate 22

Megalopterus australis Smith 1836

FIELD IDENTIFICATION 30 cm. A large, dark glossy starling with long legs and a bulky, square-tipped tail with distinct dark cross-barring. The eye is dark. It is often seen walking on the ground, and the flight is heavy.

DESCRIPTION The frons, crown, mantle and back are blue-green; the nape has a distinct blue to purple sheen, in some specimens almost forming a collar. The rump and uppertail-coverts are purple, sometimes with a bronze tinge. The lores are black, the ear-coverts and a large patch below the eye bronze, with a blue tinge around the border. Chin, throat and chest are blue-green, with purple shading in the centre of the belly, while the flanks, thighs and undertail-coverts are bluish. The wing-coverts are blue-green, with large velvety sub-terminal spots on some of the greater coverts, and a bronzy epaulet, bordered by purple. The primaries and secondaries have a blue to purple sheen, with distinct, dark cross-barring. The tail feathers are violet with very strong cross-barring, and clearly graduated in length, with the central feathers the longest. The iris is dark brown, the bill and legs black. The sexes are alike. A juvenile specimen has dull green sheen on the back and a matt black underside, without any of the purple iridescence evident in the adult (Brooke 1968). Brooke (1967b) described a female specimen with some small white feathers on the cheeks, nape and wing-coverts, and with a white tenth primary. Two other specimens were found, one had some white head feathers and a circlet of white on the neck, and some white feathers scattered on the ventral surface; the second had a patch of white feathers on the abdomen (Brooke 1968). In Kruger Park, a partially albino bird was sighted, which had the head, throat and underparts mostly white, the rest of the plumage mottled metallic-blue and white (R.J. Nuttall pers. comm.).

Birds in the eastern lowveld of South Africa, Mozambique and Swaziland seem to be effectively isolated from the rest of the species' range (Craig and Herremans 1997). This population has been described as *L. a. degener*; the status of this race requires study.

Brooke (1967b) found moulting birds from September–March, but suggested that most of the moult occurs before breeding, in September–December. Moult of the outermost primaries may be suspended and completed after breeding. Traylor (1965) reported birds in fresh plumage in January. Rudebeck (1955b) noted tail moult in a bird collected in November, but specimens from January, February and July were not moulting.

MEASUREMENTS Male (10): wing 165–195, tail 153–178, bill 26.7–29.7, tarsus 44.0–48.4. Female (10); wing 148–178, tail 137–160, bill 25.5–28.6, tarsus 42.2–45.3. Weight, unsexed (14) 74–138 g.

VOICE Very harsh, long spells of calling best described as croaking, with pauses between each group of notes (Maclean 1993, AC pers. obs.). Also a throaty, more musical call, uttered with the head flung back, bill pointed upwards and wings drooped slightly; this may be a territorial display call, as it would be given by several birds in turn, from perches spaced out in the trees (AC pers. obs.).

DISTRIBUTION AND POPULATION Burchell's Glossy Starling is found in southern Angola, western Zambia, central and eastern Namibia, Botswana, northwestern Zimbabwe and northern South Africa, ranging into adjacent eastern Mozambique and south to Swaziland. It is resident and locally common in favoured habitat.

HABITAT This is a bird of open woodland and savanna, associated particularly with camelthorn *Acacia erioloba* and avoiding miombo woodland. Absent from open plains and areas with poor tree cover; in eastern lowveld areas favours knobthorn *Acacia nigrescens* woodland.

FOOD AND FEEDING Burchell's Glossy Starlings feed on berries and fruit, also insects including locusts (Acrididae) and termites (Termitidae), feeding largely on the ground (Stark 1900). Centipedes (Scolopendromorpha) and small mice recorded, and mice (Mammalia) may be regular in the diet, as birds have been caught at bal-chatri traps for raptors, which were baited with mice (A.C. Kemp pers. comm.). Insects and cherry-sized fruit stones were noted in the stomachs of birds from Namibia (Hoesch and Niethammer 1940), *Acacia giraffae* flowers, fruit, termites, ants (Formicidae) and beetles (Carabidae) in birds from Zambia (Benson 1960). In Angola, the birds were seen feeding on *Diospyros mespiliformis* (Dean *et al.* 1987). In the Kruger National Park, South Africa, they are a familiar sight at picnic sites, where they will scavenge at the feet of visitors.

BREEDING Most nests are in tree holes, either natural holes or old barbet (Capitonidae) and woodpecker (Picidae) holes, from 2 m above the group up to 7 m. Occasionally a crevice in a cliff may be used. Nests in buildings have been reported (Stark 1900, W.R. Tarboton pers. comm.), and even in the tower of a windmill (Pickles 1989). Burchell's Glossy Starling will also use nest-boxes (WR Tarboton, pers. comm.). The nest is lined with grass, often fresh and green, and green leaves may also be brought in. Other lining material includes feathers, string, cloth, paper, snake skin and strips of clear plastic bags (W.R. Tarboton pers. comm.). The eggs are bright blue to greenish-blue, plain or with scattered red-purple spots, mainly at the thicker end; a clutch of 2–4, most often 3. They measure 27.5–31.7 x 19.8–22.1 mm (14) (Maclean 1993), weight 7.9 g (Schönwetter 1983). In captivity a male Burchell's Starling and a female Red-winged Starling mated. The nest was mud-lined, and the young bird resembled the male parent, lacking coloured wing feathers (Hopkinson 1932). The breeding season is primarily from October to January in South Africa, but there are also records from September to March (Tarboton et al. 1987), in March in Zambia (Benson et al. 1971), and January to April in Namibia and Botswana (Hoesch and Niethammer 1940, Craig

and Herremans 1997). A pair attacked a Great Spotted Cuckoo Clamator glandarius in Botswana (Pickles 1989). Burchell's Glossy Starling is parasitised by Great Spotted Cuckoo in South Africa and in Namibia (Dean and Macdonald 1972, Kemp et al. 1972). Young starlings may be raised successfully alongside single cuckoo chicks (W.R. Tarboton pers. comm.).

BEHAVIOUR Large flocks of up to 50 birds were seen in dry woodland (Hoesch and Niethammer 1940). In winter at Lake Ngami, Botswana, over 1000 birds roosted in tall *Acacia* trees, where they vocalised until well after dark. Small groups appeared to gather from a wide area, assembling on the ground before entering the roost (R.K. Brooke pers. comm.). Roosts in reedbeds may be shared with herons Ardeidae and other waterbirds. Forages on the ground in association with Cape Glossy Starlings and Greater Blue-eared Glossy Starlings; in some areas found alongside Meves' Long-tailed Glossy Starling, which Burchell's Glossy Starling will dominate at food sources.

81 SHARP-TAILED GLOSSY STARLING *Lamprotornis acuticaudus*
Plate 22

Lamprocolius acuticaudus Bocage, 1870

FIELD IDENTIFICATION 20 cm. A glossy green starling, with a pointed, wedge-shaped tail and red or orange eyes. There is a small coloured epaulet on the wing.

DESCRIPTION The crown, nape, mantle, back, and uppertail-coverts are glossy green. The ear-coverts are blue-green, the chin, throat, chest and undertail-coverts glossy green. There is some blue gloss on the belly and flanks. The wings are glossy green; an epaulet on the bend of the wing is purple tinged with bronze, and there are dark blue terminal spots on the wing-coverts. There are slight indentations on the inner webs of primaries 7–9. The tail feathers are glossy green with faint cross-barring. The iris is red, the bill and the legs black. The sexes are alike, but females may have an orange rather than red iris (Newman 1986). The juvenile plumage is matt grey with paler tips to feathers, producing a scaly appearance especially on the head; there is some gloss on the wing and tail feathers. The dorsal glossy plumage appears first, that on the belly last. In juvenile birds the iris is yellow.

Birds from southern Zaïre have been described as *L. a. katangae* on the basis of shorter tails and bills (Dirickx 1949), but there are no good grounds for recognising this race. Stresemann (1925) treated *acuticaudus* as a race of *chloropterus*. This was criticised by von Boetticher (1931b), who noted the inconsistency of using colour as a criterion in this case. He suggested that the two species might be related, but were not even congeneric in his terms. White (1948b) found *acuticaudus* and *chloropterus* in the same flocks in Zambia but saw no evidence of interbreeding, and was convinced

that they were separate species. Dirickx (1949) came to the same conclusion after reviewing the available information.

There were no specimens from June; of 49 birds, the eight showing wing moult came from August, and October to February. None were in moult during March to May (23 specimens), which suggests that moult is completed by the end of February. Traylor (1965) noted that all the specimens collected in early December were moulting, and Brooke (1968) referred to a complete moult after the breeding season.

MEASUREMENTS Male (10): wing 113–132, tail 84–105, bill 23.9–28.3, tarsus 28.5–32.4. Female (10): wing 112–131, tail 78–105, bill 23.4–26.5, tarsus 27.6–32.1. Weight of male (3) 68–73, of female (2) 65–68 g.

VOICE Birds in flocks give twittering calls, reminiscent of swallows.

DISTRIBUTION AND POPULATION Distributed from northern Namibia to southern Angola, southern Zaïre and western to northwestern Zambia, reaching the extreme southwest of Tanzania. It may be the commonest glossy starling in some areas (Chapin 1954).

HABITAT This is primarily a bird of open woodland, particularly dry miombo and mopane country.

FOOD AND FEEDING Presumably Sharp-tailed Glossy Starlings will take both fruit and insects. They were seen feeding on the fruit of *Diospyros kirkii* in Angola (Dean et al. 1987), and on *D. lycioides* in Namibia (Underhill and Brown 1997). Bowen (1931b) also reported that specimens had been collected at a fruiting tree in

Angola, feeding alongside bulbuls (Pycnonotidae) and other starlings.

BREEDING Like other glossy starlings, they nest in natural tree-holes or in cavities made by barbets (Capitonidae) and woodpeckers (Picidae), but the nest and eggs are undescribed. The breeding season is apparently from August to October in Angola (Heinrich 1958), October in Zambia (Benson et al. 1971), and November to March in Namibia (Underhill and Brown 1997). Chapin (1954) noted birds with enlarged gonads in August

in southern Zaïre. Juvenile specimens were collected in January, February, March, April, June and August.

BEHAVIOUR Flocks of up to 50 birds have been seen in Zambia (Traylor 1965), while flocks of 20 were noted in Angola (Dean et al. 1987). In Namibia, non-breeding birds form flocks of 40 or more, and are most conspicuous at this time (Underhill and Brown 1997). It is apparently resident, although Lippens and Wille (1976) referred to it as a dry-season visitor to southern Zaïre.

82 BLACK-BELLIED GLOSSY STARLING *Lamprotornis corruscus*
Plate 23

Lamprotornis corrusca Nordmann 1835

FIELD IDENTIFICATION 18 cm. A small, dark starling with a bright orange-yellow eye. It is glossy on the dorsal surface only, with the belly black, and it often appears a uniform dull black (Newman 1986).

DESCRIPTION Adult male: Crown, nape, mantle, chin, throat and upper chest glossy dark green, with some iridescent blue on the ear-coverts. The back, rump, upper and undertail-coverts, and thighs are dark green with a violet-blue gloss. The lower chest and belly is dark violet-blue with some bronzy sheen. The wing-coverts and secondaries are dark blue-green with some gloss; the alula and outer edges of the primaries are violet-blue, the tail feathers are dark violet-blue. The iris is orange-yellow, the bill and legs black. **Adult female**: Differs only in that the lower chest and belly are matt black with no gloss. The sexes are distinguishable at close range in the field on plumage characters; during the breeding season the eyes of males change to red for a variable period (Chittenden and Myburgh 1994). Juvenile birds are initially dull blackish, lacking gloss, and the iris is dark grey.

East African birds have been separated under the name *L. c. mandanus*, and Clancey (1974) claimed that this race extended as far south as the Tugela River. Another race *L. c. jombeni* was described from the interior of East Africa. However, size variation of birds on the coastal belt is clearly clinal, and extensive seasonal movements make interchange between different populations very likely. Birds from Pemba Island (**L. c. vaughani**) are clearly larger: wing of male (9 birds) 111–122 (mean 116.8), and *L. c. vaughani* also differs in the entire head being glossy purple instead of greenish. This is the only race which warrants recognition.

There is no indication of regional variation in the timing of moult, and the main moulting season is from late January to May; 58 birds showing wing moult were found amongst the 332 specimens examined. Most birds had two primary feathers growing simultaneously. Tail moult is completed within the period of wing moult, but body moult may only be completed later. Some birds showing

body moult may be found throughout the year. Juvenile birds undergo a partial moult, including only the body plumage and occasionally some rectrices.

MEASUREMENTS Male (45): wing 104–117, tail 72–90, bill 19.7–24.2, tarsus 23.3–27.3. Female (35): wing 99–112, tail 71–85, bill 19.6–22.7, tarsus 23.3–26.5. Weight of male (26) 51–68, of female (13) 46–62 g.

VOICE A noisy species, with flocks keeping up a continuous babble. The song is a sustained jumble of trilling and rather harsh piping notes, less musical to the ear than that of Cape Glossy Starling (AC pers. obs.). Pinto (1958) described the flight call as slightly nasal. Mimicry of other bird species has been reported (Pinto and Lamm 1956, Vernon 1973), and Pakenham (1936) identified notes of the Black-backed Puffback *Dryoscopus cubla*, Sombre Bulbul *Andropadus importunus*, Common Bulbul *Pycnonotus barbatus*, Dark-backed Weaver *Ploceus bicolor*, Grey-backed Camaroptera *Camaroptera brachyura*, African Paradise Flycatcher *Terpsiphone viridis*, Purple-banded Sunbird *Nectarinia bifasciata*, Diederik Cuckoo *Chrysococcyx caprius* and Cardinal Woodpecker *Dendropicos fuscescens* in the song of Black-bellied Glossy Starlings on Zanzibar. A male near Lake St Lucia, South Africa, gave perfect renditions of the calls of Square-tailed Drongo *Dicrurus ludwigii* and Common Bulbul (AC pers. obs.).

DISTRIBUTION AND POPULATION Occurs from the southern Cape Province, South Africa, northwards along the eastern coastal strip of Mozambique, Tanzania and Kenya to southern Somalia. There are few records more than 50 km inland from the coast, except in Mozambique and eastern Zimbabwe (Haroni-Lusitu region, Irwin 1981) and Kenya, where it may extend inland along the wooded Tana River as far as the slopes of Mount Kenya (Britton 1980, Lewis and Pomeroy 1989). They are also found on islands such as Inhaca, Mafia, Zanzibar and Pemba. This species is locally common, and may be abundant at times.

HABITAT This is a starling of the coastal forests and lowlands and is usually found in tall, dense vegetation; generally below 500 m and in areas of high rainfall (> 500 mm per annum). However, birds range up to 2000 m in the Meru forests and up to 1000 m in the East Usambaras, Tanzania (Zimmerman *et al.* 1996).

FOOD AND FEEDING Black-bellied Glossy Starlings are primarily frugivorous, but will take nectar, insects and other small animals. They may feed in trees or on the ground. The following fruits have been reported as food: *Ficus* sp. (Pinto and Lamm 1956, Frost 1980), *Clerodendron myricoides* (Swynnerton 1908), *Lantana* sp. (Sclater and Moreau 1933), cinnamon, *Sapium maniamum, Clausena anisata, Grevillea* sp. (Vaughan 1930), *Dovyalis longispina, Euclea natalensis, Trema orientalis, Halleria lucida, Ekebergia capensis, Apodytes dimidiata, Mimusops caffer, Sideroxylon inerme, Bridelia micrantha* (Frost 1980), *Melia azederach* (W.R.J. Dean pers. comm.), *Olea capensis, Osyris lanceolata, Acacia cyclops* (F. Dowsett-Lemaire pers. comm.), *Rapanea melanophloeos* (Koen 1992), *Morus* sp., *Harpephyllum caffrum* (Nixon 1993), *Trichilia emetica* (Frost 1980, Odgers 1993, Vernon 1993), *Phoenix reclinata* and *Acokanthera oppositifolia* (Odgers 1993). Black-bellied Glossy Starlings have been seen taking nectar from *Aloe marlothii* (Oatley and Skead 1972). They catch insects and hawk flying ants (Formicidae) and termite (Termitidae) alates (Woodward and Woodward 1899, Stark 1900, Sclater and Moreau 1933, Brooke *et al.* 1972), while Pinto and Lamm (1956) recorded small lizards (Reptilia) (presumably geckoes), Swynnerton (1908) a small snail (Mollusca), and Nixon (1992) observed birds catching reed frogs *Hyperolius* sp.

BREEDING Except for one nest in a building, all nests were in holes in trees, either natural holes or those of barbets (Capitonidae) or woodpeckers (Picidae), 2.5–6 m above the ground. A lining of grass, dry leaves and feathers has been reported (nest record cards), also hair (Maclean 1993). The eggs are pale greenish-blue, sometimes with faint brownish spots, measuring 24.2–-27.2 x 17.9–19.8 mm (36). The clutch is 2–4, most often 3 (Maclean 1993). The egg weight is 4.9 g (Schönwetter 1983). The incubation period has not been recorded, but it appears that only the female incubates, while the male perches nearby, warbling softly (AC pers. obs.). Both sexes feed the young (Pooley 1967, F. Dowsett-Lemaire pers. comm.). The nestling period is unknown, and no captive breeding records are available. There appear to be no regional differences in the timing of breeding, and 27 of 33 breeding records are from October to January, while 15 of 17 juvenile specimens were collected from December to April. There are also breeding records for August, September, February and May. Pinto (1958) collected birds with large gonads in November.

MIGRATION Curry-Lindahl (1981) categorised this species as probably migratory, although clear evidence was lacking. However, there appears to be no regular pattern of seasonal movement, although inland in Mozambique (Pinto and Lamm 1956) and in Zimbabwe (Irwin 1981) Black-bellied Glossy Starling is primarily a summer breeding visitor. At Beira, Sheppard (1909) stated that the birds arrived in November, and were then very common. At the western limits of its range in the southern Cape, it was only common when *Rapanea melanophloeos* was in fruit, which was during the winter (Koen 1992). In the eastern Cape, the birds are much more numerous in winter, although at East London there are records throughout the year (Tree 1986, C.J. Vernon pers. comm.). On Pemba Island the distinctive local race is resident, but birds on Zanzibar resemble mainland birds, and presumably interchange continues (Pakenham 1979). The presence of some birds throughout the year may conceal north-south movements along the coasts; Harvey and Howell (1987) recorded Black-bellied Glossy Starlings in all months around Dar es Salaam.

BEHAVIOUR Generally found in small flocks, of most commonly 15 to 35 birds (Tree 1986), but flocks of more than 100 birds have been recorded in some months in southern Africa (Pinto 1958, Koen 1992, C.J. Vernon pers. comm., pers. obs.), and flocks of 400 birds have been recorded in Avabuko-Sokoke Forest, Kenya (Short and Horne 1985a). Gilges (1945) noted that flocks of Black-bellied Glossy Starlings often perched, singing, at sunset in the tops of mangroves near Richards Bay, South Africa. A remarkable change in iris colour from yellow to blood-red has been reported in Black-bellied Glossy Starlings caught in mist nets (McCulloch 1963, Britton and Britton 1970). AC has also observed this colour change affecting the eye on one side of the head only, with the normal colour restored abruptly after about ten minutes. Presumably the iris is flushed with blood when the bird is under stress, but it is not known if this response plays any role in normal social behaviour. Male birds have orange-red eyes during the breeding period, with some individuals retaining this state longer than others (Chittenden and Myburgh 1994). Short and Horne (1985a) observed possible courtship behaviour when three birds from a group of seven flew down to a tree, and displayed dipping their bills and giving low calls. Pursuit flights, some of which lasted for several minutes, may be a prelude to courtship (Skead 1995). Competition for nest sites occurs, and in Tanzania both Kenrick's Starling and Waller's Red-winged Starling were seen displacing Black-bellied Glossy Starlings from a nest hole (Lack 1936). Common Starlings successfully ousted Black-bellied Glossy Starlings from a nest hole in South Africa (Dean pers. comm.), and another pair was unable to prevent Green Wood-hoopoes *Phoeniculus purpureus* from destroying their eggs (Holland 1945).

PRINCIPAL REFERENCE Craig (1989).

Lamprocolius superbus Rüppell 1845

FIELD IDENTIFICATION 18 cm. The glossy dorsal plumage, the light chestnut-brown ventral surface with a white band across the chest and the pale eye easily distinguishes this bird from all similar species.

DESCRIPTION The crown and ear-coverts are bronzy-black, the lores black. The chin, throat, chest, nape, mantle, back, uppertail-coverts and tail are glossy blue-green, with blue tones, which are most marked in the nape area. A narrow white band separates the glossy chest from the chestnut-brown belly, flanks and thighs. The vent, undertail-coverts and underwing-coverts are white. The wings are glossy metallic-green, with dark velvety-black spots on the tips of the median and greater coverts. Primary feathers 6–9 are indented on the inner web, while the outer web of primaries 5–8 is attenuated. The iris is creamy-white, the bill and legs black. The sexes are alike, but in a captive pair, the male had a noticeably wider white breastband (Restall 1968). In juvenile birds the plumage regions are clearly defined, but there is no gloss except on the wing and tail feathers. The iris is brown, the bill pale yellowish, darkening from the tip and the legs brown. A captive-bred bird was much duller than the adults on hatching, and lacked the white breastband. At seven months it had adult plumage, but the eyes were still dark, and there was yellow at the base of the bill (Lawrence 1975). For almost a year, a bird with partly white plumage was observed in the same area; its plumage was mottled green and white, with a normal chestnut-coloured belly, but with the breast band undefined (Rilling 1972). A complete albino, with pink eyes and pale legs, was sighted in a flock in Kenya (Lewis and Ogola 1989).

Birds from Tanzania reportedly have longer wings and tails, but birds of both sexes were combined in the samples (Clancey 1987). No subspecies are recognised.

Twelve of 45 specimens had wing moult, from February, April, May, August and November. This does not suggest any obvious seasonality, and there may be considerable individual variation, as implied by the extended breeding season. Van Someren (1956) stated that the first moult of the fledglings starts at four months, and is completed after about two months, but the eye colour does not change until there has been a complete change of plumage, presumably at about one year.

MEASUREMENTS Male (15): wing 115–127, tail 66–74, bill 21.2–23.4, tarsus 32–35.1. Female (15): wing 114–124, tail 65–74, bill 20.3–23.7, tarsus 30.7–35.6.

VOICE Superb Starlings have a long rambling song, at times very quiet, which in van Someren's (1956) rendering seems to consist of nearly 20 elements. He also recorded a long-drawn warning *chirr*, and a repeated *whit-chor-chi-vii* from excited birds. Erlanger (1905) described the song as

attractive, reminiscent of Common Starling, while Schuster (1926) compared it to European Robin *Erithacus rubecula*. In aviaries, the male birds sang at great length, a loosely strung series of warbles, whistles and odd notes, while females also sang, but less often (Restall 1968).

DISTRIBUTION AND POPULATION This species occurs from central Tanzania northwards throughout Kenya, in western Uganda, southwestern Sudan, southern Ethiopia and Somalia. It is widespread and abundant within this range.

HABITAT Superb Starlings generally avoid humid lowland areas, but they are found on the northern Kenya coast, and inland to 3000 m, often in very arid country, but also in cultivated areas, lakeshore woodlands and suburban gardens.

FOOD AND FEEDING Apart from scavenging around people, the birds feed largely on the ground, collecting insects such as termites (Termitidae), grasshoppers and mantids (Mantidae), moth larvae (Lepidoptera) and beetles (Carabidae). Some berries and small fruits are also taken (van Someren 1956). Superb Starlings also take nectar from sisal flowers *Agave sisalana* (Cunningham-van Someren 1974).

BREEDING Free-standing nests are built in thorn trees, but nests in tree holes and even in holes in cliffs have also been reported. Where Superb Starlings build their own nests, these are large rough structures of twigs lined with dry grass, and an entrance at one side, usually well protected by thorns and 1.5–6 m above ground (Jackson and Sclater 1938). Feathers are also used in the nest lining (Erlanger 1905). According to van Someren (1956) Superb Starlings deliberately place thorny twigs around the nest, if the tree itself is not sufficiently thorny. Nests may be in the thatch of huts, but the birds often take over nests of the White-headed Buffalo-Weaver *Dinemellia dinemelli*, even ejecting the eggs. On occasion the weavers will eject starling eggs (Huels, in Allen 1974). In Tanzania, Superb Starlings were found using the nests of Red-billed Buffalo-Weavers *Bubalornis niger* and Rufous-tailed Weavers *Histurgops rufi-cauda*, with several pairs of starlings occupying nests in a single tree (Irwin 1957). Bowen (1931a) found a nest in the side of an old vulture's nest. The eggs are a uniform dark blue, measuring 24.0–26.0 x 18.0–19.0 mm (16), weight 4.5 g (Schönwetter 1983). The usual clutch size is 4 (van Someren 1956, Archer and Godman 1961). Van Someren (1956) suggested that both adults incubated, but commented that it was difficult to be certain of the sex of the birds involved. The chicks are fed mainly on insects, particularly moth larvae (Lepidoptera), but some berries are also provided (van Someren 1956). There are numerous records of breeding in captivity, and the incubation period is 12–13 days (Restall 1968, Bartmann 1974, Lawrence 1975), the nestling period 18 (Lawrence 1975) to 24 days (Ezra 1924, Bartmann 1974). In a captive pair the female did almost all the nest-building, and only the female incubated the eggs. The female also fed the chicks much more often than the male (Restall 1968). There are breeding records for all months of the year in East Africa, but definite peaks in March–April and November–December (Brown and Britton 1980). The breeding season in Somalia is given as May and June (Archer and Godman 1961), but Phillips (1896) reported nesting in March and April. Urban and Brown (1971) gave the breeding season in Ethiopia as February to October. In southern Ethiopia, Benson (1946) found eggs in October, and chicks in March. Young birds in their first plumage were noted in April in Uganda (van Someren 1916). A Superb Starling was seen feeding a recently-fledged Great Spotted Cuckoo *Clamator glandarius* in Kenya (Trevor and Lack 1976).

BEHAVIOUR In captivity helpers at the nest have been reported by most authors. One breeder stated that the helpers were always female in his experience (R. Shanteau pers. comm.). Ezra (1924) started out with four birds, one of which was attacked by the others, and had to be removed from the aviary. The remaining three birds all took part in building the nest and feeding the chicks. Brown (1972) found that his birds bred successfully as a group of five, but were intially intolerant of other Superb Starlings in the aviary. Bartmann (1974) reported that a pair of Superb Starlings killed a third conspecific in the same aviary before they started nesting. A second clutch was laid ten weeks after the first, and the single chick from the first brood fed the second brood both in the nest and after they had fledged. Cooperative breeding was studied in the field by T. Huels, but no full account has been published. In a report by Allen (1974), the study population was described as a flock of 20 adults and juveniles, which stayed together throughout the year. There was some hierarchical organisation, but although a particular male and female were associated, other males also copulated with this female. Observations of birds running along the ground, jumping with drooping wing and out-stretched heads suggested 'some sort of nuptial display' to Granvik (1923). A female Superb Starling in captivity solicited the male by leaning forward, raising the tail and drooping and fluttering the wings. After landing, both members of the pair would cock the tail, dis-playing the white vent and undertail-coverts (Restall 1968). Van Someren (1956) also mentions and illustrates this posture, with wings lowered and a slightly lifted tail, and Schuster (1926) noted a female bending her legs and spreading the wings before copulation. Lawrence (1975) described how a presumed male bird dilated his eyes while singing, and van Someren (1956) noted that during intense excitement and calling, the pupil of the eye contracted to a mere pinpoint.

On the Tana River, Kenya, Superb Starlings were seen roosting in vacant nests of White-browed Sparrow-weavers *Plocepasser mahali* (Irvine and Irvine 1974). Bowen (1931a) observed them roosting in nests of Rufous-tailed Weavers, alongside the owners. Like other starlings, this species gathers in trees during the hottest part of the day and warbles for long periods (van Someren 1956). Superb Starlings were described as 'dancing in a ring' with Northern Anteater Chats *Myrmecocichla aethiops* and Rufous Sparrows *Passer rufocinctus* by Hayes (1982); possibly these birds were anting, or dust-bathing. Brown and Newman (1974) observed this species anting in Kenya, and anting has also been reported in captive birds by Poulsen (1956) and by Simmons (1961). In Somalia, Superb Starlings often associated with White-headed Buffalo-Weavers or Blue-eared Glossy Starlings, sometimes with Shelley's Starlings (Archer and Godman 1961). Dellelegn (1993) noted Superb Starlings foraging with small groups of Ethiopian Bush Crows *Zavattariornis stresemanni* in southern Ethiopia. In Tanzania, a pair harassed a White-naped Raven *Corvus albicollis*, swooping on its head from behind, and a flock mobbed a Spotted Eagle-Owl *Bubo africanus* (Bangs and Loveridge 1933). Archer referred to them as bold and aggressive birds, which would mob hawks, owls and snakes (Archer and Godman 1961). On the ground the birds both run and hop. They have long been 'camp followers' (Archer and Godman 1961), and are now bold scavengers around settlements and picnic sites. In Amboseli National Park, Kenya, the local vervet monkeys *Cercopithecus aethiops* have learnt to recognise and respond appropriately to the distinctive alarm calls which Superb Starlings give to aerial and terrestrial predators (Hauser 1988).

84 HILDEBRANDT'S STARLING *Lamprotornis hildebrandti*
Plate 24

Notauges hildebrandti Cabanis 1878

FIELD IDENTIFICATION 18 cm. A small starling, glossy above, brown below. It is duller than Superb Starling, and lacks the white iris and white border between the chest and the belly. It is very like Shelley's Starling, but the lower chest is much lighter brown.

DESCRIPTION The chin, throat, chest and ear-coverts are dark glossy purple. The lores are black, the crown dark glossy blue, contrasting with the chin and throat. The nape has a half-collar of bronze-green, variable in width. The mantle, back and uppertail-coverts are dark glossy blue, with some purple tones. The lower chest and upper belly are light chestnut-brown, becoming dark brown on the lower belly, vent, thighs and undertail-coverts. The lesser-coverts are dark blue with velvety-black terminal spots, the greater coverts are bronze-green with black terminal spots on the inner feathers. The secondaries are wholly bronze-green, the alula and primaries are deep blue to purple on the outer webs; the underwing-coverts are dark blue. The outer webs of primaries 5–8 are attenuated, but there is no indentation on the inner web. The tail is glossy blue-green. The iris is orange-red, and the bill and the legs are black. The sexes are alike. Juvenile plumage is initially very dull, a uniform pale chestnut-brown ventrally, with shadows of darker plumage in the chest and throat region. Dorsally the juvenile bird is a dull charcoal-grey with gloss restricted to wings and tail. The iris is brown (Zimmerman *et al.* 1996); the bill and legs were black in the specimens seen, but may be brown in younger birds.

Although only 27 birds have been examined (none from June), there were no birds in moult from July to December, whereas 13 of the 15 birds from January to May did have wing moult. Moreau (1935) found birds beginning to moult in March. This suggests that moult may be restricted to the first half of the year, but Bowen (1931a) collected moulting birds in late June and noted that immature birds were then moulting into adult plumage. Friedmann and Loveridge (1937) found that birds collected in September were in fresh plumage.

MEASUREMENTS Male (15): wing 108–122, tail 72–80, bill 20.4–23.5, tarsus 31.3–32.9. Female (6): wing 106–118, tail 64–75, bill 20.3–22.8, tarsus 29.0–32.8. Weight, female 57 g.

VOICE The flock call is a whistled *chule*, while the alarm call is rendered as *chu-ee*. The song is a low warbling phrase *chu-er chu-er chu-er cher cher chule* (Mackworth-Praed and Grant 1960); a slow sequence of creaking notes interspersed with whistles (Zimmerman *et al.* 1996).

DISTRIBUTION AND POPULATION Endemic to southern Kenya and northern Tanzania, where it is localised and uncommon.

HABITAT The birds are found in open thorn-bush country, generally between 500 and 2000 m but they are probably not resident below 1000 m (Lewis and Pomeroy 1989).

FOOD AND FEEDING Hildebrandt's Starling feeds mostly on the ground. Beetles (Carabidae), grasshoppers (Orthoptera) and seeds were recorded in the stomachs of specimens collected. Erlanger (1905) noted that the birds caught grasshoppers and other insects disturbed by his caravan.

BREEDING Nests are in tree holes, lined with a pad of hair or plant fibres. The eggs are described as white and slightly glossy, 25 x 18 mm, in a clutch of three or four (Mackworth-Praed and Grant 1960), while other eggs reportedly had linear dark markings and small brown flecks, but the identity of all of these clutches is uncertain according to Schönwetter (1983). There are apparently two breeding periods in East Africa, from March to May, and from October to December (Brown and Britton 1980). A female with a brood patch was collected in December, and there were three juvenile birds from July, one from June and one from January among the museum specimens examined. An adult Hildebrandt's Starling was seen feeding two newly fledged Great Spotted Cuckoos (Geertsema 1976).

BEHAVIOUR Hildebrandt's Starlings often feed and flock with Superb Starlings (Lewis and Pomeroy 1989).

85 SHELLEY'S STARLING *Lamprotornis shelleyi* Plate 24

Spreo shelleyi Sharpe 1890

FIELD IDENTIFICATION 16 cm. Very like Hildebrandt's Starling, but Shelley's Starling is much darker brown ventrally. Its glossy dorsal plumage and dark brown ventral plumage distinguishes it from other small glossy starlings in the area.

DESCRIPTION The crown, chin, throat and chest are all dark glossy purple — the crown is not bluer, as in Hildebrandt's Starling. There is a dull black patch which extends from the lores to the ear-coverts, separating the head and throat, and a bronzy-green collar on the nape, which is often less than 10 mm wide. The mantle, back and uppertail-coverts are a dark glossy blue. The chest, belly, thighs and undertail-coverts are a uniform dark brown. The lesser coverts are dark blue, the greater coverts bronze-green, and both are marked with black terminal spots. The secondaries are bronze-green, whereas the alula and primaries are deep blue to purple on the outer webs. The primary feathers 6–8 have attenuated outer webs, but no indentations on the inner webs. The tail is glossy blue-green. The iris is orange-red, and the bill and the legs black. The sexes are alike. Juveniles are pale chestnut-brown ventrally, while the dorsal plumage is charcoal-grey with little gloss on the wings and tail. The iris is described as brown in one specimen, pale yellowish-green in another. The bill and the legs are black. Captive-bred young birds had ashy-brown dorsal plumage and dark grey-blue eyes (Scamell 1964).

In a sample of 57 birds from all months, eight showed wing moult. Seven of these were collected between September and January and one was from June, which suggests that the main moult period is October to December. Juveniles appear to acquire adult plumage by a partial moult, which may include some rectrices and tertial remiges. Some birds retain the juvenile head plumage after this moult.

MEASUREMENTS Male (16): wing 104–115, tail 71–81, bill 19.1–23.0, tarsus 29.4–32.6. Female (7): wing 101–106, tail 64–74, bill 17.4–21.0, tarsus 26.3–31.2. Weight, female 45 g.

VOICE The song was described by Benson (1946) as a cross between the call of Superb Starling and that of White-browed Sparrow-weaver *Plocepasser mahali*.

DISTRIBUTION AND POPULATION An East African endemic, which moves seasonally between Kenya, and Somalia and southern Ethiopia, with occasional records from southeastern Sudan. It may be common within this very restricted range.

HABITAT Its usual habitat is semi-arid bushed and wooded country, in Kenya generally below 1000 m (Lewis and Pomeroy 1989).

FOOD AND FEEDING This species appears to feed less on the ground than either Superb or Hildebrandt's Starlings (Zimmerman *et al.* 1996). Lack (1985) categorized Shelley's Starling as more insectivorous than frugivorous, but there seems to be no specific information on its diet.

BREEDING Shelley's Starling nests in tree holes, 1.5–3 m above ground. There is usually a lining of grass and feathers. The eggs are generally plain pale blue, with an occasional indistinct brown freckle (Archer and Godman 1961). They measure 24.5–27.0 x 18.0 mm (28), weight 4.2 g (Schönwetter 1983). Most clutches are 4 eggs, but up to 6 have been recorded (Archer and Godman 1961). The clutch size in captivity was three, and the pair nested in a nestbox lined with feathers.

The female incubated while the male sang from a nearby perch. Both parents fed the chicks, and the nestling period was approximately 22 days (Scamell 1964). Breeding was reported in Somalia from April to June, with the birds possibly double-brooded (Archer and Godman 1961). Urban and Brown (1971) recorded breeding in Ethiopia in March, and in southern Ethiopia the birds were probably nesting in April (Benson 1946). Fledged young were recorded in July in Somalia (Clarke 1985).

MIGRATION Archer stated categorically that Shelley's Starling is a migratory species, coming north to breed and moving south for the winter within well-defined dates (Archer and Godman 1961). Benson (1946) commented on this species' sudden arrival on the breeding areas in March, and Ash and Miskell (1983) list it as an intra-tropical migrant, present in Somalia from April to September. In Tsavo, Lack (1985) recorded Shelley's Starling only in November and February–March, and it is evidently a non-breeding visitor to Kenya from October to March (Lewis and Pomeroy 1989).

BEHAVIOUR Lack (1985) often saw Shelley's Starling in flocks of up to 50 birds. Benson (1946) noted that at the onset of breeding the flocks broke up, and the birds were found singly or in pairs.

86 CHESTNUT-BELLIED STARLING *Lamprotornis pulcher* Plate 24

Turdus pulcher Statius Muller 1776

FIELD IDENTIFICATION 18 cm. The only glossy starling with coloured wing feathers; these white patches in the wings are conspicuous in flight. The dorsal plumage is glossy and the ventral plumage matt brown.

DESCRIPTION The crown and ear-coverts are charcoal-grey with a faint gloss, the lores black. The throat, chest, nape, mantle, back, uppertail-coverts, wings and tail are glossy bronze-green with some blue tones. The belly, flanks, thighs, vent, undertail-coverts and underwing-coverts are chestnut-brown. The primaries are dull white for the basal two-thirds of the inner web, producing a central white patch. Primaries 7–9 are emarginated on the inner web, 6–8 attenuated on the outer web. The iris is yellowish-white, and the bill and the legs are black. The sexes are alike. Juveniles are charcoal-grey dorsally, ventrally chestnut-brown with dark shadows on the throat and chest. Gloss is restricted to the wing and tail feathers. The iris is brown and the bill yellow, darkening from the tip; the legs are brown. Wilkinson (1982a) described an unusual individual, in which the normally glossy green feathers were dull brown with pale flecks, the dark brown areas of the remiges were dull steel-grey, and the belly was cinnamon-orange rather than chestnut. The adults commence moult in March or April, and moult is completed by December; it appears to last six or

seven months in individual birds. Primary moult is usually complete before all the secondaries are replaced. Young birds fledged between March and May apparently completed a full wing-moult by the following February; the post-juvenile moult was incomplete or interrupted in some cases. Some birds moult while breeding. It is not clear from this account whether a complete post-juvenile moult is typical of the species, and as such a moult has not been reported for any other member of the genus, this would require confirmation.

MEASUREMENTS Male (10): wing 111–123, tail 67–74, bill 23.3–26.2, tarsus 33.2–34.9. Female (10): wing 109–115, tail 65–70, bill 22.3–23.5, tarsus 32.4–35.6. Weight, unsexed (18), 51–70 g.

VOICE The call has been described as a rather pleasant *whirri whirri*, also an *earh earh* (Bannerman 1948). Bates (1934) referred to a song of 'weak, liquid notes'.

DISTRIBUTION AND POPULATION Found from Senegambia through to northern Ethiopia. The species is common over most of this region, but Nikolaus (1987) stated that numbers in eastern Sudan had decreased greatly in the past ten years. At Ennedi, Chad, this species appeared to be a rainy season visitor (Gillet 1960).

HABITAT The birds are found in dry acacia savanna and steppe, typical of the Sahel zone.

FOOD AND FEEDING Chestnut-bellied

Starlings feed primarily on the ground, and stomachs contained termites (Termitidae), beetles (Carabidae) from cow dung and *Salvadora* berries (Bates 1934). Breeding birds were observed feeding chicks on locust-hoppers (Acrididae) in Eritrea (Smith 1957).

BREEDING Nests of Chestnut-bellied Starlings may be close together, about 2–3 m above ground, with the desert date tree a favoured site. The nest is a loose ball of dry grass with a lining of feathers, in one case also a snake's skin, and an opening to one side near the top. The eggs are blue, with dark brown markings and mauve spots forming a ring about the large end (Serle 1943). Eggs measure 22.8–26.5 x 16.8–19.0 mm (34) and weigh 4.4 g (Schönwetter 1983). Clutches of 4–5 eggs were found in Nigeria (Shuel 1938), clutches of 3–4 in Sudan (Lynes 1924). In Eritrea, Smith (1957) found that the birds built their own nests or used those of Red-billed Buffalo-Weavers *Bubalornis niger*. Benson (1946) also described Chestnut-bellied Starlings using buffalo-weaver nests in Ethiopia, a few pairs to each colony. The breeding male and female contributed equally to nest-building, but only the female incubated the eggs. Young are fed by both parents and up to 12 other helpers. Captive birds brought grass and leaves into nestboxes, but did not lay eggs (Brown 1972). Breeding was recorded in June in Nigeria (Serle 1943), also in September and October (Shuel 1938). There are two distinct breeding seasons in Nigeria, from February to June, and again from September to November. Males were in breeding condition, with enlarged testes, from February to October and at least some individuals nested in both seasons. In Senegal, breeding has been recorded in all months of the year (Morel and Morel 1982, 1990) and Schifter (1986) saw nests and a fledgling being fed in December, although in the Gambia there are confirmed nesting records for June (Gore 1990). There are apparently two breeding periods in Mali as Duhart and Descamps (1963) recorded eggs in April and young chicks in November. In Niger, breeding was recorded in June and August (Giradoux *et al.* 1988), while in Burkina Faso, Thonnerieux (1988) saw nest-building in July, pairs present at nests in May and July, and a juvenile bird in July. Benson (1946) saw chicks being fed in late May in Ethiopia, and Urban and Brown (1971) gave breeding records for February, April and May. Lynes (1924) described two nesting periods in April and October for Sudan, but suggested that the same individuals were not involved, while Nikolaus (1987) gave January to June and October to November as the breeding periods. Chestnut-bellied Starling has been reported as an occasional host of Levaillant's Cuckoo *Oxylophus levaillantii* (Irwin 1988).

BEHAVIOUR Cooperative breeding in this species was first reported by Wilkinson (1978), and subsequently he studied this in detail in Nigeria. Each group, which contained at least two active breeding pairs and 6–26 non-breeders, had its own exclusive area during the breeding season, although there was some overlap of ranges. The overall sex ratio was biased in favour of males. The age of first breeding for ringed males was 2–3 years. Nest-building was carried out by the breeding pair, and occasionally the breeding male would feed the female at the nest. Other birds were only involved once there were chicks in the nest, when they fed the young, removed faecal sacs and defended the nest. Chicks were also fed and protected after leaving the nest. The same individuals helped at different nests either successively or simultaneously. Nests with more helpers are more successful, but it is not clear whether this is related to an increased food supply for the nestlings (Wilkinson and Brown 1984). In Senegal, Chestnut-bellied Starlings are usually seen in groups of 2–7, sometimes up to 20, often in association with buffalo-weavers, and occasionally with other starlings (Schifter 1986).

PRINCIPAL REFERENCES Wilkinson (1982b, 1983).

87 PURPLE-HEADED GLOSSY STARLING *Hylopsar purpureiceps*
Plate 23

Lamprocolius purpureiceps Verreaux and Verreaux 1851

FIELD IDENTIFICATION 18 cm. A short-tailed glossy starling of the forest canopy, with a glossy green body, contrasting with the dark purple head, and a dark eye.

DESCRIPTION The lores and frons are matt black. The rest of the head, chin, throat and chest are a deep, glossy purple, sharply demarcated from adjoining plumage areas. The nape, mantle, back, uppertail-coverts, belly and flanks are a glossy greenish-blue. The undertail-coverts are black with some blue sheen, and in some birds they have a bronze sheen. The wings are iridescent blue, shading to violet on the outer margins of the primaries. The tail is black with a faint purple gloss. The iris is brown, and the bill and legs are black. The sexes are alike. The juvenile is matt charcoal-grey, except for some blue gloss on the wings.

A large sample was examined, of more than 220 specimens from all months of the year. Birds in moult were recorded in every month except August, with suspended wing moult in birds from July (3), August and November. Thus no clear seasonal picture emerges, nor are there obvious regional differences, and an extended moult period with moult-breeding overlap seems likely.

MEASUREMENTS Male (10): wing 123–130, tail 72–78, bill 21.5–23.2, tarsus 24.0–26.0. Female

(10): wing 110–123, tail 65–74, bill 21.0–23.7, tarsus 23.7–25.2. Weight of male (14) 54–79, of female (4) 50–70.

VOICE The flight call is a metallic *twink*, while perched birds gave low calls like those of Lesser Blue-eared Glossy Starling (Chapin 1954). Marchant (1953) described a short, rather musical call, single or repeated two or three times. This may be the same call described by Mackworth-Praed and Grant (1973) as a few clear notes, followed by a series of half tones, then louder notes again.

DISTRIBUTION AND POPULATION Widely distributed from southern Nigeria east to Uganda and northwest Kenya, and throughout the central forested area to southwestern Zaïre. Morel and Morel (1988) list both this species and Coppery-tailed Starling for Guinea, while Thiollay (1985) reported it as rare in Ivory Coast; one of the localities given is in the extreme west of the country. However, Grimes (1987) had no records for Ghana, and for the present these records must be considered unconfirmed. The birds are locally common, with temporary concentrations at fruiting trees.

HABITAT A starling of the forest canopy, recorded at 200 m on Mt Cameroon, and at 1000 m in the Rumpi Hills (Stuart 1986); widespread in Zaïre below 1000 m (Chapin 1954).

FOOD AND FEEDING The stomachs of nine specimens contained fruit or berries. Chapin (1954) examined 13 stomachs, one of which contained a snail (Mollusca); all 13 contained berries and other fruit. Friedmann and Williams (1971) reported fruit, seeds and insect fragments in stomach contents. Fruits recorded in Gabon and Congo were *Ficus*, *Rauwolfia*, *Heisteria*, *Musanga*, *Pycanthus*, *Morinda*, *Xylopia*, *Allophyllus*, *Macaranga*, *Polyalthia*, *Trichoscypha*, as well as termites (Termitidae), grasshoppers (Orthoptera) and mantid (Mantidae) larvae (Brosset and Erard 1986, Dowsett-Lemaire 1996).

BREEDING Purple-headed Glossy Starlings nested in tree holes in Zaïre, 9 m above the ground in one case. The nest hollow was lined with small pieces of green leaves. The eggs were blue with brown spotting, denser at the larger end to form a ring, 23.5 x 18 mm; clutch size is three (Herroelen 1955). The egg weight is given as 4.0 g (Schönwetter 1983). A breeding pair was seen entering a tree hole, one carrying a small stick (Bates 1909). Breeding has been reported from Uganda in April (Brown and Britton 1980), from Cameroon in June (Bannerman 1948), although Elgood (1982) stated that there were no breeding records anywhere in West Africa. In Gabon, Purple-headed Starlings were breeding from December to February (Rand et al. 1959, Brosset and Erard 1986). Birds in breeding condition were collected between June and October in Zaïre (Chapin 1954). Nest-building was seen in June and the eggs were evidently laid in June and July (Herroelen 1955). Lippens and Wille (1976) gave the breeding season for Zaïre as from June to October in the northeast, from December to March in Kivu and from September to October at Maniema; Prigogine (1971) found birds in breeding condition from January to March, and also in May. Newly-fledged birds were recorded in Zaïre in January, June and November. Other juvenile specimens were collected in February, June and October, with immature birds collected in March, April and May. In Uganda, van Someren (1916) collected a female with an enlarged ovary in September.

BEHAVIOUR Occasionally flocks of more than 100 birds are encountered (Brosset and Erard 1986), but there are usually fewer than 20 Purple-headed Starlings in a group, and they are most often encountered in pairs or parties of four or five (Marchant 1953, Chapin 1954). They roost in dead branches at the tops of trees (Rand et al. 1959). Prigogine (1971) reported that this species occasionally joined mixed species flocks in Zaïre. When associating with other species at fruiting trees, Purple-headed Glossy Starlings were dominated by the larger Splendid Glossy Starlings and Chestnut-winged Starlings, and by hornbills (Bucerotidae), but they often foraged in the lower undergrowth, presumably taking smaller fruits (Brosset and Erard 1986).

88 COPPERY-TAILED STARLING *Hylopsar cupreocauda* Plate 23

Lamprocolius cupreocauda Hartlaub 1857

FIELD IDENTIFICATION 18 cm. A small, short-tailed glossy starling of the forest canopy; blue above, purple below, with conspicuous yellow eyes.

DESCRIPTION The crown and nape are turquoise-blue with a purple sheen. The mantle, back, and wings are plain turquoise-blue. The chin, throat, sides of the head and upper chest are purple, passing into turquoise-blue on the lower chest, belly and flanks. The uppertail-coverts and tail are glossy bronze, the undertail-coverts matt charcoal, with violet tips to some feathers. The iris is yellow, and the bill and legs black. The sexes are alike. The juvenile is matt charcoal-grey with gloss on the wings and tail only; the dorsal glossy plumage is evidently acquired first. The iris was already yellow in the specimen examined.

Thirty-five specimens were examined, from January, April–August and October–December. Those from January and April, and one bird from October show active wing moult; and another bird from January showed suspended wing moult. Overall, the sample revealed no clear seasonality. In Liberia, Rand (1951) noted wing moult in four out of five birds collected in May.

MEASUREMENTS Male (15): wing 118–129, tail

70–80, bill 20.5–22.8, tarsus 23.5–26.3. Female (13): wing 113–122, tail 65–72, bill 19.0–21.9, tarsus 21.6–24.5. Weight of male (16) 51–66, of female (6) 53–65 g.

VOICE Harsh grating calls were reported from birds in flight, while the song was a jumble of harsh notes (Walker 1939).

DISTRIBUTION AND POPULATION Occurs from Guinea and Sierra Leone to Ghana, thus west of the 'Dahomey gap' in the West African forests. This species was listed as 'near-threatened' on the basis of its restricted range, but it was considered the commonest starling in many forested areas during recent surveys.

HABITAT Primarily a bird of the canopy, recorded in primary forest, logged forest, plantations and farmbush in Sierra Leone, Ivory Coast and Ghana.

FOOD AND FEEDING Coppery-tailed Starlings were seen feeding on fruit, but also searching the foliage for insects in the mid-storey. In Sierra Leone, the fruit of *Rauwolfia* was reported from specimens collected (Walker 1939). Fruit was noted in seven stomachs of museum specimens, insects in two.

BREEDING The nest and eggs are undescribed. Birds were seen at nest holes in dead trees in October in Sierra Leone, and juveniles were observed in December. In Ghana, a pair was seen taking nesting material to a hole in a dead branch 15 m above ground in August, and adults were seen feeding three fledged young in February in Ivory Coast. Breeding in Liberia apparently occurs in October, and there is a juvenile specimen collected during March from Mt Nimba (Colston and Curry-Lindahl 1986).

BEHAVIOUR Thiollay (1985) reported flocks of up to 50 birds in the coastal forests of Ivory Coast. In Ghana, Coppery-tailed Starlings appeared to gather in the canopy tops in the late afternoon, and a flock of 23 birds was noted, while in Sierra Leone they were seen foraging in pairs or family groups. Both in Ghana and in Sierra Leone, Coppery-tailed Starlings occasionally joined mixed-species flocks foraging for insects.

PRINCIPAL REFERENCES Allport *et al.* (1989), Dutson and Branscombe (1990), Gartshore (1989).

89 AMETHYST (PLUM-COLOURED) STARLING
Cinnyricinclus leucogaster   Plate 25
Plum-coloured Starling, Violet-backed Starling

Turdus leucogaster Boddaert 1783

FIELD IDENTIFICATION 18 cm. The male is spectacularly iridescent with a pure white belly, and unmistakable. Females seen alone could be mistaken for some other species such as a thrush, but the combination of a streaky brown back, white ventral plumage with heavy streaking, and yellowish iris should permit recognition. The tail is slightly forked in both sexes.

DESCRIPTION Adult male: Head (except for black lores), chin, throat, upper chest, nape, mantle, back, rump and tail iridescent purple which depending on the light may appear black or rosy. In fresh plumage, there is a strong blue overtone, but with wear a coppery plum-colour predominates (cf. van Someren 1916). The wings are also purple, but worn primaries lack all iridescence and appear dark brown; the flight feathers are always less iridescent than the body regions. The lower chest, belly, flanks, thighs and undertail-coverts are pure white. The iris has a yellow outer ring; the bill and legs are black. **Adult Female**: lacks any iridescent plumage. The crown, nape and sides of the head are brown with dark central streaks on the feathers. The mantle, back, rump, wing-coverts, secondaries, tail and uppertail-coverts are dark brown with paler margins. Primaries are dark brown with a slight gloss when fresh, and the inner web is rufous-brown up to 1–2 cm from the tip. Chin, throat, chest, belly, flanks, thighs and undertail-coverts are white with dark central streaks, which are broadest in the chest area. There may be some buff, particularly on the chin and throat. The iris has a yellow outer ring, the bill and the legs are black. **Juvenile**: Resembles female, except for broader rufous edges to the feathers, particularly the wing-coverts. The iris is initially dark brown, with the yellow ring developing gradually. The bill and legs are dark brown, the gape yellowish, and this is still evident in the adult female. These descriptions are based on specimens from southern Africa, of the sub-species *C. l. verreauxi*.

Eastern and southern African birds, from Kenya southwards, *C. l.* **verreauxi**, are distinguished by the white outer webs of the outermost tail feathers in males, while in birds from the Arabian peninsula, *C. l.* **arabicus**, the female is dull brown above, with the tawny edges to the feathers much reduced or totally absent (Grant and Mackworth-Praed 1942). The pattern of breeding and migration supports the recognition of three sub-species.

The post-juvenile moult is incomplete, and does not include the wing feathers except for some secondaries; the first complete moult occurs at 13–14 months, when male birds acquire adult plumage. In adults, the wings and tail are moulted first, then the body moult starts. The normal duration of primary moult is 90–120 days if this is not interrupted by migration. The secondaries start moulting when primary moult is well-advanced, and feathers 5–6 are the last to be replaced, after primary moult is completed. In different populations, moult may be completed on the breeding grounds, suspended during migration, or delayed until the non-breeding area is reached. In all southern African populations, wing moult appears to take place between December and May, with some birds suspending moult while on migration. Body moult typically takes place in the months following completion of wing moult. Wing moult appears to be slightly later in Kenya, whereas in Uganda it is earlier in the local population of *C. l. leucogaster* (Traylor 1971).

MEASUREMENTS Male (10): wing 104–112, tail 61–66, bill 17.0–19.5, tarsus 21.5–23.7. Female (10): wing 95–105, tail 54–60, bill 17.0–18.6, tarsus 21.4–23.0. Weight of male (10) 39–50, of female (8) 39–56 g. All the measurements are taken from *C. l. verreauxi*.

VOICE Heuglin (1874) noted that both male and female gave soft whistles, and Priest (1936) also mentions a single, drawn-out whistle which is repeated often during the nesting season. Chapin (1954) first heard the birds call when breeding started. The male's song was compared to that of Mosque Swallow *Hirundo senegalensis*, with introductory chippering notes followed by a nasal, whining whistle *tipee-tipee-teeeuu* (Vincent 1936). Maclean (1993) noted that Amethyst Starlings are often silent, but described the song as a phrase of 9–15 twanging notes and piping calls. A male sang in the nesting tree while there were chicks in the nest (Serle 1965). In the field, the high squeaky calls are unlike those of other glossy starlings. Botz (1991) reported that whereas a captive male sang a short, stereotyped phrase, the female sang a varied song, including imitations of human whistles and the calls of other birds in the aviary.

DISTRIBUTION AND POPULATION Found throughout Africa south of the Sahara, except for the forested zone in the Zaïre basin, and the drier western and southern regions of southern Africa. They are common to abundant throughout, but in some areas their occurrence is markedly seasonal, as described below. They also occur on the southwestern corner of the Arabian peninsula.

HABITAT This is a bird of open woodland areas and riverine forest, moving extensively and often concentrated where trees are in fruit. Amethyst Starlings occur to 2100 m in the Chyulu Hills, Kenya (van Someren 1939), and may be found around clearings in lowland forest as at Bwamba, Uganda (Friedmann and Williams 1971).

FOOD AND FEEDING Fruits of *Celtis* and *Clerodendron myricoides* were found in the stomachs of birds collected in Zimbabwe, also insects (Swynnerton 1908). In West Africa, *Zizyphus* berries and winged ants (Formicidae) were reported (Bannerman 1948) and *Lannea* fruit in Cameroon (Kavanach 1977); *Ficus* and *Zizyphus* fruits, and termites (Termitidae) are mentioned for the Arabian population (Meinertzhagen 1954). Both Stark (1900) and Erlanger (1905) commented on Amethyst Starlings hawking insects in flycatcher fashion, and birds in Zimbabwe took termite alates regularly (Brooke *et al.* 1972). Sjöstedt (1910) found seeds of Fabaceae, and ants (Formicidae) in their stomachs, while Pinto (1965) also reported that most stomachs contained seeds, and some contained insects, apparently collected

from the tops of the trees. Berries of *Boscia pechuelli* and fruit of *Loranthus* were noted in Namibia (Hoesch and Niethammer 1940), and the birds are said to be fond of *Podocarpus* fruit (Mackworth-Praed and Grant 1960). *Musanga* fruit was recorded as a food item in Gabon (Brosset and Erard 1986), also *Sapium* and *Ficus* in East Africa (van Someren 1939). In summer they were found feeding on mistletoe berries (Belcher 1930), in South Africa on *Tapinanthus leendertziae* (Godschalk 1985). They will also come to gardens for mulberries *Morus alba* (Jones 1945, AC pers. obs.). Dowsett-Lemaire (1983b) saw Amethyst Starlings feeding on fruit in the same forests as Waller's Red-winged Starlings, but also feeding on insects at the forest edge and outside the forest. Amethyst Starlings are primarily arboreal, and tend to take insects off the branches or in flight, seldom feeding on the ground as other glossy starlings do. Captive birds took fruit, insectivorous bird mixture and insects, but appeared to feed the young entirely on live food (Amsler 1935, Cummings 1959, Pyper 1991).

BREEDING Amethyst Starlings nest in hollow trees, from 2 to 6 m above ground. The nest site may be close to buildings (Winterbottom 1942), and hollow fence posts are used in some areas (Becker 1980). Heights of less than 1 m and more than 10 m have also been recorded (Priest 1936). A female was observed carrying donkey dung into a nest hole, which also contained some green leaves. A male accompanied her, but did not contribute to the nest (Hoesch and Niethammer 1940). However, van Someren (1958) remarked that the male at one nest under observation contributed much more than the female. Short and Horne (1985b) saw male Amethyst Starlings collecting balls of moist elephant dung and carrying these to nesting sites on three occasions, accompanied by the female. Other observers have also reported that a layer of dry dung and green leaves often constitutes the only nesting material (Priest 1936, Jackson and Sclater 1938, Vincent 1949). In Kenya leaves of *Euclea keniensis* were identified (Ellis 1980), in South Africa *Olea* sp. (Symons 1949). Joubert (1943) described how a deep tree hole had apparently been plugged with horse dung, to form a platform on which the nest of leaves rested. Most captive birds only used leaves when nest-building, ignoring other material which was provided (Amsler 1935, Cummings 1959, Pyper 1991), but Botz (1991) reported only a sparse lining of grass and twigs in the nestbox. The eggs are pale blue, spotted with reddish-brown particularly around the thicker end (Maclean 1993), and measure 22.9–26.7 x 15.5–19.2 mm (85), weight 3.9 g (Schönwetter 1983). The clutch size is 2–4. Incubation lasts 12 days with only the female sitting, and the nestling period is about 21 days (Maclean 1993), with both adults feeding the young (Serle 1965). Incubation in captivity lasted 12–14 days, and was carried out by the female only. The nestling period was 17 days for a single chick, and both adults added more leaves to the nest during this period (Amsler 1935). In another captive brood, the chicks spent about 26 days in the nest (Botz 1991). The male fed the chicks both in the nest and after fledging, but contributed much less than the female in most cases (Amsler 1935, Cummings 1959, Pyper 1991), but in one pair the male did most of the feeding (Botz 1991).

The breeding season in southern Africa is primarily October to January (Irwin 1981, Craig 1997), in Zambia and Malawi, October and November (Benson and Benson 1977, Benson et al. 1971). In a dry year in Malawi, Dowsett-Lemaire (1983b) saw birds at the usual nest sites, but no breeding occurred. In Namibia, breeding records were sparse, and appeared to be concentrated in certain years (Becker 1980); breeding may peak in February to March, later than in the rest of southern Africa (Craig 1997). There are a few breeding records for Kenya, in March to May (Lewis and Pomeroy 1989), but Amethyst Starlings breed regularly in Tanzania in November and December (Brown and Britton 1980), where Lynes (1934) collected a young bird which he estimated at six weeks old in February. In Angola, breeding occurs from August to November (Heinrich 1958, Traylor 1963), but Chapin (1954) encountered recently fledged young in June in northern Angola. In Zaïre, this species breeds from July to November in the southeast with young noted in October, and from August to October in Kwilu (Lippens and Wille 1976). In West Africa, the few breeding records are from March to May (Mackworth-Praed and Grant 1973, Lamarche 1981, Elgood 1982, Grimes 1987), but Lowe (1937) collected a male in breeding condition in January in Ghana. Thonnerieux (1988) saw an adult with a juvenile bird in July in Burkina Faso. The Arabian population was found breeding in March and April (Cornwallis and Porter 1982). Amethyst Starlings were reportedly parasitised by a honeyguide *Indicator* sp., and there is one certain record of an egg of the Lesser Honeyguide *I. minor* in an Amethyst Starling nest (Friedmann 1955).

MIGRATION Meinertzhagen (1954) stated that the Amethyst Starling was resident in Aden. It is evidently a breeding visitor to the Tehamah mountains in North Yemen, where it was found breeding in March and April (Cornwallis and Porter 1982), but was not recorded in autumn (Brooks et al. 1987). Cave and Macdonald (1955) listed the race *arabicus* as sporadic in northeastern Sudan. Nikolaus (1987) suggested that birds in northern Sudan, recorded from April to August, all belonged to this race, which would imply migration across the Red Sea to the African mainland. The southern population is highly migratory. Winterbottom (1942) saw flocks in western Zambia in November and December, after the breeding season. His later observations indicated that birds were present at Livingstone throughout the year, but at three other sites the birds were absent for some months; peak numbers in the west to some extent coincided with no records from the east (Winterbottom 1959). Jones (1945) noted that Amethyst Starlings arrived in northern Zambia in August, were common until December, but absent after the rains. Mackworth-Praed and Grant (1950) reviewed the data available to them, and conclud-

ed that the southern race of Amethyst Starling was a breeding migrant to central and southern Angola, Namibia, Botswana, southeastern Zaïre, northeastern Zambia, Malawi, Zanzibar and Mafia islands, Mozambique, Zimbabwe and South Africa. However, it appeared to be resident in Kenya and Tanzania, partially resident in northwestern Zambia, and a non-breeding visitor to Sudan, Ethiopia, Uganda and northern Angola. Traylor's (1971) detailed study of museum material confirmed this picture, and it appears that the timing of wing moult (but not body moult) is much more constant in the different populations than the timing of breeding or migration. Thus in South Africa he found that the birds breed, then begin the moult, but most leave on migration in March or April before the moult is complete. Birds from Zimbabwe have generally completed their moult before they migrate in May, whereas starlings from Malawi and Zambia leave at an early stage of moult. Overwintering birds collected in July in Zimbabwe had new wing feathers but showed heavy body moult (Borrett 1971). Angolan birds apparently breed, then leave the area and are absent from November to March, but moult on their return in April, so that moulting takes place just after migration and before breeding (Traylor 1971). Although most birds in Malawi, Zambia and Zimbabwe are migrants arriving in September and leaving by April, there are some winter records, which suggest either that more than one population is involved, or that some birds move only locally (Benson et al. 1971, Benson and Benson 1977, Irwin 1981). Records from resident observers in Zambia suggested a partial departure of Amethyst Starlings during January, but no evidence of a northward passage at the end of the rains; there was also some indication that western Zambia held many non-breeding birds during the dry season (Aspinwall 1981). Recoveries of ringed birds at the same localities in subsequent years suggest some site fidelity in the migrants (Irwin 1981). There are few South African records outside the months October to April (Cyrus and Robson 1980, Tarboton et al. 1987, Craig 1997).

Curry-Lindahl (1981) stated that in Shaba, Zaïre, Amethyst Starlings were present from July to April, and in Serengeti Reserve, Tanzania from August to February. There was a marked passage in central Shaba in July–August and February–March, while both Kenya and Zaïre experience a marked influx of birds from April to May. Lewis and Pomeroy (1989) concluded that in Kenya the northern nominate race is a non-breeding migrant, which can appear in most months of the year, while flocks of the southern race appear in the lowlands and coastal region during March to September. At Lake Baringo, Stevenson (1983) noted small flocks each year, from May to August, occasionally in November. Van Someren (1916) collected young birds in August, and birds in moult in December in Uganda, both groups apparently *C. l. leucogaster*. They are vagrants to coastal Gabon (Brosset and Erard 1986), and irregular non-breeding visitors to Zanzibar (Vaughan 1930). North of the equator the movements are less well-defined.

Heuglin (1874) saw pairs of adults to 3000 m in Ethiopia in February and March, while in May and June there were birds accompanied by recently-fledged young. In Somalia, Amethyst Starlings were recorded only in April, May and September (Ash and Miskell 1983), while in Sudan birds of the nominate race were present from January to April and in October and November, and birds belonging to the southern race between March and May (Nikolaus 1987). Smith (1957) reported that in the east of Eritrea, Amethyst Starlings were present during the winter (October to February), and suggested that these birds might be *C. l. arabicus*. On the plateau and in the west of this region, starlings were present from March to September, but absent in winter. Thus local movements could account for the pattern seen. Surprisingly, Greling (1972) listed this species as sedentary in northern Cameroon, although he commented in the text that these were the first wet season records and that the birds carried out extensive seasonal movements. Germain *et al.* (1973) also noted massive seasonal movements, but were not certain whether these represented local movements or true migration. Bannerman (1948) quoted observers who reported Amethyst Starlings as common in the Gambia from May to October, while in Sierra Leone they were noted from December to May, and in Nigeria primarily from April to August. Elgood *et al.* (1973) stated that birds in the coastal belt of Nigeria appeared to be resident, but elsewhere Amethyst Starling was a dry-season migrant to the region south of the rivers, and a wet-season visitor to the northern savannas. It was abundant in Lagos from November to May, with the northernmost inland records in July to September (Elgood 1982). Marchant (1942) observed small flocks in the Owerri province from May to October, while for the rest of the year the birds were encountered as pairs or singletons, but they appeared to be resident. He also recognized this species as a visitor to the forest belt, where it occurred from October to April (Marchant 1953). Gatter (1988) lists the Amethyst Starling as an intra-African migrant in Liberia, and in the Gambia it is present from March to November, with no confirmed breeding

records (Gore 1990). In adjacent Senegal, all observations of Amethyst Starlings seem to come between March and August (Morel and Morel 1990). For Ghana, Grimes (1987) stated that there is a clear north-south migration, but that the movements may be more complex. In Ivory Coast, Thiollay (1985) listed it as a migrant without further details, whereas in Mali it was reported as common all year by Lamarche (1981). At Ouagadougou in Burkina Faso, Thonnerieux *et al.* (1989) described a well-marked passage of Amethyst Starlings in April–May, and again in August–September. Holyoak and Sedden (1989) recorded Amethyst Starlings in September at one locality, but not at all in November, on a trip across Burkina Faso.

BEHAVIOUR There is a record of two males and one female feeding chicks at two successive nests (Ginn 1986), but this was clearly an unusual event, and Amethyst Starlings are not cooperative breeders. In Namibia, the starlings competed vigorously for nest holes with Pied Barbets *Lybius leucomelas* and Grey-headed Sparrows *Passer griseus* (Hoesch and Niethammer 1940). In a captive pair, the male called frequently, raising first one wing and then the other in quick succession (Amsler 1935), and Cummings (1959) saw both sexes do this. Wild males perched near the nest hole will give a squeaky song and raise the wings alternately, and also lean forward, flapping both wings together one to three times (AC pers. obs.). A captive female played an active role in courtship, hopping sideways towards the male, while beating the wings rapidly (Botz 1991). It appears that wing displays play an important role in this species. The flocks often include predominantly birds of one sex, and Andersson and Gurney (1872) commented that in Namibia the males arrived first, when the birds appeared in the rainy season. However, according to Hoesch and Niethammer (1940), at the start of the rainy season large flocks were composed exclusively of females and juveniles. Communal roosting has apparently not been reported, but R.K. Brooke (pers. comm.) saw Amethyst Starlings assembling in riparian *Acacia* trees in Zimbabwe in March, and then flying off together, presumably to a roost.

90 AFRICAN PIED STARLING *Spreo bicolor*   Plate 26

Turdus bicolor Gmelin 1789

FIELD IDENTIFICATION 25 cm. A dark starling with a white belly and a pale eye; it is largely terrestrial, with a very upright stance. Distinctive within its range.
DESCRIPTION The head, throat, chest, nape, mantle, back, thighs and uppertail-coverts are dark blackish-brown, with some greenish sheen. The belly and undertail-coverts are white. The wings and tail are blackish with an oily green-gloss. The iris is white. The bill has a black upper mandible, while the lower mandible has a black

tip, but is yellow more than halfway to the tip. There is a prominent yellow wattle at the corners of the mouth. The legs are black. The sexes are alike. Juveniles have matt-black plumage, lacking gloss. The iris is brown, and only the base of the lower mandible is yellowish-white and the wattle at the corners of the gape is white. The legs are black. There is a progressive change in iris colour, and in the extent of yellow on the lower mandible, which take more than a year to attain the adult condition (Craig 1983c, Sweijd and Craig 1991).

A Pied Starling with predominantly white plumage was sighted in a flock, but it is not clear whether this bird was a true albino (van Niekerk 1996).

There is no regional variation in moult, with all records of wing moult from October to April, in a sample of more than 200 birds. Most records of tail and body moult are from January to March, and adults with wing moult have been found at active nests. The moult is relatively slow, with only one or two wing feathers growing simultaneously, and overlaps with breeding in many cases. Suspended moult has not been recorded. Adults and subadults moult at the same time, but juveniles have an incomplete moult, replacing only the body plumage and some of the rectrices (Craig 1983b).

MEASUREMENTS Male (22): wing 144–163, tail 91–108, bill 26.5–30.5, tarsus 37.6–44.4. Female (17): wing 142–155, tail 91–103, bill 25.1–29.6, tarsus 38.8–42.6. Weight of male (23) 94–113, of female (20) 93–112 g.

VOICE Adults have a harsh squawking alarm call; the shriller alarm call of chicks will often result in the whole flock mobbing the handler. The most characteristic call is a loud *wreek-wreek* given in flight, or as a flight intention call. Perched birds, including males outside the nests, give a subdued warbling call, with a wide range of musical and harsh notes, which may continue for several minutes (AC pers. obs.).

DISTRIBUTION AND POPULATION
Endemic to South Africa, Lesotho and Swaziland, with few records from the arid northwest and the eastern coastal lowlands. Its restricted distribution is probably a consequence of its origins on the inland plateau of South Africa, but it is common to abundant within this region.

HABITAT This bird is most typical of open areas dominated by grassland, to 2500 m in mountainous regions, but ranging down to the seashore in the west and south. African Pied Starlings have long been associated with agricultural areas, and are often seen on open ground around farm homesteads, on cultivated lands and near domestic stock. They may nest in buildings, and occur in villages and small towns in rural areas but are absent from larger urban settlements.

FOOD AND FEEDING The stomach contents of 105 birds included plant material, primarily seeds, from *Atriplex semibaccata, Convolvulus* sp., *Cotoneaster horizontalis, Cussonia paniculata, Cyperus esculentus, Euclea crispa, Ligustrum lucidum, Medicago sativa, Nicandra physaloides, Opuntia* sp., *Portulaca* sp., *Protasparagus laricinus, Sophora japonica* and maize. However the bulk of their diet is made up of insects, including termites (Termitidae), ants (Formicidae) and beetles (Carabidae) — up to 82 termites were found in one bird (Kok and van Ee 1990). A starling ate 120 pugnacious ants *Anoplolepis custodiens* in a single feeding spell, but fruit of *Scutia myrtina* and the slightly succulent leaves of *Lycium* sp. were also taken (Skead 1995). African Pied Starlings were among the species reported at locust swarms in the past (Thomsen 1907), and they have also been seen catching amphipods (Talitridae) from

kelp on the beach, and foraging in the rocky intertidal zone alongside Wattled and Common Starlings (Robinson *et al.* 1957). Pied Starlings often take nectar from *Aloe arborescens* and *ferox,* also from *Agave* (Oatley and Skead 1972, AC pers. obs.), and from *Sideroxylon inerme* (Skead 1995). The young are fed some fruit, including berries of *Lycium* sp., but primarily arthropods, including beetles, dragonflies, termites, caterpillars, grasshoppers (Orthoptera), centipedes, solifugids, and ticks, which may be removed from cattle; small lizards (Reptilia) have also been recorded. African Pied Starlings will take figs (*Ficus*) and grapes (*Vitus*) in gardens, and also kitchen scraps such as bread and porridge. They are often seen in association with stock, apparently feeding on insects disturbed by the animals, and regularly perch on sheep and cattle, from which they remove ectoparasites (Stark 1900, Dean and Macdonald 1981, Skead 1995). A group of birds was seen eating the flesh of toads *Bufo* sp. which had been squashed on a road (Skead 1995).

BREEDING The nests are usually in tunnels in river banks or other excavations, but African Pied Starlings will also utilize holes in buildings, in bales of hay, and rarely natural tree holes. Levaillant (1799) claimed that they often took over the nests of woodpeckers (Picidae), chasing off the builders, but this has not been confirmed by any other observers; he also described nesting in the walls of buildings, and in holes in the ground, like bee-eaters (Meropidae). Recently birds have been reported nesting on a wrecked ship, some 200 m offshore (Brooke 1995). The nests are lined with pads of grass, roots, wool, muddy bits of sedge, even paper and pieces of rope (Craig 1987, Herholdt 1987); snakeskins were also reported by Godfrey (1922). The eggs are usually bright bluegreen, either plain or with some red spotting, measuring 26.9–35.3 x 19.6–22.5 mm (131). The clutch size is 2–6, usually 4 (Maclean 1993). Haagner and Ivy (1907) reported clutches of 8–10 eggs, which they ascribed to more than one female laying in the same nest. The egg weight is 7.2 g (Schönwetter 1983). Incubation is by the female only, lasting 14–16 days (Herholdt 1987; Wilkinson *et al.* 1993). The nestling period is 23–27 days (Herholdt 1987), with both parents and helpers feeding the chicks. Breeding in the winter rainfall region of South Africa occurs from August to November, while elsewhere the main breeding season is from September to January, with a second minor peak in April and May. There are some records from all months of the year, and the birds are commonly double brooded (Craig 1983a, 1997). Pied Starlings are often parasitised by Great Spotted Cuckoos *Clamator glandarius* (Roberts 1939, Jensen and Jensen 1969, L. Coetzer pers. comm.) and also by the Greater Honeyguide *Indicator indicator* (Friedmann 1955, Jubb 1983). A Lanner Falcon *Falco biarmicus* was seen removing a nestling from a hole in a bank; a second attempt was thwarted by the starlings mobbing the falcon (van Zyl 1991).

BEHAVIOUR Cooperative breeding occurs regularly, in which up to seven other birds assist the parents in feeding the young, and may contribute the bulk of the food (Craig 1983d). A long-term study showed that helpers were primarily subadult and unmated birds, and that some individuals remained helpers over several seasons. Helpers often attend successive nests of the same breeding birds, and in several cases a helper subsequently became the mate of a bird which it had previously assisted. Allofeeding is commonly observed in the flock, and this may be associated with the distinctive coloured gape retained by adult Pied Starlings. Having found a food item, a bird will walk directly to another individual in a very upright posture, ignoring any other birds encountered, including begging juveniles. If the chosen recipient crouches and gapes, it will be fed, but should it refuse the offering, the donor will eat the food item itself. Juveniles may feed adults, and this is clearly not courtship feeding, since only one case of a bird feeding its mate (female feeding male) was observed. Subadults are the most active group in allofeeding, and this may be a means of establishing or maintaining bonds with other individuals, since in many cases the participants had been members of the same breeding group in a previous season (Craig 1988c). Jubb (1980b) described how a Pied Starling, on seeing its reflection in the hub cap of a car, went off to fetch food which it then attempted to feed to the reflection. When this failed, the bird dropped the food and attacked its image, interspersing bursts of pecking with warbled song. At close range, as during allofeeding, changes in pupil size have been noted. It appears that dominant birds contract the pupil, thus displaying a larger area of white iris to subordinate individuals. Threat displays over food items involve a head forward posture, with the tail fanned, and the wings hunched forward slightly (AC pers. obs.). Only the breeding pair fed the chicks at two nests of captive birds, whereas allofeeding was seen between members of the group (Wilkinson et al. 1993). In many areas the birds are apparently resident, but they may gather at large communal roosts which are generally in reedbeds or trees, and in some regions large nomadic flocks have been reported. Very large roosts may be formed, with more than 1,000 birds seen occupying reedbeds (Rudebeck 1955a, A.J.

Tree pers. comm.), while Godfrey (1922) quoted a report of 'thousands' roosting in a poplar copse. Every (1975) counted 1,550 African Pied Starlings flying to a reedbed roost, and noted that the largest flock contained 300 birds. The birds enter and leave the roost in small groups, calling in flight, and often following regular flight paths. A loud chorus of *squee* flight calls continues until darkness, and there may be occasional calling during the night, but when the birds leave at dawn, calling is rather sporadic. Godfrey (1922) noted that Lesser Kestrels *Falco naumanni*, sharing a roost in eucalypt trees with African Pied Starlings, responded promptly to the starlings' alarm calls. Pied Starlings often associate with Wattled Starlings, and may form mixed flocks and use the same roost sites. They may also be accompanied by Common Starlings, especially when foraging, but these two species seldom roost together.

RELATIONS WITH MAN In rural areas, the African Pied Starling is a long-standing commensal with man, and this was commented on by many early travellers in South Africa such as Thunberg (1795). They are common in small settlements, and even nested in Cape Town up to 1909 (Joubert 1945), but are not found in urbanised areas. Roberts (1939) recounted how he tried to dissuade two pairs from nesting in a church, by removing the eggs as each clutch was completed. He removed 60 eggs from one one nest, and 30 from the second, before the birds finally gave up! Local people often regard them as a nuisance and they can be destructive of fruit such as grapes, but are seldom persecuted today. However, Andersson and Gurney (1872) wrote that the flesh of this species was 'much esteemed', so it may have been hunted for the pot in the past. Levaillant (1799) also referred to Pied Starlings as very tasty at the time when the grapes were ripening, when the birds were evidently destroyed in large numbers. Others regard them with more affection; L. Coetzer (pers. comm.) recalled that his grandfather put out porridge for African Pied Starlings around the farmhouse, and a small flock regularly accompanied their benefactor when he was in the fields.

PRINCIPAL REFERENCES Craig (1985, 1987).

91 FISCHER'S STARLING *Spreo fischeri* Plate 26

Notauges fischeri Reichenow 1884

FIELD IDENTIFICATION Length 18 cm. A small grey starling with a white belly and virtually no gloss.

DESCRIPTION The crown, throat, chest, nape, mantle, back, and uppertail-coverts are dull ashgrey, with some bronze sheen on the back and rump. The lores are black and bristly. The belly, vent, thighs and undertail-coverts are white, the underwing-coverts grey with some white. Both wing and tail feathers are dull bronzy-green. These

have little gloss when worn, and the body plumage is then also much paler. The iris is creamy-white, and the bill and legs are black. The sexes are alike. No juveniles were examined, but one immature bird had a brown iris, a yellow gape and a grey tip to the bill. Young birds in the nest had bright yellow bills and dark eyes (Zimmerman et al. 1996) describe juveniles as brownish on the back with pale edges to the feathers, a yellow lower mandible and a brown iris.

Thirty-six specimens were examined from all months except December, with some birds in moult from each month except October. One bird from February showed suspended wing moult; in several instances of two birds collected on the same day, one individual showed wing moult while the other did not. It seems likely that the main moulting period is from February to July, but there is evidently a great deal of individual variation, and moult-breeding overlap may occur.

MEASUREMENTS Male (11): wing 108–116, tail 65–73, bill 22.6–24.7, tarsus 31.1–34.0. Female (11): wing 101–109, tail 59–65, bill 21.1–23.3, tarsus 31.1–32.7. Weight of male 51 g.

VOICE A distinctive, wheezy whirligig call *cree-wee-creewoo*, repeated rapidly (Fuggles-Couchman and Elliott 1946), also a loud, shrill whistle (Mackworth-Praed and Grant 1960). The song is a squeaky, metallic phrase rather like that of the Dark-backed Weaver *Ploceus bicolor* (Zimmerman *et al.* 1996).

DISTRIBUTION AND POPULATION Uncommon, but apparently resident, in southern Ethiopia and Somalia to eastern Kenya and northern Tanzania.

HABITAT The birds are found in dry, open acacia country.

FOOD AND FEEDING Fischer's Starling was once seen eating fruit, but all other food items were insects collected from the ground, mostly termites (Lack 1985). Grasshoppers (Orthoptera) and berries were noted in the stomachs of museum specimens. Nestlings were fed on butterflies (Lepidoptera) and caterpillars.

BREEDING Nests are built in thorn trees, about 2.5 m above ground. They are constructed of coarse grass, completely roofed over, with an opening above a small ramp at the side. The nests were lined with feathers. The eggs are blue with red spots (Erlanger 1905), measuring 21.0–28.0 x 16.0–19.0 mm (14), weight 4.2 g (Schönwetter 1983). There are up to 6 eggs in a clutch (Erlanger 1905). Breeding occurs in East Africa in April and May, and from September to November (Brown and Britton 1980), in Ethiopia in April and May (Erlanger 1905, Urban and Brown 1971). Chicks were found in Kenya in May.

BEHAVIOUR Cooperative breeding has been reported for Fischer's Starling, with three or four adults queuing to feed the young, and one bird seen to feed young at two different nests. The birds are generally seen in pairs or small parties, spending much their time on the ground (Fuggles-Couchman and Elliott 1946). They may form flocks with Wattled Starlings (CF pers. obs.).

PRINCIPAL REFERENCE Miskell (1977).

92 ASHY STARLING *Spreo unicolor*   Plate 26

Cosmopsarus unicolor Shelley 1881

FIELD IDENTIFICATION Length 30 cm. A grey-brown, long-tailed starling with a pale eye; unlikely to be confused with any other species within its restricted range.

DESCRIPTION The plumage is a uniform ashy-grey colour, with an oily-green sheen on the wings and rectrices; at certain angles transverse bars are visible on the rectrices. There are black, bristly feathers on the lores. The iris is yellow, and the bill and legs are black. The sexes are alike. Reichenow (1903) described the body feathers, remiges and rectrices of young birds as tipped with light brown. Juveniles newly out of the nest had pale horn-coloured bills, and dark irides with a prominent pale ring around the eye.

Single birds from January and April showed wing moult, while six birds from December were not moulting. Fifteen specimens from March, June, July, August, September and October showed no moult. Moult may thus occur before breeding, but neither moulting nor breeding seasons can be described adequately at present.

MEASUREMENTS Male (10): wing 122–130, tail 159–174, bill 23.3–25.7, tarsus 33.3–37.7. Female (8): wing 115–125, tail 138–163, bill 21.4–25.6, tarsus 33.3–35.7. Weight of male (5) 55–66, of female 62 g.

VOICE Fuggles-Couchman (1984) described the Ashy Starling as a very quiet bird. The most common call consisted of two plaintive, squeaky notes *kuri, kiwera*, the second note higher, accompanied by a light rattling of the bill. This call was sometimes preceded by two or three chuckled or warbled notes, and there was also a longer call *koora-tcheoo-chink-chink*, repeated twice. The birds give a harsh *charr* when disturbed (CF pers. obs.).

DISTRIBUTION AND POPULATION Endemic residents in the dry interior of Tanzania; there are no accepted records from Kenya (Zimmerman *et al.* 1996). Recent coastal records from Dar es Salaam may represent dry-season vagrants (Baker and Howell 1994).

HABITAT The birds occur in open woodland and wooded grassland at 1100–1800 m (Britton 1980).

FOOD AND FEEDING Ashy Starlings are apparently largely insectivorous. Feeding on termites (Termitidae) was reported by Fischer (Reichenow 1887); berries and beetles (Carabidae) were recorded in the stomachs of museum specimens. Captive birds took a commercial food mixture and fruit, but fed the young on insects.

BREEDING There are only two published breeding records, for February and March (Brown and Britton 1980), and no other field information. Birds collected in September and October had inactive gonads (Reichenow 1887). Captive birds used a nestbox, in which they laid two clutches of three eggs, which were pale greenish-blue, with tiny brownish speckles, and small reddish-brown blotches on the narrow end. The incubation period was about 14 days, and the nestling period 26–31 days; both parents fed the young.

BEHAVIOUR Ashy Starlings occur in pairs or small flocks (Zimmerman *et al.* 1996). They hop about on the ground, holding the tail at a sharp angle to the body (Irwin 1957). Schuster (1926) described the birds as running like Superb Starlings, and noted that the tail was frequently quivered. Cooperative breeding has now been observed in the field, with both parents and helpers feeding the young (N Baker, pers. comm.).

PRINCIPAL REFERENCE Wilkinson & McLeod (1991).

93 WHITE-CROWNED STARLING *Spreo albicapillus* Plate 26

Spreo albicapillus Blyth 1856

FIELD IDENTIFICATION 23 cm. A large, fairly long-tailed starling; the white crown and white wing patches in contrast to the dull dorsal plumage render it distinctive in its range.

DESCRIPTION The crown is white, the lores and ear-coverts dull grey. The nape, mantle, back and uppertail-coverts are dull bronzy-green with some gloss. The wing and tail feathers are glossy bronze-green, but the outer margins of secondaries 1–4 and their coverts are white, forming a white bar on the folded wing. The underwing-coverts are white. Primaries 6–9 have a clear indentation on the inner web, while 5–8 have attentuated outer webs. Throat, chest and flanks are dull grey with some bronzy gloss, but all these feathers have white streaks along the shaft; new feathers appear stiff and spiky. The lower belly, vent, thighs and undertail-coverts are white. The iris is pale yellow, and the bill and legs are black. The sexes are alike. Juveniles have grey-white crowns, with no gloss except on the wings and tail, while the white streaks on the ventral surface are dull and indistinct. The iris is brown, and the bill is yellow, darkening progressively from the tip; the legs are brown. Recently fledged young had yellow bills and gapes (Turner and Forbes-Watson 1976).

Smaller birds from northwest Kenya and adjacent Ethiopia were described under the name *S. a. horrensis*, but no subspecies should be recognised until the movements of the birds have been adequately recorded.

Of 33 birds examined from all months of the year, 15 were in moult, 14 of these from the period May to November, while a bird collected in March showed suspended wing moult. This suggests that moult usually occurs after the breeding season.

MEASUREMENTS Male (15): wing 147–163, tail 107–127, bill 27.4–31.0, tarsus 36.7–41.6. Female (8): wing 141–155, tail 107–122, bill 26.7–29.1, tarsus 36.8–40.0

VOICE Gives a harsh call, but birds are generally silent (Mackworth-Praed and Grant 1960); a shrill, rising call according to Zimmerman *et al.* (1996).

DISTRIBUTION AND POPULATION Found in northern Kenya, southern Ethiopia and western Somalia. They are very localised, but may be common where they do occur.

HABITAT The usual habitat is park-like thorn and acacia country, to 1500 m (Benson 1946). White-crowned Starlings often occur in open pasture lands where cattle feed (Archer and Godman 1961), and they may be found close to settlements and cultivated areas (Turner and Forbes-Watson 1976).

FOOD AND FEEDING White-crowned Starlings search for grain seeds or insects on the ground (Archer and Godman 1961). They were seen accompanying camels, and apparently catching insects which were flushed (Turner and Forbes-Watson 1976). Flocks gather at fruiting *Salvadora* trees (Zimmerman *et al.* 1996).

BREEDING Nests are built in thorn bushes about 1.5 m above ground, ball-shaped structures of grass, with a protruding side entrance (Benson 1946). Several White-crowned Starling nests have been found in a single bush. The eggs are greenish-blue with purple-red spotting, measuring 27.0–30.0 x 19.0–21.9 mm (31), weight 6.3 g (Schönwetter 1983). Clutches generally consist of 5–6 eggs, up to 9 suggests more than one bird laying in the same nest (Archer and Godman 1961). A captive pair built a very deep, almost dome-shaped nest of dry leaves, sticks and moss in a basket. The young bird was fed by both parents, and left the nest after about 25 days (Ezra 1929). Breeding was noted in Ethiopia from March to May (Benson 1946, Urban and Brown 1971), in Somalia from May to June (Archer and Godman 1961) while Clarke (1985) found a nest with chicks in May and another active nest in April; in Kenya in May (Brown and Britton 1980). White-crowned Starlings are reported as hosts of the Great Spotted Cuckoo *Clamator glandarius* in Somalia (Irwin 1988). In captivity in a large mixed starling collection, hybrids between White-crowned Starlings and Brahminy Starlings were reported (Petzsch 1951).

BEHAVIOUR White-crowned Starlings are gregarious at all times, and are often associated with White-headed Buffalo-Weaver *Dinemellia dinemelli* (Archer and Godman 1961). Dellelegn (1993) noted them foraging with small groups of Ethiopian Bush Crows *Zavattariornis stresemanni* in southern Ethiopia.

94 RED-WINGED STARLING *Onychognathus morio* Plate 27

Turdus morio Linnaeus 1766

FIELD IDENTIFICATION 30 cm. A large, long-tailed, red-winged starling with a fairly heavy bill. It has a wide distribution, and is thus most likely to be found at the same localities as other congeneric species. The mellow whistling calls are distinctive.

DESCRIPTION Adult male: Uniform glossy black, with an inky-blue sheen. All the primary remiges are chestnut-brown with a black tip, producing a large rufous patch in the wing in flight. At rest, the rufous edges of the primary feathers are clearly visible. **Adult female**: Crown, nape, sides of the head, throat and upper chest ash-grey, with some darker central streaks on the feathers particularly at the margins of the grey area. The iris is dark red, the bill and legs black. **Juvenile**: Resembles the male, but less glossy than the adults, and the iris is dark brown. The bill is also initially brown, becoming black before the change in iris colour or the appearance of a grey head in females. In captive birds, grey feathering first appeared on the head at five months (Everitt 1964).

There is clinal variation in size, with southern birds smallest with proportionately shorter tails. Birds from Ethiopia are longer-tailed and have a different moult cycle, forming a distinctive population ***O. m. rüppellii***. They intergrade with the typical population in northern Kenya.

Birds from Zimbabwe to East Africa were often placed in the race *O. m. shelleyi*, but this race was originally defined as intermediate between the nominate birds and *rüppellii*, and it cannot be demarcated satisfactorily (Craig 1988a).

Examination of more than 300 museum specimens from southern Africa showed that wing moult occurred from November to April (Craig 1983a, 1988a). Similarly Oatley and Fraser (1992) reported that in the southwestern Cape, South Africa, all 27 birds caught in January showed wing moult, whereas none of 62 birds examined between March and October was in moult; their sample did not include any birds from November or December. The timing of moult is similar in Malawi, Tanzania and southern Kenya, but Ethiopian birds moult during April to December. In Uganda, northern Kenya, southern Sudan and southern Ethiopia some birds show a mixture of morphological characters, but in all cases they follow either the southern or northern moult cycle, so that the timing of the moult seems to have only two options (Craig 1988a). Moult-breeding overlap is evident at both the population level and in individual birds caught at the nest, but the moult is relatively slow, with only one or two feathers in each wing growing simultaneously (Craig 1983a).

MEASUREMENTS Male (50): wing 142–159, tail 120–143, bill 30.0–36.5, tarsus 30.6–36.8. Female (50): wing 134–153, tail 109–139, bill 28.7–34.1 tarsus 30.6–36.0. Weight of male (67) 130–158, of female (69) 117–149 g.

VOICE Broekhuysen tabulated 15 different calls, while Rowan referred to more than 20 different song phrases, in addition to the contact calls, usually two whistled notes, and muted warbling when members of a pair were close together. Birds in flocks often produce a mixed chorus of whistles and song phrases, and harsh alarm calls are given by both pairs and by birds in flocks. The *twee-twoo* contact call is probably the most characteristic sound of this species. Threat-snapping of the mandibles and hissing was noted in a captive bird, which also produced a soft clicking sound with a closed beak, possibly a close-range signal (Rowan 1971).

DISTRIBUTION AND POPULATION This is the most widespread member of the genus, distributed from the Cape of Good Hope northwards through the eastern half of South Africa, eastern Botswana, Zimbabwe and Mozambique, eastern Zambia, Malawi, western Tanzania and Kenya to the highlands of Ethiopia and adjacent eastern Sudan, with some records from Uganda (Mt Elgon). Smith (1957) had no recent records of Red-winged Starling from Eritrea, although it was reportedly widespread in the past. Hall and Moreau (1970) mapped these records, but the only specimen from this area which has been examined proved to be a misidentified Somali Red-winged Starling, so these records may be erroneous. Common to abundant in most areas.

HABITAT Originally a bird of rocky outcrops, gorges and highland areas, the Red-winged Starling is now common in many urban areas, using buildings and other man-made structures for nesting. In Malawi, *Hyphaene* palm trees on the lake shore provide nest sites. It generally avoids arid areas, but there is some overlap with Pale-winged Starlings in the interior of South Africa (Craig and Hulley 1992). Red-winged Starling is also uncommon in coastal lowlands from Mozambique northwards. It is found to 2500 m in Ethiopia, but at higher altitudes is replaced by Slender-billed Red-winged Starling (Dorst and Roux 1973). On Mt Elgon, Red-winged Starlings have been seen above 4000 m (Granvik 1923).

FOOD AND FEEDING Fruit is eaten in large quantities, and seeds regurgitated included *Trichilia emetica, Erythrina caffra, Scutia myrtina, Melia azederach, Ficus thonningii* and *Phoenix* sp. (Vernon 1993). Stark (1900) reported that they would gorge themselves on syringa *M. azederach* berries until they could no longer fly — perhaps affected by the toxins in the berries? Cinnamon *Cinnamonum zeylanicum* berries were reported as a food item in East Africa (Sclater and Moreau 1933), and *Juniperus* in Ethiopia (Blanford 1870). Birds feed on *Cussonia paniculata, Rhus longispina, Lycium* sp. in the Karoo, South Africa (AC pers. obs.). In the Cape of Good Hope Nature Reserve, Fraser (1990) found that seeds of the introduced *Acacia cyclops* were the commonest item in faecal and regurgitated pellets of Red-winged Starlings, and 99% of the pellets contained fruit only. Other fruit species recorded were *Cassytha ciliolata, Coploon compressum, Rhus* sp. and *Lycium* sp. Red-winged Starling is thus likely to be an important dispersal agent of *Acacia cyclops*, which is an invasive alien plant in the Cape fynbos (Glyphis *et al.* 1981, Fraser 1990). Experiments with captive birds showed that seeds larger than 4 mm in diameter were regurgitated, while smaller seeds passed out in the faeces; smaller seeds are retained in the gut longer, and may thus be dispersed further (Watson 1995). At the nest, berries and *Acacia cyclops* arils, *Trema* and mulberries *Morus alba* were brought to the young. Large seeds such as those of *Diospyros pubescens, Scutia myrtina, Lycium campanulatum, Phoenix reclinata* and the introduced Australian tree *Brachychiton acerifolium* are regurgitated (Skead 1995). Animal food makes up a large part of the diet of Red-winged Starlings. Birds often hawk insects, even after dark at floodlights (Taylor 1974), and in Zimbabwe they were regular predators of termite alates (Brooke *et al.* 1972). In the Cape of Good Hope Nature Reserve, starlings caught protea beetles (Cetoniinae) and other flying insects and gleaned insects from parked motor vehicles, while beetle remains and a spider *Palystes natalius* were recorded by Fraser (1990). One specimen had only grasshoppers (Orthoptera) in the stomach (Kok and van Ee 1990), and in the past, flocks of Red-winged Starlings were seen at locust swarms in Zimbabwe (Swynnerton 1908) and in the Transvaal (Thomsen 1907). Stark (1900) stated that he had seen starlings catch mature locusts on the wing. Stinging insects such as the European wasp *Vespula germanica*, introduced to South Africa, may be eaten in significant numbers (Tribe 1991). In the intertidal zone snails *Littorina* sp. were eaten, and other unidentified molluscs (Skead 1966, Fraser 1990); Stark (1900) referred to the birds taking sandhoppers (Talitridae) and small molluscs. In the Zimbabwe highlands, Red-winged Starlings were seen feeding on freshwater crabs (Potamonidae) (Beasley 1991), and predation on lizards (Reptilia) (Mungure 1973, Beasley 1978), attacks on African Palm Swifts *Cypsiurus parvus* (Mortimer 1975) and nestling birds (Stark 1900, Taylor 1936), and feeding on carrion (Jubb 1977, AC pers. obs.) have also been reported. At the nest, adults brought grasshoppers, stick insects, caterpillars, butterflies (Lepidoptera), beetles, winged ants (Formicidae), cicadas (Cicadidae), bees (Apidae), scorpions (Scorpionidae), millipedes (Spirostreptoidea) and spiders (Araneae). The arthropod prey includes animals such as millipedes which can produce noxious secretions and are avoided by many predators. Large prey items are often broken up at an anvil site near the nest, and then delivered to the chicks piecemeal.

Oatley and Skead (1972) reported Red-winged Starlings taking nectar from *Aloe arborescens, bainesii, candelabrum, ferox, marlothii, spectabilis; Erythrina caffra, Schotia brachypetala* and *Salvia* sp. The starlings also took nectar from *Salvia africana-lutea, Leucospermum conocarpodendron* and *Mimetes fimbriifolius*, at which a feeding aggregation of 240 birds was once observed (Fraser 1990). In the Eastern Cape, birds fed on the nectar of *Protea subvestita* (Skead 1995). At such times the birds are conspicuously orange- or yellow-faced from the pollen. In East Africa, Red-winged Starlings took nectar from sisal flowers *Agave sisalana* (Cunningham-van Someren 1974). Gargett (1975) reviewed records of Red-winged Starlings associating with klipspringers *Oreotragus oreotragus* from which they removed ticks (Ixodidae), and noted that there were apparently no other records of the birds perching on large mammals. Red-winged Starlings perched on sheep were apparently using the animals as beaters and catching the insects which were flushed from the grass (Patten 1980a, Stutterheim 1980a), but in the case of cattle they regularly removed engorged ticks, particularly from the ears and under the tail (Patten 1980b, AC pers. obs.). In some cases the starlings may be taking the secretion from the pre-orbital glands of the klipspringer rather than removing ticks (Roberts 1995). Birds have also been observed gleaning ectoparasites from eland *Taurotragus oryx*, Cape mountain zebra *Equus zebra* (Fraser 1990), and impala *Aepyceros melampus* (Drummond 1991). At car parks on the Cape Peninsula, and on the University of Cape Town campus, Red-winged Starlings are familiar scavengers, which appear to eat any food discarded by humans (R. Brooke, pers. comm.).

BREEDING Ledges are favoured nest sites, today often sites on buildings; leaf bases of palms are also used. Mud is generally included in the base of the nest, with grass, rootlets and sticks forming the main structure, but other available materials may be included. A nest in a hole in a wall was made of grass and lined with horse hair, but no mud was included, whereas a nest on a ledge was much larger with an extensive mud base (Paget-Wilkes 1924). One pair took over a nest site at a waterfall previously used by *O. tenuirostris* (Dowsett-Lemaire 1983a). There is a recent record of birds nesting on the wreck of a fishing trawler, 200 m offshore (Brooke 1995). The eggs are blue with red-brown spotting, measuring 21.8–38.6 x 20.3–28.5 mm (138) (Maclean 1993), weight 9.4 g (Schönwetter 1983). There is a clutch of 2–4, usually 3 eggs. Normally only the female incubates, although Broekhuysen noted the male of one pair on the nest on three out of 33 observations, and Brown (1965) once saw a male sitting. The incubation period is typically 13–14 days , but there are also records of eggs hatching after 23–25 days. The nestling period is 22–28 days. In captivity incubation lasted 13–14 days, starting with the first egg, and the young left the nest at 22–25 days (Everitt 1964, Mare 1982). For Ethiopia, breeding was reported in April (Erlanger 1905) and possibly in October (Urban and Brown 1971); in south-eastern Zaïre, December and January (Lippens and Wille 1976). The breeding season in East Africa shows a peak in November to December and again in March, but there are records from all months except June and July (Brown and Britton

1980). At Lake Baringo, Kenya, Stevenson (1983) reported breeding from January to August, while one pair was seen feeding chicks in October (AC pers. obs.). In Zambia, birds are nesting from November to March (Benson *et al.* 1971), on Nyika Plateau in October and November (Dowsett-Lemaire 1983a), while elsewhere in Malawi there are records from November and December (Benson and Benson 1977). The main breeding season in southern Africa is September to March. The birds are commonly double-brooded, but the interval between broods is usually more than two months. Red-winged Starlings are often parasitised by Great Spotted Cuckoo *Clamator glandarius* (Jensen and Jensen 1969, Stevenson 1983). Webster (1987) reported that the cuckoo laid two eggs in a nest on the veranda of a house before the starlings had laid any eggs; both cuckoo chicks were raised.

BEHAVIOUR Allopreening, primarily of the head area, is performed by members of a pair throughout the year. Courtship feeding, often solicited by the female, occurs frequently, and Broekhuysen even saw a male beg from a female. Courtship feeding is a normal prelude to copulation, and the male will also feed the female on the nest during incubation. Regular song posts seem to be used to demarcate the territory, and some wing-stretching displays which show the rufous primaries may serve as threats. Aerial chases are frequently observed. Skead (1995) reported loud screeching during copulation. Although this species occurs in close association with man, there were no records of anting until AC saw a flock of birds, including both adults and subadults, engaged in this activity. Common Starlings were feeding in the same area, and were also seen anting. The ant species involved was the pugnacious ant *Anaplolepis custodiens*, which is widespread throughout the southern African region, and has been used in anting by other birds (Craig, in press c). Red-winged Starlings are aggressive birds, and Godfrey (1922) reported that a pair regularly displaced five Cape Glossy Starlings at a bird table. Red-winged Starlings are intolerant of other species at the nest site, and mob predators such as the African Harrier-Hawk *Polyboroides typus* in flocks. Nevertheless in some areas there may be numerous nests on a single cliff, which can resemble a colony. Pairs may roost at the nest site, but large communal roosts on cliffs or buildings are used, particularly during the non-breeding season. Winter flocks seem to be largest, and may include 500 birds or more, with temporary roost sites, such as tall trees, being used for short periods. Thomsen (1907) found Red-winged Starlings and Wattled Starlings roosting together in reedbeds in the western Transvaal, South Africa, while R. Davidson (*in litt.*) observed Red-winged Starlings and Common Mynas sharing a roost in eucalypt trees in Durban. In Zimbabwe, Brooke (1965c) found Red-winged Starlings roosting in reeds alongside weavers (Ploceinae) and Black-shouldered Kites *Elanus caeruleus*. No interactions were noted between the starlings and the kites, but when more than 200 starlings moved into a clump of Carolina poplars they apparently displaced the kites which had been roosting there. A captive bird always roosted on a high perch at night, standing on one leg (Rowan 1971). Nests may be robbed by Pied Crows *Corvus albus* (Winterbottom 1975) and African Harrier-Hawks (Thurow and Black 1981), and probably by Chacma baboons *Papio ursinus*, which can easily reach many ledges (AC pers. obs.). There is a record of an adult bird being killed by a Taita Falcon *Falco fasciinucha* (Woodall 1971).

RELATIONS WITH MAN Red-winged Starlings have taken full advantage of buildings as nest sites, which has enabled them to colonise areas where natural nest sites are lacking (Craig and Hulley 1992). In towns they will scavenge in the streets and nest in sites such as the roof over the pumps at a busy service station. Fruit-growers regard them as a pest and some birds are destroyed for this reason; Levaillant (1799) reported huge flocks in orchards and vineyards near Cape Town, where the birds caused much damage. However, they seem to be able to take advantage of any available food, and are certainly not specialist fruit eaters. At the nest the birds are often aggressive towards both man and domestic animals, with some successful nest sites being occupied for at least 35 years (Mitchell 1976). Skead (1995) had a series of pairs roosting and nesting on his farm veranda; one pair attacked the family members so vigorously while nesting that they were finally shot. With its wide distribution and ability to succeed in man-modified habitats, this must be one of the most successful African starlings.

PRINCIPAL REFERENCES Broekhuysen (1951), Craig *et al.* (1989), (1991), Rowan (1955).

95 SLENDER-BILLED RED-WINGED STARLING
Onychognathus tenuirostris   Plate 27

Lamprotornis tenuirostris Rüppell 1836

FIELD IDENTIFICATION 25 cm. A slim red-winged starling with a long, graduated tail, distinctly wedge-shaped in flight. It is most like Red-winged Starling, but is a slighter bird, with a much more slender bill.

DESCRIPTION Adult male: Crown, chin and nape are black with a greenish gloss, which is also present on the wings and tail. The rest of the plumage is purple-black. In the hand the feathers have a scalloped effect at their posterior borders. The primaries are reddish-brown, with a fairly broad band of black at the tip, so that the patch of red in flight appears central. The tail tapers sharply. **Adult female**: Crown, nape, sides of head, chin and throat dull greenish-black, with grey tips to the feathers. The lores are grey, producing a spotted effect in this region. The ventral feathers have broad grey crescents at their tips, which are much narrower on the feathers of the mantle, back and uppertail-coverts. The iris is hazel-brown, the bill black, often with a pale tip, and the legs are black. Van Someren (1922) described the juvenile bird as dull sooty-black above and below, with a bluish wash on the wings and tail.

Britton (1980) regarded Kenyan birds as intermediate between the nominate race and *O. t. theresae*, which occurs to the south and west. There are no marked differences in size or plumage characters, and the extent of movement between different populations requires study. A third race *O. t. raymondi* from Mt Kenya appears to be based on birds with slightly variant coloration. We suggest that this species should be treated as monotypic.

Of 50 specimens examined, 24 were in moult, including birds from all months of the year. Three birds with suspended wing moult were collected in June, July, and August. If this is a common occurrence, it could explain the extended moulting period.

MEASUREMENTS Male (10): wing 150–158, tail 169–178, bill 29.4–32.5, tarsus 32.2–35.2. Female (10): wing 140–148, tail 147–169, bill 28.0–31.8, tarsus 31.0–32.4. Weight of male (5) 127–142, of female (2) 113, 122 g.

VOICE The calls in flight are loud and explosive, so that the flock produces a chatter reminiscent of parrots Psittacidae (Chapin 1954). The flight call is a high-pitched *pleek*, and the flock keeps up a continuous harsh whistling and chattering.

DISTRIBUTION AND POPULATION High montane areas of eastern Africa, from the Nyika Plateau, Malawi, through Tanzania, Rwanda, Burundi, eastern Zaïre, Kenya and Uganda to Ethiopia. Locally very common in favoured habitat.

HABITAT Typical of montane forest, from 1500 to 3000 m, but may range up into alpine zone and has been seen at 5000 m, though descending to lower levels to roost.

FOOD AND FEEDING Large flocks feed on fruit at *Trema* trees. In Ruwenzori, they were observed feeding on the fruit of *Podocarpus milanjianus* (Ogilvie-Grant 1910), also *Urera hypselodendron* and wild olives *Olea africana* (Chapin 1954). In montane forests in Rwanda, Slender-billed Red-winged Starlings visited fruiting trees of *Prunus africanus*, *Ocotea michelsonii*, *Ilex mitis*, *Macaranga neomildbreadiana*, *Polyscias fulva* and *Maesa lanceolata* (Moermond et al. 1993). They stretched to reach for fruit clusters much more often than other starlings feeding in the same trees, perhaps using their long tails for balance when reaching out or down from a perch (Moermond 1992). Meinertzhagen (1937) described Slender-billed Red-winged Starlings searching for snails in lobelias on Mt Kenya, and Chapin (1954) recorded a small snail in the stomach contents of one specimen. However, they also visit *Lobelia* sp. to

feed on nectar, and appear to enhance pollination of the plants (Young 1982). Fruit of *Polyscias fulva* and *Allophylus abyssinicus* was recorded as a food item on the Nyika Plateau, and the birds caught insects on the ground and in flight, often taking insects to the nest (Dowsett-Lemaire 1983a). Gyldenstolpe (1924) saw birds feeding on the ground in old lands near villages, and Lynes (1934) described them foraging on waterweed on rocks covered by running water. Prigogine (1971) reported pupae of black flies (Simulidae), which are attached to such rocks, in the stomach contents of specimens from Zaïre.

BREEDING Slender-billed Red-winged Starlings nest singly or in small colonies in caves under waterfalls, generally at altitudes from 1300 to 2300 m with the same sites used in successive years. The nest is built by both sexes of moss on a mud base, and lined with grass. The eggs are pale blue with fine red-brown spotting, or sometimes with larger, more blotchy markings, measuring 33.5 x 32.8 mm. However, Schönwetter (1983) gives the measurements of three eggs as 32.3 x 21.9, weight 8.1 g. The clutch size is 2–4. Incubation lasts 13 days, and is by the female only, though she is fed on the nest by the male. The female alone broods the young, but both sexes feed the chicks and remove faecal sacs. The nestling period is about 23 days. The breeding season in Malawi was September to December (Dowsett-Lemaire 1983a), with nesting in the Ruwenzori Mountains, eastern Zaïre in December (Lippens and Wille 1976). Most East African breeding records come from January to March, but there are also some from August to December (Brown and Britton 1980). At cascades in Tanzania, Lynes (1934) found a colony of about ten pairs which had chicks in November, and eggs again the following January, which suggests that they are double-brooded. A male from Ethiopia in May had enlarged testes (Desfayes 1975), and Urban and Brown (1971) reported possible breeding in April. The timing of breeding may be related to water levels owing to the specific choice of nesting habitat; Chapin (1959) noted in Kivu, Zaïre, that Slender-billed Red-winged Starlings nested during the dry season.

BEHAVIOUR Brown referred to this species as 'gregarious at all times, active, excitable and noisy.' Slender-billed Red-winged Starlings always appear to roost and breed in caves under and near waterfalls, though roosts are not always used as breeding sites. The flocks may include a large component of non-breeding birds. Large flocks, up to 100 birds, were also noted on the Nyika Plateau, foraging over montane forest and grassland from 1,500 to 2,500 m (Dowsett-Lemaire 1983a). Small groups of Sharpe's Starlings are sometimes found in flocks of Slender-billed Red-winged Starlings (Ogilvie-Grant 1910). The male of a pair of Slender-billed Red-winged Starlings was observed performing a high cruising flight, accompanied by a piping call, while the female perched on top of a tree (Cheesman and Sclater 1936).

PRINCIPAL REFERENCE Brown (1965).

Onychognathus fulgidus Hartlaub 1849

FIELD IDENTIFICATION 28 cm. A large, heavy-billed red-winged starling with a longer tail than any other species likely to be found in the same habitat. The contrast between the head and body plumage of the male is clear in the field, and the red iris is conspicuous (Serle 1965).

DESCRIPTION Adult male: Glossy blue-black crown, while the nape, ear-coverts, sides of the head, chin and throat are black with a greenish gloss. The chest and belly are purple-black, while the mantle, back, wings and tail have a greenish gloss, with a purple tone on the uppertail-coverts. The primaries are reddish-brown, but there is a broad black band at the tips, so that the patch appears to be in the centre of the wing. The tail is graduated with the central feathers longest. **Adult female**: Crown, nape, chin, throat and sides of head grey, heavily streaked with glossy dark green. The iris is red, and the bill and legs black. **Juvenile**: Duller version of the male, with a brown iris.

The measurements given are all for **O. f. hartlaubi**.

The nominate race, **O. f. fulgidus**, restricted to the island of São Tomé off West Africa, is much larger (male wing 156–162, with a very heavy bill (cf Amadon 1953, plate 3). It was not recorded by Snow (1950), but was noted as common by de Naurois (1983).

Two other races have been described. **O. f. intermedius**, from Cameroon east and southwards, is reportedly intermediate in size between *fulgidus* and *hartlaubi*, but there seems to be considerable overlap.

O. f. leoninus, from Sierra Leone, was distinguished on the basis of its greenish crown (blue in other populations), but this may be an individual rather than a regional difference. Neither *intermedius* nor *leoninus* is generally recognised.

Based on 37 specimens, West African birds appear to moult from August to January, although single birds collected in March and June also had showed moult.

MEASUREMENTS Male (13): wing 117–128, tail 110–133, bill 29.1–36.4, tarsus 28.2–30.4. Female (10); wing 116–124, tail 113–129, bill 30.0–35.1, tarsus 26.0–29.1. Weight of male (13) 103–140, of female (13) 81–121 g.

VOICE Both sexes give a short, resonant call, also a whistle rather like that of orioles (Oriolidae), while the song is a double-note *churng-chuzick*, repeated several times (Chapin 1954). A quiet species, calling in flight, but seldom when perched (Brosset and Erard 1986). Marchant (1953) referred to a clear fluty *ti-ew* as the typical call, but de Naurois (1994) described the calls as grating and discordant. Harsh alarm calls were noted whenever a African Harrier-Hawk *Polyboroides typus* appeared (Maclatchy 1937).

DISTRIBUTION AND POPULATION Found from Guinea east to Uganda, south to northern Angola, also on the islands of Bioko and São Tomé, but it is absent from Príncipe (Amadon 1953, de Naurois 1994).

HABITAT Favours primary forest or old secondary forest in the lowlands, and is always in the canopy, never in scrub or undergrowth (Brosset and Erard 1986), generally below 1000 m but frequently near hills (Chapin 1954). On São Tomé, Chestnut-winged Starlings were found in forests at low and medium altitude by de Naurois (1983, 1994), but they were reported at all levels by Günther and Feiler (1985). In Nigeria, Elgood (1982) saw birds in forest clearings and wooded gardens.

FOOD AND FEEDING Fruit, berries and insects are reported in museum specimens; ten birds collected at Mt Nimba had fruit or berries in the stomach, and two had insects. A specimen from Nigeria was feeding on flowers, presumably taking nectar. Relatively large fruits such as *Dacryodes, Pycnanthus, Guibourtia, Trichoscypha* were favoured in Gabon (Brosset and Erard 1986); while oil palm-nuts *Elaeis guineensis* were also reported in villages and plantations (Rand *et al.* 1959). Fuggles-Couchman (1983) saw birds feeding on the fruit of *Maesopsis eminii*. Ten of eleven stomachs analysed in birds from Zaïre contained fruits or seeds of fruits; winged ants (Formicidae) and termite (Termitidae) alates were also recorded (Chapin 1954), and insects were noted as food items from birds from Cameroon (Germain *et al.* 1973). Chestnut-winged Starlings were seen alongside sunbirds (Nectariniidae) at the flowers of *Bombax*, presumably taking nectar; fruit, ants and beetles (Carabidae) were also reported from West Africa (Bannerman 1948).

BREEDING The first recorded Chestnut-winged Starling nest was found in Zaïre, in a palm tree where the fronds had been cut back, leaving only the broad bases. This accessible nest contained two downy young on a platform of twigs (Herroelen 1955). Serle (1965) also recorded nests in palm trees in Cameroon. A nest site in Uganda was in the underside of an African Crowned Eagle *Stephanoaetus coronatus* nest 22.5 m off the ground (Skorupa 1982). The eggs remain undescribed. Breeding was recorded in the Ivory Coast from September to December, and pairs were usually accompanied by two fledged young (Thiollay 1970). Chestnut-winged Starlings were seen at nest holes in Nigeria in January and February, but breeding was not confirmed (Pettet 1975). However, Elgood (1982) reported birds feeding young in Nigeria in February and May. In Ghana, copulation was observed in March, and nest-building in July; at one locality the same nest holes were used in October and November in consecutive years (Grimes 1987). A pair was seen entering a nest hole with dry twigs and leaf ribs in December (Kakum Forest, Ghana) (AC pers. obs.).

Breeding in west Cameroon was recorded from May to June (Serle 1981), and a February record ascribed to Neumann's Red-winged Starling probably also refers to Chestnut-winged Starling (Decoux and Totso 1988). On São Tomé the birds probably nest around September to November (de Naurois 1994). There are two nestlings from Cameroon, collected in May. Nesting occurred in Zaïre from April to September (Chapin 1954); according to Lippens and Wille (1976) from April to December north of the equator, and from October to May in the south. In the Itombe area just south of the equator, Prigogine (1971) reported breeding in November, March and April. A female from Gabon in August had an egg in the oviduct (Brosset and Erard 1986), and one from Mt Nimba had an enlarged ovary, although this August specimen also showed wing moult (Colston and Curry-Lindahl 1986).

BEHAVIOUR In Gabon, the birds were highly mobile, apparently covering very large areas, and were seldom at one site for more than a few days (Brosset and Erard 1986); local seasonal move-ments may be related to rainfall (Maclatchy 1937). Thiollay (1985) also referred to extensive movements in Ivory Coast. On Bioko, Chestnut-winged Starlings often foraged in small groups with Splendid Glossy Starlings (Eisentraut 1973). Pairs were observed on territories from April to July in Cameroon, thereafter the birds formed small flocks (Serle 1965). Groups of up to six birds were seen in Angola (Dean *et al.* 1987), two to five birds in Togo, and on São Tomé birds were encountered either singly or in flocks of up to eight individuals (Günther and Feiler 1985). Other observers did not encounter flocks at all, but always saw the birds singly or in pairs (Chapin 1954, Friedmann and Williams 1971, Germain *et al.* 1973, Britton 1980, de Naurois 1994). Small groups perched on bare branches at the tops of trees were seen apparently displaying at sunset; one bird would fly up, perform several somer-saults in the air and return to the branch, at which point a second bird would carry out the same sequence (Basilio 1963).

97 WALLER'S RED-WINGED STARLING *Onychognathus walleri*

Plate 27

Amydrus walleri Shelley 1880

FIELD IDENTIFICATION 20 cm. A short-tailed, red-winged starling of montane forest, which is smaller and more thickset than other species in same habitat.

DESCRIPTION Adult male: Crown, mantle, chest and belly dull blue-black. The ear-coverts, chin, throat and nape are glossy black with a metallic-green sheen. The primaries are reddish-brown with a broad black band at the tip, so that the red wing patch appears central. Some birds have a metallic-green crown, perhaps only in fresh plumage. **Adult female**: Crown, nape, sides of head, lores, chin and throat ash-grey, dorsally streaked with dark metallic-green. Ventrally it is dull charcoal with less gloss than the male. The iris is deep red, the bill and legs are black. **Juvenile**: Undescribed. There are three distinct subspecies.

O. w. preussi, on the highlands around Mt Cameroon and on the island of Bioko.

O. w. elgonensis, in Kenya west of the Rift Valley to Uganda, Sudan and eastern Zaïre.

O. w. walleri, from eastern Kenya south to Malawi.

O. w. elgonensis has a much shorter wing (male 114–130) and a flatter, broader bill than the nominate race. The female is grey only on the chin and throat (Zimmerman *et al.* 1996).

Data on moult are sparse, and the three populations need to be treated separately. For West Africa there were no specimens from June or August, but of the 34 birds examined, 18 were in moult, from all other months except November and December. March–April may be the mid-point of the moult. Only one of 22 *O. walleri elgonensis*

specimens was in moult, a bird collected in August. Twenty five *O. w. walleri* were birds in wing moult from October and from January to March. Friedmann and Loveridge (1937) noted that birds collected in May had fresh plumage. This suggests that the timing of moult is likely to be different in the different races.

MEASUREMENTS Male (16): wing 128–139, tail 90–103, bill 23.9–27.7, tarsus 25.0–29.5. Female (10): wing 119–133, tail 80–98, bill 23.0–24.7, tarsus 24.0–27.7. Weight of male (8) 73–92, of female 93 g.

VOICE The contact call is a clear loud whistle, used in flight and by mated pairs and also by males on song posts. A short two-note whistle is the 'flight intention' call, often used by the male to call the female off the nest, while the song is a series of clear whistled notes, each note of about one second in duration. There is also a harsh, grating alarm call like that of other *Onychognathus* species.

DISTRIBUTION AND POPULATION Three distinct populations occur, one on Bioko and in Cameroon, a second in southeastern Sudan, Uganda, western Kenya and northeastern Zaïre, and the third from Malawi through Tanzania to Kenya east of the Rift Valley. Waller's Red-winged Starlings were resident on the Kikuyu Escarpment, Kenya, but numbers fluctuated seasonally (Taylor and Taylor 1988). On the Nyika Plateau, this species was resident, with local wandering.

HABITAT A bird of mature highland forest, including small forest patches, recorded between 1000 and 2800 m in Cameroon (Stuart 1986) and in Malawi, up to 3000 m in Kenya (Zimmerman *et al.* 1996). However, on Bioko they have been found down to 200 m (Basilio 1963) and at 300 m in the East Usambaras, Tanzania (Zimmerman *et al.* 1996). Waller's Red-winged Starlings are usually found in the canopy, moving to lower levels during high winds.

FOOD AND FEEDING Fruit, particularly figs *Ficus* sp., and termites (Termitidae) were noted in the stomach contents of museum specimens, while Basilio (1963) reported fruit, spiders (Araneae) and insects from birds on Bioko. In Malawi, the fruit of *Maesa lanceolata, Podocarpus latifolius, Allophylus abyssinicus, Polyscias fulva, Ficus natalensis* and *Afrocrania volkensii* was brought to the nest, also insects (mostly winged) and chameleons *Chamaeleo goetzei*. Other fruit eaten by adults includes *Aphloia theiformis, Bersama abyssinica, Bridelia brideliifolia, B. micrantha, Celtis africana, Macranga kilimand-scharica, Maesa lanceolata, Myrica salicifolia, Prunus africana, Rhus longipes, Trichilia dregeana* and *Xymalos monospora*, all primarily 3–9 mm in diameter. Birds were seen feeding on fruit of a *Symphonia* tree in Uganda (Friedmann and Williams 1970), and they visited fruiting trees of *Ekebergia capensis, Prunus africanus, Ocotea michelsonii, Ilex mitis, Macaranga neomildbreadi-ana, Alangium chinense, Polyscias fulva* and *Maesa lanceolata* in Rwanda (Moermond *et al.* 1993). Waller's Red-winged Starlings appear to be adept at gripping thin branches so that they can get close to terminal fruit clusters, and thus seldom have to stretch to reach fruit (Moermond 1992). Cinnamon *Cinnamon zeylanicum* berries were favoured in East Africa, also *Juniperus*, and flying termites were caught on the wing (Sclater and Moreau 1933).

BREEDING Waller's Red-winged Starlings nest in holes in live or dead trees, 4 to 20 m above ground. Both sexes bring nest material of moss, bark and dead leaves to form a cup lined with thin twigs, liane fibres and bark. The eggs were described as a uniform blue-green, resembling the eggs of Spotless Starling, by Basilio (1963), but no measurements or clutch sizes have been reported. Incubation is by the female only, and is estimated at 13–16 days. Both birds feed the young on fruit and insects and remove faecal sacs, and the chicks leave the nest after 23–30 days. Breeding success is low, and predation is apparently significant. The breeding season on the Nyika Plateau extends from late August to November. In eastern Zaïre, birds breed in November, and perhaps also in March and April (Prigogine 1971). In Uganda breeding has been recorded in May, in Kenya from August to September (Brown and Britton 1980), although June nesting was also reported (Friedmann 1937), and Meinertzhagen (1937) noted birds at a nest hole on Mt Kenya in February at an altitude of over 2500 m. In Cameroon, nesting occurred from November to December (Bannerman 1948, Eisentraut 1963), although Elgood (1982) stated that there were no breeding records for West Africa.

BEHAVIOUR Sclater and Moreau (1933) described Waller's Red-winged Starlings as 'pugnacious creatures', and reported that they chased hornbills (Bucerotidae) and actually settled on their backs in flight. A pair of Waller's Red-winged Starlings regularly chased Kenrick's Starlings which were visiting a nest hole about a metre away from their nest but after several days tolerance was established between the resident pairs (Lack 1936). However, Dowsett-Lemaire (1983a) found this species to be remarkably non-aggressive, with each pair having a large home range; she estimated that non-breeding birds outnumbered breeders in the same habitat by at least three to one. Large flocks may form in the non-breeding season, with groups of more than 50 birds recorded on the Nyika plateau, and 80–100 in Kenya (Friedmann 1937, Taylor and Taylor 1988).

PRINCIPAL REFERENCES Dowsett-Lemaire (1983a–b), (1988).

98 SOMALI RED-WINGED STARLING *Onychognathus blythii*
Plate 28

Amydrus blythii Hartlaub 1859

FIELD IDENTIFICATION 28 cm. A markedly long-tailed, red-winged starling, with a longer tail than Red-winged Starling or Socotra Red-winged Starling, but smaller than the distinctive Bristle-crowned Starling.

DESCRIPTION Adult male: Uniform purple-black with some gloss. The primaries are reddish-brown, with a narrow black band near the tip, so that the wing patch extends almost to the tips of the feathers. **Adult female**: Crown, nape, sides of head, lores, chin, throat and chest plain ash-grey. The iris is reddish-brown, the bill and legs black. Mainland birds are larger and have longer tails than those on Socotra. **Juvenile**: Dark head like the male (Ogilvie-Grant and Forbes 1903).

Of eleven specimens from Socotra in January–March, seven showed wing moult. However, 12 mainland birds from these months did not show moult, whereas all twelve birds from the months April to July showed wing moult. This suggests a clear difference in timing between the two populations. One specimen from February (Socotra) has suspended wing moult.

MEASUREMENTS Male (10): wing 162–179, tail 175–194, bill 30.5–32.8, tarsus 36.8–39.9. Female (10): wing 161–170, tail 165–182, bill 28.7–31.0, tarsus 35.6–38.3. Weight, unsexed, 100 g.

VOICE Archer referred to melodious and distinctive whistles (Archer and Godman 1961). Ripley and Bond (1966) commented on 'typical *Onychognathus* alarm calls', and considered the voice harsher than that of Socotra Red-winged Starling. The usual call is *chee-chee-chee-che-woup*, a harsh *scraich* when alarmed (Ogilvie-Grant and Forbes 1903). The most frequent call in flight was a high-pitched, musical *tleep*, and a soft *chee-wee* and harsh alarm call were also noted (Porter and Martins 1996).

DISTRIBUTION AND POPULATION Endemic to Ethiopia and Somalia, with a population on the island of Socotra. Somali Red-winged Starling presumably reached Socotra from the mainland after the Socotra Red-winged Starling (Ripley and Bond 1966).

HABITAT This species is primarily a bird of high mountains in arid areas, but in some areas frequents rocky cliffs at lower altitudes.

FOOD AND FEEDING According to Archer, Somali Red-winged Starling is almost entirely a fruit-eater, favouring figs *Ficus* sp., juniper berries *Juniperus* sp. and wild olives *Olea* sp. (Archer and Godman 1961). The stomach contents of museum specimens included figs *Ficus* sp., beetles (Carabidae), and large black seeds. In Ethiopia figs, and *Juniperus* berries were noted by Blanford (1870). Fruit was taken on Socotra, especially figs and berries of the dragon's blood tree, also grasshoppers (Orthoptera) and other insects, and the birds removed ticks (Ixodidae) from the cattle (Ogilvie-Grant and Forbes 1903). Socotra birds

often perched on the backs of stock, apparently using them as beaters to disturb insects (Ripley and Bond 1966); they also foraged on the cattle, presumably removing ticks (Porter and Martins 1996).

BREEDING Nests are built in holes in cliffs or caves, but also on buildings; one pair raised five young in Archer's bathroom, and the following year birds attempted to nest on the ridge-pole of his tent! The nest was described as a loose structure of grass and a few feathers. The eggs are greenish-blue with red speckling, measuring 33.2 x 24.1 mm, clutches of 4–5 (Archer and Godman 1961). Schönwetter (1983) gives the egg measurements as 32.5 x 23.7 mm (n = 11, 30.2–35.5 x 22.0–25.0), weight 9.6 g. Breeding in Ethiopia was recorded from April to May, in September and also possibly in June (Urban and Brown 1971). Smith (1957) noted birds in Eritrea nesting on rock ledges in April. In December, adults on Socotra were accompanied by single young (Ogilvie-Grant and Forbes 1903).

BEHAVIOUR Birds on Socotra were described as very wild, usually with one of the flock on the lookout. On the ground they hopped, but did not walk. Flocks roosted on cliffs in the evening. They were sometimes seen foraging with Socotra Red-winged Starlings, but usually remained apart (Ogilvie-Grant and Forbes 1903). Flocks of at least 20 were seen regularly (Porter and Martins 1996). In Ethiopia, Blanford (1870) saw huge roosts in deep gorges.

99 SOCOTRA RED-WINGED STARLING *Onychognathus frater*
Plate 28

Amydrus frater Sclater & Hartlaub 1881

FIELD IDENTIFICATION 25 cm. It is found alongside Somali Red-winged Starling, which has a long, graduated tail, whereas the tail of Socotra Red-winged Starling is shorter and rather square-ended. Socotra Red-winged Starling is generally a smaller bird with no grey on the head in either sex.

DESCRIPTION The plumage is a uniform glossy black, except for the reddish-brown patch in the wings, which extends almost to the tips of the primaries. The iris is dark brown, the bill dark brown rather than black, and the legs black. The sexes are alike. Juvenile birds resemble the adults, but have slightly shorter tails, a greyish-black bill, and duller primary feathers (Porter and Martins 1996). The specimens are all from January, February and March; all three birds from March are in early wing moult.

MEASUREMENTS Male (5): wing 150–159, tail 137–140, bill 31.7–36.0, tarsus 37.0–38.7. Female (3): wing 149–153, tail 131–138, bill 32.6–33.8, tarsus 36.8-37.7. Weight, unsexed, 100 g.

VOICE There is a distinctive clear *pee-hoo* call,

but the alarm call is like that of Somali Red-winged Starling (Ogilvie-Grant and Forbes 1903). Ripley and Bond (1966) also mentioned the typical harsh alarm calls, but described the other calls as softer, more whistled than those of Somali Red-winged Starling. The most frequent call was a pure, far-carrying whistle *tyooo*; the alarm note a harsh *scraich* (Porter and Martins 1996).

DISTRIBUTION AND POPULATION Endemic to Socotra Island, where it probably numbers fewer than 1,000 individuals, and is currently listed as 'vulnerable' (Collar *et al.* 1994).

HABITAT The birds breed and roost in rocky areas, foraging over all parts of the island. They appear to favour wooded areas, and were also seen in town gardens (Porter and Martins 1996).

FOOD AND FEEDING The stomach contents of museum specimens included green fig pulp and grasshoppers (Orthoptera). The birds foraged like thrushes (Turdinae), searching for insects within the bushes, never on open ground nor associated with stock (Ripley and Bond 1966). Birds were seen feeding on *Zizyphus* berries, *Ficus* fruit, small red berries of *Dracaena cinnabari*, and seeds taken from the pods of a legume (Porter and Martins 1996).

BREEDING Nests were seen in natural cavities in the roof and walls of a limestone cave. They were not accessible, but appeared untidy piles of grass and small sticks (Porter and Martins 1996). The eggs are undescribed. Pairs were accompanied by a single juvenile in December (Ogilvie-Grant and Forbes 1903). In April many pairs were feeding fledglings or recently-fledged young (Porter and Martins 1996). Juvenile birds were collected in January, February and March.

BEHAVIOUR Socotra Red-winged Starling is much tamer than Somali Red-winged Starling, according to Ogilvie-Grant and Forbes (1903); however, Porter and Martins (1996) considered it to be a shyer species. They encountered the birds in pairs, or in small groups.

100 TRISTRAM'S RED-WINGED STARLING
Onychognathus tristramii
Tristram's Grackle

Plate 28

Amydrus tristramii Sclater 1858

FIELD IDENTIFICATION 25 cm. A short-tailed, red-winged starling, the only such species in its range.

DESCRIPTION The plumage is glossy black, except for the reddish-brown primary feathers with black tips. The tail is rounded, with the feathers equal in length. The female has the crown, nape, sides of head, chin and throat grey; there are dark streaks on the feathers of the posterior crown and nape and on the lower throat. The iris is brown, the bill dark brown, and the legs black. Juveniles resemble the male, with dark heads, and are less glossy than adults. Only 23 specimens were examined. Both birds from August had wing moult, but none of 17 birds from November to February showed this feature.

Southern birds have been separated as *O. t. hadramaticus*, but the size differences are slight, and the species is better treated as monotypic.

MEASUREMENTS Male (10): wing 143–155, tail 105–116, bill 30.3–33.7, tarsus 31.7–33.8. Female (10): wing 138–148, tail 100–114, bill 29.7–32.6, tarsus 31.2–34.2. Weight, unsexed (15) 115–131 g.

VOICE Harsh alarm call and musical whistles, like those of Red-winged Starling (Hofshi pers. comm.).

DISTRIBUTION AND POPULATION This is the only red-winged starling found outside of Africa, on the western Arabian peninsula from Yemen northwards to Sinai and Israel. It is common to abundant in suitable areas.

HABITAT Tristram's Red-winged Starling was formerly a bird of desolate rocky areas (Meinertzhagen 1954), but it now both feeds and nests in urban areas (Paz 1987). Physiological comparisons with Common Starling showed that Tristram's Red-winged Starling is much better able to tolerate high temperatures, which it would encounter in its desert habitat (Dmi'el and Tel-Tzur 1985).

FOOD AND FEEDING The diet was described as berries and fruit by Meinertzhagen (1954). Flocks were feeding on *Ficus nitida* and *Atriplex semibaccata*. Young in the nest were fed grapes, *Myoporum* sp, soft seeds of *Acacia* spp., *Helicella* and other small snails, grasshoppers (Orthoptera), butterflies (Lepidoptera), bees (Hymenoptera), flies (Diptera), and also dog biscuits and bread scavenged from houses. Much of this food was collected within the town of Arad, and birds breeding outside the town were also seen to visit the town to forage. Fruit of desert plants such as nitraria, *Coridia sinensis*, *Salvadora persica*, ochradenus, and grapes *Vitus* and dates *Phoenix dactylifera* was reported by Paz (1987); also various insects, including flies and bees. In North Yemen, flocks were feeding on hips of *Rosa abyssinica*, figs and fruit of *Olea chrysophylla* (Brooks 1987). Grasshoppers, beetles and seeds were noted in stomachs of museum specimens. Tristram's Red-winged Starlings sometimes pluck ticks (Ixodidae) from the hide of ibexes *Capra nubiana*, donkeys and camels (Paz 1987). Regular grooming of ectoparasites from the Nubian ibex *Capra ibex* has been described from a drinking site in Israel. Only juvenile male and female ibex were groomed, and the process followed a regular sequence, with an apparent mutual exchange of signals between the birds and the ibex. There are also reports of camels being groomed in the same way at regular sites (Yosef and Yosef 1991).

BREEDING Nests are placed in deep holes or crevices on cliffs or buildings, 6–21 m above ground. Urban nests were built of green *Tamarix* branches, sometimes with some *Acacia* leaves, and pigeon (Columbidae) feathers in the cup. No mud was included. Both male and female birds built the nest. The clutch size is 2–4. Incubation was estimated at 16 days, by the female only, while the male perched nearby and drove off other starlings and sparrows (*Passer*) which approached the nest. During the first week the female brooded the chicks; both sexes fed the young, which responded to the calls of the adults. Young birds left the nest at 28 to 31 days. The eggs are bright sky-blue, with scattered brown spots, more concentrated at the thick end (H. Hofshi pers. comm.) and measure 26.9–27.6 x 19.5–21.1 mm (5), weight 5.6 g (Schönwetter 1983). Breeding in Israel occurred from March to June, and the birds are often double-brooded. The same nest is used for the second brood, and the young are tended by the adults for about ten days after leaving the nest (Paz 1987).

MIGRATION Bigger (1931) stated that Tristram's Red-winged Starlings moved from the low, very hot summer breeding areas to cold northern wintering areas. However, there is no evidence of seasonal movements on a regular scale which justify the term migration.

BEHAVIOUR Young birds formed juvenile flocks about two weeks after leaving the nest, but still associated with their parents, and were fed by them for up to 39 days after independence. A case of infanticide was observed, in which the breeding male disappeared, and a strange male killed the chicks and subsequently courted the female (Hofshi et al. 1987b). During courtship the male fed the female insects, but allopreening was not observed. Flocks of up to 300 birds were seen in North Yemen in November (Brooks 1987).

RELATIONS WITH MAN Meinertzhagen (1954) noted that the birds could be extremely tame, and Tristram's Red-winged Starling is now a common commensal at picnic sites and holiday resorts. This may lead to changes in distribution and an increase in numbers of the species.

PRINCIPAL REFERENCE Hofshi et al. (1987a).

101 PALE-WINGED STARLING *Onychognathus nabouroup*
Plate 28

Sturnus nabouroup Daudin 1800

FIELD IDENTIFICATION 27 cm. A glossy black starling with bright orange eyes, a square tail, and conspicuous white patches in the wing in flight.

DESCRIPTION The plumage is a uniform glossy black, with the exception of the wings. The outer vane of the outer four primaries is rufous-brown, the inner vane creamy-white. On the inner wing feathers both vanes are creamy-white, but in all cases the feathers are black 20 mm from the tip, so that the white patch appears to be in the centre of the wing. At rest a narrow rufous-brown bar is visible on the folded wing. The tail feathers are approximately equal in length. The iris is bright orange-yellow, the bill and legs black. There is no sexual dimorphism, although male birds tend to be larger. Juvenile birds are less glossy and have dull brownish eyes for at least three months. Levaillant (1799) provided a fine description of Pale-winged Starling, carefully noting the differences between this species and Red-winged Starling.

Northern birds have been described as smaller with paler wings, *O. n. benguellensis*, but variation is clinal, and the species should be treated as monotypic (Craig 1988b).

Juveniles undergo a partial post-juvenile moult at about two months of age. All adults have a complete moult between November and May (based on a sample of 220 birds), and primary moult may overlap with breeding in individual birds. The moulting period does not appear to vary regionally. Wing feather replacement is relatively slow, with only one or two primary remiges growing in the same wing (Craig 1983a).

MEASUREMENTS Male (50): wing 129–156, tail 98–121, bill 26.0–31.9, tarsus 29.8–37.6. Female (42): wing 128–151, tail 90–112, bill 24.4–29.8, tarsus 29.2–37.0. Weight of male (5) 94–122, of female (13) 80–120 g.

VOICE The alarm call is a harsh *churr*, like that of Red-winged Starling, but the other calls are distinctive. In flight and prior to flying off Pale-winged Starlings give a ringing *preeoo*, to which other birds often respond by calling and flying off in turn. Perched birds of both sexes give a variety of warbling calls, reminiscent of Cape Glossy Starling; this category includes the song of the male. Interactions during group displays are accompanied by varied calls, which appear to reflect general excitement.

DISTRIBUTION AND POPULATION Pale-winged Starlings are distributed from southwestern Angola southwards through Namibia to the western interior of South Africa. At the southern and eastern limits of their range Pale-winged Starlings are frequently sympatric with Red-winged Starlings and show temporary range expansion in drought years (Craig and Hulley 1992). The birds are common to abundant.

HABITAT This is another starling of arid country, from semi-desert to desert conditions. Pale-winged Starlings roost on cliffs throughout the year, so that their activities are centred on rocky outcrops.

FOOD AND FEEDING The diet of Pale-winged Starlings in the Karoo includes dates *Phoenix reclinata*, fruit of *Diospyros lycioides* and *Cussonia paniculata*, berries of *Rhus* and *Lycium* sp., nectar and pollen from *Aloe ferox*, small insects, termite alates, butterflies and caterpillars (Lepidoptera). Insects may be caught on the ground, gleaned from the vegetation, or taken in the air by hawking from a perch (AC pers. obs.). In Namibia, the birds were seen feeding on berries of *Heeria insignis*, wild figs *Ficus* sp. and termites (Termitidae) (Hoesch and Niethammer 1940). Kok and van Ee (1990) noted that the stomach contents of seven specimens included grasshoppers (Orthoptera), beetles (Carabidae), and seeds of *Boscia albitrunca*, *Cotoneaster salicifolia*, *Crotalaria steudneri*, *Olea africana*, *Rhus lancea* and *Ziziphus mucronata*. In Namibia and at Augrabies Falls, South Africa, Pale-winged Starlings regularly perch on klipspringers *Oreotragus oreotragus* and groom ectoparasites from the antelope, which are quite tolerant of them (Tilson 1977; Jubb 1980a). They have also been seen to remove ticks (Ixodidae) from Cape mountain zebras *Equus zebra* (Penzhorn 1981), and from Hartmann's mountain zebras *Equus hart-*

mannae in Namibia (Joubert 1972). Andersson and Gurney (1872) stated that this species visits water points morning and evening.

BREEDING Nest sites are usually vertical crevices in the rock, and the nests are often extremely inaccessible, but a few cases of nesting in buildings have been reported. The nest is built of dry sticks wedged across the crevice, with a cup lined with dry grass; no mud is used. The eggs are pale greenish, spotted and smudged with pale red-brown markings, measuring 29.2–35.2 x 20.7–23.0 mm (18) (Maclean 1993), weight 8.9 g (Schönwetter 1983). The clutch size is 2–5 eggs, usually 3. The birds may be double-brooded. Both sexes build the nest and feed the young, but only the female incubates, while the male perches outside, often spending long periods in warbling song. The incubation period is estimated at 20 days, and the nestling period at 25 days. In South Africa the breeding season is October–March, varying in relation to rainfall, while in Namibia it is later, from November to April. Pale-winged Starlings are parasitised by Great Spotted Cuckoos *Clamator glandarius* (Jensen and Jensen 1969; Kemp *et al.* 1972), and they will attack cuckoos near the nest site (AC pers. obs.).

BEHAVIOUR Throughout the year Pale-winged Starlings roost in groups on cliffs, with breeding pairs generally roosting at their nest sites. They begin calling at first light, and leave in pairs or small groups after dawn. In the non-breeding season birds do not return to the roost site till

evening. R.K. Brooke (pers. comm.) saw small numbers of Pale-winged Starlings roosting on the rafters and ledges of an open building in Windhoek, Namibia. At the start of the breeding season, pairs or single birds investigate crevices, fluttering down the cliffs and displaying their white wing patches. The immediate vicinity of the nest is defended against conspecifics. Group displays occur, in which several pairs and unattached birds gather on top of the cliff, where the birds hop and posture with fluffed-up plumage. These ceremonial gatherings are most frequent prior to nesting, and take place either early in the morning or in the late afternoon. Joubert (1972) described how small flocks of Pale-winged Starlings would settle on a breeding group of Hartmann's Mountain Zebras, one or two birds per animal, and then remove ticks systematically. Sometimes the starlings were displaced by Common Drongos *Dicrurus adsimilis*, which hawked insects around the zebras, and would also take ticks off their bodies on occasion.

RELATIONS WITH MAN Along the Orange River in South Africa, Pale-winged Starlings feed on commercially-grown dates and other fruit, but most of their range is sparsely populated, and they obtain little food from man. The species is common, and birds may enter towns to feed on fruit trees in gardens and will scavenge at picnic sites in National Parks, but they very rarely nest in association with man at present.

PRINCIPAL REFERENCES Craig *et al.* (1989),

102 BRISTLE-CROWNED STARLING *Onychognathus salvadorii*
Plate 29

Galeopsar salvadorii Sharpe 1891

FIELD IDENTIFICATION 40 cm. A very large, long-tailed, red-winged starling. The long, graduated tail is an obvious field character, and the head outline with the bump of bristly feathers at the base of the bill is also distinctive at long range.

DESCRIPTION The lores and forehead are covered by a projecting crown of bristly feathers, which conceal the nostrils. There are also small bristly feathers under the chin and at the corners of the mouth. The body and wings are dark inky-black, except for the primaries, which are reddish-brown over most of their length, with black tips. The tail has some greenish gloss, and is strongly graduated with very long central feathers. At close range, the male has a deep purple tone to the head plumage. The female has a faint greenish gloss on the head and throat, with greyish feathers around the eye and ear-coverts. If the pair is seen together, the female is also recognisable by her shorter tail. The iris is a deep crimson, and the bill and legs are black. The juvenile plumage is described as much duller that that of the adult (Zimmerman *et al.* 1996).

Only 25 dated specimens were examined, with none from February, May or August; 15 birds were

in moult, with all months represented except April. This suggests an extended moult season.

MEASUREMENTS Male (12): wing 155–166, tail 232–257, bill 25.0–28.2, tarsus 36.4–40.1. Female (14): wing 146–157, tail 185–240, bill 22.1–26.8, tarsus 34.5–37.5. Weight of male 160, of female (3) 121–150.

VOICE Brown (1965) compared the chattering calls of Bristle-crowned Starling to those of Slender-billed Red-winged Starling, whereas their whistling calls were like those of the Red-winged Starling. The whistles are musical, but much higher pitched than those of Red-winged Starling (AC pers. obs.).

DISTRIBUTION AND POPULATION Endemic to Ethiopia, Somalia and northern Kenya, where it is patchily distributed, but locally common. Bristle-crowned Starlings are present at their breeding sites throughout the year at Lake Baringo (Stevenson 1983).

HABITAT Arid highlands are the typical habitat, where Bristle-crowned Starlings frequent high, rocky cliffs, which may often be close to permanent water as at Lake Turkana and Lake Baringo. The birds may enter towns and gardens, particularly to visit drinking sites (Brown 1965, AC pers. obs.). The birds are generally found below 1300 m (Zimmerman *et al.* 1996).

FOOD AND FEEDING Fruit and seeds were noted in the stomachs of museum specimens.

BREEDING Bristle-crowned Starlings nest in holes in cliffs, sometimes alongside other *Onychognathus* species as at Lake Baringo, Kenya (AC pers. obs.). The nest is built of sticks and grass, held together with mud (Urban *et al.* 1970). The eggs have not been described; the description in

Mackworth-Praed and Grant (1960) attributed to Archer in fact refers to eggs of Red-billed Oxpecker (cf. Archer and Godman 1961, p. 1416). A record of breeding in captivity provides no further information (Ezra 1931). Birds were breeding in May and June at Lake Baringo (Stevenson 1983), but a pair was also seen feeding chicks at this site in October (AC pers. obs.). Chicks were recorded in May in Ethiopia (Urban *et al.* 1970).

103 WHITE-BILLED STARLING *Onychognathus albirostris* Plate 29

Ptilonorhynchus (Kitta) albirostris Rüppell 1836

FIELD IDENTIFICATION 25 cm. A short-tailed, red-winged starling, with a conspicuous white bill. Other red-winged starlings in the same habitat are all long-tailed. The female is grey-headed.

DESCRIPTION Adult male: Uniform glossy blue-black, with a greenish gloss on the wings and tail. The primaries are reddish-brown with narrow black tips. The feathers in front of the eye are directed forwards along the white bill, covering the nostrils. The tail is rounded, with the feathers equal in length. **Adult female**: Crown, nape, sides of the head, lores, throat, chin and chest plain ash-grey. Juveniles resemble the male; the grey head of female develops later. Recently fledged young had grey heads like females, but the age of these birds was uncertain.

Twelve specimens examined included birds in moult from May, June and July. One bird from March had suspended wing moult. Erard and Prevost (1971) found that three out of five birds collected in July showed wing moult, with the outermost primaries still growing.

MEASUREMENTS Male (10): wing 148–164, tail 115–126, bill 26.5–30.1, tarsus 33.3–36.9. Female (1): wing 151, tail 115, bill 27.4, tarsus 32.3. Weight of male (2), 130, 145, of female (3) 130–135 g.

VOICE The alarm call is a harsh *charr*, while the males have a variety of short whistling calls, generally two notes *chee-up*, sometimes a low *chut*. When singing at the nest a repeated *kwit-kwit*, is accompanied by the raising and lowering of the tail. The calls are like those of Red-winged Starling, but not as melodious or drawn out.

DISTRIBUTION AND POPULATION Endemic to the Ethiopian highlands, where it can be locally common to abundant.

HABITAT The birds are found in rocky gorges and cliffs, generally between 2000 and 3000 m. In some parts of Ethiopia they also occur in towns, using man-made structures for nesting.

FOOD AND FEEDING Figs *Ficus* sp. and *Juniperus* berries were noted by Blanford (1870). Stomach contents included fruit, grasshoppers (Orthoptera), winged ants (Formicidae) and other Hymenoptera (Erard and Prevost 1971). Adults were observed hawking insects, and grasshoppers, a beetle (Carabidae) and a butterfly (Lepidoptera) were brought to the young.

BREEDING White-billed Starlings nest in holes or crevices in rocks, bridges and buildings, also on door lintels of derelict buildings. The only nest examined was constructed of grass and cereal leaf blades, and lined with plant fibres and rootlets. Apparently no mud had been used in construction. The eggs are clear turquoise-blue with small dark brown and black spots, mainly around the thick end, measuring 31.3 x 20.7 mm. Schönwetter (1983) gives the egg weight as 7.0 g. The clutch size is 2–3. Only the female was seen to incubate, but both sexes fed the young. The combined incubation and fledging periods were estimated at 35 days. The breeding season in Ethiopia was apparently from August to October; Urban and Brown (1971) also mentioned breeding in June. In Eritrea, birds were seen building in June, and apparently nesting on sheer cliffs in close association with White-collared Pigeons *Columba albitorques* (Smith 1957).

BEHAVIOUR The male sings from a perch while the female is active at the nest, and he may bring food to the female on the nest. After the breeding season small family groups are formed, but flocks of 100 birds or more roost together. White-billed Starlings bathe regularly, often at waterfalls.

PRINCIPAL REFERENCE Brown and Thorogood (1976).

Amydrus neumanni Alexander 1908

FIELD IDENTIFICATION 25 cm. A large, heavy-billed, red-winged starling with a very localised distribution. It is not usually sympatric with any similar species.

DESCRIPTION Adult male: Glossy black except for the chestnut primaries, which have narrow black tips. The feathers on the lores point forward, covering the nostrils. The iris is dark red, the bill and legs black. **Adult female**: Crown, nape, sides of the head, throat and upper chest ash-grey, with some darker streaking in the centre of the feathers. Juvenile birds resemble the male, but are duller.

There are three isolated populations.

Birds from the Jebel Marra region of Sudan are not distinguishable from those of Nigeria, Cameroon and eastern Mali, but to the west on the upper Niger river in Mali and in Ivory Coast the birds are smaller and shorter-tailed, with tail length consistently less than wing length. They are assigned to *O. n. modicus* (Craig 1988a). According to Lamarche (1981) an adult female of the nominate race had a red iris, whereas *O. n. modicus* has a brown iris; this should be investigated, as young birds would be expected to have brown irides. Bannerman (1948) also gave the iris colour of *O. n. modicus* as dark brown.

Twelve birds with wing moult were collected in March, April, June and July; of a total of 38 specimens. The moult scores suggest that wing moult may start in March, and is completed by July or August (Craig 1988a).

MEASUREMENTS Male (9): wing 155–171, tail 159–189, bill 29.3–34.3, tarsus 37.2–39.8. Female (6): wing 156–164, tail 167–177, bill 30.3–31.9, tarsus 35.8–37.3.

VOICE Neumann's Red-winged Starling has a harsh alarm note rendered as *air, air*, and a low whistle, usually given when perched (Bannerman 1948). This call was also described as a strong, fluted note (Paludan 1936). Smith (1964) heard a musical *too-whee-oo* call from a nesting pair, and also a harsh *kerr*, clearly the alarm call. Flocks in flight are reported to make a plaintive, twittering call (Bannerman 1948).

DISTRIBUTION AND POPULATION This species occurs from western Sudan (Jebel Marra) westwards to Burkina Faso and the upper reaches of the Niger River, to eastern Senegal (Morel and Morel 1990), and in southern Mauritania on the Assaba escarpment (Browne 1981). To the south it is found in Nigeria, particularly on the Jos Plateau,

and in the highlands around Bamenda in Cameroon. There are no confirmed records for Ghana (Grimes 1987), although it does occur in the north of Ivory Coast (Thiollay 1985). A localised and uncommon species, where there is suitable habitat.

HABITAT Neumann's Red-winged Starling generally occurs on rocky outcrops, inselbergs or cliffs, largely within the Sahel zone, but it may be associated with human settlements, and was found around houses at Bamako, on the river Niger, Mali (Paludan 1936). Birds were seen up to 2400 m in Sudan, and as low as 500 m in Nigeria (Bannerman 1948)

FOOD AND FEEDING Like other species, Neumann's Red-winged Starlings feed on fruit, but will also take insects. Figs *Ficus* sp., fruit of the mountain palm *Phoenix reclinata*, snails (Mollusca), ants (Formicidae) and possibly nectar of *Bombax* trees were reported by Bannerman (1948). The snails were broken up on an anvil stone.

BREEDING A nest of Neumann's Red-winged Starling in the Ivory Coast was in a cave on a rock ledge, about 5 m above the cave floor. The nest was a simple cup of straw, with three chicks being fed by both adults (Parelius 1967). Smith (1964) saw a pair feeding young on a horizontal ledge, 10 m above the ground on a vertical rock face. The eggs have not been described. The breeding season in Nigeria was April and May (Elgood 1982), and February to March in Cameroon (Bannerman 1948). Chicks were found in July in the Ivory Coast (Parelius 1967), and nesting was reported from March to September in Mali (Lamarche 1981). Nest-building was seen in July in Burkina Faso (Thonnerieux 1988). On the Jebel Marra, Lynes (1924) stated that Neumann's Red-winged Starling nested in summer (July to August).

BEHAVIOUR One bird was seen to chase off a monkey (Mammalia) which approached a fig tree, and during the breeding season Neumann's Red-winged Starlings chased bulbuls (Pycnonotidae), pipits (Motacillidae), kites (Accipitridae) and kestrels (Falconidae) from their territories. Males displayed, making short flights, and rolling and tumbling in the air. Flocks of 20–30 birds formed in November at Bamenda, Nigeria when fruit was abundant (Bannerman 1948). In Senegal, flocks were seen far from their usual rocky habitats, which suggests considerable nomadism (Morel 1985).

Poeoptera lugubris Bonaparte 1854

FIELD IDENTIFICATION 18 cm. A small, slender, long-tailed bird of the canopy, appearing blackish at a distance, with a rufous patch in the wings of females in flight. The narrow, tapered tail forms a characteristic silhouette.

DESCRIPTION Adult male: Body plumage is a uniform glossy dark blue. The wing feathers are black with some gloss on the tips, the tail feathers black with a slight sheen. The iris is yellow, and the bill and legs black. **Adult female**: Grey head with a slight blue gloss, the body plumage grey with the blue gloss more pronounced on the dorsal surface than ventrally. The tail feathers are black, the wing feathers brown, but the inner webs of the primaries have a chestnut patch. The iris is yellow, the bill and legs black. **Subadult**: Dull like the female and have markedly shorter tails; subadult male has a chestnut patch in the primaries like the female, and these feathers are replaced by adult male primaries at the first complete moult. Neumann (1920) seems to have been the first to note this peculiarity of the genus. Of the 110 specimens examined from Zaïre, some birds were in moult in every month of the year, but peak moulting activity seemed to be from November to March. Two birds from September and one from January showed suspended moult of the primary remiges. It is not clear at what age subadult males lose the female-type primaries and acquire uniform dark wing feathers.

Birds from Zaïre have been described as *P. l. major*, defined on the basis of their larger size, but Chapin (1954) regarded this race as invalid. Another race from Uganda, *P. l. webbi* has also not been recognised by later workers (Britton 1980) and this species should be treated as monotypic until geographical variation has been properly studied.

Of the birds collected at Mount Nimba, Liberia, a female in October was in early wing-moult, while another in April had almost completed wing-moult (Colston and Curry-Lindahl 1986).

MEASUREMENTS Male (10): wing 88–97, tail 121–134, bill 18.9–21.6, tarsus 18.8–20.7. Female (10): wing 86–92, tail 105–112, bill 18.8–20.5, tarsus 18.4–20.0. Weight of male (13) 35–43, of female (5) 35–39 g.

VOICE Narrow-tailed Starlings give a chirping note on the wing and when perched (Gyldenstolpe 1924). Soft, mournful cries in flight were reported by Sjöstedt (in Reichenow 1903); and melodious whistling calls were also noted in flight (Eisentraut 1963). Chapin (1954) remarked that for a starling this species was unusually silent, but that birds sometimes made a shrill, cheeping chorus in flight. Bates (1909) also reported occasional faint calls from flying birds, while Serle (1954) described the call as musical, high-pitched and explosive. The begging calls of the chicks were described as 'an airy, rhythmic squeaking', whereas the adults at the nest were only heard to utter a soft chirping note (Baranga and Kalina 1991).

DISTRIBUTION AND POPULATION Occurs from Sierra Leone eastwards to western Uganda, and through Zaïre to northern Angola in the Cabinda and Cuanza provinces. It may be locally common, and is described as resident in Gabon (Brosset and Erard 1986), and as resident in Liberia (Gatter 1988). Amadon (1953) listed this species for Bioko, but had not personally seen the specimens.

HABITAT The birds are found primarily in lowland forest, ranging out into forest patches (Chapin 1954). In Angola, Heinrich (1958) noted Narrow-tailed Starlings in coffee plantations, while in Gabon, Brosset and Erard (1986) found them to be common in secondary growth, where forest cleared for cultivation was regenerating, and in old clearings in the main forest. They were generally found below 1000 m in Cameroon (Stuart 1986), but reported to 1700 m in Uganda (Britton 1980).

FOOD AND FEEDING Several authors reported finding only fruit in the stomachs of Narrow-tailed Starlings which had been collected (Reichenow 1903, Chapin 1954, Colston and Curry-Lindahl 1986). However, Eisentraut (1963) found three butterflies (Lepidoptera) in the gullet of one specimen, and Brosset and Erard (1986) noted that the birds frequently pursued termite (Termitidae) alates and flying ants (Formicidae), and might be more insectivorous than other forest starlings. Friedmann and Williams (1970) found fruit fragments, seeds, beetles (Carabidae) and other small insect remains in the stomachs of birds collected in Uganda. At a nest, a male bird passed a large fly (Diptera) to the female, and the birds were also seen hawking insects above the canopy (Baranga and Kalina 1991). In Gabon, Narrow-tailed Starlings fed on fruits of *Musanga*, *Rauwolfia* and *Macaranga*, and also on the arils of *Pycnanthus* (Brosset and Erard 1986).

BREEDING Like other forest starlings, Narrow-tailed Starlings nest in tree holes, but they are colonial, and appear to be dependent on nest holes in dead trees provided by the colonial Naked-faced Barbet *Gymnobucco calvus* and other members of this genus; both starlings and barbets may be present at the nesting trees at the same time. This association has been reported by several observers (Sjöstedt in Reichenow 1903, Bates 1927, Houghton, Marshall in Bannerman 1948, Chapin 1954, Eisentraut 1963, Brosset and Erard 1986 and Dean *et al.* 1987). In Cameroon, Serle (1954) observed a tree which was shared 'apparently amicably' by Narrow-tailed Starlings and Grey-throated Barbets *G. bonapartei*. In Uganda, there were also no obvious interactions between these two species at a nesting tree, while elsewhere both barbet and starling nests were found in Black-and-white-casqued Hornbill

Bycanistes subcylindricus nest trees (Baranga and Kalina 1991). However, Germain et al. (1973) reported that while the starlings were tolerated by barbets in May in Cameroon, they were chased from the same tree in March, when the barbets were evidently nesting. The nests are high and inaccessible, and the nest lining has not been described. Bates (1927) felled a nest tree, and obtained three eggs 'more or less broken', pale blue-grey with scattered brown spots, more numerous at the thick end; 22 x 16 mm. The egg weight was estimated at 2.9 g (Schönwetter 1983). Females attending nests had crimped tails, which suggested that they did most or all of the incubating. Both male and female fed the young, with most of the food apparently regurgitated, as food was rarely visible in the bill (Baranga and Kalina 1991). In Cameroon, Serle (1981) recorded breeding in January, while Germain et al. (1973) saw Narrow-tailed Starlings entering nest holes in May, although breeding was not confirmed. Brosset and Erard (1986) described the breeding season for Gabon as December to March. Chapin (1954) found birds at a nesting tree in December in Zaïre, and collected a female in breeding condition.

Lippens and Wille (1976) give the breeding season as April–August in northeastern Zaïre, while Prigogine (1971) specified March and June–July at Kivu; there is a recently-fledged specimen from October. Dean et al. (1987) observed birds investigating nest holes in August in Angola, and Heinrich (1958) found a colony apparently feeding nestlings in March.

BEHAVIOUR Most observers have noted Narrow-tailed Starlings in flocks of 10–30 birds (e.g. Chapin 1954), though Gyldenstolpe (1924) reported flocks of about 100 individuals in the Ituri forest, Zaïre, in June. Prigogine (1971) noted that this species sometimes joined mixed flocks of frugivores. Baranga and Kalina (1991) observed a mixed party of starlings, Grey-throated Barbets and White-headed Wood Hoopoes *Phoeniculus bollei* foraging together. They also described a female Narrow-tailed Starling bathing and subsequently sunbathing. The birds appear to spend most of their time in the canopy, and also roost in flocks high in the trees. No courtship or territorial behaviour has been described; at the colonies pairs presumably nest in close proximity.

106 STUHLMANN'S STARLING *Poeoptera stuhlmanni*   Plate 30

Stilbopsar stuhlmanni Reichenow 1893

FIELD IDENTIFICATION 15 cm. A small, dark forest starling with a bluish tinge to the plumage, females with a chestnut wing patch in flight. Rather like the Narrow-tailed Starling, but with a shorter, less tapered tail.

DESCRIPTION Adult male: Head, nape, chin, throat and chest dark blue-black with a blue sheen. The mantle, back, rump, uppertail-coverts, belly, flanks, thighs and undertail-coverts are black with a purple sheen. Wings and tail are black, the iris has a yellow outer ring, and the bill and legs are black. **Adult female**: Head, nape, chin, throat and chest grey with a blue-grey sheen. The thighs, undertail-coverts and the centre of the belly are matt grey. Dorsally there is a faint purple gloss on the back, and a blue-grey gloss on the rump and uppertail-coverts. The wings and tail are black, but the inner webs of all the primary remiges, and the base of the outer webs of primaries 1–8 are chestnut-brown. **Subadult**: Resembles the female, and has chestnut primaries in both sexes. A juvenile from April had a creamy-white gape, and the iris is recorded as brown with a whitish outer ring. Zimmerman (1972) described the iris of an immature male as brown, while one female specimen had a yellow peripheral ring, and a brown inner ring on the iris.

From a sample of 61 specimens, it appears that wing moult is concentrated in the period from July to September, with single birds from March, April, May, November and December also moulting. There is a specimen from July with suspended moult. As in other members of the genus, male

birds acquire dark primary remiges when moulting into adult plumage.

MEASUREMENTS Male (10): wing 98–105, tail 79–89, bill 18.5–20.7, tarsus 20.0–21.8. Female (10): wing 92–102, tail 72–85, bill 17.7–19.6, tarsus 18.5–21.4. Weight of male (6) 38–46, of female (4) 35–39 g.

VOICE Lippens and Wille (1976) refer to calls 'like jays'. Jackson and Sclater (1938) noted that their trilling calls reminded him of bee-eaters, and Zimmerman (1972) commented that flocks in the canopy were very noisy, with loud trilling calls. Perched birds sing different types of song, short and loud or higher-pitched with slurred whistles (Zimmerman et al. 1996).

DISTRIBUTION AND POPULATION Found in western Kenya and Tanzania, and southwestern Uganda; it occurs to the west of the Rift Valley, whereas Kenrick's Starling is found to the east of the Rift. It also extends into eastern Zaïre, southwestern Sudan and southern Ethiopia. It is locally common within this limited range.

HABITAT Like Kenrick's Starling, Stuhlmann's Starling is a bird of the forest canopy, occurring at altitudes of 1500–2500 m, and it may wander extensively (Britton 1980, Lewis and Pomeroy 1989).

FOOD AND FEEDING Only fruit was recorded by Chapin (1954), and figs *Ficus* sp. were noted in stomachs of museum specimens. Jackson and Sclater (1938) saw this species feeding in flocks on small currant-sized fruits, alongside bulbuls (Pycnonotidae), barbets (Capitonidae) and white-eyes (Zosteropidae). In montane forests in Rwanda, Stuhlmann's Starlings were seen visiting fruiting trees of *Ilex mitis, Macaranga neomild-breadiana, Alangium chinense, Polyscias fulva* and *Maesa lanceolata* (Moermond *et al.* 1993).

BREEDING Stuhlmann's Starlings were seen entering old woodpecker (Picidae) holes (Brown 1975, Cunningham-van Someren 1975), but the sites were inaccessible and neither the nest nor the eggs have been described. Cunningham-van Someren (1975) saw both male and female visiting a nest hole 10 m above the ground, and they chased away a honey guide *Indicator* sp., a potential brood parasite. Brown and Britton (1980) listed four breeding records for this species, December in Kenya; October, February and March

in Uganda. Mann (1985) reported egg-laying in March in the Kakamega forest, Kenya. Stuhlmann's Starlings were breeding in April in the Imatong Mountains, Sudan (Nikolaus 1987), and possibly breeding in Ethiopia in March (Urban and Brown 1971). Prigogine (1971) reported young in the nest in July in Kivu, Zaïre, suggesting egg-laying in June.

BEHAVIOUR A male Stuhlmann's Starling repeatedly offered a female some object in its beak, fluttering its wings and sidling up to the female (Cunningham-van Someren 1975). It is not clear whether this represents courtship feeding, or presentation of nesting material. Prigogine (1971) stated that this species did not join mixed-species flocks.

107 KENRICK'S STARLING *Poeoptera kenricki* Plate 30

Poeoptera kenricki Shelley 1894

FIELD IDENTIFICATION 15 cm. A short-tailed, blackish starling of the forest canopy; flying females show a chestnut wing patch.

DESCRIPTION Adult male: Uniform black with a slight bronzy sheen, bill and legs black. The iris is pale yellow, the bill and legs black. **Adult female**: Grey head, throat, chest and belly, with the lores black. The wings, tail, and back are dark charcoal-grey. The inner web of primary 9, and the inner and outer webs of the other primary remiges have a central chestnut patch. A specimen labelled as a juvenile male has chestnut primaries like the female; however, according to Zimmerman *et al.* (1996), the subadult male has black primaries.

Kenyan birds have been described as a different subspecies *P. k. bensoni* on the basis of size differences, but there seems to be considerable overlap in measurements, and the species is best treated as monotypic.

Three birds collected in February showed active wing moult, and one showed suspended primary moult; there was also a bird from June in active wing moult. Other specimens from March–July, September and November were not moulting, but Bowen (1931a) collected a female in July which was moulting. As with the breeding records, there is little evidence of seasonality with such a small sample.

MEASUREMENTS Male (15): wing 99–109, tail 77–89, bill 18.6–20.7, tarsus 20.3–22.1. Female (12): wing 96–103, tail 75–84, bill 17.4–20.2, tarsus 91.1–21.5. Weight of male (4) 46–54, of female (5) 38–49 g.

VOICE The commonest call was a loud, sweet *peleep*; groups often uttered a pleasant, musical babble (Sclater and Moreau 1933).

DISTRIBUTION AND POPULATION Endemic to highland forests of central Kenya and eastern Tanzania, where it is locally common but little known.

HABITAT Kenrick's Starling is an arboreal bird of

the forest canopy in areas of rainfall >1000 mm, restricted to highlands from 900–2500 m, but apparently nomadic and occasionally visiting isolated forest patches (Britton 1980, Lewis and Pomeroy 1989). Brown (1965) noted this species in his Kenya garden only in years of high rainfall. Birds are sometimes found as low as 450 m in the East Usambaras, Tanzania (Zimmerman *et al.* 1996).

FOOD AND FEEDING Only fruit has been recorded, particularly *Ficus* sp. (Sclater and Moreau 1933, Fuggles-Couchman and Elliott 1946), but also *Trema* (Brown 1965).

BREEDING Kenrick's Starlings nest in tree holes, using old barbet (Capitonidae) or woodpecker (Picidae) holes (Brown 1965, Fuggles-Couchman and Elliott 1946). Both the male and female were seen carrying material (Lack 1936, Fuggles-Couchman and Elliott 1946), but neither the lining of the nest nor the eggs have been described. There is also no information on incubation or care of the young. Brown and Britton (1980) listed 17 breeding records, from January, March to May and July to November; they noted that all the records from September to November were from Arusha, Tanzania. Fuggles-Couchman (1984) reported unpublished records of breeding in April and October from this district. Moreau (1935) collected a male in breeding condition in February.

BEHAVIOUR Kenrick's Starlings go about in large noisy flocks (e.g. Bowen 1931a). Sclater and Moreau (1933) observed possible courtship in a party of seven birds of both sexes. The males chased the females, and then flew to a tree with nest holes, where they clung to the nest entrance, calling. Lack (1936) observed a pair of Kenrick's Starlings visiting a nest hole in the same tree as a pair of Waller's Red-winged Starlings were nesting. After frequent attacks, in which the Waller's Red-winged Starlings were dominant and the Kenrick's Starlings did not retaliate, the birds tolerated each other. The resident pair of Kenrick's Starlings tolerated visiting conspecifics, but these visitors were chased by the pair of Waller's Red-winged Starlings. At the same tree, a pair of White-eared Barbets *Stactolaema leucotis* occasionally displaced the Kenrick's Starlings.

108 SHARPE'S STARLING *Pholia sharpii* Plate 25

Pholidauges sharpii Jackson 1898

FIELD IDENTIFICATION 18 cm. A small starling of the forest canopy, dark dorsally, and pale buff ventrally; juveniles are duller with dark spotting ventrally.

DESCRIPTION The crown, sides of head, nape, mantle, rump, wings, tail, underwing-coverts, and a patch on the sides of the chest opposite the bend of the wing are glossy blue-black; this may suggest a breast-band as noted by Granvik (1923). In the hand, the blue sheen on the back contrasts slightly with the blacker head. Chin, throat and chest are cream-coloured tinged with buff. The belly, flanks, thighs and undertail-coverts are buff. The iris is yellow, and the bill and legs are black. The sexes are alike. Juveniles are matt-grey dorsally except for some sheen on the wings and tail. The chin, throat, chest and upper belly are cream-coloured with arrow-head shaped dark tips to the feathers. The iris is dark brown, and the gape is initially pale yellow. The buff wash is restricted to the thighs and undertail-coverts. The spots apparently persist longest on the chest. Brown (1972) noted two captive birds with adult plumage but dark eyes, which were presumably immature birds. On one museum specimen which still had spots present on the chest, the label noted a yellow iris.

Of 69 specimens from all months of the year, there were only four birds showing active wing moult, and five had suspended moult in the primaries, with some new and some old feathers. Of two birds collected in June at the same locality in Kenya, one showed active wing moult, the other suspended wing moult; other birds with suspended moult were collected in April (Kenya), July (Kenya, Zaïre), August (Kenya) and October (Tanzania). Birds with active wing moult were collected in Zaïre in January and March, and in Uganda in February, although this would seem to correspond with the breeding season described above. In Ethiopia, Dorst and Roux (1973) noted that Sharpe's Starlings had completed their moult by April.

MEASUREMENTS Male (10): wing 96–106, tail 63–67, bill 16.0–18.5, tarsus 20.7–22.5. Female (10): wing 92–101, tail 57–68, bill 16.0–17.8, tarsus 20.0–21.9. Weight of male (5) 40–56, of female (2) 40–42 g.

VOICE The call is a very thin, sharp noise and there is also a brief, quite soft sweet whistle. Two song phrases were distinguished, one of four notes, rather falsetto, and one of five notes reminiscent of the opening of the song of the Dark-backed Weaver *Ploceus bicolor* (Moreau and Sclater 1938).

DISTRIBUTION AND POPULATION Sharpe's Starling is found from eastern Zaïre through Rwanda, Burundi and western Uganda to southeastern Sudan, in southwestern Ethiopia, central Kenya and northern Tanzania. It is locally common.

HABITAT The birds frequent the canopy of the forests in areas above 1800 m, mostly with rainfall in excess of 1000 mm (Lewis and Pomeroy 1989). In Ethiopia, Dorst and Roux (1973) noted that this species occurred in forests at 2500 m but not in forests at higher altitudes than this, and it was absent from degraded forest habitats.

FOOD AND FEEDING Frugivorous, feeding in the canopy on *Sapium* sp. (van Someren 1939), *Olea* sp. (Beesley 1972), *Urea hypselodendron* and *Rapanea pulchra* (Chapin 1954). Fruit of *Ocotea*, and termites were noted in the stomachs of museum specimens, and Dorst and Roux (1973) observed birds hawking termites (Termitidae). They visited fruiting trees of *Ilex mitis, Macaranga neomildbreadiana* and *Polyscias fulva* in montane forest in Rwanda (Moermond et al. 1993), and birds feeding on *Polyscias fulva* usually picked fruit within reach, less often (24% of observations) stretching for it (Moermond 1992). Jackson and Sclater (1938) found Sharpe's Starlings feeding in association with Stuhlmann's Starlings, Waller's Red-winged Starlings and bulbuls (Pycnonotidae), and quoted another observer who had seen them with Slender-billed Red-winged Starlings. In captivity pears were a favourite fruit (Brown 1972).

BREEDING Nesting was observed in tree holes, with the entrance 14 m above the ground in one case (Beesley 1972). The nest and eggs are still undescribed. In eastern Zaïre, birds were in breeding condition in March (Chapin 1954), April and August (Prigogine 1971), and in Sudan Nikolaus (1987) gave the breeding months as February and April. The birds were possibly breeding in Ethiopia in March (Urban and Brown 1971), and birds in breeding condition were collected in April (Dorst and Roux 1973). Breeding in Tanzania was reported in October (Brown and Britton 1980) and a female was seen feeding nestlings in January while her presumed mate was singing (Beesley 1972). There are juvenile specimens from May, June, August, September and October, and two birds from March which show the last traces of spots on the chest.

BEHAVIOUR Van Someren (1939) noted that Sharpe's Starling was less vocal while feeding than Abbott's Starling. Taylor and Taylor (1988) also saw mixed parties of the two species feeding and singing at close quarters. They are apparently territorial during the breeding season, as Beesley (1972) described the males occupying song posts, with pairs scattered over a wide area. He noted flocks of several hundred birds at other times, the largest groups recorded; other authors have seen them in flocks of fewer than twenty birds (Chapin 1954, Cave and Macdonald 1955, Dorst and Roux 1973, Taylor and Taylor 1988), often in groups of three to eight birds (Jackson and Sclater 1938).

109 ABBOTT'S STARLING *Pholia femoralis*   **Plate 25**

Pholidauges femoralis Richmond 1897

FIELD IDENTIFICATION 17 cm. A small starling of the forest canopy, dark dorsally and on the throat and chest, otherwise creamy-white ventrally. Juveniles are duller and streaked on the ventral surface.

DESCRIPTION The head, dorsal surface, chin, throat, chest, thighs, remiges and rectrices are blue-black with a slight sheen. The belly, flanks and undertail-coverts are a dull, creamy-white. The iris is whitish, the bill and legs black. The sexes are alike. The tail feathers are almost equal in length, with the closed tail slightly forked. Juveniles are dark grey instead of blue-black; the throat and chest are yellowish-brown with darker central streaks to the feathers, and the belly feathers also have dark central streaks.

Of seven specimens from February and March, five were in moult. Three specimens from August were not moulting; none of these birds was reported to have enlarged gonads. Moreau (1935) noted that three males collected in February were in full moult, one with the testes still enlarged, and a female bird was in post-juvenile moult; these birds are in the British Museum, and thus included above.

MEASUREMENTS Male (7): wing 98–102, tail 67–72, bill 17.3–18.9, tarsus 21.8–25.3. Female (3): wing 92–99, tail 65–71, bill 18.2–18.8 tarsus 23.0–24.0.

VOICE A continuous whistling call of six notes, three ascending, then three descending, with the last note the lowest (van Someren 1939). The territorial song is high-pitched and squeaky, with some twanging notes (Zimmerman *et al.* 1996).

DISTRIBUTION AND POPULATION Endemic to highland forests of northeastern Tanzania and Kenya east of the Rift Valley. It is quite common on Mts Kenya and Kilimanjaro (Britton 1980; Lewis and Pomeroy 1989), but Collar *et al.* (1994) rated it as 'vulnerable' on the basis of its limited occurrence in protected areas.

HABITAT This starling occurs in the canopy of montane forest from 1800–2600 m (Britton 1980; Lewis and Pomeroy 1989), ranging up to 2800 m (Moreau 1935).

FOOD AND FEEDING Only fruit has been recorded. The birds were described as messy feeders, dropping many berries of *Cornus volkensii* (van Someren 1939).

BREEDING Abbott's Starling nests in tree holes, but the nest and eggs remain undescribed. There are four breeding records from Tanzania, in February, March and October (Brown and Britton 1980). Moreau (1935) collected a male in breeding condition in March.

MIGRATION Curry-Lindahl (1981) refers to this species as probably migratory, but clear evidence is lacking. However, Taylor and Taylor (1988) recorded Abbott's Starling in all months except August in their study area, although they noted a great deal of local wandering. It is likely to move in response to food availability, but true migration seems improbable.

BEHAVIOUR Van Someren (1939) saw flocks of up to 100 birds in the company of Sharpe's Starlings, and noted that Abbott's Starlings were much more vocal. Taylor and Taylor (1988) also saw the two species together, with Abbott's Starlings more numerous in flocks of up to 40 birds, and they observed that the two species fed and perched close together even when one species was singing.

110 WHITE-COLLARED STARLING *Grafisia torquata*   **Plate 31**

Spreo torquatus Reichenow 1909

FIELD IDENTIFICATION 24cm. The male appears black, with a distinctive white breastband extending up onto the sides of the neck, and a bright yellow eye. The female is grey, also appearing dark at a distance (R. Newton, in Bannerman 1948), but is paler ventrally although lacking any white.

DESCRIPTION Adult male: Uniform glossy black, except for the white patch on the upper chest which outlines a dark bib, and extends up the sides of the chest, ending sharply in line with the wings. The iris is bright yellow, the bill and legs are black. **Adult female**: Grey without gloss, but the dorsal feathers from crown to rump are tipped with blue-black, and the wing and tail feathers are dull black. A juvenile and a subadult resemble the female. Reichenow (1911) described the juvenile as grey on head and throat, with some of the throat feathers tipped white; ventrally dull brownish-grey, with the mantle and lesser coverts deep black with paler edges, producing a scaly appearance; the wing and tail feathers are black with very little gloss. This may have been a younger bird than the specimen examined. Serle (1965) collected a subadult male with brown primaries, less gloss on the ventral plumage, and the breastband flecked with grey-brown.

Specimens from January, February, March, June and December were not in moult; one bird from October and one from August showed wing moult. However, the sample is too small to draw any conclusions.

MEASUREMENTS Male (11): wing 121–133, tail 84–106, bill 21.0–23.7, tarsus 23.6–26.0. Female (6): wing 110–120, tail 76–87, bill 21.9–23.0, tarsus 22.8–24.6.

VOICE R. Newton (in Bannerman 1948) reported chirruping, and a call of three short whistled notes, and stated that both a male and a female sang a 'weak apology for a song'.

DISTRIBUTION AND POPULATION Local and uncommon in Cameroon and northern Zaïre. It does not occur in Chad, as the localities from which it was reported are in fact in the Central African Republic (Vieillard 1971), for which there are recent records (Carroll 1988). In Gabon it is apparently an non-breeding visitor and was categorised as a migrant by Brosset and Erard (1986).

HABITAT White-collared Starlings occur in open woodland rather than forest, but the birds seem to keep to the tops of high trees. They also occur in montane grasslands in Cameroon (Louette 1981).

FOOD AND FEEDING Of five museum specimens, one stomach contained insects, and four contained fruit. Berries have been reported (Bannerman 1948), and also wild figs *Ficus*, *Musanga* fruits (Chapin 1954), and fruit of *Macaranga assas* (Dowsett-Lemaire 1996).

BREEDING White-collared Starlings are presumed to nest in tree holes, but there is no recorded nesting observation. There is a juvenile specimen from May, and Lippens and Wille (1976) reported juveniles in July. Males collected in March had large testes, and birds were seen carrying twigs (Serle 1965). This suggests breeding during the first half of the year.

BEHAVIOUR Small groups of 4–10 birds were noted by Chapin (1954) and Germain *et al.* (1973) saw White-collared Starlings in pairs, once in a group of 8, but P. Herroelen (pers. comm.) recorded a flock of more than 100 birds in Zaïre in June. Blancou (1974) twice saw small groups flocking with glossy starlings (*Lamprotornis* sp.). R. Newton (in Bannerman 1948) saw a male make short circular flights from a conspicuous perch, with a female perched in a nearby tree. This appeared to be a courtship display.

111 MAGPIE STARLING *Speculipastor bicolor* Plate 31

Speculipastor bicolor Reichenow 1879

FIELD IDENTIFICATION 19 cm. Males are blue-black dorsally, and white ventrally with conspicuous white patches in the wing. Females are similar, but the head and chest are grey.

DESCRIPTION Adult male: Head, nape, mantle, rump, tail, chin, throat and upper chest glossy blue-black. The chest (apart from the black bib), belly, flanks, underwing-coverts, undertail-coverts and thighs are white. The wings are blue-black, but the bases of the primaries are white, and are visible as a patch on the folded wing. The iris is red with a yellow ring around the pupil. The bill and the legs are black. **Adult female**: Resembles the male in pattern, but the head, throat, nape and upper chest are grey, while there is a narrow band of blue-black at the ventral margin of the bib. Juvenile birds lack blue-black plumage completely, so that the head, dorsal plumage, chin, throat and upper chest are grey; the white areas are the same as those found in the adult. The wing and tail feathers are grey-brown, and the bill, legs and iris brown. Sexual dimorphism is not evident in juveniles.

A total of 46 specimens was examined, from all months. Birds with wing moult noted from the following months: January, February, April, June, July, August and December. No clear statement is possible regarding the timing of moult. Two birds, from March and October, had suspended primary moult.

MEASUREMENTS Male (11): wing 114–122, tail 77–84, bill 20.2–22.3, tarsus 27.0–30.1. Female (12): wing 105–112, tail 69–77, bill 19–23, tarsus 26.5–28.7. Weight of male 66, 69, of female (2) 61 g.

VOICE There is a shrill whistling call in flight (Mackworth-Praed and Grant 1960). In a captive pair, the male spent long periods singing. The song is described as a soft babbling, with some harsher notes (Zimmerman *et al.* 1996).

DISTRIBUTION AND POPULATION Occus in northeastern Uganda, southern Ethiopia, Somalia and Kenya, with old records from southwestern Sudan and northern Tanzania. This species is nomadic, but often locally numerous.

HABITAT The birds are found primarily in bushed and wooded country, mainly below 1200 m, in arid to semi-arid regions (Ash and Miskell 1983, Lewis and Pomeroy 1989).

FOOD AND FEEDING Magpie Starlings eat fruit, including figs *Ficus* sp. and wild tomatoes *Solanum* (van Someren 1922), and insects such as caterpillars (Haas and Nickel 1982). Captive birds took commercial food mixture, raw mince, mealworms, maggots and apple.

BREEDING Magpie Starlings nest in holes in the sides of termite (Termitidae) mounds. The nest chamber is 10–20 cm from the surface of the mound, lined with grass and green leaves (Erlanger 1905, Archer and Godman 1961). They also form small colonies nesting in holes in banks

(Haas and Nickel 1982). In captivity, a pair of Magpie Starlings lined the nestbox with no more than a few pieces of grass. The eggs are bluish green, lightly spotted all over with russet brown (Archer and Godman 1961), and measure 23.0–28.7 x 19.2–20.5 mm (29), weight 5.4 g (Schönwetter 1983). Clutches of 3–5 eggs were reported in the field (Haas and Nickel 1982), while a captive pair produced two clutches of four eggs, incubated by the female alone for about 18 days. Adults fed the young on caterpillars (Haas and Nickel 1982); in captivity both male and female fed the chicks, which left the nest after 21 days. In Kenya, nests have been found in May and June (Lewis and Pomeroy 1989); breeding may be opportunistic, in response to the availability of food (Haas and Nickel 1982). There is an old breeding record from Sudan in May (Nikolaus 1987), and a possible breeding record from Ethiopia in February (Urban and Brown 1971). In Somalia, nesting was recorded from April to June (Erlanger 1905, Archer and Godman 1961).

MIGRATION Curry-Lindhal (1981) refers to this species as a local migrant, but other authors have termed it nomadic. Archer and Godman (1961) summarised its movements in Somalia as 'north to breed and south to winter is the invariable habit.' Benson (1946) noted that most of his records were in March in southern Ethiopia, and he suggested that it arrived there to breed in February during the rains. Lewis and Pomeroy (1989) note that despite its irregular occurrence, there is some pattern to the movements of Magpie Starlings; in Kenya south of the equator there are no breeding records, and the birds have been noted only during the non-breeding period, especially from August to October. At Lake Baringo, north of the equator in Kenya, Stevenson (1983) found that Magpie Starlings were present throughout the year, although numbers varied considerably from month to month.

BEHAVIOUR Small flocks of Magpie Starlings fly about calling shrilly, and they concentrate at sites where figs and other fruit are abundant (Mackworth-Praed and Grant 1960). Groups of birds were also seen feeding on caterpillars (Haas and Nickel 1982). Birds assemble in the treetops, with flocks numbering from four or five to 20 or 30 birds (Archer and Godman 1961). Benson (1946) usually saw two or three birds together, but on one occasion recorded a group of 15.

PRINCIPAL REFERENCE Partridge (1964).

112 WHITE-WINGED BABBLING STARLING *Neocichla gutturalis*
Plate 31

Crateropus gutturalis Bocage 1871

FIELD IDENTIFICATION 20 cm. A medium-sized starling, greyish-brown with dark wings and tail, and white wing patches which are conspicuous in flight. Its flight is rather reminiscent of helmet-shrikes (Laniidae).

DESCRIPTION The crown, nape, sides of head, chin and throat are grey. The mantle feathers are brown with buff edging, the rump grey-brown as are the uppertail-coverts. Ventrally there is a small, black, wedge-shaped mark in the centre of the chest. The chest, belly, flanks, thighs and under-tail-coverts are buff-coloured, paling to white in the centre of the belly. The underwing-coverts are buff, the wing-coverts and tertials brown. The secondaries have white outer edges, forming a prominent wingbar at rest, and a wing patch in flight. The primaries and tail feathers are dark brown with a slight gloss. The iris is yellow, the bill black and the legs yellow-brown. The sexes are alike. Juveniles have a dark brown crown, mantle and wing-coverts. The chin and throat feathers, chest, upper belly and flanks have dark brown teardrop-shaped markings, while the background colour is much paler than in the adult. Wings, tail and uppertail-coverts are like those of the adult. The bill is initially yellow, blackening from the tip, the legs pale brown, and the iris bluish-grey.

Angolan birds have large whitish areas at the tips of the outer rectrices, whereas those from East Africa have only narrow pale margins (Friedmann 1930). Benson and Irwin (1966) state that Angolan birds have the longest wings and Zambian birds the shortest wings, but it is not clear if males and females were separated in their sample. Since the two populations are widely separated geographically, White-winged Babbling Starlings from East Africa have been recognised as a different race *N. g. angusta*.

There are specimens showing wing moult from December, February, April and May, while birds from July, August, October and November are not in moult. Chapin (1948) reports that Angolan birds showed wing moult in late January, suggesting that moult occurs after the breeding season.

MEASUREMENTS Male (9): wing 101–113, tail 84–92, bill 21.7–24.2, tarsus 31.3–33.7. Female (6): wing 102–110, tail 83–90, bill 22.2–24.8, tarsus 29.4–32.7. Weight of male (2) 64–72, of female 64 g.

VOICE The calls are shrill, even referred to as parrot-like, and to some observers were reminiscent of babblers (Timaliinae) (Chapin 1948).

DISTRIBUTION AND POPULATION Locally common resident in western Angola, then there is a wide gap before the birds occur again in Zambia from the Luangwa valley westwards to northwestern Malawi near the Zambian border, and in central and southwestern Tanzania. It has also been reported from southern Zaïre (Lippens and Wille 1976).

HABITAT This species occurs in open *Brachystegia* woodland with scanty undergrowth, but it is absent from much apparently suitable habitat, suggesting a relict distribution (Benson *et al.* 1971). The birds are often seen in trees, but forage on the ground.

FOOD AND FEEDING Ground foraging is confirmed by the stomach contents, which included termites (Termitidae), beetles (Carabidae) and grit, weevils (Curculionidae), and unidentified insects (Benson and Irwin 1966).

BREEDING The nests are in holes in trees, up to 8 m above the ground, lined with a pad of lichens, moss and grass. Four birds were present at one nest, but only one was seen to feed the chicks. The eggs are described as white and smooth without gloss, speckled with reddish-brown and with blue-grey undermarkings (Mackworth-Praed and Grant 1963), but the source of this information is not known, and it may be incorrect. Incubation and nestling periods are unknown. White-winged Babbling Starlings were feeding chicks in Angola in September (Dean 1974). There are juvenile specimens from Zambia from February and April,

the February bird clearly the youngest. Chapin (1948) reported male birds with enlarged testes in October and December in Tanzania, and young on the wing in Angola in January, and in Tanzania in March. Four specimens from Tanzania in November are all labelled 'breeding condition'. Benson *et al.* (1971) recorded egg-laying in Zambia in October and November. It is possible that birds in Angola breed earlier, in spring, whereas the eastern population breeds in summer.

BEHAVIOUR White-winged Babbling Starlings were found in pairs or small groups of up to seven birds in Angola in August–October. When foraging birds were alarmed, some birds would fly into trees and call, and the whole flock would move on. Although groups were present at nests, cooperative breeding was not confirmed, and the birds roosted singly. Chapin (1948) had reports of flocks of 40–50 birds in Tanzania in October–November.

PRINCIPAL REFERENCE Dean and Vernon (1988).

113 RED-BILLED OXPECKER *Buphagus erythrorhynchus* Plate 32

Tanagra erythrorhyncha Stanley 1814

FIELD IDENTIFICATION 20 cm. From its association with grazing mammals, this bird is only likely to be confused with Yellow-billed Oxpecker, and both species may be found on the same hosts. In Red-billed Oxpecker the bill is narrower and wholly red. The lower mandible lacks the prominent yellow base of Yellow-billed Oxpecker, and the yellow wattle around the eye is conspicuous at close range. The dorsal surface is uniform brown, with no contrasting paler area. Young birds have a brown patch around the eye, which seems to be lacking in Yellow-billed Oxpecker.

DESCRIPTION The plumage is dark brown, paler ventrally from the chest to the undertail-coverts, but the thighs are dark brown. The wings and tail are dark brown, the feathers of the tail stiff and pointed. The red bill is laterally flattened and slightly bulbous. The iris is yellow to reddish, with a bright yellow ring of bare skin around the eye. The legs are black, the claws sharp and curved. The sexes are alike. Newly-fledged birds have yellow bills, which become brown at about two months, changing to red by the time the birds are seven months old. The iris begins to change colour at about four months, and is completely pigmented at six or seven months (Stutterheim *et al.* 1976).

There is some geographic variation in size and coloration, but this has not been analysed thoroughly. Three subspecies have been described in southern Africa, and Mundy (1997) noted that there are three centres of distribution within the region. We prefer to treat the species as monotypic for the present.

A study in the Kruger National Park, South Africa, showed that the moult cycle for the primaries was very regular, extending from September to the end of June. The primary feathers were replaced in the

normal descendant sequence, with usually only one feather growing at a time, and moult was generally symmetrical in both wings. The average growth period for a primary feather was 34 days, giving a total estimate of 340 days for complete wing feather replacement. Secondary moult showed two foci, with moult starting at both the innermost and outermost feathers and the two waves converging to meet at the fourth secondary. Moult of the secondary feathers was less symmetrical than that of the primaries, and extended over the period January to July. Moult of the tail feathers could start before primary moult, and was usually highly asymmetrical. Two cycles of body moult occurred, from September to October and from March to April. Juvenile birds underwent a partial moult at about three months, replacing the plumage except for the wing and tail feathers by May. A complete moult then followed in September or October of the same year. In adult Red-billed Oxpeckers it appeared that body moult occurred before and after breeding, while wing and tail moult could overlap with breeding (Stutterheim 1980c). Tanzanian birds showed wing moult in December (Friedmann and Loveridge 1937). Verheyen (1953) reported moult in birds from Zaïre from May and June, but suggested that there might be two complete moults a year. A more likely explanation is that the slow progress of the moult resulted in birds with active wing moult being taken at very different seasons.

MEASUREMENTS Male (10): wing 110–125, tail 91–102, bill 19.4–21.6, tarsus 20.2–21.8. Female (10): wing 113–118, tail 81–99, bill 19.2–21.0, tarsus 19.2–21.0. Weight of male (63) 45–56, of female (57) 42–59 g.

VOICE Chicks in the nest hissed loudly at any

strange object, while a soft *tji-tji* accompanied the gaping reaction. Calls similar to those of adults were heard on day 14. A young bird in adult plumage but with a dark eye, begged from adults calling *tit-tit-tit*, though it was no longer fed (van Someren 1951). Adults give a sharp, hissing *ksss, ksss*, and a staccato twittering chorus *tsik, tsik* in flight (Maclean 1993). Van Someren (1951) described the flight call as a *trik* with the alarm call *trik-quiss*, the second part a hissing rattle. In captive birds, Neweklowsky (1974) noted a trilling call given when a bird was threatened by a conspecific, and reported two song types, one consisting of a string of soft calls, interspersed with trills and whistles, while courtship song comprised drawn-out whistling notes. The members of a pair kept in constant vocal contact when out of sight.

DISTRIBUTION AND POPULATION Red-billed Oxpecker is found from the western Central African Republic, Sudan, Ethiopia and Somalia southwards in Uganda, Kenya, Tanzania, eastern and southern Zaïre, Angola, Zambia, Zimbabwe, Mozambique, northern Namibia, Botswana and northern and eastern South Africa. Over most of its range this species has suffered reductions in numbers, due to the elimination of large game and the dipping of cattle. However, it is still common over much of East Africa. Benson and Benson (1977) considered that oxpeckers might recolonise reserves in Malawi, but noted only rare sightings in the 1970s. Red-billed Oxpecker was much more common than Yellow-billed in Caprivi, although both were dependent on cattle as hosts (Stutterheim and Panagis 1985a). In Zimbabwe both species had disappeared from some areas, and Red-billed Oxpecker was reintroduced at both Lake McIlwaine National Park (Davison 1963) and in the Matopos (Grobler 1979). However, it has not become re-established in the Matobo National Park (Mundy 1993). Stutterheim showed that the distribution of the Red-billed Oxpecker in South Africa was restricted to areas within the ranges of its preferred tick prey species *Rhipicephalus appendiculatus*, and in general to regions with an annual rainfall of 500 mm or more. The decline of this bird and its subsequent restriction to game reserves was associated with the disappearance of wild game and the practice of dipping domestic stock, initially with arsenical dips. The southern limit of the birds was the eastern Cape Province, although there are no breeding records from this region. Red-billed Oxpeckers from the Kruger Park have now been reintroduced to the Eastern Cape, with the support of local stock farmers who are using dips which are not toxic to the birds (Craig and Weaver 1990). Favourable rains in the Kruger Park led to a local increase in oxpecker numbers, apparently as a result of increased host and tick numbers (Stutterheim and Stutterheim 1980). On the other hand an increase in dipping may have caused a decline in numbers in an unprotected area (Stutterheim and Stutterheim 1981a).

HABITAT AND HOST ANIMALS Red-billed Oxpeckers are found in open savanna country, to

3000 m, where large game or domestic stock are available as hosts. Trees are probably required for breeding and roosting, although other sites may be used. Attwell (1966) provided the first comprehensive survey of oxpecker hosts. In Zambia, he observed Red-billed Oxpeckers on buffalo *Syncerus caffer*, eland *Taurotragus oryx*, giraffe *Giraffa camelopardis*, hippopotamus *Hippopotamus amphibius*, impala *Aepyceros melampus*, greater kudu *Tragelaphus strepsiceros*, black rhino *Diceros bicornis*, white rhino *Ceratotherium simum*, warthog *Phacochoerus aethiopicus*, Burchell's zebra *Equus burchelli*, roan antelope *Hippotragus equinus* and sable antelope *H. niger*, while no oxpeckers were recorded on elephant *Loxodonta africana*, hartebeest *Alcephalus lichtensteini*, lechwe *Kobus leche*, puku *Kobus vardoni*, southern reedbuck *Redunca arundinum* and waterbuck *Kobus ellipsiprymnus*. However, there were single records from other observers of Red-billed Oxpeckers perching, but apparently not feeding, on hartebeest, puku, reedbuck, tsessebe *Damaliscus lunatus* and waterbuck. Attwell saw Red-billed and Yellow-billed Oxpeckers together on buffalo, eland, hippo, rhino and impala. Red-billed Oxpeckers in Natal game reserves were sighted most often on white and black rhinos, buffalo and giraffe, with occasional records on impala, nyala *Tragelaphus angasi*, zebra, kudu and blue wildebeest *Connochactes taurinus* (Stutterheim 1980b, Stutterheim and Stutterheim 1981b). Giraffe was the most common host in the Kruger Park, followed by sable antelope, kudu and buffalo, while wildebeest, warthog and impala were rarely used. Of mammals confined in pens, eland and roan antelope were favoured, with some records on white rhino and zebra (Grobler 1980). Stutterheim (1981a) recorded feeding on all these species in the park, and also had records for nyala, black rhino and hippopotamus. The main host animals in eastern Caprivi were cattle, with a few birds seen on goats (Stutterheim and Panagis 1985b), while in Moremi Game Reserve giraffe, impala, buffalo and kudu were the major hosts, with a few birds seen on zebra, wildebeest and warthog (Buskirk 1975, Stutterheim and Panagis 1985b). Red-billed Oxpeckers in Hwange National Park, Zimbabwe, were recorded chiefly on giraffe, kudu, sable and impala (Hustler 1987). Mundy (1993) listed the top ten hosts in southern Africa as: giraffe, kudu, eland, sable, white rhinoceros, zebra, buffalo, impala and black rhinoceros. He noted sightings of Red-billed Oxpeckers on waterbuck and bushbuck *Tragelaphus scriptus* as exceptional.

In Tanzania it appeared that rhinoceroses were the chief hosts, with giraffe and eland next favourites, although Moreau had only seen Red-billed Oxpeckers on greater kudu. They were never reported on elephants, nor on smaller antelope nor carnivores (Sclater and Moreau 1933). At Lake Nakuru and in the Masai Mara Reserve birds were seen on buffalo, giraffe, waterbuck, impala, zebra, blue wildebeest and warthog (Koenig 1997). Lack (1985) found that in Tsavo the birds favoured rhino, buffalo and giraffe, but he also noted them on warthog and some antelope species. Impala is one of the few smaller antelope species which are favoured hosts, and this may be related to heavier tick burdens on this species, as discussed by Hart *et al.* (1990). On impala, they found that the oxpeckers fed on the head and neck areas. They concluded that Red-billed Oxpeckers preferred larger host species, and that this was not solely related to body surface area. Koenig (1997) also concluded that the birds favoured the larger host species, and suggested that there was a preference for hosts with manes. In Ethiopia, Mengesha (1978) recorded oxpeckers on greater kudu and lesser kudu *Tragelaphus imberbis*, Burchell's zebra, Beisa oryx *Oryx gazella*, Sommering's gazelle *Gazella soemmerringi* and warthog, as well as cattle, horses, donkeys, mules, sheep and goats. Pitman (1956) stated that horses would not tolerate the attentions of oxpeckers, but van Someren (1951) received numerous reports of Red-billed Oxpeckers feeding on horses, in some cases at wounds. Even hosts in pens are attractive to oxpeckers, and they can be trapped readily at such sites (Stutterheim 1974). Several birds perched on an elephant in Zimbabwe (Dale and Hustler 1991), but such records are rare even in areas where elephant are abundant. Chapin (1954) wrote 'The elephant is reputed to have a very sensitive skin and will not tolerate these sharp-clawed birds'; he quoted an observer, who reported that oxpeckers never stayed long on elephants when they did land on them. However, Attwell (1966) noted that Piapiac *Ptilostomus afer* were regularly associated with elephants in West Africa, perching and clambering over them, and apparently removing ectoparasites. Reviewing the few records of oxpeckers perching on elephants, Mundy and Haynes (1996) concluded that in most cases the elephants concerned were in poor physical condition and severely stressed, so that they seemed indifferent to the presence of the birds. Some host animals deliberately reject oxpeckers which land on them. Phillips (1896) commented that his pack camels swung their necks, and tried to displace the oxpeckers as soon as they landed. Giraffes sometimes shook their heads or pranced, apparently to dislodge oxpeckers, while warthogs lay down on their sides (Ade 1981). Watkins and Cassidy (1987) saw waterbucks rub their bodies against shrubs and shake their horns when Red-billed Oxpeckers attempted to settle on them; Koenig (1997) reported that at Lake Nakuru, Kenya, oxpeckers were seen on sitting waterbucks much more often than on standing animals. In a study on impala, Hart *et al.* (1990) also observed that some individual antelopes rejected oxpeckers by head tossing.

FOOD AND FEEDING Four basic feeding methods have been described: scissoring, in which the bill is opened and closed rapidly while being pushed through the hair or over the host's body at any angle; plucking, which depends on visual searching, after which food items are grabbed in the tip of the bill and pulled off with a twist of the head; pecking, with the bill closed or slightly open, after which material is picked up and swallowed, or collected by scissoring; and insect-catching, either by hawking in the air, or by stalking and snatching insects on the host (Bezuidenhout and Stutterheim 1980). The frequency of the different feeding methods is apparently related both to the prey present, and to the body surface of the host. Scissoring is the most common way of removing ticks, especially on animals with long hair where prey is detected by touch, whereas plucking is most commonly used on bare skin. Mucus and blood are often collected by scissoring, which is employed on animals with large nostrils. Warthogs seemed to be used primarily as perches for insect-catching (Stutterheim 1981a). A captive Red-billed Oxpecker would scissor on the fingers and hand, and used this feeding method to collect blood from a cut (Goodwin 1963). The diet of Red-billed Oxpeckers is predominantly ixodid ticks, also biting flies (Muscidae), and tissue and mucus from the host animal. Moreau (1933) was the first to make a careful investigation of the diet of these birds, and he found that ticks of the genera *Rhipicephalus*, *Boophilus* and *Amblyomma* were the most common items in the stomach, with a few *Hyalomma* and *Ixodes*. Blood-sucking flies (Tabanidae) made up most of the stomach contents in some individuals, and lice (Anoplura) were also recorded. Van Someren (1951) recorded the same tick genera, and large numbers of flies, as well as some lice and a few mites (Mesostigmata). Bezuidenhout and Stutterheim (1980) examined the stomach contents of birds collected in the Kruger National Park, and found up to 1,665 ticks in one bird, with *Boophilus* and *Rhipicephalus* the most important genera eaten. Relatively few flies were found, and hardly any lice or mites were present.

Captive Red-billed Oxpeckers showed a preference for *Boophilus decoratus*, *Rhipicephalus appendiculatus* and *Hyalomma truncatum*, and reduced the numbers of these species on cattle quite significantly. Experimental exposure to ticks on dipped cattle indicated that most of the chemical dips used in the past were toxic to oxpeckers, although there was no clinical response to others over a 50-day period (Bezuidenhout and Stutterheim 1980). In another study of captive birds, engorged nymphs of *Amblyomma hebraeum* and adult *Boophilus decoloratus* were favoured, but male ticks and adult females that had not fed were avoided. Red-billed Oxpeckers would also take lice from cattle. The mean daily intake was estimated as the equivalent of 12,500 larvae or 98 engorged *B. decoloratus* ticks (Stutterheim *et al.* 1988). Hair and blood are always found in Red-billed Oxpecker stomachs, but it is unclear whether the blood is derived from partly-digested ticks, or from wounds. The birds certainly utilise available wounds and may enlarge existing injuries, but do not appear to break the skin themselves (Moreau 1933, Attwell 1966, Bezuidenhout and Stutterheim 1980). Goodwin (1963) allowed a bird to take blood from a cut on his hand, and found that all visible blood was soon removed, and the pressure of the bill encouraged the flow of blood, but that there was no damage to the skin. From careful observations, Van Someren (1951) concluded that the birds opened only old injuries on domestic stock, and he noted that the wounds were kept very clean, with no infected tissue or fly larvae, while the oxpeckers appeared to take only blood and tissue fluid, not fragments of flesh. This was supported by Neweklowsky (1974) from observation of zoo birds feeding at wounds on black and white rhino. However, Mengesha (1978) claimed that Red-billed Oxpeckers did initiate wounds on tick-free stock, and that they preferred to feed on animals with such wounds. Feeding on carrion has been reported by several authors, but is evidently rare (Moreau 1933, van Someren 1951, Attwell 1966). Stick insects (Phasmatidae), grasshoppers (Orthoptera) and a few other arthropods have been recorded (Moreau 1933, Bezuidenhout and Stutterheim 1980), and the birds would catch termite (Termitidae) alates (van Someren 1951, Bezuidenhout and Stutterheim 1980). It is likely that birds feeding on hippopotamuses would remove leeches (Glossiphoniidae), but these have not been found in the stomachs of any birds collected. Olivier and Laurie (1974) noted that both species of oxpecker took only blood and tissue when feeding on hippo. Vegetable matter and grit are probably ingested incidentally while feeding, and the second-hand report of Red-billed Oxpeckers eating fruit (Bolster 1935) is probably erroneous. Jackson and Sclater (1938) described what appeared to be caterpillars or grubs being taken to the chicks, but the stomach contents of chicks from the Kruger National Park included only ticks, flies, blood and hair (Bezuidenhout and Stutterheim 1980). Young from Ethiopia also had the stomachs crammed with ticks (Erlanger 1905).

BREEDING All 43 nests found in the Kruger Park were in natural holes in trees, 1–15 m above ground. The same nest may be used in subsequent years. Lining material was hair, primarily from impala, along with dung, grass and rootlets. All birds in the breeding group participated in the search for a nest site, and brought in nesting material. The eggs are creamy-white, heavily covered in fine speckles of red-brown and lilac, measuring 22.5–26.5 x 15.8–18.6 mm (47) (Maclean 1993), weight 4.1 g (Schönwetter 1983). The clutch size was 2–5, averaging 3. Incubation began with the first egg and lasted for 12–13 days; it appeared to be carried out by the principal male and female only. Once the chicks hatched, all members of the breeding group took part in feeding the chicks and removing faecal sacs. The mean nestling period was 30 days, and the young were still fed up until 90 days old, although by then they were already feeding themselves. Of the eggs laid, 49% hatched, and only 40% produced chicks which left the nest. Sclater and Moreau (1933) found a nest at ground level, in a crack in an outcrop of stone in the middle of an open field, and Vincent (1936) described a similar nest site in a cleft in a large boulder. Both van Someren (1922) and

Henderson (1953) reported Red-billed Oxpeckers nesting in the stone wall of cattle kraals, about 1.5 m above the ground. The incubation period was 11–12 days, and the birds left the nest after 28 days. Wool pulled off the back of a sheep was used for lining the nest (Cheesman and Sclater 1936). Captive Red-billed Oxpeckers lined the nest with hay, and with hairs pulled from the ears of rhinoceros which were sharing their enclosure. The male selected the site, but both birds spent seven to eight days building the nest. The clutch was of three eggs, 24 x 17 mm and weighing 3 g. The incubation period was 13 days and the nestling period 22–27 days (Kaiser-Benz 1975). A more detailed report on the same zoo birds indicated that a juvenile seldom brought building material, and did not enter the nest during incubation. Both male and female birds incubated the eggs and brooded the young during the first week. Young birds fed themselves 21 days after fledging, and were last fed by the adults at 36 days; thereafter begging often elicited aggressive responses (Benz 1974). Red-billed Oxpeckers breed from October to March in the Kruger Park, and may raise up to three broods in a season. Temperature did not appear to be a significant factor in the timing of breeding, but rainfall influenced tick numbers on the hosts and the numbers of blood-sucking flies (Tabanidae), so that breeding was closely correlated with the first rains. This is also likely to affect dispersal of the mammalian hosts, which move around less when water is readily available, and so may remain within range of birds foraging from a nest site. Breeding in Zimbabwe occurs in November and December (Irwin 1981), and in December and February in Zambia (Benson et al. 1971). Brown and Britton (1980) listed records for all months of the year from Kenya and Tanzania east of the Rift Valley, whereas the few records from the western sector were from March to July, with one in December. Archer found nests in June and September in Somalia (Archer and Godman 1961). Benson (1946) collected eggs in March in southern Ethiopia, and juvenile birds in June and August; Urban and Brown (1971) reported breeding in Ethiopia in January, March, April, July and August. Young birds were noted in Eritrea in February (Smith 1957), and in Somalia in March (Clarke 1985).

BEHAVIOUR Cooperative breeding occurs regularly in Red-billed Oxpeckers, and was first noted by Henderson (1953) who saw three birds at a nest. In captivity, both juveniles and other adults fed the young (Kaiser-Benz 1975). Stutterheim and Stutterheim (1981b) saw five adult and two immature birds at one nest. Stutterheim suggested that young birds stayed with the parents, and helped raise subsequent broods, but had no direct proof of this. He observed both courtship feeding and copulation on the backs of the ungulate hosts, whereas the wing vibration display and open-wing display occurred only at the nest. These displays were used at nest relief, when two birds encountered each other at the nest entrance, and on disturbance such as the approach of a potential predator. They are probably derived from intention movements of flight. Cheesman and Sclater (1936) also reported copulation on the host's back, and described the male waltzing around the female with drooping wings and open bill, giving excited chattering calls. Van Someren (1958) noted a hunched threat posture, and a 'penguin-like' attitude, adopted by birds alighting alongside others. He also saw the birds dust-bathing. From observations on birds in captivity, Neweklowsky (1974) concluded that the 'penguin' posture represented submissive behaviour, and was sometimes followed by an aggressive chase. Threats involved a 'head forward' posture with wide open bill, but no fights were seen. Members of a pair kept up a 'contact song' while out of sight of each other. Captive Red-billed Oxpeckers were observed sunbathing, dust-bathing, and bathing in water, both in a bowl and from the back of a hippopotamus. They usually moved by hopping, but when courting or stalking flies would move the feet alternately. Captive birds courted on their host's back, on the ground or on a wall (Benz 1974), while others, kept apart from mammalian symbionts, courted on the branches of a tree (Lücker 1994). Courtship was always initiated by the male with his body stretched out horizontally, tail depressed, wings drooped and quivering, and bill open, uttering whistling calls. The female was initially in an upright posture, then adopted the same posture as the male, who responded by spreading the wings out sideways, and the pair circled about, quivering their wings while the male gave the courtship song. The female solicited by raising her tail and standing still; the male then mounted with beating wings and the bill directed downwards (Benz 1974). Competition for nest holes does occur and in the Kruger National Park Red-billed Oxpeckers interacted with Burchell's Glossy Starlings, Cape Glossy Starlings and Southern Grey-headed Sparrows *Passer diffusus*, all of which could displace them from holes during the searching phase. The oxpeckers appeared to defend only the nest hole, and no evidence of territoriality was observed. Once the hole was occupied, they usually defended it successfully against other species, but one nest under construction was usurped by a Burchell's Glossy Starling, and a Striped Kingfisher *Halcyon chelicuti* took over a nest containing eggs. In captive birds, one pair aggressively defended the nest area against conspecifics, whereas another pair in the same enclosure showed no evidence of territorial behaviour (Benz 1974). Birds perched on hosts sometimes squatted down with one wing open (Sclater and Moreau 1933, van Someren 1958), which probably represents sunbathing rather than maximising contact with the host's skin. Oxpeckers clamber up and down the host, propped up by the tail rather like woodpeckers (Picidae); when disturbed, they commonly move to the far side of the animal, and are reluctant to leave it. They may even return to the bodies of animals which have been shot. Early travellers noted that game, in particular rhinos, responded to the alarm calls of the birds, which thus served as an early warning system for their hosts. Van Someren (1951, 1958) remarked that

Red-billed Oxpeckers often favoured a particular animal in a herd, despite the close proximity of other tick-ridden animals. When defecating, the birds raised their tails and shot the excrement well clear of the host. A captive bird would greet its keeper, holding its body very upright with the head and neck sleeked and swayed slightly from side to side, while the feathers of the belly and rump were erected (Goodwin 1963).

Resightings of marked birds suggest a home range of about 27 km^2, with only one bird sighted as much as 8 km from the trapping site (Stutterheim 1981b). While breeding, colour-marked birds were seen within 7 km^2 of the nest. Flocks of Red-billed Oxpeckers in Kenya roosted in crevices in trees, cliffs or stone walls (van Someren 1956), while Red-billed Oxpeckers in Moremi Game Reserve, Botswana, roosted in tall palms *Hyphaene benguellensis*, and were never seen perched on mammals (Stutterheim and Panagis 1985b). In Gorongosa National Park, Mozambique, a group of birds also roosted in a palm tree, and at Lake Ngami, Botswana, each party of oxpeckers roosted separately in an *Acacia* tree (R.K. Brooke pers. comm.). Both van Someren (1951) and Pitman (1956) also reported that the birds roosted in trees, and would wait outside kraals until the cattle emerged in the morning. Dowsett (1968) reported one instance of this species roosting on buffalo at night in Zambia, but this is evidently exceptional, or perhaps the birds involved were misidentified. Captive birds left their rhino hosts at dusk, and roosted in bushes in the enclosure (Neweklowsky 1974). In Uganda, Red-billed Oxpeckers were seen in flocks with Wattled Starlings (van Someren 1916). A Gabar Goshawk *Micronisus gabar* stooped at oxpeckers on a giraffe in Zimbabwe; the birds responded by moving to the other side of the host. A group of oxpeckers mobbed the hawk when it pursued an individual bird (Ade 1981).

ECTOPARASITES Two tick species, *Amblyomma hebraeum* and *Boophilus decoloratus* which are eaten by adult Red-billed Oxpeckers, have been found on the nestlings, and both are occasionally found attached to adult birds. The feather mite *Pterodectes buphagi* is present on most adults, and the feather louse *Sturnidoecus* sp. is also common, but hippoboscid flies were very seldom recorded (Stutterheim 1977).

RELATIONS WITH MAN As far as domestic stock are concerned, the activities of oxpeckers have not always met with approval: 'they have, on the one hand, been credited with performing services of the utmost value in cleaning cattle of ticks, and they have been heartily damned for making, and keeping open, wounds and carrying disease from one beast to another. In general the natives with whom I have discussed the 'Shash' are in favour of the birds; while the European stock-owners would gladly see their extermination, as, indeed, follows upon extensive cattle-dipping' (Sclater and Moreau 1933, p 209). Cheesman and Sclater (1936) reported that they would keep the saddle-galls of pack mules open, pecking at the wounds and drinking the blood.

Jackson and Sclater (1938) blamed them for heavy losses of pack donkeys, whose sores were aggravated to the point where the animals were useless. The explorer Baker stated that he employed boys to chase these pests away from his pack animals (cited in Shelley 1906). Van Someren (1951) paid particular attention to complaints about wound-feeding, but concluded that healthy animals were seldom attacked, and that the birds could easily be kept away from a wound by coating it with thick grease or Stockholm tar, after which it would soon heal. However, Mengesha (1978) reviewed the relations of Red-billed Oxpeckers with stock in Ethiopia, and concluded that they were harmful to stock rather than beneficial.

PRINCIPAL REFERENCES Stutterheim (1982a–c).

114 YELLOW-BILLED OXPECKER *Buphagus africanus* Plate 32

Buphagus africanus Linnaeus 1766

FIELD IDENTIFICATION 20 cm. Oxpeckers are normally encountered clinging to the bodies of cattle or large wild herbivorous mammals. Yellow-billed Oxpeckers are grey-brown overall, but in flight the pale lower back and rump is the best character for separating this species from Red-billed Oxpecker. The bill of Yellow-billed Oxpecker is red towards the tip and yellow at the base. At close range the eye is red, but lacks a coloured wattle. In young birds, both bill and eye are dark brown but the pale rump is evident in birds of all ages (Stutterheim *et al.* 1976).

DESCRIPTION The plumage is dark brown, paler below from the upper chest to the undertail-coverts, but creamy-fawn on the rump and upper-tail-coverts. The wings and tail are dark brown. The central rectrices are the longest, all the feathers are stiff and very pointed. The bill is heavy, laterally flattened, bulbous near the tip, and with a very broad base to the lower mandible, which is yellow whereas the tip is red. The iris is red, the legs black, with notably sharp and curved claws. The sexes are alike in plumage. Just after fledging, birds have yellow bills and a narrow yellow ring around the eye. These features are brown in older immature birds, which are also darker in plumage than adults. The age at which bill and iris change colour is not known. Dowsett (1965) collected a newly-fledged young bird, with a pale yellow bill, fading to lemon-coloured at the gape, and a uniform dark iris. The dorsal plumage was finely barred black, the rump buffy and the ventral parts more orange than those of the adult.

Birds from the southern Congo basin are smaller and darker with a grey rump, and are generally treated as a distinct subspecies **B. africanus langi**. The differences in coloration and bill size on which *B. a. megarhynchus* was based have not been confirmed by other workers, and this race is not recognised. Southern birds are larger, but such variation does not warrant recognising *B. a. haematophagus*.

There are no field data on moult; of 50 museum specimens from all months, 21 showed wing moult. All birds from February, March and April were in moult. One specimen from April had interrupted wing moult but active tail moult, while another from August had interrupted wing moult with active head and body moult. This suggests a slow moult, extending over much of the year, as found in Red-billed Oxpecker.

MEASUREMENTS Male (10): wing 115–127, tail 90–107, bill 19.3–22, tarsus 21.6–24.1. Female (10): wing 118–123, tail 92–101, bill 18.4–21.6, tarsus 20.5–22.8. Weight of male (2) 57–60, of female (5) 53–71 g.

VOICE A hissing, cackling *kriss, kriss* is the main call (Maclean 1993), also a reedy rattling (Zimmerman *et al.* 1996).

DISTRIBUTION AND POPULATION The original range of the Yellow-billed Oxpecker extended from Senegal to Sudan, southwards in Uganda, Kenya, Tanzania and eastern Zaïre to Zambia, Angola, Namibia, Botswana, Zimbabwe and northeastern South Africa. Where both oxpecker species occur in southern and eastern Africa, the Yellow-billed Oxpecker seems to be less common and is much more abundant from western Uganda westwards. Throughout its range it is dependent on the availability of hosts. Although Belcher (1930) reported this species as quite numerous on cattle in some areas, Benson and Benson (1977) had no records over the previous 20 years, and it is still very rare in Malawi. Priest (1936) recorded some sightings in Zimbabwe from correspondents, but did not encounter the birds himself. Irwin (1981) assumed that Yellow-billed Oxpecker had been more widespread formerly, but stated that it was now limited to protected areas with large ungulate populations, notably Hwange National Park. In the Caprivi area, Yellow-billed Oxpeckers appeared to be uncommon and nomadic (Stutterheim and Panagis 1985a). In Zimbabwe they were re-introduced to McIlwaine National Park (Davison 1963) and to the Matobo National Park (Grobler 1979). Woodward and Woodward (1899) noted that this was a rare species in Natal, and by about 1915 Yellow-billed Oxpecker was extinct in South Africa, except for a few records of vagrants (Stutterheim and Brooke 1981). The decisive factors in its decline seem to have been the destruction of buffalo and rhino populations, followed by the 1896 rinderpest epidemic which decimated both cattle and buffalo *Syncerus caffer*, and the subsequent introduction of toxic dips for domestic stock. However, from 1979 the birds began to reappear in the northern sector of the Kruger

National Park, and by 1985 breeding had been recorded. Many buffalo herds had Yellow-billed Oxpeckers on them, as revealed by aerial censuses of the large mammals (Hall-Martin 1987, Whyte *et al.* 1987). It is assumed that these birds originated from southeastern Zimbabwe, and may have moved south following cessation of cattle dipping in rural areas during the war in Zimbabwe. Yellow-billed Oxpeckers have now also been successfully reintroduced to several game reserves in Natal, where breeding has since been reported (Lockwood 1986, 1988, Stutterheim and Panagis 1988). Elgood (1982) noted that in Nigeria, Yellow-billed Oxpecker numbers had diminished drastically in areas where cattle were dipped regularly, and in Ghana the only records came from Mole National Park, where the birds were uncommon (Grimes 1987). Its status was noted as rare in Ivory Coast (Thiollay 1985), but common in the Gambia and northern Senegal (Morel and Morel 1990).

HABITAT AND HOST ANIMALS Occurs in open savanna, wherever potential host animals are available, but it is more localised than Red-billed Oxpecker. Schifter (1986) noted that in northern Senegal since the extermination of large game, Yellow-billed Oxpeckers were seen exclusively on domestic stock such as donkeys. In Mali, the birds were noted on cattle, buffalo, hartebeest *Alcephalus lichtensteini*, tsessebe *Damaliscus lunatus*, roan antelope *Hippotragus equinus*, giraffe *Giraffa camelopardis* and eland *Taurotragus oryx* (Lamarche 1981). Cattle and donkeys are the main hosts in Nigeria (Elgood 1982), while both game and cattle were utilised in Cameroon (Louette 1981). Buffalo were the primary hosts in Gabon, while a bushbuck *Tragelaphus scriptus* ran off head-tossing on the approach of a flock of oxpeckers (Maclatchy 1937). Donkeys and cattle were utilised in Angola, while in National Parks the birds were feeding on buffalo and roan antelope (Günther and Feiler 1986, Dean *et al.* 1987). Chapin (1954) reported buffalo, hippo, eland and zebra *Equus* sp. as regular hosts in Zaïre. In the Masai Mara Reserve, Kenya, Koenig (1997) saw Yellow-billed Oxpeckers on buffalo, giraffe, impala *Aepyceros melampus* and zebra. In Zambia, Attwell (1966) observed Yellow-billed Oxpeckers on buffalo, eland, giraffe, hippo *Hippopotamus amphibius*, impala, greater kudu *Tragelaphus strepsicaros*, black *Diceros bicornis* and white rhinos *Ceratotherium simum*, roan antelope, sable antelope *Hippotragus niger*, warthog *Phacochoerus aethiopicus*, blue wildebeest *Connochaetes taurinus* and zebra, sometimes on the same animal as Red-billed Oxpeckers. There were single records from other observers of birds on lechwe *Kobus leche* and sitatunga *Tragelaphus spekei*. In Botswana and eastern Caprivi, the only hosts recorded were cattle, buffalo and giraffe (Buskirk 1975, Stutterheim and Panagis 1985b). The birds showed a preference for buffalo and white rhino in Zimbabwe, with giraffe, zebra and eland used quite often, sable antelope regularly, and impala, kudu and warthog very rarely (Grobler and Charsley 1978). Giraffe accepted newly-released Yellow-billed Oxpeckers in McIlwaine National Park, whereas both zebra and eland rejected them (Davison 1963). In Hwange National Park, Zimbabwe, their primary hosts were buffalo, and only Yellow-billed Oxpeckers were recorded on black and white rhinos (Hustler 1987). Buffalo appear to be the primary host in the Kruger National Park (Whyte *et al.* 1987), but Yellow-billed Oxpeckers reintroduced to the Matobo National Park have survived despite the culling of all the buffalo (Mundy 1993); later studies showed that they favoured large-bodied hosts, but when using smaller animals such as impala concentrated on herds and avoided solitary individuals (Mooring and Mundy 1996a). Some birds were seen to perch on elephant *Loxodonta africana* in Zimbabwe (Dale and Hustler 1991, Mundy and Haynes 1996), and Yellow-billed Oxpeckers were seen alongside Red-billed Oxpeckers on kudu (Campbell 1989). Mundy (1993) listed the top ten hosts of this species in southern Africa as: buffalo, white rhinoceros, eland, giraffe, kudu, zebra, black rhinoceros, roan antelope and hippopotamus.

FOOD AND FEEDING The distinctive bill shape of the Yellow-billed Oxpecker has led some authors to suggest that it feeds in a different way to the Red-billed Oxpecker (e.g. Irwin 1981). However, observations on captive birds showed that both species used the same feeding methods, namely scissoring, plucking, pecking, and insect catching. Yellow-billed Oxpeckers spent less time away from the host animal, and made more use of plucking and wound-feeding. When offered a selection of tick species in different stages of engorgement, they showed a high preference for *Boophilus decoloratus* and *Rhipicephalus simus* adult ticks. Generally, engorged females were taken before males or unfed females. The oxpeckers also removed lice *Damalina bovis* from cattle, and under experimental conditions were able to clean heavily infested animals completely over a period of weeks. Engorged ticks measuring 8 x 12 mm were the largest items the birds could swallow whole; if larger ticks were offered, the birds would puncture the integument, consume the contents of the body, and then remove and eat the empty shell of the tick. The daily food intake was estimated at 13,600 larvae or 109 engorged female *Boophilus decoloratus* ticks (Stutterheim *et al.* 1988). A study of the relationship between Yellow-billed Oxpeckers and impala in Zimbabwe showed that the birds favoured those parts of the body where ticks were most abundant, and most of the hosts tolerated their activities. Tolerant impala reduced their own grooming activities by up to 36%, indicating the benefit gained from the attendant oxpeckers (Mooring and Mundy 1996b). Woodward and Woodward (1899) observed Yellow-billed Oxpeckers wound-feeding on cattle, and resorted to shooting the birds. A bird shot near domestic pigs in West Africa had only fleas *Haematopius suis* in its stomach (Germain *et al.* 1973). The stomach contents of a nestling included a good deal of hair, apparently from buffalo, a seed, and insect fragments, but no ticks (Dowsett 1965). On hippo, Yellow-billed Oxpeckers fed entirely on blood and tissues from wounds (Olivier and Laurie 1974).

BREEDING Nests are in tree holes, 2–7 m above ground, lined with hair plucked from host animals. A nest in Zimbabwe had a base of dry grass, with a thick pad of hair and soft grass with a few feathers (Vincent 1949). Chapin (1954) quoted reports from Zaïre of Yellow-billed Oxpeckers nesting in the tower of a church alongside Rock Pigeons *Columba guinea*, and under the sheet-iron roof of a mission building. The eggs are white with reddish-brown speckling, 26 x 18 mm, weight 4.5 g. The incubation period is 13 days, the nestling period about 25 days (Mundy and Cook 1975). Clutch size is 2–3 eggs. Schönwetter (1983) gives the egg measurements as 22.8–26.6 x 15.9–18.3 mm (12), weight 3.9 g. In Senegambia breeding occurs from June to September (Morel and Morel 1982, Gore 1990), and from April to August in Nigeria (Shuel 1938, Elgood 1982). Breeding in Sudan occurs in May (Nikolaus 1987). For East Africa there is no clear pattern, with records from December to June, and in October (Brown and Britton 1980). In Rwanda, birds were breeding from March to April, in Zambia in December (Benson *et al.* 1971), and from September to March in Zimbabwe and Botswana (Irwin 1981, Mundy 1997). Dark-billed juvenile specimens were collected in April, May and September in East Africa, while there were others from November-January and May–June in which the bill was changing colour. This species has also been bred successfully in captivity (Lockwood 1988).

BEHAVIOUR Yellow-billed Oxpeckers in Nigeria were found roosting in trees, often in the company of other starlings such as Long-tailed, Greater Blue-eared and Lesser Blue-eared Glossy Starlings (Mundy and Cook 1975). In southern Africa they were found roosting on giraffe or cattle at night by Stutterheim and Panagis (1985b), who also cited records of birds roosting on kudu and roan antelope. In Zambia, Dowsett (1968) found the birds on buffalo at night, and summarised similar reports from other areas. Kudu and sable antelope were used by roosting birds in Zimbabwe (Thomson 1982). Near a nest hole, a bird was seen quivering its wings while perched on a tree trunk (Smith 1964); a similar display has been reported for Red-billed Oxpecker (see above). Dowsett (1965) reported that a group of four adults was feeding nestlings, and cooperative breeding is evidently regular in this species as in Red-billed Oxpecker. Mundy and Cook (1975) saw three adults at a nest with chicks. Under captive conditions Yellow-billed Oxpeckers always dominated Red-billed Oxpeckers in aggressive encounters, and were apparently able to exclude the other species from preferred roosting and feeding sites (Stutterheim *et al.* 1988). In a captive immature bird, Chapin (1954) noticed that the eye colour was sometimes scarlet, sometimes orange, as though the colour varied with the blood supply. Another captive bird would adopt a horizontal posture when approached, fluttering its wings, and on occasion would show the same response to its own reflection (Goodwin 1963).

BIBLIOGRAPHY

Abdulali, H (1947) The movement of the Rosy Pastor in India [*Pastor roseus* (L.)]. *J. Bombay Nat. Hist. Soc.* 46: 704–708.

—, (1967) The birds of the Nicobar Islands, with notes on some Andaman birds. *J. Bombay Nat. Hist. Soc.* 64: 139–190.

Adamson, B (1953) Notes on the Green Glossy Starling (*Lamprocolius chalybeus*). *Avicult. Mag.* 59: 46–53.

Ade, B (1981) Wankie observations. *Bokmakierie* 33: 15–19.

Adret-Hausberger, M and Jenkins, PF (1988) Complex organisation of the warbling song of Starlings. *Behaviour* 107: 138–156.

AICRP (1992) *Research highlights of AICRP on Agricultural Ornithology.* Andhra Pradesh Agricultural University, Hyderabad.

Akhmedov, KP (1957) The mynah, its agricultural importance in Tadjikistan and methods of encouraging artificial nesting. *Uchen'iye Zap. Stalinabad Zh. pedagog. Inst.* 1: 101–113 [In Russian].

Akhtar, SA (1990) Altitudinal range extension of the Brahminy Myna *Sturnus pagodarum* in Chushul, Ladakh. *J. Bombay Nat. Hist. Soc.* 87: 147.

Al-Dabbagh, KY, Mohammed, SM and Jiad, JH (1992) First breeding records of Palm Dove *Streptopelia senegalensis* and Starling *Sturnus vulgaris* in Iraq. *Sandgrouse* 14: 53–54.

Ali, S (1963) On the alleged inferiority of the Southern Grackle (*Gracula religiosa indica*) as a talking bird. *J. Bombay Nat. Hist. Soc.* 60: 455–456.

— and Ripley, S D (1972) *Handbook of the birds of India and Pakistan,* Vol. 5. Oxford University Press, Oxford.

Allen, PM (1974) Lecture – 9th September 1974. *E. Afr. Nat. Hist. Soc. Bull.* October: 138.

Allport, GA, Ausden, H, Hayman, PV, Robertson, P and Wood, P (1989) The conservation of the birds of Gola Forest, Sierra Leone. ICBP Study Report No. 38. ICBP, Cambridge.

Altenburg, W and von Spanje, T (1989) Utilization of mangroves by birds in Guinea-Bissau. *Ardea* 77: 57–74.

Amadon, D (1943) The genera of starlings and their relationships. *Am. Mus. Novit.* 1247: 1–16.

— (1953) Avian systematics and evolution in the Gulf of Guinea. *Bull. Am. Mus. Nat. Hist.* 100: 393–452.

— (1956) Remarks on the starlings, family Sturnidae. *Amer. Mus. Novit.* 1803: 1–41.

— (1962) Family Sturnidae, in *Check-list of birds of the world.* Vol. XV. Museum of Comparative Zoology, Cambridge, Mass.

Amsler, M (1935) The breeding of the Amethyst Starling. *Avicult. Mag.* 13: 295–300.

Andersson, CJ and Gurney, JH (1872) *Notes on the birds of Damara Land and the adjacent countries of South-west Africa.* John van Voorst, London.

Andrews, IJ (1995) *The birds of the Hashemite Kingdom of Jordan.* Andrews, Musselborough.

Anon (1988) Unusual bird sightings. *Bird Observations* 674: 38–39.

Anon (1992a) Photographic debut for a Pacific starling. *National Geographic* June 1992.

Anon (1992b) Bali starling increase. *Wingspan* December 1992: 8.

Anon (1996) Hercules C130: the emergency services were badly informed. *Le Monde* 8 October 1996.

Anon (1998) Bali Starling. *World Birdwatch* 20: 4

AOU. (1983) *Check-list of North American Birds.* 6th Edition. American Ornithologists' Union, Lawrence, Kansas.

Ara, J (1953) The mating habits of the House-crow (*Corvus splendens*) and Pied Myna (*Sturnus contra*). *J. Bombay Nat. Hist. Soc.* 50: 940–941.

Archawaranon, M (1994) Reproductive strategies of the Hill Myna in Thailand. *J. Orn.* 135: 3.

Archer, G and Godman, EM (1961) *The birds of British Somaliland and the Gulf of Aden.* Vol. IV. Oliver and Boyd, London.

Ash, JS (1984) Bird observations on Bali. *Bull. Br. Orn. Club* 104: 24–35.

Ash, JS and Miskell, JE (1983) Birds of Somalia: their habitat, status and distribution. *Scopus Suppl.* 1: 1–97.

Ashworth, D and Parkin, DT (1992) Captive breeding: can genetic fingerprinting help? *Symp. Zool. Soc. Lond.* 64: 135–149.

Aspinwall, DR (1978) Movement Analysis Charts. Comments on Lesser Blue-eared Starling. *Zambian Orn. Soc. Newsl.* 8(6): 67.

— (1981) Movement Analysis Charts. Comments on Amethyst Starling. *Zambian Orn. Soc. Newsl.* 11(9): 115–117.

— (1986) Movement Analysis Charts. Comments on Wattled Starling. *Zambian Orn. Soc. Newsl.* 16(1): 4–7.

Atkinson, RJC (1956) *Stonehenge.* Hamish Hamilton, London.

Attwell, RIG (1966) Oxpeckers, and their associations with mammals in Zambia. *Puku* 4: 17–48.

Bährmann, U (1964) Über die Mauser des europäischen Stars (*Sturnus vulgaris* L.). *Zool. Abhand. (Dresden)* 27: 1–9.

Baker, ECS (1926) *The fauna of British India,* Vol. 3. Taylor and Francis, London.

Baker, NE and Howell, KM (1994) Unusual movements of Afrotropical birds in the Dar es Salaam area. *Proc. VII Pan-Afr. Orn. Congr.*: 163–168.

Baker, RH (1951) The avifauna of Micronesia, its origin, evolution and distribution. *Univ. Kansas Publ., Mus. Nat. Hist.* 3: 1–359.

Bangs, O and Loveridge, A (1933) Reports on the scientific results of an expedition to the southwestern highlands of Tanganyika Territory. III Birds. *Bull. Mus. Comp. Zool.* 75: 143–221.

Bannerman, DA (1932) Account of the birds collected (i) by Mr G.L. Bates on behalf of the British Museum in Sierra Leone and French Guinea; (ii) by Lt.-Col. G.J. Houghton, RAMC, in Sierra Leone, recently acquired by the British Museum. Part II. *Ibis* 13th ser. 2: 217–261.

— (1948) *The birds of tropical West Africa.* Vol. VI. Oliver and Boyd, Edinburgh and London.

Baranga, J and Kalina, J (1991) Nesting association between Narrow-tailed Starlings *Poeoptera lugubris* and Grey-throated Barbets *Gymnobucco bonapartei.* *Scopus* 15: 59–61.

Barber, ME (1880) Locusts and locust birds. *Trans. S. Afr. Phil. Soc.* 1(3): 193–218.

Bartmann, W (1974) Eine Volierenbrut des Dreifarbenglanzstars (*Lamprespreo superbus*). *Gefied. Welt* 98: 21–22.

Basilio, A (1963) *Aves de la isla de Fernando Po.* Coculsa, Madrid.

Bates, GL (1909) Field notes on the birds of southern Kamerun, West Africa. *Ibis* 9th ser. 3: 1–74.

— (1926) [Mr GL Bates described a new genus of starling from N.W. Cameroon]. *Bull. Br. Orn. Club* 46: 104–105.
— (1927) Notes on some birds of Cameroon and the Lake Chad region: their status and breeding times. *Ibis* 12th ser. 3: 1–64.
— (1934) Birds of the southern Sahara and adjoining countries in French West Africa. Part V. *Ibis* 13th ser. 4: 685–717.
Bayliss-Smith, TP (1972) The birds of Ontong Java and Sikaiana, Solomon Islands. *Bull. Br. Orn. Club* 92: 1–10.
Beasley, A (1978) Red-winged starling preying on lizard. *Honeyguide* 95: 44.
— (1991) Red-winged starlings: unusual nests, and preying on crabs. *Honeyguide* 37: 17–18.
Becker, P (1980) Der Amethystglanzstar (*Cinnyricinclus leucogaster*) als Brutvogel in Südwestafrika. *Mitt. Ornithol. Arbeitsgr. S.W.A. wiss. Ges.* 16(1–2): 1–2.
Beecher, WJ (1978) Feeding adaptations and evolution in the starlings. *Bull. Chicago Acad. Sci.* 11: 269–298.
— (1985) In quest of starlings. *Bull. Field Mus. Nat. Hist.* September: 16–21.
Beehler, BM and Bino, R (1995) Yellow-eyed Starling *Aplonis mystacea* in Central Province, Papua New Guinea. *Emu* 95: 68–70.
— Pratt, TK and Zimmerman DA (1986) *Birds of New Guinea.* Princeton University Press, Princeton.
Beesley, JSS (1972) A breeding record of Sharpe's Starling *Cinnyricinclus sharpii* in the Arusha National Park. *E. Afr. Nat. Hist. Soc. Bull.* January: 12–13.
Belcher, DF (1930) *The birds of Nyasaland.* Technical Press, London.
Bell, HL (1972) Notes on the Yellow-faced Myna. *Emu* 72: 110.
— (1975) Avifauna of the Ninigo and Hermit Islands, New Guinea. *Emu* 75: 77–84.
— (1982) A bird community of New Guinean lowland rainforest. 3 Vertical distribution of the avifauna. *Emu* 82:143–162.
— (1984) New or confirmatory information on some species of New Guinean birds. *Australian Bird Watcher* 10: 209–228.
— (1986) Occupation of urban habitats by birds in Papua New Guinea. *Western Found. Vert. Zool.* 3: 1–48.
Bell, K (1984) Breeding the Golden-breasted Starling *Cosmopsarus regius*. *Avicult. Mag.* 90: 34–35.
Bellingham, M and Davis, A (1988) Forest bird communities in Western Samoa. *Notornis* 35: 117–128.
Bennun, L, Frere, P and Squelch, P (1990) Blue-eared Glossy Starlings *Lamprotornis chalybaeus* and Wattled Starlings *Creatophora cinerea* associating with livestock. *Scopus* 14: 29–30.
Benson, CW (1946) Notes on the birds of southern Abyssinia. *Ibis* 88: 444–461.
— (1953) Breeding of *Lamprotornis mevesii mevesii* (Wahlberg). *Ostrich* 24: 121.
— (1959) Some additions and corrections to a 'Check list of the birds of Northern Rhodesia'. *Occ. Pap. Nat. Mus. Sth. Rhod.* 23B(2): 257–285.
— (1960) Some additions and corrections to a 'Check list of the birds of Northern Rhodesia'. *Occ. Pap. Nat. Mus. Sth. Rhod.* 24B(3): 343–350.
— (1962) Some additions and corrections to a 'Check list of the birds of Northern Rhodesia'. *Occ. Pap. Nat. Mus. Sth. Rhod.* 26B(4): 631–652.
— (1982) Migrants in the Afrotropical Region south of the equator. *Ostrich* 53: 31–49.
—, and Benson, FM (1977) *The birds of Malawi.* Montfort Press, Limbe.
—, Brooke, RK, Dowsett, RJ, and Irwin, MPS (1971) *The birds of Zambia.* Collins, London.
—, Colebrook-Robjent, JFR and Williams, A (1977) Contribution à l'ornithologie de Madagascar. *Oiseau Rev. fr. Orn.* 47: 167–191.
—, and Irwin, MPS (1966) The *Brachystegia* avifauna. *Ostrich Suppl.* 6: 297–321.
Bentz, P-G (1987) Sjeldne fugler i Norge i 1985. *Var Fuglefauna* 10: 91–95.
Benz, M (1974) Beiträge zur Fortpflanzungsbiologie des Rotschnabelmadenhackers, *Buphagus erythrorhynchus* (Stanley). *Zool. Garten* 44: 144–167.
Bernis, F (1960) Migración, problema agrícola y captura del Estornino Pinto (*Sturnus vulgaris*). *Ardeola* 6: 11–100.
Berry, PSM (1976) Some further Luangwa Valley observations. *Bull. Zambian Orn. Soc.* 8(2): 41–44.
Bertram, B (1968) Hill Mynas breeding in artificial nests in the Garo Hills District of Assam, India. *Avicult. Mag.* 74: 181–181.
— (1969) Hill Mynas and the trade in them from India. *Avicult. Mag.* 75: 253–255.
— (1970) The vocal behaviour of the Indian Hill Myna, *Gracula religiosa*. *Anim. Behav. Monogr.* 3 (2): 79–192.
— (1976) The voice of the Indian Hill Myna (*Gracula religiosa*) in the wild. *J. Bombay Nat. Hist. Soc.* 71: 405–413.
Bezuidenhout, JD and Stutterheim, CJ (1980) A critical evaluation of the role played by the red-billed oxpecker *Buphagus erythrorhynchus* in the biological control of ticks. *Onderstepoort J. Vet. Res.* 47: 51–75.
Bigger, WK (1931) Migrations of *Cinnyris* and *Onychognathus* in Palestine. *Ibis* 13th ser. 1: 584–585.
Blaber, SJM (1990) A checklist and notes on the current status of the birds of New Georgia, Western Province, Solomon Islands. *Emu* 90: 205–214.
Blaker, M, Davies, SJJF and Reilly, PN (1984) *The atlas of Australian birds.* Melbourne University Press, Melbourne.
Blancou, L (1974) *Grafisia torquata* en Afrique central. *Oiseau Rev. fr. Orn.* 44: 90.
Blanford, WT (1870) *Observations on the geology and zoology of Abyssinia.* MacMillan & Co., London.
Bocage, JVB du (1871) Aves das posseões portuguegas da Africa occidental. *J. Sci. Math. Phys. nat.* 3: 266–277.
Boetticher, H von (1931a) Beiträge zur Systematik der Vögel II. Die verwandtschaftlich-systematische Stellung der Webervögel (Ploceidae) zu den Finkenvögeln (Fringillidae) und Staren (Sturnidae). *Senckenbergiana* 13: 147–153.
— (1931b) Ist *Heteropsar acuticaudus* (Boc.) eine Rasse von *Lamprocolius chloropterus* (Swains.)? *Anz. Ornith. Ges. Bayern* 2(3): 138–140.
— (1940) Die Glanzstare Afrikas. *Anz. Ornith. Ges. Bayern* 3(3): 86–91.
— (1951) Gattungen und Untergattungen der afrikanischen Glanzstare, sowie anderer Starvögel (Sturnidae). *Zool. Anz.* 147: 195–200.
Bohner, J, Chaiken, ML, Ball, GF and Marler, P (1990) Song acquisition in photosensitive and photorefractory male European starlings. *Hormones Behav.* 24: 582–594.
Bolster, RC (1935) Abnormal diet of the Red-billed Oxpecker and Bronze-tailed Glossy Starling. *Ostrich* 6: 50–51.
Bonaparte, C-L (1854) Notes sur les collections rapportées en 1853, par M.A. Delattre, de son voyage en Californie et dans le Nicaragua. *Compt. Rend. Hebd. Séances Acad. Sci.* 38: 378–389.
Boosey, EJ (1959) Four glossy starlings. *Game bird breeders', pheasant fanciers' and aviculturalists' gazette* 8(2): 62–64.

Borret, RP (1971) The Amethyst Starling in winter in Rhodesia. *Ostrich* 42: 81–82.
— (1973) Notes on the food of some Rhodesian birds. *Ostrich* 44: 145–148.
Botz, K (1991) Zuchterfolg beim Amethystglanzstar *Cinnyricinclus leucogaster*. *Trochilus* 12: 70–71.
Bourlière, F (1953) Sur le comportement de *Gracupica nigricollis*. *Oiseau Rev. fr. Orn.* 23: 261–264.
Bowen, WW (1931a) East African birds collected during the Gray African Expedition – 1929. *Proc. Acad. Nat. Sci. Philad.* 83: 11–79.
— (1931b) Angolan birds collected during the Gray African Expedition – 1929. *Proc. Acad. Nat. Sci. Philad.* 83: 263–299.
Bradley, D and Wolff, T (1956) *Birds of Rennell Island.* Danish Science Press, Copenhagen.
Brandt, JH (1962) Nests and eggs of the birds of the Truk Islands. *Condor* 64: 416–437.
Brazil, MA (1990) *The birds of Japan.* Black, London.
Bregulla, HL (1992) *Birds of Vanuatu.* Anthony Nelson, Oswestry.
·Britton, PL (ed.) (1980) *Birds of East Africa.* East Africa Natural History Society, Nairobi.
—, and Britton, H (1970) Eye colour of the Black-bellied Glossy Starling. *E. Afr. Nat. Hist. Soc. Bull.* November : 46.
Broekhuysen, GJ (1951) Some observations on the nesting activities of the Redwing Starling, *Onychognathus morio*, and especially the feeding of the young. *Ostrich* 22: 6–16.
—, Schmidt, R and Martin, J (1963) Breeding of Wattled Starling *Creatophora cinerea* in the southern Cape Province. *Ostrich* 34: 173–174.
Brooke, RK (1965a) On the breeding of *Lamprotornis mevesii* (Wahlberg). *Bull. Br. Orn. Club* 85: 139–141.
— (1965b) Ornithological notes on the Turancungo district of Mocambique. *Arnoldia (Rhodesia)* 10(2): 1–13.
— (1965c) Roosting of the Black-shouldered Kite *Elanus caeruleus* (Desfontaines). *Ostrich* 36: 43.
— (1967a) On the moults and breeding season of the Long-tailed Starling *Lamprotornis mevesii* (Wahlberg). *Bull. Br. Orn. Club* 87: 2–5.
— (1967b) On the plumage (including a partial albino), moults and breeding season of *Lamprotornis australis* (Smith). *Bull. Brit. Orn. Club* 87: 60–61.
— (1968) More of the plumages, moults and breeding seasons of southern African starlings. *Bull. Br. Orn. Club* 88: 113–116.
— (1971) An aberrant *Lamprotornis mevesii* with comments on the limits of the genus *Lamprotornis*. *Bull. Br. Orn. Club* 91: 20–21.
— (1989) Possible effects of locust swarms on the birds of western Bushmanland in March 1989. *Promerops* 190: 10.
— (1995) The wreck of the Otori Maru No. 8 as a bird breeding site. *Promerops* 218: 9.
—, Grobler, JH, Irwin, MPS and Steyn, P (1972) A study of the migratory eagles *Aquila nipalensis* and *A. pomarina* (Aves: Accipitridae) in southern Africa, with comparative notes on other large raptors. *Occ. Pap. natn. Mus. Rhod.*B 5(2): 51–114.
Brooks, DJ (1987) Feeding observations on birds in North Yemen. *Sandgrouse* 9: 115–120.
— Evans, MI, Martin, RP and Porter, RF (1987) The status of birds in North Yemen and the records of the OSME Expedition in autumn 1985. *Sandgrouse* 9: 4–66.
Brosset, A and Erard, C (1986) Les oiseaux des régions forestières du nord-est du Gabon. Vol 1: Écologie et comportement des espèces. *Rev. Ecol. Suppl.* 3: 1–289.
Brough, T (1969) The dispersal of Starlings from woodland roosts and the use of bio-acoustics. *J. Appl. Ecol.* 6: 403–410.
— and Bridgeman, C J (1980) An evaluation of long grass as a bird deterrent on British airfields. *J. Appl. Ecol.* 17: 243–253.
Brown, JL (1987) *Helping and communal breeding in birds.* Princeton University Press, Princeton NJ.
Brown, LH (1965) Redwinged Starlings of Kenya. *Jl. E. Afr. Nat. Hist. Soc.* 25: 41–56.
— (1975) Breeding of Stuhlmann's Starling and Narina's Trogon. *E. Afr. Nat. Hist. Soc. Bull.* April: 44–45.
—, and Britton, PL (1980) *The breeding seasons of East African birds.* East Africa Natural History Society, Nairobi.
—, and Newman, KB (1974) "Anting" in African passerine birds. *Ostrich* 45: 194–195.
—, and Thorogood, KM (1976) Ecology and breeding habits of the White-billed Starling *Onychognathus albirostris* in Tigrai, Ethiopia. *Bull. Br. Orn. Club* 96: 60–64.
Brown, P (1972) Notes on some African starlings. *Avicult. Mag.* 78: 15–18.
Browne, PWP (1981) New bird species in Mauritania. *Malimbus* 3: 63–72.
Bruch, K (1983) Gelungene Zucht des Smaragdglanzstars (*Coccycolius iris*). *Trochilus* 4: 56–57.
Buden, D W (1996) Rediscovery of the Pohnpei Mountain Starling (*Aplonis pelzelni*). *Auk* 113: 229–230.
Buskirk, WH (1975) Substrate choices of oxpeckers. *Auk* 92: 604–606.
Buzun, VA (1987) The colonial structure, some forms of behaviour and the enemies of the Rose-coloured Starling in the eastern Crimea. *Vestnik Zooligii* 5: 61–63 [In Russian].
Byrd, GV (1979) Common Myna predation on Wedge-tailed Shearwater eggs. *Elepaio* 39: 69–70.

Cain, AJ and Galbraith, ICJ (1956) Field notes on the birds of the eastern Solomon Islands. *Ibis* 93: 100–134, 262–295.
Cambrony, M and Motis, A (1994) Statut de l'Étourneau Unicolore *Sturnus unicolor* en Languedoc-Rousillon en 1993. *Alauda* 62: 135–140.
Campbell, NA (1989) Both species of oxpecker on greater kudu. *Honeyguide* 35: 26.
Capanna, E and Geralico, C (1982) Karyotype analysis in ornithological studies: II The chromosomes of four species of African birds (Nectarinidae, Ploceidae and Sturnidae). *Avocetta* 6: 1–9.
Carroll, RW (1988) Birds of the Central African Republic. *Malimbus* 10: 177–200.
Cave, FO and Macdonald, JD (1955) *Birds of the Sudan.* Oliver and Boyd, Edinburgh.
Chalmers, M L (1986) *Annotated checklist of the birds of Hong Kong.* Hong Kong Bird Watching Society, Hong Kong.
Chapin, JC (1916) Four new birds from the Belgian Congo. *Bull. Am. Mus. Nat. Hist.* 35: 23–29.
— (1932) The birds of the Belgian Congo. Part I. *Bull. Am. Mus. Nat. Hist.* 65: 1–756.
— (1948) *Neocichla gutturalis* (Bocage) is a starling. *Auk* 65: 289–291.
— (1954) The birds of the Belgian Congo. Part IV. *Bull. Am. Mus. Nat. Hist.* 75B: 1–846.
— (1959) Breeding cycles of *Nectarinia purpureiventris* and some other Kivu birds. *Ostrich suppl.* 3: 222–229.
Cheesman, RE and Sclater, WL (1936) On a collection of birds from North-Western Abyssinia. Part IV. *Ibis* 13th ser. 6: 163–197.

Cheke, AS (1987) An ecological history of the Mascarene Islands, with particular reference to extinctions and introductions of land vertebrates. In: Diamond, A W (ed) *Studies of Mascarene Island birds*. Cambridge University Press, Cambridge.

Cheng, TH (1987) *A synopsis of the avifauna of China*. Paul Parey, Hamburg and Berlin.

Chittenden, H and Myburgh, N (1994) Eye colour change in Black-bellied Starlings. *Birding Sthn Afr.* 46: 117.

Chiurla, E H and Martìnez, M M (1995) Observaciones sobre el Estornino Crestado (*Acridotheres cristatellus*) en el sudeste de la provincia de Buenos Aires. *Nuestras Aves* 31: 24–25.

Chudhoury, A (1991a) Distribution of the Orange-billed Jungle Myna *Acridotheres javanicus* Cabanis in north-east India. *J. Bombay Nat. Hist. Soc.* 88: 286–287.

— (1991b) New for Assam: the White-vented Myna. *Bull. Oriental Bird Club* 13: 20–23.

Clancey, PA (1958) The generic status of the Superb Starling *Spreo superbus* (Rueppell) and its allies. *Durban Mus. Novit.* 5(10): 137–138.

— (1974) On the validity and range of *Lamprotornis corruscus mandanus* Van Someren, 1921. *Bull. Br. Orn. Club* 94: 113–116.

— (Ed.) (1980) *SAOS checklist of southern African birds*. Southern African Ornithological Society, Johannesburg.

— (1987) Subspeciation in the Afrotropical Superb Starling *Lamprotornis superbus*. *Bull. Br. Orn. Club* 107: 25–27.

— and Holliday, CS (1951) A systematic revision of the races of *Lamprotornis nitens* (Linnaeus) endemic to the South African subcontinent. *Ostrich* 22: 111–116.

Clapp, GE (1987) Kites and other birds feeding on caterpillar infestations in poinciana trees *Delonyx regia* in Popondetta, Papua New Guinea. *Muruk* 2: 73–75.

Clark, CC, Clark, L and Clark, L (1990) "Anting" behavior by Common Grackles and European Starlings. *Wilson Bull.* 102: 167–169.

Clarke, G (1985) Bird observations from northwest Somalia. *Scopus* 9: 24–42.

Clark, L and Mason, JR (1985) Use of nest material as insecticidal and anti-pathogenic agents by the European starling. *Oecologia* (Berl.) 67: 169–176.

— (1988) Effect of biologically active plants used as nest material and the derived benefit to Starling nestlings. *Oecologia* (Berl.) 77: 174–180.

Clergeau, P (1981) Dynamique des dortoirs d'étourneaux *Sturnus vulgaris* dans le Bassin de Rennes. *Alauda* 49: 13–24.

Clunie, F (1976) Jungle Mynah "anting" with a millipede. *Notornis* 23: 77.

Coates, BJ (1970) The Common Starling – a bird new to New Guinea. *Papua New Guinea Bird Soc. Newsletter* 59: 2.

— (1985) *The birds of Papua New Guinea*, Vol. 1. Non-passerines. Dove Publications, Alderley, Queensland.

— (1990) *The birds of Papua New Guinea*, Vol. 2, Passerines. Dove Publications, Alderley, Queensland.

— and Bishop, K D (1997) *A guide to the birds of Wallacea*. Dove Publications, Alderley, Queensland.

Cole, DT (1963) Cape Glossy Starling nesting in pipe. *Bokmakierie* 15: 20.

Colebrook-Robjent, JFR and Greenberg, DA (1976) Great Spotted Cuckoo *Clamator glandarius*: first breeding record for Zambia and a new host species. *Ostrich* 47: 229–230.

Collar, NJ and Andrew, P (1988) *Birds to watch: the ICBP world check-list of threatened birds*. ICBP, Cambridge.

Collar, NJ, Crosby, MJ and Stattersfield, AJ (1994) *Birds to watch 2: the world list of threatened birds*. BirdLife International, Cambridge.

Colston, PR and Curry-Lindahl, K (1986) *The birds of Mount Nimba, Liberia*. British Museum (Natural History), London.

Cooper, J and Underhill, LG (1991) Breeding, mass and primary moult of European Starlings *Sturnus vulgaris* at Dassen Island, South Africa. *Ostrich* 62: 1–7.

Cooper, P (1976) Wattled Starlings feeding in Kenya coffee trees. *Honeyguide* 87: 31.

Cornwallis, L and Porter, RF (1982) Spring observations of the birds of North Yemen. *Sandgrouse* 4: 1–36.

Cortès, JE (1982) Nectar feeding by European passerines on introduced tropical flowers at Gibraltar. *Alectoris* 4: 26–29.

Counsilman, JJ (1971) *Some aspects of the behaviour of the Indian Myna, Acridotheres tristis tristis (L.)*. MA thesis, University of Aukland.

— (1974) Waking and roosting behaviour of the Indian Myna. *Emu* 74: 135–148.

— (1977) Visual displays of the Indian Myna during pairing and breeding. *Babbler* 1: 1–13.

Cox, P A (1982) Vertebrate pollination and the maintenance of dioecism in *Freycinetia*. *Amer. Nat.* 120: 65–80.

Craig, AJFK (1983a) Moult in southern African passerine birds: a review. *Ostrich* 54: 220–237.

— (1983b) The timing of breeding and wing-moult of four African Sturnidae. *Ibis* 125: 346–352.

— (1983c) A Pied Starling study. *Safring News* 12: 8–11.

— (1983d) Co-operative breeding in two African starlings, Sturnidae. *Ibis* 125: 114–115.

— (1985) The distribution of the Pied Starling, and southern African biogeography. *Ostrich* 56: 123–131.

— (1987) Co-operative breeding in the Pied Starling. *Ostrich* 58: 176–180.

— (1988a) The timing of moult, morphology, and an assessment of the races of the Red-winged Starling. *Bonn. zool. Beitr.* 39: 347–360.

— (1988b) The status of *Onychognathus nabouroup benguellensis* (Neumann). *Bull. Br. Orn. Club* 108: 144–147.

— (1988c) Allofeeding and dominance interactions in the cooperatively breeding Pied Starling. *Anim. Behav.* 36: 1251–1253.

— (1989) A review of the biology of the Black-bellied Starling and other African forest starlings. *Ostrich Suppl.* 14: 17–26.

— (1992) The distribution of the Wattled Starling in southern Africa. *Ostrich* 63: 31–37.

— (1996) The annual cycle of wing-moult and breeding in the Wattled Starling *Creatophora cinerea*. *Ibis* 138: 448–454.

— (1997) European Starling, Indian Myna, Pied Starling, Black-bellied Starling, Glossy Starling, Greater Blue-eared Starling, Plum-coloured Starling, Red-winged Starling, Pale-winged Starling. In: Harrison, JA, Allan, DG, Underhill, LG, Brown, CJ, Tree, AJ, Parker, V and Herremans, M (Eds), *The atlas of southern African birds*. BirdLife South Africa, Johannesburg.

— (In press a) Evolutionary trends in southern African glossy starlings (*Lamprotornis*). *Ostrich* .

— (In press b) A phylogeny for the African starlings (Sturnidae). *Ostrich* .

— (In press c) Anting in Afrotropical birds: a review. *Ostrich*.

—, and Hartley, AH (1985) The arrangement and structure of feather melanin granules as a taxonomic character in African starlings (Sturnidae). *Auk* 102: 629–632.

— , and Herremans, M (1997) Wattled Starling, Long-tailed Starling, Burchell's Starling. In Harrison, JA, Allan, DG, Underhill, LG, Herremans, M, Tree, AJ, Parker, V and Brown, CJ (eds.) *The atlas of Southern African birds.* BirdLife South Africa, Johannesburg.

—, and Hulley, PE (1992) Biogeography and sympatry of Red-winged and Pale-winged Starlings in southern Africa. *J. Afr. Zool.* 106: 313–326.

—, Hulley, PE, and Walter, GH (1989) Nesting of sympatric Red-winged and Pale-winged Starlings. *Ostrich* 59: 69–74.

—, Hulley, PE, and Walter, GH (1991) The behaviour of Palewinged Starlings, and a comparison with other *Onychognathus* species. *Ostrich* 62: 97–108.

—, and Weaver, A (1990) The relocation of the Redbilled Oxpecker. *Bee-eater* 41 (4): 58–61.

Craig, P, Morrell, T E and So'oto, K (1994) Subsistence harvest of birds, fruit bats and other game in American Samoa, 1990–1991. *Pacific Science* 48: 344–352.

Cramp, S and Perrins, CM (eds.)(1994) *The birds of the western palearctic.* Vol. 8. Oxford University Press, Oxford.

Crandall, LS (1949) Notes on seasonal changes in *Creatophora cinerea*, the Wattled Starling. *Zoologica, NY* 34: 103–106.

Crosby, M (1990) The reintroduction of the Bali Mynah. *Birding World* 3: 256.

Cummings, WD (1959) Breeding of the Amethyst Starling at the Keston Foreign Bird Farm, 1958. *Avicult. Mag.* 65: 44–46.

Cunningham-Van Someren, GR (1974) Sisal flowers, nectar and birds. *E. Afr. Nat. Hist. Soc. Bull.* August:104–107.

— (1975) Breeding of Stuhlmann's Starling *Poeoptera stuhlmanni. E. Afr. Nat. Hist. Soc. Bull.* May: 12.

Curry-Lindahl, K (1981) *Bird migration in Africa.* Academic Press, London and New York.

Cuthill, I and Hindmarsh, A M (1985) Increase in Starling song activity with removal of mate. *Anim. Behav.* 33: 326–328.

Cyrus, D and Robson, N (1980) *Bird atlas of Natal.* University of Natal Press, Pietermaritzburg.

Dale, J and Hustler, K (1991) Oxpeckers use elephants in Hwange National Park. *Honeyguide* 37: 18.

Davey, P (1982) Albinism in the Blue-eared Glossy Starling. *E. Afr. Nat. Hist. Soc. Bull.* Sept/Oct: 77.

Davidar, ERC (1991) Common Myna *Acridotheres tristis* (Linn.) fishing. *J. Bombay Nat. Hist. Soc.* 88: 287.

Davidson, P, Stones, T and Lucking, R (1995) The conservation status of key bird species on Taliabu and the Sula Islands, Indonesia. *Bird Conservation International* 5: 1–20.

de Iongh, H (1983) Is there still hope for the Bali Mynah? *Tigerpaper* 10: 28–32.

— , HH, Komara, A, Moeliono, M, Soemarto, P, Soebrata, S, Spliethoff, PC and Sunarja, IS (1982). A survey of the Bali Mynah *Leucopsar rothschildi* Stresemann 1912. *Biological Conservation* 23: 291–295.

de Schauensee, RM (1928) Plumages of the Wattled Starling. *Auk* 45: 217.

de Schauensee, RM (1984) *The birds of China.* Oxford University Press, Oxford.

de Wiljes, EA (1957) Iets over de Djalak Putih (*Sturnus melanopterus*) als "displaced person" in Bandung. *Penggar Alam* 37: 31–36.

Davison, E (1963) Introduction of ox-peckers (*Buphagus africanus* and *B. erythrorhynchus*) into McIlwaine National Park. *Ostrich* 34: 172–173.

Dawson, A (1994) The effects of daylength and testosterone on the initiation and progress of moult in Starlings *Sturnus vulgaris. Ibis* 136: 335–340.

Dean, WRJ (1974) Breeding and distributional notes on Angolan birds. *Durban Mus. Novit.* 10: 109–125.

— (1978) Plumage, reproductive condition and moult in non-breeding Wattled Starlings. *Ostrich* 49: 97–101.

—, Huntley, MA, Huntley, BJ and Vernon, CJ (1987) Notes on some birds of Angola. *Durban Mus. Novit.* 14: 43–92.

—, and Macdonald, IAW (1972) *Lamprotornis australis*: a new host of *Clamator glandarius. Ostrich* 43: 66.

—, — (1981) A review of African birds feeding in association with mammals. *Ostrich* 52: 135–155.

—, and Vernon, CJ (1988) Notes on the White-winged Babbling Starling *Neocichla gutturalis* in Angola. *Ostrich* 59: 39–40.

Decoux, J-P and Totso, RC (1988) Composition et organisation spatiale d'une communauté d'oiseaux dans la région de Yaoundé. *Alauda* 56: 126–152.

Deignan, HG (1945) *The birds of northern Thailand.* U S Natl. Mus. Bull. 186.

— (1954) The glossy starlings (*Aplonis*) of Borneo. *Sarawak Mus. J.* 6: 129–132.

Delacour, J (1947) *Birds of Malaysia.* MacMillan, New York.

— and Mayr, E (1946) *Birds of the Philippines.* MacMillan, New York.

Dellelegn, Y (1993) Observations on the Ethiopian Bush Crow *Zavattariornis stresemanni* in Yabello, southern Ethiopia. *Proc. VIII Pan-Afr. Orn. Congr.:* 469–474.

Delpy, KH (1972) Über den Grünschwanzglanzstar (*Lamprotornis chalybeus*). *Gefied. Welt* 96: 124–125.

Dement'ev, GP and Gladkow NA (1960) *Birds of the Soviet Union,* Vol. 5. Israel Program for Scientific Translations, Jerusalem.

Demey, R and Fishpool, LDC (1991) Additions and annotations to the avifauna of Côte d'Ivoire. *Malimbus* 12: 61–86.

Desfayes, M (1975) Birds from Ethiopia. *Rev. Zool. Afr.* 89: 505–535.

Devasahayam, S and Rema, J (1991) Acacia seeds – a new food source for birds at Calicut. *Newsletter for Birdwatchers* pp 12–13.

Dhanda, SK and Dhindsa, MS (1996) Breeding performance of Indian Myna *Acridotheres tristis* in nestboxes and natural sites. *Ibis* 138: 788–791.

Dhindsa, MS (1980) Bank Myna, *Acridotheres ginginianus* (Latham): a good predator of house-flies, *Musca domestica* L. *Science and Culture* 46: 294.

— (1984) Status of the avian fauna in Punjab and its management. In: Atwal, A S, Bains, S S and Dhindsa, M S (eds.) *Status of wildlife in Punjab.* Indian Ecological Society, Ludhiana.

Dhondt, A (1976) Bird observations in Western Samoa. *Notornis* 23: 29–43.

Diamond, JM (1972) Avifauna of the Eastern Highlands of New Guinea. *Publs. Nuttal Orn. Club* 12: 1–438.

Dickinson, EC, Kennedy, RS and Parkes, KC (1991) *The Birds of the Philippines.* Check–list No. 12. British Ornithologists' Union, Tring.

Dirickx, HG (1949) Description d'un nouveau Sturnidae du Congo belge. *Rev. Zool. Bot. Afr.* 42: 302–306.

Dittami, J (1983) Notes on Blue-eared Glossy Starlings, *Lamprotornis chalybaeus*, at Nakuru, Kenya. *Scopus* 7: 37–39.

— (1987) A comparison of breeding and moult cycles and life histories in two tropical starling species: the Blue-eared Glossy Starling *Lamprotornis chalybaeus* and Ruppell's Long-tailed Glossy Starling *L. purpuropterus. Ibis* 129: 69–85.

Dmi'el, R and Tel-Tzur, D (1985) Heat balance of two starling species (*Sturnus vulgaris* and *Onychognathus tristramii*) from temperate and desert habitats. *J. comp. Physiol.* 155B: 395–402.

Donnelly, BG (1966) Editorial. *Bee-eater* 17(4): 2.

— (1967) Editorial. *Bee-eater* 18(1): 4.

Dorst, J and Roux, F (1973) L'avifaune des forêts de *Podocarpus* de la province de l'Arussi, Ethiopie. *Oiseau Rev. fr. Orn.* 43: 269–304.

Downer, A and Sutton, R (1990) *Birds of Jamaica.* Cambridge University Press, Cambridge.

Dowsett, RJ (1965) On a nest of the Yellow-billed Oxpecker *Buphagus africanus* in Zambia. *Bull. Brit. Orn. Club* 85: 133–135.

— (1967) Breeding biology of *Lamprotornis mevesii* (Wahlberg). *Bull. Br. Orn. Club* 87: 157–164.

— (1968) Oxpeckers *Buphagus* spp. on game animals at night. *Bull. Br. Orn. Club* 88: 130–132.

— and Forbes-Watson, AD (1993) *Checklist of birds of the Afrotropical and Malagasy regions. Vol. 1: Species limits and distribution.* Tauraco Press, Liege.

Dowsett-Lemaire, F (1983a) Studies of a breeding population of Waller's Red-winged Starlings in montane forests of south-central Africa. *Ostrich* 54: 105–112.

— (1983b) Ecological and territorial requirements of montane forest birds of the Nyika Plateau, south-central Africa. *Gerfaut* 73: 345–378.

— (1988) Fruit choice and seed dissemination by birds and mammals in the evergreen forests of upland Malawi. *Rev. Ecol.* 43: 251–285.

— (1996) Avian frugivore assemblages at three small-fruited tree species in the forests of northern Congo. *Ostrich* 67: 88–89.

— and Drummond, D (1991) Red-winged starlings on impala. *Honeyguide* 37: 16–17.

Draffan, R (1977) Notes on the Yellow-faced Myna – *Mino dumontii*. *PNG Bird Soc. Newsletter* 133: 8–9.

—, Garnett, S T and Malone, G J (1983) Birds of the Torres Strait; an annotated and biogeographical analysis. *Emu* 83: 207–234.

Dubale, MS and Patel, G (1975a) Adaptations for food getting in Sturnidae. 1: study of osteological elements. *Pavo* 10: 8–20.

—, — (1975b) Adaptations for food getting in Sturnidae. 2: myology. *Pavo* 10: 80–105.

Dubinin, NP (1953) Forest birds in the lower part of the Ural river valley. Part 1. *Trudy Inst. Lesa Akad. Nauk SSSR.* 18: 3–126 [In Russian].

Duckworth, JW, Evans, MI, Safford, RJ, Telfer, MG, Timmins, RF and Zewdie, C (1992) A survey of Nechisar National Park, Ethiopia. ICBP Study Report No. 50. ICBP, Cambridge.

Duhart, F and Descamps, M (1963) Notes sur l'avifaune du delta central nigerien et régions avoisinantes. *Oiseau Rev. fr. Orn.* 33 (no. spec.): 1–106.

du Pont, JE (1971) *Philippine birds.* Delaware Museum of Natural History, Greenville.

— (1976) *South Pacific Birds.* Delaware Museum of Natural History, Greenville.

— and Rabor, D S (1973) South Sulu archipelago birds. *Nemouria* 9: 1–63.

Dupont, PR (1930) The Common Mynah (*A. tristis*) as a pest in Seychelles. *J. Bombay Nat. Hist. Soc.* 34: 806–807.

Durrer, H and Villiger, W (1967) Bildung der Schillerstruktur beim Glanzstar. *Z. Zellf.* 81: 445–456.

—, — (1970) Schillerfarben der Stare (Sturnidae). *J. Orn.* 111: 133–153.

Dutson, G and Branscombe, J 1990. Rainforest birds in south-west Ghana. ICBP Study Report No. 46. ICBP, Cambridge.

Dyer, R (1971) Partial albino starling. *E. Afr. Nat. Hist. Soc. Bull.* October: 161.

Dymond, N (1994) A survey of the birds of Nias Island, Sumatra. *Kukila* 7: 10–27.

East, R and Pottinger, RP (1975) Starling (*Sturnus vulgaris* L.) predation on grass grub (*Costelytra zealandica* (White) Melolonthinea) populations in Canterbury. *N. Z. J. Agric. Res.* 18: 417–452.

Eck, S (1976) Die Vögel der Banggai-Inseln, inbesondere Pelengs. *Zool. Abh. Staatl. Mus. Tierk.* Dresden 34: 53–100.

Eddinger, RC (1967) A study of the breeding behaviour of the Mynah (*Acridotheres tristis* L.). *Elepaio* 28: 1–5, 11–15.

Eens, M (1997) Understanding the complex song of the European Starling: an integrated ethological approach. *Advances in the study of animal behaviour.* 26: 355–434.

Eens, M and Pinxten, R (1990) Extra-pair courtship in the Starling *Sturnus vulgaris*. *Ibis* 132: 618–619.

— and — (1996) Female European Starlings increase their copulation solicitation rate when faced with the risk of polygyny. *Anim. Behav.* 51: 1141–1147.

—, — and Verheyen, R F (1989) Temporal and sequential organisation of song bouts in the European Starling. *Ardea* 77: 75–86.

—, — and — (1991a) Organisation of song in the European Starling: species specificity and individual differences. *Belg. J. Zool.* 121: 257–278.

—, — and — (1991b) Male song as a cue for mate choice in the European Starling. *Behaviour* 116: 210–238.

— and Verheyen, RF (1992) No overlap in song repertoire between yearling and older starlings *Sturnus vulgaris*. *Ibis* 134: 72–76.

Eguchi, K, Yamagishi, S and Randrianasolo, V (1993) The composition and foraging behaviour of mixed-species flocks of forest-living birds in Madagascar. *Ibis* 135: 91–96.

Eisentraut, M (1963) *Die Wirbeltiere des Kamerungebirges.* Paul Parey, Hamburg and Berlin.

— (1973) Die Wirbeltierfauna von Fernando Po und Westkamerun. *Bonn. zool. Monogr.* 3: 1–428.

Elgood, JH (1982) *The birds of Nigeria.* British Ornithologists' Union, London.

—, Fry, CH and Dowsett, RJ (1973) African migrants in Nigeria. *Ibis* 115: 375–411.

Elkin, JA, Mann, C F and Ozog, AC (1993) Black-collared Starling *Sturnus nigricollis*, a species new to Borneo and the Sundas. *Forktail* 8: 155.

Elliott, CCH (1990) The migrations of the Red-billed Quelea *Quelea quelea* and their relation to crop damage. *Ibis* 132: 232–237.

Ellis, M (1980) The use of dung and leaves by nesting African starlings. *Avicult. Mag.* 86: 111–112.

Emison, WB (1992) The importance of remnant vegetation to the Blue Bonnet in north-western Victoria. *Aus. Bird Watcher* 14: 159–164.

Engbring, J and Ramsey, FL (1989) *A 1986 survey of the forest birds of American Samoa.* US Fish and Wildlife Service, Department of the Interior.

—, — and Wildman, V J (1990) *Micronesian forest bird surveys, the federated states: Pohnpei, Kosrae, Chuuk and Yap.* US Fish and Wildlife Service, Department of the Interior, Washington DC.

Erard, C and Prevost, J (1971) Notes on some Ethiopian birds. *Bull. Br. Orn. Club* 91: 21–25.

Erlanger, C von (1905) Beiträge zur Vogelfauna Nordostafrikas. *J. Orn.* 53: 670–756.

Etchècopar, RD and Hüe, F (1964) *Les oiseaux du Nord de l'Afrique, de la Mer Rouge aux Canaries.* Société Nouvelle des Editions Bubée, Paris.

— and — (1983) *Les oiseaux de Chine, de Mongolie et de Corée. Passereaux.* Société Nouvelle des Editions Bubée, Paris.

Evans, PGH (1986) Ecological aspects of wing moult in the European Starling *Sturnus vulgaris. Ibis* 128: 558–561.

— (1988) Intraspecific nest parasitism in the European Starling. *Anim. Behav.* 36: 1282–1294.

Evans, SM, Fletcher, FJC, Loader, PJ and Rooksby, FG (1992) Habitat exploitation by landbirds in the changing Western Samoan environment. *Bird Conservation International* 2: 123–129.

Everitt, C (1964) Breeding the Red-winged Starling. *Avicult. Mag.* 70: 133–135.

Every, B (1975) Some impressions of the Karroo avifauna. *Bee-eater* 26(1): 6–7.

— (1981) Notes from 'Bokvlei'. *Bee-eater* 32(4): 38–39.

Ezra, A (1924) The gregarious nesting of the Superb Glossy Starling (*Spreo superbus*). *Avicult. Mag.* 2: 168–170.

— (1929) Breeding the White-capped Starling (*Heteropsar albicapillus*). *Avicult Mag.* 7: 175–176.

— (1931) Successful breeding of *Galeopsar salvadorii* and *Leucopsar rothschildi. Avicult. Mag.* 9: 305–306.

— (1933) Breeding Rüppell's Starling (*Lamprotornis purpuropterus*). *Avicult. Mag.* 11: 357–358.

Fairon, J (1975) Contribution à l'ornithologie de l'Aïr (Niger). *Gerfaut* 65: 107–134.

Fauth, PT, Krementz, DG and Hines, JE (1991) Ectoparasitism and the role of green nesting material in the European starling. *Oecologia* 88: 22–29.

Feare, CJ (1976) Communal roosting in the mynah *Acridotheres tristis. J. Bombay Nat. Hist. Soc.* 73: 525–527.

— (1984) *The Starling.* Oxford University Press, Oxford.

— (1985) The humane control of urban birds. *Universities Federation for Animal Welfare Symposium,* pp. 50–62.

— (1986) Behaviour of the Spotless Starling *Sturnus unicolour* Temm. during courtship and incubation. *Gerfaut* 74: 3–11.

— (1989) The changing fortunes of an agricultural bird pest: the European Starling. *Agric. Zool. Rev.* 3: 317–342.

— (1991) Intraspecific nest parasitism in Starlings *Sturnus vulgaris:* effects of disturbance on laying females. *Ibis* 133: 75–79.

— (1993) European Starlings drinking nectar. *Wilson Bull.* 105: 194.

— (1994a) Common Mynas drinking sea water. *J. Bombay Nat. Hist. Soc.* 91: 144–145.

— (1994b) Changes in numbers of Common Starlings and farming practice in Lincolnshire. *Brit. Birds* 87: 200–204.

— (1995) The role of agricultural change in integrated bird pest management. In: JA Bissonette, JA and Krausman, PR (eds.) *Integrating people and wildlife for a sustainable future.* The Wildlife Society, Bethesda, pp.376–380.

— (1996) Studies of West Palearctic birds: the Common Starling. *Brit. Birds* 89: 549–568.

— and Burnham, SE (1978) Lack of nest site tenacity and mate fidelity in the starling. *Bird Study* 25: 189–191

— and Constantine, DAT (1980) Starling eggs with spots. *Bird Study* 27: 119–120.

— and Gill, EL (1997) First record of the Wattled Starling *Creatophora cinerea* in the Seychelles. *Scopus* 19: 118–119.

— and Kang, N (1992) Allocation of *Sturnus melanopterus* to *Acridotheres* (Sturnidae). *Bull Br. Orn. Club.* 112: 126–129.

— and McGinnity, N (1986) The relative importance of invertebrates and barley in the diet of Starlings *Sturnus vulgaris. Bird Study* 33: 164–167.

—, Allan, JR and Gretton, A (1994) Dispersed communal roosting in Common Mynas. *J. Bombay Nat. Hist. Soc.* 91: 455–457.

—, Douville De Franssu, P and Peris, SJ (1992) The starling in Europe: multiple approaches to a problem species. *Proc. Vertebrate Pest Conference* 15: 83–88.

—, Spencer, P L & Constantine, D A T (1982) Time of egg-laying in starlings. *Ibis* 124: 174–178

Ferrer, X, Motis, A and Peris, SJ (1991) Changes in the breeding range of starlings in the Iberian Peninsula during the last 30 years: competition as a limiting factor. *J. Biogeography* 18: 631–636.

Finch, BW (1986) The *Aplonis* starlings of the Solomon Islands. *Muruk* 1: 4–16.

Finsch, O (1899) Das genus *Gracula* Linn. und seine Arten nebst Beschreibung einer neuen Art. *Notes Leiden Mus.* 21: 1–21.

Fischl, J and Caccamise, DF (1987) Relationships of diet and roosting behavior in the European Starling. *Am. Midl. Nat.* 117: 395–404.

Fish and Wildlife Service (1985) Revised list of migratory birds. *Department of the Interior Federal Register* 50: 13,703–13,722.

Fisher, HI (1950) The birds of Yap, western Caroline Islands. *Pacific Science* 4: 55–62.

Fleck, E (1894) Das Vogelleben Deutsch-Südwestafrikas und dessen Schauplatz. *J. Orn.* 42: 353–415.

Fliege, G (1984) Das Zugverhalten des Stars (*Sturnus vulgaris*) in Europa: eine Analyse der Ringfunde. *J. fur Ornithol.* 125: 393–446.

Foster, MS (1975) The overlap of moulting and breeding in some tropical birds. *Condor* 77: 304–314.

Fraser, MW (1990) Foods of Red-winged Starlings and the potential for dispersal of *Acacia cyclops* at the Cape of Good Hope Nature Reserve. *S. Afr. J. Ecol.* 1: 73–76.

Friedmann, H (1930) The geographic variations of *Neocichla gutturalis* (Bocage). *J. Wash. Acad. Sci.* 20: 434–435.

— (1937) Birds collected by the Childs Frick expedition to Ethiopia and Kenya Colony. Part 2. Passeres. *Bull. U.S. Nat. Mus.* 153: 1–56.

— (1955) The honeyguides. *Bull. U.S. Natn. Mus.* 208: 1–292.

—, and Loveridge, A (1937) Notes on the ornithology of tropical East Africa. *Bull. Mus. Comp. Zool.* 81: 1–413.

—, and Northern, JR (1975) Results of the Taylor South West African Expedition 1972 ornithology. *Los Angeles County Mus., Contrib. Sci.* 266: 1–39.

—, and Williams, JG (1970) The birds of the Kalinzu Forest, southwestern Ankole, Uganda. *Los Angeles County Mus., Contrib. Sci.* 195: 1–27.

—, — (1971) The birds of the lowlands of Bwamba, Toro Province, Uganda. *Los Angeles County Mus., Contrib. Sci.* 211: 1–70.

Frost, PGH (1980) Fruit-frugivore interactions in a South African coastal dune forest. *Acta XVII Congr. Inter. Orn.*: 1179–1184.

Fuggles-Couchman, NR (1983) On the occurrence of *Onychognathus fulgidus* the Chestnut-winged Starling in Tanzania. *Scopus* 7: 98–99.

— (1984) The distribution of, and other notes on, some birds of Tanzania – Part II. *Scopus* 8: 81–92.

—, and Elliott, HFI (1946) Some records and field-notes from north-eastern Tanganyika Territory. *Ibis* 88: 327–347.

Fuller, E (1987) *Extinct birds.* Viking/Rainbird, London.

Gadjil, M (1972) The function of communal roosts: relevance of mixed roosts. *Ibis* 114: 459–462.

Gallagher, MD and Woodcock, MW (1980) *The birds of Oman.* Quartet Books, London.

Gallego, S and Balcells, E (1960) Nota biologìa sobre Estornino Negro (*Sturnus unicolor*) en Lugo (NW de España). *Ardeola* 6: 337–339.

Gargett, V (1975) Association between Red-winged Starlings *Onychognathus morio* and Klipspringers *Oreotragus oreotragus. Bull. Br. Orn. Club* 95: 119–120.

— (1984) Great Spotted Cuckoo in Botswana. *Honeyguide* 30: 76.

Gartshore, ME (1989) An avifaunal survey of Tai National Park, Ivory Coast. ICBP Study Report No. 39. ICBP, Cambridge.

Gatter, W (1988) The birds of Liberia (West Africa). A preliminary list with status and open questions. *Verh. orn. Ges. Bayern.* 24: 689–723.

Gaugris, Y, Prigogine, A and Vande Weghe, J-P (1981) Additions et corrections à l'avifaune du Burundi. *Gerfaut* 71: 3–39.

Geertsema, AA (1976) Great Spotted Cuckoo parasitising Hildebrandt's Starling. *E. Afr. Nat. Hist. Soc. Bull.* July/August: 85.

Geikie, A (1912) *The love of nature among the Romans.* John Murray, London.

George, JC (1976) Physiological adaptations in the Rosy Pastor wintering in India. *J. Bombay Nat. Hist. Soc.* 71: 394–404.

Germain, M, Dragesco, J, Roux, F and Garcin, H (1973) Contribution à l'ornithologie du Sud-Cameroun. II Passeriformes. *Oiseau Rev. fr. Orn.* 43: 212–259.

Gibbs, D (1996) Notes on Solomon Island birds. *Bull. Br. Orn. Club* 116: 18–25.

Gilges, W (1945) Notes on the birds around Richards Bay – Zululand. *Ostrich* 16: 102–108.

Gillet, H (1960) Observations sur l'avifaune du massif de l'Ennedi (Tchad). *Oiseau Rev. fr. Orn.* 30: 99–134.

Gilliard, ET (1949) A study of the Coleto or Bald Starling (*Sarcops calvus*). *Amer. Mus. Novitates* 1429: 1–6.

— and LeCroy, M (1966) Birds of the Middle Sepik Region, New Guinea. *Bull. Amer. Mus. Nat. Hist.* 132: 247–275.

Ginn, HB and Melville, DS (1983) *Moult in birds.* BTO Guide 19. British Trust for Ornithology, Tring.

Ginn, PJ (1986) Birds using helpers at the nest. *Honeyguide* 32: 45.

Giradoux, P, Degauquier, R, Jones, PJ, Weigel, J and Isenmann, P (1988) Avifaune du Niger: états des connaissances en 1986. *Malimbus* 10: 1–140.

Glutz von Blotzheim, UN (1962) *Handbuch der Vögel Mitteleuropas.* Akademische Verlagsgesellschaft, Wiesbaden.

Glyphis, JP, Milton, SJ and Siegfried, WR (1981) Dispersal of *Acacia cyclops* by birds. *Oecologia* 48: 138–141.

Godfrey, R (1922) Birds of the Buffalo Basin, Cape Province, V. *S. Afr. J. Nat. Hist.* 3: 37–49.

Godfrey, WE (1986) *The birds of Canada.* National Museums of Canada, Ottawa.

Godschalk, SKB (1985) Feeding behaviour of avian dispersers of mistletoe fruit in the Loskop Dam Nature Reserve, South Africa. *S. Afr. J. Zool.* 20: 136–146.

Gonzales, PC and Rees, CP (1988) *Birds of the Philippines.* Haribou Foundation for the conservation of Natural Resources, Manila.

Goodwin, D (1963) Some behaviour of a captive red-billed oxpecker. *Avicult. Mag.* 69: 113–117.

Gore, MEJ (1990) *Birds of The Gambia.* (2nd rev. ed.) British Ornithologists' Union, London.

Gramet, P and Dubaille, E (1983) Les nouvelles aires d'hivernage de l'Étourneau Sansonnet, *Sturnus vulgaris*, sur la façade maritime ouest, étudiées en fonction de l'Èvolution agronomique. *Académie d'agriculture de France, Séance du 13 Avril.* pp 455–464.

Grant, CHB and Mackworth-Praed, CW (1942) A new race of Violet-backed Starling from Arabia. *Bull. Br. Orn. Club* 63: 7.

Grant, GS (1982) Common Mynas attack Black Noddies and White Terns on Midway Atoll. *Elepaio* 42: 97–98.

Granvik, H (1923) Contribution to the knowledge of the East African ornithology. *J. Orn.* 71 (Sonderheft): 1–280.

Greling, C de (1972) Sur les migrations et mouvements migratoires de l'avifaune éthiopienne, d'après les fluctuations saisonnieres des dénsites de peuplement en savane soudanienne au nord Cameroun. *Oiseau Rev. fr. Orn.* 42: 1–27.

Green, RH (1983) The decline of the Eastern Rosella and other Psittaciformes in Tasmania concomitant with the establishment of the introduced European Starling. *Records Queen Victoria Mus.* 82: 1–5.

Gregory-Smith, R (1985) Introduction and spread of the Common Myna in Canberra. *Adjutant* 15: 10–14.

Greig-Smith, PW (1982) Behaviour of birds entering and leaving communal roosts of Madagascar Fodies *Foudia madagascariensis* and Indian Mynas *Acridotheres tristis. Ibis* 124: 529–534.

Grimes, LG (1976) The occurrence of cooperative breeding behaviour in African birds. *Ostrich* 47: 1–15.

— (1987) *The birds of Ghana.* British Ornithologists' Union, London.

Grindley, JR (1964) Wattled Starling (*Creatophora cinerea* (Menschen)) caught at sea. *Ostrich* 35: 124.

Grobler, JH (1979) The re-introduction of oxpeckers *Buphagus africanus* and *B. erythrorhynchus* to the Rhodes Matopos National Park, Rhodesia. *Biol. Conserv.* 15: 151–158.

— (1980) Host selection and species preference of the Red-billed Oxpecker *Buphagus erythrorhynchus* in the Kruger National Park. *Koedoe* 23: 89–97.

—, and Charsley, GW (1978) Host preferences of the Yellow-billed Oxpecker *Buphagus africanus* in the Rhodes Matopos National Park, Rhodesia. *S. Afr. J. Wildl. Res.* 8: 169–170.

Gruson, ES (1976) *A checklist of the birds of the world.* Collins, London.

Günther, R and Feiler, A (1985) Die Vögel der Insel São Thomé. *Mitt. zool. Mus. Berlin* 61, *Suppl. Ann. Orn.* 9: 3–38.

—, — (1986) Zur Phänologie, Ökologie und Morphologie angolanischer Vögel (Aves). Teil II: Passeriformes. *Abhand. staatl. Mus. Tierk. Dresden* 14: 1–29.

Gupta, RC and Bajaj, R (1991) On the nest lodging and its composition in respect of Pied Myna, *Sturnus contra contra* Linnaeus. *Geobios* 18: 149–155.

Guy, P (1976) An unusual long-tailed glossy starling. *Honeyguide* 85: 40.

Gwinner, E (1977) Photoperiodic synchronization of circannual rhythms in the European Starling (*Sturnus vulgaris*). *Naturwissenschaften* 64: 44–45.

Gyldenstolpe, N (1924) Zoological results of the Swedish expedition to Central Africa, 1921. Vertebrata, I Birds. *K. Svensk. Vet.-Ak. Handl.* Series 3, vol. 1(3): 1–326.

Haagner, A and Ivy, RH (1907) The birds of Albany Division, Cape Colony. *J. S. Afr. Orn. Un.* 3: 76–116.

Haas, V and Nickel, E (1982) Breeding of Magpie Starlings *Speculipastor bicolor* in Kenya. *Scopus* 6: 41.

Hadden, D (1981) *Birds of the North Solomons.* Wau Ecology Institute, Handbook No. 8, Wau, Papua New Guinea.

Hagemeijer, WJM and Blair, JM (1997) *The EBCC atlas of European breeding birds.* Poyser, London

Hails, CJ (1984) Bird pests, management techniques and the status of bird pests in Singapore. Unpub. report to the Ministry of National Development, Singapore, 28pp.

— (1985) Studies of problem bird species in Singapore: I. Sturnidae (mynas and starlings). Unpub. report to the Ministry of National Development, Singapore, 97 pp.

— (1987) *Birds of Singapore.* Times Editions, Singapore.

Hall, BP (1960) The ecology and taxonomy of some Angolan birds. *Bull. Brit. Mus. (Nat. Hist.)* 6: 367–453.

—, and Moreau, RE (1970) *An atlas of speciation in African passerine birds.* British Museum (Natural History), London.

Hall-Martin, AJ (1987) Range expansion of the Yellow-billed Oxpecker *Buphagus africanus* into the Kruger National Park, South Africa. *Koedoe* 30: 121–132.

Hamilton, JB (1959) A male pattern baldness in wattled starlings resembling the condition in man. *Ann. N.Y. Acad. Sci.* 83: 429–447.

Haneda, K and Ushiyama, H (1967) Life history of the Red-cheeked Myna (*Sturnus philippensis*) II. Breeding season (2). *Jap. J. Ecol.* 17: 49–57 [In Japanese].

Harrison, C and Greensmith, A (1993) *Birds of the world.* Dorling Kindersley, London.

Harrison, CJO (1963a) "Open-billed allopreening" by Rothschild's Grackle *Leucopsar rothschildi.* Ibis 105: 118–119.

— (1963b) The displays of some starlings (Sturnidae) and their taxonomic value. *Ardea* 51: 44–52.

Harrison, T and Smythies, B E (1963) The Grey-backed or Chinese Starling *Sturnus sinensis* in Borneo. *Ibis* 105: 268.

Hars, D (1991) Le Martin Triste *Acridotheres tristis,* une espèce exotique installé à Dunkerque (nord) depuis 1986. *Héron* 24: 289–292.

Hart, BL, Hart, LA, and Mooring, MS (1990) Differential foraging of oxpeckers on impala in comparison with sympatric antelope species. *Afr. J. Ecol.* 28: 240–249.

Hartby, E (1969) The calls of the Starling (*Sturnus vulgaris*). *Dansk. Orn. Foren. Tidsskr.* 62: 205–230.

Hartert, E (1929) Birds collected during the Whitney South Seas Expedition. VIII. Notes of birds from the Solomons. *Amer. Mus. Novitates* 364: 1–19.

Hartlaub, G (1859) Monographische Übersicht der Glanzstaare (Lamprotornithidae) Africa's. *J. Orn.* 7: 1–36.

— (1874) Die Glanzstaare Afrika's. *Abh. Ver. Bremen* 4: 35–98.

Harvey, WG and Howell, KM (1987) Birds of the Dar es Salaam area, Tanzania. *Gerfaut* 77: 205–258.

Hashiguchi, D and Ueda, K (1990) The Grey Starling as a fruit-eater: analysis of regurgitated seeds. *Strix* 9: 55–61[In Japanese].

Hashisuka, M and Udagawa, T (1950) Ornithology of Formosa. *Quart. J. Taiwan Mus.* 4: 1–180.

Hauff, P (1991) Zur Geschichte der nierderländischen Vogeltöpfe. *Mitt. Zool. Mus. Berl. 67 Suppl: Ann. Orn.* 15: 147–151.

Hausberger, M, Jenkins, PF and Keene, J (1991) Species-specifity and mimicry in bird song: are they paradoxes? A re-evaluation of song mimicry in the European starling. *Behaviour* 117: 53–81.

Hauser, MD (1988) How infant vervet monkeys learn to recognize starling alarm calls: the role of experience. *Behaviour* 105: 187–201.

Hayes, J (1982) Notes on bird behaviour. *E. Afr. Nat. Hist. Soc. Bull.* March/April: 40–41.

Hector, JM (1989) An economic analysis of potential Starling damage in Western Australia. Discussion paper 3, Agricultural Protection Board of Western Australia, 14pp.

Heinrich, G (1958) Zur Verbreitung und Lebensweise der Vögel von Angola. Systematischer Teil II. *J. Orn.* 99: 399–421.

Henderson, GH (1953) Southern Red-billed Oxpecker *Buphagus erythrorhyncha caffer.* Ostrich 24: 132.

Henry, GM (1971) *A guide to the birds of Ceylon.* Oxford University Press, Oxford.

Herbert, EG (1923) Nests and eggs of birds in central Siam. *J. Nat. Hist. Soc. Siam* 6: 81–123.

Herholdt, JJ (1987) Observation of the incubation and nestling period of the Pied Starling *Spreo bicolor,* with notes on nestling growth. *Mirafra* 4: 75–77.

Herremans-Tonnoeyr, D, Herremans, M and Smith, PA (1995) Birds feeding on protective capsules of Mopane psyllids. *Babbler* 29/30: 34–35.

Herroelen, P (1955) Notes sur quelques nids et oeufs inconnus d'oiseaux africains observés au Congo Belge. *Rev. Zool. Bot. Afr.* 52: 185–192.

— (1987) Over de rui van de Rose Spreeuw, *Sturnus roseus.* Gerfaut 77: 99–104.

Heuglin, MT von (1874) *Ornithologie Nordost-Afrika's.* Fischer, Cassell.

Hindmarsh, AM (1984) Vocal mimicry in starlings. *Behaviour* 90: 266–273.

Hiraldo, F and Herrera, CM (1974) Dimorfismo sexual y diferenciación de edades en *Sturnus unicolor* Temm. *Doñana, Acta Vertebrata* 1: 149–170.

Hoesch, W (1936) Nester und Gelege aus dem Damara-land. *J. Orn.* 84: 3–20.

—, and Niethammer, G (1940) Die Vogelwelt Deutsch-Südwestafrikas namentlich des Damara- und Namalandes. *J. Orn.* 88: Sonderheft.

Hoffenberg, AS, Power, HW, Romagnano, LC, Lombardo, MP and McGuire, TR (1988) The frequency of cuckoldry in the European Starling (*Sturnus vulgaris*). *Wilson Bull.* 100: 60–69.

Hofshi, H, Gersani, M and Katzir, G (1987a) Urban nesting of Tristram's Grackles *Onychognathus tristramii* in Israel. *Ostrich* 58: 156–159.

— (1987b) A case of infanticide among Tristram's Grackles *Onychognathus tristramii*. *Ibis* 129: 389–390.

Holland, FH (1945) [Letter to the editor]. *Ostrich* 16: 178.

Hollom, PAD, Porter, RF, Christensen, S and Willis, I (1988) *Birds of the Middle East and North Africa*. Poyser, London.

Holmes, P (1979) *The report of the ornithological expedition to Sulawesi, 1979*. P Holmes, Ruislip, 97 pp.

Holub, E and von Pelzein, A (1882) *Beitraege zur Ornithologie Suedafrikas*. A Hoelder, Vienna.

Holyoak, DT and Sedden, MB (1989) Distributional notes on the birds of Burkina Faso. *Bull. Br. Orn. Club* 109: 205–216.

Holyoak, DT and Thibault, J-C (1984) Les oiseaux de Polynésie orientale. *Mem. Mus. Natl. d'Hist. Naturelle, Ser.A*. 127: 1–209.

Hölzinger, J (1992a) Der Rosenstar (*Sturnus roseus*) als Brutvögel in Griechenland – eine Zusammenfassung. *Kartierung mediterr. Brutvögel* 7: 17–25.

— (1992b) Der Rosenstar (*Sturnus roseus* [L. 1758]) 1988 Brutvögel bei Kavala (Nordgriechenland): Beobachtungen zum Auftreten und zur Ernährung. *Kartierung mediterr. Brutvögel* 7: 3–8.

Hoogerwerf, A (1963) Some subspecies of *Gracula religiosa* (Linn.) living in Indonesia. *Bull. Br. Orn. Club* 83: 155–158.

— (1965) Notes on Indonesian birds with special reference to the avifauna of Java and the surrounding small islands (III). *Treubia* 26: 211–291.

— and Hellebrekens, WPJ (1967) A further contribution to our oological knowledge of the island of Java. *Zool. Verh. Leiden* 88: 1–165.

Hopkinson, E (1932) More additions to breeding records. *Avicult. Mag.* 10: 319–326.

Howard, R and Moore, A (1980) *A complete checklist of the birds of the world*. Macmillan, London.

Hüe, F and Etchècopar, RD (1970) *Les oiseaux du Proche et du Moyen Orient*. Boubée et Cie, Paris.

Huels, TR (1981) Cooperative breeding in the Golden-breasted Starling *Cosmopsarus regius*. *Ibis* 123: 539–542.

Hughes, A and Turner CG (1975) Breeding and behaviour of Rothschild's Mynah *Leucopsar rothschildi* at the National Zoological Park, Washington. *Int. Zoo Yearbook* 15: 116–120.

Hustler, K (1987) Host preference of oxpeckers in the Hwange National Park, Zimbabwe. *Afr. J. Ecol.* 25: 241–245.

Inskipp, T, Lindsey, N and Duckworth, W (1996) *An annotated checklist of the birds of the Oriental Region*. Oriental Bird Club, Sandy.

Inskipp, C and Inskipp, T (1991) *A guide to the birds of Nepal*. A & C Black, London.

Irvine, G and Irvine, D (1974) Down on the Tana. *E. Afr. Nat. Hist. Soc. Bull.* December: 158–159.

Irwin, MPS (1953) Notes on some birds of Mashonaland, Southern Rhodesia. *Ostrich* 24: 37–49.

— (1957) Some field notes on a collection of birds from Tanganyika Territory. *Ostrich* 28: 116–122.

— (1981) *The birds of Zimbabwe*. Quest, Salisbury.

— (1988) Order Cuculiformes. In: Fry, CH, Keith, S and Urban, EK (Eds). *The birds of Africa*. Vol. III: 58–104. Academic Press, London.

— and Benson, CW (1967) Notes on the birds of Zambia: Part IV. *Arnoldia (Rhodesia)* 8(3): 1–27.

Ivanov, AI (1969) *The birds of the Pamir-Alay Mountains*. Nauka, Leningrad [In Russian].

Jackson, FJ and Sclater, WL (1938) *The birds of Kenya Colony and the Uganda Protectorate*. Vol. 3. Gurney and Jackson, London.

Jacot Guillarmod, A, Jubb, RA and Skead, CJ (1979) Field studies of six southern African species of *Erythrina*. *Ann. Missouri Bot. Gard.* 66: 521–527.

Jahn, H (1942) Biologie der Vogel Japans. *J. Orn.* 90: 7–302.

Jamieson, IG and Craig, JL (1987) Critique of helping behaviour in birds: a departure from functional explanations. *Perspec. Ethol.* 7: 79–98.

Jenkins, JM (1983) The native forest birds of Guam. *Ornithological Monographs* 31: 1–61.

Jennings, M (1991) New breeding species. *Phoenix* 8: 2

Jensen, RAC, and Jensen, MK (1969) On the breeding biology of southern African cuckoos. *Ostrich* 40: 163–181.

Jepson, P (1993) Recent ornithological observations from Buru. *Kukila* 6: 85–109.

Jior, RS, Dhindsa, M S and Toor, H S (1995) Nests and nest contents of the Bank Myna (*Acridotheres ginginianus*). *TigerPaper* 22: 25–28.

Jones, CG (1996) Bird introductions to Mauritius: status and relationships with native birds. In: Holmes, J S and Simons, J R (eds.) *The introduction and naturalisation of birds*. Stationery Office, London, pp 113–123.

Jones, H (1945) Notes on some birds of the Northern Rhodesia copperbelt. *Ostrich* 16: 176–183.

Jones, PJ and Tye, A (1988) A survey of the avifauna of São Tomé and Principe. ICBP Study Report No. 24. ICBP, Cambridge.

Joubert, E (1972) The social organisation and associated behaviour in the Hartmann Zebra *Equus zebra hartmannae*. *Madoqua* ser. 1(6): 17–56.

Joubert, HJ (1943) Some notes on birds. *Ostrich* 14: 1–7.

— (1945) Starlings and others. *Ostrich* 16: 214–215.

Jubb, RA (1952) Some notes on birds of Southern Rhodesia. *Ostrich* 23: 162–164.

— (1977) "Old Wheezie". *Diaz Diary* 43: 4.

— (1980a) Birds feeding on ectoparasites. *Diaz Diary* 77: 4.

— (1980b) Some window and wheel-tapping birds. *E. Cape Naturalist* 69: 11.

— (1983) Note on the greater honeyguide. *Diaz Diary* 116: 10–11.

Kaiser-Benz, M (1975) Breeding the Red-billed Oxpecker *Buphagus erythrorhynchus* at Zurich Zoo. *Int. Zoo. Ybk* 15: 120–123.

Kang, CL, Chan, WK, Feare, CJ, Wells, DR and Kang, N (1994) The relationship between mynas: an application of DNA sequencing. *J. Orn.* 135: 33.

Kang, N (1989) *Comparative behavioural ecology of the mynas, Acridotheres tristis (Linnaeus) and A. javanicus (Cabanis) in Singapore*. PhD thesis, National University of Singapore.

— (1991) The mynas (*Acridotheres* spp.) of Singapore. *Nature Malaysiana* 16: 98–103.

— (1992) Radiotelemetry in an urban environment: a study of mynas (*Acridotheres spp.*) in Singapore. In Priede, IG and

Swift, SM (eds.) *Wildlife telemetry. Remote monitoring and tracking of animals.* Ellis Horwood, Chichester.

—, Sigurdsson, JB, Hails, CJ and Counsilman, JJ (1990) Some implications of resource removal in the control of mynas (*Acridotheres spp.*) in Singapore. *Malayan Nature Journal* 44: 103–108.

— and Yeo, VYY (1993) Roost site selection and the waking and roosting behaviour of mynas in relation to light intensity. *Malayan Nature Journal* 46: 255–263.

Kannemeyer, M (1951) [Nesting habits of the Cape Glossy Starling]. *Bee-eater* 2(2): 10.

Karlsson, J (1983) *Breeding of the Starling.* PhD Thesis, University of Lund.

Kavanagh, M (1977) Foods of some Cameroonian birds. *Bull. Nigerian Orn. Soc.* 13(44): 145.

Kazakov, BA (1976) New and rare birds in the south-west part of Rostov region. *Ornitologiya* 12: 61–67 [In Russian]`   .

Kekilova, AF (1978) Food of some passerines in Murgab Valley (Turkmeniya) during spring and autumn migration. *Tez. Zoolshch. 2. Vsesoyuz. Konf. Migr. Ptits* 1: 29–30 [In Russian].

Kemp, AC, Kemp, MI, Jensen, RAC, and Clinning, CF (1972) Records of brood parasitism from central South West Africa. *Ostrich* 43: 145–148.

Kerpez, TA and Smith, NS (1990) Competition between European Starlings and native woodpeckers for nest cavities in Saguaros. *Auk* 107: 367–375.

Khera, S and Kalsi, RS (1986a) Diurnal time budgets of the Bank Myna *Acridotheres ginginianus* (Sturnidae) during pre-laying, laying and incubation periods. *Pavo* 25: 25–32.

— (1986b) Waking and roosting behaviour of the Bank Myna, *Acridotheres ginginianus*, in Chandigarh and surrounding areas. *Pavo* 24: 55–68.

Kidd, E (1978) Some notes on the birds of Brunei. *Brunei Mus. J.* 4: 115–164.

King, B, Woodcock, M and Dickinson, EC (1975) *A field guide to the birds of South-east Asia.* Collins, London.

Kinsky, FC and Yaldwyn, JC (1981) The bird fauna of Niue Island, south-west Pacific, with special notes on the White-tailed Tropic Bird and Golden Plover. *Nat. Mus. New Zealand, Miscellaneous Series* No. 2: 1–49.

Klatt, DH and Stefanski, RA (1974) How does a mynah bird imitate human speech? *J. Acoust. Soc. Am.* 55: 822–832.

Koen, JH (1992) Medium-term fluctuations of birds and their potential food resources in the Knysna Forest. *Ostrich* 63: 21–30.

Koenig, WD (1994) Two new bird-mammal associations from Kenya, with comments on host use by Wattled Starlings. *Ostrich* 65: 337–338.

— (1997) Host preferences and behaviour of oxpeckers: co-existence of similar species in a fragmented landscape. *Evol. Ecol.* 11: 91–104.

Kok, OB and van Ee, CA (1990) Dieetsamestelling van enkele voëlsoorte in die Oranje-Vrystaat en Noordwes-Kaap. 3. Lede van die Sturnidae-familie. *Mirafra* 7(1): 18–25.

Koike, S (1988) Breeding ecology of the Red-cheeked Myna *Sturnus philippensis. Strix* 7: 113–148 [In Japanese].

— (1992) Intersexual relationship of a trigynous group of the Red-cheeked Myna *Surnus philippensis. Strix* 11: 151–156 [In Japanese].

Komdeur, J (1996) Breeding of the Seychelles Magpie Robin *Copsychus sechellarum* and implications for its conservation. *Ibis* 138: 485–498.

Korelov, MN, Kuz'mina, MA, Gavrilov, EI, Kovshar', AF, Gavrin, VF and Borodikhin, IF (1974) *The birds of Kazakhstan, vol. 5.* Nauka, Alma Ata. [In Russian].

Kotagama, S and Fernando, P (1994) *A field guide to the birds of Sri Lanka.* Wildlife Heritage Trust of Sri Lanka, Colombo.

Kovshar', AF (1966) *The birds of the Talasskiy Alatau mountains.* Kaynar, Alma Ata [In Russian].

Kramer, G (1930) Bewegungstudien an Vögeln des Berliner Zoologischen Gartens. *J. Orn.* 78: 257–268.

Kraus, K (1985) Beobachtungen zum Verhalten und zur Brutbiologie des Schmalschnabelstars (*Scissirostrum dubium* Latham, 1802). *Trochilus* 6: 71–79.

Kunkel, P (1962) Zur Verbreitung des Hüpfens und Laufens unter Sperlingsvögeln (Passeres). *Z. Tierpsychol.* 19: 416–439.

Kuroda, N (1959) Field studies of the Grey Starling, *Sturnus cineraceus* Temminck. 2. Breeding biology (part 3). *Misc. Rep. Yamashina Inst. Ornithol. Zool.* 13: 31–48 [In Japanese].

— (1960) Research on the winter roost-mortality in the Grey Starling. *Misc. Rep. Yamashina Inst. Ornithol. Zool.* 2: 99–122 [In Japanese].

— (1961) Ontogeny of behaviours in the Grey Starling. *Misc. Rep. Yamashina Inst. Ornithol. Zool.* 3: 83–112 [In Japanese].

— (1962) Winter roost distribution and feeding dispersal of the Grey Starling in Kanto Plain. *Misc. Rep. Yamashina Inst. Ornithol. Zool.* 3: 144–154 [In Japanese].

— (1963a) Adaptive parental feeding as a factor influencing the reproductive rate in the Grey Starling. *Res. Popul. Ecol.* 5: 1–10.

— (1963b) The molting of young Gray Starlings. *Misc. Rep. Yamashina Inst. Ornithol.* 3: 260–273.

— (1964a) The comparative analysis of breeding rates of rural and urban Grey Starling colonies in Tokyo area; the second report (part 1). *Misc. Rep. Yamashina Inst. Ornithol. Zool.* 4: 1–30.

— (1964b) Comparative analysis of breeding rates of rural and urban Grey Starling colonies in Tokyo area: the second report (part 2). *Res. Popul. Ecol.* 6: 1–12.

— (1973) Fluctuation of winter roosting flock of *Sturnus cineraceus* at Koshigaya and the roost change to Omatsu in summer. *Misc. Rep. Yamashina Inst. Ornithol. Zool.* 7: 34–55.

— (1975) A probable pair bond confirmation in Grey Starling. *Misc. Rep. Yamashina Inst. Ornithol. Zool.* 7: 564–565.

Lack, D (1936) On the pugnacity at the nest of a pair of *Onychognathus walleri walleri. Ibis* 13th ser. 6: 821–825.

Lack, P (1985) The ecology of the land-birds of Tsavo East National Park, Kenya. *Scopus* 9: 2–23, 57–96.

— and Quicke, DLJ (1978) Dietary notes on some Kenyan birds. *Scopus* 2: 86–91.

Lamarche, B (1981) Liste commentée des oiseaux du Mali. *Malimbus* 3: 73–102.

Lamba, BS (1963) The nidification of some common Indian birds IV. The Common Myna (*Acridotheres tristis* Linn.). *Res. Bull. Panjab Univ.* 14: 11–20.

— (1981) A queer nesting site of Bank Myna *Acridotheres ginginianus. J. Bombay Nat. Hist. Soc.* 78: 605–606.

Langrand, O (1990) *Guide to the birds of Madagascar.* Yale University Press, New Haven & London.

— and Sinclair, JC (1994) Additions and supplements to the Madagascar avifauna. *Ostrich* 65: 302–310.

Lawrence, KJ (1975) Breeding the Superb Spreo. *Foreign Birds* 39: 8–11.

Layard, EL and Sharpe, RBS (1884) *The birds of South Africa.* Quaritch, London.

Leader, PJ (1995) Crested Mynah kleptoparasitising Chinese Pond Heron Chicks. *Hong Kong Bird Report* 1995: 253–254.

LeCroy, M (1981) Records of *Aplonis* starlings on the Sepik. *PNG Bird Soc. Newsletter* No. 179–180: 10.

— (1995) Further observations of *Aplonis* starlings feeding on insects. *Muruk* 7: 47–48.

— and Peckover, W S (1983) Birds of the Kimbe Bay area, West New Britain, Papua New Guinea. *Condor* 85: 297–304.

—, —, Kulupi, A and Manseima, J (1984) Bird observations on Normanby and Ferguson, D'Entrecasteaux Islands, Papua New Guinea. *Wildlife in Papua New Guinea* No. 83/1: 1–7.

Lekagul, B and Cronin, EW (1974) *Bird guide of Thailand.* Kuruspha, Bangkok.

— and Round, PD (1991) *A guide to the birds of Thailand.* Saha Karn Bhaet, Bangkok.

Lever, C (1987) *Naturalised birds of the world.* Longmans, London.

Levaillant, F (1799) *Histoire naturelle des oiseaux d'Afrique.* Vol. II. J.J. Fuchs, Paris.

Lewis, AD and Ogola, MF (1989) Four aberrantly plumaged birds observed in Kenya. *Scopus* 13: 114.

— and Pomeroy, D (1989) *A bird atlas of Kenya.* AA Balkema, Rotterdam.

Lippens, L and Wille, H (1976) *Les oiseaux du Zaïre.* Lanoo, Tielt.

Liversidge, R (1961) The Wattled Starling (*Creatophora cinerea*) (Menschen). *Ann. Cape Prov. Mus.* 1: 71–80.

Liversidge, R (1975) Beware the exotic bird. *Bokmakierie* 27: 86–87.

— (1968) Bird weights. *Ostrich* 39: 223–227.

Lockwood, G (1986) Yellow-billed Oxpeckers and a lot of bull. *Bokmakierie* 38: 73–74.

— (1988) Oxpeckers: a success story. *Bokmakierie* 40: 119–120.

Lombardo, MP, Power, HW, Stouffer, PC, Romagnano, LC and Hoffenberg, AS (1989) Egg removal and intraspecific brood parasitism in the European Starling (*Sturnus vulgaris*). *Behav. Ecol. Sociobiol.* 24: 217–223.

Long, JL (1984) *Introduced birds of the world.* David and Charles, London.

Lorenz, K (1949) Die Beziehung zwischen Kopfform und Zirkelbewegung bei Sturniden und Icteriden. In: Mayr, E and Schuz, E (Eds). *Ornithologie als biologische Wissenschaft. (Festschrift von Erwin Stresemann).* Pp: 153–157. Carl Winter, Heidelberg.

Louette, M (1981) The birds of Cameroon. *Verhand. Kon. Acad. Wetens. Lett. Schone Kunsten Belg.* 43 (163): 1–295.

Lowe, WP (1937) Report on the Lowe-Waldron expeditions to the Ashanti forests and northern territories of the Gold Coast. Part III. *Ibis* 14th ser. 1: 830–864.

Lücker, H (1994) Zucht des Rotschnabelhadenhackers. *Gefied. Welt* 118: 9–10.

Lundberg, P and Eriksson, L-O (1984) Postjuvenile moult in two northern Scandinavian Starling *Sturnus vulgaris* populations evidence for difference in the circannual time-program. *Ornis Scand.* 15: 105–109.

Lynes, H (1924) On the birds of north and central Darfur. *Ibis* 11th ser. 6: 648–719.

— (1934) Contribution to the ornithology of southern Tanganyika Territory. *J. Orn.* 82: Sonderheft.

Maccarone, AD (1987) Evidence for resource-based communal roosting by European starlings. *Bird Behav.* 7: 49–57.

Macdonald, JD (1973) *Birds of Australia.* A H and A W Reed, Sydney.

MacKay, VM and Hughes, WM (1963) Crested Mynah in British Columbia. *Canadian Field Naturalist* 77: 154–162.

MacKinnon, J (1990) *Field guide to the birds of Java and Bali.* Gadjah Mada University Press, Bogor.

— and Phillipps, K (1993) *The birds of Borneo, Sumatra, Java and Bali.* Oxford University Press, Oxford.

MacKinnon, K and Mackinnon, J (1991) Habitat protection and re-introduction programmes. *Symp. zool. Soc. Lond.* 62: 173–198.

Maclatchy, A-R (1937) Contribution à l'étude des oiseaux du Gabon méridional. *Oiseau Rev. fr. Orn.* 7: 311–364.

Maclean, GL (1993) *Roberts' birds of southern Africa.* John Voelcker Bird Book Fund, Cape Town.

Mackworth-Praed, CW and Grant, CHB (1950) On the migratory movements of the southern race of the violet-backed starling. *Ibis* 92: 402–404.

—, — (1960) *Birds of eastern and north eastern Africa.* Vol. 2. Longmans, London.

—, — (1963) *Birds of the southern third of Africa.* Vol. 2. Longmans, London.

—, — (1973) *Birds of western and west-central Africa.* Vol. 2. Longmans, London.

Magarry, A (1987) Observations on Metallic or Shining Starlings (*Aplonis metallica*). *North Queensland Naturalist* No. 188: 7.

Mahabal, A and Vaidya, VG (1989) Diurnal rhythms and seasonal changes in the roosting behaviour of Indian Myna *Acridotheres tristis* (Linnaeus). *Proc Indian Acad. Sci. (Anim. Sci.)* 98: 199–209.

—, Bastawade, DB and Vaidya, VG (1990) Spatial and temporal fluctuations in the population of Common Myna *Acridotheres tristis* (Linnaeus) in and around an Indian city. *J. Bombay Nat. Hist. Soc.* 87: 392–398.

Majumdar, N (1978) On the taxonomic status of the Eastern Ghats Hill Myna, *Gracula religiosa peninsularis* Whistler and Kinnear, 1933 [Aves: Sturnidae]. *J. Bombay Nat. Hist. Soc.* 75: 331–333.

Manikowski, S (1984) Birds injurious to crops in West Africa. *Tropical Pest Management* 30: 379–387.

Mann, CF (1985) An avifaunal study in Kakamega Forest, Kenya, with particular reference to species diversity, weight and moult. *Ostrich* 56: 236–262.

Marchant, S (1942) Some birds of the Owerri Province, S. Nigeria. *Ibis* 14th ser. 6: 137–196.

— (1953) Notes on the birds of south-eastern Nigeria. *Ibis* 95: 38–69.

Mare, JJ (1982) Breeding the Red-winged Starling *Onychognathus morio. Avicult. Mag.* 88: 191–192.

Marien, D (1951) Notes on some Asiatic Sturnidae (birds). *J. Bombay Nat. Hist. Soc.* 49: 471–487.

Martin, WK (1996) The current and potential distribution of the Common Myna *Acridotheres tristis* in Australia. *Emu* 96: 166–173.

Mason, GW and LeFroy, HM (1912) The food of birds in India. *Mem. Dep. Agric. India ent. Ser.* 3: 1–371.

Mat, HA and Davison, GWH (1984) Communal roosting and foraging in a population of Common Mynas. *Sains Malaysiana* 3: 231–238.

Mauersberger, G and Möckel, R (1987) Über Arealerweiterungen bei vier Vogelarten im kaukasischen Raum. *Mitt. Zool. Mus. Berl., Suppl.: Ann. Orn.* 63: 97–111.

Mayr, E (1931) Birds collected during the Whitney South Sea Expedition. XIII. A systematic list of the birds of Rennell Island with descriptions of new species and subspecies. *Amer. Mus. Novitates* 486: 1–29.

— (1942) Birds collected during the Whitney South Sea Expedition. XLVIII Notes on Polynesian species of *Aplonis*. *Amer. Mus. Novitates* 1166: 1–6.

— and Greenway, F C (1962) (eds.) *Peters checklist of the birds of the world, Vol. 15*. Mus. Comp. Zool. Cambridge, Massachusetts.

McClure, HE (1974) *Migration and survival of the birds of Asia*. United States Army Medical Component, SEATO, Bangkok.

McCormack, G (1997) Cook Islands – an oceanic oasis. *World Birdwatch* 19: 12–16.

McCulloch, D (1963) Colour change in the iris of the Black-bellied Starling *Lamprocolius corruscus*. *Ostrich* 34: 177.

McCulloch, MN (1991) Status, habitat and conservation of the St Helena Wirebird *Charadrius sanctaehelenae*. *Bird Conservation International* 1: 361–392.

McLelland, J (1981) Digestive system. In: King, AS and McLelland, J (Eds). *Form and function in birds*. Vol. 1: 69–181. Academic Press, London.

Medway, Lord and Wells, DR (1976) *The birds of the Malay Peninsula*. Vol. 5. Witherby, London.

Mees, GF (1996) *Geographical variation in birds in Java*. Publications of the Nuttall Ornithological Club, No 26, Cambridge, Massachusetts.

— (1997) On the identity of *Heterornis senex* Bonaparte. *Bull Br. Orn. Club*. 117: 67–68.

Meier, G (1988) Erfahrungen bei der Pflege von Jallastaren (*Sturnopastor contra jalla*). *Trochilus* 9: 84–88.

Meijer, T (1991) The effect of a period of food restriction on gonad size and moult of male and female Starlings *Sturnus vulgaris* under constant photoperiod. *Ibis* 133: 80–84.

Meinertzhagen, R (1937) Some notes on the birds of Kenya Colony, with especial reference to Mount Kenya. *Ibis* 14th ser. 1: 731–760.

— (1954) *Birds of Arabia*. Oliver and Boyd, Edinburgh.

Mengesha, YA (1978) A study of oxpecker-mammal symbiosis in Ethiopia. *E. Afr. Agric. For. J.* 43: 321–326.

Menon, V (1994) The trade in Hill Mynas in India. *TRAFFIC Bull.* 14: 81–882.

Merkel, FW (1978) Sozialverhalten von individuell markieren Staren – *Sturnus vulgaris* – in einer kleiner Nistkastenkolonie. *Luscinia* 43: 163–181.

Meyer, AB and Wigglesworth, LW (1898) *The birds of Celebes and neighbouring islands*. Vol. 2. Friedländer and Sohn, Berlin.

Meyer, HF (1959) Great Spotted Cuckoo parasitizing a hole-nesting species in Southern Rhodesia. *Ostrich* 30: 85.

Michaelis, HJ (1977) Der Grünschwanzglanzstar. *Falke* 24: 70–71.

Midya, S and Brahmachary, RL (1991) The effects of birds upon germination of banyan *(Ficus benghalensis)* seeds. *J. Trop. Ecol.* 7: 537–538.

Milon, P, Petter, J-J, and Randrianosolo, G (1973) Oiseaux. *Faune Madagascar* 35: 1–263.

Milsom, TP and Horton, N (1995) *Birdstrike – an assessment of the hazard on U.K. civil aerodromes 1976–1990*. Central Science Laboratory, Slough.

Milstein, P and Newman, KB (1981) Field differentiation in the blue-eared glossy starlings. *Bokmakierie* 33: 11–12.

Mirza, ZB (1982) New bird record for Pakistan. *Pakistan J. Zool.* 14: 238.

Mishra, RM, Bhatnagar, S and Sharma, M (1987) Studies in the dispersal ecology of *Azadirachta indica* Juss. *Geobios* 14: 212–216.

Miskell, J (1977) Cooperative feeding of young at the nest by Fischer's Starling *Spreo fischeri*. *Scopus* 1: 87–88.

Mitchell, CS (1976) Prolonged use of a nest and nest-site by Red-winged Starlings. *Honeyguide* 86: 35.

Moermond, TC (1992) Feeding behaviour of central African fruit-eating birds. *Proc. VII Pan-Afr. Orn. Congr.*: 391–396.

— ka Kajondo K, Sun, C, Kristensen, K, Munyaligoga, V, Kaplan, BA, Graham, C and Mvukiyumwani, J (1993) Avian frugivory and tree visitation patterns in a Rwanda montane rain forest. *Proc. VIII Pan-Afr. Orn. Congr.*: 421–428.

Moeed, A (1976) Foods of the Common Myna (*Acridotheres tristis*) in central India and in Hawkes Bay, New Zealand. *Notornis* 23: 246–249.

Mooring, MS and Mundy, PJ (1996a) Factors influencing host selection by yellow-billed oxpeckers at Matobo National Park, Zimbabwe. *Afr. J. Ecol.* 34: 177–188.

— (1996b) Interactions between impala and oxpeckers at Matobo National Park, Zimbabwe. *Afr. J. Ecol.* 34: 54–65.

Moreau, RE (1933) The food of the Red-billed Oxpecker, *Buphagus erythrorhynchus* (Stanley). *Bull. Ent. Res.* 24: 325–335.

— (1935) A contribution to the ornithology of Kilimanjaro and Mount Meru. *Proc. zool. Soc. Lond.* 1935: 843–891.

— (1966) *The bird faunas of Africa and its islands*. Academic Press, London.

—, and Sclater, WL (1938) The avifauna of the mountains along the Rift Valley in north central Tanganyika Territory (Mbulu District). *Ibis* 14 ser. 2: 1–32.

Morel, GJ (1985) Les oiseaux des milieux rocheux au Sénégal. *Malimbus* 7: 115–119.

—, and Morel, M-Y (1982) Dates de reproduction des oiseaux de Sénégambie. *Bonn. zool. Beitr.* 33: 249–268.

—, — (1988) Liste des oiseaux de Guinée. *Malimbus* 10: 143–176.

—, — (1990) *Les oiseaux de Sénégambie*. ORSTOM, Paris.

Morrison, A (1980) A note on Javanese aviculture. *Avicult. Mag.* 86: 108–110.

Mortimer, J (1975) Red-winged Starlings preying on Palm Swifts. *Honeyguide* 82: 44.

Motis, A (1985) Biologia de la reproduccion de *Sturnus vulgaris* i de *Sturnus unicolor* en l'área de simpatria de les comarques del Segriá i les Garrigues. Tesinas de Licenciatura, Facultad de Biología, Universidad de Barcelona.

— (1992) Mixed breeding pairs of European Starling (*Sturnus vulgaris*) and Spotless Starling (*Sturnus unicolor*) in the north-east of Spain. *Butll. G.C.A.* 9: 19–23.

Mountjoy, DJ and Lemon, RE (1991) Song as an attractant for male and female European starlings, and the influence of song complexity on their response. *Behav. Ecol. Sociobiol.* 28: 97–100.

Moynihan, M (1978) An "ad hoc" association of hornbills, starlings, coucals, and other birds. *Terre Vie* 32: 557–576.

Mundy, PJ (1993) Notes on oxpeckers. *Honeyguide* 39: 108–112.

— (1997) Red-billed Oxpecker, Yellow-billed Oxpecker. In: Harrison, JA, Allan, DG, Underhill, LG, Brown, CJ, Tree, AJ, Parker, V and Herremans, M (Eds), *The atlas of southern African birds*. BirdLife South Africa, Johannesburg.

— and Cook, AW (1975) Observations of the Yellow-billed Oxpecker *Buphagus africanus* in northern Nigeria. *Ibis* 117: 504–506.

272

— and Haynes, G (1996) Oxpeckers and elephants. *Ostrich* 67: 85–87.

Mungure, SA (1973) Nest of Red-wing Starling *Onychognathus morio*. *E. Afr. Nat. Hist. Soc. Bull.* April: 52.

Murphy, ME and King, JR (1991) Nutritional aspects of avian moult. *Acta XX Congr. Int. Ornithol.*: 2186–2193.

Naik, NL (1970) Wing pterylography of some starlings. *Pavo* 8: 45–74.

— and Naik, RM (1969) On the plumages and moults of some Indian starlings. *Pavo* 7: 57–73.

Naik, VR (1987) Nest of the Pied Myna *Sturnus contra* Linnaeus. *J. Bombay Nat. Hist. Soc.* 84: 210.

Nakamura, H (1986) Ecological studies of the beech forest bird community in Kayanodaira Heights. *Bull. Inst. Nature Educ. Shiga Heights, Shinshu Univ.* 23: 9–29.

Narang, ML and Lamba, BS (1982) A contribution to the food habits of Grey-headed Myna, *Sturnus malabaricus malabaricus* (Gmelin). *Indian J. Forestry* 5: 24–29.

— and ——(1984) A contribution to the food habits of some Indian birds (Aves). *Rec. Zool. Survey India.* Occasional Paper No 44, 76pp.

Naurois, R de (1969) Peuplements et cycles de reproduction des oiseaux de la côte occidentale d'afrique. *Mem. Mus. Nat. Hist. natur.* ser. A 56: 1–312.

— (1983) Les oiseaux reproducteurs des îles de São Tomé et Principe: liste systematique commentée et indications zoogeographiques. *Bonn. zool. Beitr.* 34: 129–148.

— (1994) *Les oiseaux des îles du Golfe de Guinée.* Instituto di Investigaçâo Científica Tropical, Lisbon.

Nechaev, VA (1975) The biology of the Grey Starling *Spodiopsar cineraceus* (Temm.) in Primûrye. *Trudy Biol. Pochv. Inst.* 29: 63–82. [In Russian.]

Neumann, O (1904) [Über die Roflugelglanzstare]. Deutsche Ornithologische Gesellschaft. Bericht über die April-Sitzung 1904. *J. Orn.* 52: 567–569.

— (1920) Neue Gattungen und Unterarten afrikanischer Vögel. *J. Orn.* 68: 77–83.

Neweklowsky, W (1974) Beobachtungen an Rotschnabelmadenhackern, *Buphagus erythrorhynchus* (Stanley). *Zool. Garten* 44: 121–143.

Newman, KB (1971) Birds eating ants. *Bokmakierie* 23: 29–31.

— (1986) Identifying glossy starlings. *Bokmakierie* 38: 84–86.

Nikolaus, G (1987) Distribution atlas of Sudan's birds with notes on habitat and status. *Bonn. zool. Monogr.* 25: 1–322.

Nixon, A (1992) Black bellied Starling eating reed frogs, *Hyperolius* sp. *Bee-eater* 43: 12–13.

— (1993) Food of Blackbellied Starlings. *Bee-eater* 44: 9.

Nixon, RD (1971) Population dynamics in four species in Port Elizabeth in 1970. *Bee-eater Suppl.* 2: 1–2.

Nowak, RM and Paradiso, JL (1983) *Walker's mammals of the world.* 4th Edition. Johns Hopkins University Press, Baltimore and London.

Oatley, T and Fraser, M (1992) Red-ringed Red-winged Starlings. *Safring News* 21: 43–49.

—, and Skead, DM (1972) Nectar feeding by South African birds. *Lammergeyer* 15: 65–74.

Oberholser, HC (1905) Birds collected by Dr. W.L. Abbott in the Kilimanjaro region, East Africa. *Proc. U.S. Nat. Mus.* 28: 823–936.

— (1930) A new genus of African starlings. *Sci. Pub. Cleveland Mus. Nat. Hist.* 1: 81–82.

Odgers, JA (1993) More on the feeding habits of the Black-bellied Starling. *Bee-eater* 44: 31–32.

Ogilvie-Grant, WR (1910) Ruwenzori Expedition reports. 16. Aves. *Trans. Zool. Soc. Lond.* 19: 253–480.

— and Forbes, HO (1903) Aves. In: Forbes, HO (Ed.) *The natural history of Sokotra and Abd-el Kuri.* Pp 19–72. RH Porter, London.

Olivier, RCD and Laurie, WA (1974) Birds associating with hippopotamuses. *Auk* 91: 169–170.

Oustalet, E (1879) Description d'une nouvelle espèce de merle bronze (*Coccycolius iris*). *Bull. Soc. Philom. Paris* ser. 7 vol. 3: 84–86.

Page, N and Oatley, TB (1979) Indian mynas feeding on ticks. *Lammergeyer* 27: 50.

Paget-Wilkes, AH (1924) Notes on the birds of the Grahamstown district, Cape Province, South Africa. *Ibis* 11th ser. 6: 720–763.

Pakenham, RHW (1936) Field-notes on the birds of Zanzibar and Pemba. *Ibis* 13th ser. 6: 249–272.

— (1979) *The birds of Zanzibar and Pemba.* British Ornithologists' Union, London.

Paludan, K (1936) Report on the birds collected during Professor O. Olufsen's expedition to French Sudan and Nigeria in the year 1927; with field notes by the collector Mr Harry Madsen. *Vidensk. Medd. Dansk Naturh. Foren.* 100: 247–346.

Pandey, DN (1991) Nesting habitat selection by the Pied Myna *Sturnus contra* Linn. *J. Bombay Nat. Hist. Soc.* 88: 285–286.

Parasara, UA, Parasharya, BM and Yadav, DN (1990) Studies on the nestling food of the Bank Myna, *Acridotheres ginginianus* (Latham). *Pavo* 28: 37–42.

Parelius, DA (1967) A nest of *Onychognathus morio neumanni* in the Ivory Coast. *Bull. Nigerian Orn. Soc.* 4(13–14): 40.

Parish, D and Prentice, C (1989) Chestnut-cheeked Starling *Sturnus philippensis*: a first record for mainland South-East Asia. *Bull. Br. Orn. Club* 109: 107–108.

Parkes, KC (1952) The races of the Bald Starling of the Philippines. *Condor* 54: 55–57.

Parmelee, A (1959) *All the birds of the Bible.* Lutterworth Press, London.

Parrack, JD (1973) *The naturalist in Mallorca.* David and Charles, London.

Parsons, JJ (1960) Sobre la caza a gran escala del Estornino Pinto (*Sturnus vulgaris*) en España. *Ardeola* 6: 235–241.

Partridge, WR (1964) Breeding the Magpie Starling (*Speculipastor bicolor*). *Avicult. Mag.* 70: 196–198.

— (1966) Breeding the Golden-crested Myna (*Mino coronatus*). *Avicult. Mag.* 72: 128–129.

Pascual, JA (1992) *Reproducción y alimentación del Estornino Negro (Sturnus unicolor) en un rebollar.* PhD thesis, University of Salamanca.

— (1993) Ocupación de distintos modelos de nidal por el Estornino Negro (*Sturnus unicolor*). *Doñana Acta Vertebrata* 20: 165–178.

Patel, JR, Yadav, D N, Mathew, K L and Parasharya, B M (1992) The food of nestling Brahminy Myna *Sturnus pagodarum* (Gmelin). *Pavo* 30: 109–117.

Patten, G (1980a) Red-winged Starlings (R745). *Wits Bird Club News* 111: 24.

— (1980b) Ectoparasites eaten from host mammals. *Wits Bird Club News* 109: 13.

Pavey, CR (1991) Comments on the range, seasonality and behaviour of some north Queensland birds. *Sunbird* 21: 13–18.

Paxton, M and Cooper, T (1986) Wattled Starlings breeding at Rietfontein, Etosha. *Lanioturdus* 22: 37–40.

Paz, U (1987) *The Birds of Israel*. Christopher Helm, London.

Peck, B (1983) Breeding notes for 1983. *Avicult. Mag.* 89: 146–151.

Peckover, WS (1975) Yellow-faced Myna (Grackle) *PNG Bird Soc. Newsletter* 109: 3.

Pek, LV and Fedyanina, TF (1961) Rose-coloured Starling. In Yanushevich, A I (ed.) *The birds of Kirghiziya. Vol. 3*. Academy of Sciences of the Kirghiz SSR, Frunze [In Russian].

Penry, EH (1979) Early and late dates for Splendid Starlings (*Lamprotornis splendidus*). *Bull. Zambian Orn. Soc.* 11: 36–38.

Penzhorn, BL (1981) Association between birds and mountain zebras. *Ostrich* 52: 63–64.

— (1982) A partial albino Cape Glossy Starling. *Ostrich* 53: 205.

— and Cassidy, R (1985) A partial albino long-tailed starling. *Bokmakierie* 37: 92.

Perdeck, AC (1967) The Starling as a passage migrant in Holland. *Bird Study* 14: 129–152.

Peris, SJ (1980a) Biologìa del Estornino Negro (*Sturnus unicolor* Temm.). *Ardeola* 25: 207–240.

— (1980b) Biologìa del Estornino Negro (*Sturnus unicolor*). II. Dieta del pollo. *Doñana, Acta Vertebrata* 7: 249–260.

— (1981) Tamaño del bando y comportamiento alimenticio del Estornino Negro (*Sturnus unicolor* Temm.). *Studia Oecologica* 2: 155–169.

— (1983) Criteria for age determination in the Spotless Starling (*Sturnus unicolor*): cranial pneumatisation and tarsal colour. *J. Orn.* 124: 78–81.

— (1984a) Nidificación y puesta en el Estornino Negro. *Salamanca, Revista provincial de estudios* 11–12: 175–234.

— (1984b) Descripción y desarrollo del pollo del Estornino Negro. *Ardeola* 31: 3–16.

— (1988) Postjuvenile and postnuptial moult of the Spotless Starling (*Sturnus unicolor*). *Gerfaut* 78: 101–112.

— (1991) Ringing recoveries of the Spotless Starling *Sturnus unicolor* in Spain. *Ring. Migr.* 12: 124–125.

—, Motis, A, Martinez-Vilalta, A, and Ferrer, X (1991) Winterquartiere und Winterbestand des Stars (*Sturnus vulgaris*) in Spanien während der letzen 30 Jahre. *J. Orn.* 132: 445–449.

Perumal, RS, Subramaniam, TR and David, PL (1971) Studies on the birds visiting CSH-1 sorghum and the extent of bird damage. *Andhra Agric. J.* 18: 205–207.

Peterjohn, BG, Sauer, JR and Link, WA (1994) The 1992 and 1993 summary of the North American breeding bird survey. *Bird Populations* 2: 46–61.

Pettet, A (1975) Breeding behaviour of *Clamator glandarius* at Ibadan. *Bull. Nigerian Orn. Soc.* 11: 34–40.

— (1977) Seasonal changes in nectar-feeding by birds at Zaria, Nigeria. *Ibis* 119: 291–308.

Petzsch, H (1951) Über den wissenschaftlichen Wert von Wirbeltierbastarden aus zoologischen Gärten. *Zool. Garten* 18: 183–196.

Phillips, EL (1896) On birds observed in the Goolis mountains in northern Somaliland. *Ibis* 7th ser. 2: 62–87.

Pickles, R (1989) Burchell's Starlings breed in borehole tower. *Babbler* 18: 40–42.

Pinto, AA da R (1958) A contribution towards the study of the avifauna of the island of Inhaca. *Bol. Soc. Estudos Prov. Mocambique* 112: 29–62.

— (1965) Contribuiça~o para ó conhecimento da avifauna de regia~o nordeste do distrito do Moxico, Angola. *Bol. Inst. Invest. Cient. Angola* 1(2): 53–249.

— and Lamm, DW (1956) Contribution to the study of the ornithology of Sul do Save (Mozambique). Part III. *Mem. Mus. Dr Alvaro de Castro* 4: 107–167.

Pinxten, R and Eens, M (1990) Polygyny in the European Starling: effect on female reproductive success. *Anim. Behav.* 40: 1035–1047.

—, — (1994) Male feeding of nestlings in the facultatively polygynous European Starling: allocation patterns and effect on female reproductive success. *Behaviour* 129: 113–140.

—, Eens, M and Verheyen, RF (1989a). Polygyny in the European Starling *Sturnus vulgaris. Behaviour* 111: 234–256.

—, —, — (1991a) Brood parasitism in European Starlings: host and parasite adaptations. *Acta XX Congressus Internationalis Ornithologici*, pp 1003–1011.

—, —, — (1991b) Conspecific nest parasitism in the European Starling. *Ardea* 79: 15–30.

—, —, — (1994) Communal breeding in the European Starling: evidence from DNA fingerprinting. *Auk* 111: 482–486.

—, —, Van Elsacker, L & Verheyen, R F (1989b). An extreme case of polygyny in the European Starling *Sturnus vulgaris. Bird Study* 36: 45–48.

Pitman, CRS (1956) Oxpeckers. *Zoo Life* 11: 21–25.

Pizzey, G (1980) *A field guide to the birds of Australia*. Collins, Sydney.

Plowes, D (1944) Nesting of Cape Glossy Starling. *Ostrich* 15: 70–71.

Pooley, AG (1967) Some miscellaneous ornithological observations from the Ndumu Game Reserve. *Ostrich* 38: 31–32.

Porter, RF and Martins, RP (1996) The Socotra Starling *Onychognathus frater* and Somali Starling *O. blythii. Sandgrouse* 17: 151–154.

Potts, GR (1967) Urban Starling roosts in the British Isles. *Bird Study* 14: 35–42.

Poulsen, H. (1956) A study of anting behaviour in birds. *Dansk orn. Foren. Tidsskr.* 50: 267–298.

Priest, CD (1936) *The birds of Southern Rhodesia*. Vol. IV. William Clowes, London.

Prigogine, A (1971) Les oiseaux de l'Itombe et de son hinterland. *Mus. Roy. Afr. Centr. Sci. Zool.* 185: 1–298.

— (1983) Contribution aux migrations de *Lamprotornis splendidus bailundensis. Gerfaut* 73: 193–195.

— and Benson, CW (1979) The mysterious movements of *Lamprotornis splendidus bailundensis. Gerfaut* 69: 437–446.

Pringle, VL (1971) Nesting colony of Wattled Starlings. *Bee-eater* 22(1): 2–3.

Proud, A (1987) Some summer records from north-west Somalia. *Scopus* 11: 41–43.

Prys-Jones, RP (1991) The occurrence of biannual primary moult in passerines. *Bull. Br. Orn. Club* 111: 150–152.

Pyle, P, Howell, SNG, Yunick, RP and Desante, DF (1987) *Identification guide to North American passerines*. Slate Creek Press, Bolinas.

Pyper, S (1991) Breeding the Amethyst Starling. *Avicult. Mag.* 97: 144–146.

Querengässer, A (1973) Über das Einemsen von Singvögeln und die Reifung dieses Verhaltens. *J. Orn.* 114: 96–117.

Raffaele, HA (1989) *A guide to the birds of Puerto Rico and the Virgin Islands.* Princeton University Press, Princeton.

Rahman, MK and Hussain, KZ (1988) Notes on the breeding record of the Common Myna, *Acridotheres tristis* Linnaeus. *Bangladesh J. Zool.* 16: 155–157.

Rand, AL (1936) Distribution and habits of Madagascar birds. *Bull. Am. Mus. Nat. Hist.* 72: 145–499.

— (1942) Results of the Archbold Expeditions No. 42, birds of the 1936–1937 New Guinea Expedition. *Bull. Amer. Mus. Nat. Hist.* 79: 289–366.

— (1951) Birds from Liberia. *Fieldiana, Zool.* 32(9): 561–653.

—, Friedmann, H and Traylor, MA (1959) Birds from Gabon and Moyen Congo. *Fieldiana, Zool.* 41(2): 221–411.

Reichel, JD and Glass, PO (1990) Micronesian Starling predation on seabird eggs. *Emu* 90: 135–136.

Reichenow, A (1879) Neue Vögel aus Ostafrika. *Orn. Centralbl.* 4: 107–114.

— (1887) Dr. Fischer's ornithologische Sammlungen während der letzten Reise zum Victoria Njansa. *J. Orn.* 35: 38–78.

— (1893) Diagnosen neuer Vogelarten aus central-Afrika. *Orn. Monatsber.* 1: 29–32.

— (1900) Neues aus Deutsch-Ostafrika. *Orn. Monatsber.* 8: 98–100.

— (1903) *Die Vögel Afrikas.* Vol. 2. Neumann, Neudamm.

— (1909) Neue Arten von Kamerun. *Orn. Monatsber.* 17: 140.

— (1911) Die ornithologischen Sammlungen der zoologisch-botanischen Kamerun-Expedition 1908 und 1909. *Mitt. zool. Mus. Berlin* 5: 203–258.

Restall, R (1968) The Superb Spreo Starling (*Spreo superbus*). *Avicult. Mag.* 74: 113–123.

Richard, BR (1975) Breeding the long-tailed glossy starling *Lamprotornis mevesii purpureus* at the Jersey Zoological Park. *Rep. Jersey Wildl. Preserv. Trust* 11: 39–40.

Richmond, CW (1897) Descriptions of ten new species of birds discovered by Dr W.L. Abbott in the Kilimanjaro region of East Africa. *Auk* 14: 154–164.

Riddiford, N, Harvey, PV and Shepherd, KB (1989) Daurian Starling: new to the Western Palearctic. *Brit. Birds* 82: 603–612.

Riekert, B and Clinning, C (1985) The use of artificial nest boxes in the Daan Viljoen Game Park. *Bokmakierie* 37: 84–86.

Riley, JH (1929) A review of the birds of the islands of Siberut and Sipora, Mentawi Group (Spolia Mentawiensia). *Proc. U.S. Natl. Mus.* 75: 1–45.

Rilling, G (1972) Albinism in a Superb Starling and a topi. *E. Afr. Nat. Hist. Soc. Bull.* April: 63.

Rinke, D (1986) Notes on the avifauna of Niuafo'ou Island, Kingdom of Tonga. *Emu* 86: 82–86.

Ripley, SD (1944) The bird fauna of the West Sumatran islands. *Bull. Mus. Comp. Zool.* 94: 307–429.

— (1983) Habits of the Bank Myna, *Acridotheres ginginianus*. *J. Bombay Nat. Hist. Soc.* 80: 219.

— and Rabor, DS (1958) Notes on a collection of birds from Mindoro Island, Philippines. *Peabody Mus. Nat. Hist. Bull.* 13: 1–83.

— and Bond, GM (1966) The birds of Socotra and Abd-el-Kuri. *Smithson. Misc. Coll.* 151(7): 1–37.

—, Saha, SS and Beehler, BM (1991) Notes on birds from Upper Noa Dihing, Arunachal Pradesh, Northeastern India. *Bull. Br. Orn. Club* 111: 19–28.

Risdon, D (1990) Breeding the Royal Starling. *Avicult. Mag.* 96: 89–91.

Rivero, EM, Lartigau, B, Caridad, PH and Llorens, PR (1996) Registro concreto de nidificación del estornino pinto (*Sturnus vulgaris*) en la Argentina. *Nuestras Aves* 34: 46.

Roberts, A (1922) Review of the nomenclature of South African birds. *Ann. Transvaal Mus.* 8: 187–272.

— (1932) Migration of African birds. *Ostrich* 3: 97–109.

— (1939) Swifts and other birds nesting in buildings. *Ostrich* 10: 85–99.

Roberts, PJ (1982) Post-juvenile moult of Rose-coloured Starling. *Brit. Birds* 75: 38–40.

Roberts, SC (1995) Gleaning in klipspringer preorbital glands by Red-winged Starlings and Yellow-bellied Bulbuls. *Ostrich* 66: 147–148.

Roberts, TJ (1992) *The birds of Pakistan.* Vol. 2. Oxford University Press, Oxford.

Robertson, I (1992) New information on birds in Cameroon. *Bull. Br. Orn. Club* 112: 36–42.

— (1993) Unusual records from Cameroon. *Malimbus* 14: 62–63.

Robiller, F and Gerstner, R (1985) Zucht des Smaragdglanzstars (*Coccycolius iris*). *Gefied. Welt* 109: 158–159.

Robinson, J, Robinson, C St C and Winterbottom, JM (1957) Notes on the birds of the Cape L'Agulhas region. *Ostrich* 28: 147–163.

Rochard, JBA and Horton, N (1980) Birds killed by aircraft in the United Kingdom, 1966–1976. *Bird Study* 27: 227–234.

Rowan, MK (1955) The breeding biology and behaviour of the Redwinged Starling *Onychognathus morio*. *Ibis* 97: 663–705.

— (1971) Adventures of a Red-winged Starling. *Bokmakierie* 23: 74–76.

Rowley, I (1976) Cooperative breeding in Australian birds. *Proc. XVI Int.Orn. Congr.* pp 657–666.

Rudebeck, G (1955a) Some observations at a roost of European Swallows and other birds in the south-eastern Transvaal. *Ibis* 97: 572–580.

— (1955b) Aves I. In: Hanstrom, B, Brinck, P and Rudebeck, G (Eds). *South African animal life: results of the Lund University expedition in 1950–1951.* Vol. II: 426–576. Almqvist and Wiksell, Stockholm.

Rustamov, AK (1958) *Birds of Turkmenistan.* Vol. 2. Academy of Sciences of the Turkmen SSR, Ashkhabad [In Russian].

Ruthke, P (1971) Nächtlicher Gesang von Einfarbstaren (*Sturnus unicolor*) am Schlafplatz. *Vogelwelt* 92: 191.

Safford, RJ (1996) A nesting colony of Yellow-eyed Starlings *Aplonis mystacea*. *Emu* 96: 140–142.

Sagitov, AK, Belyalova, L E and Fundukchiev, S E (1990) Distribution of the Common Myna (*Acridotheres tristis tristis*) in central Asia and Kazakhstan. *Sovremennaya Ornitologiya* 1990: 86–91 [In Russian].

Salikhbaev, KS and Bogdanov, AN (1967) *Fauna of the Uzbek SSR Vol. 2, Birds Part 4.* Fan, Tashkent [In Russian].

Sandhu, PS and Toor, HS (1984) Some pestiferous birds in agriculture and their management in Punjab. In: Atwal, AS, Bains, SS and Dhindsa, MS (eds.) *Status of wildlife in Punjab.* Indian Ecological Society, Ludhiana.

Sane, S (1983) *Some aspects of the wildlife/pet trade in India.* Bombay Natural History Society, Bombay.

Satheesan, SM, Grubh, RB and Pimento, RJ (1990) An updated list of bird and bat species involved in collision with aircraft in India. *J. Bombay Nat. Hist. Soc.* 89: 129–132.

Sawyer, RCJ (1982) Breeding the Splendid Starling *Lamprocolius splendidus splendidus. Avicult. Mag.* 88: 189–191.

Scamell, KM (1964) The breeding of the Shelley's Starling. *Avicult. Mag.* 70: 198–200.

— (1969) Breeding the Spotted-winged Stare (*Saroglossa spiloptera*). *Avicult. Mag.* 75: 262–265.

Schenk, J (1907) The Rose-coloured Starling in the Hortobagy in 1907. *Aquila* 14: 252–275 [In Hungarian].

— (1931–34) Die Brutinvasion des Rosenstars in Ungarn in den jahren 1932 und 1933. *Aquila* 28–31: 136–153.

Schifter, H (1986) Beiträge zur Ornithologie des nordlichen Senegal. *Ann. Naturhist. Mus. Wien* 87B: 83–116.

Schlee, MA (1993) Breeding biology and behaviour of captive Bank Mynas, *Acridotheres ginginianus* (Latham). *Zool. Garten N. F.* 63: 126–142.

Schleussner, G (1990) Experimentelle Induktion sektoraler Handschwingenmauser bei adulten männlichen Staren (*Sturnus vulgaris*). *J. Orn.* 131: 151–155.

Schodde, R (1977) Contributions to Papuasian ornithology. VI. Survey of the birds of southern Bougainville Island, Papua New Guinea. *Division of Wildlife Research Technical Paper No. 34*: 101 pp.

Schönwetter, M (1983) *Handbuch der oologie* 37: 591–622. Edited and revised by W. Meise. Akademie-Verlag, Berlin.

—, Dittami, JP and Gwinner, E (1985) Testosterone implants affect molt in male European Starlings, *Sturnus vulgaris. Physiol. Zool.* 58: 597–604.

Schuster, L (1926) Beiträge zur Verbreitung und Biologie der Vögel Deutsch-Ostafrikas. III. *J. Orn.* 54: 709–742.

Sclater, WL (1930) *Systema avium Aethiopicarum*. British Ornithologists' Union, London.

—, and Moreau, RE (1933) Taxonomic and field notes on some birds of north-eastern Tanganyika Territory. Part IV. *Ibis* 13th ser. 3: 187–219.

Scott, RE (1965) First-year Starling retaining juvenile flight feathers and comments on post-fledging moult. *Bull. Br. Orn. Club* 85: 66–67.

Seibels, B (1996) In situ conservation of the Bali Mynah: no easy task. *AZA Regional Conference Proceedings* 1996, pp 361–362.

Sengupta, S (1968) Studies in the life of the Common Myna, *Acridotheres tristis tristis* (Linn.) 1. Breeding biology. *Proc. Zool. Soc. Calcutta* 21: 1–27.

— (1976) Food and feeding ecology of the Common Myna. *Proc. Ind. Nat. Sci. Acad.* 42: 338–345.

— (1982) *The Common Myna*. Chand, New Delhi.

Serebrennikov, MK (1931) Die Rosenstar (*Pastor roseus* L.), seine Lebensweise und ökonomische Bedeutung in Uzbekistan (Turkestan). *J. Orn.* 79: 29–56.

Serle, W (1943) Field observations on some north Nigerian birds. *Ibis* 14th ser. 4: 1–47.

— (1954) A second contribution to the ornithology of the British Cameroons. *Ibis* 96: 47–80.

— (1965) A third contribution to the ornithology of the British Cameroons. *Ibis* 107: 230–246.

— (1981) The breeding seasons of birds in the lowland rainforest and in the montane forest of West Cameroon. *Ibis* 123: 62–74.

Sharpe, RB (1891) On the birds collected by Mr. F.J. Jackson during his recent expedition to Uganda through the territory of the Imperial British East African Company. *Ibis* 6th ser. 3: 233–260.

Shelley, GE (1889) On the birds collected by Mr. H.C.V. Hunter, F.Z.S., in eastern Africa. *Proc. Zool. Soc. London* 1889: 356–372.

— (1906) *The birds of Africa.* Vol. V. Part I. RH Porter, London.

Shelton, L (1982) In: News and views. *Avicult. Mag.* 88: 58–59.

Sheppard, PA (1909) A list of, and notes on, birds collected and observed in the district of Beira, Portuguese S.E. Africa. *J. S. Afr. Orn. Un.* 5: 24–49.

Shi-chun, L, Xi-Xuo, L, Xuo-Kuang, T and Yao-Hua, S (1975) On feeding habits of the Rose-coloured Starling (*Sturnus roseus*) and its effects on locust population density. *Acta Zool. Sinica* 21: 71–77 [In Chinese].

Shirota, Y, Sanada, M and Masaki, S (1983) Eye-spotted balloons as a device to scare Grey Starlings. *Appl. Ent. Zool.* 18: 545–549.

Short, LL and Horne, JFM (1985a) Notes on some birds of the Arabuko-Sokoke forest. *Scopus* 9: 117–126.

—, — (1985b) Notes on some birds of Ol Ari Nyiro, Laikipia Plateau. *Scopus* 9: 137–140.

—, — (1988) Order Piciformes. Indicatoridae, honeyguides. In: Fry, CH, Keith, S and Urban, EK (Eds). *The birds of Africa.* Vol. III: 486–512. Academic Press, London.

—, — and Muringo-Gichuki, C (1990) Annotated checklist of the birds of East Africa. *Proc. west. Found. vert. Zool.* 4(3): 61–246.

Shuel, R (1938) Further notes on the eggs and nesting habits of birds in northern Nigeria (Kano Province). *Ibis* 14th ser. 2: 463–480.

Sibley, CG and Ahlquist, JE (1974) The relationships of the African sugarbirds (*Promerops*). *Ostrich* 45: 22–30.

—, — (1984) The relationships of the starlings (Sturnidae: Sturnini) and the mockingbirds (Sturnidae: Mimini). *Auk* 101: 230–243.

—, — (1990) *Phylogeny and classification of birds.* Yale University Press, New Haven and London.

Sibley, CG and Monroe, BL Jr (1990) *Distribution and taxonomy of birds of the world.* Yale University Press, New Haven and London.

—, and — (1993) *Supplement to the distribution and taxonomy of the birds of the world.* New Haven, Yale University Press.

Sieber, J (1978) Freiland Beobachtungen und Versuch einer Bestandsaufnahme des Bali-stars *Leucopsar rothschildi. J. Orn.* 119: 102–106.

— (1980) Lappenstare: Gemeinschaftsnestbau. *Gefied. Welt* 104(1): 10–11.

— (1983) Nestbau, Brut und Jungenaufzucht beim Balistar (*Leucopsar rothschildi*). *Zool. Garten N. F. Jena* 53: 281–289.

Simmons, KEL (1961) Some recent records of anting in passerine birds. *Avicult. Mag.* 67: 124–132.

— (1966) Anting and the problem of self-stimulation. *J. Zool., Lond.* 149: 145–162.

— (1986) *The sunning behaviour of birds.* Bristol Ornithological Club, Bristol.

Simwat, GS and Sidhu, AS (1974) Developmental period and feeding habits of Bank Myna, *Acridotheres ginginianus* (Latham) in Punjab. *J. Bombay Nat. Hist. Soc.* 71: 305–308.

Singh, J, Sidhu, AS, Dhindsa, MS and Saini, HK (1990) The effect of fodder cuttings on larval population, disease incidence and bird predation of *Helicoverpa armigera* in berseem. *Ann. Biol.* 6: 153–159.

Siu-Ying, L (1940) A preliminary report on the foods of the Chinese Crested Mynah in Foochow. *Biol. Bull. Fukien Christian University, Foochow* 2: 95–98 [In Chinese].

Sjöstedt, Y (Ed.) (1910) *Wissenschaftliche Erbebnisse der schwedischen zoologischen Expedition nach dem Kilimandjaro, dem Meru und den umgebenden Massaisteppen Deutsch-Ostafrikas 1905–1906.* 1 Band, Abteilung 1–7. Palmquist, Stockholm.

Skead, CJ (1995) *Life-history notes on East Cape birds 1940–1990.* Vol. 1. Algoa Regional Services Council, Port Elizabeth.

Skead, DM (1966) Birds frequenting the intertidal zone of the Cape Peninsula. *Ostrich* 37: 10–16.

Skorupa, JP (1982) East African breeding records for *Cossypha cyanocampter* and *Onychognathus fulgidus. Scopus* 6: 46–47.

Smith, HG and Schantz, T von (1993) Extra-pair paternity in the European Starling: the effect of polygyny. *Condor* 95: 1006–1015.

Smith, KD (1957) An annotated checklist of the birds of Eritrea. *Ibis* 99: 1–26.

— (1965) On the birds of Morocco. *Ibis* 107: 493–526.

Smith, VW (1964) Further notes on birds breeding near Vom, northern Nigeria. *Nigerian Field* 29: 161–174.

Smythies, BE (1960) *The birds of Borneo.* Malayan Nature Soc., Kuala Lumpur.

— (1981) *The birds of Burma.* Malayan Nature Soc., Kuala Lumpur.

Snow, DW (1950) The birds of São Tomé and Principe in the Gulf of Guinea. *Ibis* 92: 579–595.

— (1981) Tropical frugivorous birds and their food plants: a world survey. *Biotropica* 13: 1–14.

Sody, HJV (1930) De broedtijden der vogels in West en Oost Java. *Tectona* 33: 183–198.

— (1992) On habitat utilization in various south Asian starlings. *Mitt. Zool. Mus. Berl.* 68 Suppl. Ann. Orn. 16: 115–123.

Sontag, WA (1978) Notizen zu Nestbau, Zucht(versuchen) und Verhalten in der "Brutpflegephase" beim Lappenstar, *Creatophora cinerea* (Meuschen). *Zool. Garten* 48: 235–244.

— (1979a) Über Lebens und Balzgewohnheiten des Lappenstars. *Gefied. Welt* 103: 70–72, 84–85.

— (1979b) Beobachtungen zum nicht-epigamen Verhalten des Lappenstars, *Creatophora cinerea* (Meuschen). *Bonn. zool. Beitr.* 30: 367–379.

— (1979c) Remarks concerning the social behaviour of Wattled Starlings, *Creatophora cinerea* (Meuschen). *J. Nepal Res. Centre* 2/3: 263–268.

— (1980) Gefangenschaftsstudien zum Sozialverhalten und zur Soziologie des Lappenstars *Creatophora cinerea* (Meuschen) (Sturnidae). *Z. Kölner Zoo* 23: 33–39.

— (1981a) Einige Beobachtungen und Bemerkungen zum Leben des Lappenstars, *Creatophora cinerea* (Meuschen). *Gefied. Welt* 105: 41–42.

— (1981b) Zur Rolle des Flügels im Ausdruck des Lappenstars *Creatophora cinerea* (Meuschen). *Zool. Garten* 51: 337–342.

— (1984) Die äusseren Differenzierungen am Kopf, agonistisches Verhalten und Statusanzeige beim Lappenstar *Creatophora cinerea* (Meuschen). *Verh. Dtsch. Zool. Ges.* 77: 335.

— (1985) Gesangsformen unterschiedlicher Information biem Pagodenstar (*Sturnus pagodarum*, Sturnidae) und ein Vergleich dieses Phänomens bei anderen Vogelarten. *Verh. Dtsch. Zool. Ges.* 78: 216.

— (1985a) Song and courtship of the Wattled Starling *Creatophora cinerea. Malimbus* 7: 129–135.

— (1985b) Zur Funktion des Gesangs bei Sturniden (Staren). *Luscinia* 45: 181–200.

— (1985c) Die morphologische Besonderheiten am Kopf des Lappenstars *Creatophora cinerea* (Meuschen) und ihre biologische Funktion. *Proc. Intern. Symp. Afr. Vertebr., Bonn* 1985: 395–406.

— (1989a) Der Flügel als Ausdrucksorgan bei Vögeln. Der Fall des Lappenstars *Creatophora cinerea*, einer afrikanischen Starenart. *Luscinia* 46: 125–163.

— (1989b) Zur Raumnutzung zweier systematisch nahestehender Stare (*Leucopsar rothschildi* und *Gracupica nigricollois*) unter kontrollierten Bedingungen. *Verh. Dtsch. Zool. Ges.* 82: 291.

— (1990) Species, class and individual characteristics in the African Wattled Starling, *Creatophora cinerea. Bonn. zool. Beitr.* 41: 163–169.

— (1991) Habitatsunterschiede, Balzverhalten, Paarbildung und Paarbindung beim Lappenstar *Creatophora cinerea. Acta Biol. Benrodis* 3: 99–114.

Stark, AC (1900) *The birds of South Africa.* Vol. 1. RH Porter, London.

Stepanov, EA (1987) Food supplies and coloniality in the Rose-coloured Starling (*Pastor roseus*) in central Kazakhstan. *Ornitologiya* 22: 118–123 [In Russian].

Stevenson, H (1866) *The birds of Norfolk.* Vol. 1. Matchett and Stevenson, Norwich.

Stevenson, T (1983) *The birds of Lake Baringo.* Sealpoint Publicity, Nairobi.

Sticklen R (1981) Nesting association between Eclectus Parrots and Shining Starlings, Iron Range, QLD. *Bird Observer* No. 597: 87.

Storer, TI (1931) Known and potential results of bird and animal introduction with especial reference to California. *Monthly Bulls. Dept. Agric. Calif.* 20: 267–273.

Stouffer, TC, Romagnano, LC, Lombardo, MP, Hoffenberg, AS and Power, HW (1988) A case of communal nesting in the European Starling. *Condor* 90: 241–245.

Stresemann, E (1912) Description of a new genus and species of birds from the Dutch East India islands. *Bull. Br. Orn. Club* 31: 4–6.

— (1940) Die Vögel von Celebes. *J. Orn.* 88: 1–135.

— (1925) Ueber einige *Lamprocolius*-Arten. *J. Orn.* 73: 147–161.

— and Stresemann, V (1966) Die Mauser der Vögel. *J. Orn.* 107: Sonderheft.

Stuart, SN (Ed.) (1986) *Conservation of Cameroon montane forests.* International Council for Bird Preservation, Cambridge.

Studer-Thiersch, A (1969) Das Zugverhalten schweizerischer Stare *Sturnus vulgaris* nach Ringfunden. *Ornithol. Beob.* 66: 105–144.

Stutterheim, CJ (1974) Ringing and colour-marking the Red-billed Oxpecker in the Kruger National Park. *Safring News*

3(2): 11–15.

— (1977) Ectoparasites of the Red-billed Oxpecker in the Kruger National Park. *S. Af. J. Sci.* 73: 281.

— (1980a) Sheep as animated perches. *Wits Bird Club News* 109: 13.

— (1980b) Symbiont selection of red-billed oxpecker in the Hluhluwe-Umfolozi game reserve complex. *Lammergeyer* 30: 21–25.

— (1980c) Moult cycle of the Red-billed Oxpecker in the Kruger National Park. *Ostrich* 51: 107–111.

— (1981a) The feeding behaviour of the Red-billed Oxpecker. *S. Afr. J. Zool.* 16: 267–269.

—, — (1981b) The movements of a population of Red-billed Oxpeckers (*Buphagus erythrorhynchus*) in the Kruger National Park. *Koedoe* 24: 99–107.

— (1982a) Past and present ecological distribution of the Red-billed Oxpecker (*Buphagus erythrorhynchus*) in South Africa. *S. Afr. J. Zool.* 17: 190–196.

— (1982b) Breeding biology of the Red-billed Oxpecker in the Kruger National Park. *Ostrich* 53: 79–90.

— (1982c) Timing of breeding of the Red-billed Oxpecker (*Buphagus erythrorhynchus*) in the Kruger National Park. *S. Afr. J. Zool.* 17: 126–129.

—, and Brooke, RK (1981) Past and present ecological distribution of the Yellow-billed Oxpecker in South Africa. *S. Afr. J. Zool.* 16: 44–49.

—, Mundy, PJ and Cook, AW (1976) Comparisons between the two species of oxpecker. *Bokmakierie* 28: 12–14.

—, and Stutterheim, IM (1980) Evidence of an increase in a Red-billed Oxpecker population in the Kruger National Park. *S. Afr. J. Zool.* 15: 284.

—, — (1981a) A possible decline of a Red-billed Oxpecker population in the Pilansberg Complex, Bophuthatswana. *Ostrich* 52: 56–57.

, — (1981b) Observations on the redbilled oxpecker in Mkuzi Game Reserve and Nxwala State Land. *Lammergeyer* 31: 1–4.

Stutterheim, IM, Bezuidenhout, JD and Elliott, EGR (1988) Comparative feeding behaviour and food preferences of oxpeckers (*Buphagus erythrorhynchus* and *B. africanus*) in captivity. *Onderstepoort J. vet. Res.* 55: 173–179.

—, and Panagis, K (1985a) The status and distribution of oxpeckers (Aves: Passeriformes: Buphagidae) in Kavango and Caprivi, South West Africa/Namibia. *S. Afr. J. Zool.* 20: 10–14.

—, — (1985b) Roosting behaviour and host selection of oxpeckers (Aves: Buphaginae) in Moremi Wildlife Reserve, Botswana, and eastern Caprivi, South West Africa. *S. Afr. J. Zool.* 20: 237–240.

—, — (1988) Capture and transport of oxpeckers *Buphagus erythrorhynchus* & *B. africanus* from the eastern Caprivi Strip, SWA/Namibia. *Madoqua* 15: 251–253.

Summers, RW (1989) Starlings excavating nest holes in sand dunes. *Scott. Birds* 15: 181.

— and Feare, CJ (1995) Roost departure by European Starlings *Sturnus vulgaris*: effects of competition and choice of feeding site. *J. Avian Biol.* 26: 289–295.

— Westlake, GE and Feare, CJ (1987) Differences in the physical condition of starlings at the centre and periphery of roosts. *Ibis* 129: 96–102.

Svensson, L (1992) *Identification guide to European passerines*. 4th edition. Svensson, Stockholm.

Sweijd, N and Craig, AJFK (1991) Histological basis of age-related changes in iris color in the African Pied Starling (*Spreo bicolor*). *Auk* 108: 53–59.

Swynnerton, CFM (1908) Further notes on the birds of Gazaland. *Ibis* 9th ser. 2: 1–107.

Symons, HG (1949) The nesting of the Plum-coloured Starling. *Ostrich* 20: 167–168.

Takenaka, M and Takenaka, S (1994) Distribution patterns and characteristics of Grey Starling *Sturnus cineraceus* summer roosts in the eastern Kanto area. *Jap. J. Ornithol.* 43: 11–17.

Tarboton, WR, Kemp, MI and Kemp, AC (1987) *Birds of the Transvaal*. Transvaal Museum, Pretoria.

Taylor, JS (1936) Birds in the garden. *Ostrich* 7: 45–48.

— (1951) Nesting habits of the Cape Glossy Starling (*Lamprocolius nitens phoenicopterus* Sw.). *Bee-eater* 2(1): 8.

Taylor, PB and Taylor, CA (1988) The status, movements and breeding of some birds in the Kikuyu Escarpment. *Tauraco* 1: 72–89.

Taylor, RH (1974) The use of floodlights by Red-winged Starlings for catching insects after dark. *Ostrich* 45: 32–33.

Temme, M (1979) Notes on the Violet-backed Starling (*Sturnus philippensis*) in Manila/Philippines. *Orn. Mitt. Gottingen* 31: 86–87.

Thiede, W and Thiede, U (1971) Zur Brutbiologie des Rostbackenstars. *Bonn. Zool. Beitr.* 22: 261–274.

Thiollay, J-M (1970) Récherches écologiques dans la savane de Lamto (Côté d'Ivoire): le peuplement avien, essai d'étude quantitative. *Terre Vie* 24: 108–144.

— (1985) The birds of Ivory Coast: status and distribution. *Malimbus* 7: 1–59.

Thomsen, F (1907) Locust birds in the Transvaal. *J. S. Afr. Orn. Un.* 3: 56–75.

Thomson, GM (1922) *The naturalisation of plants and animals in New Zealand*. Cambridge University Press, London.

Thomson, TS (1969) Breeding the Purple-headed Glossy Starling. *Avicult. Mag.* 75: 6–8.

Thomson, WR (1975) Long-tailed Starlings and Great Spotted Cuckoos at Chipinda Pools. *Honeyguide* 81: 35–36.

— (1982) Oxpeckers roosting on game animals. *Honeyguide* 110: 46–47.

Thonnerieux, Y (1988) État des connaissances sur la reproduction de l'avifaune du Burkina Faso (ex Haut Volta). *Oiseau Rev. fr. Orn.* 58: 120–146.

—, Walsh, JF and Bortoli, L (1989) L'avifaune de la ville de Ouagadougou. *Malimbus* 11: 7–40.

Thunberg, KP (1795) *Travels in Europe, Africa and Asia, made between the years 1770 and 1779*. F & C Rivington, London.

Thurow, TL and Black, HL (1981) Ecology and behaviour of the Gymnogene. *Ostrich* 52: 25–35.

Tilson, RL (1977) Pale-winged Starlings and klipspringers in the Kuiseb Canyon, Namib Desert Park. *Ostrich* 48: 110–111.

Tomek, T (1984) Materials to the breeding avifauna of the People's Democratic Republic of Korea. *Acta Zool. Cracov.* 27: 19–46.

Toor, HS and Ramzan, M (1974a) A study on grapes lost to birds. *Punjab Hort. J.* 14: 46–48.

— and — (1994b) Seasonal food and feeding habits of the birds of the Punjab – 1. *Journal of Research, Ludhiana* 11: 191–196.

Tosh, FE, Doto, IL, Beecher, SB and Chin, DTY (1970) Relationship of starling-blackbird roosts and endemic histoplasmosis. *Amer. Rev. Resp. Dis.* 101: 283–288.

Trail, PW (1994) Distribution and status of mynas in American Samoa. *Elepaio* 54: 19–21.

Traylor, MA (1963) Check-list of Angolan birds. *Publ. Cult. Co. Diam. Angola* 61: 1–250.

— (1965) A collection of birds from Barotseland and Bechuanaland. *Ibis* 107: 357–384.

— (1971) Molt and migration in *Cinnyricinclus leucogaster*. *J. Orn.* 112: 1–20.

Tree, AJ (1986) Blackbellied Starling project. *Diaz Diary* 151: 15.

— (1997) Lesser Blue-eared Starling. In: Harrison, JA, Allan, DG, Underhill, LG, Brown, CJ, Tree, AJ, Parker, V and Herremans, M (Eds), *The atlas of southern African birds*. BirdLife South Africa, Johannesburg.

Trevor, S and Lack, P (1976) Great Spotted Cuckoo parasitising Superb Starling. *E. Afr. Nat. Hist. Soc. Bull.* May/June: 50.

Tribe, GD (1991) Red-winged starlings feeding on the European wasp. *Plant Protection News* 23: 7.

Trollope, J (1987) British softbill imports – some observations. Part I: Corvidae to Coerebidae. *Avicult. Mag.* 93: 171–173.

Turner, DA and Forbes-Watson, AD (1976) Status of the White-crowned Starling *Spreo albicapillus* (Blyth) in Kenya. *Bull. Br. Orn. Club* 96: 58.

Tyagi, AK and Lamba, BS (1984) A contribution to the breeding biology of two Indian Mynas. *Recs. Zool. Surv. India* 55: 1–108.

Umeda, N, Okanoya, K, Nakamura, K and Furuya, I (1993) Operant conditioning of the Grey Starling, *Sturnus cineraceus*. *Jap. J. Ornithol.* 41: 9–16 [In Japanese].

Underhill, LG and Brown, CJ (1997) Sharp-tailed Starling. In: Harrison, JA, Allan, DG, Underhill, LG, Brown, CJ, Tree, AJ, Parker, V and Herremans, M (Eds), *The atlas of southern African birds*. BirdLife South Africa, Johannesburg.

—and Zucchini, W (1988) A model for avian primary moult. *Ibis* 130: 358–372.

Uno, H, Ohno, Y, Yamada, T and Miyamoto, K (1991) Neural coding of speech sound in the telencephalic auditory area of the mynah bird. *J. Comp. Physiol.* 169A: 231–239.

Urban, EK and Brown, LH (1971) *A checklist of the birds of Ethiopia*. Haile Selassie I University Press, Addis Ababa.

—, Buer, CE and Plage, GD (1970) Four descriptions of nesting, previously undescribed, from Ethiopia. *Bull. Br. Orn. Club* 90: 162–164.

Uys, CJ (1977) Notes on Wattled Starlings in the Western Cape. *Bokmakierie* 29: 87–89.

van Balen, B and Gepak, VH (1994) The captive breeding and conservation programme of the Bali Starling (*Leucopsar rothschildi*). In Olney, P J S, Mace, G M and Feistner, A T C (eds.) *Creative conservation: interactive management of wild and captive animals*. Ch. 24: 420–430.

van Bemmel, ACV and Voous, KH (1951) On the birds of the islands of Muna and Butung, S E Celebes. *Treubia* 21: 27–104.

van den Berg, AB (1982) Moults and basic plumages of Rose-coloured Starling. *Dutch Birding* 4: 136–139.

— and Bosman, CAW (1986) Supplementary notes on some birds of Lore Lindu Reserve, central Sulawesi. *Forktail* 1: 7–13.

van der Merwe, F (1984) 'n Nalatenskap van Rhodes: Europese Spreeus verdring gryskopspegte. *African Wildl.* 38: 152–157.

van der Zon, APM (1980) Bali's endangered white starling. *Oryx* 9: 345–349.

Vande Weghe, J-P (1973) Les periodes de nidification des oiseaux du parc national de l'Akagera au Rwanda. *Gerfaut* 63: 235–255.

van Helvoort, B (1987) Status and conservation needs of the Bali Starling. *Bull. Oriental Bird Club* 5: 9–12.

—, Soetawidjaja, MN and Hartojo (1985) *The Rothschild's Mynah (Leucopsar rothschildi) – a case for captive or wild breeding?* International Council for Bird Preservation, Cambridge.

van Marle, JG and Voous KH (1988) *The birds of Sumatra*. Check-list No. 10. British Ornithologists' Union, Tring.

van Niekerk, DJ (1996) Albino Pied Starling *Spreo bicolor* (Sturnidae) with some notes on albinism in the Motacillidae. *Mirafra* 13(1): 9–10.

van Someren, VD (1951) The red-billed oxpecker and its relation to stock in Kenya. *E. Afr. Agric. J.* 17: 1–11.

— (1958) *A bird watcher in Kenya*. Oliver and Boyd, London and Edinburgh.

van Someren, VGL (1916) A list of birds collected in Uganda and British East Africa, with notes on their nesting and other habits. Part II. *Ibis* 10th ser 4: 373–472.

— (1922) Notes on the birds of East Africa. *Novit. Zool.* 29: 1–246.

— (1924) [Description of a new subspecies of *Cosmopsarus*]. *Bull. Br. Orn. Club* 44: 70–71.

— (1939) Birds of the Chyulu Hills. *J. E. Afr. Uganda Nat. Hist. Soc.* 14: 15–129.

— (1956) Days with birds. *Fieldiana, Zool.* 38: 1–520.

Van Zyl, AJ (1991) Unusual falcon hunting behaviour. *Gabar* 6: 68.

Vaughan, JH (1930) The birds of Zanzibar and Pemba. *Ibis* 12th ser. 6: 1–48.

Vaughan, RE and Jones, KH (1913) The birds of Hong Kong, Macao and the West River or Si Kiang in south east China, with special reference to their nidification and seasonal movements. *Ibis*, series 10, 3: 17–76, 163–201, 351–384.

Vaurie, C (1959) *The birds of the palearctic fauna. Passeriformes*. Witherby, London.

Verheyen, R (1953) *Exploration du Parc National de l'Upemba. Fascicule 19. Oiseaux*. Institut des Parcs Nationaux du Congo Belge, Bruxelles.

Verheyen, RA (1994) Some observations on intraspecific brood parasitsm in the Spotless Starling. *J. fur Ornithol.* 135: 136.

Vernon, CJ (1973) Vocal imitations by southern African birds. *Ostrich* 44: 23–30.

— (1993) Gluttonous starlings raid Natal mahogany. *Bee-eater* 44: 9.

Vieillard, J (1971) Données biogéographiques sur l'avifaune d'Afrique centrale. *Alauda* 39: 227–248.

Vincent, AW (1949) On the breeding habits of some African birds. *Ibis* 91: 313–345.

Vincent, J (1936) The birds of northern Portuguese East Africa. *Ibis* 13th ser. 6: 48–124.

von Plessen, B (1926) Verbreitung und Lebensweise von *Leucopsar rothschildi* Stres. *Ornithologisches Monatsberichten* 34: 71–73.

Walker, GR (1939) Notes on the birds of Sierra Leone. *Ibis* 14th ser. 3: 401–450.
Walsh, JF, Cheke, RA and Sowah, SA (1990) Additional species and breeding records of birds in the republic of Togo. *Malimbus* 12: 2–18.
Walter, H and Demartis, AM (1972) Brutolichte und Okologische Nische Sardischer Stadtvögel. *J. Orn.* 113: 391–406.
Wang, S, Zheng, B and Yang, L (1983) Record of the nest and eggs of 11 species of birds in Xishuangbanna of Yunnan. *Zool. Res.* 4: 238 and 308 [In Chinese].
Ward, P (1968) Origin of the avifauna of urban and suburban Singapore. *Ibis* 110: 239–254.
— (1971) The migration pattern of *Quelea quelea* in Africa. *Ibis* 113: 275–297.
—, and Zahavi, A (1973) The importance of certain assemblages of birds as "information centres" for food finding. *Ibis* 115: 517–534.
Warner, R (1968) The role of introduced diseases in the extinction of the endemic Hawaiian avifauna. *Condor* 70: 101–120.
Watkins, BP and Cassidy, RJ (1987) Evasive action taken by waterbuck to Red-billed Oxpeckers. *Ostrich* 58: 90.
Watling, D (1975) Observations on the ecological separation of two introduced congeneric mynahs (*Acridotheres*) in Fiji. *Notornis* 22: 37–53.
— (1982) *The birds of Fiji, Tonga and Samoa.* Millwood Press, Wellington.
— (1983) Ornithological notes from Sulawesi. *Emu* 83: 247–261.
Watson, J (1995) Seed dispersal by birds: Redwinged Starlings as agents for dispersal. *Bee-eater* 46: 45–49.
—, Warman, C, Todd, D and Laboudallon, V (1992) The Seychelles Magpie Robin *Copsychus sechellarum*: ecology and conservation of an endangered species. *Biol. Conservation* 61: 93–106.
Wavertree, Lady (1930) Further notes on the breeding of the royal starling and black-winged grackle. *Avicult. Mag.* 4th ser. 8: 327–328.
Webb, CS (1951) The Wattled Starling. *Avicult. Mag.* 57: 79–82.
Webster, K (1987) Observations on breeding at Rookwood, Queenstown (3126DD) district. *Bee-eater* 38: 20.
Weitzel, NH (1988) Nest site competition between the European Starling and native breeding birds in northwestern Nevada. *Condor* 90: 515–517.
West, CC and Pugh, PB (1986) Breeding and behaviour of Rothschild's Mynah. *Dodo* 22: 84–97.
West, MJ and King, AP (1990) Mozart's starling. *Am. Sci.* 78: 106–114.
—, Stroud, AN and King, AP (1983) Mimicry of the human voice by European Starlings: the role of social interaction. *Wilson Bull.* 95: 635–640.
Whistler, H (1923) The Spotted-wing Starling (*Psarogolossa spiloptera*, Vigros). *J. Bombay Nat. Hist. Soc.* 29: 290–292.
— (1928) *Popular handbook of Indian birds.* Gurney and Jackson, London.
Whitaker, JIS (1898) On a collection of birds from Morocco. *Ibis* Ser. 7; 4: 592–610.
White, CMN (1943) Field notes on some birds of Mwinilunga, Northern Rhodesia. *Ibis* 85: 127–131.
— (1948a) Weights of some Northern Rhodesia birds. *Ibis* 90: 137–138.
— (1948b) *Lamprocolius acuticaudus* in Northern Rhodesia. *Ibis* 90: 136–137.
— (1962) *A revised check list of African shrikes, orioles, drongos, starlings, crows, waxwings, cuckoo-shrikes, bulbuls, accentors, thrushes and babblers.* Government Printer, Lusaka.
— and Bruce, MD (1986) *The birds of Wallacea.* Check-list No. 7. British Ornithologists' Union, Tring.
Whitehead, SC, Wright, J and Cotton, PA (1996) Measuring the impact of parental foraging by Starlings (*Sturnus vulgaris*) on soil invertebrate prey availability: an enclosure experiment. *Oikos* 76: 511–521.
Whyte, IJ (1981) Anting in Blue-eared Glossy Starlings. *Ostrich* 52: 185.
—, Hall-Martin, AJ, Kloppers, JJ and Otto, JPAduT (1987) The status and distribution of the Yellowbilled Oxpecker in the Kruger National Park. *Ostrich* 58: 88–90.
Wickler, W (1966) Flügelhochstellen als Landesignal von *Lamprotornis* (Sturnidae). *J. Orn.* 107: 87–88.
Wildash, P (1968) *Birds of South Vietnam.* Tuttle, Tokyo.
Wiles, GJ, Aguon, CF, Davis, GW and Grout, DJ (1995) The status and distribution of endangered animals and plants in northern Guam. *Micronesica* 28: 31–49.
— and Masala, Y (1987) Collapse of a nest tree used by Finch-billed Mynas *Scissirostrum dubium* in north Sulawesi. *Forktail* 3: 67–68.
Wiley, JW (1986) Status and conservation of raptors in the West Indies. *Birds of Prey Bull.* 3: 57–70.
Wilkinson, R (1978) Co-operative breeding in the Chestnut-bellied Starling *Spreo pulcher*. *Bull. Nigerian Orn. Soc.* 14: 71–72.
— (1982a) A colour variant of *Spreo pulcher* at Kano, Nigeria. *Malimbus* 4: 49.
— (1982b) Social organisation and communal breeding in the Chestnut-bellied Starling (*Spreo pulcher*). *Anim. Behav.* 30: 1118–1128.
— (1983) Biannual breeding and moult-breeding overlap of the Chestnut-bellied Starling *Spreo pulcher*. *Ibis* 125: 353–361.
— (1984) Variation in eye colour of Blue-eared Glossy Starlings. *Malimbus* 6: 2–4.
— (1988) Long-tailed Glossy Starlings *Lamprotornis caudatus* in field and aviary with observations on co-operative breeding in captivity. *Avicult. Mag.* 94: 143–154.
— (1996) Cooperative breeding in captive Emerald Starlings *Coccycolius iris*. *Malimbus* 18: 134–141.
—, and Brown, AE (1984) Effect of helpers on feeding rates of nestlings in the chestnut-bellied starling *Spreo pulcher*. *J. Anim. Ecol.* 53: 301–310.
—, and McLeod, W (1991) Breeding the Ashy Starling at Chester Zoo. *Avicult. Mag.* 97: 163–166.
—, —, and Longford, D (1993) Some observations on the breeding of African Pied Starlings at Chester Zoo. *Avicult. Mag.* 99: 182–185.
Williams, TD, Dawson, A and Nicholls, TJ (1989) Sexual maturation and moult in juvenile Starlings *Sturnus vulgaris* in response to different daylengths. *Ibis* 131: 135–140.
Williamson, P and Gray, L (1975) Foraging behaviour of the Starling. *Condor* 77: 84–89.
Willimont, LA (1990) A case of competition between European Starlings and West Indian woodpeckers on Abaco, Bahamas. *Florida Field Nat.* 18: 14–15.
Wilmers, TJ (1987) Competition between Starlings and Kestrels for nest boxes: a review. *Raptor Research Rep.* 7:

156–159.

Wilson, GT (1975) A second non-iridescent Long-tailed Starling. *Ostrich* 46: 185.

Wilson, PR (1973) *The ecology of the Common Myna (Acridotheres tristis L.) in Hawkes Bay.* PhD thesis, University of Wellington.

Winter, SV and Sokolov, EP (1983) The Daurian Starling, *Sturnia sturnina* (Pall.) in the Middle Amur region. *Trudy zoolog. Inst. Leningr.* 116: 61–71 [In Russian].

Winterbottom, JM (1942) A contribution to the ornithology of Barotseland. *Ibis* 14th ser. 6: 337–389.

— (1959) Notes on the status of some birds in Northern Rhodesia. *Ostrich* 30: 1–12.

— (1975) Notes on the South African species of *Corvus*. *Ostrich* 46: 236–250.

Witherby, HF, Jourdain, FCR, Ticehurst, NF and Tucker, BW (1938) *The handbook of British Birds. Vol. 1.* Witherby, London.

Wolters, HE (1975–82) *Die Vogelarten der Erde.* Paul Parey, Hamburg.

Won, P-O (1961a) *Avi-mammalian fauna of Korea.* Institute of Agriculture, Suwon, Korea [In Korean].

—(1961b) An observation on the birds utilizing nest-boxes in Korea – with special reference to relation of birds to forestry practice. *Korean J. Zool.* 4: 21–28.

— and Woo, HC (1957) Ecological notes on *Sturnia sturnina* Pallas from the view points of forestry protection. *Bull. Forestry Exp. Sta. (Seoul)* 6: 111–127 [In Korean].

Woodall, PF (1971) Bird notes from the northern Sengwa Gorge, Rhodesia. *Ostrich* 42: 148–149.

Woodward, RB and Woodward, JDS (1899) *Natal birds.* Davis, Pietermaritzburg.

Wright, J and Cuthill, I (1992) Monogamy in the European starling. *Behaviour* 120: 262–285.

Yom-Tov, Y, Imber, A and Otterman, J (1977) The microclimate of winter roosts of the Starling *Sturnus vulgaris*. *Ibis* 119: 366–368.

Yosef, R and Yosef, D (1991) Tristram's grackles groom Nubian ibex. *Wilson Bull.* 103: 518–520.

Young, TP (1982) Bird visitation, seed-set, and germination rates in two species of *Lobelia* on Mount Kenya. *Ecology* 63: 1983–1986.

Zaias, J and Breitwisch, R (1990) Molt-breeding overlap in Northern Mockingbirds. *Auk* 107: 414–416.

Zeleny, L (1969) Starlings versus native cavity–nesting birds. *Atlantic Nat.* 24: 158–161.

Zimmerman, DA (1972) The avifauna of the Kakamega Forest, western Kenya, including a bird population study. *Bull. Am. Mus. Nat. Hist.* 149: 255–340.

—, Turner DA and Pearson DJ (1996) *Birds of Kenya and Northern Tanzania.* Christopher Helm, London.